THE EXCEPTIONAL INDIVIDUAL

FOURTH EDITION

Charles W. Telford
San Jose State University

James M. Sawrey
Austin Peay State University

Prentice-Hall, Inc., Englewood Cliffs, New Jersey 07632

Library of Congress Cataloging in Publication Data

Telford, Charles Witt.
The exceptional individual.

  Bibliography: p.
  Includes index.
  1. Exceptional children—Education. I. Sawrey,
James M., joint author. II. Title.
LC4031.T4 1981   371.9   80-19230
ISBN 0-13-293878-2

editorial / production supervision and interior design: CATHIE MICK MAHAR
cover design: RD GRAPHICS
manufacturing buyer: EDMOND W. LEONE

Printed in the United States of America

10 9 8 7 6 5 4 3 2 1

PRENTICE-HALL INTERNATIONAL, INC., *London*
PRENTICE-HALL OF AUSTRALIA PTY. LIMITED, *Sydney*
PRENTICE-HALL OF CANADA, LTD., *Toronto*
PRENTICE-HALL OF INDIA PRIVATE LIMITED, *New Delhi*
PRENTICE-HALL OF JAPAN, INC., *Tokyo*
PRENTICE-HALL OF SOUTHEAST ASIA PTE. LTD., *Singapore*
WHITEHALL BOOKS LIMITED, *Wellington, New Zealand*

CONTENTS

INTELLECTUAL EXCEPTIONALITY   203

7   The Gifted and Highly Creative   204

8   Low Levels of Cognitive Development (Mental Retardation)   244

THE SENSORIALLY HANDICAPPED   334

MOTOR AND COMMUNICATION HANDICAPS   417

12   Orthopedic and Other Physical Impairments   418

13   Communication Disorders   454

BEHAVIORAL AND EMOTIONAL DISORDERS   487

PREFACE

Concern for the handicapped has increased tremendously in the past two decades. Almost daily, new court decisions, legislative acts, and new programs affecting the handicapped are announced. Many of the disabled are now being served who were not served before, in ways that are both new and promising. The handicapped are participating increasingly in all aspects of society and are actively involved in programs designed for their benefit. Exceptional people have been propelled "out of the closet." This change is manifesting itself in the educational procedures known as "mainstreaming."

Throughout the 1970's and into the '80's the integration of children with special needs into the regular programs continues to be the focus of concern in the field of special education. The establishment of special institutions, schools, and classes for these children were well-intentioned and presumably more effective ways of providing special services for individuals with handicaps. It was seldom recognized that these procedures also served the establishment by removing troublesome individuals from the regular classrooms and from the mainstream of society and had a number of unanticipated deleterious side-effects.

In the 1960's these arrangements began to be questioned on many fronts. "What is special about these segregated classes and schools?" "Are the teaching-learning procedures really different in these special facilities?" "Are they more effective educationally than the regular classes?" These questions typified the educational concerns. In addition, social action groups raised social, political, and ethnical questions concerning the side effects of segregated facilities, such as: "What are the effects of segregating and labeling these individuals?" "Is the stigmatization of these people increasing their handicaps?" "Doesn't the stereotyping and stigmatizing of these handicapped individuals function as a 'self-fulfilling prophecy' "? "Are purely educational considerations determining the selection of these children?" "How about the ethnic, cultural, and social class bias in the tests and other devices used for selection purposes?"

Social action groups, parents, and their legal representatives began to claim that the handicapped were experiencing discrimination in ways analagous to the disadvantaged ethnic groups, lower social classes, and women. As a result of the combined effects of legislative acts, court decisions, moral imperatives, and philosophical commitments, the trend toward mainstreaming as the most normalizing and least restrictive educational arrangement for the handicapped keeps rolling.

Partly as a reflection of these movements and concerns, we have made the following changes in this, the fourth edition of our book. We have increased the emphasis on the more purely educational as contrasted with the medical, social, and psychological aspects of exceptionality. We have a separate chapter dealing with the ethical and legal concern of exceptional individuals. We also have devoted a chapter to the various factors that facilitate or retard the development of human potential. This chapter systematizes and expands a variety of topics previously scattered throughout the book and treated less systematically.

We have deleted the chapters on the bicultural individual and the aged. However, some of the material previously treated in these chapters is integrated into other chapters. The deletion of these chapters and the reintroduction of a chapter on personal-social deviance were the result of suggestions given by users of the book.

We have retained the following features which characterized the three previous editions:

the consistent use of a cultural frame of reference in defining exceptionality and in identifying and dealing with the problems of exceptional people and their families;

the handling of the problems of exceptional people as essentially the magnified problems of individual differences among people in general;

the emphasis on the generality of most of the problems of exceptionality;

and our use of the terms *exceptionality* and *exceptional people* rather than *exceptional children,* reflect our conviction that exceptionality is often more the problem of the entire family and culture—the tone of which is set by the adults—than it is the property of a unique individual.

The acceptance of a dominantly cultural frame of reference in dealing with exceptional people results in an emphasis on the relative nature of the deviations and a recognition of the extent to which the problems of exceptionality cut across categories. For this reason the early chapters of the book deal with those problems common to exceptional people in general, irrespective of the nature or origin of their exceptionalities.

While our emphasis is on contemporary concepts and practices, we have also tried to view these in terms of their predecessors. Today's ideas do not spring full-blown from creative minds. They have their historical roots and their natural histories. Historical perspective is necessary for the understanding, appreciation, and evaluation of current concepts and practices. In a limited way we have tried to provide this perspective.

This book is intended for use at the upper division level as an introduction to the problems of exceptional people. It is intended as a survey for people who will specialize in one of the specific areas of exceptionality and for the prospective or current teacher, principal, supervisor, superintendent, occupational therapist, physical therapist, nurse, or physician who will work with a wide variety of deviant individuals but who will not become a specialist in the field.

Every book has many hidden contributors. Our wives, Una Mae Sawrey and Aldene E. Telford, have contributed through their encouragement, their tolerance of our neglect of family responsibilities, and their critical reading of the manuscript. Ms. Emi Nobuhiro typed most of the manuscript and helped in many other ways during its development.

CHARLES W. TELFORD

JAMES M. SAWREY

INTRODUCTION TO EXCEPTIONALITY

PART

CHAPTER 1

SOME BASIC SOCIAL AND PSYCHOLOGICAL CONSIDERATIONS

Individual differences are universal. No two individuals are exactly alike, and the differences between the extremes of human variability are tremendous. There are authentic cases of otherwise normal adult males ranging in height from below two to over nine feet. Individual differences in weight are relatively just as great. Differences in physique range all the way from the perfection of the superbly developed and highly tuned athlete to the totally dependent hospitalized "crib" or "basket" case. Speech facility varies from the precise and melodious through the guttural and scarcely recognizable to meaningless noises and cries. People range intellectually from the extremely gifted (IQ's as high as 200 have been reported) to the totally custodial. The sensory acuity of individuals varies from the totally blind and deaf at one extreme to people with hyperacute sensitivity at the other. The personality and emotional adjustments of people range from the highly self-actualized and well-organized superior individuals to the completely disorganized and deteriorated chronic psychotics. In every dimension of human development, aptitude, and achievement, the extent of individual differences is tremendous.

We begin with a panoramic view of the great diversity of people labeled exceptional. This preview will also indicate the wide range of reactions and modes of adjustment to exceptionality.

WHAT IT MEANS TO BE EXCEPTIONAL

Giftedness: High Levels of Cognitive Development

early promise
unrealized

William James Sidis's father began training his son before he was two years of age. William was able to read and spell before he was three years old. At three and a half he was able to write. When he saw his father using the typewriter he asked to be shown how to operate the machine. In six months he was able to type. When the boy was five his father gave him several calendars to help him develop the concept of time. By studying these, the boy was able to devise his own method of predicting on what day of the week any date would fall. At the age of five he also was able to read Russian, French, and German. After entering the first grade, he passed through several grades in six months. A year later, with the aid of a skeleton and a textbook, he knew enough about the structure of the human body to pass a medical student's examination on the subject. By the age of ten he knew algebra, geometry, trigonometry, and calculus. At the age of nine he passed the entrance examination at Harvard but was not allowed to matriculate until the age of eleven. Less than a year later, he delivered an original lecture before the Harvard Mathematical Club on the fourth dimension. William astounded the seventy-five assembled scholars.

These spectacular exploits inspired all sorts of glowing predictions for his future. However, he seems to have spent the rest of his life trying to hide from the publicity he neither sought nor wanted. As a young man he became embittered and disillusioned and developed an extreme aversion toward his father, whom he blamed for the shambles of his life. His childhood enthusiasm for learning disappeared. He fled from one low-paying job to another and lived in dismal quarters. He died of a cranial hemorrhage July 17, 1944 at the age of forty-six, apparently destitute and unemployed. William's history gave rise to the *Sidis fallacy*—the belief that such exceptional talent rarely matures and becomes productive. However, this belief has been disproven repeatedly. An examination of William's life indicated that he was not a victim of intellectual precocity and educational acceleration, but instead, a casualty of extreme parental exploitation and emotional deprivation (Montour, 1977).

early promise
realized

John Stuart Mill began the study of Greek at the age of three. By the time he was eight he had read Plato, Xenophon, and Herodotus and was studying algebra and geometry. At twelve he was studying logic and reading Aristotle in the original. The following year he began the study of political economy and at sixteen published several controversial articles in the field. He lived a full and highly productive life as logician, philosopher, political scientist, and psychologist as well as diplomat and member of Parliament. He died at the age of sixty-seven while still a productive scholar and politician (Packe, 1954).

MENTALLY RETARDED: LOW LEVELS OF COGNITIVE DEVELOPMENT

mild mental retardation

We began to suspect that something was wrong when our son was still babbling and had no speech when he was two years old. We thought he might be mentally retarded and were quite convinced of the fact when he was four. However, two clinics centered on his speech limitation and felt that he had only had a speech problem. Our pediatrician thought that he was just a spoiled child. He really was not officially identified as mentally retarded until he was eight years old. After our son was identified as retarded, we were fortunate in having access to a good class for the mildly mentally retarded. Our son is now making progress. Even though academically he is very slow, he ice skates well, he can row a boat and play baseball. He now perceives himself as a reasonably normal teenager. Although his speech is poor, he continues to develop and will probably be able to function independently in society. He is now in a work-study program learning to become a carpenter's helper.

a degree of social independence

"I now pronounce you husband and wife." The words are familiar, but a generation ago this marriage could not have taken place. Although these people had managed to master the skills necessary for independent living, restrictive legislation and public prejudices would have stood in their way, for Norma and George are mentally retarded. The successes that these two people have achieved are due to a fortunate combination of circumstances. These included parents who began very early to prepare their children for eventual independence although without realizing what they were doing. Because the parents were busy and active, it became imperative for them to make their handicapped children independent as early as possible. Teaching the children to travel by themselves was done as much to provide the adults with greater freedom as to provide the children with mobility and independence. Much of the children's early independence training came about as a reaction by the parents against the prospect of being tied down for the rest of their lives.

When the children were "travel-trained" their parents no longer had to transport them to and from every function they attended. Participating in group activities provided the children with an active social life and also freed their parents several afternoons a week. As they grew older, the movement toward group homes for the retarded made it possible for Norma and George to live in a setting where they could become still more independent. They met, fell in love, and decided to get married.

Today parents can begin early independence training realizing that it may be the start of a long-range plan by which their handicapped children may be able to move out of the home to protected group living, possibly to their own apartments, and even to marriage. The progress of Norma and George is also made possible by sweeping legislative changes concerning the handicapped as well as fundamental changes in the ways the handicapped are perceived by themselves and by others. Although many prejudices concerning the disabled remain, enough progress has been made that Norma and George and millions like them can now see themselves, and be seen by others, as people capable of living independent and even productive lives.

ORTHOPEDIC DISABILITIES

one step toward freedom

My world really changed when my physical therapist, Miss Hanson, showed me a ridiculous looking contraption which might have been a sweatband with an additional strap going up over the head and a long stick with a tip on the end fastened in front. I was shown a picture of a boy typing with this contraption on his head. I looked at the device and the picture sullenly, and wondered what it had to do with me. I was told that it was a headstick which might make it possible for me to write. Miss Hanson asked me if I was willing to try. I nodded skeptically.

Up until this time I had been an impossible child. I was sullen, uncooperative and rebellious. Physically, I was completely uncoordinated. Even after ten years of speech, physical, and occupational therapy, I still could not walk, talk, or use my hands. I had practically given up hope.

After reluctantly agreeing to try a headstick, I was taken back to my classroom and put in a straight-backed chair with arms. I was tied in to keep me from toppling onto the floor. Miss Hanson put the headstick on her head and demonstrated its use. She then put it on me, placed a typewriter on a table in front of me, and told me to turn the machine on. To my surprise, I was able to do so quickly. She then told me to start writing the alphabet and I did. At her suggestion, I then wrote my name. I couldn't believe it! The other children all came over to share my victory. I was no longer mute! My journey out of solitary confinement had begun.

I was given directions for exercises to strengthen the muscles of my neck. I religiously did my neck exercises both at home and at school until my neck was the best developed part of my body. I also learned to turn the pages and follow the lines of a book with my headstick. It was like a dream come true! I worked hard for I had at last broken the silence which had imprisoned me all my life (adapted from Rusk, 1978).

severe multiple handicaps

Our son Julius is now four years old. Not until he was three and had been to more than a dozen clinics and specialists did we obtain a positive diagnosis, and we were able to accept it. Julius is mentally retarded and has cerebral palsy. At nine months he was unable to sit up, crawl, or control his body in any purposeful way. At twelve months he started having seizures. With medication his seizures are now under control. He has been in a regular physiotherapy program for a year and has made considerable progress. He was able to crawl on all fours after six months of therapy and is now standing by himself. We are all anxiously awaiting his first solo step!

EPILEPTIC DISORDERS

equal rights to employment

For the first time, George had been told right out by a small manufacturing concern where he had sought work that they would not hire him because he was an epileptic. He felt discouraged, frustrated, and angry. He considered filing a civil rights discrimination suit against the company. However, he had one more company on his list and decided to give it a try. The manager-owner of the company interviewed him, went over his job application, inquired about his medical background, and hired him. George had fully expected to be back on the street again when the interviewer learned that he was an epileptic. Later, when George asked his boss why he had hired him, the reply was, "You had the skills, experience, and attitude we were looking for and to discriminate against someone because of a medical problem is as bad as discriminating against someone because of race." Besides, his boss added, "it is illegal to do so."

Eight times in the previous month this intelligent, competent, and articulate machinist had been told "sorry" by interviewers.

They would first become curious about the medical background noted on his application; then, on finding that he was an epileptic, their curiosity would turn to rejection and George would be back on the street again.

Up until about a year ago, George had never revealed that he had epilepsy because the condition had never been diagnosed. He had first experienced a series of blackouts, and then, a little over a year ago, while working, he had three separate seizures. He entered a hospital for observations and a diagnosis of epilepsy was made. Although the doctors are not sure what caused the condition, he had sustained a head injury in a car accident four months before his blackouts began. Head injuries are a major cause of epilepsy in adults. With proper medication his seizures seemed to be completely under control and he left the hospital.

Although George had a doctor's statement that his seizures were under control and he had been free of seizures for nearly a year, as soon as prospective employers heard the word *epilepsy* they would get "this weird look in their eyes" and ask questions which implied that "they thought that my mental condition was not quite right."

George went to work for his new boss. However, on his second day at work he had a convulsion, following which he was dazed and confused. He was sure that the seizure resulted from the tension and pressure of starting a new job, which he needed badly, and the strain of moving into a new apartment at the same time. Fortunately, his boss was understanding, sent him home and told him he hoped that he would be back soon. He went back to work three days later and has been free of seizures ever since.

AUDITORY IMPAIRMENT

caught in the criminal-legal system

Two policemen picked up a teenage boy on an assault complaint. When they stood him against a wall to frisk him he kept turning around and looking at them. They said he was resisting arrest. The boy reached for his pocket where he had a notebook and pencil. Thinking he was reaching for a gun, one of the cops placed a hammer-lock on him and placed him in handcuffs. All the time the boy made noises but said nothing. When they read him his rights he asked no questions nor did he make any demands. He just gestured with his hands, grunted, and shook his head. The policemen were sure he was either mentally retarded or psychotic.

At the station, when the boy was being booked, a clerk in the office wasn't so sure. He was reminded of his brother who was deaf. When the clerk began using sign language, the boy's face lit up and he began signing in return. Apparently the boy had tried to get a woman to write out directions to an address he was trying to find. The woman had misunderstood his advances and called the police. When the situation was explained and the facts verified, the boy was sent home.

No one knows how many hearing-impaired persons are innocently snared in the nation's legal system. Unfortunately very few deaf people know their rights in such situations. In 1975, Congress voted seed money to set up "protection and advocacy" programs in each state. Today, if you are deaf and accused of a crime and need an interpreter the courts are required to provide one. While all fifty states have statutes requiring that the deaf be provided with interpreters in criminal cases, in civil cases, many states have no such statutes.

a case of delayed diagnosis

According to his mother, four-year-old Sam was stubborn and deliberately disobedient. He used banging on the furniture, stomping his feet, and screaming to get attention. He was destructive and completely unmanageable. According to the psychologist, he was "untestable," "uncooperative," and "unable to socialize" in any way. He communicated by grunting and screaming. He had repeated temper tantrums. The only positive signs were that he watched other children closely and imitated them a great deal. However, he reacted to other children in overly aggressive ways.

Acting on a suggestion by the psychologist, Sam's vision and hearing were tested and he was found to be "profoundly hearing-impaired." He had been deaf for the first four years of his life and no one knew it!

VISUAL IMPAIRMENT

a pianist who happens to be blind

"I am not a blind jazz pianist," he insists, "I am a pianist who plays jazz and happens to be blind." The speaker is George Shearing. George was born blind but for over three decades has been a jazz musician, concert pianist, composer, and at the age of sixty still plays over a dozen symphonic concerts a year.

George practices for his concerts with his wife, who is sighted. Since musical scores in Braille are very few and exceedingly cumbersome, he learns most of his pieces by listening to tapes. He says that the score of Bach's Well-Tempered Clavier in Braille is about the size of six suburban telephone directories. George has produced over 100 jazz compositions. He says he has always wanted people to regard him as a *pianist* rather than as a *blind pianist*.

simulated blindness

I found my fork on the left side of my plate and I decided to start with the potatoes I knew were in the center of my plate. I scooped where I thought the potatoes were, put the fork to my mouth, and discovered there was no food on it. I tried again and got a mixture of carrots and potatoes. Well, at least I got something to my mouth! I continued eating from the same general area of my plate until I could find no more potatoes. I then explored another region of my plate but could get nothing on my fork. I then decided to try my spoon and after several attempts managed to get two peas in my mouth. I then tried for some salad but my fork kept coming up empty. On feeling around the outside of my plate I discovered I had succeeded in pushing most of the salad off the plate onto the table.

How about trying for some meat! I felt the meat with my hand in order to locate it and then succeeded in cutting it. When I got the piece of meat to my mouth I discovered it was so big I could not get it into my mouth. Cutting again, I did better and was able to get a piece of meat an appropriate size into my mouth. I felt along the table for my glass. Grasping it, I realized for the first time how smooth, cold, and beautiful it felt.

No, I was not blind! I was a member of a class dealing with the handicapped and had agreed to eat one meal while blindfolded in order to experience at first hand some of the problems encountered by the blind when faced with such a simple thing as eating a meal.

Some other things I became aware of in the course of the meal. My first feeling when deprived of vision was of being alone and detached. I was inclined to cease talking with others and withdraw into my own world. I could hear people talking but experienced them more as disembodied voices such as might issue from a radio than as real live persons. When I wanted to speak to someone close I was inclined to touch them so as to assure myself that they were really there. I also became more aware of the sounds around me. While eating I concentrated on the texture, taste, and odor of the food, qualities I had not fully taken in when I could see.

Trying to eat a meal without the use of sight gave me a new realization of the problems faced by the blind. I found eating without sight to be very difficult, time consuming, and frustrating.

a case of
dyslexia

My family realized that I was having serious trouble from the first year in school. I seemed to be unable to learn to read. When the reports started coming from school, my parents began looking for help. Psychologists, child-guidance people, psychiatrists—all tested, probed, and theorized. Everyone agreed that something was wrong but no one could say just what. The first real insight came one summer when my family insisted that I attend a summer program for children with serious reading problems. I did not want to go, but to my surprise, I had a good time. I got to know a lot of other kids who seemed quite normal but, like me, could not read. Somehow that seemed to help. My teacher tested me and said I had an IQ of 120. When he explained what that meant, I didn't believe him.

That summer I began to feel a little better about myself and did learn to read a little. In the sixth grade I was assigned to a special education class in another school. All the kids who attended that school were "different." Some were emotionally disturbed, some were mentally retarded, and some, like me, had special educational problems. We were all picked up by a bus and taken to the special school. I was always afraid my friends would see me on that bus with the other kids. It really wasn't so bad at the school. The teacher really cared and I began working harder. We also did arts and crafts work and I found that I was good at crafts. The other kids said they liked what I did. I also earned a letter at track. I always could run fast. In high school I am back in the regular classes except that when there is reading or writing to be done, I go to a special resource room where assignments are read to me.

At home one of my parents also reads my assignments to me. Sometimes they read into a tape recorder and I can listen to it by myself. My parents also help with my other assignments. When I have to answer questions, they read them aloud and I answer orally while they write down what I say. Sometimes I dictate into a tape recorder and later my sister types up what I have dictated.

I learned the name of my condition—dyslexia—before I could pronounce it. I have learned that my condition is not uncommon. I get some consolation from the fact that I may be like Leonardo da Vinci, who many people think had dyslexia, and Nelson Rockefeller, who certainly did. I understand there are colleges that have centers to help people like me. My counselors say I have plenty of ability to do college work. However, I am still worried. How can I make a living if I cannot read any better than a third or fourth grader? What if I am smart—when I can't read!

a case of developmental immaturity or inherent defect

We have been told that our boy has a learning disability, more specifically, a perceptual handicap. Over the past three years he has been given every conceivable type of test—motor, sensory, intelligence, and neurological. We have spent hundreds of hours having him creep, crawl and roll, sleep in a certain fashion, practice visual pursuit movements and eye-hand coordinations. He has been on several special diets—some eliminating all artificial additives, others rich in trace minerals; now he is taking megavitamins. Nothing has seemed to help. His second grade teacher tells us to let the child alone. According to her, his problem is a developmental immaturity and eventually he will stop writing backwards, reversing his letters, and will begin to read. Right now we are at our wit's end. Please help us!

EMOTIONAL DISTURBANCE

a case of autism

Our ten-year-old daughter is an autistic child. We were first told by our family physician that she was severely mentally retarded. However, while she functioned much like a mentally retarded child, somehow she didn't fit the pattern. We were then told that she was brain damaged, but doctors were unable to find positive evidence to support this. She was unable to sit up at nine months. However, at ten months she suddenly began sitting up. Physically, she continued to progress but speech failed to develop and she was entirely indifferent to other people. At two years of age we took her to a clinic where she was given a thorough examination and was diagnosed as autistic. When she was four years old we put her in a nursery school with a teacher who understood autistic children. This teacher convinced us that our daughter was not mentally retarded and could learn and we began systematically working with her at home. When she was six, we placed her in a private day school for severely disturbed children. This school was educationally rather than clinically oriented. They said, "Let's start with the child where she is and go on from there, without probing her background and how she got that way." She has adjusted well to her new school and seems to be making significant progress.

recovery from childhood schizophrenia

Mary had been unable to function in either nursery school or kindergarten. She was terrified by the other children and would scream and cry when they approached her. After several clinical evaluations, Mary was given a diagnosis of childhood schizophrenia. At seven years of age Mary was placed in a special class for emotionally disturbed children. For the entire year she constantly engaged in bizarre behavior. For example, she would either flee from the room or try to hide under her chair whenever strangers approached. When another child reached out to touch her she would shrink away and scream. If another child told her to quit screaming, she would hold her head in her hands and repeat, "I scream! I scream! I scream!"

After a year in school Mary could read at first grade level and perform simple arithmetic calculations. Gradually Mary came to tolerate physical contact with the other children and the group began to give her some support. When another child tried to upset her by telling her that there was a spider under her chair, the boy sitting next to her told her with a brushing motion that he had frightened it away and she needn't be afraid. The other children began to accept Mary's bizarre behavior without undue concern. The therapist explained to Mary that her unusual behavior was frightening to the others and she seemed to understand this. The teachers and therapist assured Mary that her fears were understandable and acceptable and that they would not abandon her, irrespective of her thoughts and feelings. Mary's bizarre behavior decreased noticeably over the next six months. The other children were more comfortable with her and became more supportive. When told that her behavior on the playground embarrassed the others she cried. This was the first time she had been observed to cry because of anything but fear. Mary's schoolwork improved and her symptoms gradually subsided. After four years Mary was placed in a regular class and was able to handle it. She subsequently graduated from high school.

These are all exceptional individuals. The cases described are not intended to be representative of the entire population of people in need of special educational, occupational, and social treatment. They are intended, rather, to give some idea of the great diversity of people conventionally designated as exceptional.

WHEN THE OTHER PERSON SURPRISES US

In terms of a rough set of norms, people build a large set of expectancies concerning others. We expect most people to be "normal," and when our expectancies are not realized we develop additional categories to fit deviations from the normal. Deviant persons and activities become categorized as "abnormal." We develop different expectancies for the abnormal in general as well as for specific types of abnormalities. These categories and related expectancies provide a certain degree of predictability in social interactions. People are disconcerted when their expectations are not realized; social forces are exerted to bring norm violators into line with those expectancies. Norm violators are unpredictable, and this unpredictability increases the costs of social interactions.

The social concerns manifested toward mental handicaps derive, in part, from our uncertainties as to the nature, causes, and treatment of mental disorders. We are uncomfortable in the presence of uncertainties and the general public perceives mental deviates as unpredictable, unreliable, and prone to violent and antisocial behavior.

PRESCIENTIFIC CONCEPTIONS OF DEVIANT PEOPLE

Although the existence of deviant human behavior and development aroused curiosity and focused interest on normal behavior and development, mystical and supernaturalistic interpretations of deviations persisted long after naturalistic explanations of the more ordinary behavioral events and developmental sequences had been generally accepted. It seems that belief in evil or benign spirits as the cause of deviant behavior has been evident from the beginning of recorded history. The substitution of naturalistic for supernatural explanations of the unusual in human behavior and development has been a slow process and is not complete even today. The tremendous popularity of the book and movie *The Exorcist* indicates that a large segment of the general population still either believes in or is intrigued by demonological interpretations of deviant human behavior.

People are always uncomfortable with uncertainties. Consequently, the occurrence of a bizarre or baffling event evokes a search for explanations that allow the individual to make sense of the event. Once having hit upon an acceptable account of the observed event, the person passes easily and without awareness of the process from "possibility" to "probability" to "certainty." Today, many modern equivalents of the sorcerer, witch doctor, or native healer are ready to offer explanations and provide advice to persons seeking help for mental or physical health problems.

QUALITATIVE VERSUS QUANTITATIVE CONCEPTIONS OF THE DIFFERENCES BETWEEN EXCEPTIONAL AND NORMAL PEOPLE

The substitution of a naturalistic for a supernatural explanation of the origins and nature of the deviant characteristics of an individual did not solve the problem of the nature of the exceptional person. In some respects, the demonological conception of the exceptional person was a qualitative as contrasted with a quantitative one.

A qualitative conception of exceptional individuals is that they constitute separate and, in many ways, distinct categories or classes of people. As separate categories of people, they are considered to have traits and characteristics which make them fundamentally different from the general run of humanity. The titles of certain books and courses—the "psychology of" the gifted, the mentally retarded, the blind, the deaf, women, blacks, or chicanos—suggest that there is a separate kind or brand or category of psychology which "explains" these categories of people and that such explanations are fundamentally different from the "psychology of" normal people. Such a view implies that a separate and unique set of conceptual categories or ways of thinking is required to understand and deal with exceptional individuals. They are supposed to learn, perceive, think, and adjust in ways which are unique to them; therefore they cannot be understood in terms of those principles of learning, thinking, perceiving, and adjusting which have been derived from and are applicable to normal people. The trend of thinking over the last hundred years has been away from qualitative conceptions, and toward a quantitative frame of reference.

The quantitative conception of exceptionality holds that the differences between the deviant groups, on the one hand, and the normal, on the other, are differences only of degree and not of kind. Thus the perceptual, conceptual, learning, and ideational processes of all people—whether normal or deviant—are fundamentally the same. We all learn, retain, recall, perceive, think, and make personal and social adjustments according to the same general principles and patterns, but some of us do these things faster, better, more accurately, or more appropriately than others. In its extreme form, the quantitative conception of the mentally retarded is that they are intellectually inferior to the normal by designated amounts, as roughly indicated by test performances, school achievement, and social competence, and that they are essentially normal in ways unrelated to intellectual competence. Except as a consequence of their intellectual deficiences, their personalities, characters, physical characteristics, and social characteristics are normal—or, at least, their deviations from the normal in these respects are not necessarily or inherently a part of their intellectual deficiencies. The notion that the cognitive and linguistic development and functioning of the handicapped are qualitatively similar to those of the nonhandicapped but may be at a slower rate and/or level of development is accepted by most but not all researchers in the field.

In the next chapter we shall document that individuals who are significantly deviant in physique, intellect, behavior, or beliefs are subject to a variety of internal and external stresses as well as socially- and self-imposed restrictions which make them more vulnerable and more likely than normals to develop over-defensive, aggressive, or withdrawal patterns of behavior. These behavior patterns, however, are found among every segment of the population, and are not peculiar to the deviants.

The current tendency to lump several conventional categories of handicapped into a single grouping labeled *Developmental Disabilities*, the belief that the "habilitation" of mental deviates should be based on a "developmental" rather than on a "defect" model, and the pleas for "normalization" are all consistent with the belief that differences between the normal and the handicapped are largely quantitative rather than qualitative in nature. When special education is perceived as simply providing better educational opportunities, as a part of general education, for children with special learning needs, it tends to decategorize the handicapped and encourages people to perceive these children as normal individuals with certain learning problems.

If disproving the qualitative conception of the difference between the disabled and the normal is difficult, eradicating the widespread acceptance of the idea will be even harder. When a disabled person achieves commensurately with a normal person despite the handicap, he or she is perceived as overcompensating. The overdependency of a similarly disabled person is also seen as a direct expression of the defect. Much of what the deviant individual does is seen as a manifestation of the deviancy. When a blind, deaf crippled, or mentally retarded individual gets into trouble or has an accident, the difficulty is readily ascribed to the defect. The same experiences of normal people are seen either as situation-evoked or as ordinary events in a normal life requiring no explanation.

Few people can accept that a handicapped person's under- or over-achievements can arise from ordinary motives and serve the identical functions in his or her life as they do in the lives of ordinary people. The belief that the achievements of the handicapped require some unique explanation is so widespread that such people are expected and required to develop a special rationale to explain their "normal" behavior, a special philosophy to account for their achievements. The handicapped are expected to have a unique philosophy to explain why they want the same things as the nonhandicapped and work for them in similar ways. Handicapped individuals respond to these expectancies by stating their philosophies, which are largely reflections of the prevalent stereotypes concerning their particular disability. When the behavior of deviant persons violates our expectations, we often "de-normalize" them by imbuing them with special powers to account for their unexpected acts. The blind are said to have a sixth sense; the person deprived of any sense is believed to have a compensatory hyperacuity of the other senses. The notion that deviants—particularly psychotics and the blind—have access to realities that are closed to other people is an old and persistent one.

While it is often legally and administratively necessary to use independent quantitative criteria to identify exceptional individuals, the final test of the validity of these criteria is social usefulness. If deficiencies in adaptive behavior and an IQ of below 70 are accepted as the arbitrary criteria of mental retardation for placement in special classes, but it is found that many children with IQs of 75 can profit equally by placement in such classes, the 70 limit loses much of its usefulness as a criterion. It then becomes necessary either to change the limit or to expand the criterion so as also to take into consideration demonstrated school achievement and physical and social maturity. The audiometric criterion for deafness or partial deafness and the visual acuity criterion for blindness or partial sightedness are meaningful and valid only insofar as experience proves that individuals thus designated are correspondingly handicapped educationally, socially, and vocationally. The judgments of specialists as to the degree of exceptionality represented by the orthopedically handicapped, the speech defective, and the socially and emotionally maladjusted are validated to the degree that individuals so identified do require, and are found to profit by, special education and treatment specifically designed for them. Because of the priority given to the pragmatic social criteria, the term *exceptional individual* usually refers to those people who differ from the average to such an extent that they are perceived by society as requiring special educational, social, or vocational treatment. True, such criteria lack specificity and vary from culture to culture and from one generation to another, but they seem to be the most meaningful yet suggested. Such a relative, social conception of the exceptional individual finds quantitative criteria to be useful only insofar as they correlate with the social. If it is found that all or most of the test-identified exceptional children also meet the educational and social criteria, test performance can be used for identification purposes. But when educational methods and requirements change, when social demands vary, and when occupational opportunities are modified, the tests' usefulness will also change.

Critics find considerable fault with a definition of the exceptional individual as that person who deviates from the norm in physical, mental, emotional, or social characteristics to such a degree that he or she requires special social and educational services to develop his or her maximum capacity. In actual practice, a combination of traditional practice, cultural values, social needs, and even political pressures determines what dimensions and degrees of individual differences are sufficiently significant for something to be done about them.

the variable nature of social criteria of exceptionality In a primitive culture, where survival and effectiveness depend upon one's skill in hunting, physical handicaps are serious defects, whereas the inability to learn to read, write, calculate, and handle abstract concepts is much less significant. Where individual and tribal survival and prestige are determined by sensory acuity and by physical agility, strength, and endurance, physically defective infants may be abandoned even though they may be intellectually superior. In an agricultural community which is sparsely settled and unmechanized, a psychotic, mentally retarded, or socially inadequate individual may be a problem to his immediate family without becoming a matter of general social concern. The rural boy who fails to learn in school can still do useful work under the supervision of his parents and siblings and can become a contributing member of the family.

Variations among people are universal, but society determines which deviations will be considered disabilities or assets, impairments or enhancements of personal worth. Assets and disabilities are dictated as much by the tasks a culture demands or expects of its members and by the meanings it attaches to deviations from the norm as by the objective facts of exceptionality.

Today's increasing social concern for extreme intellectual deviates (the mentally retarded, the intellectually gifted, and the creative) is, in part, a reflection of our cultural expectancies and values. A discussion of the reasons for the increasing social problems of mental retardation and current interest in the gifted and the creative will point up the cultural frame of reference within which all categories of exceptional children are perceived.

In present-day America, the need for unskilled and semiskilled workers is rapidly declining, while the demand for professional, managerial, scientific, and technically trained workers is increasing. The bulk of the work requiring good hands and a strong back is being automated, and knowledge is being substituted for strength. Inventiveness, creativity, and intellectual activity are becoming the real human assets. An advanced industrial culture requires a well-educated, creative, and adaptable labor force. Today's young students can expect to see a complete technological revolution during the course of their lifetimes. The jobs they might hold today will probably not exist when they are fifty. As adults they may well be working with processes not yet developed and using machines still to be designed. In such a highly automated and rapidly changing industrial society, the need is for people to invent, design, install, monitor, and service equipment. Someone who offers manual dexterity, brute strength, and endurance is no longer truly productive. Adaptability rather than a specific skill, creativity rather than rote information, the capacity for change rather than a given fund of information in one limited area are the assets valued by such a culture. The concept of a position or industrial occupation as a specialized activity is being replaced by an emphasis on the more general and abstract occupational and professional aptitudes. The greater plasticity and adaptability characteristic of higher intelligence are becoming imperative.

One result of these cultural changes is that mentally and/or educationally retarded individuals, for example, are increasingly becoming a social liability. Even the farm is changing. The demands of scientific farming, the rational use of complicated modern farm machinery, the pressures of mechanized, large-scale, efficient production have forced the marginal farmer and farm worker out of the market. The reduction in the absolute number of farm laborers, as well as the even greater decrease in their relative number, have driven hordes of marginal farm workers, tenants, and owners to the cities, where they gravitate to the slums and swell the ranks of the urban culturally disadvantaged.

In the urban centers, persons with marginal intelligence come to the attention of the educational, public health, police, and public welfare agencies designed to help them, their intellectual limitations become obvious, and public concern is aroused. With increasing numbers of people being labeled as intellectually marginal and inadequate in terms of the social and occupational demands of the culture, the need for special assistance increases tremendously. Handicaps are always relative to the social context. A mental or physical aberration becomes a handicap only when it becomes a barrier to one's potential for work, play, or self-realizing within the context of one's life.

AREA OR MODE OF DEVIATION

The conventional classification of exceptional individuals is the *area* or *mode* of primary deviation. This is a qualitative type of classification. The modes or areas selected for consideration reflect the current cultural values of the society. We have selected five general areas or modes of deviation for primary consideration.

intellectual and academic deviance We shall deal with intellectual deviations in both directions from the mean. On the lower end of the scale of intelligence and scholastic aptitude are the mentally retarded, the borderline, the dull, and those with more specific learning disabilities. At the high end of the intellectual scale are the gifted. Creative and potentially creative persons, although they probably do not possess the same kind of exceptionality as the intellectually gifted and the retarded, are probably a subgroup of the gifted, but they will be considered separately because of the current interest in them. A certain minimum of intellectual capacity is necessary to be creative, but creativity seems to correlate only moderately with general intelligence. Therefore we will deal with the creative and the intellectually gifted as two overlapping, but not identical, categories.

sensory deviance The sensorially exceptional—the hard-of-hearing and the deaf, the partially sighted and the blind—constitute a second area of exceptionality. There are, of course, people who have no sense of pain (analgesia), who lack all sensitivity in local skin areas (cutaneous anesthesia or anaphia), and who have no sense of smell (anosmia). There may also be people without a sense of taste, or gustatory sensitivity, and without motor sensitivity, or kinesthesis, although the authors have never heard of them. Such conditions are exceptional in a statistical sense and often constitute medical and psychological curiosities, but they do not pose social problems and therefore are not typically considered in discussions of exceptionality.

motor deviance The third mode of exceptionality is in the motor area. In this group we shall consider the crippled, or orthopedically handicapped, and the speech defectives. While no one will question that the first subgroup are principally motor deviants, many will insist that most speech disorders are functional rather than organic in nature. However, speech defects have their motor aspects, and we shall subsume them under the motor deviants rather than placing them in a class by themselves.

behavioral and personality deviance The fourth area or mode of exceptionality is the general behavioral and personality category. This mode resists definition and delimitation even more than the intellectual, sensory, and motor modes of deviation. We can, of course, conceive of a theoretically normal range of emotional and personality adjustment. This normal range of adjustment grades imperceptibly into the minor personality maladjustments, which in turn pass into the more serious disturbances—the neuroses and the psychoses. The simplest view of the fundamental nature of the personality maladjustments is a quantitative, social-learning conception. Its proponents consider personality deviations to be the end results of the process of social learning. Psychosis and neurosis are thought to be understandable in terms of excessive anxiety, frustrations, conflict, and repression, which are basic processes common to all people. The personally distressing and social handicapping neurotic and psychotic manifestations are considered to be the end results of the many defensive mechanisms which develop as a consequence of the individual's attempts to handle life's stresses. There are, of course, other ways of viewing personality maladjustments. The 1970s and 1980s have witnessed an increasing public concern with problems of mental health and mental illness.

social deviance The social deviant has traditionally been the primary concern of law enforcement agencies. Juvenile delinquents and adult criminals are, by definition, social deviants. However, society has become increasingly aware of the existence of subcultural groups—ethnic minorities and the economically disadvantaged—who, for a variety of reasons, deviate so far from the dominant social norm that they constitute educational and social problems. The bulk of these people live in poverty, and when cross-cultural studies are made of such people the world over, they seem to possess sufficient common characteristics to cause one to wonder if there does not exist a worldwide "culture of poverty."

THE OVERLAPPING OF AREAS OR MODES

The enumeration of discrete categories of exceptional individuals oversimplifies the facts of life. Many, or even most, exceptional people are exceptional in more than one area. Everyone knows of people who are both blind and deaf. Most individuals with cerebral palsy have speech, sensory, or intellectual defects in addition to their motor handicaps, and it is very difficult for an extremely physically, sensorially, or mentally handicapped individual not to become, to some degree, a social or personality deviant. People who are handicapped in one way may also excel in another. The cripple may be a genius or an artist.

In 1977 there were over 10,000 children enrolled in schools and classes for the multiply handicapped in the United States. It is conservatively estimated that 25 percent of all deaf children in the United States have at least one additional disability (Flathouse, 1979).

The problems of the multiply handicapped are not simply additive in nature (the sum of the problems imposed by the individual disabilities) but are synergistic because of the dynamic interaction of the handicaps. This interaction of disabilities results in the appearance of unique developmental and behavioral patterns that cannot be attributed either to single factors or to their additive effects. For example, hearing loss in a mentally retarded child drastically reduces the child's informational input, contributing to further depression and delay in the development of functional cognitive abilities. This, in turn, impairs the use of any residual hearing, thus instituting a debilitating cycle.

Although little consensus exists concerning the numbers of multiply handicapped individuals in the population, there is agreement that this population is increasing rather than decreasing. This increase is generally attributed to improved prenatal care, reduced infant mortality, and the prolongation of the life of children at risk because of their handicaps (Flathouse, 1979).

Obviously, an almost infinite number of possible combinations of abilities and disabilities will be found in a typical population. One of the primary tasks of this book is to indicate the relationships commonly found among the many modes of socially significant deviations. We shall attempt to unravel some of the genetic and organic factors, social determinants, and relationships among these deviations.

It is obvious that there is no consistency in our selection of the particular areas and direction of deviation for consideration. We deal with both the exceptionally bright and the exceptionally dull, but we limit ourselves to the negative deviants, the handicapped, in all the other areas.

Why are we not just as concerned with the child who has *superior* sensory or motor capacities as we are with the child who has a motor or sensory handicap? There are several partial answers to this question. One is that physically superior people do not constitute social problems; they do not cause trouble. We also are not aware of any possible public costs or social losses resulting from our failure to develop and capitalize on the supernormal abilities of these individuals. Perhaps our society is such that it cannot profit significantly from the superior sensory and motor capacities of its citizens. The telescope and the microscope have so extended the limits of human vision that the difference between the average person and the person with the most acute vision is relatively unimportant. It may be that artificial devices—amplifiers of sensory capacities—and the natural adaptability of the sense organs can bring the sensory aptitude of all but a small percentage of people above a certain minimum, and that differences above this level are not socially and economically critical.

In a way, we do recognize and reward motor facility, even though the physically and athletically superior are not usually considered in texts on exceptional children. In college, and to a lesser degree in high school, we hire and pay large salaries to people who follow the athletic records of prospective students, scout their games, and actively recruit, train, and coach them. We award the selected students scholarships purely on the basis of athletic aptitude; we provide special housing, "training tables," tutoring services, and special medical care, to ensure that they will remain in school and will either maintain or increase their athletic prowess. Uniforms, equipment, and accessories are given to them. Athletic teams are provided with special transportation over great distances, so that they can compete with other, similarly subsidized teams. Special post-season games are held in exotic places to provide the teams with vacation trips at public expense. Star performers receive special awards, testimonial dinners, and public acclaim. And the termination of the athlete's collegiate program may be the beginning of a professional career with similar monetary and social rewards.

Without labeling them as such, we do provide very special programs for the physically superior. But such programs are seldom rationalized, like the programs for the intellectually talented, in terms of the "development and utilization of human resources." Intercollegiate athletic programs are considered part of the physical education program, but the principal justifications for such programs are monetary reward, personal and institutional prestige, and entertainment.

Some interest has recently developed in individuals who are above average in terms of personality integration and social adjustment. Mental health is still largely conceived of as an absence of mental illness, but there have been several attempts to define superior social and personal adjustment. There have also been some studies of the antecedents of superior mental health. However, we do not yet have enough relevant information to justify the inclusion of individuals with superior social ability and personality in our discussions of exceptional people. Similarly, we consider the problems of the culturally disadvantaged without giving comparable attention to the culturally advantaged.

THE TREND TOWARD NONCATEGORIZING

Three large-scale movements, now in progress, minimize traditional categories of deviants. One is the deinstitutionalization movement—the transfer of a large percentage of the psychiatric population from institutions to the local community. Another is *mainstreaming*—the return of many school children from their special classes to the regular classrooms. The third movement, which is also involved in the other two, consists of widespread attempts to reduce the deleterious effects of categorizing and labeling deviants. The net effect of these three trends has been a proposal to deal with all deviants noncategorically. While we are in sympathy with this general trend, it does have limitations. We have stressed that all the handicapped, and to a degree all deviants, have much in common. However, some treatment, educational, social, and vocational problems are unique to several of the conventional categories.

Blind persons have unique problems learning to read and becoming independently mobile. The deaf have special problems in learning to speak via the visual, cutaneous, and kinesthetic senses. The limited motor potential of the orthopedically handicapped and the deviant speech of the stutterer pose problems requiring unique approaches.

Many service needs are category-related. This means that categorical specialists are still needed to design, administer, and monitor special instructional, training, and care programs for these persons. Certainly, groupings should be on the basis of the individual's care, training, and educational requirements rather than the conventional medical, psychological, social welfare, and legal categories.

A 1979 survey indicated that the majority of states continue to use the traditional or similar categories in the identification and education of exceptional children. As a result of this survey, these authors conclude that there is no national movement away from the traditional categories; on the contrary, there appears to be an increase in new categories (Garrett and Brazil, 1979).

TERMINOLOGY

There is relatively little standardization of terminology in the field of exceptionality. Only recently terms such as *insane, blind, deaf, crippled,* and *criminal,* as well as the term *feebleminded* and its subdivisions—*moron, imbecile,* and *idiot*—were used to refer to various categories of exceptional individuals. The present tendency is to substitute less stigmatizing, gentler, and less emotionally toned terms for the older ones which have acquired connotations of helplessness and hopelesness.

Mental deficiency was first substituted for *feeblemindedness;* still more recently, *mental retardation* has become the term approved by the American Association on Mental Deficiency (Grossman, 1977). It is recommended that degrees of retardation be indicated by the terms, *mild, moderate, severe,* and *profound.* However, in educational contexts, the term *educable* refers to the level called *mildly retarded* by the American Association, and the educators *trainable* group roughly approximates the *moderately retarded* as defined by the Association. The matter is further complicated because the educators often refer to the educable and the trainable as "mildly" and "severely" retarded, respectively, thus departing from the Association's recommendations.

The National Association for Retarded Citizens refers to the three degrees of retarded as *marginally dependent, semidependent,* and *dependent,* respectively.

The search for less stigmatizing and more appropriate terms continues. For example, the conventional terms have changed from *culturally deprived,* to culturally disadvantaged, to *culturally deviant or culturally different* to *bicultural.*

In the interest of euphoniousness the mentally retarded and the intellectually gifted are sometimes referred to as individuals with low and high levels of cognitive development, respectively.

The development of generic, less stigmatizing categories to replace the older, specific categories of disabilities is reflected in the relatively new designation *developmental disability.* Originally the developmentally disabled populations were specified as the mentally retarded, cerebral palsied, epileptic, and autistic. However, the more recent formulation is noncategorical and functional, emphasizing the severity and chronic nature of the disability and the services needed rather than diagnostic categories. In essence, a developmental disability is defined as a severe, chronic disability, attributable to mental and/or physical impairment, which results in substantial limitations of adaptive behavior in certain designated areas of human activities.

The terminology used for the other categories of the exceptional is not quite so involved. However, it is considered better to speak of the *orthopedically handicapped* than of the *crippled*. Although it is more awkward, the blind are often called the *sightless* or the *visually impaired*. The deaf or the partially deaf have become the *aurally handicapped*. The older terms *lunatic* and *insane* have been replaced by *psychotic* and *personality deviants*, which cover a broad, indefinite spectrum of deviant behavior in the same general area.

Originally, these categories of deviant people were all referred to as *disabled* or *handicapped*. However, when the intellectually superior were included along with the intellectually and physically handicapped, the term *exceptional* was adopted to refer to the entire group. This nonspecific designation, having no connotations of inferiority or inadequacy, is now used to refer to any or all of the deviant categories, although the general public often objects to this usage because the term is often understood in terms of its common dictionary definition as "uncommon; hence, superior." Occasionally, we find the terms *unusual child* or *special child* used in place of *exceptional child*.

While the renaming of old categories partly reflects changing conceptions and greater precision in definition and classification, to a greater extent it reflects our cultural emphasis on the democratic belief that all people are created equal and our attempt to avoid the connotations of inherent inferiority which eventually accrue to the terms applied to groups of people perceived as handicapped. Although labels are necessary for certain purposes, there is a tendency to use them as little as possible because of the stigmas attached to many of them. This is discussed more fully in the following chapter. Paradoxically, the more we learn about exceptional people, the less confident we become about our ability to classify them usefully.

SUMMARY

The study of deviant people is really a study of all humankind. The problem of exceptional people is a part of the larger problem of individual differences in general. Prescientific conceptions of the origins and nature of the more extreme forms of development deviation and behavioral aberration tended to be supernatural and mystical. Later, the handicapped were regarded as separate categories of human beings. Deviants were considered basically different from other people, and their behavior was explained by special theories and concepts distinct from those used to understand the behavior of "normal" people. Current conceptions are quantitative, holding that the differences between the normal and the exceptional are of degree only. The emphasis today is on the large core of normality found in every deviant individual. Understanding handicapped children means first understanding them as children, and only then understanding the ways in which their deviations may influence their development and behavior.

The basic social, psychological, and educational needs of exceptional children are identical with the needs of all children and can be met in much the same general ways. Only the specifics differ. Regardless of category or nature of their handicap, all have the same needs as the nonhandicapped. These include the need to learn and develop one's potential, to accept oneself, to be accepted and have rewarding relationships with others, to acquire self-help and occupational skills, to understand the world in which they live, and to enjoy living to the maximum extent possible.

There are probably few psychological experiences peculiar to exceptional people. The basic motivations for affection, acceptance, and approval exist whether the IQ is 50 or 150, whether the body is beautiful or a caricature, whether the movements are graceful or made awkward and incoordinate by crippling disease or accident, whether speech is melodious or guttural. These exceptional children, like any others, can be comfortable and secure when they feel that they are accepted, appreciated, and liked. They will be equally uneasy and insecure when they are rejected and depreciated. Disability increases the probability of occurrence of certain frustrations and conflicts for the disabled, but these experiences are not unique to disabled persons. They simply experience them more often than do their nondisabled peers.

Strengths and weaknesses are found in varying degrees in all categories of people, the advantaged as well as the disadvantaged, the normal and the abnormal, the deviant and the nondeviant, and in all ethnic groups.

Deviations are conceived of as having several aspects: area (sensory, motor, intellectual, emotional, social); intensity (degree of the deviation, from mild to severe); and extensity (the range of behavior that is affected). The visibility or obviousness of a deviation also influences its personal and social significance.

REFERENCES

Flathouse, V.F., "Multiply Handicapped Deaf Children and Public Law 94-14,"*Exceptional Children*, 1979, *45*, 560–65.

Garrett, J. E. and N. Brazil., "Categories Used for Identification and Education of Exceptional Children," *Exceptional Children*, 1979, *45*, 291–92.

Grossman, H. J., ed., *Manual on Terminology and Classification in Mental Retardation* (Washington, D.C.: American Association on Mental Retardation, 1977).

Montour, K., "William James Sidis, The Broken Twig," *American Psychologist*, 1977, *32*, 265–79.

Packe, M. St. J., *The Life of John Stuart Mill* (New York: Macmillan, 1954).

Rusk, W. L., "Journey Out of Silence," *The Exceptional Parent*, Oct. 1978, *8*(5), 17–18.

SUGGESTIONS FOR STUDENTS AND INSTRUCTORS

1. Discuss the validity and significance of the distinction between a "disability" and a "handicap."

2. Defend the proposition: "When quantitative differences between people become sufficiently extreme they really become qualitative ones."

3. Cite instances of handicaps that are particularly relative to their social or cultural contexts.

ADDITIONAL READINGS

McNamara, J. and B. McNamara, *The Special Child Handbook* (New York: Hawthorn Books, Inc., 1977). A wealth of information concerning all types of exceptional children.

Landau, E. D., S. L. Epstein, and A. P. Stone, eds., *The Exceptional Child Through Literature* (Englewood Cliffs, N. J.: Prentice-Hall, 1978). Seventeen well-chosen stories portraying the personal side of persons with major disabilities and of the gifted.

SELECTED FILMS

The Exceptional Child. (60 minutes) (B & W) Time-Life Films, 43 W. 16th St. New York, N.Y. Depicts the diverse types of exceptional children.

A Matter of Convenience. (15 minutes) The Stanfield House, 900 Euclid, Santa Monica, Calif., 90035. Young blind skiers and amputees demonstrate and discuss the difference between a disability and a handicap.

Faces of Courage. (18 minutes) The Minnesota Society for Crippled Children and Adults, 3915 Valley Road, Golden Valley, Minn., 55422. Four handicapped individuals discuss their feelings about their handicaps.

ORGANIZATIONS AND AGENCIES

American Coalitions of Citizens with Disabilities
1224 Dupont Circle Bldg., Room 308
Washington, D. C. 20036

Bureau of Education for the Handicapped
Office of Education
Department of Health, Education, and Welfare
400 Maryland Avenue, S.W.
Washington D. C. 20202

Closer Look
National Information Center for the Handicapped
1201 Sixteenth Street, NW
Washington, D. C. 20037

The Council for Exceptional Children
1920 Association Drive
Reston, Va. 22091

Directory of Organizations Interested in the Handicapped
Committee for the Handicapped
1028 Connecticut Avenue
Washington, D. C. 20036

(A detailed list of 107 organizations and the names and addresses of many more. Single copies are free.)

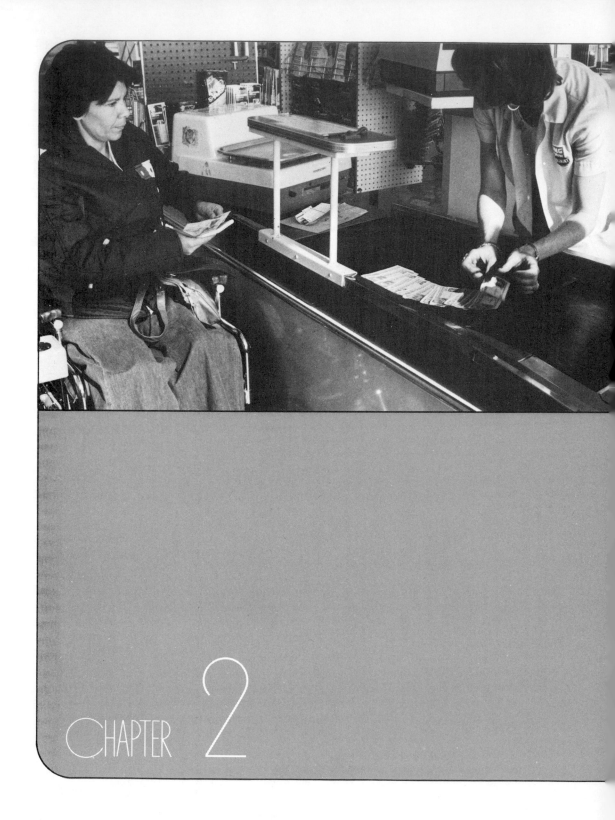

CHAPTER 2

EXCEPTIONALITY AND STIGMATIZATION

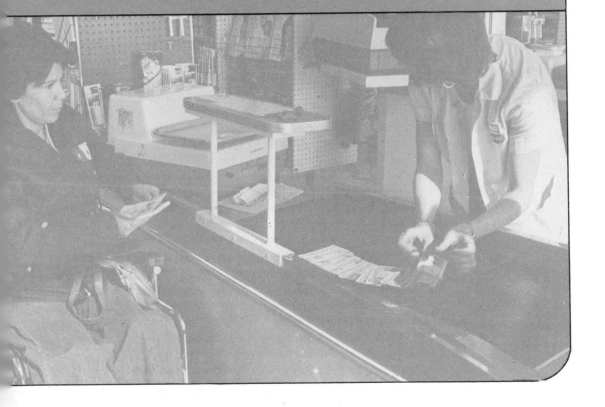

Historical changes in our ways of conceptualizing mental and behavioral exceptionality support the general proposition that the way a problem is perceived and defined largely determines what is or is not done about it. Conversely, what is done about a personal or social problem assumes a certain conceptual framework concerning its origins and causes. When mental defects were considered to be the result of demonological possession, their treatment was the province of the clergy—the priests and priestesses. Treatment was designed to drive evil spirits from the body.

Within a moralistic framework mental and behavioral disabilities were perceived as moral defects. They were punishments for sins, either one's own or one's parents'. Treatment consisted of preachments and exhortations encouraging the afflicted individual to "strengthen the will," "overcome the unnatural passions," or "get rid of evil thoughts."

The supernatural and moralistic concepts of mental exceptionality were gradually replaced by what has come to be known as the *medical model*. According to this concept behavioral, ideational, and emotional disabilities were perceived as *illnesses* to be dealt with in the same way as the conventional physical disorders.

Disease is considered something within the person and treatment is directed at diagnosing the ailment and applying the appropriate treatment. The aim of clinical or educational intervention is to change the person for the better by medical, educational, or psychotherapeutic intervention (Abrams and Kodera, 1978). The clinically oriented medical and educational concepts are often referred to as *person-centered* in contrast to the psychologically derived *social-learning* and the more sociological *conspiratorial-labeling* concepts which are perceived as *situation-oriented*.

People sponsoring the social-learning concept of exceptionality believe that the most disadvantaged exceptional individuals have failed adequately to "solve the problems of living." They experience "developmental disabilities" rather than personal defects. The inadequate behaviors of people labeled handicapped are learned, maintained, and altered by precisely the same processes as those involved in the more "normal" adjustment patterns. According to the social-learning theorists, if all people can be provided with appropriate learning opportunities, living conditions, and vocational opportunities, their handicaps will largely disappear.

The conspiratorial-labeling concept perceives disadvantaged exceptional people as the victims of a corrupt or "sick" society. Labels are attached to troublesome categories of people to justify segregating, institutionalizing, and dehumanizing them under the guise of treatment. Troublesome individuals are assigned to socially useful stigmatized categories and are then classed as incompetents because of their "illnesses." The illness-incompetence label evokes the appropriate expectancies and behavior by teachers and students, attendants and "patients." This closes the cycle of the self-fulfilling prophecy. According to the conspiratorial concept, we should stop blaming the victim—the disadvantaged exceptional person—and concentrate on the reformation of society, the true culprit (Sagarin, 1976).

Most people today recognize that none of these extreme positions is acceptable. The fundamental but infinitely complex task is to unravel and understand the interactive outcomes of the physical and social environmental circumstances of the individual's life and the conditions and potentialities of the person. We treat this problem more fully in a later chapter. In this chapter we are concerned primarily with the problem of categorizing, labeling, stigmatizing, and the self-fulfilling prophecy.

REACTIONS TO EXCEPTIONALITY

Over the past three decades a long series of experiments has shown that people who perceive themselves as markedly different from the norm of their reference group become concerned about their differentness (Asch, 1952; Freedman and Doob, 1968; Maslach, 1974). For example, when normal subjects are consistently fed fictitious information indicating that their performances are markedly different from the norm of their reference group, they begin to feel and act like truly exceptional individuals. Furthermore, even though the evidence indicates only that their performances differ from the norm, with no clues whatever as to whether their performances are relatively high or low, good or bad, desirable or undesirable, the subjects act consistently as though their deviant performances are undesirable and stigmatizing.

For example, in experimental situations, subjects made to feel deviant preferred associating with other deviants more than did nondeviants. Their preference for other deviants held true even when the other deviants were unlike themselves. Persons made to feel deviant but whose deviancy was unknown to others minimized social contacts and avoided being conspicuous in situations where their deviancy might become obvious. Deviants were found to be treated better by similar deviants than they were by nondeviants. Deviancy was found to be an important determinant of how a person is treated. In experimental situations where subjects were given free choice of subjects upon whom to bestow rewards or punishments, nondeviants chose known deviants more often for punishment than for reward, while deviants chose other deviants more often for reward than for punishment. The findings indicate that the deviant subject is strongly concerned about minimizing the deviancy and behaves in ways that will produce this effect. In studies of social influence, these same researchers found that the deviant is excessively concerned about possible mistreatment and is therefore reluctant to expose his or her differentness publicly. The more intimate and threatening the situation, the greater this reluctance becomes.

These studies represent the laboratory counterparts of the formation of clubs, social groups, and subcultures by various deviant groups such as the blind, deaf, homosexuals, and drug addicts as well as by many minority ethnic, religious, and political groups. Some of these will be described and discussed in later chapters.

The experimental evidence, as well as anecdotal evidence and self-observation, all indicate that individuals who are markedly exceptional in physique, behavior, or beliefs are subject to a variety of internal and external pressures to reduce the extent or perceptibility of their differentness. Feelings of exceptionality have important effects on the individual's behavior independent of the dimension of deviancy or the social evaluation of the differentness. Everyone who feels deviant is to some extent affected in similar ways and is motivated to behave in similar ways. Although most people prefer not to be exactly the same as the norm of their reference groups, they also prefer not to be too different. Exactly where individuality turns into anxiety-arousing deviancy varies tremendously for different people, circumstances, and dimensions. However, at some point most people begin to be concerned about their deviancy.

In addition to exceptionality as such, each dimension or category of deviancy carries with it an assortment of social and personal meanings and values. While each category and degree of differentness can be considered to be either positive or negative in value, it seems necessary to assume that, on balance, deviation is considered dominantly negative. This seems to follow from the experimental findings, already reported, in which statistically "normal" subjects who were fed information which made them believe that they were deviant, with no specification of the personal or social significance of their differentness, behaved in the same way as do people who are deviant in personally and socially devalued ways. Thus it seems from anecdotal evidence, research studies, and introspection that deviancy itself causes people to be concerned about possible diminished social acceptance, personal devaluation, or actual mistreatment because of their deviancy.

Except in the controlled conditions of the laboratory, significant deviancy involves social evaluations and consequences of a negative or positive sort, self-judgments of a similar type, and sometimes institutionalized and legalized sanctions, prohibitions, and punishments.

It is clear that extreme deviancy is a matter of concern both to the deviant and to others. A common core of attitudes and expectancies with reference to the handicapped as a group seems to cut across all categories of the disabled.

However, there are some unique components associated with the various types of exceptionalities as well as differences in the relative strength of the attitudes and beliefs. Parish, Dyck, and Koppes (1979) found that the gifted, normal, and physically handicapped categories of individuals were more positively evaluated than were the mentally retarded, learning disabled, and emotionally disturbed. The preceding categories are listed in the order of increasing negativity of evaluation.

Probably this status hierarchy of disabilities is what makes people prefer one label to another. For example, sophisticated parents may seek centers or diagnosticians more likely to give a preferred diagnosis or label. Of course, in addition to preferring a "higher status" diagnosis, parents may find one diagnosis or label more acceptable than another because it implies hope of improvement or because it suggests that they are not to blame. Thus, a diagnosis of "minimal brain injury incurred at birth" is preferable to "mental retardation of unknown etiology" because the former is physical rather than mental, it relieves the parent of blame, and it provides an apparently simple explanation of the child's behavioral deficiencies.

Since all the categories of exceptional people considered in this book, except the gifted and the creative, are handicapped and hence negatively valued, the rest of this chapter will be devoted to the psychological and behavioral consequences of stigmatizing exceptionality.

VARIABLES CONTRIBUTING TO TOTAL DEVIANCE

Three factors that account for the total effects of organic or behavioral deviance can be distinguished. First, there are first-order effects, limits imposed by the inherent nature of the deviation. Midgets, the orthopedically handicapped, the blind, the deaf, and the albino are organic deviants who have certain limitations imposed by the very nature of their deviance. Their behavioral repertoires remain limited in certain ways, irrespective of social attitudes and expectations or their self-evaluations. The second factor (a second-order effect that influences the deviant's behavior) is society's evaluations of and expectations for such individuals and the extent to which society has deviced and made available to such people alternative ways of behaving to compensate for the means closed to them by the nature of their deviance. The individual's total handicap may be diminished or increased by these social factors. The third factor (another second-order effect contributing to the deviant person's total handicap) is the individual's self-evaluation and expectations. If, as many people believe, people's self-concepts are formed largely from a distillation of other people's evaluations of them, the second and third factors are intimately related.

Ever since Walter Lippman (1922) popularized the concept over a half century ago, social stereotyping has been dominantly perceived as arbitrary and deleterious in its effects. However, it seems clear that classifying, categorizing, and stereotyping are inevitable components of cognitive development. Stereotyping is closely related to the development of perceptual and conceptual categories and to the psychology of predictions. A major component of cognitive development consists in abstracting characteristics and rules and grouping experiences into useful classes and categories (Rosch and Lloyd, 1978).

Young children learn the differences between men and women, adults and children, tall and short people, thin and fat people, black and white people, doctors and lawyers, and so forth in a never-ending series of classes and subclasses depending upon the society's cultural demands, the child's personal needs, and the level of cognitive development. The evolution of a wide variety of abstract rules as well as perceptual and conceptual categories is a fundamental and universal learning experience.

Some categories of experience involve relatively invariable distinguishing characteristics. Some of these are number concepts and numerical calculations, as well as many scientifically defined categories (inanimate vs. animate things, plants and animals, horses and cows). However, many social concepts and categories are not strictly defined and are based on probabilities or general trends (honesty as related to social class, general competence as related to physical size, personality characteristics as related to sex and race).

Categorizing and classifying are ways in which people handle the infinite complexities of their worlds. Our senses take in much more raw information than the human processing system can handle. Given people's limited capacity for decoding and assimilating incoming information, cues are attended to selectively, perceived, and acted upon in terms of the individual's previous experiences with persons or things having the same or similar characteristics. Sensory input is assimilated selectively into the person's existing repertoire of categories, or *schema*. The existing schema (organized meanings and behavioral expectancies) contribute to the coherent and systematic selection of the most relevant component of the available information and make it comprehensible and manageable. If we continued through life experiencing the world as it actually is, our perceptual universe would forever remain infinitely complex and constantly changing. Since no two things are exactly alike and no one thing is ever twice the same, a photographically sensed world would remain in a state of constant flux. Without some ordering and classifying it would remain, in a sense, totally unknowable (Tsujimoto, Wilde, and Robertson, 1978).

It is obvious that information, as well as beliefs, attitudes, and expectations, does not arise spontaneously. Perceptual and conceptual categories and behavioral expectations are developed, verified, and modified in at least four overlapping ways (Bandura, 1978). The first and most obvious way is by direct observation of the consequencies of one's own acts, including feedback from other people. For example, mother, sister, nurse, and baby sitter all provide warm, nurturant care while father, brothers, and other males seldom do so; thus one concludes that females are solicitous of others' welfare while males are not.

Second, information concerning perceptual and conceptual categories is extracted from vicarious experience. We observe the behavior of others and draw inferences from observing the effects of their actions. We see others avoiding contact with the crippled, blind, deaf, and the mentally retarded and we behave similarly on the assumption that such individuals are undesirable or inappropriate associates.

Third, when we read, hear others express opinions, and see movies portraying certain groups in stereotyped ways (women as warm, nurturant, and dependent and men as autonomous and independent; blacks as menial and subservient and whites as dominant and upper class) we classify these groups in conceptual categories.

Thus, children develop definite conceptions of classes of people or ethnic groups different from their own. Even without direct contact with members of certain ethnic, religious, or social categories, children form definite mental images in terms of which they act.

Fourth, in addition to direct personal experiences, the observation of others, and other social sources of information, people also draw logical inferences concerning individuals and groups which extend beyond their firsthand or vicarious experiences. For example, when we find that certain groups of people who are socially devalued are also deviant in color or physique from the more highly valued groups, we infer that other groups of people who are deviant in similar ways are also to be devalued (all dark-colored versus light-colored people).

As the result of perceived regularities in behavior or characteristics, as well as in the other ways indicated, we develop categories and behavioral expectancies. We then relegate newly perceived persons or things to these categories. We then "know" the newly perceived person or thing in terms of the characteristics that define the relevant category (small, mature, white, Jewish, physician—father). In this way we make our world—particularly our social world—more stable, more predictable, and more manageable.

When individuals are assigned to a certain category we attribute to them the presumably stable and enduring dispositions and characteristics defining that class of people. We then feel able to understand them and predict their future behavior without having to know each on an individual basis. We also use these beliefs and expectations to guide our interactions with these people.

SOME VALUE COMPONENTS

An additional component of each person's development consists in generalizing ideas as to what "ought to be"—what the person would like to be (the ideal person), as well as "what is"—what kind of a person he or she is (self-concept). Because they develop so gradually and largely without the person's awareness, it is easy to infer that these concepts about human nature, both ideal and real, are enduring aspects of human life—some sort of psychological universals. However, it seems clear that these concepts actually are historically derived and culturally determined. The extent to which current and/or recommended practices assume these values as self-evident verities is also difficult to realize. Value judgments also apply to human categories. Categories of people are not only cognitively defined groupings; they also come to have values and feelings associated with them. Classes of people and the characteristics they display or have assigned to them come to be perceived as good or bad, desirable or undesirable. Thus handicaps and disabilities may come to be "bad" while normality is "good." In the past, and to some degree today, people have viewed physical and mental disabilities as evidence of some obscure moral defect. The assumed relationship between virtue and happiness, on the one hand, and between wickedness and punishment, on the other, is so strong that when the second condition is present the first is assumed.

A wide variety of psychological processes is involved in stabilizing, maintaining the predictability, and reducing the complexity of our perceptual worlds. These same processes support and sustain the stigmatized categories with which we are particularly concerned. For example: (1) We selectively attend to, perceive, assimilate, retain, and recall information consistent with our already existing beliefs. Thus our perception of a particular person tends to be distorted in the direction of greater conformity to existing categories and stereotypes. (2) We interact with others in ways that favor confirmation of our expectancies. We ask questions that search preferentially for evidence that the category to which we have assigned the individual is appropriate. Our biased interactions, in turn, tend to constrain the behavior of the other person in ways that provide stereotype-confirming evidence (Tsujimoto, 1978). (3) Stereotype-confirming instances have greater impact than do disconfirming instances. Consequently, we overestimate the number of ways in which a given person conforms to our expectancies (Snyder, Tanke, and Bercheid, 1977). (4) In judging similarities we look for common rather than distinctive features and characteristics. This emphasis on similar rather than distinguishing characteristics favors the perpetuation of social stereotypes (Snyder and Swann, 1978). (5) When people's acts are grossly inconsistent with the category to which we have assigned them, a review of our perceptions and past interactions with them may result in our reinterpreting these observations in ways which are more consistent with the category.

For example, on learning that a friend is a homosexual, we selectively recall and reinterpret past events and interactions in ways consistent with our stereotype of gay individuals. The person's past is selectively rewritten and reconstructed to support our new categorization and expectations. Thus perceptual categories and stereotypes influence information processing, current as well as past, in ways consistent with and supportive of present beliefs and expectancies. Retrospective recall and reinterpretation help maintain the stereotype and also support the conviction that the person was really acting this way all the time. And so, in the interests of preserving a stable and predictable social world, we create and perpetuate stereotypes of people that lead to erroneous as well as correct inferences and expectations about others.

Thus, when "normal" people believe that the mentally ill, orthopedically handicapped, blind, deaf, and mentally retarded are helpless and incapable of learning to support themselves, treatment of these people may fail to provide opportunities for acquiring and exercising competencies that would enable them to become independent. In this way stereotypic beliefs may be self-actualizing and contain the germ of the self-fulfilling prophecy. (6) The categorization of persons into distinct groups is sufficient to produce an in-group versus an out-group relationship. When this occurs we tend to ascribe a greater overall similarity between ourselves and the in group (normals) as compared with the out group (handicapped). We also are more attracted to members of the in group (Wilder, 1978). Out-group stereotypes are generally less favorable than are in-group stereotypes. Even the same traits may be evaluated positively for the in group and negatively for the out group (loyalty versus clannishness). The attribution processes operate to the advantage of the in group. For example, when an in-group member acts in a positive way, a positive, enduring personal trait is postulated to explain the behavior (helping someone in need is attributed to altruism). However, when an out-group member acts in a similar way, the behavior is dismissed as resulting from environmental circumstances (helping another is attributed to social pressures). Negative behaviors are likely to be interpreted in opposite ways for in and out groups (Stephan, 1977).

When we insist that categories and prejudices are the outcome of "normal" perceptual-cognitive processes we are not saying that they have no deleterious effects. They undoubtedly do. Most people subscribe to the principle that people should be judged as individuals rather than in terms of color, race, sex, age, or religion—all group designations. However, categorizing leads us to treat individuals in terms of the real or assumed norm of a group rather than in terms of their unique characteristics as individuals. Stereotypes function as guides to action as well as channels for the evoking and expression of affect. The process of inferring the characteristics of an individual from the presumed characteristics of the group perpetuates the vicious cycle of stereotyping. Traits are attributed to the individual because of group membership and our belief in the stereotype is strengthened because we have found another person with the stereotypical characteristics.

Because of the universality of categorizing and labeling and their association with stigmatization, these processes have been claimed to be the primary roots of the denigration and social rejection of the handicapped. Labeling is often used interchangeably with stigmatization—the assigning of negative traits to people. It is often used to account for the inappropriate assigning of people to segregated, low-status facilities or special classes. In addition, as a result of the inevitable labeling and stigmatizing involved, agencies such as special schools and classes, residential institutions, and prisons, designed to treat, rehabilitate, and reduce the disadvantage of the individuals concerned, have been charged with direct responsibility for either creating or increasing the deviancies they were designed to remedy.

The notion that labeling is the root of the stigmatization and rejection of the handicapped has been extrapolated from and finds its principal support from the socio-psychological study of criminal behavior. Within the criminal justice system, behavioral deviance is law-breaking. Society defines criminally deviant behavior by establishing laws and rules, the breaking of which constitutes criminal behavior.

Although the primary criminal deviance is law-breaking itself, society's perception and labeling of violators and their subsequent treatment often result in the violator continuing a criminal career appropriate to the label. Criminals tend to behave in accordance with their new social role, leading to further deviance and stigmatization. The criminal career is perceived largely as a function of labeling, stigmatization, and differential treatment with their accompanying social and self-expectations.

From the sociological consideration of law-breaking, the concern with labels has spread to disfavored or disadvantaged categories of individuals such as the psychotic, the mentally retarded, and the physically disabled. Interest in labeling has focused on the ways in which society develops and manifests its expectations, and behaviors which arise and are maintained, once the deviant person is identified and labeled. These expectations and modified behaviors induce secondary deviance which is considered to overshadow the primary norm violations.

The psychotic, mentally retarded, orthopedically handicapped, the blind, and the deaf do violate social expectations of "normal" behavior. They are devalued as "handicapped" and this may encourage them to assume and play a dependent or "sick" role. They also elicit a wide variety of deviant expectations and reactions in other people. However, the extent of the secondary deviances induced by legally or educationally defined handicaps is often quite different from those induced by the criminalization of such activities as homosexuality, prostitution, and drug addiction.

Despite some claims to the contrary, identification and official labeling of individuals as mentally retarded or psychotic does not lead to the stigmatizing effects of deviancy to the degree that it does in behavior labeled "criminal." Identification, social isolation, rejection, and unofficial labeling are found in situations and circumstances where labels per se can hardly be a factor that directly influences the situation.

UNOFFICIAL LABELING AND STIGMATIZATION

As we have stated, the development of perceptual and conceptual categories of people is inevitable. Related to this is the attachment of evaluative judgments and feelings to these categories. Words used to describe, identify, categorize, and label a person inevitably carry evaluative connotations as well as denotative meanings. Relatively affectively neutral words such as *unemployed, poor,* and *obese,* while primarily descriptive of a person's condition, also have value connotation (good or bad, desirable or undesirable). The stigmatization of socially devalued individuals and/or acts is impossible to avoid. The facts of socially devalued deviancy are apparent to all sharing these underlying values and do not depend upon official labeling. Three incidents in the life of one of the authors (C. W. T.) are pertinent to this observation.

The "village idiots" were well known to all the residents of the small community (population 500) where he was reared. Three members of one family were generally recognized as belonging to this category. This was not because of the low status of the entire family, for the parents and two other siblings were recognized as quite normal. The three mentally deficient children were never officially identified or labeled in any way, but this did not prevent their unofficial labeling. Another individual in the same community, less severely deficient, was also the victim of unofficial labeling. On one occasion, several young men were considering some venture and the village wag started to count the members present: 1, 2, 3, 3½—the ½ was the village "half-wit," a mildly mentally retarded individual. Everyone laughed at the characterization, which was funny, but also very cruel! The fact of the boy's stigmatized deviancy was apparent to all in the community.

The third incident occurred when the writer was taking a course in mental testing during the early years of the testing movement. One course requirement was the administration of twenty-five individual Binets and one group test. Rewarding the first child with five cents for taking the Binet resulted in an ample supply of volunteers for the individual test. However, gaining access to an appropriate group was not so easy. After several turn-downs, the writer obtained permission from the principal of the local high school to test a group. On reporting to his office, the writer was referred to an unoccupied classroom where individuals to be tested would assemble. The hour proved to be the general convocation period, and the principal was sending designated children to the room one at a time. As they strolled in, they looked around inquiringly and asked why they had been sent. They were told to take seats and when they were all there, an explanation would be given. The early comers kept up an active conversation as to what it all meant. Finally, when about half the group was assembled, one of the first boys to enter the room said, "Oh, I know, we are all the dumbbells!" He was right and the others agreed. The principal had picked out the "slow learners" to be tested. None had been given mental tests and they were not segregated or otherwise officially designated or labeled. However, they were self-labeled, and also categorized by their peers.

Unofficial labeling precedes the corresponding official process and mediates many of the same effects. Judging from the available evidence, recent attempts to eliminate the stigma of special-class placement in school have not been particularly successful. Almost without exception, the studies that originated with G. O. Johnson in 1950 and have continued down to the present (Jones, 1977) have shown: (1) that intelligence-test-defined mentally retarded children in regular classes are uniformly informally labeled and sociometrically either isolated or actively rejected by their peers; (2) that the physically integrated mentally retarded school children are not more socially accepted by their peers than are comparable segregated mental retardates; and (3) that retarded children in the new "open" ungraded classroom situation are rejected as often, and in one study (Gottlieb and Budoff, 1973) more often, than are comparable children in an integrated regular "walled-in" single-grade classroom. J. Gottlieb and M. Budoff found that the mentally retarded children in both these integrated-classroom situations were more rejected by peers than were segregated mildly mentally retarded children.

It has also been found that simply de-labeling educable mentally retarded children and integrating them within the mainstream of a newly opened elementary school where the children and teachers were unaware of their previous segregation did not alter their negative behavior patterns, their self-perceptions, nor their peers' negative judgments (Gampel, Gottlieb, and Harrison, 1974).

In another study, children expressed a more favorable attitude toward a competent than an incompetent child. Paradoxically, however, an academically incompetent child who was not labeled as retarded evoked negative attitudes, especially from boys, whereas an equally incompetent child who was labeled retarded evoked positive attitudes. The mentally retarded child who reacted competently was responded to in the same way as a nonlabeled or "normal" child. Children are more tolerant and accepting of incompetent behavior from a peer who is not expected to perform well (mentally retarded) than from a child for whom there is no obvious explanation for poor performance. For this reason, integrated, unlabeled mentally retarded children evoke more negative reactions from their nonretarded classmates than do comparably retarded segregated (labeled) children. The label provides a basis for an understanding and acceptance of the incompetent children which does not apply to the non-labeled. The nonretarded respond differently to the deviant child when they can account for the deviance in some way—as with a label (Budoff and Siperstein, 1978).

The research evidence of the prepsychotic or prelabeled status of the mentally ill is less satisfactory than is that concerning the mentally re-tarded. However, available evidence indicates that mentally ill persons are not solely the prisoners of the stereotype and the social policies and prac-tices resulting from their being labeled, as some people have contended. The "myth" of mental illness has often been presented as a modern in-vention. However, the conditions encompassed by this term have appar-ently been found in every society known to us. The major categories of mental illness are known in all cultures, although the terms applied to them and the theories concerning them differ sharply from our own. Western psychiatrists, native healers, and medicine men alike identify a person with overt psychotic symptoms as abnormal. Mental disorders are identified even when the language has no distinctive label for the cate-gory. The signs and symptoms of mental deterioration and derangement are recognized in practically all societies. The absence of formal diagnosis and labeling does not abolish the behavior or category. What does differ cross-culturally are conceptions concerning etiology and differences in so-cial management.

In many societies, the patient's immediate or extended family or the local community of neighbors assumes the responsibility for the affected individual's care and protection. J. W. Eaton and R. J. Weil (1955) lived in and studied the incidence of mental illness and mental retardation in a relatively isolated and closely knit community of Hutterites. It was be-lieved that mental disorders were practically nonexistent in such com-munities. However, Eaton and Weil found people displaying all the symptoms of mental disorders and mental retardation. What did differ from the larger surrounding culture was that such individuals were en-couraged to participate in the normal life of the Hutterite community as much as possible, and the entire community assumed responsibility for their care and protection. The deviant individuals were known by all the people in the community, and their limitations were accepted without their being labeled or rejected. Only rarely did they become residents of a state hospital and consequently statistics. The favorable mental health record of the Hutterites was the result not of the absence of potential "patients," but rather of the unique communitywide attitudes and ways of handling the problem.

THE SELF-FULFILLING PROPHECY

We have already indicated that perceiving individuals in terms of categories always contains the germs of the self-fulfilling prophecy, the basic idea of which is that our perception of a situation may change the situation to fit our perception. One of the most blatant examples of this mechanism is the situation of blacks in America. In perspective, it is clear that as the result of unique historical conditions, slavery in America took the form of chattel slavery and assigned blacks to an inferior category of humanity. Although official slavery has been abolished, the assumptions and attitudes that it nurtured and the prejudices, expectations, and discriminatory practices that it produced have persisted. For example, since blacks "are" intellectually inferior, and poorly motivated, it is a waste of money to try to educate them in the same way as whites. So blacks have been provided with less financial support for their schools and poorly trained teachers who shared the low expectations of the culture. Sure enough, blacks' achievements proved to be below those of whites. The belief resulted in the condition, and the condition perpetuated the belief.

The primary message of the women's liberation movement in America is that women, like blacks, have been the victims of culturewide stereotyping which has functioned as a self-fulfilling prophecy. The historical origins of the current cultural stereotypes of "woman's role" and "masculine behavior" are not so well known as the sources of our attitudes toward blacks. Perhaps they are so remote in time, so diffuse and varied in their sources, and so pervasive in the culture that the recognition of their existence and the identification of their roots become very difficult.

It seems clear that American society, which places a high value on competence and achievement, provides greater rewards for the "male" characteristics of independence and mastery than it does for the "female" characteristics of dependency and submissiveness. Consequently, females can receive positive social reinforcement either by adopting male characteristics, such as competence and independence, or by fitting into the more stereotyped role that society has structured for women. For the male, only the conventional male role provides consistent positive reinforcement.

The culturally perpetuated expectancy concerning the sexes is internalized in early childhood, becomes a component of one's self-concept, and powerfully conditions each individual's aspirations and expectations. To accept both the black–white and the male–female stereotypes, one must be reared in a society in which the differences postulated by these stereotypes are components of a self-evident system of beliefs.

The self-fulfilling prophecy (expectancy effect) has been invoked to explain the disappointing performances of children in special compensatory education programs and the limited success of many other special education programs. It has been used by frustrated spokespersons for the socially disadvantaged because it shifted the blame from the handicapped individual and the social planner to the teacher, the schools, and society.

However, it remained for the widespread publicity given to R. Rosenthal and L. Jacobsen's *Pygmalion in the Classroom* (1968) to bring the concept of the self-fulfilling prophecy out of the realm of academics and into real life. As a result of this study, most research on the topic has focused on learning in the classroom. Rosenthal and Jacobsen claimed that providing teachers with fictitious information purporting to indicate which of their students had much greater potential than they were using, which would probably be late bloomers, and which would show considerable improvement during the school year produced the reality. The results of the study were alleged to show that the high expectations and supposedly different treatment provided designated students resulted in their making significantly greater improvement than comparable children not so designated. This study has been widely quoted and all sorts of inferences drawn from it, many of which, while containing some elements of truth, resulted in some far-reaching but unwarranted conclusions.

One result of this study was to overemphasize the behavioral effects of official labeling and stigmatization. The study seemed to say that children in general do poorly because teachers expect them to do so. The mentally retarded function as they do because test scores reinforce the teachers' expectations of low achievement and help rationalize the minimal efforts exerted in their behalf. The children succumb to these expectations, cease trying, and thus close the circle to make the expectation become the reality. If we would stop testing, assigning low IQs to, stigmatizing, and then segregating these children into special classes, and would instead anticipate high achievement from them, they would respond to these high expectations.

Because of the great significance of Rosenthal and Jacobsen's results, were they to prove genuine and amenable to generalization, repeated attempts were made to replicate the study, largely without success. Subsequent studies have shown that most teachers are able to identify children with inappropriately assigned, inflated test scores and high predictions of probable achievement. Living with these children day to day, with constant evaluative input, they receive information that completely overshadows the results of a faulty test-derived evaluation. An externally imposed expectation is readily canceled when it contradicts the continual flow of information relative to the student's potential and achievement. J. B. Dusek (1975) made a comprehensive survey of the published studies in which teachers either were told that certain identified students should do well and significantly improve academically, or were given specific false test scores or trait assignments, to determine the degree to which this information would bias teachers' judgments and/or influence the students' performances. After a critical examination of the available evidence, Dusek concluded that the research evidence offers little or no support for these propositions.

A good deal of evidence indicates, however, that teachers, like all others, do categorize and stereotype children on the basis of culturewide attitudes and expectations. Some of these category-related attitudes and expectations involve such variables as sex, social class, race, and ethnic group. Culturewide stereotypes and social expectations can become self-fulfilling prophecies, particularly when they are inculcated early in life and receive widespread support from society. Studies of the various factors operative in assigning children to special education classes have brought to light several of these stereotyping expectations.

Not all teacher-student expectations constitute handicapping stereotypes. Dusek (1975) surveyed the relevant literature and found that teachers' self-generated expectations are positively related to student achievement. On further inquiry, he found that teachers' expectations often resulted in different treatment of students, reflecting the teachers' perception of the most effective ways of teaching children with differing aptitudes and needs, rather than prejudicial stereotyping. Teacher expectations may be beneficial when they lead to different treatment designed to meet the child's individual needs and characteristics.

For example, informing a teacher that a given child is mentally retarded may evoke several alternative expectancies, such as:

1. The child cannot learn; therefore, the only thing to do is to baby sit and keep the child out of mischief and reasonably happy.

2. The child will learn slowly but will master appropriate material if it is presented more slowly, repeated more often, and richly illustrated.

3. The child will have difficulty in mastering much conventional academic material and will need a supportive environment to prevent frustration and discouragement.

4. This child will learn in essentially the same way as "normal" children if material is selected and presented in ways that are appropriate to his or her level of competence.

Only the first of these expectations is negative and fits the Rosenthal and Jacobsen claims. The other three assumptions and expectations all deal with the most effective way to teach a child with low scholastic aptitude. In each, it is assumed that appropriate expectations will lead to superior learning (Guskin, 1978).

Children placed in special or homogeneous classes are presumably segregated for their own good. These specialized, high-cost programs are designed to provide for the unique educational needs of exceptional children so as to reduce the extent of their handicap and make it possible for them more nearly to realize their potential. Most people concerned with selecting children and certifying their eligibility for placement in special facilities, programs, and sections are reasonably competent, well-intentioned people, sincerely interested in providing exceptional children with the best possible education. In practice, however, many informal and unacknowledged selective factors operate in the actual placement of children in special education classes. Children certified as eligible by committees who screen candidates for special-class or special-school placement almost universally are initially referred by teachers. Children referred as possibly mentally retarded, educationally handicapped, neurologically impaired, or emotionally disturbed are so nominated for a variety of reasons. For example, a child technically within one of these categories has an increased probability of being referred for possible removal from the regular class if, in addition to his primary disability, he is also male rather than female, lower- rather than middle- or upper-class, black rather than white, and hyperactive or delinquent rather than docile and well-behaved. Practically every school system has more equally handicapped children in regular classes, with no special provision for their education, then in special classes and/or schools. The likelihood of a child's being transferred back into a regular class from the special class or school decreases as the child's number of socially devalued characteristics increases.

It will be unfortunate if the discrediting of the data and claims of the Rosenthal and Jacobsen study leads to the wholesale discarding of a concept that has considerable validity and usefulness in a broader social context. Experimental evidence as well as general observation indicates that one barrier to achievement is lack of motivation, and one component of achievement motivation is expectation of success. A person does not try unless he believes that he has a reasonable prospect of success. Teachers must have confidence in their students. Certainly teachers who believe that their students cannot learn, do not wish to learn, and have unconcerned parents are poor teachers. Similarly, the child who, for whatever reason, is convinced that he or she cannot learn or that it is not worthwhile to try must somehow have these expectations modified as a necessary prerequisite for learning.

Since the stigmatization effect seems to be most amenable to social control, many recent developments in the area of mental health, special education, and rehabilitation have been designed to minimize stigmatization. The increasing tendency to eliminate or reduce the segregation of deviants into institutions and special classes is an effort to reduce their stigmatization. The constant renaming of negatively valued conditions and behavioral categories is sustained partly by this motive. Renaming deviancies in the personality realm as *mental illness, maladjustment,* and *inadequacies in personal-social living* is partly a reflection of different ways of conceptualizing the conditions, but it is also an attempt to divorce these disorders from the negative connotations of *lunacy, insanity,* and *psychosis.* We previously indicated that *mild, moderate,* and *severe mental retardation* have replaced *feebleminded, moron, imbecile,* and *idiot* for similar reasons. However, these efforts are only partly successful, and the reason for their limited success is fairly clear.

Although cultures differ considerably in the dimensions of behavior considered of major significance, the existence of a scale of prestigious and shameful differentness is a universal feature of social life. In any group of people who share a set of values in terms of which they develop social norms, those who do not adhere to these norms are deviants and become socially stigmatized. When the deviancies are sufficiently extreme and social reactions to the deviancies exceed critical limits, the deviants become segregated from the normals. The deviancies become stabilized and take on added significance when the affected individuals are labeled and given formal status.

Official labeling serves a number of useful primary purposes but also has many unintended secondary consequences. Descriptive and classificatory systems are used as designations of specific clusters of symptoms (behavioral syndromes). They are economical of time and energy in summarizing, giving meaning to, and communicating with others about symptoms, etiologies, and processes. The primary reason for assigning people to professionally defined categories is to facilitate the development of relevant hypotheses concerning the treatment of those persons. Labeling a behavior syndrome as indicative of mental illness, mental retardation, epilepsy, orthopedic handicaps, legal blindness, deafness, or learning disorders has a series of consequences designed to benefit individuals by giving them the right to appropriate treatment. The only legitimate justification for official labeling and categorizing is that it leads to more effective treatment. The questions raised by many workers in the field of mental health are: Can more effective treatment be provided without categorizing and labeling? If not, then how can we retain the benefits derived from categorizing the handicapped while diminishing the negative consequences of categorizing?

ARGUMENTS AGAINST OFFICIAL LABELING

Official labeling attaches a disability label to the handicapped individual which results in a generalized devaluation and a restructuring of the individual's opportunities as well as social and self-expectations. The individual becomes a prisoner of his or her own reputation. Categorizing people emphasizes their differentness, and because we see an individual as different in one negatively valued way, our perception of the many ways in which he or she is like the unimpaired is blurred. People in trouble and in need of assistance can be given such help without artificial, arbitrary categorization. The "help" provided under the guise of treatment and hospitalization often does more harm than good.

Specifically defined and delimited categories discriminate against people who do not fall within the categories but who are equally in need of help. All human beings in need of assistance should be entitled to such help, whether or not they fall within the prescribed categorical limits. Providing special assistance only to special categories of the disabled results in the multiplication of such categories and the assigning of people to these groups, rather than focusing on the social circumstances and processes that cause the disabilities. It concentrates on the rehabilitative treatment of mental health rather than on the prevention and life-enhancing potential of mental-health practices and policies. The persistence of medically-oriented categories and labels has perpetuated the person-problem orientation that militates against making needed social changes in dealing with stigmatized deviants.

ARGUMENTS FOR OFFICIAL LABELING

Unofficial categorizing and labeling are inevitable, precede the corresponding official processes, and mediate many of the effects ascribed to the official labels. Official categorization and labeling are necessary or helpful in identifying clusters of symptoms characterizing clinical entities. They provide a shorthand professional descriptive nomenclature which is useful in conceptualizing and transmitting information about patients and processes. Descriptive categories and labels are also necessary for setting administratively and legally as well as professionally—or personally—dictated requirements for admission to "patient" status. Legally and administratively authorized financial and care benefits are limited to those who "fit the category." For example, special financial aid and educational assistance are provided people who are legally blind, deaf, orthopedically handicapped, mentally retarded, or mentally ill. Failure to be officially certified precludes an individual's obtaining such help. Defining behavioral disorders as "mental illness" or some equivalent term may be necessary before people with such conditions can be covered by medical and hospital insurance benefits. A categorical label may open doors for those in need of assistance.

Conventional labels serve as rallying points for mobilizing people and resources. Practically all voluntary organizations—golfers, antique car buffs, societies for crippled children, or the Epilepsy Foundation of America—are organized in terms of categorical interests. Even though such groups prefer less stigmatizing labels for their categories, the terms have emotional appeal vital in mobilizing constituencies, initiating movements, promoting legislation, and planning programs. Decategorizing the handicapped may decrease the commitment and involvement of these groups.

SOME POSITIVE SIGNS

Because of the widespread concern with arbitrary categories, labels, and stigmas many things have been done to minimize the use, as well as the deleterious effects, of labeling. Many of the archaic stigmatizing terms have been discarded and replaced by more acceptable ones such as *developmentally disabled* and *people with special needs*. Some states are financing special programs and additional help for the handicapped on a noncategorical basis. Integration of the handicapped into the mainstream of society and the retention of more children in regular classes will do much to minimize their differentness and the necessity for formal labels. More and more, labeling is being used only when it is necessary to identify and obtain appropriate special services, treatment, or particular needs.

In addition, the general public is being educated to cease equating a person with an exceptionality. To the degree that we cease thinking and speaking of a *blind* musician, a *deaf* mechanic, a *crippled* lawyer, or an *epileptic* author and refer to them simply in terms of their professional affiliations or employment, we will minimize the effects of categorical labels. When it seems necessary to indicate a handicap it can be minimized by giving it a secondary emphasis—a musician who is blind, a brilliant lawyer despite his deafness, an author who is epileptic. We can also use the handicapping category only when it is relevant to the interpersonal or professional relationships involved. The emphasis should remain on the individual as a person and only secondarily on the fact that he or she is also educationally, physically, or sensorily handicapped. When we refer to a person as "a cripple," "an autistic," "a psychotic," "an epileptic," or "a deviant," the person is equated with the disability; the person becomes a category and is thereby dehumanized. Some evidence indicates that society's harsh judgments on many categories of people just because they are different are decreasing.

THE MINORITY STATUS OF EXCEPTIONAL INDIVIDUALS

In many ways, handicapped people perceive themselves as an oppressed minority because, like many ethnic minorities, they are subject to a set of circumstances and social pressures that restrict their lives. This widespread discrimination imposes a kind of group identity on the many categories of the disabled which sets them apart from the nondisabled.

The nondisabled majority tend to maintain a certain social distance, often treating the disabled as outsiders. Many normal people feel uncomfortable in the presence of a disabled individual. They find it very difficult to accept and mingle with the disabled as they do with other people, and since they have the greater prestige and power, they can restrict the opportunities of the handicapped. Nearly two-thirds of a sampling of college students stated that they would not marry an amputee (one leg), and half would not date such a person. Nearly three-fourths would not date a deaf person (Rusk and Taylor, 1946). The handicapped thus are often forced either to associate with one another or to become socially isolated. They are frequently segregated—physically, psychologically, and socially. Disabled persons sensing social discrimination gravitate to their own kind who can accept them without reservations. And, like members of a minority racial group, they resent their group identification, even though they feel more comfortable there. Noreen Linduska indicates in her autobiography, *My Polio Past,* that she first resisted new group identifications by refusing to answer letters from her readers who had disabilities, but gradually came to realize that she had slipped into a different category of society (the disabled) even though she did not like it.

Identification with a group of similarly disabled people has some advantages. Within such a group the individual is, to a degree, protected from the frustration, conflict, anxiety, and disappointment which might result from trying to compete with and gain acceptance from the more able majority. Within the world of the disabled one may find understanding and acceptance, friendship and love, respect and status in a way which is impossible while remaining a marginal person in the culture of the more able majority. The disabled are no longer motivated to act "normal."

In the larger urban centers there are many organizations and clubs for particular types of exceptional people, particularly the blind and the deaf. In New York City, for example, the Union League of the Deaf rents an entire building for its use. The deaf publish journals and newspapers, own an insurance company, and periodically hold a World Conference of the Deaf and a World Deaf Olympics. They have a church and largely take care of their social work. They have even lobbied *against* additional income tax exemptions for the deaf similar to those allowed the blind. In this respect the deaf are behaving like many minority racial groups.

Some social and behavioral deviants develop subcultures that, like the ethnic and racial ghettos, constitute havens where the individuals can live openly and with mutual support and insist that they are just as good as anyone else.

The disabled, like disadvantaged ethnic groups, experience vocational discrimination. While vocational outlets for the disabled may be realistically circumscribed, restrictions are often extended to areas where the limitations are not inherently confining. Failure to graduate from high school, for example, may prevent a person from even being considered for a job requiring only manual labor; the absence of significant physical defects may be a prerequisite for employment in a company which has jobs in which many disabilities would not be at all handicapping. Unrealistic requirements close the doors of employment to many of the disabled. In the 1960s and 1970s about 20 million working-age people in the United States described themselves as disabled. If we accept this estimate, it means that about 10 percent of the total working-age population are disabled. It is estimated that more than half of all working-age disabled adults who could work are jobless. Prejudicial stereotyping of the disabled who do work often keeps them in menial and blind-end jobs (Gliedman and Roth, 1980).

And, as we have already mentioned, the disabled are subject to the consequences of group stereotyping. Like minority racial and ethnic groups, persons with disabilities are often discriminated against on a wholesale basis.

Disabled people are supposed to feel and act inferior, and other people expect them to act accordingly. People see in others what they expect to see and resist modifications of these expectancies. People also tend to respond to others according to how they expect others to respond to them. The person with a disability who acts in a normal or superior manner is considered to be compensating or overcompensating for inferiority. Individuals are perceived in terms of the presumed characteristics of the group to which they are assigned. H. Chevigny, in his autobiography (1946), indicates that when he became blind, people expected him to act like a tragic figure. They are disconcerted and disbelieving when a blind person insists that he is not a tragic figure. In the same way, people are disturbed when members of disadvantaged ethnic groups fail to act inferior and even indicate that they feel as worthy as any other group. People are expected to keep their places and play the roles dictated by cultural stereotypes! When reality violates our expectations, we try to normalize reality by fitting it into our most appropriate perceptual categories.

In the early 1970s, as the political and social activities of the minority ethnic groups was declining, people with various types of handicaps began organizing a civil rights movement of their own. A new generation of organized groups such as the American Coalition of Citizens with Disabilities and Mainstream Inc. have joined with the older groups to lobby and participate in protest movements and demonstrations in support of better services, as well as changes in housing, public buildings, and transportation, where formidable barriers are posed to their mobility. They have also worked for an end to the prejudicial stereotyping and job discrimination that have often proved more restrictive than the basic handicaps themselves.

In the seventies the disabled and their relatives enlisted the support of legislators and legal advocates to obtain passage of landmark legislation which has resulted in what some have called a "quiet revolution" in disability. Accordingly, handicapped individuals have become increasingly vocal in the past few years. They have become cognizant of their rights to education, employment, public transportation, and access to buildings, all associated with a fuller and more useful life. The handicapped are asserting their right to share the world of the nonhandicapped.

However, the rallying cries of the various liberation movements of the 1960s and 1970s, such as "Sexual Equality," "Gay Power," "Chicano Power," and "Black is Beautiful," cannot be matched by the chronically disabled. We do not hear "It's Good to be Blind," "Up with Multiple Sclerosis," or "Long Live Diabetes." There is no common basis for positive identification. The handicapped are still the *de*formed, the *dis*abled, the *dis*eased, the *ab*normal, and above all, the *de*viants or the *in*valids. All of these designations have negative connotations.

DENIAL VERSUS ACCEPTANCE OF A DISABILITY

The person with a disability, and those who work with the disabled, have problems in two related areas. One involves capacities and aptitudes, abilities and disabilities. The second has to do with levels of motivation and the setting of realistic levels of aspiration. The problem of abilities and disabilities can be attacked with tests and other measuring devices. Medical, psychological, educational, and sociological testing instruments and rating devices make it possible to indicate roughly the extent of organic, educational, psychological, and social impairment.

However, the problem of establishing realistic levels of aspiration in the social, personal adjustment, educational, and occupational areas is much more complex. It not only involves individuals themselves, particularly their self-concepts, but also families, schools, and communities—indeed, their whole society. The point of crucial impact of all of these social influences is the individual's self-concept, which is largely a distillation of other people's evaluations. Persons come to conceive of themselves as adequate or inadequate as they see themselves reflected in the evaluations of others.

Because so many disabled people's lives tend to revolve about their disabilities rather than their abilities, their self-concepts are often unrealistically low. Consequently, their self-expectations, levels of aspiration, and general motivational levels are unnecessarily diminished. Recognizing this, many people are motivated and encouraged by others to *deny* the fact of their disability. When an entire culture puts a high premium on a given ideal state, there is a great deal of reinforcement of behavior which conceals, minimizes, or denies the existence of deviations from that ideal. To associate with the normal on their terms, to act normal, to compete with the normal, then becomes the ideal pattern of one's life. The person with a disability observes that the rewards in this world go, not to the person who accepts those limitations which are seemingly dictated by his or her condition, but to the individual who either refuses to accept the disability as a handicap or who strives for the cultural ideal despite the condition.

Because of the advantages of being considered normal, almost every person who is able to do so will "pass" on certain occasions. People with epilepsy under control, the hard-of-hearing person, and the partially blind can and often do pass for normal. Homosexuals, drug addicts, and prostitutes, as social deviants, conceal their identities (pass) with the general public, and particularly with the police, but in various ways disclose their identities to special classes of people—clients, connections, pushers, and fellow-members. One solution to the problem of denial versus acknowledgement of a deviancy is to divide one's world into an in group who "know" and a larger group within which the handicapped individual passes. Nonperceptible handicaps may be known only to one's doctor and immediate family. Those in the know protect the handicapped in passing. Those sharing a common stigma often provide mutual aid in passing. Homosexual overtures are made in ways nonhomosexuals will not recognize. Ex-prisoners and ex-mental patients assist one another in concealing their previous status to people on the "outside."

However, certain genuine limitations are not to be denied. The blind person cannot enjoy the beauties of the landscape. The use of auditory cues is denied to the deaf. The trainable child cannot master calculus. To expect these people to strive for such goals is asking them to try for the impossible. To deny completely the existence of a disability requires that the person act as if the condition did not exist. And to do this, the individual, as well as those about him, must pretend that he is something or someone other than himself. He must become an actor, and acting twenty-four hours a day is hard work. Concealment indicates shame and involves strain. Despite eternal vigilance and constant work, the person with a disability often cannot get away from the disability. The individual who by words or actions says, "Treat me just like a nondisabled person, no matter what!" often finds himself or herself in impossible situations.

For example, the blind host who elects to deny his blindness may be faced with the problem of pouring cocktails for his guests. None of the alternatives open to him permit him to act like a seeing person. The usual way for a blind person to fill a glass is to hook one finger over its edge and then pour until the liquid reaches the finger. In this way the glasses can be uniformly and properly filled. However, this method is not available to the person who is acting like a sighted individual; besides, some people object to having another person's fingers in their cocktails. Another method, which follows the pattern of the sighted, is to pour the liquid from a sufficient height so that it makes a noise as it flows into the glass. The fullness of the glass can be estimated from the change in sound and the weight of the glass as it fills. But this method is not very accurate; it is hazardous to pour from a distance without visual guidance and difficult to judge when the glass is properly filled. There is no practical way for a blind person to fill glasses as do the sighted.

Again, persons who are hard of hearing may try to act as if their hearing were normal. They try to listen hard. They must never say "What?" They watch other people's faces and gestures for cues. In dimly lit rooms they pretend to be in reverie or asleep. They develop ways to get people to repeat without actually asking them to. They invent humorous stories to account for mistakes which result from failure to hear accurately. They fake daydreaming, absentmindedness, boredom, and indifference. In situations where hearing is difficult, they talk all the time. Frances Warfield (1948) gives a vivid autobiographical account of these and other defensive maneuvers of a partially deaf individual who tries to deny her disability. A post-polio adolescent who denied his orthopedic handicap, Raymond Goldman (1947), would swim early in the morning to prevent others from seeing his legs. When girls were present, he would not walk. When his braces were first fitted, he hated them and refused to wear them. When he was in the fifth grade he took his cue from a telephone repairman and referred to his braces as "tree-climbers."

One solution to the problems posed by socially devalued deviancy is to accept the reality of the deviancy but to deny the stigma, diminish the stigmatizing effect by pointing out the greater defects in "normals," or insist that the deviant individuals really possess special positive values. The Garveyites, the Black Muslims, and other black separatists have propounded a militant segregationist or secessionist ideology for the blacks of America. Black separatists emphasize the special values, distinguishing characteristics, and unique contributions of their kind. They flaunt stereotypical attributes such as color (black is beautiful), distinctive dress ("native" costumes and "natural" hair style), and articles of diet ("soul food"). The orthopedically handicapped sometimes develop the concept of the greater defects in supposedly "normal" people. The outwardly healthy and robust body hides an inwardly crippled and corrupt mind. The blind see the normally sighted as having eyes but failing to see. They are blind to the real meanings and significances of the things they experience. People with normal ears are deaf to the pleas of other people. The socially devalued deviant may convert the stigmatized component into a symbol of superiority. This effect can be facilitated by a derogation of the "normal" referent group.

The price of passing is high and the effort is often futile. When a person must constantly be vigilant to deny a disability, it becomes the central focus of life. Such persons may resort to partial social isolation to help conceal the defect and thus fend off possible discovery.

If denial is not feasible, what about accepting one's disability? Mental hygienists insist upon the virtues of acceptance of oneself as a prerequisite of mental health. But acceptance of one's disability involves a lowering of one's level of aspiration and a renunciation of many of the goals of the nondisabled. In a culture which places a high value on either the normal or the ideal, the acceptance of one's disability often carries with it an acceptance of a generally inferior status—a devaluation of the disabled individual as a person.

Acceptance of one's handicap includes the acknowledgement of the contaminated aspects of one's social identity. The acknowledgement of the handicap implies acceptance that some of one's attributes warrant social derogation. If persons accept all the implications of a disability, they may so succumb to the condition that they become just as unrealistic as the person who elects to deny a disability. When the disabled person concludes, because of his condition, that "it is not worthwhile to live," when he tries "to go into hiding and never show his face for the rest of his life," when he feels so sorry for himself that he expects others to do for him many things that he can well learn to do for himself, he is succumbing to his disability.

Goffman (1963) points out the paradox that when handicapped individuals are urged to accept themselves and either explicitly or implicitly are told that as members of the genus they are entitled to full acceptance and respect from others as whole people, they are also told that they are different and that it is foolish either to deny or ignore this difference. The normal's acceptance of the handicapped is always conditional. Satisfactory social relationships between normals and deviants depend upon the latter voluntarily refraining from "cashing in" on the claim of acceptance beyond the point that normals find comfortable. Positive relationships depend upon the implied promise that the extended credit of complete acceptance will never be fully used.

Goffman also shows that a previously stigmatized person does not attain complete acceptance as a whole human being following remediation or repair of a defect. The full restoration of function does not typically result in acquisition of fully normal status. The change of status is from someone with a defect to someone with a history of having corrected a defect, but the stigma of having been defective persists. The "reformed" alcoholic and the "cured" drug addict are still perceived as more vulnerable and less complete human beings than are individuals with no such histories of deviancy.

Any show of anger by an ex-convict or an ex-psychotic is seen as a direct expression of a basic criminal or psychotic nature. A sarcastic remark to a companion, a heated argument with a spouse, or a sudden change in mood is perceived as a manifestation of defectiveness. These same responses by a nonstigmatized person are seen as the normal reactions of ordinary people, signifying nothing in particular.

In this connection it may be helpful to make clearer certain distinctions which have long been implicit and are now becoming explicit in our thinking concerning the disabled. Just as we found the distinctions between the concepts of disability and handicap to be useful, similar distinctions between *denying* one's disability and *coping* with it, on the one hand, and between *accepting* one's limitations and *succumbing* to them, on the other, may be equally helpful.

ACCEPTING A DISABILITY WITHOUT SUCCUMBING TO IT

How to accept one's limitations without succumbing to them is the problem. To accept one's disability and oneself as a person with a disability requires a clarification of what one can and cannot do. When this is achieved, the individual renounces the goals that are closed and concentrates on the achievement of the possible. When a person is able to say to herself and to others, "This is my limitation; these things I cannot do," she eliminates much uncertainty and ambiguity from her life. She is now free to study the requirements of new or different situations realistically and objectively in terms of her abilities and disabilities. Acceptance does not require that the status quo be rationalized in a Pollyannaish way as the most desirable, nor does it require a flight into apathy, egocentricity, or hypochondria. The disability can be perceived as inconvenient and limiting without being debasing, and the person can strive to improve her condition in a realistic way.

CHANGING REALITIES

Opportunities for the handicapped far exceed the dreams of most people only a few years ago. Realistic levels of expectation for the disabled a generation ago are no longer realistic. Whereas "acceptance" previously meant acquiescence to a limited access to the mainstream of life and the exclusion of most disabled people from the everyday opportunities available to the nonhandicapped, this is no longer true. The stress on *realistic acceptance* as the key concept in the adjustment of the handicapped symbolized the limited opportunities afforded them. However, although we still have far to go, dramatic changes have taken place. Today the handicapped are becoming effectively involved in programs and agencies designed for their welfare. Disabled people serve on the boards of the agencies whose services they use. They have become advocates and activists in their own interests. Today many of the handicapped can realistically insist on receiving the same or equivalent social, educational, and vocational opportunities afforded the nonhandicapped. Acceptance no longer means it is useless to try, but does include, together with increased opportunities, the recognition that they, like all people, may fail to realize fully their goals.

One difficulty with charitable agencies and individuals who are dominantly sentimentally helpful in their approach to people with disabilities is that they may unwittingly reinforce a tendency toward succumbing. Pity and charity, as approaches to rehabilitation, often do not focus on acceptance and coping. The more helpless and dependent the individual, the more he or she is worthy of sympathy, compassion, pity, and charity—but these may operate to reinforce dependent behavior.

COPING WITH A DISABILITY

The difficulties which arise from denying the existence of a disability have already been indicated. Concealing the disability does not eradicate it. The too strenuous striving for acceptance by others negates itself. Denial grows out of the individual's lack of self-acceptance, and acceptance of one's limitations is a prerequisite to coping with them. Having accepted a disability without succumbing to it, individuals no longer need to deny their limitations; they are free to cope with life to the best of their abilities. Coping involves making the most of what one has, and arranging one's life according to one's abilities. The person deprived of vision copes by learning to read and write in Braille, learning to type, and learning to use a cane or a seeing-eye dog. He acquires those skills which are open to him. He investigates and makes use of all of the educational and social facilities that are available, he does not disregard the difficulties (that would be denial), nor is he overwhelmed by them (that would be succumbing). But *how* to cope with one's disability without denying its existence and *how* to accept an infirmity without succumbing to it are two major problems of the disabled.

When disabled persons cannot get away from a disability, the question becomes how they can best get along with it. Overcompensating in the area of one's disability, even when possible, may drive the individual to outward success, but not to personal adjustment. Only when a person feels guilty about a disability does that person have something to disprove or make up for. Only when one feels especially bad in one respect must he or she be especially good in another to counterbalance it. The successful person copes with the problems of status by engaging in activities in which the prospects of satisfactory achievement and personal satisfaction are greatest, rather than by feeling compelled to do better in the area of the disability (in order to deny the handicap) or in a closely related area (in order to make up for the deficiency). For the person with serious disabilities to insist on competing and winning over the nonhandicapped may mean that the individual has not adjusted to the infirmity and is over-motivated to achieve in this particular area just to prove the extent to which it does matter—the extent to which it is overvalued.

Wright (1974) has dichotomized a series of attitudes and practices which encourage either coping or succumbing behavior on the part of the handicapped. These are summarized and paraphrased below:

ENCOURAGEMENTS TO COPING

1. Emphasizing what the individual can do
2. Perceiving the person's basic self as worthwhile
3. Seeing the handicapped individual as playing an active role in planning and living his life
4. Valuing even minor accomplishments in themselves, not because they attain or exceed a norm
5. Perceiving the limiting and negative components of the self as manageable
6. Managing limitations by ameliorating them to the degree practical and then living on satisfactory terms with the inherent limitations

ENCOURAGEMENTS TO SUCCUMBING

1. Emphasizing the individual's limitations rather than his assets
2. So overvaluing the defective components of the self that the person has an unrealistically low social and self-image
3. Seeing the handicapped person as passively directed and helped by others
4. Evaluating accomplishments in terms of external norms
5. Seeing the person's limitations as overwhelming
6. Giving up in the face of difficulties

Ideally, handicapped persons see themselves as full human beings who at worst happen to be excluded from a limited area of social or occupational life. They are not types or categories but unique human beings, in the same way as the nonhandicapped. They should fulfill the obligations of the nonhandicapped as fully as they can, stopping short only when the effort required to overcome or deny defectiveness increases its obviousness.

Many individuals who advocate a "normalizing" concept for the handicapped believe that the disabled have suffered from a paternalism on the part of their well-intentioned able-bodied friends. This paternalistic attitude has typically taken the form of a medical model. Such a concept perceives the handicapped as chronic patients entitled to the same tolerant understanding and treatment provided the victims of any serious disease. One trouble with this concept is that the role of a patient in our society is in many ways similar to that of a child. Patients are expected to obey the edicts of the professionals and devote their energies to getting well. However, disabled persons are perceived not only as helpless because they are sick, but doubly helpless because they are unable to master the task of getting well. Many more active members of the civil rights movement for the disabled believe that some of the campaigns in their behalf, such as the annual cerebral palsy and muscular dystrophy telethons, perpetuate a paternalistic medical model of the handicapped.

The attempts of whites in America to help blacks reflect this dilemma. When whites display attitudes of tolerance, understanding, and acceptance of blacks, when they overlook or excuse defects and delinquencies in blacks that they condemn in whites, their attitudes carry inevitable overtones of condescension. The whites seem to be saying, "These blacks are children. They have to go through this stage in growing to maturity, and so we have to overlook their deficiencies." This kind of talking down to blacks often results in needed help being rejected because its acceptance demeans the recipients. For example, some blacks have opposed programs of school integration because of the implication that black children (inferiors) must be with white children (superiors) in order to be well educated. (Note that even "tolerance" has overtones of magnanimous condescension. We never speak of being tolerant of people we think of as superior to ourselves.)

PROVIDING ASSISTANCE TO THE DISABLED

The perennial dilemma faced by those who would help the disabled or the disadvantaged is how to render assistance without generating dependencies. When a normal, socially advantaged, emotionally sensitive individual has intimate contact with an organically impaired or socially disadvantaged person, his or her reactions are likely to be a mixture of sympathetic concern, compassionate involvement, and social guilt, which he or she is motivated to reduce. Emotionally motivated and sustained nurturant assistance is likely to reinforce dependency and perpetuate a self-derogating role which the proferring of assistance implies. Self-humiliation and condescension are not constructive components of a helping relationship. The helping hand and the forgiving attitude may imply, "We must be tolerant and understanding with these inadequate people. We, unlike them, must be patient, accepting, and forgiving." Such attitudes only reinforce the acceptance of inferiority. On the other hand, making impossible demands and expecting normal or superior performance from a truly handicapped person makes failure and disappointment inevitable.

"Helpful" people with the best of intentions can unwittingly violate a variety of cherished liberties and prerogatives. For example, in the guise of proferring help, people can be intrusive (invade other people's privacy), coercive (deprive them of autonomy), and moralistic (try to make others "good" like we are).

SUMMARY

The practice of categorizing and stereotyping racial and handicapped groups has generally been viewed as pathological in origin and detrimental to the categorized individuals. However, categorizing of persons and things having common characteristics is intrinsic to cognitive development. Because of an overload of sensory input it becomes necessary to develop perceptual and conceptual categories in order to deal with the vast amount of available data. The main function of categorizing is to reduce the complex world to a more simple and manageable structure. Race and sex as well as various physical, mental, and behavioral characteristics are obvious variables in terms of which people are categorized.

Of course, categorizing and streotyping do have deleterious effects. They can lead to stigmatizing certain categories of people and, under some circumstances, become a self-fulfilling prophecy. As the result of categorizing, in-group differences are minimized and out-group differences are exaggerated. Because of this, exceptional individuals tend to be perceived in terms of their differentnesses rather than in terms of their commonalities with the nonexceptional.

Concern over the deleterious effects of categorizing, stereotyping, labeling, and the self-fulfilling prophecy reached their zenith during the 1960s and early 1970s. During this period, some people believed that the stigmatization resulting from official labeling largely "explained" the handicaps of many categories of exceptional people. However, the bulk of the research studies on the topic indicate that the self-fulfilling prophecy in the form originally postulated does not function as claimed. Teachers are constantly modifying their expectancies and teaching procedures as the result of student performances. Labels and initial information such as test scores do not induce permanent attitudes and expectancies, as originally claimed. Categorizing and labeling become self-fulfilling prophecies only when social expectancies are all-pervasive and operate over long periods of time. The process of becoming a handicapped person is the result of a complicated interaction process that includes the inherent disability, social and self-evaluation of the disability, unofficial labeling, formal labeling, and the total effect of these on the individual's self-expectations.

Exceptionality has both positively and negatively valued components. Individuals want to be different in certain ways and resist efforts to deny them their individuality. However, when deviance becomes extreme, it is generally perceived negatively, induces anxiety, and initiates activities designed to reduce the person's differentness.

The total behavioral consequences of negatively valued differentness include those emanating from (1) the inherent limitation imposed by the disability, (2) social attitudes and expectations as well as the compensations available to the exceptional individual, and (3) the exceptional individual's self-image, aspirations, and self-expectations.

Programs designed to reduce the stigma of exceptionality must deal with social values and attitudes, official and unofficial labeling, and legislative and court actions. Devalued exceptional people, like disadvantaged ethnic minorities, experience social and vocational discrimination, develop and withdraw into separate subcultures, and are excessively stereotyped. The problems of exceptionality are the problems of all humanity. People are not helped if their exceptionalities are ignored when these deviancies are relevant to treatment, training, or educational procedures, on the one hand, or when they are classified, labeled, and treated in terms of medical or psychological categories irrelevant to education and treatment, on the other.

Denial of a disability (acting as if it does not exist) is distinguished from *coping* with a disability (developing the most adequate substitute alternatives). *Accepting* a disability (learning to live with it) is differentiated from *succumbing* to it (being overwhelmed by the threat).

REFERENCES

Abrams, K. and T. L. Kodera, "Expectancies Underlying the Acceptability of Handicaps: The Pervasiveness of the Medical Model," *Southern Journal of Educational Research,* 1978, *12,* 7–20.

Asch, S., *Social Psychology* (Englewood Cliffs, N. J.: Prentice-Hall, 1952).

Bandura, A., "The Self System in Reciprocal Determinism." *American Psychologist,* 1978, *33,* 344–358.

Budoff, M. and G. N. Siperstein, "Low-income Children's Attitudes Toward Mentally Retarded: Effects of Labeling and Academic Behaviors," *American Journal of Mental Deficiency,* 1978, *82,* 474–79.

Chevigny, H., *My Eyes Have a Cold Nose* (New Haven, Conn.: Yale University Press, 1946).

Dusek, J. B., "Do Teachers Bias Children's Learning," *Review of Educational Research,* 1975, *45,* 661–84.

Eaton, J. W. and R. J. Weil, *Culture and Mental Disorders* (New York: Free Press, 1955).

Freedman, J. L. and A. N. Doob, *Deviancy: The Psychology of Being Different* (New York: Academic Press, 1968).

Gampel, D. H., J. Gottlieb, and R. H. Harrison, "A Comparison of Classroom Behavior of Special Class EMR, Integrated EMR, Low IQ, and Nonretarded Children," *American Journal of Mental Deficiency,* 1974, *79,* 16–21.

Gliedman, J., and W. Roth. *The Unexpected Minority: Handicapped Children in America,* (New York: Harcourt Brace Jovanovich, 1980).

Goffman, E., *Stigma: Notes on the Management of Spoiled Identity* (Englewood Cliffs, N. J.: Prentice-Hall, 1963).

Goldman, R., *Even the Night* (New York: Macmillan, 1947).

Gottlieb, J., and M. Budoff, "Social Acceptability of Retarded Children in Nongraded Schools Differing in Architecture," *American Journal of Mental Deficiency,* 1973, *78,* 15–19.

Guskin, S. L., "Theoretical and Empirical Strategies for the Study of the Labeling of Mentally Retarded Persons," in N. R. Ellis, ed., *International Review of Research in Mental Retardation,* vol. 9 (New York: Academic Press, 1978).

Johnson, G. O., "A Study of the Social Position of Handicapped Children in the Regular Grades," *American Journal of Mental Deficiency,* 1950, *55,* 60–86.

Jones, R. A., *Self-Fulfilling Prophecies: Social, Psychological, and Physiological Effects of Expectancies* (Hillsdale, N.J.: Lawrence Erlbaum Associates, 1977).

Linduska, N., *My Polio Past* (Chicago: Pellegrini and Cudahy, 1947).

Lippman, W., *Public Opinion* (New York: Harcourt Brace, 1922).

Maslach, C., "Social and Personal Bases of Individuation," *Journal of Personality and Social Psychology,* 1974, *29,* 411–25.

Parish, T. S., N. Dyck, and B. M. Koppes, "Stereotypes Concerning Normal and Handicapped Children," *Journal of Psychology,* 1979, *102,* 63–70.

Rosch, E. and B. B. Lloyd, eds., *Cognition and Categorization* (New York: Halsted Press, 1978).

Rosenthal, R. and L. Jacobsen, *Pygmalion in the Classroom* (New York: Holt, Rinehart and Winston, 1968).

Rusk, H. A. and E. J. Taylor, *New Hope for the Handicapped* (New York: Harper and Row, 1946).

Sagarin, E., "The High Cost of Wearing a Label," *Psychology Today,* 1976, *9*(10), 25–32.

Snyder, M. and W. B. Swann, "Hypothesis-Testing in Social Interaction," *Journal of Personality and Social Psychology,* 1978, *36*, 1202–12.

Snyder, M., E. D. Tanke, and E. Bercheid. "Social Perception and Interpersonal Behavior: On the Self-fulfilling Nature of Social Stereotypes," *Journal of Personality and Social Psychology,* 1977, *35*, 656–60.

Stephan, W. G., "Stereotyping: The Role of In Group—Out Group Differences in Causal Attribution for Behavior," *Journal of Social Psychology,* 1977, *101*, 255–66.

Taylor, M. C., "Race, Sex, and the Expression of the Self-Fulfilling Prophecies in a Laboratory Teaching Situation," *Journal of Personality and Social Psychology,* 1979, *37*, 897–913.

Tsujimoto, R. N., "Memory Bias Toward Normative and Novel Traits," *Journal of Personality and Social Psychology,* 1978, *36*, 1391–1401.

Tsujimoto, R. N., J. Wilde, and D. R. Robertson, "Distorted Memory for Exemplars of a Social Structure: Evidence for Schematic Memory Processes," *Journal of Personality and Social Psychology,* 1978, *36*, 1402–14.

Warfield, F., *Cotton in My Ears* (New York: Viking, 1948).

Wilder, D. A., "Reduction of Intergroup Discrimination Through Individuation of the Out-Group," *Journal of Personality and Social Psychology,* 1978, *36*, 1361–74.

Wright, B. A., "An Analysis of Attitudes and Effects," *The New Outlook for the Blind,* 1974, *68*, 108–18.

SUGGESTIONS FOR STUDENTS AND INSTRUCTORS

1. Discuss the advantages and disadvantages of both the "medical" and "social-learning" models of mental and behavioral handicaps.

2. Discuss the positive and negative consequences of categorizing people.

3. Discuss the proposition: "We react to the world in terms of what we believe it to be, rather than what it really is."

4. Discuss the relative validities of the "self-fulfilling prophecy" in such conditions as brain damage and drug addiction.

5. Discuss the proposition: "So long as society has a scale of values, persons categorized as possessing certain characteristics will be stigmatized."

ADDITIONAL READINGS

Goffman, E., *Stigma: Notes on the Management of Spoiled Identity* (Englewood Cliffs, N.J.: Prentice-Hall, 1963). A very good discussion of the origins and manifestations of social stigmatization.

Windsor, P., *The Summer Before* (New York: Harper and Row, 1973). A fictionalized personal account of two runaways who flee from an unsympathetic and repressive society only to join an equally unaccepting subculture.

SELECTED FILMS

Unlearning Prejudice. (30 minutes) Anti-Defamation League of B'nai B'rith, 315 Lexington Avenue, New York, N.Y. Discusses the acquisition and reeducation of prejudice.

Being. (21 minutes) ACI Films, 35 West 45th Street, New York, N.Y. 10036. Indicates the difficulties a paralyzed young man faces in establishing friendships that are not based on pity.

ORGANIZATION

Society for the Rehabilitation of the Facially Disfigured
550 First Avenue
New York, N.Y. 10016

CHAPTER 3

THE DEVELOPMENT OF HUMAN POTENTIAL

In a broad sense, this chapter is concerned with the causes of the tremendous differences in the rate and ultimate levels of human development and functioning. However, causation is not a simple concept. For example, to the average person, the tubercle bacillus is *the cause* of tuberculosis. However, virtually all of us are exposed to live tubercle bacillus, but relatively few of us have or have had active tuberculosis. The presence of the bacillus is a necessary but not a sufficient condition for the development of the disease. Also involved are genetic susceptibility and a host of less specific factors such as personal habits, nutrition, and general health as well as temporary and fluctuating factors such as fatigue, stress, and even emotional state at the time of exposure. All of these and possibly more are involved in the total causal complex. When we are dealing with levels of intellectual, social, emotional, motivational, and general behavioral status, the causal factors are still more complex and interrelated.

Probably no one grows up in an environment that permits the fullest realization of his or her potential. In fact, we do not know how to identify such an environment. We are much better at indicating conditions that produce impairments than we are at specifying the circumstances that foster superior development and performance. However, we shall indicate here the present state of our information concerning the circumstances that promote both the dignity of and fulfillment of the potential of all people, with particular reference to the handicapped.

It is axiomatic that human development and performance result from the interactive effects of three groups of factors. One group consists of the individual's capacity or power—the enabling component. While *capacity* is the term most commonly used to refer to this component, we prefer the term *power*. Capacity connotes a static or fixed component, whereas the enabling component is constantly changing.

The power factor includes a variable genetic component interacting with the accumulative effects of the individual's lifetime experiences. What one is capable of doing, in addition to one's hereditary potential, is tremendously influenced by the totality of one's learned repertoire of motor and cognitive skills, information, and attitudes.

In addition to his or her skill and ideational repertoire, each person also acquires a wide variety of attitudinal and motivational predispositions which either facilitate or retard subsequent learning. These constitute the second category of factors. Potential does not generate its own motivation. Motivation determines the degree to which the power factor is activated and utilized in the interest of desired goals. Another obvious factor determining behavior is the external situation in which people find themselves.

Although we often separate these components for discussion purposes, they are not separate and distinct factors. For example, internal personal factors, current environmental influences, and behavioral outcomes all operate as interlocking determinants of one another. Personal power and motivational levels induce expectations concerning the outcomes of anticipated acts. The environmental effects created by these actions (success or failure, movements toward or away from desired goals), in turn, alter expectations. People evoke different reactions from others by such physical characteristics as size, facial features, sex, dress, and general attractiveness. The differing social treatment afforded individuals because of these stimulus characteristics affects such personal internal factors as self-expectations and self-image. These internal factors, in turn, modify actions in ways which either sustain or alter the environmental impact of such things as social biases and stereotypes. Since all of these components are reciprocally related, the search for simple or ultimate determiners is futile. Let us briefly consider the perennial nature-nurture problem.

NATURE VS. NURTURE—LEARNING TO ASK THE RIGHT QUESTIONS

In historical perspective it is clear that early attempts to deal with the relative contribution of heredity and environment to human development were greatly oversimplified. Up until the last decade, the pendulum swung back and forth between extreme geneticism, on the one hand, and extreme environmentalism, on the other. When it was discovered that certain human characteristics were transmitted from one generation to another as unit characteristics and that these unit characteristics were determined by the presence or absence of certain genes in the germ cells, a period of extreme geneticism began. This emphasis was dominant from the 1920s to the 1940s.

In the latter decade a number of studies demonstrated that environment exerted a significant effect on the level of intellectual functioning of foster children. The types of homes in which foster children were raised had a significant effect on their adult level of functioning. These studies initiated a swing from extreme geneticism to an environmental emphasis, which continued until the 1950s and 1960s, when many workers seemed to deny that genetic factors played any significant role in determining people's intellectual levels.

In retrospect, much of the heated controversy of this period seems to have consisted of setting up a straw man in the form of extreme genetic determinism and then proceeding to take refuge in extreme environmentalism. However, it soon became clear that extreme geneticism and extreme environmentalism were both untenable positions. The answer to the question, "Is this characteristic inherited or acquired?" could only be, "It is neither. No trait can exist without the combined effects of both genetic and environmental factors."

We next moved to another level of questioning, which was to prove equally untenable. Granted that heredity and environment are always involved in the origin and development of human traits, which of the two is the more important? It soon became clear that this question was equally meaningless. Trying to answer it is like trying to determine which is the more important of the two blades of a pair of scissors. Reduce one to a zero and the other becomes a zero. We can never say that one is more important than the other.

At a still higher level of complexity, we began asking such questions as, "Even though, in an absolute sense, we cannot say that either genetic or environmental factors are the more important in human development, can't we say that one or the other contributes *more to human trait variances* (the extent to which people differ from one another in specified ways)?" We are still trying to deal with the nature-nurture question within this context. However, many workers in the field are convinced that asking the overall question of the degree to which environmental and genetic factors determine variances in human traits is the wrong question. In order to deal with it we must be specific about what characteristics we are talking about, the specific population we are dealing with, the kinds of genetic mechanisms involved, under what environmental circumstances, and at or during what periods of life. All this sounds quite complicated and it undoubtedly is. Perhaps some specific examples will make the meaning of this statement clearer.

Heritability measures, obviously, will vary with the trait. Skin and eye color and body physiques will show higher heritabilities than will conventional indices of intelligence, and these, in turn, will show higher degrees of genetic determination than will measures of personality and attitudinal traits. Human nature is neither immutably fixed nor unlimited plastic. Some traits are environmentally pliable while others are relatively resistant. Given environmental differences may produce little differences in one genetic strain (one population) but big differences in another.

It is no longer possible to assume that the heritability of traits obtained with one category of subjects or at one age yields valid information with reference to other populations or age groups. The heritability indices obtained for intelligence and several personality traits are lower for adults than for children. This may be due to the relaxing of certain environmental controls in adulthood which increases the environmental variances impinging on the subjects (Dworkin, Burke, and Maher, 1976).

In many instances, age-related variables dramatically influence development. The elimination of galactose from a galactosaemic infant (one unable to metabolize glactose) or phenylalanine (one of the amino acids) from the diet of a PKU child, who is unable to metabolize this substance, will make the difference between an individual who will develop quite normally and one who is severely mentally retarded. The elimination of these constituents of the diet from such children will have no noticeable effect on development and level of intellectual functioning when delayed beyond childhood. In many similar conditions the effects of environmental variables are age- and population-specific.

Despite the complexities of the ordinary hereditary-environmental interactions, there are certain conditions which we can justifiably say are *primarily* either genetic or environmental in origin. Several hundred exceptional syndromes of development result from the presence or absence of single genes (McKusick, 1979). In these conditions the deviant development will always occur despite tremendous environmental differences. The departures from normal development are very extreme while the impact of environmental variations on the affected characteristics are relatively very small. In these cases we feel quite certain in assigning the preponderant influence to heredity. An estimated 10 percent of live-born infants have some form of genetic variation that plays a significant role in producing handicap (Scriver, Laberge, and Fraser, 1978).

On the other hand, there are equivalent developmental exceptionalities which can be attributed to environmental factors. For example, severe brain injury, cerebral infections, the ingestion of high levels of toxin, asphyxia, and radioactivity *in utero* may result in the severe impairment of mental and physical function. In such cases, even with normal or superior genetic endowment, the environmental factors so lower the individual's level of functioning that genetic factors are relatively unimportant. In these cases we feel quite comfortable in referring to them as environmentally caused.

However, most of the physical, mental, and personality traits of psychological and educational importance are intermediate between these extremes in terms of their nature versus nurture determination. In most cases, hundreds of genetic determiners interact in dynamic ways with a similar large number of environmental factors in determining human development and performance.

In a theoretically completely permissive, freely competitive society with no social inheritance and with full equality of opportunity and unrestricted mobility, levels of competence would be largely determined by the relevant genetic differences. Conversely, in completely rigid caste cultures we have a self-perpetuating system of inequality which is entirely social in origin. Social dictates are total, irrespective of genetic variations within or between castes. Deprivation or affluence continues indefinitely and unchanged from one generation to another, irrespective of inherent genetic differences.

With such a complex set of genetic-environmental-age-competence interactions it is clear that each population and each individual will require a different environment for maximum development. Except for identical twins, no two individuals are, or probably ever have been, genetically alike. Each person is genetically unique and similarly, each person has a unique environment. Unique genes and unique environments interact in the development of each person in unique ways. When we arbitrarily classify and categorize people we disregard this uniqueness. One cardinal principle of education, recognized in theory, but long disregarded in practice, is that each pupil, for maximum development, requires a unique environment and individual treatment. The best opportunity for one is not the best opportunity for all. Of course, one reason why uniqueness in treatment is not realized in practice is that we do not know enough. This lack of relevant information is making the realization of individualized educational programs for the handicapped, as mandated by law, very difficult.

ENVIRONMENTAL VARIABLES

For purposes of discussion we will consider three overlapping groups of environmental variables which are important in the development of human potential. One category consists of the more purely physical ones. A second group we will call *familial-cultural* and the third are the *social-structural* components of the environment.

PHYSICAL-ENVIRONMENTAL VARIABLES

The more purely physical components of one's environment include the obvious: clothing, food, shelter, and medical care. Clothing should be adequate and appropriate to one's age, sex, and peer group. Clothing serves not only to cover one's body and to regulate temperature, but is also important in contributing to social acceptance and self-perception. Adequate food, both quantitatively and qualitatively, is essential to maximum development. Housing not only provides shelter but ideally, also provides room for individual family members to read, study, and meditate relatively undisturbed. Preferably, housing will be in an area relatively free of physical threat and environmental pollutants.

For maximum effect medical care and advice should be continuously available for both prevention and remediation. Care should cover the prenatal and natal periods and extend over the entire life span. Preventive measures include such things as advice about and monitoring of diet, exercise, and that lifestyle considered most appropriate for each individual. It will, of course, also cover such things as immunizations and the minimizing of accidents and infections. It is obvious that the availability and utilization of these physical environmental factors are related to such things as socioeconomic status, ethnic membership, and family practices as well as personal idiosyncrasies.

FAMILIAL-CULTURAL VARIABLES

Familial-cultural-ethnic factors are tremendously important determiners of the particular constellation of human traits that will be nurtured and developed in a given individual. Extensive studies agree that the repertoire of skills, information, attitudes, and values with which children enter school are the most important predictors of how they will do in school. At each successive educational level, differences in achievement remain highly correlated with these entry characteristics and additional achievements merge with and are powerfully influenced by them. The ways in which educational advantage and disadvantage are perpetuated from one generation to another are not well understood but a broadly-held belief is that familial attitudes and practices with reference to such things as self-perceptions, internal versus external control, authoritarian versus democratic orientation, individuation versus conformity, dependence versus independence, competition versus cooperation, and immediate versus delayed gratification of needs are important determiners of a person's motivational systems. The tremendous differences in rates of educational and socioeconomic advancement of the various ethnic groups in American society are usually explained in terms of such variables.

A recent study found that the earnings of European-born, legally admitted Americans are about 10 percent lower than native-born Americans at the end of their first five years of residence here. After ten years they earn, on the average only about 4 percent less. When they have been here twenty and thirty years, they earn 6 percent and 13 percent *more* respectively than their native-born counterparts. When the U.S.-born sons of white immigrants have about the same educational level as do the sons of native-born whites, they have 5 percent *higher* earnings.

In contrast to these remarkable achievements of European-Americans, Mexican-Americans earn nearly 25 percent less than do other white males of the same generation. The average earnings of American blacks continue to be far below that of whites (Berman, 1978).

No doubt, significant ethnic and cultural differences do exist in the values, expectations, and life styles that different groups espouse. One cultural heritage may impart to a child a feeling of strength and worth, a high resolve with reference to intellectual and vocational achievements, and a sense of pride in accomplishments, while a different culture does none of these things. In contemporary America a Jewish boy is much more likely to graduate from college than is a Gentile boy of equal ability and socioeconomic status. On the other hand, an American-born child of Italian ancestry is less likely to attend and graduate from college than is the average American child of comparable socioeconomic level and ability (Halsey, Flaud, and Anderson, 1961).

Each child acquires a certain cultural heritage that powerfully conditions his or her attitudes, values, and levels of aspiration.

We have had relatively little success singling out which particular cultural components reinforce each other cross-culturally and which ones are handicapping. Some very divergent cultures that seem to be ideal candidates for marked incompatibility apparently do not function in this way, whereas people coming from countries whose cultures appear compatible to the culture to be adopted prove to be markedly handicapped. Consonant and dissonant cultural components seem to differ with different societies. Thus equal cultural disadvantage may arise from different cultural components. An examination of some representative ethnic groups will demonstrate the nature of some of these differences.

some positive components of japanese culture Superficially, the Japanese would seem to be ideal candidates for the category of culturally disadvantaged in America. Japanese language, culture, religion, and family organization seem to be very different from their American counterparts. The background of the typical Japanese immigrants to America was rural peasant. Their vocational background was that of subsistence farming. They came to the United States with only temporary residence in mind. They established and maintained special part-time schools to perpetuate their native language, religion, and culture. They were members of a highly visible, socially deviant group. They met prejudice, discrimination, and restrictive legislation in America. However, in a comparatively short time the Japanese have attained a surprisingly high level of education; they have moved from unskilled migrant farm laborers to renters; and finally, as the legal restrictions concerning land ownership were removed, they became highly competent, independent farmers. As the social barriers were lowered, they also became successful business and professional people. In both education and income the Japanese rank higher than all other identifiable ethnic groups as defined by the United States census; more than 50 percent of Japanese children of college age are attending college. This percentage places the Japanese well ahead of WASPs (Yee, 1976).

Although they differ in many respects, there is apparently a significant compatibility—not necessarily identity—between the value systems of the Japanese and the American culture which has made it possible for the Japanese-American to progress rapidly in current American society. Some of these compatibilities are the personal characteristics of diligence and hard work, a belief in the importance of attaining and maintaining a good personal and family reputation in the community, and an unquestioned expectation that children will fulfill their obligations to self, family, and race. The Japanese emphasis on strong communal and family ties and their style of life have resulted in a low rate of identified and diagnosed mental illness (Yee, 1976). Nair (1970), in a comparative study of farming practices in the United States, Japan, and India, claims that the small Japanese farmer has not essentially changed the skillful and diligent practices of five hundred years ago. She claims that their practices derive from the purest "Protestant" work ethic, although they have never known Calvin, Knox, or Luther. Maybe the alleged ethic is neither uniquely American nor uniquely Protestant.

the jewish advantage The Jewish characteristics which seem to work to their advantage in contemporary American culture are (1) a strong, closely knit family and communal organization; (2) a passion for education and upward socioeconomic mobility; (3) a long-range time orientation; and (4) broad and liberal humanitarian interests.

Studies have repeatedly documented the strengths of the Jewish family. The Jews have a low incidence of families broken by desertion, separation, or divorce. Child neglect is virtually nonexistent, and the rate of juvenile delinquency is low. If anything, Jewish children suffer from maternal overprotection. Intermarriage between Jews and non-Jews is comparatively rare; disapproval of intermarriage is remarkably strong, even among the American-born. Jewish parents favor residence in predominantly Jewish neighborhoods in order to increase the probability of intra-faith marriage for their children. In America the closeness of the Jewish family has never restricted the child's achievement. The Jewish family participates symbolically in the accomplishments of its members. The Jewish child is also a part of a community that is rapidly moving upward, and so he or she experiences no conflict between individual achievement and occupational mobility, on the one hand, and family or communal loyalty, on the other. Jewish mobility is a socially approved mass phenomenon.

Jewish tradition and culture have always placed a high value on education. Intellectual attainments carry high prestige. The preschool Jewish boy receiving religious instruction is already a serious student. "Parents will bend the sky to educate their sons," is an old Jewish saying. It is therefore not surprising that the Jews have displayed a passion for education unparalleled in American history. The free city colleges of New York were largely Jewish by the turn of the century. With the increasing prosperity of the Jewish community, the admissions officers of the high prestige universities became busily engaged in devising ways of keeping the Jewish segment of their student bodies down to what they considered reasonable proportions. At one time the professional schools—notably the medical schools—set tight quotas for Jewish students. The Jews have become the best educated ethnic group in America. At times they have been overeducated in proportion to the vocational opportunities open to them. The brute facts of discrimination maintained the bans on higher levels of employment long after they had been lowered within the educational institutions. This meant that highly educated Jews often were unable to obtain employment in areas for which they were well trained and qualified.

Although the Jewish family is closely knit and family identifications are high, the entire Jewish community is in many respects the important social entity. The present and future status of all Jews is the really significant variable. The accomplishments of the individual Jew are meritorious in themselves, they add to the prestige of the individual, and reflect credit on the family; but more important, they enhance the status of all Jews. The entire community—and all Jews, in a very real sense—participates in the achievements of its members. One generation sacrifices to educate and push the next generation up the ladder, with the expectation that this generation will pass along the advantage with an additional increment to the next. Parental and community gifts and benefits for young people are not given in anticipation of reciprocal gifts in the present, but rather are expected to elicit corresponding assists to each succeeding generation. Thus assistance progresses in an ascending spiral and not only blesses the giver and helps the recipient but, more significantly, enriches the community and the entire ethnic group. The emphasis on the desirability of prolonged formal education—the benefits of which accrue to the family, to succeeding generations, and to the community—reflects a long-range time orientation, an extreme form of a delayed-gratification pattern. Thus we find many components of traditional Jewish family and communal life contributing to the motivation of the individual. These cultural values instilled in the developing child account largely for the fact that a Jewish boy is much more likely to graduate from college than is an Anglo-American boy, who in turn is more likely to graduate from college than is an Italian-American, Puerto Rican, or Afro-American of comparable social and intellectual levels (Halsey and others, 1961).

the spanish-american's handicap Spanish-American immigrants to the United States are concentrated in two areas—Puerto Ricans in the New York metropolitan area and Mexican-Americans in the southwestern United States.

The economic disadvantage of Puerto Ricans in New York City is comparable to that of blacks. The per-family income of Puerto Ricans in 1960 was 63 percent of the median income of all New York families. In this same year, 5 percent of all New York males, 6.9 percent of all non-white males, and 9.9 percent of all Puerto Rican males were unemployed. One-half of all the families in the city receiving supplemental aid from the Department of Welfare were Puerto Rican. They constituted one-half of the home-relief cases and one-third of the aid-to-dependent-children cases (Glazer and Moynihan, 1963).

Many Puerto Ricans leave school at the earliest possible age. In 1960, 18 percent of the elementary school pupils, 17 percent of the junior high school students, and only 8 percent of the high school students were Puerto Ricans. This indicates a high dropout rate below the high school level. The proportion of Puerto Ricans in the academic high school was only 5 percent in 1960. However, Puerto Ricans have fared better than blacks in terms of upward economic and social mobility, although they still constitute a big group of the ethnically disadvantaged.

Puerto Rican family life has some strengths as well as some apparent weaknesses. In some ways the native Puerto Rican family is similar to that of the European peasant. It is patriarchal and authoritarian. The husband demands respect and obedience from wife and family. The marriages, unlike those of European peasants, however, include many consensual, or common-law, marriages. Consequently, as among the blacks, about one-third of the births have been technically illegitimate. The consensual marriage is unstable and is made even more so by the existence of additional mistresses and the considerable sexual adventurism of Puerto Rican men.

The position of children in the Puerto Rican family is better than the marriage practices suggest. Most observers report that mothers are very much attached to their children, often loving them to the point of overprotection. Although men might have children by a number of women, they typically take responsibility for all of them. The custom of having godparents (coparents) for each child provides a second set of parents to take over the responsibility of parenthood when necessary. Children may be overprotected; certainly, they are seldom abandoned, rejected, or neglected.

Whether because of less prejudice and discrimination or because of different personal and social motivations, the prognosis for improvement in the status of Puerto Ricans seems to be better than for blacks. In 1960 there were an estimated four thousand Puerto Rican-run businesses in New York City, considerably more than the much larger black population has established, even though the major black migration considerably preceded that of the Puerto Ricans. The 1960 census showed more Puerto Ricans than blacks in the category of "managers, officials, and proprietors."

The cultural disadvantage of the Mexican-Americans, like that of the Puerto Ricans, results more from their having cultural traits that handicap them in American society than from enforced segregation, prejudice, and discrimination. Many Mexican-American communities reproduce in a modified form the barrio of Mexico. People from the same villages in Mexico have settled together in the same localities and maintained a life similar to that found in Mexico. Inhabitants of the Mexican-American community share strong feelings of kinship and a feeling of separation from the English-speaking community.

Families and godparents are the most important social ties among the people of the Mexican-American community. The extended family, including grandparents, aunts, uncles, and cousins, is closely tied together and provides mutual aid and counsel. Four kinds of godparents are recognized, one for each of the sacraments—baptism, first communion, confirmation, and marriage. These godparents enter into a special social and religious relationship, not only with their godchild, but also with the child's parents. This relationship formalizes friendship, extends the size of the kinship group, and enhances neighborhood solidarity.

The Mexican family is authoritarian and patriarchal. Both parents express deep affection and concern for their children. Men are expected to have extramarital amorous adventures, often of a rather permanent sort, but like the Puerto Ricans, they accept responsibility for their illegitimate offspring. Children are seldom deserted, nor do they lack care and affection.

The cultural disadvantage of the Mexican-Americans manifests itself in, or derives from, poverty, low levels of educational achievement and social status, and little expectation that their level or that of their children will improve. The studies intended to clarify the nature of these disadvantages have not been very helpful, but the better controlled ones indicate that the attitudes of Mexican-American children toward education and social advancement are generally considered to be less positive than are those of Anglo-American children even when the groups are matched for socioeconomic level, intelligence, age, grade, and sex (Demos, 1962).

Social class also significantly differentiates the Mexican-American from most other families. The educational and occupational level of Mexican-American parents remains quite low, even among families that have resided in the United States for three generations. Moreover, the father's occupation improves only slightly with each succeeding generation. Maybe the realities of a culture of poverty perpetuate Mexican-American children's low level of confidence in their ability to fulfill their parents' aspirations for them.

the disadvantaged black americans The problems of the disadvantaged blacks in America have been studied more extensively than have those of any other ethnic group, and the historical and social roots of their peculiar status are fairly well known. Slavery took the unique form of chattel slavery in response to the uneasy situation in which one person owned another person's body as well as his or her labor in an absolute and total sense. This condition had no precedent in English tradition or in common law. Since Roman times English society had known only free men and serfs. The problem of the uncertain status of the person who was neither a free man nor a serf was solved by defining the slave as chattel property which, like one's horse or land, had no inherent rights.

Thus blacks as chattel slaves came to be considered inherently inferior. Since blacks were thus lacking in the capacities for education and for functioning as free men, slavery was justified as necessary for the blacks and an obligation of the whites. Slavery became "the white man's burden." Thus a set of beliefs concerning blacks in America grew up and was perpetuated more as a set of self-evident assumptions than as a result of conscious formulation. The treatment of blacks that developed within the framework of these beliefs made them into dependent, uneducated beings who seemed indeed incapable of exercising the prerogatives and obligations of freedom. Thus the vicious circle was closed and became a self-fulfilling prophecy.

All the major studies of race problems in America agree that the primary source of the racial dilemma is the social and psychological legacy of slavery and the caste system it involved. The assumption of inherent black inferiority, a rationalization for the caste system, has produced a vicious circle which is a crippling black dependency and feelings of inferiority which are proving very resistant to change. The consequences of the assumption of innate black inferiority have trapped blacks and whites alike.

SOCIAL-STRUCTURAL VARIABLES IN DEVELOPMENT

To a considerable degree, social institutions designed to further the development of citizens are the crystallization of implicit belief systems. The original free universal education intended to prove equality of opportunity for all children consisted of a single curriculum imparted to all in a like fashion. This, in effect, meant an education for those children able to attend and profit by the one program provided. When it was discovered that schools differed tremendously in the resources they commanded, equality came to be conceived in terms of equality of resources. This concept was the basis for court decisions which declared that separate schools for blacks and whites were acceptable so long as they were equal—the famous "separate but equal" doctrine. Court decisions declaring unconstitutional the use of local property taxes as the principal financial support for schools, since this method did not provide an equality of resources to all children, were also based on this concept. Rich districts were able to raise several times as much money for school purposes as were poor districts. This resulted in gross inequities in the allocation of educational resources.

When the more equal distribution of educational resources failed to change significantly the educational achievements of the less advantaged social class and ethnic groups, *compensatory* programs were instituted. Additional resources were allocated to those children who failed to achieve at the same rate as the more advantaged children. These practices implicitly define equity in terms of equality of results.

Increasingly, it is becoming clear that social organizations and institutions provide citizens with differential access to the educational and vocational means of achieving culturally valued goals. Since educational systems screen admissions, allocate status, and regulate entry into most segments of the labor force, educational inequalities have widespread social and economic consequences.

Some characteristics of social organizations and practices that tend to diminish the handicap of people with disabilities as well as maximize the development of the inherent potential of all people are as follows:

1. Tolerance for a wide range of mental, physical, and behavioral traits with a minimum of stereotyping and labeling. The permissible range of behavior should be limited only to the degree that one's personal freedom does not threaten or unduly restrict other people's freedom.

2. The allocation of resources and the development and use of educational and vocational training programs based on individual needs, irrespective of social class, race, color, sex, or disability.

3. Individuals judged on the degree to which they are developing in the direction of personal betterment and social effectiveness, rather than in terms of fixed norms and standards.

4. A pluralistic society, the components of which have enough in common to enable all citizens to work and live together in reasonable harmony and still maintain their individual, ethnic, and subcultural identities according to their individual preferences.

FAMILY INFLUENCES ON MOTIVATIONAL LEVEL

Family, ethnic, religious, cultural, and subcultural motivational influences are all intertwined. To some degree, social and religious factors operate via the family. However, family attitudes, value systems, and levels of aspiration may deviate from the prevailing social patterns and exert forces independent of them. To a large degree, the ultimate educational attainments and achievements of the children represent the family aspirations come true. Prevailing climates of opinion and the levels of expectancy displayed in the home can do much to nurture and sustain high educational achievement. The encouragement in the home of educational achievement may not be sufficient, but certainly it is one of the more necessary conditions of high educational attainment. Children are, to a large degree, the carriers of the attitudes and aspirations of their parents.

Studies comparing the parents of lower social class children who are high achievers and who express high levels of aspirations and expectations with comparable parents of low achievers with low levels of expectation, while not always in agreement, tend to show the following about parents of high achievers:

1. Parental aspirations and expectations for their children are the overriding influence. The families of the high achievers definitely and consciously exert pressure on their children to do well and expect them to succeed.

2. The parents of the high achievers are well aware of social hierarchies, consider the occupational world to be stratified educationally, and feel their own lack of education to have been their own major handicap.

3. The parents of the high achievers make demands and have expectations for their children which are clearly defined.

4. The families of high achievers are concerned with independence training. They expect their children to assume responsibilities and display mature behavior at an earlier age than do the parents of the low achievers.

In contrast, the parents of low achieving, low aspiring children of comparable socioeconomic status showed the following characteristics:

1. They accept the scheme of things and their place in it fatalistically. They consider themselves lucky to have jobs and expect their children to be much like them. That is the way life is!

2. They live largely in the present. They have no long-range plans for themselves or for their children.

3. They have only vague conceptions of formal education beyond high

school and have not seriously considered the possibility of higher education for their children (Kahl, 1953; Halsey and others, 1961).

ATTRIBUTION PROCESSES

The proposition that people's beliefs concerning themselves and the world around them significantly influence their behavior seems self-evident. Social and self-expectations and personal aspirations have long been central concepts accounting for the motivation and achievement of all people, but particularly the handicapped. When we perceive situations and causal relationships as real, they become real in terms of their consequences. Beliefs have consequences irrespective of their truth or falsity. When failure leads to a perception of a low probability of future success, motivation to achieve is decreased and, in an extreme situation, may be a disaster. Success increases one's anticipation and expectation of success in future performances, and an increased expectation of success is followed by improved performance. Failure has the converse effect.

In addition, the perceived *reasons* for one's successes and failures are important in determining future performance. In everyday situations, people assign causes to their own and others' behavior. Assigning such causes ascribes meaning to behavior and enables people to feel that they can or cannot predict and control their world. A body of information and explanatory principles has evolved to account for the processes involved in making these causal inferences.

One basic principle established by research is that behavior change and its maintenance are facilitated when these modifications are perceived as caused by oneself to a greater extent than when these same events are attributed to external causes. In other words, a person's belief in the relative importance of intrinsic and extrinsic factors in controlling one's life have been found to be significant in the development of a wide variety of behavioral traits, including the initiation and maintenance of behavior change (Lahle and Berman, 1979).

The handicapped have difficulties in developing and maintaining satisfactory self-concepts and in appropriately assigning causes to their activities. As compared with the nonhandicapped, they receive more contradictory messages from their environment as to their relative competences, their successes and failures, who they are and what they are, what they can do and what they cannot do, and who or what controls their lives. The social roles of all but the most severely handicapped persons are likely to be ambiguous. As disabled individuals their paths are often narrowed, either realistically or in terms of social expectations, and social demands are reduced to a minimum. Certain components of their environment tell them to accept their disability by renouncing many of the goals of the nondisabled. However, equally powerful social forces drive the handicapped to deny their differentness. They soon discover that achievement rather than renunciation is the route to acceptance and esteem. They observe that the rewards go predominantly to those who, rather than accepting their disabilities, achieve in spite of them. Recently the importance of the ways in which people perceive themselves and others has been extensively researched in the name of *attribution processes.*

A substantial body of research evidence indicates that people tend to take personal credit for meritorious behavior and to attribute behavior with negative outcomes to others or to external causes over which they have no control. By taking credit for good acts and denying blame for bad outcomes, individuals protect their own self-esteem and public images. This same self-serving bias manifests itself in other attribution processes. Following failure, people tend to attribute their own behavior to external causes while they attribute similar failure by others to more internal personal characteristics. Negative self-attributions that would undermine the individual's self-esteem are avoided (Bradley, 1978).

There are also some significant differences in the behavioral consequences of our perception of two types of external and internal factors as the principal causes of our successes and failure. Since ability is a relatively stable and dependable personal characteristic, success which is seen as due to one's inherent abilities (a personal trait) results in a feeling of self-satisfaction and an expectation of further successes. (I am competent and can succeed.) When success is perceived as the result of supreme effort it similary induces a feeling of self-satisfaction but, since effort is variable and unstable, there is less expectancy of constant future success. (I can succeed if I try very hard.)

When success is perceived as the result of the task being easy, mastery is not accompanied by self-congratulation nor an expectation of future success on tasks of ordinary difficulty. When success is perceived as the result of pure chance, neither self-satisfaction nor continued striving follow. The success perceived as due to ability is most rewarding and promising; success due to extreme effort also results in self-satisfaction but with less promise. Success perceived as due to a low level of task difficulty carries no particular self-satisfaction and a little expectation of continued success, while success considered to be due to luck carries not only no self-satisfaction but also less chance of future success.

Corresponding consequences can be deduced for failure perceived as due to internal factors (ability or effort) or to such uncontrollable external factors as task difficulty, chance, or a hostile environment (Bar-Tal, 1978).

Research studies comparing the attribution patterns of groups of people who differ in achievement motivation and in output have supported these theoretical considerations in the following ways:

1. Individuals who attribute outcome to effort work harder and longer than do those who attribute outcome to ability.

2. The less persistent children are at a task, the greater is the tendency for them to take less responsibility for both success and failure.

3. Children who persevere least tend to attribute outcomes to luck or uncontrollable external factors rather than effort.

4. Children rated or assessed as helpless place less emphasis on the amount of effort required for success.

5. There is evidence that some experiences with failure prepare individuals to cope with future failure by immunizing them against the deleterious effects of subsequent failure. Carefully manipulated successes and failures can escalate effort. Errorless learning renders children less able to deal with subsequent errors and failure. Children with a high sense of personal control are more resistant to the debilitating effects of failures than are the more externally-oriented children (Thomas, 1979).

6. It has been found that providing students with instructions, information, and feedback concerning their relative successes in learning tasks which encourage them to make ability attributions for success and lack of effort attributions for failure (both internal factors) increase achievement motivation and performance (Bar-Tal, 1978).

It should be emphasized that any procedures which instill unrealistic perceptions in students will be self-defeating. Practices designed to modify the perceptions and expectations of learners should establish realistic perception of abilities and emphasize the importance of effort as compared with uncontrollable external factors in achievement. These goals, it seems obvious, can best be achieved in individualized educational programs where students can start from where they are and be given tasks commensurate with their abilities. In such situations success can realistically be attributed to ability and effort and failure to lack of effort—attributions that maximize feelings of self-satisfaction, task-persistence, and expectations of continued success. Neither extreme internality nor externality of control are conducive to most appropriate behavior. The critical factor is the congruence between the individual's perception of the locus of control and the specific situations involved.

Teachers and students alike have long observed that repeated failures in learning and performance are usually accompanied by feelings of frustration, defeat, and sometimes hopelessness. This has always been recognized as a significant factor in the underachievement of the handicapped. In fact, special classes for the mentally retarded and now mainstreaming of these same students were designed to counteract this phenomenon.

More specifically, in the 1890s the minister of education in France observed that a small percentage of the students in the beginners' classes were unable to progress in the normal way and became progressively more retarded in achievement as they were passed from grade to grade. By the time these children were judged incapable of progressing at the expected rate they had become frustrated, discouraged, and often had ceased trying. The minister of education planned to establish special classes for these slow learners where they would be in small groups, receive more individualized instruction, and be able to progress at their own rates. It was felt that if children who would experience special learning problems could be identified before they had failed repeatedly, the resulting hopelessness and subsequent underachievement could be prevented. As a result, Alfred Binet was asked to devise some means of identifying these vulnerable children early in their school careers so that learning tasks appropriate to their stages of development could be assigned. This would provide these children with a reasonable number of success experiences, permit them to progress at their own rates, and consequently prevent them from underachieving.

As a result, Binet developed the first scholastic aptitude test to assist in the better education of children with special learning problems. It is interesting to note that we have come full circle in dealing with this problem. Special classes were designed to minimize the degree to which such noncognitive factors as low self-concepts and expectations, experiences of repeated failure, and one's perception of the causes of successes and failures contributed to the low achievements of children with special learning problems. The mainstreaming of the handicapped is designed to achieve these same things.

When the disadvantaged see themselves as living in and controlled and restricted by a hostile world, they have little incentive for trying to improve themselves. A general bias in people's understanding of the causes of behavior fosters this belief. An impressive array of research studies indicates the existence of a self-serving bias in the way people perceive events.

People tend to attribute their positive behavior to their dispositions (I contribute to charities because I am a considerate person) while attributing their negatively-valued acts to external factors (I hit him because he was threatening to hit me). We take credit for our good acts and find the causes for our bad acts in the environment. More specifically, people generally attribute their own successes to ability and effort (internal factors) but blame their failures on bad luck or uncontrollable external conditions or events (Bradley, 1978).

This same self-serving bias operates in our perception of others. We are inclined to attribute other people's failures to their inherent dispositions (internal factors) and their successes to luck or favorable circumstances (external factors). Our attitudes shape our behavior and, in turn, our attitudes are shaped by behavioral outcomes (Lahle and Berman, 1979). For example, discrimination against an innocent victim leads people to derogate their victims and thus justify their actions. The derogation of the victim then increases the tendency to discriminate further (Ross and Sicoly, 1979).

LEARNED HELPLESSNESS

Attribution processes are obviously involved in the phenomenon known as "learned helplessness." Since the middle 1960s a large number of experiments show that a variety of animals (dogs, cats, rats, and humans) experience marked disruptions of behavior following prolonged exposure to unsolvable problems or unavoidable punishment. For example, whereas naive dogs quickly learn to avoid or escape electric shock by jumping over a barrier in a shuttle-box, dogs that first received a series of shocks they could neither avoid nor escape (an unsolvable problematic situation), showed marked deficits in subsequently acquiring a shuttle-box escape response.

The effects of analogous uncontrollable events, such as trying to solve problems with no solutions or repeated failure on problems that are too difficult for the individual, have been studied in humans with comparable results. This phenomenon has usually been interpreted in terms of attribution processes and its accompaniments. In the face of repeated attempts and continuing failure the learner perceives that there is no relationship between his or her responses and outcome—nothing solves the problem, avoids the punishment, or produces rewards. This results in a marked reduction in motivation to try, as well as feelings of frustration and hopelessness.

Several studies with humans have found that learned helplessness has several dimensions and various determiners. Helplessness may be generalized across situations or may be specific to a particular situation. It may be temporary or permanent. The student who constantly fails academically may give up trying in this area but remain highly competitive in athletic or social situations where successes are more frequent. People experiencing repeated failures make a series of inferences or attributions concerning their meaning. The consequences of repeated failures vary according to whether the failures are perceived as due to personal or environmental factors. Externals display greater helplessness in comparable situations. Within groups predominantly internal in orientation, failure perceived as due to lack of ability is likely to be more stable and global than comparable failures perceived as due to lack of effort. Failure perceived as due to a hostile or nonresponsive environment is more global and permanent than similar experiences perceived as the result of poor luck. When the relevant attributions are both stable and global the situation is perceived as most hopeless.

In working with the mentally retarded the author (C.W.T.) has always been impressed with the marked difference in general behavior of the typical six-year-old child with a mental age of six and the average twelve-year-old mentally retarded child with the same mental age. The latter, compared with the former, is lethargic and passive, must be continually urged to try, is quite unresponsive and lacking in spontaneity. In many ways these children fit the picture of experimentally induced learned helplessness which is global and permanent.

As we have already indicated, research studies, as well as general observation, indicate that it is possible to prepare individuals for failure and to prevent the more extreme consequences of failure. The results of these studies have obvious implications for vulnerable handicapped children. Immunization effects have been achieved in the lower animals as well as in humans by providing a pretreatment scheduled pattern of successes and failures. In a typical study different groups of subjects experienced 50 or 100 percent successes or no pretreatment in a series of situations before being presented with a similar solvable, but difficult, learning problem. A marked immunization effect was found for the 50 percent success groups but none for the 100 percent groups (Jones, Nation, and Massad, 1977; DeVellis, 1977). Klein and Seligman (1976) were successful in reversing the feelings of helplessness and clinically diagnosed depression by similar "success therapy." These findings are consistent with the results of operant conditioning in which a given response on the part of the learned is followed by rewards always, never, or sometimes. Much greater persistence of positive responding has been found consistently with a partial reinforcement schedule. This would follow from the tenets of attribution theory. However, attribution theory can be overgeneralized. It would follow from attribution theory that if a person desired a certain outcome and believed that a·given act would be followed by that outcome he or she would act accordingly. In fact, this does not always happen.

RATIONALITY VERSUS IMPULSIVITY

Adults as well as children often act irrationally even when they "know better." A series of research studies have verified the observations that people often prefer an immediate lesser reward to a more valuable delayed one. Of course, the choice of the more immediate lesser reward may be rational if the immediate reward is perceived as certain while the delayed one is more problematical. In such cases the more certain immediate reward is more subjectively valuable than is the less certain delayed one. On the other hand, the delay versus immediate gratification choice may involve a conflict between immediate impulse gratification and rational utility consideration (impulse control).

The evidence seems to support the conflict interpretation. For example, in one study kindergarten children were given a choice between a piece of candy now or two pieces tomorrow. They also were asked to indicate which choice they thought a "very smart" or a "very stupid" kindergarten child would make. The results show that the children attributed much more delay to the "smart" than to the "stupid" child. However, the percentages of children actually giving delayed responses and assigned to the "stupid person" category were identical (49 percent). While the children attributed delay of satisfaction to a "smart" individual, they themselves displayed no more delay than they attributed to the "stupid" child. A much higher incidence of delay choices was attributed to the "smart child" than the children themselves displayed. The tendency toward immediate gratification competes with, and often overcomes, the recognized rational decision to delay reward (Nisan and Koriat, 1977).

Underachieving children with special learning difficulties have been found to make choices that are more irrational and impulsive than their high achieving peers. They also differ in their time orientation.

COGNITIVE TEMPO

Cognitive tempo, or reflection-impulsivity, is the degree to which an individual considers alternative hypotheses in the solution of problems. In problem-solving that involves response uncertainty, rapid but inaccurate responding is termed impulsive, whereas a reflective tempo is characterized by slow and accurate responding.

A long series of researches have consistently demonstrated that children with high impulsive tempos are inferior to more reflective children in a wide variety of cognitive and perceptual-motor processes. Impulsive children have greater difficulty in inhibiting movements, are less able to process information, perform less well on perceptual and discrimination learning tasks, and are less effective in search strategies (Digate, Epstein, Cullinan and Switzky, 1978).

Additional research has related cognitive tempo to performance on a wide variety of achievement tests. In classroom situations, teachers rate impulsive children as less attentive and less able to concentrate on school tasks. Impulsivity is related to school failure. Children identified as eligible for special educational programs are characterized by high impulsivity. Several studies have demonstrated that reflectivity-impulsivity can be significantly modified by procedures specifically designed for this purpose.

Procedures that have been found effective in modifying impulsivity include: (1) required delay, (2) direct instruction, (3) self-verbalization, (4) differentiation training, (5) modeling, and (6) response consequences.

In required delay situations, the teacher can elicit an appropriate delay before responding by simple instructions or by timing the responses so as to insure that the students refrain from responding to a problem for a predetermined amount of time. This procedure has been found to improve the performances of mentally retarded and other categories of disadvantaged children with learning difficulties.

Children in several studies have shown reduced impulsivity as a result of simple instruction and practice in systematically scanning the various alternatives before rendering a judgment. Children can be taught to generate alternative responses when these are not present or obvious, then consider each in turn, gradually narrowing the possibilities before finally selecting one.

Hyperactive and impulsive children have reduced their impulsivity by learning to talk to themselves when considering alternatives. This seems to induce caution and make for more careful and deliberate procedures. These self-verbalizations may vary from specific self-instructional procedures to simply saying to themselves, "Slow down," or "Check all the rest before choosing."

Differentiation training consists of teaching children to look for subtle differences rather than responding in terms of superficial, easily recognized similarities or differences.

Exposure to reflective models—either their peers or their teacher—has been found to modify impulsivity. Modeling plus self-verbalization has been found to be more effective than either alone.

Immediate corrective feedback, either verbal or nonverbal, which provides learners with direct evidence of the relative appropriateness of their choices, significantly decreases impulsivity (Digate and others, 1978).

In complex learning tasks which take some time to complete, it is difficult to provide intermediate or partial success sufficient to sustain effort. This is particularly true of the young and the handicapped whose time orientation is short. The learner often makes many nonproductive responses (errors) and success is so delayed that the relationship between the appropriate responses and the end result is not recognized. In such situations, it is helpful to provide intermediate social rewards in the form of encouragement and evidence of progress toward the goal when this is not obvious to the learner. It is also difficult to maintain the proper balance between assistance and forebearance by the adult in charge. For example, in teaching the handicapped child such self-help skills as dressing and eating, the adult is greatly tempted to give up trying to teach and dress or feed the child to save time and energy and to get the task done.

THE REALITIES OF LIFE AND COGNITIVE STYLES

For a variety of reasons handicapped persons live disproportionately in the lower socioeconomic levels of society. To a considerable degree, people get sick and acquire disabilities because they are poor; they become poorer because they are handicapped, and they then become even more handicapped because they are poorer. Consequently, in addition to their primary disability, the handicapped experience a number of additional physical, social, and economic disadvantages. To a marked degree they are less able to command the resources required to obtain the advantages enjoyed by their more favorably situated nonhandicapped peers. Many of the social realities of the lives of the socially disadvantaged and the handicapped shape such things as their internal (dispositional) versus external (situational) orientation, reflective versus impulsive responses, immediate versus delayed gratification patterns, and self-blame versus blaming others for failures.

The ultimate penalty of economic disadvantage as well as personal handicap is less that of physical privations than the permanent narrowing of the individual's perceptions of the possibilities in the world, some of which are reality-based. de Lone (1979) has documented the extent to which the offspring of poor parents with little education and with intermittent or dead-end employment will be unlikely to advance significantly above the socioeconomic status of their parents. For example, according to de Lone, the sons of successful professional men with salaries in the upper tenth of all incomes in America are twenty-seven times more likely, as adults, to earn an income in this same category than are the equally intellectually competent sons of unskilled laborers with incomes in the lowest tenth of the population. The sons of the latter have only one chance in eight of earning even a median income as adults and will probably have at least four years less formal schooling than their more affluent peers. The poor realistically perceive little opportunity for higher education as well as for well-paying and meaningful employment. This disadvantage has several accompaniments, many of which relate to such things as self-concepts, aspirations, expectations, and attribution processes.

The time orientation of disadvantaged lower-class children is likely to be quite different from that of their middle-class counterparts. The future of lower-class children is more likely to be an indefinite, vague area with promises of rewards and punishments too remote and uncertain to have much motivating force. The life patterns of these children do much to develop short time orientations which encourage impulsivity rather than reflectivity, and immediate rather than delayed gratification patterns. Discipline is typically in terms of immediate punishments or rewards designed to obtain momentary compliance. Life includes a series of sudden short-term tensions and momentary reliefs. Individuals do not frustrate themselves for long periods of time and the general patterns of life discourage planning with reference to long-range goals.

Family routines often lack the structure and predictability found in the typical middle-class family. Meals may be irregular; food is eaten when and in whatever amount available. Not only are the availability of food, clothing, shelter, and heat unpredictable, but changes in the family make-up may take place without warning. Other people move in with the family, children may switch from one family to another, parents separate and reunite, siblings leave home for work and return when out of work. The typical lower-class child's life is characterized by constant shifting more than is that of average middle-class children. Consequently, lower-class individuals perceive chance, or luck, and such external environmental factors as job availability, being at the right place at the right time, and the influence of powerful people and social institutions as the major controlling influences in their lives. Thus the realities of disadvantaged individuals' lives contain many elements that lead to the development of an external rather than an internal orientation, blaming others rather than self-responsibility, impulsivity rather than reflectivity, and immediate rather than delayed gratification patterns.

Handicapped individuals experience many of these same circumstances as well as others which are not socioeconomically related. In an earlier chapter we indicated how the very definition of disability encourages people so labeled to adopt the role of the sick person with its childlike behavior and dependency. By playing the sick role disabled people retain the special attention, sympathy, diminished responsibility, and special privileges that sickness entails. Anyone working with the disabled is amazed at the tremendous range of reactions and adjustments made to physical and mental disabilities. The same limitations that lead many individuals to helplessness and complete dependency inspire others to a high degree of autonomy and independence. There is general agreement that the ways the families and society view and treat disabled individuals tremendously affect not only their self-perceptions and expectations but also their chances of functioning at their optimum level. There are no simple formulas for achieving this, but to be truly helpful, one must provide support and assistance so as to nurture the development of competence, self-respect, and independence. Help and assistance should not be imposed on the disabled as on passive individuals. They should be administered in ways that assist the individuals to develop skills they can acquire and to use their own capacities as autonomous beings. Successes should be their successes and thus help them develop more positive concepts about themselves and their powers.

To encourage an internal rather than an external frame of reference, self-responsibility, and a delayed gratification orientation, learning tasks should be so related to the learner's abilities that a reasonable percentage of success is possible. Feedback from the process should be immediate and complete. Social feedback should emphasize that success proves that effort pays off, and should indicate that the important thing is how it makes the learner feel—he or she should feel pride in his or her successes and confident that future progress is possible.

For maximum effect success and self-satisfaction cannot be tied to fixed goals. Success and failure should always be relative to the current state of the learner and the direction of change rather than its amount. For the totally disabled with multiple handicaps, success may be slight improvement in basic sensory, motor, or language functions which make the individual less of a burden on others and minimally able to communicate some basic needs. For another person, success may consist in developing a minimum degree of self-sufficiency in mobility and language. On a higher level, success will be in terms of learning more subtle motor-personal-linguistic functions which make possible participation in social and vocational pursuits. On the highest level, success may be in terms of the reduction of one's interpersonal conflicts, and the development of social and vocational skills so as to maximize personal satisfaction and self-actualization.

SUMMARY

People's performances are the result of the interaction of their current potential, their motivations, and the opportunities provided by their environment. Genetic and environmental factors are both involved in every aspect of development and performance. Historically we have seen the pendulum swing back and forth between the extremes of hereditarianism and environmentalism. Successively, we have posed the nature-nurture questions as: Is this characteristic inherited or acquired? Is heredity or environment more important in human development? What are the relative contributions of heredity and environment to human development? The answers to these questions have been: No characteristic is ever entirely inherited or acquired; it is always both. Neither heredity nor environment can be said to be more important than the other as determiners of human development. It is also impossible to assign specific weights to genetic and environmental determiners of development and performance. Today we perceive the most appropriate nature-nurture question to be something like the following: To what extent is this specific trait environmentally pliable or resistant? In order to deal with the nature-nurture problem meaningfully we have to specify the population or individuals, the specific traits or characteristics, the environmental circumstances, and the life periods involved.

Unique genetic factors and unique environments interact in the development of each unique individual. We cannot say that human nature is either immutably fixed or unlimitedly plastic. Individual traits can vary from being highly resistant to variations in the environment to being highly modifiable.

Environmental factors involved in the development of human potential include the physical, the familial-cultural, and the social-structural. The physical factors include such things as prenatal environment, birth complications and trauma, diet, exposure to toxic agents, level of medical care, and general environmental enrichment or deprivation.

Family and culture are critical determiners of many of the most significant motivational factors such as the way individuals perceive themselves and other people, as well as their beliefs concerning the nature and source of the principal constraints on their development and performances. Family and culture instill many of the basic values, expectations, and beliefs that become important determiners of achievement. Social class, caste, ethnicity, as well as membership in one of the categories of the handicapped can all impose powerful constraints on achievement motivation.

Handicapped individuals and members of socially disadvantaged groups depend upon others more than do the more favored groups for their life maintenance and welfare. Consequently their life circumstances predispose them to believe that external factors such as social institutions, powerful individuals or groups of individuals, or "luck" are the basic agents controlling their lives. The principal controlling factors are perceived as being in the environment rather than within themselves. On the other hand members of the more favored groups are more inclined to believe that the world is orderly and therefore potentially controllable. They also are more inclined to believe that their behavior is the result of their personal characteristics and capabilities rather than external environmental circumstances. The degree to which people believe that their behavior is controlled by external environmental or internal personal factors has been found to be correlated with a variety of personal social traits. In general, "internal" individuals who expect to exert personal control of their actions and are responsible for the consequences of their actions manifest higher levels of personal adjustment, and more positive life styles. They more actively seek information, and are less responsive to external pressures.

Child-rearing practices, teaching methods, and social welfare procedures which stress independence training, personal responsibility, and the appropriate matching of learning tasks to individuals' capacities so that a reasonable probability of success is always present are conducive to the development of an internal frame of reference.

REFERENCES

Bar-Tal, D., "Attributional Analysis of Achievement-Related Behavior," *Review of Educational Research,* 1978, 259–71.

Berman, P., "Does the Melting Pot Still Meld?" *Forbes,* Oct. 31, 1978, *122*(9), 63–75.

Bradley, G. W., "Self-Serving Biases in the Attribution Process: A Reexamination of the Fact or Fiction Question," *Journal of Personality and Social Psychology,* 1978, *36*, 56–71.

de Lone, R., *Small Futures: Children, Inequality, and the Limits of Liberal Reform* (New York: Harcourt Brace Jovanich, 1979).

Demos, G. D., "Attitudes of Mexican-American and Anglo-American Groups Toward Education," *Journal of Social Psychology,* 1962, *57,* 249–56.

DeVellis, R. F., "Learned Helplessness in Institutions," *Mental Retardation,* 1977, *15,* 10–13.

Digate, G., M. H. Epstein, D. Cullinan, and H. N. Switzky, "Modification of Impulsivity: Implications for Improving Efficiency in Learning for Exceptional Children," *The Journal of Special Education,* 1978, *12,* 459–68.

Dworkin, R. H., B. W. Burke, and B. A. Maher, "A Longitudinal Study of the Genetics of Personality," *Journal of Personality and Social Psychology,* 1976, *34,* 510–18.

Glazer, N., and D. P. Moynihan, *Beyond the Melting Pot* (Cambridge: M.I.T. Press, 1963).

Grey, D. A., "Effects of Frequency and Probability of Reward on Choice," *Psychological Reports,* 1978, *42,* 543–49.

Halsey, A. H., J. Flaud, and C. A. Anderson, eds., *Education Economy and Society* (New York: Free Press, 1961).

Jones, S. L., J. R. Nation, and P. Massad, "Immunization Against Learned Helplessness in Man," *Journal of Abnormal Psychology,* 1977, *86,* 75–83.

Kahl, J. A., "Educational and Occupational Aspirations of 'Common Man' Boys," *Harvard Educational Review,* 1953, *23,* 348–66.

Klein, D. C. and M. C. P. Seligman, "Reversal of Performance Defects and Perceptual Defects in Learned Helplessness, and Depression," *Journal of Abnormal Psychology,* 1976, *89,* 11–26.

Lahle, L. P. and J. J. Berman, "Attitudes Cause Behavior: A Cross-Legged Analysis," *Journal of Personality and Social Psychology,* 1979, *37,* 315–21.

Larned, D. T. and D. Muller, "Development of Self-Concept in Grade One Through Nine," *Journal of Psychology,* 1979, *102,* 143–55.

McKusick, V. A., *Mendelian Inheritance in Man: Catalog of Autosomal Dominant, Autosomal Recessive and X-Linked Phenotypes,* rev. ed. (Baltimore: Johns Hopkins Press, 1979).

Nair, K., *The Lonely Furrow: Farming in the United States, Japan and India,* (Ann Arbor, Michigan: University of Michigan Press, 1970).

Nisan, M. and A. Koriat, "Children's Actual Choices and their Conception of the Wise Choice in a Delay-of-Satisfaction Situation," *Child Development,* 1977, *48,* 488–94.

Ross, M. and F. Sicoly, "Egocentric Bias in Availability and Attribution," *Journal of Personality and Social Psychology,* 1979, *37,* 322–36.

Scriver, C. R., C. L. Laberge, and F. C. Fraser, "Genetics and Medicine: An Evolving Relationship," *Science,* 1978, *200,* 946–52.

Thomas, A., "Learned Helplessness and Expectancy Factors: Implications for Research in Learning Disabilities," *Review of Educational Research,* 1979, *49,* 208–21.

Yee, A. H. "Asian Americans in Educational Research," *Educational Researcher,* Feb. 1976, *5*(2), 5–8.

SUGGESTIONS FOR STUDENTS AND INSTRUCTORS

1. Why are the extreme positions of geneticism and environmentalism considered equally untenable today?

2. What types of nature-nurture questions are considered appropriate today?

3. Why is it almost impossible to separate the effects of the physical and sociocultural variables that influence development in population studies?

4. Discuss the various meanings of human equality.

ADDITIONAL READINGS

Scobey, M. M. and G. Graham, eds., *To Nurture Humaneness* (Washington, D.C., Association for Supervision and Curriculum Development, NEA, 1970). Indicates how our notions about human nature and the assumptions of social institutions manifest themselves in educational ways.

Willis, J. W., J. Crowder, and J. Willis, *Guiding the Psychological and Educational Growth of Children* (Springfield, Ill.: Charles C.Thomas, 1975). A practical guide to aid in promoting the psychological and educational needs of children.

SELECTED FILMS

Green Valley Grandparents. (13 minutes) (B & W) Center for Southern Folklore, 3756 Mimora Ave., Memphis, Tenn. 38111. Mutual benefits deriving from contacts between senior citizens and disabled children.

Dehumanization and the Total Institution. (15 minutes) Studio One Animation, 1220 Glenwood Avenue, Minneapolis, Minnesota. This film alerts people to the human rights of institutionalized people.

ORGANIZATIONS AND AGENCIES

National Genetics Foundation
250 W. 57th Street
New York, N.Y. 10019

Closer Look
National Information Center for the Handicapped
Box 1492
Washington, D. C. 20013

Human Growth Foundation
Maryland Academy of Science Bldg.
601 Light Street
Baltimore, M.D. 21230

Council for Exceptional Children
1920 Association Drive
Reston, V. A. 22091

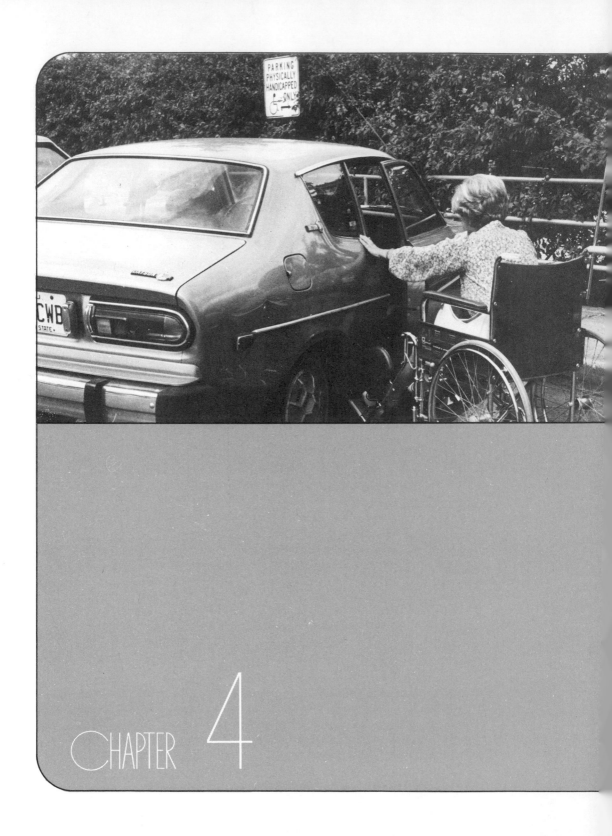

CHAPTER 4

SOME ETHICAL AND LEGAL CONSIDERATIONS

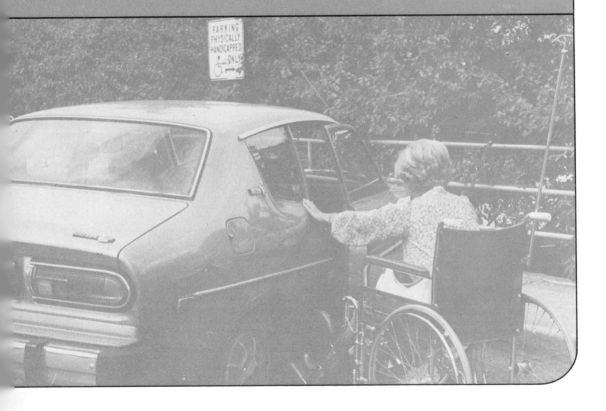

Social attitudes concerning the education, care, and rehabilitation of deviant individuals, and public provision for them, are largely a reflection of a set of more general, culturewide beliefs and attitudes concerning the obligations of society as a whole to its individual citizens. Ever since the 1930s, the trend in the United States has shifted toward increasing responsibility of society to provide environmental circumstances conducive to the development of good physical and mental health, to make it possible for every adult to become gainfully employed, and to provide maximum opportunities for the development of one's potential. The assumptions basic to the providing of universal opportunities for educational advancement, vocational outlets, and self-actualization for the "normal" have been expanded to include all people simply because as human beings they are worthy of respect and consideration and are deserving of the entire range of opportunities previously afforded only to a part of the population.

The promise of universal educational opportunities has usually meant, in practice, one educational program available to all those able and willing to profit by it. The inability of deviant individuals, and groups of individuals, to take advantage of the programs provided because of sensory, motor, emotional, or intellectual limitations was explained in terms of demoniacal possession, retribution for parental sins, inborn perversity, punishment for individual delinquencies, inherent moral weaknesses, defective genes, or the inevitable accidents of normal life, according to the prevailing beliefs of the times—not as a result of society's failure to provide programs and opportunities appropriate to the special needs of these people. In the apportioning of blame for the social failures of deviant citizens, the responsibility was predominantly that of the deviant. In a less moralistic framework, the question was, "Why isn't this person able to take advantage of the opportunities which society provides?" rather than, "Why doesn't society provide educational, rehabilitative, and vocational facilities and programs appropriate to this individual's needs?"

The climate of the times that progressively has provided more adequately for the blind, the deaf, the orthopedically handicapped, the mentally deficient, and the emotionally disturbed has expanded to a similar concern for the culturally disadvantaged (Afro-Americans, American Indians, Mexican-Americans, Puerto Ricans, many rural whites, and ghetto dwellers of all colors and ethnic origins). Studies of the culturally disadvantaged have disclosed that large segments of the population were born into and reared under circumstances which inevitably imposed handicaps upon them. Furthermore, it is now evident that these handicapping circumstances were created and perpetuated by the practices arising from the basic assumptions and beliefs of the larger society.

Society increasingly has assumed the obligation of providing help for all individuals and groups who for whatever reason require assistance. It has also become concerned with changing those conditions, practices, and erroneous beliefs that contribute to the handicaps of these people.

The emergence of a widespread concern for handicapped and disadvantaged people has resulted in the state's assuming increasing responsibility for extending the rights and privileges of full citizenship to all people. This extension of responsibility has manifested itself in the civil rights movement, the war on poverty, Head Start and many related programs, and judicial decisions extending the rights, privileges, and immunities once available only to the affluent or knowledgeable to all citizens. Many Supreme Court decisions that have been widely criticized as coddling or protecting the criminal are really designed to extend to the poor, the ignorant, and the disadvantaged the same legal protections and rights previously available only to the more advantaged segments of the population. When the Court insists that all persons taken into custody as criminal suspects must be informed of their rights concerning self-incrimination and legal counsel, it is simply making available to the lowliest citizen of the nation the same protections and privileges previously enjoyed only by the more advantaged segments of the population. The well-informed, the better educated, and the more affluent criminals, with legal counsel prompting them at each critical point, know that they need not give self-incriminating testimony and are able to obtain legal counsel

and advice. The ignorant bowery wino, the poorly informed first of-
fender, and the disadvantaged delinquent are not aware of their legal
rights and privileges and consequently may be convicted and punished,
not because they are guilty, but because they are ignorant, ill-informed,
or poor.

The recent redefinition of mental illness as failure in social living,
and the development of a communitywide public health approach to
those problems of personal and social maladjustment previously viewed
as purely personal afflictions, have accompanied increasing public concern for deviant and, particularly, disadvantaged people. There is increasing professional and public recognition of the existence of a complicated and thorny set of interrelationships among poverty, unemployment,
crime, physical illness, emotional disturbance, personality disorganization,
mental deficiency, and educational retardation.

One manifestation of the changing climate is the increase in public
espousal of humanistic as well as humanitarian values. Historically, special programs for the handicapped—the blind, the deaf, the orthopedically handicapped, the mentally deficient, and the emotionally disturbed—were designed to reduce the level of dependency of the disabled,
on the one hand, and to express humanitarian concern for people less
fortunate than ourselves, on the other. Rehabilitative and educational
procedures were designed to increase the productive efficiency of disabled individuals and thus make them less of a financial and personal
burden on society.

Programs for the intellectually gifted and the potentially highly creative were conceptualized as maximizing the superior individual's contributions to society. The aptitudes and capacities of superior people were
conceived as community assets to be used to the fullest possible extent so
as to maximize their value to the state. In the 1960s a surge of interest in
the intellectually superior and the creative individual was motivated, at
least in part, by the "space race" and the belief that it was necessary to
use the intellectual potential of these people to the maximum if we were
to make the scientific and technological advances necessary to attain or
maintain national superiority.

To a degree, people were seen as a national commodity to be managed for maximum productivity. The intellectual capacities of citizens
constituted tools for the realization of personal, but more importantly, social and nationalistic goals. Education has always served a dual function.
It contributes to self-actualization on the one hand and to socialization
and increased public worth on the other. Recently, the goal of education
has been conceptualized more in terms of self-realization and less in
terms of productive efficiency. The failure of any individual to realize his
or her potential is seen more as a personal disappointment than as a social loss.

SOME VALUE CONSIDERATIONS

How a society handles the problems posed by the presence of handicapped and disadvantaged minorities reflects its fundamental conception of the nature and worth of the individual and its basic assumptions concerning its communal obligations to the individual. Americans have traditionally seen themselves as devoid of social class bias and their society as uniquely open and fluid. For the most part, they have taken the oft repeated statement that all people are born free and equal as factual. They have assumed that making free public education available to all citizens provided equality of educational opportunity to all people.

Over the last generation Americans have become acutely aware of the discrepancy between their philosophical commitments and preachments on the one hand and their practices on the other. They are discovering that uniformity of opportunity is not necessarily equality of opportunity. Supplying unlimited numbers of free books to all children does not provide educational opportunity equally to blind, trainable mentally retarded, and sighted children of normal mentalities. Educational opportunities equivalent to those provided to normal children by ordinary educational procedures require that alternatives be provided to deviant individuals that are as appropriate to their special characteristics as the ordinary school curriculum and methods are to the average child. The freedom and equality to which all people are entitled are those of equity in law, and equal rights to life and self-realization. The ideal of maximum opportunities for each person in terms of his or her unique constellation of traits and characteristics is replacing that of uniformity of opportunities. Each person has equal rights to dignity, courtesy, respect, and the maximum possible provision for him to develop whatever potential he has, not because these will make him a more productive being and a more socially acceptable person, but because these are his birthright as a human being. The notion of maximum opportunity for self-realization for all requires the use of all resources available to capitalize on the assets and minimize the deficits of each individual. Optimum human development rather than maximum productivity becomes the primary goal of educational and rehabilitative efforts. Of course, only on the level of concrete goals and specific programs and procedures can such an abstract tenet be realized.

In Chapter 1 we indicated that the assets and liabilities of exceptional individuals are determined as much by the tasks and demands of society as by the objective fact of the type and degree of exceptionality. However, the relative degree of fit between a given person's aptitudes and the requirements of the culture is only part of the story. In addition to the social and vocational utility of a person's aptitudes, values also accrue to many essentially nonrelevant personal characteristics.

Despite the democratic contention that physique is a superficial characteristic which has little influence on our judgments of others, incidental observation, as well as a long series of research studies, have demonstrated that physical appearance is an important determiner of social acceptance and success. The existence of a multi-billion-dollar cosmetic industry, plastic surgery, and the fashion industry is evidence of a widespread concern with physical appearance. Physical beauty, as a social stereotype, shows remarkable uniformity across age, sex, intellectual level, and socioeconomic status (Langlais and Downs, 1979). Even in nursery school, more attractive children, as judged by adults, are more popular with their peers and are perceived as having more socially desirable personal characteristics, better academic potential, and better social relationships than their less attractive counterparts (Karris, 1977). Attractive people are seen as more deserving of reward and more readily elicit voluntary help from others than otherwise comparable but less attractive people (Adams, 1977). In simulated court situations, attractive or high-status victims or defendants receive more favorable treatment than do comparable less attractive or low-status persons (Stephan and Tully, 1977). It seems clear that we all form impressions and make judgments about others on the basis of their physical attractiveness, and that we make more favorable attributions to good-looking than to unattractive people. An actor simulating a hippie is much more likely to be reported for shoplifting by other shoppers than is the same actor simulating a "straight" person. Attractiveness operates to evoke positive responses from others and those who evoke more positive responses also emit more (Adams, 1977).

Thus, physically attractive persons attract others, who then engage in a benign escalation cycle where each overpays the other in a series of reciprocal exchanges. This is one form of the self-fulfilling prophecy. It has also been shown that individuals are evaluated more favorably when they simply associate with physically attractive persons. It seems clear that, while most underlying traits bear no necessary relationship to physical beauty, people make inferences and display expectancies which result in advantages to those blessed with a "whole" body and physical attractiveness; conversely, an increment of social disadvantage accrues to those persons who are physically deviant in ways perceived as unattractive. There is evidence that people perceived as having valued behavioral characteristics, such as competence, and favorable personality characteristics are also judged to be physically attractive. Thus the "beauty equals good" stereotype is bidirectional (Gross, 1977; Hickling, Noel, and Yutzler, 1979; Owens and Ford, 1978). Those persons who both give and receive more socially positive responses, develop greater potential for satisfactory adjustment. Thus a cultural value—body wholeness and physical beauty—becomes an important determiner of personal-social worth.

Marred physical beauty, such as facial disfigurement, without physical limitations, carries with it a social stigma and is generalized to indicate personal and social inadequacy much more than is an invisible defect, such as surgically uncorrectable congenital heart disease, a progressive disability resulting in a shortened life span and restricted educational, vocational, and recreational activities. The cultural ideal of physical wholeness and physical attractiveness means that visible disabilities generally produce more negative reactions and social discrimination than more disabling invisible disabilities (Karris, 1977). Other social values are also intertwined with basic aptitudes in determining the total assets or disabilities of a person. Social stereotypes also function as value-laden norms in the intellectual and behavior realm. The ideal of "a sound mind in a sound body" is still a norm in most societies. With widespread literacy and technological developments, physical strength and agility become less important, while intellectual ability and academic skills are more highly valued. As society places greater value on superior intellect, it necessarily stigmatizes and rejects those who do not have it. A person with low intellect becomes one with an "unsound mind." If intellectual ability were valued on a par with artistic skill, manual dexterity, or athletic prowess, it would be a good thing to have, but individuals would not be particularly stigmatized or ostracized when they lack it. However, so long as "brainpower" is an important personal measure, efforts by parents and teachers of the less endowed to devalue it will be largely futile. Ego-deflating personal comparison in terms of intellectual capacities is an inevitable part of contemporary society. Children can hardly see themselves as adequate individuals simply because their parents and/or teachers say they are, when the rest of society is continually telling that they are not. In the larger social context, their very identities often revolve around the thing which they lack. Of course, parents can improve the situation by putting less emphasis on academic grades, by underplaying intellectual prowess and academic achievements. They can insist that other achievements are equally valid measures of personal worth and success. However, when the child asks, "Why can't I read?" or "Why do the other kids call me a dummy?" it doesn't help much to say, "I love you anyway." Mental soundness and superiority along with physical soundness and attractiveness are important cultural values which influence the status and treatment accorded deviants.

Another cultural value, which overlaps the supremacy of intellectual aptitudes, is that characterized as the middle-class Protestant ethic, even though it is found in its purest form in some societies and persons who are poor, non-Christian, and who have never heard of Calvin or Knox (Nair, 1970). In essence this value makes productivity the measure of personal worth. It idealizes the virtues of independence, self-reliance, diligence, and hard work. In terms of this value, the individuals who, because of physical or mental defect or weakness of character, are non-productive and dependent upon others for their livelihood or care, are devalued as persons.

The problems of devalued deviants are as much matters of philosophical values and consequent social practices as they are of the objectively defined deficits of the individuals. Attitudes, values, and expectations are as important as physical restraints and internal limitations in determining the total handicap of a person with a disability.

In those societies where citizens are perceived as autonomous beings with certain inherent rights, the obligation to control their lives and actions in ways compatible with the corresponding rights of others is also recognized. In order to keep an acceptable balance between personal rights and social obligations, thousands of laws and codes of conduct are enacted and enforced in various ways.

These rights and obligations are considerably modified, however, when applied to the young, the mentally infirm, and the incompetent. The personal rights of these people are often abrogated or relegated to parents, guardians, institutions, or to the courts. However, the longstanding concern with civil and personal rights of the less advantaged minorities has recently been extended to the handicapped. This concern has resulted in a wide variety of legislative acts and court decisions extending many of the rights enjoyed by the nonhandicapped to persons with disabilities. Court and legislative actions increasingly incorporate the view that all people, handicapped or not, are autonomous, self-determining individuals who are responsible for their own actions to the maximum degree possible. These official acts reflect current social values which, in turn, influence who we consider handicapped, what services we think they are entitled to, and who is responsible for providing these services. Legislative acts and court decisions both reflect and mold social values and beliefs.

CHANGING CONCEPTIONS OF EQUAL EDUCATIONAL OPPORTUNITIES

Since the founding of our nation, it has been considered the obligation of the states to provide all school-age children with a tax-supported common education. Accordingly, a common school pattern and a uniform curriculum were provided for all. It was considered the responsibility of the individual students to take advantage of this opportunity and acquire the basic educational skills. Equality of opportunity meant a common school experience for all.

In 1896 the United States Supreme Court held that educational equality did not necessarily mean the same for all, at least in terms of facilities. Separate educational facilities could exist for particular classes of children as long as they remained "equal." This court decision established the "separate but equal" principle, which prevailed until 1954, when the Supreme Court declared that racial segregation, in itself, constituted inequality of educational opportunity. Thus began the nationwide movement to integrate the races in educational facilities.

When the additional educational opportunities provided by racial integration did not significantly reduce the educational deficits of black and other disadvantaged minority children, a new concept began to emerge. Equality of education began to mean "equality of results" rather than equality of opportunities. It seemed obvious that equality of results required unequal input. Thus we had a period of compensatory education. Many programs were designed to compensate for the disadvantages suffered by certain ethnic and social groups. Although it is nearly twenty years since these programs were started, their results are still in dispute. A host of evaluative studies have produced conflicting results, but on the whole, the results have been disappointing, although not sufficiently so to terminate the programs. What did seem clear is that curricular changes, regrouped children, and increased expenditures were not decisive in bringing about equality of results.

The compensatory education concept actually had been in practice for decades in the establishment of special classes and/or schools for the handicapped, and similar judgments have been made concerning its efficacy in this context. It has generally been conceded that the smaller classes, specially trained teachers, and additional funds provided for special classes for the handicapped, particularly the mentally retarded, have not reduced the handicap of the segregated children. Consequently a new concept of equality of educational opportunities for the handicapped is evolving without being so labeled. This might be called "a free and appropriate education based on individual needs." The newest groups seeking the right to a free and appropriate education individually designed to reduce their deficits significantly, if not to produce full equality of results, are the various groups designated as handicapped—the blind, the deaf, the orthopedically handicapped, the mentally retarded, as well as many with less specific, but no less real, special learning needs. Their numbers are estimated at from 8 to 10 million and they comprise some 15 percent of the school-age population. They, like the ethnic minorities and the poor, have endured a long history of segregation, discrimination, and misunderstanding.

During the 1970s a series of landmark decisions and legislative acts went a long way toward establishing the right to a free and individually appropriate education for all, irrespective of the nature and degree of handicap. These acts and ensuing regulations are still defining more precisely the dimensions of a "free and equally appropriate public education" for all. We shall briefly summarize this legislation as it relates to the handicapped.

As the result of a large number of legislative acts and rulings as well as judicial decisions and orders, the following legal rights of handicapped children have been established (see Hooker, 1978 and Burgdorf, 1979 for complete citations and additional references):

1. the right to a free, appropriate education for all children (the principle of zero rejects).

2. the right to placement in the least restrictive environment.

3. the right to nondiscriminating evaluation procedures.

4. the right of due process of law.

THE PRINCIPLE OF ZERO REJECTS

In 1971 the United States District Court of the Eastern District of Pennsylvania decreed that the state must provide all mentally retarded children with access to publicly supported education. Two years later the courts of the District of Columbia rendered a similar decision in behalf of all handicapped children. Since then, it has been established that all children, regardless of handicap, are entitled to a free, appropriate education. Any practice which excludes children from the regular educational program without providing alternative programs denies these children the rights of due process and equal protection of the law as provided in the federal constitution. The failure of schools to provide the handicapped with an appropriate education cannot be excused by the claim that there are insufficient funds. This constitutional right must be afforded all children despite the greater expense involved. Furthermore, systematic procedures shall be instituted for locating all handicapped children.

AN APPROPRIATE EDUCATION

Legislative acts have defined an "appropriate education" for a handicapped child as an individualized education program to be developed jointly by the child's teachers, the parents or guardians, a special education representative, and whenever appropriate, the child. The individualized education program shall include a determination of the child's present educational levels, a statement of short-term as well as annual goals, the nature and anticipated duration of the special services to be provided, and a periodic evaluation of the degree to which the stated objectives are being realized. Such an evaluation shall be made at least annually.

THE LEAST RESTRICTIVE ENVIRONMENT

The deinstitutionalization and mainstreaming movements were initiated by a coalition of people with radically different philosophies. They were facilitated and then mandated by legislative acts and court decisions.

The deinstitutionalization of the mentally ill resulted partly from the extensive use of a wide variety of newly developed drugs which reduced the psychotic states of a large group of hospitalized patients to a point where they could leave the psychiatric institutions and live either at home or in group housing situations. The deinstitutionalization movement was sanctioned by fiscal conservatives because it was less expensive and approved by liberals because they perceived institutional life as dehumanizing and as doing more harm than good.

The movement away from separate schools and special classes for the handicapped was similarly motivated. Available evidence (none of it very good) seemed to show that children with special educational needs (principally the mentally retarded) did just as well academically when in regular classrooms as when they attended special segregated classes or schools. Liberals were convinced that the labeling and stigmatization resulting from special class placement did the students more harm than good. Conservatives thought that keeping the handicapped in the regular classrooms (mainstreaming) would reduce the costs of educating them.

Most states now have laws and regulations supplementing the national legislation requiring the education or treatment of the handicapped in regular classes or in the local communities to the extent permitted by the nature and severity of the handicap. The special needs of the handicapped range from lifelong total care in an institution for the most severely handicapped, through full-time special school or special class placement with part-time attendance in a special class or treatment center, to regular classroom attendance with minimal assistance supplied by a special resource teacher.

Legislation mandating education in the least restrictive environment does not use the popular term *mainstreaming*. It does not require that all handicapped children be educated in the regular classroom. It does not abolish any existing educational program or setting. Education may take place in a special class, special institution, hospital, or home, either full or part time. It requires only that the handicapped be educated with the nonhandicapped "to the maximum extent appropriate." The least restrictive environment has reference to the "unique needs of each individual child." The legislation also requires that when a child is moved from one setting to another which is more restrictive, the accompanying documents must show cause and indicate why the child was unable to participate in the less restrictive setting.

Nondiscriminatory Testing and Evaluation

The issue of valid and nondiscriminatory assessment and placement of the educationally handicapped has centered on the claims of misclassification, mislabeling, stigmatization of the handicapped, and the "self-fulfilling prophecy." A series of court actions and legislative acts have highlighted the following alleged adverse effects of previous testing and evaluation procedures:

1. the preponderance of ethnic minority children in special education classes.

2. the assignment of children to special education classes resulting in their being labeled, isolated, rejected, and stigmatized.

3. the assignment of labels, resulting in stereotyping, which in turn led to lowered social and self-expectations and contributed to a self-fulfilling prophecy.

4. the fact that many mildly retarded children so identified and segregated neither needed nor benefited from such placement.

Early litigation concerning inappropriate testing and placement took place in California where Mexican-Americans and blacks accounted for a greatly disproportionate share of children in the classes for the educable mentally retarded. Class-action suits which were brought against school districts and the State Board of Education claimed that the placement procedures involved were biased and prejudicial and resulted in many Mexican-American and black children being inappropriately placed in classes for the mentally retarded. Such misplacement, it was alleged, carried with it a stigma and a "life sentence of illiteracy."

As a result of these and similar suits and court actions a widespread antitesting movement has developed and is still influential. Court judgments and legislative acts have greatly restricted the use of conventional tests and the use of test scores in the identification and placement of children in special programs for the handicapped. As a result, most school systems are now required to use both verbal and nonverbal tests, individually administered in the child's preferred language. In addition, test scores must be evaluated in relation to the child's developmental history, cultural background, and school achievement.

Since it was recognized that the mislabeling and misplacement of handicapped children occurred not only as a result of inappropriate testing and evaluation procedures but also because of arbitrary and inappropriate decisions and acts of school personnel and school boards, court decisions and legislation have provided a long list of rather specific "due process" procedures to protect student and parental rights.

DUE PROCESS REQUIREMENTS

The legal basis for most court decisions and legislative acts mandating due process procedures are the due process clauses of the Fifth and Fourteenth Amendments of the United States Constitution (Kotin and Eager, 1977). The federal rulings and state regulations usually require the following to meet the due process standard in the evaluation and educational placement of handicapped children.

1. Parents shall receive notice prior to evaluation, placement, or changes in placement of the handicapped child.

2. The written notice and oral interpretations shall be given in the primary language of the home. If the primary language of the home is not English, parents have the right to an interpreter/translator.

3. Educational progress and placement must be reviewed periodically with prior notice to the parents, an invitation to the parents to participate, a description of the procedures to be used, a report of the findings and recommendations of the review team shortly after completion of the review, and a reiteration of the procedures and rights provided at the initial evaluation.

4. Parents or guardians must be provided with an opportunity to obtain an impartial due process hearing, to examine all relevant records, and to obtain an independent educational evaluation of the child.

5. Whenever a decision of the board is contested to the point that a formal hearing is requested, the hearing must be conducted in an objective way by an impartial hearing officer or neutral review board.

6. When such hearings are held, the parents have the right to receive prior notice of the hearing, to be permitted to review all relevant records, to be represented by counsel, to bring in witnesses and cross-examine all witnesses, to present their own evidence including the results of independent evaluations and recommendations, to receive a complete record of the proceedings and, if dissatisfied, to appeal the decision.

7. Procedures must be instituted to protect the rights of the child when the parents or guardians are not known, are unavailable, or when the child is a ward of the state by providing an individual (not an employee of the state or local educational agency) to act as a surrogate for the parents or guardian.

COMPREHENSIVE REHABILITATION LEGISLATION

The federal Rehabilitation Act of 1973 and the subsequent 1978 amendments, in effect, legislate civil rights for all disabled citizens. Discrimination of all types against the handicapped by agencies receiving federal funds is unlawful. This legislation contains provisions to ensure basic human and civil rights for all handicapped individuals whether their disability be mental, physical, or emotional. It emphasizes that assistance shall be given handicapped individuals to facilitate their becoming active and productive members of society. It covers children as well as adults.

In many ways the national rehabilitation legislation and additional laws passed by the states parallel the provisions of the Education for All Handicapped Children Act (PL 94-142) passed by Congress in 1975.

In general, legislation concerning the handicapped provides that

1. no otherwise qualified handicapped person shall, because of his handicap, be discriminated against in any program or activity receiving federal financial assistance.

2. vocational education shall be made available to the handicapped with specially designed instruction to meet the unique needs of each person, at no cost to the parents or student.

3. each public agency shall insure that its handicapped children have available to them the same variety of educational programs and services, including vocational education, as are available to the nonhandicapped.

4. each public agency shall provide nonacademic and extracurricular services so as to afford handicapped children an equal opportunity for participation in them. These services and activities include counseling, health services, transportation, athletics, recreation, special interest groups, and employment.

5. states shall expend at least 10 percent of their total federal educational allotment on vocational education for handicapped persons.

6. where a vocational educational program is deemed appropriate for a handicapped person that program shall be an individualized education program.

7. employers doing business with the federal government shall take affirmative action to recruit, hire, train, and promote handicapped individuals.

The federal act also provides that rehabilitation programs must include individualized written programs. It similarly mandates an annual review of each individual's rehabilitation program, and specifies that severely handicapped persons shall receive special consideration.

During the 1950s and 1960s considerable attention and extensive legislation focused on those groups and individuals deprived of educational opportunities and employment because of racial, sex, or age discrimination. During the 1970s the protection and opportunities afforded these groups have been extended to the physically and mentally handicapped. The emphasis has shifted from opportunities and services provided because of sentimental or charitable considerations to services as a matter of constitutional and legislative rights.

The right to education has been expanded to include the right to treatment, to rehabilitation, to employment, to the vote, and the right to enjoy many other rights previously denied to many categories of handicapped.

The section of the Rehabilitation Act dealing with discrimination against the disabled has been repeatedly challenged and regularly upheld in the courts. However, in June 1979 the U. S. Supreme Court limited the scope of the act when it held that a college of nursing in North Carolina was within its rights when it refused admission to a woman who was hearing-impaired to the extent that she had to rely largely on lip-reading to understand others. The court held that this impairment could prevent a nurse from responding effectively to a patient in certain critical situations. While the court ruled very narrowly, some fear that the ruling may discourage qualified handicapped people from applying to professional schools and encourage some schools to avoid compliance with the law.

SOME ETHICAL AND MORAL ISSUES

Passing laws and issuing legal mandates do not necessarily provide the benefits these acts are intended to confer. Social attitudes, values, and expectations, as well as social and political power, are as important as legal statutes. Legislation concerning the handicapped has greatly expanded the school's role as a social agency. It has similarly extended industries' social obligations. Laws now tell educators and employers that greatly expanded educational and vocational opportunities must be provided the handicapped. It also indicates how these must be provided, what the specific responsibilities of the schools and employers are, how parents are to be involved, and specifies that the civil and legal rights of the handicapped shall not be infringed.

The impact of these laws will not be confined to the handicapped. The nonhandicapped and their parents will become concerned over possible inequities arising from the implementation of these acts. Persons suffering from borderline conditions may be concerned that they are being discriminated against because they fail to qualify for the special services provided for the officially-designated handicapped. The parents of the lesser or nonhandicapped may demand more authority and involvement in the programs provided for their children. There may be demands for individualized education programs for the less handicapped, for the gifted, and possibly, all others in between. We may hear charges of "reverse discrimination" because of the differential costs of the special and regular programs. The nonhandicapped and their parents can be expected to test their strengths, their due process rights, and demand "equal treatment." We may expect to hear more about accountability on the part of all schools and programs. When budgets are tight and programs must be cut there may be a tendency to maintain the legally-mandated special programs at the expense of those for the nonhandicapped. And when it becomes necessary to withhold benefits from one person in order to provide special services to another, ethical as well as legal issues are sure to arise.

The question of equality of opportunities versus equality of treatment versus equality of results, the equitable allocation of scarce resources, the consequences of mainstreaming on the nonhandicapped as well as the handicapped all involve critical ethical issues. For example: When the destructive behavior or excessive time required to produce minimal improvement in the handicapped deprive the other children of an equivalent share of the limited time and resources, how shall the welfare of the two groups be weighted?

If there is one theme running through recent legislation, court decisions, and general discussions it is an emphasis on the enhancement of the life of the handicapped individual, rather than the payoff to society or to particular institutions or the effects on the nonhandicapped. For example, the courts have said that the fact that it takes several times as much money to provide an appropriate education, or vocational training, or public transportation for the handicapped as for the nonhandicapped is no reason for not providing these things.

The Ethics of Behavioral Intervention

The care and treatment of the handicapped have always reflected prevailing attitudes and philosophy concerning human existence and human worth. It is common knowledge that the extermination of some categories of the handicapped was practiced in many societies during certain historical periods. Presumably, these practices went unquestioned as being in the best interests of the societies.

As long as the procedures involved in the care and treatment of people with special problems are reasonably consistent with current cultural or subcultural practices they are accepted as reasonable and useful. When the medicine man expels evil spirits from disturbed individuals, when the theologian exhorts others to be less sinful, when the mentally infirm are institutionalized, and when children with severe educational problems are placed in special classes, the goal is to change these people in ways considered desirable by techniques believed to be effective. So long as these procedures are reasonably consistent with prevalent mores, current concepts, and acceptable theories, their appropriateness and efficacy are taken for granted. However, when the basic assumptions underlying these practices become explicit, and when programs for the modification of human beings are consciously planned, quantitatively evaluated, compared with alternatives, and when their rational foundations become clear, many moral and ethical questions arise. Ethical issues have been raised most often in connection with incompetents and institutionalized persons, and with the use of drugs and behavior modification techniques. Some of the ethical questions most often raised are: By what right does one person exert control over another? Most people would agree that controls are appropriate when necessary to prevent injury to the person or to others but how about their use for the mere convenience of others? Who are the appropriate authorities and agencies to exert such controls, when law and order are not at stake? (Parents, teachers, self-appointed groups, physicians, welfare agencies?) What limits should be placed on the use of such behavioral controls? How much coercion is acceptable and under what circumstances is coercion appropriate?

Everyone influences or controls to some degree the activities of others in ways they consider to be appropriate and effective. Most of these controlling forces are a part of normal social interaction. Parents, siblings, and peers are perpetually involved in such interacting controls. Teachers, clergy, salespersons, lawyers, and politicians spend much of their professional lives influencing the behavior of others in ways they consider to be desirable. These professionals are perceived as successful to the degree that they are able to get others to modify their behavior in specified ways. The control of others, either consciously and systematically or in haphazard ways, is universal. Only the formal, institutionalized programs of reform, rehabilitation, treatment, and education, which are amenable to evaluation, have come to be challenged on both legal and ethical grounds. Are the consciously planned and organized programs of behavior modification and biofeedback less ethical than the unplanned and often inconsistently administered controls sanctioned by tradition?

One assumption often overlooked by those who criticize formal programs of behavior modification is that traditional practices designed to control or modify behavior are the safest and most effective ones. However, history provides many examples of long-standing customary practices which have subsequently been found to do more harm than good. Medical practice provides many examples. For centuries it was believed that fevers resulted from the overstimulation of the body by an excess of blood and toxins. Consequently, extensive bleeding and purging were done to remove the excess blood and toxic substances from the body.

Critical evaluation of these practices proved them to be more dangerous than the conditions they were believed to cure. Although a time-honored adage, "Spare the rod and spoil the child," is still accepted by many people, the bulk of the evidence indicates that physical punishment of children is associated with high levels of aggressive behavior later in life and with child abuse in adults.

The prevention of severe mental and physical impairment has quite universally been approved and remains a laudable goal. However, many ethical issues arise as technological advances in biology and medicine open new possibilities. Genetic screening and counseling are two of the least controversial of these advances. By means of family histories and individual tests parents or potential parents can be informed of the probabilities of their offspring being defective. Parents aware of the potential outcomes and options can then make their choices concerning contraception and/or abortion. In addition, abnormalities of many types in a fetus can be detected through amniocentesis (the examination of cells recovered from the placental fluid). When abnormalities are discovered, the parents then have the option of having an abortion. How much persuasion or coercion is it ethical to use in counseling individuals with defective genes or the parents of a defective fetus? Should they be provided with information concerning the nature of the impairment in a completely unbiased and nondirective fashion and be left to make the decision by themselves? Or should they also be informed of the costs to themselves and/or to society of providing lifelong care for such a child and of their social responsibilities? Should they be told that, since the procedures are expensive and involve some risk, genetic screening or amniocentesis will be done only if they are willing to forego having children or to agree to an abortion provided the conception or birth of a severely handicapped child is highly probable?

How about the ethics of failing to take the drastic steps necessary to make possible the survival or to prolong the life of a newborn with varying degrees of mental or physical impairment? Should the same standards apply to the handicapped as to the nonhandicapped? In some such situations, the courts have said that the handicapped shall not be discriminated against. In at least one case the court has said that where two siblings are equally acceptable as kidney donors, the parents cannot select the handicapped sibling to be the donor rather than the nonhandicapped solely on the basis of the handicap. The handicapped are entitled to all the privileges and immunities of the nonhandicapped. How about mentally competent, handicapped individuals who insist that they, rather than their nonhandicapped siblings, be the donors of body organs because they see themselves as worth less to their families or to society than their unimpaired siblings? At what point does the violent and destructive behavior of a mentally retarded, psychotic, or hyperactive individual justify placing the person in a restricted situation such as an institution? How about providing the handicapped with their equal share of available resources when matters of appearance and social norms are the primary consideration? Should skin care, hair styling, clothing in the current style, orthodontic care, and plastic surgery be provided equally to the handicapped and the nonhandicapped? Should we require the performance of a relatively risk-free but very expensive operation on a nonhandicapped infant but not on a handicapped one? With limited financial and human resources, should individuals with a greater probability of either contributing to society or being less of a burden on society be given special preference? How about the relative "rights" of the handicapped individual versus the nonhandicapped siblings and parents? How about the rights of the parents of a sexually active, mildly mentally retarded girl to have her sterilized versus the right of the girl to decide for herself? Is it fair to deprive nonhandicapped siblings of their equal share of the family's time and money in order to meet the excessive requirements of the handicapped?

Most people accept the moral obligation of society to do what it can to prevent or ameliorate severe mental and physical impairment in its citizens. Today more and more citizens are accepting the corollary obligation to do what they can to enhance the quality of human life. To be consistent, both of these obligations would require citizens to support studies to determine whether current practices are doing more harm than good. They should also support efforts designed to determine the relative effectiveness of alternative procedures and practices. Controlled studies are necessary if harmful procedures are to be supplanted by more promising ones. The hope of preventive and effective treatment programs can be realized only through support for and participation in research on the social, psychological, biological, and physical factors contributing to health and illness.

Current discussions concerning the ethics of research and practice in this area focus on the dangers of atomic radiation, genetic engineering, and the "right to die with dignity." Many feel that the potential for abuse is so great in these and related areas that further investigations should be prohibited. The assumption is that by not investigating these sensitive areas we can avoid making difficult ethical decisions. However, the cessation or prevention of investigations involves the same critical moral and ethical decisions as does the decision to proceed with them.

The limitations of our programs for the prevention of physical and mental defects are imposed more by the tremendous gap in knowledge than by our failure to apply what is known. The decision not to do research which might result in reducing the pain and suffering and defectiveness of a large segment of the population involves major moral and ethical issues.

Do the recipients of the benefits of previous research in which others have participated have any obligation to participate in additional research studies which may be of benefit to others? Thousands of individuals, but for previous research on metabolic disorders such as phenylketonuria, would be severely mentally handicapped. Do such individuals or their families have any special moral obligation to support or participate as subjects in additional studies which may be of equal benefit to others?

The Problem of "Free and Informed Consent"

A major ethical problem involved in research using human subjects is that of "informed consent." Because of recent highly-publicized instances of soldiers, prisoners, and institutionalized handicapped persons serving as subjects in experiments with real or potential dangers without, in some cases, realizing that they were doing so, there is considerable agitation to somehow safeguard the due process rights of such people. As a result, most of the professions using human subjects in research have either legal restrictions or voluntary codes of ethics defining permissible or desirable practices related to informed consent.

Most such codes require the "free and informed consent" of normal adults. On the surface, this seems quite simple and straightforward. In practice, however, "free" consent may result from a good deal of biased information and covert pressure. Let us take a case of a tissue donor. The question of actually signing a consent form is only raised after a series of positive minor decisions and acts of compliance. The prospective donor has agreed to be considered as a possible subject. He or she has submitted to a preliminary briefing as to what is involved, and has come to the hospital and donated blood and tissue samples for testing. Most of the information and instructions provided assume that ultimately consent will be given. Doubts concerning the wisdom of donating are minimized. The long and complicated procedures tend to make the assumption of consent the most plausible one. Contacts with professionals and technicians, all of whom assume the same thing, exert considerable conformity pressure. When doubts are expressed, the individuals are often urged to talk with past donors. Names of people who have been approached and refused to donate are not given. The testimonies of previous donors and the "passing" of successive tests gradually define the situation as an "opportunity" to donate. Rather than making a sacrifice and granting a special favor, the question becomes a matter of being good enough to donate. Most donors, in retrospect, never really recall the point at which all the pros and cons were objectively weighed and a clear decision reached. By the time they are told that they are eminently suitable as a donor they felt already committed to the act. The providing of the "full information" had really all pointed in one direction and was persuasive and coercive in a covert way. The decision in many cases is far from the reality of being the result of a freely and completely informed judgment.

Critical ethical and legal questions are raised when the "free and informed consent" involves the severely mentally handicapped who are judged incapable of understanding the situation. It is generally considered appropriate and legal for parents, guardians, or a court with appropriate jurisdiction to give consent. If a subject is incapable of giving consent should parents or surrogates give such consent if the procedure (1) is required for the life or well-being of the subject, (2) if it holds some prospect of being of direct benefit to the individual, or (3) if it involves no, some, or considerable risk for the individual but promises to provide benefit to others? Appropriate references and further discussion of these ethical issues are found in McGough and Carmichael, 1977; Eisenberg, 1977; and Hardman and Drew, 1978.

SUMMARY

In the last decade the attention that was previously focused on those deprived of educational, social, and employment opportunities because of race, sex, or age has been extended to the physically and mentally handicapped.

Recent policy changes, as seen in legislation and court decisions, reflect shifts in the direction of humanitarian rather than institutional or economic values. The general principle of developing one's potential and enhancing the life of the handicapped and the disadvantaged has become the central focus of concern. This reflects a more humane conception of children in particular and of people in general and a more specific recognition of the state's obligation to them. The original concern with the physical welfare of people has been expanded to include an obligation to provide for their psycho-social development and contribute to better lives. The concepts and practices subsumed under such terms as deinstitutionalization, mainstreaming, normalization, least restrictive environment, right to education and/or treatment, and decategorization reflect shifts in attitudes and practices toward atypical individuals and groups.

The two laws that have done the most to further the basic educational, civil, and human rights of all disabled individuals are the Rehabilitation Act of 1973 and the Education of All Handicapped Children Act of 1975.

The Education for All Handicapped Children Act (commonly known as Public Law 94–142) requires that every state and its localities, if they are to continue to receive funds under this act, make available a free, appropriate public education for all handicapped children between the ages of three and eighteen. This was to begin by the September 1978 school year. The act further mandates the extension of such education to all children from ages three to twenty-one by September 1980.

Handicapped children, as defined by this act, are "mentally retarded, hard of hearing, deaf, orthopedically impaired, other health impaired, speech impaired, visually handicapped, seriously emotionally disturbed or children with specific learning disabilities who, by reason thereof, require special education and related services."

An "appropriate" education is to be achieved through the development of a written individualized education program (IEP). The law requires that only four persons be involved in its development: the parents or guardians, the teacher or teachers of the child, a representative of the local education agency, and, whenever appropriate, the child. The IEP is designed to assure that, when a child requires special education, the education will be appropriate to his or her special learning needs.

The Vocational Rehabilitation Act Amendment of 1973, and the subsequent 1978 amendment, constitute a basic civil rights provision designed to prohibit discrimination against the handicapped.

In many ways, the national rehabilitation legislation, as well as additional laws passed by the states, parallel the provisions of the Education of All Handicapped Children Act of 1975. In addition to prohibiting discrimination in employment, the law requires employers to take affirmative action in employing and training qualified handicapped and to make reasonable accommodations for them.

Some of the more difficult moral issues involving the handicapped include the ethics of genetic counseling, amniocentesis, contraception, and abortion. Decisions concerning the fair distribution of limited resources to the handicapped and the nonhandicapped and obtaining consent for treatment and research all involve ethical issues for which there are no definitive answers.

REFERENCES

Adams, G. R., "Physical Attractiveness, Personality, and Social Reactions to Peer Pressure," *Journal of Psychology,* 1977, *96,* 287–94.

Burgdorf, R. L., ed., *The Legal Rights of Handicapped Persons: Cases, Materials, and Text* (Baltimore, Md.: Paul H. Brookes, 1979).

Eisenberg, L., "The Social Imperatives of Medical Research," *Science,* 1977, *198,* 1105–10.

Gross, A. E. and C. Crofton, "What is Beautiful is Good," *Sociometry,* 1977, *40,* 85–90.

Hardman, M. L. and C. J. Drew, "Life Management Practices with the Profoundly Retarded: Issues of Euthanasia and Withholding Treatment," *Mental Retardation,* 1978, *16,* 390–96.

Hickling, E. J., R. C. Noel, and F. D. Yutzler, "Attractiveness and Occupational Status," *Journal of Psychology,* 1979, *102,* 71–76.

Hooker, C. P., ed., *The Courts and Education. The Seventy-seventh Yearbook of the National Society for the Study of Education,* part 1 (Chicago, Ill.: The University of Chicago Press, 1978).

Karris, L., "Prejudice Against Obese Renters," *Journal of Social Psychology,* 1977, *101,* 159–60.

Kotin, L. and N. B. Eager, *Due Process in Special Education: A Legal Analysis* (Cambridge, Mass.: Research Institute for Educational Problems, 1977).

Langlais, J. H. and A. C. Downs, "Peer Relations as a Function of Physical Attractiveness: The Eye of the Beholder or Behavioral Reality," *Child Development,* 1979, *50,* 409–18.

McGough, R. S. and W. C. Carmichael, "The Right to Treatment and the Right to Refuse Treatment," *American Journal of Orthopsychiatry,* 1977, *47,* 307–20.

Nair, K., *The Lonely Furrow: Farming in the United States, Japan, and India* (Ann Arbor: University of Michigan Press, 1970).

Owens, G. and J. G. Ford, "Further Considerations of the 'What is Beautiful' Finding," *Social Psychology Quarterly,* 1978, *41,* 73–75.

Stephan, C. and J. C. Tully, "The Influence of Physical Attractiveness on the Decisions of Simulated Jurors," *Journal of Social Psychology,* 1977, *101,* 149–50.

SUGGESTIONS FOR STUDENTS AND INSTRUCTORS

1. In what way is the "beauty equals good" relationship bidirectional?

2. Discuss the proposition, "We cannot legislate morality."

3. How does current legislation define "an appropriate education"?

4. Discuss the variables to be considered in deciding which is the least restrictive environment for a particular person.

5. Indicate what level of mental development or chronological age you consider necessary for an individual to be able to give "informed consent."

ADDITIONAL READINGS

Kotin, L. and N. B. Eager, *Due Process in Special Education: A Legal Analysis* (Cambridge, Mass.: Research Institute for Educational Problems, 1977). A good summary of new legislation and court decisions relating to special education.

Mearig, J. S., *Working for Children: Ethical Issues Beyond Professional Guidelines* (San Francisco, Calif.: Jossey-Bass, 1978). This book covers the legal rights of children and the responsibilities and moral decisions faced by professional people who work with them.

SELECTED FILMS

Equal Protection of the Law. (30 minutes) BFA, 2211 Michigan Avenue, Santa Monica, Calif. Portrays the difficulties involved in integration.

ORGANIZATIONS AND AGENCIES

Mental Disability Legal Resource Center of the Commission on the Mentally Disabled
American Bar Association
1800 M Street, N.W.
Washington, D. C. 20036

Architectural and Transportation Barriers Compliance Board
Room 1004, Switzer Building
Washington, D. C. 20201

Western Law Center for the Handicapped
849 South Broadway, Suite 206
Los Angeles, Calif. 90014

National Center for Law and the Handicapped
1236 N. Eddy Street
South Bend, Ind. 46617

National Center for Law and the Deaf
Gallaudet College
Florida Avenue and Seventh Street, N.E.
Washington, D. C. 20002

CHAPTER 5

THE CARE AND EDUCATION OF EXCEPTIONAL INDIVIDUALS

Too often yesterday's fond hopes, which lead to today's approved practices, become tomorrow's evils. Most social and educational reform movements begin as reactions to existing evils. An initial sense of outrage and indignation provides the impetus and sustaining motivation for reform. Strength is generated by focusing the attack on existing evils. However, the history of reform movements indicates that programs designed to protect people from neglect and abuse do not assure positive benefits.

For example, placement in residential institutions in the 1800s was perceived as the humane alternative to the neglect experienced by mentally incompetent individuals who remained in their communities or to the terrible abuse which they received in jails and almshouses. Humanitarian appeals and the claim that the mentally disabled were as deserving of treatment as the physically ill resulted in a tremendous growth of residential institutions for mental defectives. However, the mental hospitals—the hope of the 1800s—became the "snake pits" of the 1900s and the special classes and schools for the handicapped came to be perceived as settings in which labeling and stigmatizing had a more catastrophic impact on the segregated students than did their inherent impairments. Institutionalization and special class placement of the handicapped, it was claimed, did more harm than good and should be discontinued. A National Research Council committee spent four years studying problem children and their families in America and recommended that all the large custodial institutions that housed the mentally retarded, emotionally disturbed, physically handicapped, and delinquent children be abolished (Gaylin, 1977).

Consequently, "deinstitutionalization," "normalization," and "mainstreaming" became the rallying cries of the 1960s and 1970s. Predictably, deinstitutionalization and mainstreaming were done without providing adequately for more effective alternatives. As a result, we have experienced a counterreaction against the housing of thousands of formerly institutionalized persons in hostile local communities without adequate housing, supervision, or treatment. A comparable situation developed when handicapped children were hurriedly mainstreamed back into the regular classes from which they were originally moved because their educational needs were not being met.

successful main-streaming

How was I ever going to manage with Craig in my room? If this was mainstreaming, I wanted none of it! Craig's mother had told me that I might have a little trouble with him as he had never been away from home before and, "Oh yes, you may have to help him when he goes to the bathroom." An understatement, if there ever was one! Craig not only could not go to the bathroom by himself, he couldn't feed himself, speak understandably, or go up and down stairs. For the first three days Craig spent most of the time either in my lap or sitting in a chair at my knee. It was obvious that something had to change if, in addition to taking care of Craig, I was going to deal with my additional twenty-one first-graders.

I quickly sent out an SOS for every specialist in the school—the principal, the nurse, the social worker, the medical consultant, the learning disability teacher, and the speech therapist. They were all sympathetic but not very encouraging. The learning disability teacher could take Craig for half an hour each day. The speech therapist could work with him three times a week. But "mainstreaming" meant that Craig was going to spend the bulk of his time in my room! I wondered what kind of people had ever instituted such an impossible program.

I soon discovered that if I was going to find time to eat my own lunch, Craig would either have to learn to feed himself or someone else would have to help him. I asked one of my best students to help Craig eat. I soon had twenty-one eager teacher's aides! They were all helping teach Craig to go up and down stairs, to go to the bathroom, to eat, and to talk.

As the weeks went by, the other children were as excited about Craig's progress as I was. Yesterday he said his name and today he ate his soup without spilling! At show-and-tell, Craig mostly mumbled, but the whole class listened carefully to see if he would use one of the words they had taught him. When at Thanksgiving time Craig was able to say, "To Grandma's house we go" over and over in a recognizable fashion, the entire class applauded, while he beamed.

By the end of the year Craig was able to speak a dozen recognizable phrases, read thirty words, count to twenty, eat by himself, and go up and down stairs. These accomplishments would never have been possible without the assistance of Craig's parents who worked closely with me. His speech therapist, special education teacher, and most of all, Craig's twenty-one classmates contributed immeasurably to Craig's successful mainstreaming.

a main-
streaming
failure: how
not to do it

"The first year of educational mainstreaming for Beth has been a total disaster." This is the opinion of Beth's mother. Beth, a mentally retarded ten-year-old, had been mainstreamed into a regular public school first grade. Her parents felt that her adjustment and progress in the regular first grade were far below that attained in a comparable period in the special preschool she had attended for two years previously. They felt that she had not learned anything during the year and that she had regressed in her self-help skills. They believed this lack of progress reflected a total lack of interest and preparation on the part of the school personnel. Mr. and Mrs. Wright had visited the school the spring before Beth was to enter. In spite of this forewarning, little seemed to have been done to prepare for Beth's entry.

The principal had not anticipated any special problems with Beth. Since her teacher was experienced and flexible it was assumed that their usual procedures for easing new children into the first grade would be sufficient. The principal felt sure that the teacher, with the help of a resource teacher, could deal with any special problems that might arise. It was thought best not to set up a "self-fulfilling prophecy" by alerting all the school personnel and making elaborate preparations.

The principal, teacher, and special services personnel all were unprepared for the amount of time and energy required by a student like Beth. According to Beth's mother, when she went to the school she felt that very little planning had been done about Beth's special program. Everything seemed to be done on a day-to-day basis. The teacher appeared completely baffled by Beth, but insisted that they could work out a program for her. Beth has been unhappy from the first day of school and her general behavior has been worse—at home as well as at school.

Beth's sister, Sarah, has also suffered this year. The other children teased her about her sister. According to Sarah, the other children sometimes imitate Beth's way of talking and then laugh about it. Mrs. Wright thinks Sarah should protect and do more for Beth. Her husband disagrees and thinks that Sarah should not assume the burden of Beth's problems. He doubts that Beth will ever be able to deal with the demands of the regular class.

At a conference of the parents, the principal, and Beth's teacher, the school staff people were apologetic about what had happened. The principal and the teacher didn't appreciate the preparation and additional assistance Beth would require. The principal agreed that he had not taken the time to have the kind of discussion with the parents that would have been helpful. Beth's teacher said she had been promised a teacher's aide. However, since she was not sure how she was going to use her she hadn't filed a formal request. She indicated that while all the first-grade children have self-care problems, she was unprepared for the extent of Beth's needs. She acknowledged that she should have asked for more help from the special education personnel but she had always found it easier to handle her own problems rather than working out some type of collaboration.

The teacher and the principal apologized to Beth's parents and hoped that they could make a new start the following fall and do better. Mr. and Mrs. Wright are both convinced that mainstreaming was a mistake for their daughter.

SOME ALTERNATIVES TO THE INSTITUTION

The deinstitutionalization movement is not new. As early as 1916 a Jewish orphanage in New York established an auxiliary group home to help prepare orphaned adolescent girls for normal home and community living. During the 1930s social legislation was passed in the United States to provide financial aid to families with dependent children, child welfare services, public adoption agencies, and foster home care as alternatives to orphanage care for neglected and dependent children. As a result, the number of children in orphanages was reduced by half in the next two decades. However, the number of institutionalized delinquents, mental deficients, and mentally ill continued to increase (Gula, 1974).

In the late 1950s and early 1960s a major drive began for the development of group homes and similar community facilities as alternatives to custodial institutions. The 1970s have seen the beginning of comprehensive community-based human-services systems for social service and health delivery. While these broad human service systems are still in the conceptualization and planning stage, they are perceived as an alternative to the proliferation and fragmentation of human service facilities which still prevail in the United States. This fragmentation of services is largely the result of the funding of services according to categories of disabilities by federal, state, and local appropriating and governing bodies.

The movement to blanket the conventional categorical service facilities (mental illness, mental retardation, blindness, deafness, delinquency, and so on) into a broad coordinated service system may be facilitated by several concurrent developments. Among these are class-action lawsuits establishing constitutional rights to effective services for all the handicapped, and the concern with the effects of labeling and stigmatizing individuals (one of the secondary consequences of providing services by categories). The advocacy groups working for specific categories such as minority ethnics, homosexuals, prisoners, females, and the more conventional categories of the handicapped are discovering that they have much in common; they may eventually combine their efforts in favor of broad service systems. In the meantime, less comprehensive national, state, and local efforts at establishing the more conventional community services as alternatives to institutionalization continue.

Our discussion of the deinstitutionalization and mainstreaming movements has focused on the mentally retarded and the emotionally disturbed because these groups have been the focus of recent concern. However, most of the components of the models proposed for attaining these ends for mental deviates have long been part of the programs available to the physically handicapped. While there has been considerable discussion of the relative merits of the residential versus the special class for the blind, the deaf, and the orthopedically handicapped, the questions have centered on the types and categories of children who could be most effectively educated in these respective settings. Institutionalization was never the norm. Long before the current deinstitutionalization movement got under way, residential schools for children in these categories were decreasing in importance, and special classes in day schools were increasing. The deinstitutionalization of the bulk of these handicapped children began long ago.

Most special educational classes for these categories of handicapped were also partially integrated. Most frequently, a special teacher had the major responsibility for the handicapped, but integrated the children into regular classes to the extent that it was feasible. Partial integration was also the most common administrative arrangement for the educable mentally retarded at the high school level. Completely self-contained classes for the mentally retarded were largely confined to the elementary grades. In the compartmentalized high school, the mentally retarded typically studied industrial arts, home economics, music, art, and physical education along with the "normal" students. They were segregated only in their home rooms and in more academically demanding courses. Thus, many components of the current normalization or mainstreaming movement have long been part of most conventional special education programs. Among the facilities that have functioned as alternatives to the residential institution are day hospitals, day care centers, foster and adoptive homes, halfway houses, group homes, and sheltered workshops.

DAY HOSPITALS OR DAY TREATMENT CENTERS

Day hospitals have been used principally for psychiatric patients who need intensive treatment and who are able to spend their nights elsewhere—usually in their homes. Day hospitals are less expensive than the usual residential facility, and they keep the patient related to home and community rather than separated and isolated from them. The first such hospital was established in Moscow in 1932. Since that time similar facilities have been established in many countries. In 1960, 5,000 patients a year were receiving care in twenty-six American day hospitals (Winich, 1960); California has established several such centers (MacMillan and Aase, 1964).

The day hospital reduces the likelihood that the patient will become over-dependent on institutional life. Many individuals adapt to institutional life too readily. They feel secure in the hospital and become fearful of a return to their homes and community. The day hospital reduces the "hospitalization effect." Experience indicates that some patients respond to treatment more readily in a day hospital than they do in a residential setting which offers total care.

The day hospital also seems to incur less stigma than does the regular psychiatric facility, partly because the patients continue to live at home and partly because legal commitment is avoided. Day hospitals must be in or near larger population centers and have adequate public transportation.

In addition to physical therapy, pharmacotherapy, and individual and group psychotherapy, there is usually provision for occupational therapy, school classes, libraries, and recreation. Occupational training or retraining is also offered in almost all day centers. Patients may be transferred to outpatient departments, halfway houses, day care centers, or other facilities upon completion of treatment, or, when they do not respond or are judged to be too ill for the day hospital, they may be transferred to a custodial institution. The day hospital has been used more for adults than for children. One study reports that only 10 percent of the patients were below the age of twenty. Day hospitals have also been used primarily for the more seriously emotionally disturbed patients—the neurotics and psychotics (Kramer, 1960).

Day Care Centers for the Handicapped

The disabled child who is either too young or too severely handicapped to take advantage of the special education and other training programs of the community often places a tremendous strain on the personal and financial resources of the family. When such children remain isolated at home, they also lack the social contacts and experiences which are necessary for maximum development. To lessen the burden on the family and to provide some social contacts for these children, day care centers have been established in most larger communities. Private day care centers have been operating for many years, and publicly supported agencies have recently been established (Jew, 1974).

The original day care programs provided physical care alone, but more recently self-help and socialization training have been added. Several states have established nursery school programs for preschool mental retardates.

The advantages of day care centers for the handicapped are: (1) the parents are relieved of the twenty-four-hour task of caring for the handicapped child; (2) nonhandicapped siblings will not be neglected because the excessive demands of the handicapped child will be diminished; (3) the rest of the family can live a more normal social life because the emotional strain is diminished and a more wholesome family atmosphere facilitated; (4) the parents may be able and willing to keep the child at home instead of placing him or her in an institution or boarding home; and (5) the training received in such centers may raise the child's level of functioning to the point where he or she can attend special classes, become partially self-supporting, or at least be less of a burden to others. Day care centers for many types of the handicapped stand midway between the traditional outpatient clinic and inpatient hospital services. The day care facility provides more constant and intensive supervision, care, and treatment than does an outpatient service. It combines care, treatment, and rehabilitation. In some cases, a single administrative organization may operate an inservice unit, a day care program, an outpatient department, and, either on its own or in cooperation with other agencies, vocational rehabilitation services.

Outpatient Clinics

Another community-based facility serving the disabled which is expanding rapidly is the outpatient clinic. Individuals no longer requiring the supervision and intensive treatment of the residential facility or the day care center may report to an outpatient clinic daily or weekly, as required, for treatment or counseling. The community outpatient clinic may serve as a diagnostic center, as a limited treatment facility, and as a referral agency.

The future will probably witness still more significant changes in the development of comprehensive community-based services for exceptional people. Many such centers, to provide for all the needs of the handicapped, including preventive, diagnostic, and rehabilitative care and consultative and educational needs, are now in operation, and still more are being planned.

FOSTER CARE

Foster care is a social service provided to families who are temporarily unable to care for their children or as a way station for children who will be put up for adoption. Children enter the system through their parents, who voluntarily surrender them to a local child care agency, or the courts, which award custody to either a public or private agency in cases of neglect or abuse. The agencies are then supposed to place the child in a temporary home. This home may be a private family, group residence, or institution. Some agencies try to move their children quickly out of the system but many do not and what was supposed to be a temporary shelter often becomes a permanent one. As a result, in 1977 there were some 400,000 children in foster homes by child care agencies in the United States (McTaggart, 1977). The Child Welfare League of America estimates that foster children stay in care for an average of from four to six years. They also claim that if the parents do not take a child back within eighteen months, they never do.

Children remain so long in this system for several reasons. One is monetary. Foster care is subsidized by state and federal agencies and these payments are structured so that it pays agencies to keep the children as long as possible. Another reason is that social workers have traditionally considered many of these children—especially the handicapped—to be unadoptable. However, more than half of a random sampling of prospective adoptive parents were found to be willing to take these children. The North American Coalition on Adoptable Children has placed large numbers of handicapped children—even the severely handicapped (McTaggart, 1977).

ADOPTION SERVICES FOR THE HANDICAPPED

At one time moderately or severely handicapped children were considered unadoptable. However, most of these children are now referred to as hard-to-place children, and many are being adopted. Many such adoptions are facilitated by the Adoption Resource Exchange of North America (ARENA), a clearing-house organized and operated by the Child Welfare League of America to help agencies find homes for their hard-to-place children. Any licensed adoption agency may register without charge children for whom they are unable to find homes, and approved families who are willing to accept a hard-to-place child can do likewise. From this information, families and children are tentatively matched and referred to local agencies for further consideration and action.

While many agencies are phasing out their adoption services because of the shortage of infants, others are accepting for placement more of the hard-to-place children—minority ethnic group children, older children, and the handicapped. Handicapped children whose adoption has been facilitated through ARENA include those with dwarfism, mental retardation, blindness, deafness, cardiac disorders, epilepsy, emotional disturbances, speech defects, hyperactivity, and albinism. Many children previously "lost" in foster homes and institutions are now being "found" and placed for adoption. Some agencies see the current imbalance between available infants and adoptive applicants as an opportunity to extend their services to those children and families who have been largely overlooked in the past. Today's definition of an adoptable child as "any child in need of a permanent family who can benefit by family life" (Gallagher, 1972) makes this feasible.

In the early 1970s, black groups protested the adoption of black children by whites, with the result that a practice that had risen sharply in the 1960s fell off sharply during the next decade (Ladner, 1977).

One development which has enlarged the categories of adoptable children and adoptive families is that of subsidized adoptions (Gallagher, 1972). Financial reimbursement makes possible the adoption of handicapped children by otherwise acceptable parents who cannot afford to assume the financial responsibilities involved. By the mid-1970s, thirty-nine states and the District of Columbia had passed subsidized adoption legislation to provide a subsidy for children who are handicapped (Kravik, 1975). Such financial assistance often enables a family to adopt a child requiring special medical, nursing, or psychiatric care, or educational-rehabilitation programs. Organizations are becoming increasingly active in promoting the interests of children who are awaiting adoption and in providing post-adoptive services to adopted children and their adoptive families.

HALFWAY HOUSES

Sometimes the boarding home is used much like a dormitory in a residential institution. The halfway house provides a facility for older adolescents and adults in which handicapped persons may live for varying periods of time preparatory to going out into the community entirely on their own. People residing in such facilities may be working in a sheltered workshop or on competitive jobs; they may be receiving vocational rehabilitation or simply seeking employment. The halfway home is typically an intermediate step for individuals who will soon return to the community following a period of institutionalization; but, like family care and the boarding home, it can serve as an alternative to institutionalization.

The halfway house, as an aftercare facility which has been used primarily for discharged patients, is designed to assist the patient's transition from hospital to community life. It is used for alcoholics, criminals, the mentally ill, and juvenile delinquents. It facilitates the movement of individuals from a dependent existence in an institution in which they received total care to the free community, by providing an intermediate situation—a more independent, but still relatively simple life in a supervised residential facility. Vermont has established a network of such houses as a transitional facility between the state mental hospital and a rehabilitation agency. The halfway house provides a sheltered social environment in which new roles and behaviors can be tried and developed. Most provide professional counseling and supervision. The period of residence is typically limited to from three months to a year.

Similar facilities in rural settings are sometimes known as "work camp houses." In such settings, jobs are available on the grounds and the residents are usually there twenty-four hours a day.

GROUP HOMES

While halfway houses in the past were primarily pre- or post-institutional facilities, many group homes today are part of the broad deinstitutionalization movement. Group homes are operated for the emotionally disturbed, the mentally retarded, actual or potential delinquents, alcoholics and ex-alcoholics, and drug addicts and ex-addicts, detached from earlier pre- or post-institutional connections. Group homes, like halfway houses, provide residential care, supervision, counseling, and/or therapy for a broad class of deviant individuals.

Group homes have been established in large family dwellings, apartments, high-rises, and public housing units. Their quality varies greatly, and many have been criticized for several reasons. Some programs lack dedicated leadership, sufficient funds, and public support. One fear is that such community facilities place potentially dangerous mental defectives and delinquents free on the streets. As we mentioned earlier, in some cases deinstitutionalization has meant precipitously moving the mentally ill and mentally deficient from "back wards" to "back alleys" without needed resources and services.

A recent court ruling focuses on this problem. A 1970 National Institute of Mental Health study reported that 56 percent of the 3,600 patients in the St. Elizabeth Hospital in Washington, D.C.—once regarded as the finest mental institution in the United States—did not belong in the hospital and would be better off in alternative care facilities. In 1974 a class-action suit was filed in the U.S. District Court. Judge Aubrey Robinson ruled in *Dixon* v. *Weinberger* that the federal government must provide alternative care facilities such as nursing homes, foster homes, and halfway houses for St. Elizabeth's inpatient population capable of living in such community-based settings. Judge Robinson stated that a full range of treatment must be made available to those placed in these residential facilities (Schaar, 1976).

VOCATIONAL REHABILITATION PROGRAMS

All the states of the United States provide vocational rehabilitation programs for disabled adults. The public program of vocational rehabilitation had its beginnings in World War I, was started officially in 1920, and has expanded tremendously since World War II. Many state rehabilitation programs have recently been expanded to include mentally retarded and psychiatrically disabled adults, as well as the physically handicapped. Rehabilitation personnel are also cooperating with the schools. They take those individuals who either finish the school program or exceed the age limits for school attendance and provide them with additional vocational training, counseling, and supervision.

To be eligible for the services of the Vocational Rehabilitation Agency, the person must be substantially handicapped as a result of a physical or mental disability; must be of employable age by the time the rehabilitation services are completed; and must show promise of becoming employable or of attaining a higher level of vocational adequacy as a consequence of the service. These requirements limit the program to adults and older adolescents and to those with milder handicaps.

The vocational rehabilitation agencies have no training facilities of their own, but purchase such services from existing sources. The financial help provided by this service has facilitated the development of training centers, sheltered workshops, and on-the-job training programs for the handicapped. Anyone can refer a handicapped person to a local vocational rehabilitation office. The vocational rehabilitation program includes evaluation (medical, psychological, and vocational), training (school, sheltered workshop, or on-the-job), and eventual job placement. All these services are provided at no direct cost to the client.

SHELTERED WORKSHOPS

As the name indicates, a sheltered workshop is a facility providing training or employment geared to the capacities and needs of people who cannot satisfactorily be trained or employed in normal competitive job situations because of special disabilities. Such workshops are found in public and private residential institutions and as independent endeavors in the community. Like the vocational rehabilitation programs, they are primarily for adults.

Individuals working at sheltered employment may, at the lowest level, spend their days in the workshop, keeping busy. Even with maximum assistance and supervision, these people produce little of economic importance, although they act like ordinary employed adults. The workshop serves somewhat the same function for these people that the day care center does for younger children. The work done by individuals with greater aptitude—the "sheltered employable" group of persons—can contribute significantly to their support. People functioning on this level may be partially self-supporting in the workshop, but they can probably never compete in an ordinary environment. Individuals with greater potential— the "deferred employable" group—use the sheltered workshop purely for training, preparatory to their placement in ordinary employment. On this level, the sheltered shop mediates between idleness and regular employment. The workshop is primarily a means of controlling the stress on the workers and of assisting handicapped people to increase their self-sufficiency. The shop often provides training in skills which can be used in other jobs; in addition, it may inculcate general work habits, attitudes, and self confidence which, it is hoped, will carry over to future employment even in different jobs. It is assumed that the disabled person in a sheltered workshop can develop a "work personality" consisting of punctuality, cooperative work habits, and desirable ways of relating to authority, as well as favorable attitudes toward a job, a boss, fellow workers, and earnings.

People in sheltered workshops may make new things for sale, repair or recondition used articles for resale, or contract or subcontract work from private industry. Such workshops have long provided employment and training for the auditory, visually, and orthopedically handicapped; more recently, some workshops have also accepted the mentally retarded and the mentally ill. Many separate workshops have also been established solely for the mentally retarded or emotionally disturbed. In 1960 there were more than 600 sheltered workshops in the United States. Over 100 of these were operated by one organization, Goodwill Industries (Olshansky, 1960).

SOCIAL AND RECREATIONAL PROGRAMS

The handicapped child, like every other child, needs a social life and recreation. The overprotection provided in some homes, the failure of ordinary groups and organizations to accept the handicapped, and the inherent limitations of the uniquely disabled necessitate special provision for the social and recreational needs of the handicapped. In communities where special educational programs, training facilities, vocational programs, and occupational outlets for the disabled either are not available or are very limited, recreational and social programs may provide the handicapped with their sole opportunities for social contacts.

While many handicapped individuals can participate in the regular social and recreational programs of the community, many others cannot. Recreational programs for the handicapped may not differ markedly from those provided for the general public, but it often is necessary to provide some special equipment, training, and supervision. In addition to regular, supervised playground activities and group games, these programs may include conducted field trips, day and summer camps, social groups, and clubs. The programs are often provided or sponsored by city or school recreational departments, voluntary groups and agencies, churches, the YWCA and YMCA, the Boy Scouts and the Girl Scouts, and similar organizations.

One type of cooperative self-help organization contributing to the recreational and social life of some types of handicapped adults is the ex-patient club. Such clubs were first started in England in 1940. By 1959 an estimated seventy clubs were operating in the United States, the largest concentration of such clubs being in California (Olshansky, 1960).

RESPITE CARE

One of the early Respite Home Programs was developed by the Hartford Regional Center (an agency of the Connecticut Department of Health, Office of Mental Retardation) to provide temporary care to enable families with handicapped children to take vacations, to cope with emergencies, or just to find temporary relief from the constant stress of caring for a handicapped individual. The respite program is a community-based, family-centered alternative to institutional care. Temporary care (not exceeding thirty days) is provided a handicapped child in the home of another family—a "respite family." Social workers screen prospective respite families, match natural and respite families, and provide back-up and emergency services when needed. Emergency medical services are also available. When such a placement seems desirable, the social worker arranges a preplacement visit in the home of the respite family; the natural parents, the child, and the coordinator are present. If both families are agreeable, the contract for the period of care is signed. The fees ($10 a day for the first two days and $5 a day thereafter) are paid by the natural parents to the respite family. Funds are available for the care of children whose parents cannot afford the cost (Case, Fitzgerald, and Ficarro, 1975). Many other locations now provide respite care for the handicapped.

When the California state residential facilities for the mentally retarded operated school programs, many children enrolled in these schools spent their summer vacations at home with their families. Since this left space available in the institutions, other mentally retarded children were accepted for temporary placement to permit their families to be free for vacations and other activities, just as do the respite care facilities today.

HOME TRAINING AND COUNSELING PROGRAMS

Most parents of handicapped children lack the knowledge and skills needed to train them effectively. Yet home training services, although they are an essential part of a comprehensive program for the disabled, are available in few communities. The John Tracy clinic in Los Angeles provides information concerning home training techniques for the parents of deaf children; it conducts a nursery school for deaf children and special training classes for parents; and it has hundreds of parents enrolled in its correspondence course. Similar services are provided by the Chicago Hearing Society and Clinic. The Volta Bureau in Washington, another good source of information for parents, also teaches special educational techniques to parents of deaf children. Similar sources of information and training are available to the families of the blind. The National Association for Retarded Children, which has its headquarters in New York and has many state and local affiliates, serves as a clearinghouse for information about the mentally retarded. The United Cerebral Palsy Association, Inc., and its local affiliates perform a similar function for victims of cerebral palsy. The United States Children's Bureau in Washington, D.C., is a good source of information on all types of exceptional children.

The counseling facilities available to the parents of the mentally retarded and most of the other categories are still quite inadequate. Clinic staffs, private physicians, city and county health officials, social workers, nurses, and school personnel all provide some counseling and information for parents of exceptional children, but this is usually sporadic and not followed up. Most parents need and welcome assistance in understanding the significance of their child's condition and would benefit from more information and counseling about handling and training the child.

One agency, whose historical exclusive function has been the placement of children who needed separation from their parents, has recently developed a program of home services designed to keep such children at home (Goldstein, 1973). This agency accepts the fact that long-term treatment is inevitable in most such cases. Treatment includes not only conventional casework, counseling, and sometimes psychotherapy, but also the development of personal-social, homemaking, child care, and vocational skills. The social work job becomes that of "parenting" both children and parents. Social workers share in planning and carrying out many ordinary daily tasks and activities, providing many direct, concrete supportive services. Fewer than 5 percent of the children served by this program have required separation from their parents. The program involves long-term treatment—children have received treatment for as long as five and a half years at a cost of approximately $1,000 per year per child.

The exceptional person needs special counseling and guidance. Achieving self-understanding, establishing goals consistent with one's abilities and disabilities, and making realistic life plans are major problems in everyone's life, but they are especially critical and difficult for the exceptional individual. While there seems to be nothing distinctive and unique about the personalities of exceptional people, the handicapped do have more severe adjustment problems and are thus in greater need of counseling. The evaluation of the aptitudes of exceptional children is difficult, and their educational programs are often different. Their vocational opportunities are unique, and the need for specially trained counselors is great.

EDUCATION OF THE GENERAL PUBLIC
CONCERNING EXCEPTIONAL CHILDREN

One of the greatest needs of exceptional people is for increased public awareness, acceptance, and understanding of exceptionality—particularly of disabling exceptionality. In the first place, unless a substantial part of the public recognizes the needs of the handicapped, the disabled will not be provided with the necessary facilities, programs, and opportunities. Second, unless the general public understands the nature of the difficulties and the needs of the various types of disabled persons, even the available resources and opportunities may be denied them.

Handicapped persons do not need sympathy and pity. They need understanding and acceptance as persons with certain limitations. There is little use in training a handicapped child to become socially adept and aware if fearful and anxious neighbors will not let their children play with her. It is not helpful to teach her to play games, or to sing and dance, if she remains socially unacceptable. Occupational and vocational training programs are wasted if employers will not give the handicapped an opportunity to demonstrate their competence. Many a business person will send a handicapped child to summer camp but not employ him when he grows up. There has been a significant increase in public awareness and understanding of the disabled, but there is still much to be done and too few agencies to do it.

FROM SPECIAL CLASSES TO MAINSTREAMING

In the century since the first special classes were established in the United States, segregated special classrooms or schools have been the most popular administrative arrangements for educating the handicapped. However, during the last two decades two movements have changed the nature of special education in America. One of these has been the *right to education* or *zero reject* trend. Until recently, large numbers of children were excluded from school programs because they were "too something-or-other"—too mentally deficient, too emotionally disturbed, too crippled, or too unmanageable. However, since recent legal decisions have enunciated the legal right to education, many children previously excluded from school have been provided with special programs.

Changing social attitudes have also facilitated this trend. The inclusion of more and more of the mentally retarded in the school program is fairly typical. In most states, provision for the mentally retarded has followed a common course over the past thirty years. First, additional funds (usually in the form of special state aid) were made available to school districts which elected to provide special programs for the mildly mentally retarded (the educable mentally retarded). Next, it was made mandatory for school districts to provide such programs. A decade later, the same sequence of events—first permissive and then mandatory programs—resulted in the establishment of similar provisions for the moderately retarded (the trainable mentally retarded). Still more recently in some states, special programs for the severely mentally retarded have been provided under educational auspices.

Recent legal decisions and legislation have both reflected and accelerated the movement to require that all children, regardless of handicap or level of functioning, have access to appropriate education and/or training. The courts have said, in effect, that none of the conventional reasons for exclusion from school—no money, no room, no facilities, no teachers, or low aptitude for learning—could be used to justify the withholding of education from certain categories of children. If communities do not have at their disposal the additional money necessary to provide teachers, space, equipment, and transportation for these new students, they must reallocate the available resources currently assigned exclusively to other categories of children.

Another movement that is changing the nature of special education in America was mentioned earlier: providing services on a noncategorical basis and retaining the deviant child in the regular classroom with supplementary instructional assistance and support provided by specialized personnel—popularly referred to as mainstreaming. The current emphasis on noncategorical treatment and mainstreaming was brought about by a series of events including:

1. the failure of research studies to establish the effectiveness of special classes for the handicapped.

2. a realization of the inadequacy of medically and psychologically defined diagnostic categories for educational purposes.

3. studies indicating that many educationally and aptitude-irrelevant factors, such as race, social class, personality characteristics, and manageability, were operative in special class placement.

4. a realization of the deleterious effects of officially categorizing and labeling, a traditional prerequisite for providing needed educational assistance.

5. court judgments and legislation of the type already discussed.

Some Philosophical Assumptions

One of the most basic assumptions underlying the current trends is that every human being—handicapped or not—is entitled to the fullest measure of the available educational resources. Society, via its educational system, has the obligation to devise programs and provide treatment tailored to meet the deviant child's individual needs, rather than simply to sort children according to the degree that they fit existing programs and techniques, excluding those who do not fit. It is also assumed that mainstreaming will foster the valuing rather than the stigmatization of human differences.

Labeling and segregating the deviants increases their distinct categorization and stigmatization. Consequently, keeping them in the regular classroom should increase the mutual understanding and acceptance of normal and deviant. Public policies and educational practices should encourage not mere tolerance, but a positive valuing of differences. They should encourage respect for individuality and an appreciation of the differing talents of persons who are different physically, mentally, linguistically, and culturally.

Handicapped children are expected to profit from exposure to developmentally more typical peer models and from opportunities to learn adaptive ways of interacting socially with their more normal peers. However, research on the efficacy of integrated programs in these areas has shown that these positive outcomes do not necessarily result from such arrangements. In most integrated school settings, levels of peer interaction and imitation between handicapped and nonhandicapped classmates are consistently minimal unless specific procedures are instituted to bring this about (Donaldson and Martinson, 1977).

If we can extrapolate from studies of racial integration, it seems that having handicapped and nonhandicapped children work and play together, to the maximum degree possible, is the best way to improve their attitudes and behavior. A survey of the relevant studies has shown that conducting human relations workshops for school personnel and having students discuss race relations in class also help, but by far the strongest influence on students' attitudes and behavior is working and playing in mixed groups (Slavin and Madden, 1979).

The fact that social class, race, and handicap are, to a degree, interrelated complicates the problem of peer acceptance of the handicapped. We have previously indicated that, for a variety of reasons, the handicapped come disproportionately from disadvantaged ethnic groups and from the lower socioeconomic classes. Race, social class, and handicap when combined are more than additive in their effects on peer attitudes and acceptance.

Although research evidence as to their effectiveness is lacking, simulation activities, trying out artificial aids and appliances, having discussions with handicapped individuals, viewing movies, videotapes, slides, and reading printed material dealing with the handicapped, as well as class discussions concerning the variety, nature, and special problems of the handicapped are all being used to assist the nonhandicapped to understand the problems of others. Simulation activities are limited only by the ingenuity of the teachers and the time and facilities available. They can include such things as having the children move about the room or the school yard, or eat a meal, while blindfolded to simulate blindness. To approximate poor vision, sandwich bags can be folded and placed over the eyes, and students can then be requested to write, read, and walk up or down stairs. Listening to a class with plugs in their ears and trying to understand a film presentation without the sound can simulate the problems of deafness. To approximate difficulties in motor coordination, participants can wear heavy gloves while trying to button a coat, tie their shoes, or pick up a coin. Poor gross motor coordination can be simulated by tying the ends of a cord to the ankles and walking while keeping the cord taut. Similar arm restrictions can be obtained by tying the upper part of the arms to the body, thus permitting movements only at the elbow and wrists. Going up and down stairs skipping a rope, or dancing with the shoelaces tied together may approximate other limitations.

Exposure to and limited experiences with the aids and appliances of the handicapped are often used prior to or subsequent to the entrance of a handicapped child into the classroom. Braille equipment, hearing aids, travel canes, wheelchairs, walkers, and crutches can be borrowed from hospitals, rehabilitation centers, or supply houses. Contacts can vary from simply observing the appliances and handling them, to actually trying them out for short periods of time. The more adventurous students may find it challenging to try out the aids and appliances in simulated handicapping situations.

The awkwardness of the inexperienced nonhandicapped as compared with the adeptness of the handicapped in manipulating and using the aids and appliances will indicate to the former that handicaps are relative to the individual's capacities in terms of the demands of the particular situation, and are not solely conditions within the person. The greater adeptness of the handicapped children may also be something to enhance their social and self-images.

Devising situations and experiences equivalent to such mental handicaps as autism and mental retardation is more difficult. However, some components of the language limitations of the more severely handicapped can be simulated by limiting speech to two-word combinations and using words with no more than two syllables. Having the students ask for common things and give instructions with these linguistic limitations may be instructive. When the language limitations are broken, the listeners may be instructed to look blank and ignore all requests untill the same things are restated within the prescribed limitations.

These activities are all designed to instill positive attitudes and encourage social interaction with handicapped individuals, thus increasing the likelihood of establishing mutually satisfying reciprocal activities. In helping children to understand better their handicapped classmates, we have to locate the disabled somewhere between the extremes of "These children are really just like us" and "These children are basically different from us." The first minimizes or denies differences—both those that are truly handicapping and those that are superficial. The second proposition overgeneralizes the differences—even those that are truly handicapping.

Children need to be made aware of the universality and significance of individual differences without equating "sameness" with "being good" and "differentness" with "being bad." All people are similar in their need to be accepted, appreciated, treated with respect, and so on. Differences are in terms of size, physique, and in the things they can or cannot do, and the special aids they may or may not need.

One assumption of the mainstreaming movement is that the purposes of special education are no different from those of regular education. The focus is on the individual and his or her optimum development in an open society. The goal of all programs for the handicapped is to provide the disabled with the physical, intellectual, and social skills needed to live, learn, and work in the community with the least special support from others. Current thinking emphasizes the continuity between the handicapped and the nonhandicapped. While the handicapped, by definition, depend upon others for their maintenance and welfare, we all depend upon others for these same things to a greater or lesser extent. These needs are extreme for everyone in infancy and for many in old age. To a large extent, our attitudes toward the handicapped reflect our general philosophies concerning human worth.

If we value a society tolerant of all disabilities and supportive of people with special needs, we will favor integration to the maximum degree possible. We will work for a society where handicapped and nonhandicapped grow up, attend school, socialize, and work together. A society which is highly tolerant of a wide range of abilities will place less emphasis on competitive success and more on the improvement of each individual.

A commitment to the concepts of normalization and mainstreaming should not gloss over the reality and significance of differences. Special education exists in recognition of these differences. It provides something unique and different, or above and beyond, that which we do for the nonhandicapped. We teach oral speech and sign language to the deaf, we teach Braille and independent mobility to the blind. But probably 75 percent of what we do for children with special needs we do also for the nonhandicapped as a part of general education. Sometimes the more extreme advocates of normalization seem to be saying, "If we just treat the handicapped like the nonhandicapped, their disabilities will disappear." Special programs and services for the handicapped exist because more than this is required if these individuals are to optimize their personal development as well as their ability to function in society.

SOME PROPOSED PROGRAM CHANGES

Specific programs for exceptional children can best be understood as a part of larger programs and movements. Community services for troubled and handicapped children in the United States have always been inadequate. The rapid growth of large custodial residential institutions for dependent, delinquent, retarded, and emotionally disturbed children occurred largely because no alternatives were available. The multi-billion-dollar expenditures for these institutions, which increased each year, diverted funds from potentially more effective community resources. Beginning in the early 1960s and gathering momentum in the 1970s, a concerted movement arose to develop nationwide community services as alternatives to custodial and other segregated facilities.

THE FRAGMENTATION OF SERVICES

Commissions which have surveyed the services available for exceptional individuals have uniformly been appalled by the disarray. The dispersion of responsibility among dozens of overlapping and sometimes competing agencies, the fragmentation of services, and the frequency with which persons in need of services become lost in the system have been documented repeatedly. The confusion is equally dismaying when seen from the inside by the families involved, as well as by the handicapped themselves. It is often difficult for families or individuals to learn what services are available. The handicapped may be referred endlessly from agency to agency, never receiving comprehensive evaluation or assistance. All agree that the old system—or lack of it—is costly, ineffective, and sometimes does more harm than good.

INTEGRATED HUMAN SERVICE SYSTEMS

In the 1970s several events indicated that the movement to establish a set of nationwide comprehensive community-based service systems was taking root. Already established systems which involve this concept are the community mental health centers and the regional mental retardation centers; there are proposals for new social service and health delivery systems. Each of these combine traditional service systems to establish more comprehensive community-based services. Several ambitious programs of this type have already been launched. Most of the states have established coordinating offices for human resources. These offices usually include all, or several, of the following conventional departments: welfare, corrections, mental health, mental retardation, and physical health. We currently seem to be moving toward programs providing a wide range of coordinated human services systems including instruction, counseling and support for parents in their homes, medical and legal services, day care services, emergency shelters and temporary facilities, foster homes, hostels, group and halfway houses, rehabilitation services, sheltered workshops, day hospitals, night hospitals, hospitals for intensive care, convalescent and nursing homes, outpatient care, categorical and noncategorical self-contained special classes, partially and completely integrated school classes, and short- and long-term custodial institutions. Such an array of integrated services should enable the parents of a child with special needs to register the child at birth; the system would then assume lifetime responsibility for providing the services needed to assist or replace the family in caring for the child. Registration should occur as soon as the handicapping condition is suspected.

A genuinely comprehensive public services program requires that society accept responsibility for the total welfare of all its citizens. Although such programs will be involved in preventing personal waste and human misery and increasing personal competence, they are also concerned with those experiences, conditions, and institutions that promote, nurture, and perpetuate self-realization and social effectiveness.

When intervention in the form of support or treatment becomes necessary, the usual objective is to maintain the deviant individual as close to his or her intimates in the family and community as possible. When an individual becomes unable to maintain him or herself without additional help, a spectrum of services is used; a series of increasingly supportive levels of intervention which will ordinarily be kept at a minimum, oriented toward gradually decreasing levels of support leading to the client's return to home and/or community.

The first level of sustaining support is the client's primary group, usually the family. The goal of the first level of intervention is to maintain the individual in the home or, if necessary, to remove him from this setting and then return him as soon as possible. The person's intimates need to be involved in the treatment process from beginning to end.

The second level of support involves the more active participation of a caseworker or paraprofessional. This person assists the family members in providing the additional support necessary, determines if, and when, additional treatment is necessary, and then follows through on these needs.

When a higher level of intervention seems necessary, outpatient care by higher-level professionals may be provided. When sustaining on an outpatient level is deemed insufficient, a still higher level of intervention involving semiprotective or total-care institutionalization may be necessary. The overriding principle involved is that the most appropriate treatment should be provided in the least restrictive alternative situation.

SOME CHARACTERISTICS OF CURRENT EDUCATIONAL PROGRAMS

Even a cursory survey of the current literature indicates that a large number of mainstreaming programs are in operation. While these programs vary widely in administrative organization and variety of services provided, they have enough common features to warrant some generalizations.

A Hierarchy of Auxiliary Services

Special education under mainstreaming becomes a set of services facilitating the tailoring and monitoring of educational programs to meet individual needs, rather than a device for sorting children according to the degree that they fit existing programs.

The minimal service provided within such a hierarchy consists of observing the child referred for special consideration, surveying existing records, conferring with the regular classroom teacher, and suggesting the use of procedures and resources already available. At a slightly higher level, it will be necessary to provide a new program specifically for the child with learning problems. At this level, observation of the child is supplemented by formal and informal testing. The auxiliary personnel (school psychologist, resource teacher, speech therapist, or the like) assist the regular teacher in academic diagnosis, program planning, and supply any needed additional instructional resources. At this level, the child stays in the regular classroom but receives supplementary, diagnostic, and instructional services.

At a somewhat higher level of special services intervention, the child leaves the regular class for special assistance, either to receive tutoring or to spend small portions of each day with a resource teacher. Very often, the tutoring or other special assistance is provided in a resource room or center. *Consulting room, floating room, headquarters room,* and *learning center* are alternative terms sometimes used for these service areas. When the learning problems are more acute, part-time assignment to a special class may occur. At this level, the major responsibility for the child may be with either the regular or the resource teacher, depending upon the amount of auxiliary instruction provided. The regular and resource teachers both instruct the child and are jointly responsible for the child's progress.

When the child's needs are considered to be so unique or extreme that the combined regular teacher–resource teacher efforts are insufficient, either part-time or full-time special-class placement may be required. Despite the best auxiliary services, the mainstreaming of all children is not possible. Some extreme deviants will always need separate and markedly different educational facilities, even closed residential institutions.

Under a system of special services intervention, the individuation of instruction is emphasized. School psychologists and other auxiliary special education personnel participate in assessing each child's assets and limitations, devising individualized programs which will capitalize on the assets and maximize the student's learning and personal-social development. Tests are used not so much to make comparisons with other children or with a norm as to set up realistic specific educational objectives and subsequently to determine the degree to which these objectives have been attained in preparation for the next steps. Such tests used to monitor progress are known as *criterion-referenced* as contrasted with the more conventional *norm-referenced* tests. Representative samples of the educational tasks selected from the relevant instructional areas are organized into a criterion-referenced test. Test information is then used to evaluate the child's progress toward instructional objectives and to locate him so as to select or design his next instructional tasks appropriately.

SOME NEW CHALLENGES POSED BY MAINSTREAMING

Although current legislation establishes a free, appropriate education as a basic right of handicapped children, it does not mandate mainstreaming. However, it takes a decidedly positive view of the benefits of contacts between the handicapped and the nonhandicapped. Handicapped children are to be educated in a minimally restrictive appropriate setting and for many of them, this will be the regular classroom. Integration of the handicapped into the regular classroom poses many new problems for both the regular and special teachers.

In the past several decades, teachers—principally elementary school teachers—have relied on special education programs to relieve them of many of their most difficult students. It may well be that the availability of special classes for exceptional children has resulted in the regular teachers' making only token efforts to meet the special needs of these students. With social workers, school psychologists, psychiatrists, and special educational specialists available, the solution of every troublesome educational and behavior problem was to refer the problem child to the appropriate specialist. If most of these troublesome children remain in or are returned to the regular classroom, both regular and special teachers must meet new challenges and learn to play new roles.

When the principal solution for special learning problems was to refer the children for possible placement in special classes, there was considerable motivation for classroom teachers to refer such children. However, if most of these children are now to remain in the regular classes even when referred for special help, there will be a greater reluctance to make such referrals. When a child is referred by a classroom teacher, that teacher immediately becomes involved in making observations and special reports, filling out referral forms, and attending conferences to determine whether the special services are needed or appropriate for the child. If the child is considered eligible for special education auxiliary services, the regular teacher then becomes involved in setting up appropriate goals, devising an individual education plan for the child, being partially responsible for carrying out the program, and being held partially accountable for the program's results. This is a very time-consuming process, and most teachers will think twice before referring many children who are borderline in terms of their perceived needs. They will often elect not to refer such children and continue doing what they can for the individuals without assuming the additional burdens imposed by formal referral, devising, administering, monitoring, and being held responsible for the outcomes of the individualized education programs. While the statement of educational objectives and the individual education programs do not constitute a contract, dissatisfied parents can ask for revisions of the program or invoke due process procedures if they believe that the school is not making appropriate efforts to implement the program and attain the stated objectives.

Of course, parents have the right to refer their children for diagnostic evaluation as to their eligibility for special educational services. If such children are found eligible, an individual education program must be instituted for them. However, as in the past, most of the referrals will probably continue to be teacher initiated.

We should remember that special classes were established for children, many of whom had been sitting year after year in classes learning very little except to expect failure and to hate school. Although these children were physically present, they were socially and psychologically segregated. If the new mainstreaming is to do better than regular class instruction has done for these children in the past, a major restructuring of the roles of both regular and special teachers are in order.

One matter of great concern to classroom teachers is the additional work load posed by the presence of handicapped children in the regular classrooms. In many areas of the country classrooms are overcrowded and teachers already have the tremendous task of meeting the needs of from thirty to forty regular students. The additional problems posed by the presence of a child who is deaf or blind, or one who is both deaf and cerebral palsied, or one who is blind and borderline mentally retarded will seem overwhelming to many regular classroom teachers.

Demands and expectations in the special class were adapted to the special behavioral and intellectual limitations of the children. The demands and procedures of the regular class remained unchanged—those who failed to meet them were removed. Mainstreaming will require accommodation to and tolerance for a much wider range of performances and behaviors than has been true in the past. If these exceptional children are to remain in the regular classrooms many special auxiliary services will be required to modify the maladaptive behavior and performance levels to more acceptable levels and increase the tolerance levels of the regular students and school personnel.

It would seem to be axiomatic that the handicapped should not be returned to regular classes until the regular teachers are trained to teach them and are willing to have them. Competence and positive attitudes are both necessary. Massive efforts will be required to train teachers in the requisite skills. Federal legislation does mandate in-service training for special and regular teachers and over $8 million dollars have been granted the states for this purpose. However, most school administrators insist that this is grossly inadequate. The short workshops and institutes usually provided have done little to meet the need. Everyone seems to agree that we need massive in-service training programs and corresponding adjustments in teacher training and certification requirements. The new programs will require a major revamping of the training programs for both regular and special education teachers as well as school psychologists if they are to play the new roles expected of them.

For a long time attitudes will remain the most serious impediment to effective mainstreaming. They are also the hardest to modify. Current studies indicate that the closer one gets to the actual operational level of the mainstreaming programs the greater is the uncertainty and anxiety concerning them. Judges, legislators, social reformers, state officials, and district administrators are most enthusiastic. Building principals are less certain and classroom teachers are the most ambivalent.

According to one teacher, "To adequately meet the educational needs and legal requirements of the one deaf child who has been assigned to my class would require 50 percent of my teaching time, leaving 50 percent for the thirty-four other students." All teachers talk about the class size problem. Certainly a great deal more has to be done to adjust class sizes and to prepare both special and regular teachers to work together to meet the needs of a wide variety of children with different disabilities. The mainstreaming of a sizable percentage of handicapped children will require redesigning, not only of special education, but of many aspects of regular education as well.

The classroom teachers are going to be faced with children whose educational objectives may be quite different from those of the nonhandicapped. For example, in traditional programs for the educable mentally retarded, high priority has been given to the development of vocational and social skills to enhance the person's transition from school to a job setting. Will this continue to be an objective within general education or are we to assume that since the mentally retarded are to be "normalized," the academic goals of general education are also appropriate for the mentally retarded? Are we really committed to a wide variety of educational goals for the handicapped or do we simply accept lower levels of performance in the regular academic areas, promoting and graduating the handicapped along with their more competent peers, without distinctive labeling? How about competence testing? Of course, the legally mandated individualized education programs are supposed to provide for all of these contingencies. However, many teachers question whether anyone has the special skills and information necessary to devise programs so individualized as to meet both the educational and vocational needs of these special children. They feel that a great many specialized procedures and techniques will be required; such things as special materials, self-contained instructional packages, expertise in behavior controlling techniques, and instructional strategies must be made available to both regular and special teachers.

We must recognize that persons with mental handicaps, by definition, do not learn and develop normally in response to normative procedures. For the most part, children become designated as developmentally disabled, mentally retarded, or learning disabled only after normal educational experiences have proven to be either inadequate or inappropriate. Do we have available the specialized procedures and techniques to normalize these individuals?

Although many fiscal conservatives favored deinstitutionalization and mainstreaming because they thought these procedures would be cheaper, this will probably not be true. Implementing the new programs will require large sums of money. The source and adequacy of these funds is a major concern of educators. Congress appropriated $315 million for the school year 1977–78. It also *authorized* annual increases, reaching $3.2 billion in 1982. However, the amounts actually made available are determined by Congress and the president on a year to year basis and few people expect these initial commitments to be kept. Actual funding may be sporadic and inadequate, but the legal requirements are permanent. Many fear that funds from other programs will be diverted in order to maintain the legally-mandated special programs when funds become scarce. Irrespective of the funds available, school districts must meet the law's provisions or be subject to prosecution for violating the handicapped children's civil rights.

It is estimated that the implementation of the new program will require 250,000 additional special education personnel. The hiring of additional special education teachers often arouses resentment on the part of the regular teachers, who may be faced with layoffs because of decreasing enrollments and limited budgets. Getting qualified teachers is also complicated by the priorities specified by federal legislation. First priority must go to those handicapped children who are now receiving no education; next in line are those whose current education is deemed inadequate. The law also mandates that every state conduct a thorough search for handicapped children who have been overlooked, a mandate that will greatly increase the number of handicapped children in the educational system.

Recruiting and training qualified teachers is a formidable task. Special education is not a glamorous area of teaching and requires people with a special type of dedication, particularly when they must work with many of the severely handicapped previously excluded from the educational system because they were considered ineducable.

Despite the widespread use of the term, "mainstreaming" does not appear in the Education for All Handicapped Children Act which is largely responsible for the great expansion of the program. The key concept of the act is that handicapped children are to be educated in a *minimally restrictive appropriate environment*. It additionally specifies that *to the maximum extent appropriate* the handicapped are to be educated with the nonhandicapped. The handicapped are to be placed in special classes, special schools, or other segregated facilities only when the nature or severity of the handicap is such that education in the regular classes, even with the aid of supplementary services, is not feasible.

The wording of the act encourages people to stop thinking of handicapped children as a homogeneous group for whom a single educational facility or program will suffice. The prescribed procedures require that the individual children's needs be specified and services then provided which best meet these needs in *the least restrictive setting*.

The idea of a hierarchy of educational settings can be extended to living settings and work situations as suggested by the tabulation which follows:

A CONTINUUM OF LIVING, WORKING, AND LEARNING SETTINGS

living circumstances	educational programs	work settings
1. Independent living in home or apartment	1. Regular class and curriculum	1. Full employment after regular preparation
2. Semi-independent living with minimal assistance	2. Regular class plus resource teacher	2. Full employment following special training for the handicapped
3. Group living with supervision	3. Special class with some time in the regular class	3. Work-study program leading to full or limited employment
4. Day or night living with professional care	4. Self-contained special class	4. Workshop training and experience leading to full or limited employment
5. Complete institutional care	5. Special residential school	5. Sheltered workshop employment of unlimited duration
		6. Occupationally untrainable—completely dependent

MAINSTREAMING IS NOT NEW

Mainstreaming is a new term for an old practice. Even when the institutional, special school, and special class populations were at their maximum, there were far more handicapped children in the mainstream. Practically all of the educable mentally retarded and the children with learning disabilities who constitute the bulk of the educationally handicapped attended regular classes for extended periods of time before being segregated in special classes. At all times more children who technically met the minimum requirements for special educational placement remained in the regular classes than were referred and officially designated as handicapped.

Typically, students in these categories are identified only after they have attended regular classes for several years and have failed to learn. After several years of repeated failure, someone—usually the current teacher—decides that a given child will continue to experience greater and greater educational deficits unless some special help is given. When the teacher makes a formal referral, the child's educational history is brought together with test performances and other relevant information and a decision is made—first as to the child's eligibility for special class placement. If the educational retardation and mental test scores are sufficiently low, the student may be eligible for placement in a special class for the mentally retarded. If educational retardation is extreme but intelligence test scores are within the normal range, the child may be eligible for a class for the learning disabled. In any case, special class placement occurs only after these children have spent several years in the regular classroom. Mainstreaming is not new for these children.

Some degree of mainstreaming has always been experienced by these same categories of children at the junior and senior high school levels, where classes are departmentalized. Typical programs for mentally retarded or learning disabled students at these levels provides for them to attend some classes with regular students. These classes are generally considered to be less intellectually demanding, including physical education, art, music, shop work, home economics, and typing. These students usually like classes such as mathematics, English, and science in special classes taught by a special education teacher who also functions as advisor and coordinator of the program. Thus, depending upon the special abilities and disabilities of each student, the handicapped can be mainstreamed anywhere from 100 percent to a very small percentage but practically never 0 percent of the time.

Clearly, both legislators and educators perceive of mainstreaming as only one of several alternatives available as programs for the handicapped. Where mainstreaming is feasible, it may take place to varying degrees. A 1977 survey indicated that in typical programs designated as "mainstreamed", the handicapped spent about 50 percent of their time in regular classes (MacMillan and Semmel, 1977).

IMPLEMENTATION OF THE LEGALLY-MANDATED IEP

The concept of individualized instruction is not new. Historically, we have had the Batavia Plan, The Dalton Plan, and the Winnetka Plan for general education. More recently, a program called Individually Prescribed Instruction (IPI) has been used in several hundred schools in the United States and in several foreign countries (McLaughlin, 1972). The child-centered, individualized program which most closely approximates the IEP requirements within special education has been called the diagnostic/prescriptive approach (Safer, Morrissey, Kaufman, and Lewis, 1978). In many ways, the IEP represents a formalization of the diagnostic/prescriptive approach to teaching.

As indicated in an earlier chapter, PL 94–142 requires that every handicapped child receiving special education services must have an IEP. This program is developed or approved by a representative of the local educational agency, the child's teachers, the child's parents or guardians, and when deemed appropriate, the child. The program should contain statements of the child's current level of performance, short-term objectives and annual goals, the specific services to be provided, the dates for initiation and projected duration of the special services, the extent to which special services are to be provided to the child, and the extent of the child's participation. The specific criteria to be used in verifying that the objectives have been attained and a periodic review of the programs at least annually must also be provided.

Much of the ambivalence expressed by school administrators and teachers toward mainstreaming has centered on the IEP. One reason for this concern is that widespread adoption of the individualized approach has never actually occurred in the classrooms and teachers have had very limited experience with it. In most instances individualized programming remains a concept with which all teachers are familiar but which is only minimally an operational reality.

The implementation of the law will require several changes. First, formal plans for the educational assessment of the children and their progress must be made. The formulation of the plans involves a large number of people to develop and state specific short- and long-term goals, meet and work with parents, keep complete records to document the implementation of the program, and indicate the progress being made.

Second, since each child may be working toward different goals and progressing at different rates, implementation will require classroom reorganization. More individualized instruction will often require that individual work centers or areas be established and supplied with self-instructional materials and worksheets. Aides, student assistants, and adult volunteers will have to be used more extensively in the classroom. Consequently, teachers will spend considerable time coordinating and supervising their activities.

Third, the program will also require much more sharing of duties, authority, and responsibilities than in the past. Special and regular educational teachers, principals, supervisors, school psychologists, and other support personnel, as well as the parents, and in some instances, the handicapped students themselves must all share in the duties and responsibilities.

Finally, accountability on the part of school personnel is provided for by the prescribed procedures so as to insure that each program is effectively implemented in accordance with the IEP document.

CHANGES IN TEACHER ROLES

It seems clear that the classroom teachers are going to spend more of their time in noninstructional activities. They will be involved in making formal educational assessments, formulating short- and long-term goals, notifying parents and obtaining their consent concerning prospective program changes, attending IEP meetings, and keeping detailed records of student progress. Teachers will spend considerable time working with aides, volunteers, or student assistants assigning tasks, explaining procedures, supervising and coordinating their schedules. Teachers certainly will engage in much more programming, record keeping, and supervisory activities than they are accustomed to.

Many teachers feel uncomfortable with the extensively shared responsibilities the program involves. They feel that they are losing a great deal of autonomy as teachers and have much less control over classrooms and students. Many people not responsible for classroom instruction will play significant roles in planning programs for which the teachers will be held largely accountable.

Teachers often express concern over their increased accountability to outsiders. The federal law certainly implies accountability and teachers feel that this will mean that continuous and measurable progress by all students is expected. Many teachers are concerned that students' progress under the IEP may be used as a measure of the teacher's performance. It may also be used by federal or state authorities to monitor compliance with the law.

Teachers participating in IEP programs claim to work longer hours than do their regular education peers. The principals and directors of special education confirm the teachers' claims. One study found that the average amount of time a teacher spends in formulating and writing an IEP was about eleven hours (Safer and others, 1978). The estimated number of hours reported as spent in job-related activities ranges from fifty-five to sixty-seven per week. Even those teachers who strongly support the program are dismayed about the time required. Implementation of the individualized program seems to be subsidized to a great extent by the teachers' good will and dedication.

Teachers and administrators are in agreement that a wide variety of special support resources are required for the new programs. These resources include: organized assessment systems and materials related to specific educational objectives, a variety of suggested sequences of objectives, a wealth of instructional materials cross-referenced to educational objectives, and standardized record-keeping forms. All of these can reduce the amount of teacher time and effort required by the programs.

Many school districts have adopted, or developed, standard batteries of assessment instruments that can be quickly administered and scored. These instruments allow a child's performances to be translated into specific objectives which are sequenced in a series. This can be fairly easily done in such basic educational skill areas as reading and arithmetic. Objectives need to be highly specific and accompanied by appropriate criteria for evaluation purposes. For example, once a child's current level of performance in a given skill area has been determined, the teacher can select an appropriate objective from the continuum of skills and achievement levels and attach a copy of the objective and sequences to the child's permanent program plan. Instructional materials can be cross-referenced to objectives so that teachers can select commercial or district-generated materials appropriate for a given objective.

A set of standard forms for planning and record keeping are also essential. These forms should parallel the planning process, feed directly from one stage to another, and be maximally useful for recording both short- and long-range objectives and planning, as well as for daily or weekly instructional planning. A tremendous literature is appearing to assist schools instructionally and considerable commercial forms and aids are becoming available (Turnbull, Strickland, and Brantley, 1978).

In most districts teachers are given several hours of daily teacher-aide time. In addition, community volunteers, student interns, or assistants provide help in instruction, data collection, and recording, depending upon their experience and training. Consultive assistance is also considered essential. Typically a school psychologist and other specialists work on a continuing basis with both the regular and special education teachers. Many schools have regular meetings of the entire education staff to exchange information, discuss practices, and make plans for dealing with special problems.

The legislative mandates have provided a new impetus to individualized educational planning. This legislation places the responsibility for the programs on the state, the district, and the school administration as well as on the teacher. This division of responsibility will promote both administrative and monetary commitments. The legislative mandate will assist in getting the required resources from fiscal-conscious school boards, school administrators, and state legislators.

SUMMARY

Ever since the first residential institutions and special classes were established for the handicapped, such segregated environments have been the most popular setting for caring for, treating, and educating such persons. However, during the last two decades, increasing discontent with these segregated facilities has emerged and many alternative arrangements have been proposed and implemented. The deinstitutionalization movement came about partially as the result of widespread recognition that, in many cases, the segregated institutions were doing more harm than good. Innumerable investigations over a century disclosed that such institutions, created for the good of their residents, had repeatedly come to be characterized by classic patterns of neglect, isolation, and dehumanization. The ever-increasing cost of such facilities together with their chronic overcrowding, understaffing, and insufficient funding led to a search for less expensive alternatives.

The alternatives to large mental hospitals have been community mental health centers, small local facilities, placing of previously institutionalized patients in group homes, and maintaining the handicapped in their own homes. Alternative educational programs for the handicapped retain the deviant child in the regular classroom and provide supplemental support to the regular classroom teacher. This practice is usually referred to as *mainstreaming*.

The current emphasis on mainstreaming has been brought about partly as the result of:

1. the equivocal results of research reports dealing with the effectiveness of the segregated programs.

2. a realization that categorizing and official labeling may add appreciably to the diagnosed handicap.

3. the increased awareness of the biasing effects of race, social class, sex, and educationally irrelevant behavioral characteristics, which have resulted in inappropriate placement of many individuals in segregated facilities.

4. court judgments concerning institutional and special class assignments and the rights of patients and exceptional children to appropriate psychiatric and/or educational treatment.

Many people believe that the swinging of the pendulum toward the elimination of all such segregated facilities may be subjecting many of the handicapped to even more painful and frustrating experiences in the name of "normalization." Today the question is not "to segregate or not to segregate" but rather, "What is the least restrictive and most normalizing setting in which this individual's personal and educational needs can be met?" It seems clear that this will require a continuum of services with many program alternatives, including noncategorical resource rooms, learning centers, categorical rooms and/or teachers, special classes, and segregated residential facilities. It is not yet clear what extent and nature of handicapping conditions can be effectively accommodated in the mainstream of the school, community, and family, even with the support of resource or itinerant teachers, learning centers, and community mental health resources.

REFERENCES

Case, R., A. S. Fitzgerald, and J. M. Ficarro, "Respite Care," *Exceptional Parent,* 1975, *5*(1), 7–11.

Donaldson, J. and M. C. Martinson, "Modifying Attitudes toward Physically Disabled Persons," *Exceptional Children,* 1977, *43,* 337–41.

Gallagher, V. M., "Adoption in a Changing Society," *Children Today,* 1972, *1*(5), 2–6.

Gaylin, J., "Our Endangered Children: It's a Matter of Money," *Psychology Today,* May 1977, *10*(12), 94–95.

Goldstein, H., "Providing Services to Children in Their Own Homes," *Children Today,* 1973, *2*(4), 2–7.

Gula, M., "Community Services and Residential Institutions for Children," *Children Today,* 1974, *3*(6), 15–17.

Jew, W., "Helping Handicapped Infants and Their Families," *Children Today,* 1974, *3*(3), 7–10.

Kramer, B. W., "The Day Hospital: A Case Study," *Journal of Social Issues,* 1960, *16,* 14–19.

Kravik, P. J., "Adopting a Retarded Child: One Family's Experience," *Children Today,* 1975, *4*(5), 17–21.

Ladner, J. A., *Mixed Families: Adopting Across Racial Boundaries* (New York: Anchor-Doubleday, 1977).

MacMillan, D. L. and W. L. Semmel, "Evaluation of Mainstreaming Programs," *Focus on Exceptional Children,* 1977, *9*(4), 1–14.

MacMillan, T. M. and B. H. Aase, "Analysis of the First 500 Patients at the San Diego Day Treatment Center," *California Mental Health Research Digest,* 1964, *2,* 11.

McLaughlin, W. P., "Individuation of Instruction," *Phi Delta Kappan,* 1972, *53,* 378–81.

McTaggart, L., "The Scandal in Foster Care," *Parade,* Sept. 18, 1977, 15–16.

Olshansky, S., "The Transitional Workshop: A Survey," *Journal of Social Issues,* 1960, *16,* 33–39.

Safer, N. D., P. A. Morrissey, M. J. Kaufman, and L. Lewis, "Implementating IEP: New Teacher Roles and Requisite Support Systems," *Focus on Exceptional Children,* March 1978, *10*(1), 1–20.

Schaar, K., "Community Case Ordered for D. C. Mental Patients," *APA Monitor,* 1976, *7*(2), 1.

Slavin, R. C. and N. C. Madden, "School Practices that Improve Race Relations," *American Educational Research Journal,* 1979, *16,* 169–80.

Turnbull, A. P., B. B. Strickland, and J. C. Brantley, *Developing and Implementing Individualized Education Programs* (Columbus, Ohio: Merrill Publishing, 1978).

Winich, C., "Psychiatric Day Hospitals: A Survey," *Journal of Social Issues,* 1960, *16,* 8–13.

SUGGESTIONS FOR STUDENTS AND INSTRUCTORS

1. Discuss the distinction between physical and psycho-social segregation and integration.

2. Indicate which you consider to be the most formidable barriers to successful mainstreaming.

3. To what degree is mainstreaming a new name for an old practice?

ADDITIONAL READINGS

Schifani, J. W., R. M. Anderson, and S. J. Odie, eds., *Implementing Learning in the Least Restrictive Environment: Handicapped Children in the Mainstream* (Baltimore, Md.: University Park Press, 1980). A comprehensive view of the problems of mainstreaming.

Guralnick, M. J., ed., *Early Intervention and the Integration of Handicapped and Nonhandicapped Children* (Baltimore, Md.: University Park Press, 1978). Another examination of the issues and rationale of integrated programs.

SELECTED FILMS

To Live On (29 minutes) J. E. G. Hess Productions, Franklin Lake, N. J., 07417. A documentary about a school for watchmaking employing the handicapped. Complete independence for the students is the goal of the school.

A Question of Attitude (12 minutes) Australian News and Information Bureau, 636 Fifth Avenue, New York, N. Y. Portrays the reluctance of many firms to employ the handicapped.

ORGANIZATIONS AND AGENCIES

President's Committee on Employment of the Handicapped
Department of Labor
1111 20th Street, N. W.
Washington, D.C. 20210

National Industries for the Severely Handicapped
4350 East West Highway
Suite 1120
Washington, D.C. 20014

American Association for the Education of the Severely/Profoundly
Handicapped
P. O. Box 15287
Seattle, Wash. 98115.

CHAPTER 6

FAMILY AND PERSONAL PROBLEMS OF EXCEPTIONAL PEOPLE

THE DYNAMICS OF FAMILY RELATIONS

Just as people with different stigmas must face similar problems and adjust to them in similar ways, the problem of a family with a mentally retarded, blind, deaf, orthopedically handicapped, or epileptic child is an instance of a universal experience—how the family copes with unexpected disappointment and trauma. Family crises, frustrated ambition, and occasional high levels of stress are experiences common to most families. Likewise, the basic problem faced by the families of exceptional individuals is essentially that of all families—how to cope with the problems of living in ways that will enhance rather than hinder family members' growth and development. The behavior of the deviant is shaped by the actions and attitudes of others, and the adjustments of the family of an exceptional child can either limit and distort or encourage and facilitate the child's potential for growth.

When working with the handicapped, it is easy to focus attention so completely on the defective individual that we forget he or she is a member of a family and that the family may be as much a casualty as is the handicapped member.

family problems—a case study

Jerry, eight years old, has cerebral palsy. His parents have filed for a divorce. How did it come about? To go back to the beginning: According to Jerry's mother, she didn't really want a baby. "I knew something was wrong during my pregnancy. Sometimes I think this is God's punishment, although I really know that is crazy," she reported. When the initial state of shock wore off, the mother took over. She never asked anyone what she should do; she just plunged in to work with her son. She read everything she could find on cerebral palsy and became an authority on the topic. Initially the husband approved and was proud of her.

Slowly but surely the entire family life became organized around Jerry and his special needs. This did not bother the husband until he noticed that their daughter was badly in need of new clothes. When he asked his wife to buy their daughter some new clothes, she gave him a blank stare but said and did nothing. The husband finally asked his sister to help his daughter buy some new clothes. The wife became angry and complained to her sister-in-law about her spoiling the girl and how useless the husband was around the house.

For a while after his son's birth, the husband tried doing things for the handicapped child. However, he decided it would be better if Jerry tried to do more for himself, and began doing less for him. The wife took up the slack by doing more and more for her son. The husband felt that the only way he could be useful to his family was to earn more money. Consequently, he began working longer hours, and weekends as well. After a few years he gradually came to the realization that their marriage had come to an end. They no longer did anything together—never went out or visited friends, and no longer had any sex life. Half the time the wife slept in Jerry's room. At other times, husband or wife or both were too tired.

The wife was at her son's call twenty-four hours a day. At his slightest sign of distress she would rush to his side. When Jerry was seven the family moved to a house in the suburbs, nearer the hospital. The husband did not complain, even though it increased his commuting time from twenty minutes to an hour. A year later, he came home one evening, told his wife it was all over, and asked for a divorce.

The divorce came as a surprise to everyone. There had been no fighting, quarreling, or bickering. The wife was too preoccupied and tired to be involved with her husband, and the husband had ceased bothering her. Although the request for a divorce came as a shock to the wife, in some ways she was relieved by it. For a long time the husband had been just one more mouth to feed and one more person to work for and clean up after. Their divorce settlement was amicable; very little explanation was given to other people.

About a year later, the former husband married again and took his daughter to live with him and his new wife. The former wife offered no objections to this arrangement. She was still completely wrapped up in Jerry, and had little time or energy to spend with her daughter.

This case is an extreme example of the problems common to families with severely handicapped children. It is very difficult to provide the handicapped child with the extra care and money required and at the same time not to deprive the other family members of their rightful share of attention, time, and affection. Another mother admitted, "My own divorce did not result from my son's deafness, but rather from my response to his deafness. I jumped so headlong into my son's problems and the problems of the deaf that I completely neglected my family and marital obligations, which led to the break-up of our marriage."

MARITAL STRESS IN FAMILIES OF THE HANDICAPPED

There are no marital problems peculiar to the parents of the handicapped. However, in addition to the stresses and strains characteristic of the average family situation, the parents of the disabled have additional pressures. Although the majority of parents of the handicapped are able to cope with the extra problems, the number of desertions and divorces is considerably above that of the general population. One study of 142 familes, each having a child with spina bifida (a failure of the vertebrae to close around the spinal cord), found that the divorce rate where a child survived with this condition was nine times higher than for comparable "normal" families. It was only three times higher for families in which the child did not survive. Marriages following a prenuptial conception that resulted in a spina bifida child were especially vulnerable, increasing the divorce or separation rate by 50 percent (Tew, Lawrence, Payne, and Townsley, 1977). Research studies support the common sense observation that a handicapped child adds greatly to the strains on a marriage. These strains manifest themselves in ways other than divorce: minor marital problems, suicide, and alcoholism are much more prevalent in families of handicapped children (Block, 1978).

every child deserves a loving family—a case study

Our son is nine years old, cerebral palsied, and mentally retarded. He is unable to walk or talk and is only minimally able to communicate his needs. According to our doctor, the lack of oxygen during a long and complicated delivery produced severe damage to his nervous system. It was difficult to absorb the initial shock of the realization that we had a child who was severely handicapped both physically and mentally. However, as the initial numbness wore off, our love for our handicapped child began to assert itself. Today I am firmly convinced that parents' genuine love for their children, whether handicapped or nonhandicapped, is essential for the child's welfare and for the family's mental health. We have always been totally involved in our children's lives and we have seldom been separated from them.

We do not believe that the presence of our handicapped boy has been in any way detrimental to our two other children. They have developed quite normally. They do not hesitate to bring their friends to our house. They discuss their handicapped brother with their friends freely and without apology. I think they are more mature and compassionate because they have a handicapped brother.

Three days a week we take our boy to an intensive training center where he receives training in elementary basic life skills. We know that he will always be dependent upon others for almost total care. However, we share the conviction of the people at the center that learning to feed himself is better than having someone else feed him and being able to sit upright in a chair is preferable to lying in a crib for the rest of his life. The family had a special celebration when he was able to eat his first meal without help. We were all thrilled when he was first able to stand up while holding onto his chair.

When patience and loving care bring even minimal improvement in a severely mentally and physically disabled child, it leaves one with a feeling of warmth and pride. Of course, we wish that our boy were normal but he is ours. We only hope that every parent of a handicapped child can experience the degree of positive regard for their child that we do for ours (adapted from Hosey, 1973).

there is also a dark side

Another parent's reactions are condensed and paraphrased as follows: "I felt a great relief when I learned that some other parents of handicapped children were unable to love—some even hated—them. After nearly ten years of feeling guilty because I was unable to find medical help, an educational program, or a place in society for our multiply handicapped daughter, I at last have decided that there is nothing more that I can, or should, do for her. She remains unresponsive to others. She cannot return my love and any love that I had for her as an infant has long ago dried up. I do not love her and she does not love me! I keep asking myself why I do not love her and can find no answer. However, after learning that other parents, in their more candid moments, are able to admit to this 'side' of their reactions to their handicapped children, I have been relieved of my great burden of guilt. I have decided that I will pretend no more! I will continue to take care of my daughter to the best of my abilities but I will no longer be overwhelmed because I cannot fulfill the parental obligation of loving her."

While there are almost as many different patterns of reaction to evidence of inadequacy in one's offspring as there are parents with such children, certain types of reactions are sufficiently common to warrant description. Some of the more common reactive patterns to the advent of a defective child into a family are realistic coping with the problem; denial of the reality of the handicap; self-pity; ambivalence toward or rejection of the child; projection of the difficulty as the cause of the disability; feelings of guilt, shame, and depression; and patterns of mutual dependency.

None of these reactions is peculiar to parents in general or to the parents of defective children; they are the common reactions of normal people to frustration and conflict. The average parent will, in the course of a lifetime, display or experience these reactions to nondisabled children as a part of normal life processes, and it is helpful to the parents of handicapped children to be aware of the universality of their reactions. Many parents of deviant children not only experience feelings of guilt and shame but feel guilty and ashamed of themselves for doing so. That is in addition to feeling guilty, they feel guilty about feeling guilty. Such guilt is a secondary source of emotional disturbance to parents who are already overladen emotionally. The presence of a handicapped child in the family constitutes an additional stress, and defensive reactions are likely to occur more often and to a greater degree in such families than in families all of whose members are reasonably normal.

One source of conflict is that the presence of a severely handicapped child in a family arrests certain components of the family cycle. The severely disabled child may permanently occupy the social position of the youngest child in the family. This child does not develop the independence and autonomy of adulthood. This is often the situation in the family with a severely mentally retarded child. There the parental role is fairly constant regardless of the child's birth-order position; the severely mentally retarded individual is the permanent infant and never emerges from his or her infantile or childish status. One sibling of such a child had the following to say:

a sibling's view

I came to be aware of my sister's condition only gradually. As I grew older I realized that she was decidedly different. She developed very slowly, so even though I was two years older than her, I was soon much larger and more mature in every way. She has been almost a perpetual infant. We have always referred to her as "the baby." My sister's condition never really was explained to me. I can recall my mother telling me that my sister was sick and that she would probably never be really well. Not until I was nearly grown did I learn that she was severely retarded as the result of a rubella infection contracted before she was born. Her mental capacity is less than one year. Presently, she is institutionalized in a state hospital. My parents see her about once a week. I see her once every month or two. For some reason, I find the visits becoming more and more difficult. My sister is very happy where she is and it really makes no difference to anyone, except my parents, whether I see her or not.

coping realistically with the problems of the exceptional child Because of our concern with the problem parent as well as the problem child, we can easily overlook that many parents are able to cope in a healthy and constructive way with the problems presented by the presence of a defective child. Many people meet the initial decisions and the additional stresses in a realistic, well-integrated way, just as they meet the other crises and stresses in their lives.

For example, a twenty-two-year-old congenital quadruple amputee with prostheses describes his family's treatment of him as follows:

In my estimation my treatment by my family couldn't have been better. I have two sisters, both older than myself. My parents agreed completely on how I was to be treated. However, it seems that my father took the lead in setting the general tone concerning my treatment. As long as I can remember, he insisted that I do everything that I could do—and no funny business!

Very early he explained my handicap to me. He told me that there were certain things I probably could not do, but that I *could* do most things. He always insisted that I try practically everything. I was always given specific duties around the house. I performed all the normal duties—helping set the table, carrying out the garbage, and running errands.

My sisters, taking their cue from my parents, never let me get away with anything. They were certainly aware of my handicap, but hardly ever referred to it. They assumed that I was essentially normal and that I would do everything until it was positively demonstrated that I could not. When I finally told them that I couldn't do something, they usually accepted it as a fact. In school, there were no special classes or teachers. However, my father explained to my teachers how I was treated at home and told them to do likewise. My teachers accepted that I could not write at the blackboard. My first grade teacher immediately informed me that I was going to learn to write. I was sure that I would never be able to. However, she taped a piece of paper to my desk, placed a pencil in my clamp, and said, "Now write." I eventually learned to write and to type. This was just a normal school with an understanding teacher.

When I came home from school and asked my father why people stared at me, he simply told me, "It's because you have clamps for hands and artificial legs which make you limp."

I liked sports and played as much as possible. Of course I was a miserable player. When I was nine or ten I told my father that I was going to be a professional athlete. He sat me down and told me that someday I would realize that I would never be a professional athlete. He said that I would have to learn to use my head more than my arms and legs.

I never recall blaming anyone else for my disability. I was told that it was really no one's fault—it had just happened. Of course I used to fantasize and dream that I had normal arms and legs. I never saw my wheelchair in a dream. I was a great athlete and won games—but all in my dreams. I have never been sensitive about my disability. When a child asks me about my hands and his parents try to shut him up, I usually tell them to let him ask. Then I answer the questions and explain it to both the child and the parents.

denial of the child's disability Except for the most obvious disabilities, most parents react with some denial to evidence of their child's inadequacy. Powerful social and personal forces motivate a parent to do so. The cultural stereotype of the ideal child, the parents' expectation that their offspring will successfully play the roles that society and parents assign the child, the parents' hopes that their child will attain or surpass their accomplishments all contribute to their "it just can't be so" reaction when the child is apparently defective. Because parents identify with their children, participate in their successes and failures, bask in their reflected glory, and are belittled by their shortcomings, they inevitably experience a loss of self-esteem when one of their offspring is less than expected. A defect in the child is seen as partly that of the parent.

When the initial realization of an infant's defectiveness comes suddenly and traumatically, the more unconscious defensive reactions may occur. One mother actually believed that she had *only imagined* that she had held her physically deformed, day-old child in her arms when the nurse took the infant back to the nursery. Later she was unable to recall the first six weeks at home with her defective child. One father reports that when asked how many children he had, he would say "two." He actually had three but the third was a badly deformed thalidomide child. One father of a thalidomide infant was unable to take a second look at his deformed infant for three days. Another parent says, "I stumbled in darkness for three years searching for . . . I do not know what. It was so painful to carry this secret dread that something was wrong with my son, wanting to know, yet fearing to hear the actual words spoken. I felt I was living somewhere alone on an island. For a long time I was unable to read anything about mental retardation. I started to read Pearl Buck's book about her own mentally retarded daughter but quickly put it aside— something in me would not let me read or think about it" (Gregory, 1972). Acceptance is seldom a one-time act of faith; it is not that simple. Acceptance often starts as a fleeting thing, a continuous, ever-changing process which fluctuates at different levels at different times and in different contexts.

One mother said, "The time immediately after the birth of my child with multiple congenital defects was the loneliest time of my life. I felt that neither encouraging family and friends nor competent and sympathetic doctors could really help, for none of these had ever given birth to such a child" (Ouellet, 1972).

Another parent has suggested that "adapting and coping are more realistic goals than acceptance. Anger, resentment, and guilt at having a disabled child and distress concerning the situation are to be expected and may continue indefinitely. Parents can adapt to the situation and cope with the problems of a handicapped child without becoming resigned to it and happy with the circumstances" (Eisenpreis, 1974).

One mother says, "As we moved along with Kathryn there were many episodes which stand out as if they were still frames in a motion picture. Each episode marked a new idea or a confirmation of a suspicion, producing what some call the 'Aha!' response. Each one moved me along a road now paved with convictions" (Bennett, 1974).

The parents of a physically disabled child seem to identify more completely with their child's physique than do the parents of the nonhandicapped. It is not surprising that perceptual distortion, misinterpretation of evidence, and all the defenses in one's repertoire will be used to deny evidence of inferiority in one's offspring. Sometimes this denial takes the form of a prolonged trek from doctor to doctor and clinic to clinic, in search of a more favorable diagnosis. Failing this, the parents claim that the specialists are all wrong. Any parent knows his or her child better than all the professionals!

Denial certainly operates as a protective device and may serve a necessary function at a certain stage in parental adjustment. Parental ambitions and expectations are threatened by evidence of a child's impairment. Denial serves to protect the parents' self-esteem and image of themselves. Denial affords parents additional time to become adjusted to the pain and disappointment which build up as changes in expectations and self-regard occur.

Sympathetic friends, relatives, and even professional people often unwittingly support the parents' denial of their child's inadequacy. They stress the child's assets and minimize limitations. They emphasize the difficulties of diagnosis, the uncertainties of developmental trends, and the limitations of our knowledge. There are no certainties in this world! Telling a parent bluntly and with certainty that he or she has a defective child is a hard task for any counselor and is often postponed, or temporized, or modified in the hope that it will be easier on the parents and in the certainty that it is easier on the counselor.

Many parents never progress beyond the stage of partial acceptance. They may accept the diagnosis but reject its prognostic implications. How about the miracle drugs, a new operation, a novel form of psychotherapy, a radically new diet, or unlimited amounts of parental love? Parenthetically we might mention that the most recent evaluation of the many drug and dietary treatments of mental retardation for which positive claims have been made concludes that, despite great enthusiasm on the part of their proponents, no such programs have been demonstrated effective.

self-pity Except when the parents are able to assume and maintain a realistic and objective attitude toward their child's disability, some feelings of self-pity are likely to be experienced: "What a terrible thing to happen to me," "Why did this happen in my family?" "What have I done to deserve this?" The threat to the parents' and the family's prestige represented by the presence of a defective child looms large in most middle- or upper-class households.

When the emotional reaction is extreme, the devout relgionist may question fundamental religious beliefs. "How could a benign Diety permit such a thing to happen? Why did He do this to me?" As the result of such questioning and doubt, the parent may become embittered and atheistic. Other people find solace in their religious beliefs. Although the evidence is conflicting, some studies find Catholic mothers, who are generally more religious than Protestants, to be more accepting of their defective children than are comparable non-Catholics (Zuk, 1962, Boles, 1959).

One mother describes her mixed emotions as follows:

> I am sure that it is only after we have lived through our anger, grief, doubts, and self-torture, and recognized these reactions for what they are, that we can really go on to positive action. For years I thought I was the only one who felt guilty and ashamed of my thinly disguised hostile feelings and death wishes. Not until I met with other parents and heard them compile their reactions—alarm, anger, anxiety, anguish, bewilderment, bitterness, denial, depression, disbelief, despair, and even impulses to destroy the child—did I realize that these were universal experiences. I then became unashamed to admit that I had experienced every one of them and

> was finally able to transform them into positive action. I have finally attained the place where I am able to discuss my emotions frankly with other people.

ambivalent feelings toward the handicapped Even the best parents feel ambivalent toward their normal children. Parental attitudes, while dominantly positive, always have overtones of resentment and rejection. The restriction of activities, the additional responsibilities, the minor disappointments of parenthood, the anxieties, and the irritations which are a normal part of the bearing and rearing of offspring inevitably produce ambivalent parental reactions. Parents accept and love, but they also reject and dislike their children.

One parent describes these reactions as follows:

> *It seems clear that many parents of severely handicapped children never completely recover from shock, denial, and rejection to acceptance and positive adjustment. The negative reactions of rejection, guilt, bitterness and resentment never disappear entirely but remain submerged just below the surface and show themselves in various ways. These contradictory feelings and conflicting emotions often remain unresolved. When parents feel that the burden imposed by their handicapped child must always take precedence over their own needs and desires, they feel cheated and betrayed. They never really "get over" the negative reactions to their child and their resentment toward the situation in which they feel entrapped.*
>
> *When the birth of a severely handicapped child is first "accepted" it is assumed that all obstacles can be overcome if they just try hard enough—all problems are solvable. However, gradually they come to see this as a myth. Bit by bit and little by little the realization that they are faced by a succession of problems—a lifetime commitment—destroys the myth. Beneath the "well adjusted" and "accepting" exterior, rejection, resentment, and bitterness remain dormant. Most parental reactions do not progress through a neat developmental sequence ending in mature coping and acceptance (adapted from Searl, 1978).*

Inevitably, the negative components of this ambivalence will be accentuated when the child is handicapped. These negative reactions vary all the way from the conscious and overt wish that the child would die or had never been born to repressed, unacknowledged, veiled, and symbolic hostility and rejection. In any case, ambivalent feelings give rise to guilt reactions, which in turn often result in overprotection, oversolicitousness, and a parental life of martyrdom—an attempt to deny or compensate for the hostile feelings of which the person is ashamed.

One parent says, "After a period of mourning and denial, a state of relative acceptance occurred. However, while feeling proud of my mature acceptance of my child's limitations, I now see the school band marching and it suddenly strikes me that my child will never do that and I cry. In church, all the other children march in on Children's Day and her father carries in my child. I curse silently at the unfairness and cry again."

Parental ambivalences are often involved in the *treatment* of disabled offspring. Trying to find and tread that narrow path between withholding the realistically necessary care and assistance, on the one hand, and doing too much and nurturing helplessness and overdependency, on the other, is always difficult. In trying to find this path, many parents are more demanding and less tolerant of excuses from their disabled child than they are of their normal offspring. When the disabled child asks the parent to do something for him, the parent hesitates and asks, "Can he do it for himself?" She often does not do for the disabled child many things that she does immediately and without question for her more able offspring because she is less aware of the dangers of instilling overdependencies in the latter.

projection Projection is a common defense against feelings of anxiety. Anxiety concerning personal guilt, or unacceptable feelings of resentment and hostility, can be diminished by blaming someone other than oneself for the threatening situation. Parents made anxious by the conditions arising from the handicapped child will often project the causes of the child's deficiencies onto convenient scapegoats. Resentment and hostility may be directed at the other children, the spouse, the doctor, the teacher, the counselor, or society in general. Professional people working with such parents can expect to serve as the innocent victims of this process. Unprovoked attacks against others often represent displaced hostility resulting from the chronic frustrations engendered by the defective child. One mother who has had such experiences reports:

> When I discovered that because of our child's condition we were labeled and stigmatized as a family, I experienced a deep resentment against society, doctors, psychologists, teachers, and people in general. This resentment was directed principally toward those who were closest to me—my husband, mother, father, and my other children. My escape from the hurt, confusion, and resentment was to become involved in programs of positive action. I joined our local Mental Health Association and became active in getting a special school program established for emotionally disturbed (autistic) children. I started to "reach out" and look at all handicapped children and adults. Only then was I able to do something other than blame and blame and blame. Yes, we need laws, but you cannot legislate informed concern and love, and that is what it takes. We need to stir ourselves, to stir our friends and neighbors, our schools and our government in these terms. Please hold my hand, lest I forget!

guilt, shame, and depression Guilt and shame are components of several of the reaction patterns already discussed. However, they are sufficiently important in themselves to warrant further discussion. Shame, as used here, refers to the "What will other people think and say?" reaction, whereas guilt refers to the individual's feelings of self-reproach or self-condemnation. Shame is more other-people oriented; guilt, more self-directed. Shame involves the expectation of ridicule or criticism from others, while guilt involves self-blame, personal regret, and a feeling of decreased personal worth. Shame and guilt both involve anxiety, and popular usage does not differentiate them. Empirical studies indicate that guilt and anxiety, as indicated by self-report, are highly correlated (Laxer, 1964). Feelings of guilt, or self-blame, with their accompanying anxiety and lowered self-concept, result in depression. Shame and its accompanying anxiety, on the other hand, may protect the self-concept by directing hostility outward.

Some feelings of guilt or shame are common experiences of the parents of handicapped children. When the parental reaction is dominantly that of shame, the threat to one's personal prestige and the family's social status looms, often realistically, like an ever-present shadow. *Actual* social rejection of the child with a disability ranges all the way from a slight uneasiness on the part of the neighbors when they are in the presence of the disabled individual to thinking of the handicapped person as subhuman and dangerous. The parents of disabled children are aware of many beliefs centering on the sins of the parents and "bad blood," as well as such notions as that parental neglect or carelessness are possible causes of many disabilities, particularly when the etiology is either obscure or unknown.

The anticipation of social rejection, ridicule, and loss of prestige, when extreme, may result in an immediate and drastic solution to the problem. To avoid social rebuffs, some parents try to withdraw from social participation. Other parents assume the role of martyr to allay any suspicion of lack of parental concern or parental inadequacy as a possible cause of the child's defect. By devoting one's entire life to the child, the parent says to the world, "See what a dedicated and devoted parent I am! How can anyone suggest that the child's difficulties arise from my carelessness or inadequacy?"

Attempts at immediate foster home or institutional placement of the defective child may be the parental reaction to the threat of social ostracism. Less drastic attempts to keep the child from public exposure are a common reaction. The defective child, in either case, becomes the traditional skeleton in the closet, the forgotten child. The fear of social disclosures may force parents to prefer private to public institutional placement even when they can ill afford the additional expense.

Some complications involved in institutional placement are suggested by the parent who said, "I was relieved when we finally placed our son in a residential home—then I felt guilty for feeling relieved."

Every institution housing the severely disabled—particularly the psychotic and the severely mentally retarded—contains a sizable group of children who are never visited by their parents or other relatives. The writers have been impressed by the large number of severely handicapped children in the higher-priced private institutions whose families reside in distant parts of the country. Many children in private institutions in California, for example, come from outside the state, some from New York, Pennsylvania, and Florida. The only contact many of these families have with their children is to send a Christmas present, possibly a birthday present, and mail a monthly check to the institution. The implication is that these children are the forgotten ones and that excessive distance from home is an advantage to the family. Private institutions with ambiguous names, such as Pleasant Hill Manor, The Pines, Yorktown Hall, or The Hudson Country School, are often preferred to public institutions whose names are indicative of the types of children enrolled.

Feelings of guilt and self-accusation, like shame, may result in a parental life of martyrdom. However, the martyrdom resulting from shame is an attempt to prove to other people that the parent is competent and adequate, while the same behavior motivated by guilt is directed at defending the parental *self-concept*. The guilt-motivated parent is trying to deny or compensate for feelings of hostility and rejection. Overconcern, oversolicitousness, excessive care, and protection are ways in which parents may reassure themselves that they are good parents. Showering the child with presents, clothes, and other material things, sacrificing to send the child to expensive schools and to provide care beyond the child's needs may be motivated by the parents' need to prove to themselves what good and devoted parents they are. Some parents find solace in the rewards of martyrdom.

The guilt-ridden parent is always in danger of giving the child more protection than the realities of the situation demand. Of course, the handicapped child *realistically* requires more protection than does a normal child. The parent with little, if any, prior experience with the disabled does not know how much extra care and protection the child requires. It is therefore easy for the parent to rationalize the expenditure of enormous amounts of time, energy, and money, and the bestowal of excessive affection and care, which really represent compensations for feelings of rejection.

Feelings of depression are frequent experiences of either shame- or guilt-laden people. Grief reactions typical of the loss of a loved one are to be expected. Whenever anxiety mounts and the stresses of life seem overwhelming, despondency and depression are likely to ensue.

patterns of mutual dependency An earlier section mentioned the interaction and circularity of effects in family relationships. Parent and child, most often mother and disabled child, develop self-perpetuating patterns of mutual dependency. We have indicated the ways in which the parent—particularly the overanxious parent—can foster overdependency in the handicapped child. Less obvious is that the parent can become almost equally dependent on the disabled child. Whenever a parent invests a large part of herself, both materially and emotionally, in the care of a handicapped child, a condition of circular dependency can easily develop. Such children, either through their real needs or their parents' exaggeration of their needs, become dependent on the parents. The parents, in turn, need the excessive care and dependency of the children to prove their adequacy as parents. At times the excessive supervision, protection, and care provided by the oversolicitous parent increases and perpetuates the child's dependency. These reciprocal needs may be perpetuated indefinitely. By devoting so much of their time and energy to the handicapped child, parents invest so much of themselves in the project that their entire lives become centered in the child. When this occurs, parents may actually resist efforts to relieve them of the burden because of the void it would leave in their lives. Sometimes the handicapped child's lack of motivation is the result of an adult-fostered dependency and immaturity which is sustained by the neurotic satisfaction the parent derives from the child's dependency. The child, in turn, feels secure within the protecting parental arm. There is evidence that when such a neurotically sustained relationship involving a severely handicapped child has persisted for several years, it is very difficult to reverse.

Neurotic dependency can also develop in the disabled member of a dyad. This is particularly true when a predisposed adult develops a disability. A paralyzing stroke may accentuate or crystallize processes of surrender, dependency, and resignation already in progress. The neurotically inclined adult can exaggerate his incapacities, relinquish activities he is capable of doing, become more demanding of others, and institute a cycle of functional dependency. A chronically "hurt" child can learn to use hurt as a weapon. The cycle is self-perpetuating in more than one way. The failure to use one's remaining physical capacities results in their atrophy, which in turn increases the organic disability and the real dependency. There is a dynamic interplay of physiological, psychological, and social factors in all aspects of exceptionality.

SIBLINGS' REACTIONS TO THE EXCEPTIONAL CHILD

Evidence indicates that the siblings largely adopt the parents' attitudes toward the disabled child (Klein, 1972). When the parents view the defective child with shame or hostility, the siblings do likewise. When the family has been helped by counseling, the presence of a young mentally retarded child need not have an adverse effect on teenage siblings. The family may be so concerned with an obviously handicapped child, however, that a less obviously deviant sibling who is more seriously emotionally disturbed and more in need of help may be overlooked.

When the nonhandicapped siblings are required to supervise, care for, defend, and protect the handicapped child, resentment often develops. When the defective child receives excessive attention and affection, when the additional expense incurred by the deviant child deprives the others of educational and recreational opportunities, the resentment is aggravated. The overprotection of the handicapped is often accompanied by varying degrees of neglect of the other children. The siblings and their possessions may suffer directly at the hands of a demanding, hyperactive, and destructive handicapped child. Some sibling problems are illustrated in the following comments, adapted from S. D. Klein (1972).

a brother who happens to be handicapped

As a kid, I did not realize that there was anything really wrong with my brother. I found his crutches and wheelchair fun to play with. It was only when other kids made fun of him that I began to realize that he was handicapped. My parents strove very hard to make him seem normal. They asked me to help him but they never suggested that he was sick or abnormal. Then all of a sudden, we started taking him to the hospital. Once a week my mother and I would sit in the hospital waiting room for hours and hours. I saw other children and marveled that they were so different.

Then, one time, several doctors went with my brother into an adjoining room and it suddenly dawned on me that they were all concerned about his condition. One of the doctors brought my mother an X ray photograph of his short leg. I looked at it with her and said, "Mama, that is someone's foot, only a part of it goes down like this, and this part is missing." At that moment it dawned on me—that was really my brother and he was defective.

I think we all feel like protecting and defending our handicapped siblings. My brother went to a special school so I was never in school with him. However, when I was in the seventh grade some guy who did not know me was talking in the back of the bus about how dumb my brother was. He said you could make him do anything and all that kind of stuff. I walked back to the kid and slugged him in the face. I was really mad but he, of course, could not understand what was happening. From then on, I was always protecting my brother from something—from teasing, from fights, and from other kids trying to take advantage of him. I knew that many things I did were foolish but you can't help getting emotionally involved. One day, one of my friends told about some other kids who had picked on my brother and how sorry he felt. Then he turned to me and asked, "What did happen to your brother to make

> him that way?" "Don't ask me that, and the next person who asks
> that will get punched in the face," I retorted. Even when I said that,
> I knew that it was foolish, but it had made me mad. I felt strange
> about the whole thing and now wonder if my reactions were not the
> result of my own lack of understanding.

Practically every systematic study of exceptional people and their families stresses the need for more and better counseling. In their fervent search for solutions to their dilemma, the parents of exceptional children are perpetually looking for counsel.

The Goals of Parental Counseling

The goals of counseling are essentially the same irrespective of who is being counseled. The nature of the information imparted, the ways in which the person is informed, and the methods used may vary, but the purposes of counseling remain constant. Counseling goals are intellectual, emotional, and behavioral in nature.

In the intellectual realm, the parents of exceptional children need information concerning the nature and extent of the child's exceptionality—diagnostic information. They want to know the probable cause of their child's condition—etiological information. They require information concerning facilities and services available for the care, treatment, and education of these children—information concerning remediation. They should be informed of what the future may hold for the handicapped child, as well as of the specific programs most appropriate to the needs and capacities of their child—prognosis.

However, the imparting of information is seldom enough. The purely intellectual or factual approach to problems involving emotionally-laden relationships is notoriously insufficient in itself. People's feelings often carry more weight than do their intellects. Therefore, it is just as important to help parents with their attitudes and feelings as it is to provide them with adequate information. Counselors must concern themselves with the parents' fears and anxieties and their feelings of guilt and shame. They should attempt to reduce the emotional vulnerability of the family members. While the strains and tensions suffered by the family of the exceptional child cannot be eliminated, it is often possible to increase their ability to tolerate tension. Adequate counseling will also result in modified behavior by parents. Every counseling program should involve specific plans for the family and the handicapped child.

The goals of counseling for the parents of exceptional children are considerably more modest than are those of psychotherapy. Counseling is not intended to change the personality of the counselee. It is intended to help reasonably well-integrated people understand and deal more adequately with the problems growing out of the presence of the deviant child in the family. Work with the families of handicapped children is closer to social work than to psychotherapy. It is more concerned with environmental manipulation and the handling of practical problems than with the personalities of the family members.

Parental Dissatisfactions with Counseling

Attending meetings of parents of the handicapped, one has the impression that dissatisfaction with their experiences with professional people is almost universal. One mother characterized her conferences with professionals as "a masterful combination of dishonesty, condescension, misinformation, and bad manners" (Bennett, 1974). Hardly anyone seems pleased with the way he or she found out about the child's handicap and what could be done about it. Clients and professionals alike blame each other for this dissatisfaction. On the one hand, professionals point out that people blame the bearer of bad news, that what parents hear and what professionals say are often distinctly different, that purely descriptive diagnostic information is perceived by parents as "blaming the parent," and that parents often expect the impossible, as indicated by statements such as "If he would only tell me what my child's condition *really is,* I'm sure I could deal with it" and "I felt there was some sort of key and if he would just give it to me, it would reveal the secret of her recovery."

Parents, in turn, claim that most doctors know very little about many categories of exceptionality, that they are more pontifical than helpful, and that they avoid telling the parents what they know or believe by temporizing or giving vague hints and irrelevant observations which only distract and confuse. Parents also complain that doctors provide diagnostic information either in highly technical jargon or in purely pejorative terms, and that too often the parents are either told nothing beyond "You have a big problem there!" or are pressured to accept premature simple solutions—"Institutionalize the child."

Nothing is to be gained by attempting to apportion blame for this state of affairs. Certainly, some parents are not informed and others are tactlessly informed of their child's disability. Professionals can be insensitive to parents' feelings and unresponsive to their needs. They can either under- or overestimate the parents' capacity and readiness to understand and accept the child's disability and the realities of the situation.

Parents furious at the treatment they have received at the hands of some professionals tell other parents, and they all learn to distrust professionals. Parental hostilities, in turn, repel the professionals and reinforce their beliefs concerning parents. Professionals are human, too, and often respond to hostility with counter-hostility. Thus these two groups, who need each other's cooperation, are driven apart, What parents tell other parents is important. One parent with a bad experience tells others about it, leading them to expect similar experiences.

SOME ELEMENTARY PRINCIPLES OF PARENTAL COUNSELING

Interested readers and prospective professional counselors should consult the professional literature on family counseling. We shall present only a list of suggestions for the nonprofessional counselor who either elects to or must counsel the parents of exceptional children. Many different professional people counsel the parents of the handicapped—physicians, psychologists, social workers, school administrators, teachers, speech and occupational therapists, and physical therapists—and few of these people are professionally trained counselors.

the importance of listening Most counselors, particularly teachers, talk too much. They have faith in the efficacy of instruction and exhortation, and they commonly assume that beliefs and actions derive directly from information and that people behave inappropriately simply because they don't know any better. To be effective, however, counseling must be appropriate to the feelings, attitudes, and personality of the counselee, as well as to his or her intellectual and informational level. The only way to determine the counseling needs of a given person is to let him tell you, and the best way for him to tell you is in his own way.

In the intial interview the counselees should be permitted to lead. They should do most of the talking and dominate the interview. If both parents are present—as they should be—much can be learned by permitting and encouraging them to talk about their problem child, the nature of the problems with which they want to help, what has been done for the child, the plans they have made, and their expectations.

Avoid questions that can be answered with a simple yes or no. Rephrasing what has been said and using such phrases as, "Tell me more," or "Anything else?" encourage amplifications and more complete replies.

Permitting the counselees to tell their stories in their own ways provides clues to the stage of thinking they have attained in their concern for their children. It will indicate whether they are still concerned about diagnosis or the acceptance of diagnosis. The terms they use and their general vocabulary may indicate the level of sophistication and understanding they have attained. A listener can usually form some idea of the speaker's feelings and attitudes—the degrees of guilt, conflict, and confusion the counselees are experiencing.

the problem of terminology Most parents of exceptional children are laypeople who do not understand professional jargon. Communication must be in terms the counselee can understand. If the parents talk first, the counselor learns their vocabulary and the terms that they find acceptable. Laypeople often perceive professional terminology, even when they understand it, as stigmatizing and threatening. If parents refer to their child as a "slow developer" or as "nervous" or "handicapped," the counselor can adopt and use these terms in discussing the child. Their meaning will become clearer as the exact nature of the child's condition becomes clearer. Terms such as *crippled, moron, psychotic, feebleminded,* or even *mentally retarded* and *orthopedically handicapped* may well be set aside in an attempt to determine specifically the child's developmental status— what he can and cannot do. As we pointed out earlier, the fact that a disability exists—whether it be a language deficiency, an orthopedic handicap, a disorganization of personality, or mental retardation—may be less significant than the degree of the disability and the extent to which the person is handicapped by the deficiency.

Professionals will improve their relationships with parents by treating each handicapped person as an individual rather than as a "case," no matter how unusual and interesting. Referring to a child by name, or at least as "your daughter" or "your son," makes the person something more than a statistic. If the patient is an infant, holding it in a respectful and caring way during the discussion conveys to the parents the fact that the professional considers the baby human and worthy of concern and acceptance. In this context, one parent said, "Although it is now nineteen years since my child with Down's Syndrome was born, it is still painful for me to recall the coldness, the brutality and the inhumanity of the manner in which my doctor held my daughter by the nape of her neck, like a plucked chicken, and pointed to her typical mongoloid features" (Pender, 1975). The counselor should be interested in learning about the abilities and disabilities and the unique characteristics of the individual under study, rather than in simply classifying, categorizing, and labeling.

the problem of acceptance The counselor will remember that while his or her primary concern is for the exceptional child, the parents are also emotionally disturbed. They are in conflict. They have feelings of shame and guilt. They are subject to terrific social pressures and are vulnerable to criticism. Many parents have developed self-defeating and blind-alley resolutions of their conflicts. Their attitudes and practices may actually be aggravating their child's condition.

Merely to judge, disapprove of, or condemn parental attitudes and practices does not help, however. Overt or implied criticism of parental practices only adds to the emotional load of people who are already overwhelmed by their problems. Criticism from the counselor therefore is often met with hostility; the parents become defensive and invite counter-hostility. Understanding, acceptance, and empathy are fundamental requirements of a helpful counseling relationship. Unconditional acceptance of the family as worthy and deserving of regard and assistance—the parents as well as the exceptional child—is a requisite of a helping relationship.

To be warm and sympathetic, to be understanding and helpful without fostering overdependence, is one of the challenges of counseling. To help parents to a better understanding of themselves, their child, and their relationships, yet not take over by providing too much advice and assistance, is a critical task. If the counselor is to be most effective, the parents must see that it is primarily their problem and that no one else can solve it for them.

A nonjudgmental, noncondemning, accepting, and understanding attitude toward people does not imply uncritical endorsement and support for whatever is done or proposed. The ultimate goal is to formulate and carry through plans which will most benefit the exceptional child, and with which the family can live at peace. The consequences of current or proposed practices can be suggested, alternatives can be proposed, and appropriate plans can be sanctioned. Additional information can be supplied in such a way as to reinforce certain behavior and discourage others without rejecting or disapproving the individuals involved.

the importance of counseling the entire family Some reasons for counseling the entire family have already been listed. Another important reason is that it facilitates communication among family members. It is very difficult for a mother—for it is usually the mother who is counseled—to go home and restate, explain, interpret, and answer questions concerning a long and involved counseling session, the nature of which she may only partially understand. Selective perception and memory distortion preclude accurate reporting. Emotional tension may be making communication between family members difficult. Effective communication among family members may even have broken down.

The advent of a child belonging to one of the familiar disability syndromes such as Down's Syndrome (mongolism), whose condition is usually recognized at birth, poses special counseling problems. Recognizing that the parents have the right to know, professionals usually give diagnostic information as soon as possible after the delivery. If a couple is left to learn about their infant's condition from someone other than their physician, their relationship with the doctor, as well as with other professionals with whom they might consult, is jeopardized. Whatever their race, religion, or socioeconomic status, learning that their newborn infant is seriously defective is a traumatic experience. Parents need all the support and assistance they can be given. Therefore, the initial diagnostic information should be presented to both parents. Some counselors prefer to discuss the child's condition with the father before they go in together to talk with the mother. They also try to arrange to have a close friend or relative present when the initial diagnostic information is conveyed, if the father is not available. It is felt that the vulnerable new mother should not be alone at this time.

Conferences involving the entire family may reopen avenues of communication and help unite the members in the interest of making plans for the exceptional person's welfare. The emotional isolation in which each suffers in silence, is afraid to express fears, and is reluctant to precipitate the issue is too often a part of the burden imposed on the nondisabled family members.

Effective planning and execution involve the whole family. When all the concerned family members participate in counseling, conflicting beliefs and attitudes come to light, and differences in opinion can be ventilated and possibly reconciled. Family members are more likely to share responsibility and cooperate for a common goal if all are involved in the discussion and planning. Unfortunately, counseling of the entire family is not yet the general practice.

the importance of feelings and attitudes Feelings are often stronger than admonitions and logical decisions. Self-pity, anxiety, guilt, and shame are primarily feeling states. While some parents act inappropriately because they do not know any other way to act, far more act less adequately than their information dictates because of anxieties, hostilities, and guilt feelings. It is therefore essential that counseling be as concerned with feelings and attitudes as with giving information and making formal plans. Parents need help in clarifying their feelings. They need assistance in wandering through their emotional mazes. When deep-seated emotional disturbances and emotional disorientation are present, however, the problems may be beyond the reach of the ordinary teacher, counselor, physician, or school psychologist, and long-term psychotherapy may be necessary.

Parents can be encouraged to express their feelings by such questions as, "How do you feel about it?" or "And what was your reaction?" and by avoiding critical or moralistic observations or comments. It is also well not to overload the parents with information and press for critical decisions too soon. Accept parental concerns as real. To simply tell them to "Stop worrying," or "You worry too much," or "You are overanxious" may imply that you do not accept either the reality or seriousness of the situation or that you consider the parents to be either chronic worriers or neurotic.

Feelings and attitudes must often be dealt with before the parents can progress to the point of planning rationally for their child. Confused, frightened, and grieving parents should neither be offered stereotyped solutions nor be pressed for lifetime decisions. Frightened and bewildered by the diagnosis, they may welcome an opportunity to escape the problem when a solution such as foster-home or institutional placement is suggested. However, if it is acted upon, they soon discover that the initial placement of the child does not solve the problem. They begin to wonder whether the child would not have done better if he had stayed at home, they experience guilt over their apparent rejection of their infant, and they feel betrayed by the doctor who suggested placement. The feelings and conflicts which are aroused at the birth of a defective child are not resolved when the doors of the institution or foster home close behind the baby. Rather than making any major decisions, the more immediate problem is to help the family deal with the acute grief and chronic sorrow they are experiencing. This cannot be done in one or two short discussions.

When the diagnostic information has been imparted, the parents' comments and questions should be solicited. The counselor should be willing and able to accept critical questions and expressions of doubt, as well as a wide variety of emotional reactions. The parents should be encouraged to discuss the matter between themselves and return to continue the discussion. If they are in need of immediate assistance in caring for the child, they can be told how to contact a public health nurse or social worker. Some parents go through a long period of denial and mourning before acceptance reaches the point where they can mobilize their resources and begin serious, long-range planning.

the place of interpretation in counseling Interpretation can occur at several different levels. At one level, it may be largely a matter of providing information. All parents need information. However, information often requires interpretation; as we indicated earlier, the meaning of the facts of a disability is more important than the presence of the condition.

Some people need self-understanding more than an understanding of the handicapping condition of their child. Some parents need help but do not realize it; others realize they need assistance but cannot ask for or accept it; some seek advice but are unable to follow it. Many parents agree to plans they are unable to carry out. Parents, like all other people, often contradict what they say by what they do. All such people can profit by a greater understanding of themselves and their needs. They need to be interpreted to themselves.

Interview questions may point up gross inconsistencies. Questions of concern may be discussed without probing parental defenses too deeply. Interpretation in depth is hardly practical in counseling which stops short of psychotherapy. Defense mechanisms have value for the individual. To probe deeply and deprive an individual of her defenses without carrying through and helping her to substitute a more adequate adjustment may do more harm than good.

The interpretations of the average counselor will provide information which is as complete and accurate as possible. They will dispel misconceptions. However, even the latter may be carried too far. When the actual causes of the handicapped child's condition are unknown, parents often develop very positive beliefs about its etiology. These beliefs have considerable value for the parents, for the parents can discuss their child's condition frankly and openly when they are able to present the alleged causes as the real ones. In such cases, so long as the belief does not result in inappropriate treatment for the child, the belief may represent a useful fiction which is just as well left undisturbed.

imparting diagnostic information One function of counseling is to help parents realize the nature and extent of their problem as early as possible. Many valuable years are often lost because of failures either in diagnosis or in parental acceptance of the factors or implications of diagnostic information. The parents of exceptional children often say, "Why didn't someone tell us?" or "If we had only known sooner!" In many cases these parents had been told in various ways, but their ears were not open. Parental attitudes have to develop to a certain level before there is receptivity to the facts and implications of threatening diagnostic information. Understanding and acceptance of diagnosis cannot be forced. Time is required, and counselors can only present the available data as completely and as honestly as possible and hope for its eventual acceptance.

Test data and general impressions must be stated in the counselee's terms. Exact test scores are seldom disclosed. Intellectual status and achievement are usually most meaningful when they are stated in terms of approximate mental age or school grade equivalents. Asking the parents to indicate their estimates of the child's level is often helpful. When the parents' estimate is in approximate agreement with intelligence test scores and other evidence of achievement, a simple confirmation of the parental judgment may be sufficient. When the data are discrepant, additional information may be needed. When parents are reluctant to accept diagnostic information no matter how complete, the counselor may supply the names of several other specialists or agencies from which the parents may select those with whom they wish to consult. One diagnosis or one statement of a diagnosis is seldom enough. It is normal for most parents to want to shop around. Many parents need to nurse their doubt and maintain their defenses until they are able to dispense with them. The initial rejection of many diagnoses and their implications is to be expected. Only the parents can make the critical decisions. Counselors can only assist in the process.

It will facilitate acceptance and action if the parents can be involved every step of the way. If the parents are involved in the diagnosis and in planning educational or treatment procedures, the question of the parents' "right to know" will never arise. Providing parents with copies of diagnostic reports and decisions made concerning their child will give them an opportunity to discuss and better understand the information. Today, parents have the legal right of access to such information.

Acceptance of a realistic diagnosis is furthered by accenting positive assets rather than the liabilities of the exceptional individual. The handicapped person is typically under special study because of his disability, and his limitation tends to be the overshadowing fact of his life. But every person has some positive attributes, and diagnosis should be as concerned with what the person *can* do as with what he cannot do. Plans which are built around what the child is able to do and formulated to take maximum advantage of his abilities may be more palatable to the parents than plans which are dominated by the child's disabilities.

the importance of plans Specific plans for the exceptional child should be considered as early as possible. Sometimes an early shift in emphasis from diagnosis to what can best be done for the child immediately will indirectly bring acceptance of an implied status while resistance to an explicit statement is still great. Parents are often able to accept the facts of the child's present level of functioning while rejecting their implications for the child's future attainments.

When the parents have not sufficiently accepted the realities of the child's status to be able to make long-range plans, they may still be receptive to suggestions for dealing with the problems of living on a day-to-day basis. Plans which make use of the family and community resources to meet the child's immediate needs may then gradually be extended to the more remote ones.

The typical starting point for planning is the parents' conception of their child's future. A plan which they have considered, together with alternatives suggested by the counselor, is the beginning. Planning for the future is a continuing process and is never complete. Plans are realized one step at a time and need constant revision in light of the individual's progress. If the parents leave a conference with nothing more than a commitment to attend a meeting of parents with similar problems and exchange information and plans with these parents, they have taken an important first step. Reading suggested literature on their child's condition may be an additional small step toward making long-range plans for their child.

keeping expectations "realistic" In an earlier chapter we indicated that people working with the handicapped find it difficult to tread that narrow path between being too protective and too demanding—expecting either too much or too little. Matching expectations with reasonable possibilities involves (1) maintaining expectations and demands at a sufficiently high level to challenge the person to achieve and to become independent, and (2) keeping expectations sufficiently realistic that each person has a good chance of succeeding and is also protected from total failure. A belief in the possibility of improvement by students and instructors and parents is crucial for effective learning. Individuals should be provided with a good chance to learn and succeed but they should also be protected against a high probability of total failure. Since the realities of yesterday are not the realities of today for the handicapped, who can say what the realities of tomorrow will be? This uncertainty makes the setting of appropriate goals difficult.

As compared with previous times, the handicapped today are receiving a lot of public attention. This mass media are giving them extensive coverage and are helping to destroy some of the old myths concerning the limitations of the disabled. However, there is a danger that they may promote some complementary myths. The news media tend to make folk heroes out of handicapped individuals who have achieved greatness.

Of course, everyone knows about Helen Keller who, despite being both blind and deaf, graduated from Radcliffe with honors and went on to become an internationally famous author and lecturer. Most people perceive Franklin D. Roosevelt as the ultimate in superior adjustment to disability. After becoming a virtual paraplegic, he went on to become the only president who was ever elected to serve four terms in office. Currently, Max Cleland, who lost both legs and a forearm in Vietnam, is head of the Veteran's Administration. Today's local paper features a UPI story about Richard Chavez receiving the first W. Clement Stone Award, which recognizes people who have overcome great adversity. Technically, Chavez is 100 percent disabled. However, he has become a state licensed private investigator and manages a school for disabled people which employs a staff of twenty-two. He also serves on the Department of Rehabilitation Appeals Board and is a member of the California State Committee for Employment of the Handicapped.

Two folk heroes in the field of athletics are Glenn Cunningham and Wilma Rudolph. Cunningham's legs were burned so severely as a child that his doctors predicted that he would never walk. He not only learned to walk, however, but became an all-time great as a runner, competing in the 1932 and 1936 Olympics and winning 38 AAU titles. Wilma Rudolph was crippled with polio and confined to bed for four years as a child. Despite this, she became the first American woman to win three gold medals as a runner in Olympic competitions.

These success stories carry three messages, only the first two of which are true. The first message is that handicapped people can learn, improve themselves, and even become more than their disabilities seem to permit. Many more can become lovers, spouses, parents, and be reasonably happy. Second, some can even attain greatness. Third, if these individuals can attain greatness, so can all of the handicapped, if they will only aim high enough and try hard enough. Have we not been told by the development-of-human-potential people that "the human potential of every person is infinite?" It follows from these considerations that the failures of the disabled to achieve greatness are their fault or their families'. They have failed to realize their potential. They have just not tried hard enough and therefore feel guilty because of their failure. This is just as mythical as the belief that the handicapped are helpless. Of course, publicizing the remarkable achievements of handicapped individuals does have its positive side. Since the handicapped are defined in terms of their limitations, publicizing their superior achievements focuses attention on possibilities, even though they may be within the range of relatively few. It also helps to de-stereotype the handicapped, emphasizing that the range of abilities and achievements among the handicapped is just as great as it is among the nonhandicapped.

group counseling Group counseling ranges all the way from an informal exchange of information and experiences among a group of parents with common problems to formal counseling by a trained and experienced leader. Group counseling directed by a leader can range from lecture, lecture and discussion, directed discussion, or free discussion to directive or nondirective psychotherapy.

Group guidance, counseling, and psychotherapy were originally used and justified because they saved the time of counselors and psychotherapists, who are in such short supply. However, experience indicates that working with groups may have some unique advantages over individual counseling or psychotherapy. Recently there has been a tremendous growth in group approaches to many training, guidance, counseling, and psychotherapeutic problems.

The parents of mentally retarded children, often under considerable environmental stress, are confronted with day-to-day problem behavior. One study evaluated the relative effectiveness of behaviorally-oriented and reflective group counseling. The members of the behaviorally-oriented counseling group were taught the principles and applications of techniques for dealing with specific child-rearing problems. The members of the reflective-oriented group were provided opportunities to discuss their feelings and problems, while the leaders conveyed the importance of feelings of empathy, acceptance, and understanding in dealing with their children. In terms of six success criteria, the behaviorally-oriented program resulted in significantly more improvement than did the reflective model (Tavormina, 1975). The evidence indicated that parents of the mentally retarded profited most by instruction and training in dealing with the specific problems they faced in rearing their children.

Some of the advantages of group counseling of the parents of exceptional children are:

1. The group gives the parents emotional support. Groups of people with common experiences and similar needs feel free to express their feelings, attitudes, and beliefs. The group identification which typically develops as the result of shared experiences and common feelings seems to lessen the individual's emotional burden. The mere discovery that many other reasonably normal and adequate parents have similar conflicts and frustrations helps many parents to put their own problems in a different perspective.

In the group situation parents are free to proceed at their own rate. They can bring up and focus on problems that are most significant to them. In group discussion they are able to clarify their ideas and feelings. Self-pity, guilt, and shame diminish when parents discover that others have shared and surmounted their problems.

2. In the group situation, parents educate one another. The typical group of parents of exceptional children have, *in toto*, accumulated a tremendous amount of information about exceptional children and the resources available for their diagnosis, care, and treatment. They are able to save one another a tremendous amount of time, money, and emotional stress by the exchange of information and experiences. And parents are generally more receptive to information, advice, and counseling coming from people like themselves than they are to the same information provided by professionals.

3. Programs for action are more likely to succeed as the result of group endeavors than when individuals act alone.

Many times the greatest service that a counselor can provide the parents of exceptional children is to put them in touch with a local group of parents, and perhaps to follow through and see that they meet with the group at least once. Such parents can also profit from membership in the state and national organizations concerned with exceptional people.

counseling as a continuing process Whenever possible, counseling services should be continuously available. Parents who are not receptive to counseling at one time may be so later. The problems of exceptional children change with their age. A program for a handicapped child which is adequate so long as the child is of school age must be replaced by another when he or she is older. Changes in the family constellation bring new problems. While the aim of counseling is to help the parents help themselves, an overdependency on counselors is discouraged. Parents should leave counseling with the feeling that they can return if subsequent problems become overwhelming.

THE SELF-HELP ORGANIZATIONS

Paralleling professionally organized and directed group counseling, a self-help movement has grown in the United States. Some of these groups were started in the 1930s, but their tremendous growth has occurred largely in the last two decades. Two general types of self-help are distinguishable. One type is composed of the deviant individuals themselves who have the same problems and are seeking help from one another; Alcoholics Anonymous, Gamblers Anonymous, Neurotics Anonymous, Overeaters Anonymous, Recovery Inc., and Synanon are illustrative of this group. The second type consists of family members or friends of the persons with the primary personal-social problems; Alanon, Alateen, and

Parents of Retarded Children are examples of organizations of this type. Almost every category of deviants has organizations of both types.

While the functions of the two categories overlap, the latter type more often engages in advocacy, social action, and program development, whereas the former is more likely to focus on its more immediate problems. A tremendous number of people are involved in these programs. One survey of self-help organizations for the physically handicapped alone found over 1,200 such groups in the United States (Massachusetts Council of Organizations of the Handicapped, 1973). In 1973, Alcoholics Anonymous reported a membership of 405,858 in 14,037 chapters in the United States (Jaques and Patterson, 1974).

Except for those with multiple handicaps or the extremely debilitating conditions, almost every person with a problem can find a group of people with the same problem, ready to help. These groups can be located by contacting the local Family Services organization, city or county health agencies, or by writing to The Self-Help Institute, Northwestern University, Evanston, Illinois, 60201.

Many of the values of such self-help groups are the same as those provided by professionally organized group counseling and psychotherapy:

1. gaining facts and information concerning their conditions and problems

2. exchanging information concerning ameliorative and coping devices

3. providing mutual motivation and support

4. receiving feedback from others to assist in evaluating one's status and progress

5. gaining a group identification that reduces one's feelings of isolation and alienation

6. obtaining satisfaction from members' mutual altruistic concern.

THE CHILD-ABUSING PARENT

When stresses exceed the parents' endurance levels, it is inevitable that they will direct their resentment and hostility at the child. When this hostility becomes overt, the result may be a battered or abused child.

"When my husband was here, we fought all the time. Now he is gone and there is only me and the baby. The baby cries and whines so much I can hardly stand it. His incessant demands for attention drive me wild. I need someone to talk to—someone to listen to my troubles—someone to help. Yes, even someone to fight with is better than being totally alone. At times I feel completely frustrated. I get so wrought up that I can't see. I don't know what I am doing. I grab the baby and shake him until he gets blue in the face. Afterward, I am so ashamed and wonder how I could do such a thing. Being a parent, destitute, and alone is the worst situation in the world. I cry out for help and no one answers."

While child abuse is not primarily a problem of the deviant child or parent, deviancy in either may be a contributing cause or a consequence of the abuse. Child abuse involves a vulnerable child, a predisposed abusing parent, and a stress situation which triggers the abuse (Zeskind and Lester, 1978). Other things being equal, a handicapping condition in a child will significantly increase the level of family stress. The increased ambivalence in parental feelings engendered by a child who is handicapped increases the probability that such a child will become a scapegoat for overt acts of resentment and hostility. Finally, child abuse often results in head injury, which involves a likelihood of brain damage. One study estimates that 28 percent of battered children with head injuries suffer permanent brain damage (Brandwein, 1973); in this researcher's opinion, child abuse is a significant cause of mental retardation. D. Zadnik (1973) claims that many children are visually impaired or blinded by child abuse. One study of fifty-one cases of child abuse found that one-quarter of the children were low-birth-weight infants (Klein and Stern, 1971), more likely than infants of normal birth weight to suffer from a multiplicity of problems. Such problem children add to the parents' burden and are vulnerable in two ways: They are vulnerable as objects of overt hostility, and since they are more fragile they are also more likely to be damaged by physical abuse. However, most abused children are not handicapped (Shanas, 1975).

CHARACTERISTICS OF THE CHILD-ABUSING PARENT

Child-abusing parents come from all socioeconomic levels. However, the reported cases (the only ones studied) come disproportionately from families experiencing economic and social stress. Abusing families also have a high incidence of unstable marriages, separation, and divorce as well as of minor criminal offenses. The abused child is often the outcome of an unwanted pregnancy. The families are commonly described as "multiproblem families" in which an interplay of socioeconomic, mental, physical, and emotional factors condition the abuse (Shanas, 1975; Garbarino and Crouter, 1978).

Abusing parents themselves, as children, were often neglected or abused either physically or emotionally. They were reared and treated in much the same way that they treat their own children. They are reacting to their children in keeping with their own experiential history of cruelty and lack of love. In addition, abusing parents often make unrealistic demands on their children. When the child's performance fails to meet their high level of expectations, they justify the abuse as a proper disciplinary measure and strongly defend their right to use physical force (Green, Gaines and Sandgrund, 1974).

At one time a high incidence of neurotic or psychotic behavior was assumed to be characteristic of abusing parents. Today the consensus seems to be that, while direct and deliberate murder of a child often indicates a frankly psychotic parent, few abusing parents are clinically psychotic or neurotic. They are most often characterized as "lacking in impulse control" (Spinetta and Rigler, 1972).

E. J. Merrill (1962) has identified three clusters of traits characteristic of abusing parents: (1) Such parents are beset with a generalized and pervasive hostility and aggressiveness usually directed at the world in general but sometimes focused on a vulnerable child. (2) Such parents are characterized by rigidity, compulsiveness, and perfectionism. They expect their children to be clean, orderly, and obedient far beyond their years. These parents insist that they are entirely right in the ways they treat their children and defend their right to act as they do. They seem to be concerned primarily with their own pleasures and blame the children for the troubles they are having. (3) Child-abusing parents may be immature, passive, dependent, moody, unhappy, and despondent. Generally passive and unaggressive, they occasionally break out with uncontrolled violence directed toward their children.

Since the battered child syndrome was first recognized in the 1950s, considerable progress has been made in dealing with the problem. A Child Abuse Prevention and Treatment Act was passed by Congress and signed by President Gerald Ford on January 31, 1974. It established a National Center on Child Abuse within the Office of Child Development of the Children's Bureau. By April 1975 the bureau had awarded grants and contracts totaling $4.5 million to increase and improve services for the prevention, identification, and treatment of child abuse and neglect (News and Reports, *Children Today,* 1975). All fifty states now have child abuse report laws which require physicians to report suspicious cases.

When victims of child abuse are simply returned to their parents, one-third of them will subsequently be seriously injured or even killed. Consequently, many communities now provide psychiatric and/or counseling services for the parents and protection and care for the children. For example, San Francisco has an Extended Family Center which serves families referred by the courts and by public health, mental health, and social welfare agencies. The state of Florida has a "hot line" which has been receiving about 20,000 calls a year in cases of child abuse and/or neglect. In Oregon, a volunteer group—the Child Abuse Study Committee,

Inc.—is focusing on the area of public education. The United States Office of Education is awarding grants for the development of models for teacher training (Shanas, 1975).

THE RESPONSIBILITIES OF EDUCATORS

School personnel—teachers, counselors, and school psychologists—are often able to identify and report cases of child abuse. Formerly, school people were often reluctant to report suspected cases because they feared personal or legal reprisals. They were also fearful of becoming involved in grievance hearings and court proceedings. However, most states have enacted legislation which encourages and expedites the reporting of suspected cases of neglect or abuse, and relieves the informants of personal liability. In most cases, this legislation *requires* the reporting of suspected cases by hospital employees, doctors, and day care workers as well as school personnel. The usual procedure is for a written statement to be filed with an appropriate social agency. The social agency investigates and if the reports are considered to be unfounded, those reporting are so notified and all the relevant records are destroyed. When the evidence indicates that abuse has probably occurred the appropriate law enforcement agencies intervene.

Some communities have established a toll-free telephone child abuse line for the use of all citizens wishing to report instances of child abuse. These calls can be anonymous. There are facilities for vulnerable parents who feel so overwhelmed by critical home situations that they need advice and assistance in warding off possible child abuse. There are also several hundred local chapters of Child Abuse Anonymous in the United States. Patterned after Alcoholics Anonymous, the members of this organization assist each other by counseling, providing mutual support, and obtaining professional help when needed.

PARENTS AS CHILD ADVOCATES

Citizen advocacy movements for the handicapped resemble similar civil rights movements. In contrast to other ways of helping people, advocacy movements attempt to change human service agencies and the ways in which they function. In an earlier chapter we indicated some of the limitations of charity as a way of helping people. Appeals in the name of charity communicate pity toward the recipients, romanticize their special natures and needs, keep the recipient in a dependent situation, and momentarily relieve suffering without altering its root causes. Charity does not solve personal or social problems; it may only delay or diminish their impact and divert efforts from more effective long-range programs.

Another, more sophisticated way of helping people is by providing professional services. This approach has an "experts know best" frame of reference. Clients receive services which others consider to be most appropriate on a take-it-or-leave-it basis. This is the traditional medical model.

Still another way of helping people is to become an advocate. The advocate concentrates on achieving the needed human services as a right. Advocacy assumes that institutions and social attitudes create or contribute to human abuse, neglect, and injustice. During the past two decades organized groups—principally parent groups—have become very effective pressure groups working to increase and improve the services provided exceptional children.

At first these parent groups tended to be local in their orientation. However, more and more of them have fused into state, regional, and national organizations, combining the force of numbers with information, persuasion, and political power to promote public action. These groups focus on providing appropriate services for the handicapped as a right.

These groups have learned to use the methods found effective by civil rights advocates. These include demonstrations designed to publicize issues, obtain short-term goals, and create a sense of group solidarity. Making demands, another familiar tactic, may take the form of presenting a bill of rights or list of grievances to the appropriate authorities. Demands in the name of the handicapped are effective public education tools because these individuals have traditionally been powerless. Symbolic acts can focus attention on an issue or injustice. For a handicapped person to refuse to be the poster child of the year may focus attention on the need for social change rather than charity as the way to meet the needs of the handicapped. Because it is unexpected and unusual, the symbolic act has considerable impact. Probably the most effective advocacy has been in the interest of legislation and administrative policies. Legal advocacy has produced extensive legislation, as detailed in an earlier chapter. This legislation has crystalized efforts designed to further the deinstitutionalization, mainstreaming, and normalizing procedures so prominent today. Implicit in these movements are new ways of thinking about human services. Instead of privileges, advocates speak of rights. The existence of advocacy groups and organizations brings to both the handicapped and their families the realization that they are not alone in their struggle for change (Bilken, 1976).

The recently-organized National Committee for Citizens in Education is primarily an advocacy organization. It distributes a free Parent Rights Card which advises parents of their rights under existing laws, publishes handbooks, conducts parent-training programs, provides a twenty-four hour hotline, and investigates the implementation of laws affecting schools.

Assert and maintain your right to know and to be involved. Since you are the primary planner, decision-maker, advocate, and monitor for your child, insist that you be treated as such. Your success in doing this will depend upon how well informed you are and your ability to work and cooperate with the other people involved. Resistance to your inclusion in the decisions concerning your child can be met by persuasion, by insisting that you know many things about your child that the others do not know, and finally, be insisting on your legal rights.

Obtain and retain copies of your child's records. If possible, make tape recordings of diagnostic and interpretive conferences. Keep records of visits with dates, addresses, persons present, and if other records are not available, your recollections and understandings of what was said and recommendations made.

Become informed. Familiarize yourself with the professional literature and terminology used by specialists in the area of your child's exceptionality. Make sure that you understand the terminology used by professionals. If in doubt, ask them to translate into lay language and give examples of what they mean. Talk with as many professionals as you can. Talk with other parents, join parent groups, and share your information with them. Visit, observe, and ask questions about programs that may be of help to your child.

Work hard at trying to de-stigmatize the category to which your child belongs. Insist on and impart to your child and others the notion that differentness is not bad. Encourage the idea that these deviants are individuals with certain special problems, rather than defective persons. Do not hide your child just because he or she is different. It is important for both you and your child to learn to cope with the inevitable questions and/or stares of others.

Help your child become maximally independent. Do not do for him, and do not permit others to do for him, those things he can do or learn to do for himself. Firmness and the setting of limits combined with patience and persistence are as necessary for the development of the handicapped as for the nonhandicapped.

Give your child as normal a life as possible. Think in terms of what she *can* do rather what she cannot do. It is easy to be so impressed with limitations that you fail to see possibilities.

Your problems are not unique. The problems of the parents of exceptional and nonexceptional children are basically the same. It is of course necessary for the parents of exceptional children to exert special effort in dealing with the increased emotional and physical strain engendered by the child's differentness. Fear, anguish, anger, and resentment vie with faith, hope, and love in the matrix of all parent-child relationships. It is harder for the latter to overbalance the negative emotions which have a greater likelihood of cropping up because of the exceptional circumstances of the deviant child.

THE PARENTS' ROLE IN EDUCATIONAL PLANNING

The law spells out the parents' rights to be participants in all decisions concerning their children's educational programs. These rights include the diagnostic evaluation, IEP development, and due process procedures.

diagnostic evaluation Prior to involvement in the IEP, parents should:

1. get in touch with the appropriate school administrator. Parents have the right to refer their child for a diagnostic evaluation. No child can be excluded from school because of a handicap.

2. investigate the availability of services. Remember that programs are available for children as young as three years.

3. consider getting an outside evaluation. If you are dissatisfied with the evaluation made by the school, you are entitled to an outside evaluation.

IEP development When the IEP is being developed the parents should:

1. attend all meetings held to plan the child's IEP.

2. bring a special outside child advocate to a conference whenever you feel it advisable. Many parent organizations of the handicapping specialties have advocates prepared to give assistance.

3. feel free to discuss all relevant information about your child.

4. be satisfied that the program is tailored to meet the special needs of your child. Be sure that the child is being placed in the least restrictive environment.

5. remember that your signature on the IEP document does not end your involvement in the program.

6. be aware that continued participation in teachers' conferences, and at least one formal evaluation of the child's progress each year, with the IEP updated accordingly, are expected.

due process As indicated in an earlier chapter, whenever you, as parents of a handicapped child, feel that your child is not receiving the services required by law, you can submit a written request for a hearing to the local superintendent of schools. The superintendent is then required to call a conference with school representatives. If the matter is not resolved to your satisfaction, a hearing panel is formed and a hearing is conducted. You are entitled to a copy of the panel's decision within forty-five days. If you are not satisfied with the panel's findings and recommendations, you may appeal the decision to the state superintendent of public instruction, and if still dissatisfied, you have the right to bring a civil court action.

SOME UNRECOGNIZED HEROES

We all recognize and applaud the single act of heroism—rescuing the elderly woman from a burning building or saving a drowning child. However, we seldom recognize that it takes equivalent courage, infinite patience, and everlasting perseverance to be a good parent to severely handicapped children. The rescue operations required by these children are matters of daily tedium punctuated by a succession of minor crises, rather than matters of high drama.

Many people who are able to mobilize their sources and make the supreme effort required to meet crises of short duration are completely unable to endure the repeated pin pricks, incessant demands, and many disappointments that are part of the prolonged care of a disabled child. Very often, the daily and even hourly routines of medication, special diets, and eternal vigilance are more than one can bear. Being patient with an impulsive, hyperactive, and destructive child is a perpetual drain on one's reserves. Giving the same answer or repeating the same instructions for the tenth time and frequently changing diapers for the mentally retarded incontinent boy tries the patience of the most dedicated. Long waits in clinics and doctor's offices or innumerable conferences with principals, teachers, speech therapists, physiotherapists, and psychologists may go on year after year with no end in sight. The ceaseless demands and pressures and conflicting emotions may keep the strongest of parents perpetually tired. When they become tired, bored, irritated, and resentful of the tedious, repetitive, and never-ending tasks, they feel guilty and this further confuses them. Certainly being able to meet these situations and maintain a reasonable degree of hope requires just as much heroism as rushing into a burning house to rescue a child (adapted from Stewart, 1978, p. 126).

SUMMARY

The individual exceptional child can best be understood in terms of the entire family constellation. Family and child exert reciprocal effects on each other, and changes in either affect both. Parental and family reactions to the advent of a child with a disability do not differ in kind from people's reactions to other types of stress. Parental reactions to the problems of the exceptional range from complete denial to realistic coping with the situation. Self-pity, ambivalence, projection, guilt, shame, depression, self-punishment, and the development of patterns of mutual dependency are common parental reactions to the presence of a less-than-adequate child in the family.

The general reactions of children to a handicapped sibling largely reflect those of the parents, but must always be considered in counseling the families of exceptional children. Working with the families of exceptional children involves no unique counseling techniques or principles. However, the nonprofessional counselor is admonished to heed these precepts:

1. Let the counselee talk.

2. Use the terminology of the counselee.

3. Accept the counselee as an individual but do not necessarily approve of and endorse his ideas, practices, and plans.

4. See both parents, preferably the entire family.

5. Deal with feelings and attitudes as well as with intellectual matters.

6. Keep interpretation on a fairly elementary and superficial level.

7. Give diagnostic information according to the individual's ability to understand and accept it.

8. Include specific plans for the future.

9. Remember that group counseling is often useful for the parents or families of exceptional children.

10. Keep your door open. Counseling should be a continuing process.

Suggestions for parents include:

1. Assert and maintain your right to know and to be involved in all plans and decisions concerning your handicapped child.

2. Become informed concerning the category of your child's disability.

3. Help your child to become maximally independent.

4. Give your child as normal a life as possible.

5. Remember that your problems are not unique just because your child is deviant.

REFERENCES

Bennett, J. M., "Proof of the Pudding," *The Exceptional Parent*, 1974, *4*(3), 7–12.

Bilken, D., "Advocacy Comes of Age," *Exceptional Children*, 1976, *42*, 308–15.

Block, J., "Impaired Children," *Children Today*, 1978, 7(6), 2–6.

Boles, G., "Personality Factors in the Mothers of Cerebral-palsied Children," *Genetic Psychology Monographs*, 1959, *59*, 159–218.

Brandwein, H., "The Battered Child: A Definite and Significant Factor in Mental Retardation," *Mental Retardation*, 1973, *11*(5), 50–51.

Eisenpreis, B., "My Child Isn't Like That," *The Exceptional Parent*, 1974, *4*(2), 5–9.

Garbarino, J. and Crouter, A., "Defining the Community Context for Parent-Child Relations: The Correlates of Child Maltreatment," *Child Development*, 1978, *49*, 604–16.

Green, A. H., R. W. Gaines, and A. Sandgrund, "Child Abuse: Pathological Syndrome of Family Interaction," *American Journal of Psychiatry*, 1974, *131*, 882–86.

Gregory, R. W., "Family Forum," *The Exceptional Parent*, 1972, *2*(2), 30.

Hosey, C., "Yes, Our Son is Still With Us," *Children Today*, 1973, *2*, 14–17.

Jaques, M. E. and K. M. Patterson, "The Self-help Group: A Review," *Rehabilitation Counseling Bulletin*, 1974, *18*(1), 49–58.

Klein, S. D., "Brother to Sister: Sister to Brother," *The Exceptional Parent*, 1972, *2*(1) 10–15; (2), 26–27.

Klein, M. and L. Stern, "Low Birth Weight and the Battered Child Syndrome," *American Journal of Diseases of Children*, 1971, *122*, 15–18.

Laxar, R. M., "Relation of Real Self-rating to Mood and Blame and Their Interaction in Depression, *Journal of Consulting Psychology, 1964, 28,* 539–548.

Massachusetts Council of Organizations of the Handicapped, Inc., *A Directory of Organizations of the Handicapped in the United States* (Hyde Park, Mass.: 1973).

Merrill, E. J., Physical Abuse of Children: An Agency Study; in V. De-Francio, ed., *Protecting the Battered Child* / (Denver: American Humane Association, 1962).

Ouellet, A. M., "Michelle: A Long Way to Kindergarten," *The Exceptional Parent*, 1972, *2*(2), 31–33.

Pender, B., "A Parent's View," *Children Today*, 1975, *4*(1), 34–35.

Searl, S. J., "Stages of Parental Reactions," *The Exceptional Parent*, 1978, *8*(2), 27–29.

Shanas, B., "Child Abuse: A Killer Teachers Can Help Control," *Phi Delta Kappan,* 1975, *56*(7), 479–82.

Spinetta, J. J. and D. Rigler, "The Child-abusing Parent: A Psychological Review," *Psychological Bulletin,* 1972, *77,* 296–304.

Stewart, J. C., *Counseling Parents of Exceptional Children* (Columbus, Ohio: Charles E. Merrill Co., 1978).

Tavormina, J. B., "Relative Effectiveness of Behavioral and Reflective Group Counseling with Parents of Mentally Retarded Children," *Journal of Consulting and Clinical Psychology,* 1975, *43,* 22–31.

Tew, B. F., K. M. Lawrence, H. Payne, and K. Townsley, "Marital Stability Following the Birth of a Child with Spina Bifida," *British Journal of Psychiatry,* 1977, *131,* 77–82.

Zadnik, D., "Social and Medical Aspects of the Battered Child with Visual Impairment," *The New Outlook for the Blind,* 1973, *67,* 241–50.

Zeskind, P. S. and B. M. Lester, "Acoustic Features and Auditory Perceptions of the Cries of Newborns with Prenatal and Perinatal Complications," *Child Development,* 1978, *49,* 580–89.

Zuk, G. H., "The Cultural Dilemma and Spiritual Crises of the Family with a Handicapped Child," *Exceptional Children,* 1962, 405–8.

SUGGESTIONS FOR STUDENTS AND INSTRUCTORS

1. Indicate the types of marital conflict most likely to be intensified by the birth of a handicapped child.

2. What are the positive as well as negative components of parental denial of a child's disability?

3. Discuss the notion that parents go through a definite sequence of stages from denial to acceptance of a child's disability.

4. Discuss the proposition: "Counseling should help others understand their problems and become aware of alternative courses of action rather than solve their problems."

5. Discuss the question, "What are realistic expectations?"

ADDITIONAL READINGS

Moprik, S. I. and J. A. Agard, *Handbook for Parents of Handicapped Children* (Cambridge, Mass., Abt Books, 1978). A good practical guide.

St. Cyr, M., The Story of Pat (Paramus, N.J.: Paulist Press, 1970). A first-hand account of a mother's experiences with a brain-damaged, crippled, and mentally retarded daughter.

Gold, P., *Please Don't Say Hello* (New York: Behavioral Publications, Inc.,

1975). The mother of an autistic child describes the strange and frightening world of a severely disturbed child and its effects on other children.

Selected Films

Mental Retardation—The Long Childhood of Timmy. (58 minutes) (B&W) McGraw-Hill Text Film, 330 W. 42nd Street, New York, N. Y. Graphic portrayal of the emotional impact of a Down's Syndrome child on the family.

Stress—Parents with a Handicapped Child. (30 minutes) Contemporary Films, 330 W. 42nd Street, New York, N. Y. The parents of five handicapped children speak frankly about their problems and worries.

Organizations and Agencies

Disabilities Rights Center, Inc.
1346 Connecticut Avenue, N.W.
Washington, D. C.

National Committee for Citizens in Education
Suite 410
Wilde Lake Village Green
Columbia, Md. 21044

INTELLECTUAL EXCEPTIONALITY

PART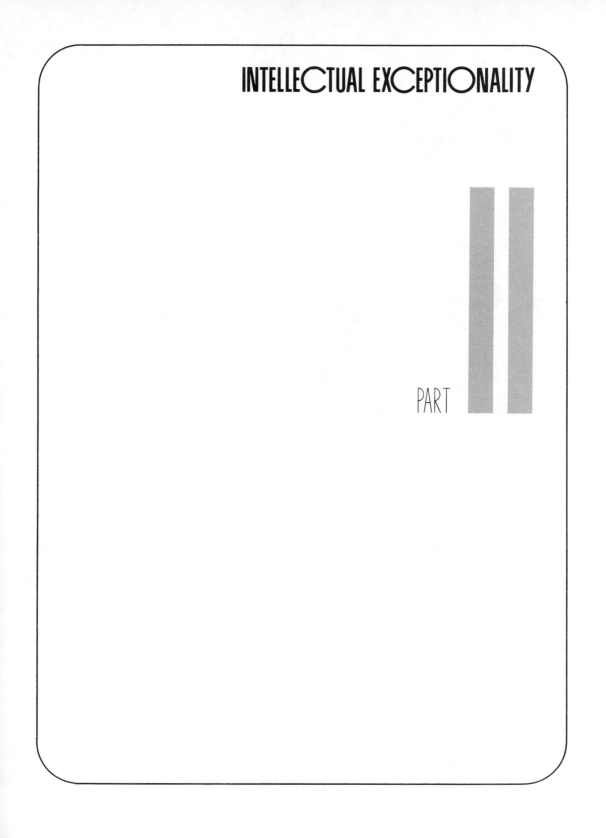

CHAPTER 7

THE GIFTED AND HIGHLY CREATIVE

The specific nature of outstanding ability demanded by society tends to vary over the years, but the demand for the contributions of the intellectually superior is always high. The ever-increasing complexity of society and the expanding horizons of scientific investigation have emphasized the necessity for early identification and training of the very brilliant. It is theorized that early identification and subsequent training will help bring about more complete use of their potential for making significant contributions to the culture and also will be of personal benefit to the brilliant themselves. The contributions of the very bright portion of the population should enhance the quality of existence for all. Concern for the human condition will not allow us to overlook or fail to develop this potential for human betterment.

SOME BACKGROUND

Concern for the identification and training of the gifted is not recent. Plato wanted to discover the most able youth so that they might be educated for state leadership and suggested tests of native ability for their selection.

The scientific investigation of the gifted readily can be traced to F. Galton's (1869) reports of his genetic and statistical studies of the gifted. These were really the first quantitative studies of human abilities.

Galton attempted to show that people's natural abilities derived from inheritance in much the same way as did such features as height and other physical attributes. Carefully examining the biographies of individuals of outstanding achievement, he concluded that the principal elements contributing to achievement were "ability, zeal, and readiness to work." He felt that each of these was in part a result of inheritance, but that the most important factor was the "gift of high ability." He devoted his book to the study of the ability of gifted people. From his studies he recognized two kinds of ability. The more important one was a single "general ability" that was basic to all thoughts and actions. A number of "special aptitudes," each of limited scope, were also recognized, but Galton insisted that these special factors were of secondary importance and contributed only slightly to the attaining of eminence. He asserted that without a special gift for a particular kind of achievement one would not achieve in that area, but that to become great in a given area one needed a high degree of general ability. He emphasized the great versatility that he found in the early years of the future genius. According to Galton, those of outstanding ability to achieve possess a greater *quantity* of their particular abilities. They possess the same *qualities* as do others, but they have them in greater quantity.

Much interest was aroused by these reports and by subsequent investigations of social influences on the gifted as well as the role of genetic factors in giftedness (Ward, 1906; Cattell, 1915). Reports of leadership, mental health, and ability were made, and genius was presented as superior mental ability by L. M. Terman (1904, 1905, 1906).

With the advent of the Binet tests, it was soon discovered that the range of performance on intelligence tests was great and that those scoring very high on the tests, indeed, exceptional. Early investigations by Terman and others (1915, 1925) initiated the attack on many of the then current beliefs about the brilliant and on the attitudes toward them. The reports of Terman and others (1925) constitute an important landmark in the investigations of giftedness. He investigated more than a thousand gifted children and reported on their development and behavior. These children were studied well into adulthood, and these investigations have provided a large volume of data about the gifted (Terman and Oden, 1947, 1959; Oden, 1968). Investigations of the gifted have been numerous, and a substantial body of literature in this area has accumulated (Stanley, George, and Solano, 1977; Passow, 1979).

Creativity has been an area of considerable concern over the past few decades. Previous research that might now be called investigation of creativity was conducted under different topic headings, and reported in the psychological literature under such labels as "insight," "imagination," "artistic ability," and "special abilities."

Many people believe that our culture is becoming less and less tolerant of independent or socially divergent behavior. The social and cultural dangers of overconformity in both the ideational and overt behavioral realms have been emphasized by social theorists. The rewards for conformity, and the relative absence of rewards for independent thinking and acting, have been a possible stifler of individuality and a deterrent to self-expression (Sawrey and Telford, 1975).

Recent technological advances have made it possible to solve within minutes problems that previously would have taken years. Electronic computers and data processing equipment not only have taken the drudgery out of certain kinds of problem solution, but they have made it possible for people to formulate problems that heretofore could not even be considered. Human ingenuity can now be applied to using machines to perform further analyses, the results of which may lead to still further hypotheses to be investigated. The electronic age seems more and more to reject people as performers of routine tasks and solvers of routine problems. Machines can perform a great number of tasks and solve many problems with much greater efficiency than can people. Such a technological culture, if it is to continue its growth, demands less of human physical energy and more of ideational processes. Unique ideas, and original problems and new ways of solving them, are the grist of an innovating society. At the same time, we cannot allow our lives and our culture to become as mechanistic and controlled as our very efficient technology must be. Humans must be the controllers of the technology, not vice versa. Continued social, political, industrial, and educational progress is dependent, in large part, on the creativity of the members of society.

Creativity, in part at least, is dependent upon intellectual prowess and will be considered along with and as a part of giftedness. We shall present a generalized view of the gifted and creative, their problems, and their promise.

PROBLEMS OF DEFINITION AND TERMINOLOGY

Definitions of intelligence have been offered by a great number of investigators. These definitions have perhaps reflected the divergence of interests and theoretical orientations of persons interested in intelligence as much as they have contributed to any clarification of the concept. The way in which intelligence is defined is at least a partial determinant of the way in which the intellectually gifted or exceptionally intelligent will be defined. It is to be expected, then, that uniformity of definition of the exceptionally brilliant will not be found. This problem is further confounded when the same criterion is used differently by various investigators. This is the case in attempting to delineate the exceptional.

In Terman's notable investigations, the IQ as measured by the Stanford-Binet intelligence test (Terman and others, 1925) was the criterion used. The minimum score originally set for the gifted was 140, although some children scoring as low as 135 were later included in his group. Subsequently, other investigators have employed other scores as being the minimum for the gifted child. Perhaps the most popular figure has been an IQ of 130 but IQs lower than 130 have been used to select children for special classes. A. O. Heck (1953) indicated that an IQ of 125 was an approximate point for determining admission to classes for the intellectually superior, and children with IQs of 120 whose performance is consistently outstanding in areas of value to society have been considered eligible for special classes (Otto, 1957).

The use of the IQ in defining the gifted had the advantage of objectivity. It also could be applied relatively early in life. This gave it an advantage over the earlier definitions, which categorized the gifted as those who had achieved outstanding stature in one of the professions and thus identified them after their education and training were completed. Although L. S. Hollingworth (1931) asserted that the IQ was the only way to identify gifted children with certainty, using it as the sole basis has come under severe attack. Children from low socioeconomic backgrounds and from certain ethnic backgrounds tend not to score well on verbal tests and may be excluded when such instruments are used as the basis for selection. Some children who do not score exceptionally high on intelligence tests later tend to excel in music and the arts. To include these individuals, the definition of the gifted was broadened to include the "talented" and those whose performance is consistently remarkable in some potentially valuable activity (Witty, 1958). Further elaboration of the definition to include creativeness as a part of giftedness has evolved.

The profusion of definitions of the gifted is great. W. Abraham (1958) reported that one of his students uncovered 113 different definitions of the gifted while preparing a term paper. Despite this diversity and the confusion in terminology, there is some general agreement as to who constitutes the exceptional. The recently recognized shortcomings of conventional intelligence tests and the IQ derived from their administration probably has not greatly reduced the use of the IQ as a convenient frame of reference for thinking about the gifted. Most investigations of the gifted, talented, and creative have dealt with individuals with high IQs (Passow, 1979), although included among the gifted are those who achieve at exceptional levels in special areas (Stanley, 1979).

Definitions of creativity are numerous, and they vary according to the particular emphasis given to the concept. If one focuses on the process or processes of creating, the resulting definition might be at variance with that of one who focuses on the end product of creative endeavor. If one is concerned with the personal or phenomenological aspects of behavior, the definition will include behavior and feelings that were unique to a particular individual under specified conditions. If the focus of concern is the socially significant and unique responses of individuals, an external frame of reference evolves and leads to a different kind of definition, one which involves a comparison with some cultural norm.

For a response to a problem to be termed original, the probability of its occurring must be low (Maltzman, 1960; Mednick, 1962). I. Maltzman has added that it must also be relevant to the situation; S. Mednick that it must also be useful. By these standards, a person may be highly original, but not qualify as highly creative. This is obviously true as these concepts are considered by Mednick. Maltzman contends that creativity depends not only on originality, but also on societal recognition and approval. And because creativity depends on society's approval, he contends that originality is the facet of creativity most readily investigated in the laboratory.

J. P. Guilford (1959) distinguished between originality and creativity on the basis of his factor analytic investigations of creativity. Originality is one of several traits contributing to creativity. Creativity is a more general trait that includes not only originality, but flexibility, fluency, and motivational and temperamental traits as well.

Personal or phenomenological definitions of creativity involve novelty or uniqueness, but place it in a personal frame of reference. A product may be creative if it is new or novel to the individual involved, if it is that person's creation, if it is expressive of him or herelf rather than dictated by someone else. It need be neither useful nor unique in itself. Its social recognition and cultural impact may be zero, but if it is a unique personal experience, it is creative (Maslow, 1959, 1970; Rogers, 1959; Barron, 1968). A. H. Maslow (1970) distinguished between *special-talent* creativeness of the Mozart type and the creativeness of all people. He indicated that creativeness is a universal human characteristic, that each person has originality or inventiveness with unique characteristics. The creativeness of the self-actualized person he compared to the naive creativeness of unspoiled children. All people possess the potential for creativeness at birth, but most lose it as they become acculturated. J. G. Nicholls (1972) has discussed, in some detail, the concept of creativity as a normally distributed trait.

Those who use a cultural frame of reference insist that a creative product must be novel to both the individual and the society and that, in addition, it must be useful. To be called "creative," an activity must result in something that is culturally, as well as individually, novel and useful (Torrance, 1962).

Before adequate educational programs or personal guidance for the gifted, talented, and creative can be instituted, these individuals must be identified in some manner. If gifted students require different curricula and methods of instruction than do average students, these people must be discovered so that appropriate measures can be taken for their academic welfare. The same thing is true in the personal and social realms. If development of the gifted as persons is to receive unique consideration, they must be known to those who can make the necessary provisions.

For educational purposes, a systematic program for identification can be developed. Classroom teachers can use measuring devices with all of their students as a first crude step. Such a preliminary screening program can save time and effort, and reduce the complex task of final selection by well-trained personnel.

Tests of achievement can be employed systematically in the school. Those who score high enough above the norms for their age or grade to be considered outstanding can be further examined. However, tests of educational achievement do not detect the individual who has the *potential* for high-level achievement but who is not achieving at a rate beyond that of his or her classmates. Such tests have been employed very successfully in the identification of school children curently achieving at high levels in specific fields such as mathematics (Stanley, 1977, 1979).

Group tests of intelligence can be employed as a rough device to discover those individuals who are not achieving at a high level. At the same time, those who are achieving at high levels but do not score high on the group tests of intelligence can be referred for more intensive investigation.

Reliance on group tests of intelligence for initial identification is sometimes necessary because of the lack of adequately trained personnel. When this procedure is employed, several dangers are encountered (Martinson and Lessinger, 1960; Pegnato and Birch, 1959). R. A. Martinson and L. M. Lessinger found that less than half of a group of 332 pupils scoring over 130 on the Stanford-Binet scored as high as 130 on a group test of intelligence. C. V. Pegnato and J. W. Birch reported similar findings: to identify 92 percent of those scoring above 135 on an individual test, it was necessary to consider all who had exceeded 115 on the group test. This discrepancy between the results of employing group and individual intelligence tests points up the necessity for thorough examination if the detection procedures are to be effective.

Individual intelligence tests are to be administered by trained individuals. Interpretation of test results is not a routine matter. The trained psychologist has available the use of more valid measuring instruments than does the untrained individual. The psychologist also has had special training in the interpretation and use of such scores once they have been derived. The sophistication of trained psychologists makes their services in this area imperative. They have knowledge of a variety of tests and testing devices, and can make better estimates of the procedures to be used in an individual evaluation.

Despite the recently recognized shortcomings of conventional intelligence tests, scores on the instruments are employed, at least as early screening devices, to identify populations containing many of the potentially gifted, talented, and creative. Batteries of intellectual tests and measures of special ability are now being employed as opposed to the single measures of intellectual functioning employed earlier (Robinson, Roedell, and Jackson, 1979). Additionally, measures of special abilities are used to identify those individuals who do exceptionally well in specific areas such as mathematics (Stanley, 1979).

An interesting attempt to identify the gifted by evaluating school children's creative responses has been reported (Martinson and Seagoe, 1967). In this investigation a high-IQ group (Stanford-Binet IQ mean = 142.7) produced more products that were rated as creative than did a lower-IQ group (mean = 107.5). The traditional IQ proved to be a better predictor of creative production than did a measure of divergent thinking!

School grades also have been employed as a rough device for screening. As a generalization, it is safe to say that students who obtain a preponderance of A and B grades are more likely to be gifted than are those who get lower grades, but school grades reflect many things besides achievement. (It has already been indicated that achievement measures, by themselves, are not adequate.) High grades are sometimes given to increase morale and motivation, and biases are bound to creep into the situation as a result of personality, as well as of social and cultural factors involved in the complex schoolroom situation.

Teachers' ratings and peer nominations have also been used. When teachers have been asked to designate the children in their classes who are gifted, however, they have not been able to do so very accurately. This is particularly true when no operational definition of giftedness is supplied and each teacher is left free to use personal judgment in determining giftedness. One investigation (Pegnato and Birch, 1959) found that teachers did not refer about 55 percent of the children who were later found to be gifted by the criteria established by the investigators. Thirty-one percent who were not gifted by the criteria employed were referred. If checklists of behavioral characteristics of the gifted are supplied, however, the teachers' ratings improve. Peer nominations by elementary school children have been found to correlate highly with teacher nominations (Granzin and Granzin, 1969). The Maryland State Department of Education suggests recommendations by self, staff, parents, peers, and others as initial screening devices in identifying children of high levels of ability and performance. They also recommend the use of a behavioral checklist and encourage the appropriate placement of students selected for the visual and performing arts based on their potential as well as their demonstrated proficiency in their area of talent. Rather extensive lists (Abraham, 1958; Kough and DeHaan, 1955) cite characteristic behavior of the gifted, either defined by the constructors of the lists or based on large numbers of investigations of the characteristics of gifted individuals. Precocity in a number of physical and intellectual areas combined with breadth of activities and interests are usually indicative of giftedness.

The value to the culture of stimulating, directing, and educating the brilliant is so great that the importance of the task of identifying them should not be underestimated. The use of the best available techniques for this purpose is to be encouraged. A variety of procedures can be employed and the best trained personnel available should employ them.

CREATIVE CHILDREN

If the characteristics of children who will later become highly creative adults can be determined, it may be possible to provide them, at a very early age, with experiences that will develop the positive characteristics and minimize those that lead to low productivity and creativity. A great deal of effort has been expended in attempts to discern the cognitive (Kogan, 1973) and other personality variables in children that might be predictive of adult creativity. Tests designed to measure various aspects and correlates of creativity in children have been developed and some follow-up studies of children have been carried out (Torrance, 1977). These studies indicate that measures of creative thinking ability better predicted creative achievement than did measures of intelligence and educational achievement. However, scores obtained on the Torrance tests of creative thinking and scores on intelligence tests are rather highly correlated. These tests (Torrance, 1966) have been used rather widely as measures of creativity. Among the tasks are an ask-and-guess test, a product-improvement test, an unusual-uses test, and a just-suppose test. These tests present problems that emphasize unusual or clever ideas. The battery also contains the picture-construction test, the incomplete-figures test and the parallel-lines test. There are four scoring criteria for the Torrance tests: fluency—the number of relevant responses made; flexibility—the number of shifts from one category of meaning to another; originality—the infrequency of the responses offered; and elaboration—the detail and specificity of the responses. All of the tasks call for the production of divergent solutions, multiple possibilities, and some type of thinking theoretically involved in creative behavior. L. M. Terman and M. H. Oden's (1959) follow-up studies of gifted children at adulthood have indicated that the highly *intelligent*, as determined by IQ, tend to become highly productive adults, but we do not know whether these individuals were creative either as children or as adults.

Children who were early identified as being highly creative have been reported to evidence high levels of creative activity in follow-up investigations up to twelve years later. Their creative endeavors cover a broad spectrum of activities (Torrance, 1979).

An elaborate battery of tasks has been developed by J. P. Guilford and his associates (Guilford and Merrifield, 1960) for the assessment of creativity. Guilford has attemped a factorial analysis of the intellect and its measurement. In his presidential address to the American Psychological Association (1950), he outlined a group of objections to existing measures of intellect and indicated that the "structure of intellect" was complex, and required a variety of measures. He hypothesized that the thinking abilities involved in creativity were those he had defined as "divergent productions and transformations," as opposed to the "convergent functions" that he indicated were being measured by the then-current measures of intellect. Although Guilford has subsequently modified his thinking on this issue, much emphasis was given to *convergent versus divergent thinking*. Guilford's subsequent designation of components of creative thinking includes not only divergent productions, but the redefinition of abilities of the convergent-production category of his structure of intellect as well as sensitivity to problems which fall in his "evaluation" category. Thus a great number of thinking abilities are designated as involved in creativity, and a goodly number of tests have been designed for their measurement (Guilford, 1959; Guilford and Merrifield, 1960; Taylor and Holland, 1962).

J. W. Getzels and Jackson (1962) used five different measures of creativity in their research. Some of their ideas were borrowed from Guilford, and others were of their own creation. One measure was a word-association test in which subjects were required to give as many definitions as possible of a fairly common word, such as *bolt* or *sack*. The score depended on the absolute number of definitions and the number of different categories into which they could be placed. A second measure was a uses-of-things test. This test is similar to tests used by Guilford in his studies of cognitive ability. The subject gives as many uses as possible for a common object, such as a brick or a toothpick, and is scored on the basis of both the number and the originality of the uses given. "Brick can be used as a bed warmer" is a more original answer than "bricks can be used to build houses." A third measure was the hidden-shapes test, from a previously developed test battery (Cattell, 1956). In this test, the subject is shown a card with a simple geometric figure on it and is then required to find that figure hidden in a more complex form or pattern. A fourth measure was a fables test, in which the subject is presented with short fables from which the last line is missing, and is required to compose three different endings for each: a "moralistic" one, a "humorous" one, and a "sad" one. The score depends upon the number, appropriateness, and originality of the endings. A final test was termed *make-up problems*. In this situation, the subject is presented with a number of complex paragraphs. Each paragraph contains many numerical statements, and the subject is required to make up as many mathematical problems as possible with the information given. The score depends on the number, appropriateness, complexity, and originality of the problems.

IQ AND CREATIVITY

Many reports of limited relationships between creativity and intelligence have been made by generalizing from samples containing a restricted range of both intelligence and creativity. The meaning of correlation under such circumstances is difficult to discern. It has long been known that the IQ, above a given level, is essentially unrelated even to such an intellectually challenging area as collegiate success. Many factors are involved including, health, motivation, study habits, and family finances. On the other hand, unless there is a certain minimum level of measured intelligence, academic failure becomes highly predictable. There *are* individual differences among the highly intelligent. Restriction of the range of one variable does not equally restrict other variables, even though they are highly correlated in the general population. Creativity, if it is a complex of individual differences among the highly intelligent, should not be expected to correlate highly with IQ. The study of individual differences is most desirable, and studies of individual differences among the highly intelligent, including creativity as a variable, are to be encouraged. The concept of creativity should enhance our knowledge of people and their performances, but enthusiasm for it should not be carried to the point of making it into a panacea for the woes of society. The implied, and sometimes stated, abandonment of the concept of general intelligence may be a matter of throwing the baby out with the bath water. Although it may well be true that we must look beyond the limits of the IQ to understand creativity (Guilford, 1950), it does not follow that intelligence can be ignored in our quest for such understanding. Creativity has been defined as involving social usefulness, and it appears logical that most of the useful creative ideas are likely to come from the most intelligent. High intelligence does not guarantee creative activity, but low intelligence certainly militates against it.

CORRELATIONAL INVESTIGATIONS AND SPECULATIONS

It has been estimated, as the result of correlational studies of creativity and intelligence among subjects designated highly creative, that the correlation between the two variables is low but positive (Barron and others, 1965). In these instances, the range of both creativity and intelligence has been restricted. The amount of restriction of ranges varies from one investigation to the next, and the exact curtailment of range of creativity is really not known. For highly creative writers, the correlation between IQ and creativity has been estimated to be around .40 (Barron, 1963). In a study of architects designated as creative, a correlation of near zero is reported, but the author speculates that, over the entire range of creativity and intelligence, there is a positive relationship between the two variables (MacKinnon, 1962). From a study of the upper 1 percent of high school students, it has been estimated that intelligence has little or no relationship to creative performance in arts and science (Holland, 1961). In addition to the problem of curtailment of range, it has been pointed out that creativity in a given area may require different abilities from creativity in another. Among architects, creativity may reflect the ability to engineer structural innovations, in which case it should be a correlate of intelligence. But if creativity depends on new artistic designs, intelligence would probably be less important (McNemar, 1964). The kind of creativity involved, then, may be a factor in the degree of correlation to be expected. Highly creative writers were reported to have an average IQ of about 140. Creative writers apparently are very bright! From groups of so restricted a range of intelligence, conclusions about the general relationship of intelligence and creativity cannot be drawn.

Users of tests of creative thinking for elementary school children and adolescents have reported little relationship between scores on such measures and scores on tests of intelligence (Torrance, 1962; Getzels and Jackson, 1962). The extensive investigation of Getzels and Jackson (1962) has been cogently criticized by a number of other workers (De Mille and Merrifield, 1962; Marsh, 1964; McNemar, 1964; Ripple and May, 1962). Their statistical procedures and manner of describing their research have been attacked. They used, as a measure of creativity, the sum of scores of five tests of creativity. Using their reported data, Q. McNemar (1964) discerned that creativity and the IQs in their sample correlate to the extent of .40. This r has been greatly attenuated by the usual measurement errors, by the restriction of the IQ range (the mean was 132), and by the variety of intelligence test scores employed. McNemar concluded that their creativity tests and intelligence tests have far more common variance than is indicated by the authors' report. Getzels and Jackson's use of Chi Square as a statistical procedure has been criticized by R. W. Marsh (1964) because of Chi Square's insensitivity to interaction. Marsh concluded that the IQ may still be the best single criterion for creative potential.

An empirical demonstration of the possible effect of restriction of the range of IQs has been reported by R. E. Ripple and F. B. May (1962). By correlating Otis IQs and scores on creative thinking tests administered to several seventh-grade groups, homogeneous or heterogeneous with respect to their IQs, they demonstrated that the low correlation of these measures reported by other investigators may well be due in part to the restricted range of the IQs in their samples. F. Barron (1968) asserts that beyond a minimum IQ, creativity is not a function of intelligence as measured by IQ tests. A minimum IQ would appear to be about 120, which has to be considered a rather high IQ.

An unfortunate designation of the groups investigated and reported by Getzels and Jackson has contributed to the confusion. Basically, they reported on two groups of adolescents. One group was composed of individuals scoring in the top 20 percent on measures of intelligence but not in the top 20 percent on measures of creativity. The other group scored in the top 20 percent on measures of creativity, but not on measures of intelligence. They excluded those who were in the top 20 percent on both. The group scoring in the top 20 percent on measures of creativity but not on intelligence was labeled *high-creative* group, and the other group was labeled the *high-IQ* group. The mean IQ of the high IQ group was 150, whereas the mean IQ of the high-creative group was 127. Now an IQ of 127 most certainly is not as high as an IQ of 150, but it is still a high IQ when the total range is considered; their high-creative group was still fairly bright. The labeling of the two groups as *high-IQ* and *high-creative* has probably contributed to the tendency to overlook their high level of intelligence.

The correlation between IQ and creativity obtained in an extensive investigation of a carefully chosen sample of 7,648 fifteen-year-old boys and girls in Project Talent (Shaycoft and others, 1963) was reported to be .67. This *r* becomes .80 when corrected for attenuation (McNemar, 1964).

It would seem that the extent of the relationship between IQs and measured creativity depends on the nature of the tests of creativity employed, among other things. The nature and size of the relationship remains speculative, however. It would appear that the early speculations that the relationship is slight may have been exaggerated and may have led to considerable confusion. Creativity of certain kinds may be highly related to intelligence, while creativity in certain other areas may be less highly dependent on intelligence. That some intelligence is essential for the production of cultural, scientific, technological, or artistic innovation would appear obvious.

Most researchers consider creativity to constitute a cluster of traits resembling and, to some extent, overlapping general intellectual ability. Studies of creative individuals have indicated that creative activity, like intellectual productivity in general, is the result of a dynamic interaction among a group of characteristics including a certain minimum of intellectual ability together with such things as high drive, cognitive flexibility, open-mindedness, and tolerance of ambiguity. Although there is practically no correlation between intelligence test scores and creativity among individuals judged highly creative by their peers, no one doubts that over the entire range of intelligence, from the mentally retarded to the most intellectually gifted, a positive relationship exists.

sociability and creativity Highly creative individuals are not high in sociability. In general, the creative person is neither asocial nor antisocial; he or she simply has less than normal regard for the pleasant security of positive peer approval. The threat of negative evaluation or social rejection is not cause for personal alarm. The creative individual is much more inner- than outer-directed, and can be a minority of one without being unduly disturbed. Such a person may be more sensitive to the demands of a problem than to the evaluations of the social environment. The highly creative person does not value "togetherness" highly, is not greatly concerned with smooth interpersonal relations, and consequently may be perceived as asocial or antisocial.

CHARACTERISTICS OF THE GIFTED

In discussing the characteristics of the gifted as a group, there is always the danger of falsely assuming that individual differences among them are small. There are many differences between one highly intelligent individual and the next, which are not to be ignored when considering the gifted as a group. To assume homogeneity among the gifted would be to ignore the fact that the restriction of any one variable does not have an equally restrictive effect on other variables, even though they may be highly correlated. For example, if a group of people, all of whom are six feet or over in height, is selected for investigation, it is true that there will be also some selection on the basis of weight. Tall people tend to weigh more than short ones. But the restriction of the variability of weight will not be as great as the restriction imposed on height, even though the two are positively correlated.

Variability in factors other than general intelligence is to be expected among the gifted as a group. Among the gifted will be found the short, tall, active, and lethargic, as well as high achievers, low achievers, those with special talent, and those who are highly creative. It should be remembered, in reading the following paragraphs, that the intellectually superior are being considered as a group and that the characteristics indicated are not all applicable to each and every gifted person.

PHYSICAL CHARACTERISTICS

As a group, the gifted tend to exceed the average on measures of physical traits (Terman et al., 1925; Witty, 1930; Miles, 1954). B. S. Burks, D. W. Jensen, and L. M. Terman (1930) report that a study of Terman's gifted group showed them to have superior ratings on thirty-four anthropometric measures, including height, weight, and general physical development. Witty's (1930) six-year investigation of another group of gifted children found them to be of better than average bodily development. Superior neuromuscular capacity (Monahan and Hollingworth, 1927) and infrequent physical defects (Jones, 1925) among children of superior intelligence have been reported.

Terman and P. A. Witty both secured health histories of their samples. Consistently, health examinations showed that the general physical health of both the children and their parents was better than average. The children were slightly heavier at birth. They cut their first tooth about two months earlier, and walked and talked about two months earlier than the average child. The children in these investigations were more precocious in speech development than they were in other areas. Later development seems to follow an accelerated program, and pubescence is reached earlier by the gifted.

Both major and minor physical defects are found less frequently among groups of gifted children than among the unselected population. They are, in general, fine physical specimens who enjoy good growth and health. These findings, when they were first reported, were in sharp disagreement with popular opinion. It had been thought that the brilliant were typically frail and weak. Research has indicated that, in fact, they are likely to be large, robust, and healthy.

SEX

The question of whether giftedness occurs more frequently in girls or boys really has not been satisfactorily answered. In some investigations of children with high IQs, an excess of boys over girls is reported. Terman and others (1925) found 121 gifted boys and 100 gifted girls in a sample of 643 preschool and elementary school children. A. M. Jones (1925) reports a similar finding. M. D. Jenkins (1936) reported an excess of girls over boys in a Negro population. The adequacy of the sampling procedures in all these studies can be questioned, if they are to be used to investigate the frequency of the sexes among the gifted. In the Terman studies, volunteers were permitted and teachers were asked to nominate individual students for examination. Such a procedure apparently produces a disproportionately large number of boys. Some evidence of this can be garnered from the fact that when all children of given birth dates were examined in Scotland, the sample was found to contain a ratio of 4 boys to 5 girls with IQs of 140 and over (MacMeeken, 1939). Other investigators using samples more adequate for this purpose have reported similar findings (Lewis, 1940). After reviewing a number of investigations, C. C. Miles (1954) and Terman and L. E. Tyler (1954) concluded that there appeared to be consistent difference in the frequency of the sexes among the gifted, and that the sex ratios found depended on the content of the test used.

In view of the conflicting data, it would seem safe to assume that no large discrepancy exists in the frequency with which the sexes occur among the gifted. This is particularly true in view of the fact that the experiences of the sexes become more and more divergent with age, so that we cannot be certain of the fairness of a given test for both sexes. E. E. Maccoby and C. N. Jacklin (1974) have made a thorough examination of sex differences and intellect. Early examination of intelligence is contaminated by different development schedules for the sexes and the lower reliability of the scales at the earlier ages. Men and women do not appear to differ on measures of global intelligence; however, they do appear to differ with respect to some specific abilities.

Sex differences in mathematical ability are not found with consistency until the end of the elementary school years, although sex differences in geometry skills have been reported as early as age nine (Mullis, 1975). By the end of the secondary school years, young men appear to be quite superior to young women with respect to mathematical reasoning ability. Males in general exceed females on tests of spatial relationships (Anastasi, 1958) and their abilities appear to be innate (Bock and Kolakowski, 1973). Possibly spatial relationship abilities are highly related to mathematical reasoning and this might be used to account, in part, for the observed differences in mathematical abilities. However, these differences may be due to differential socialization and learning experiences as well.

Females are found to be superior to males on measures of verbal ability before age three and after age eleven (Maccoby and Jacklin, 1974). Consistently, more boys than girls are found to have reading problems in schools. A good review and discussion of gifted and talented women is that of Callahan (1979).

sex role of the creative person Creative males consistently tend to score higher in femininity than do their less creative peers on tests designed to indicate the relative strength of the masculine and feminine components of personality. This shift toward femininity in creative males results from their conforming less rigidly to the traditional male sex role than does the average male. The creative male is able to develop and manifest intellectual and cultural interests that are either male or female without feeling threatened. The creative male is able to participate in and give expression to both masculine and feminine traits. He is less completely identified with and limited by his male identification, and in this sense he is also more independent of the culturally imposed stereotype of masculinity and femininity than are his more rigidly sex-typed male contemporaries.

EDUCATIONAL ACHIEVEMENT

The importance of educational achievement among the intellectually superior has been emphasized. The highly superior can make considerable and significant contributions to the culture, and it is felt that they must become educated to a relatively high degree to maximize their productivity and possibly to ensure their personal happiness and welfare.

The results of research on the educational attainment of the gifted indicate that, as a group, they achieve highly in most areas. They do not tend to be one-sided, as had been thought. They tend to be remarkably versatile, and their accomplishments in educational areas are found to be rather universally high. This tends to refute the old supposition of the compensation of abilities. The mass of research data indicates that there is no compensating area of weakness for the areas of demonstrated strength in educational achievement.

Early studies of the school progress of the gifted have been in general agreement that they make rapid strides in academic areas (Terman and others, 1925; Witty, 1940). Terman reports that three out of five of his gifted group attended kindergarten before entering the elementary grades at an average of six years and three months. This was in the early 1920s, when kindergartens were not as prevalent as they are currently. One out of ten in his sample was placed in the second grade on beginning school, and one out of five skipped half of the first grade. By the end of grade school, his group was found to have skipped one entire grade. Still, the gifted children were found to be below the placement that would be made on the basis of mental age. This is commonly found among gifted children in school. It has been pointed out (Miles, 1954) that if the average gifted child were promoted according to mental age (MA), he or she would be at least 2.8 years advanced by the age of seven and 5 or more years accelerated by the age of eleven. This would seem to be an unwarranted expectation of performance by these students, however. It has been pointed out that the MA progressively overestimates the potential of students as their IQ increases, and that this may be due to the lack of opportunity to receive either school or life experiences essential to performance at their level of MA.

Whether the achievement of the gifted is assessed by the grades assigned to their schoolwork or by achievement tests, the results tend to be the same (Witty, 1940). They tend to excel in the academic aspects of education. Teachers rate them as superior in such areas as reading, arithmetic, grammar, science, literature, composition, history, and geography. They excel to a lesser degree in areas that are not correlated so highly with intelligence, such as penmanship, shopwork, sewing, and art. The gifted tend to receive a larger proportion of As and Bs than do students of average intellectual ability. This seems to hold true even when the children have been accelerated and are competing for grades with older classmates (Barnette, 1957; Shannon, 1957).

On standardized tests of achievement, the gifted consistently score higher than their classmates of average intellectual ability. Terman and others (1925) pointed out that the measured achievement of the gifted in grade school correlates more highly with intelligence when age is held constant than it does when years of attendance in school are used. Correlations between achievement and intelligence have been found to be higher for moderately superior children than for highly superior children (Cohler, 1941; Johnson, 1942). This is to be expected in view of the increasing overestimation of achievement as IQ increases. When classroom instruction is about the same (Hollingworth and Cobb, 1928) or when groups with lower IQs receive special coaching (Hildreth, 1938), the differences in IQ continue to affect the achievement scores. Those with high IQs tend to retain their superior status on measures of achievement, especially on tests measuring more complex abilities.

Having an exceptionally high IQ does not guarantee the possession of any particular special ability, and recent attention has been given those with exceptional talent in particular fields. A notable exploration in this area has been the Study of Mathematically Precocious Youth (SMPY) (Stanley, 1979; Stanley, George, and Solano, 1977). This Johns Hopkins University project attempts to identify at an early age those children who reason mathematically extremely well. Tests of mathematical reasoning ability were administered to high scoring students from the elementary grades on an achievement test battery. In an early group, 49 percent of the boys and 30 percent of the girls tested from grades seven, eight, and nine were found to score higher than the average college-bound male twelfth grader. These youngsters and others similarly selected were given special instruction in mathematics and were able to make amazingly rapid progress, completing two and three years of the usual mathematics curriculum in a year or less.

The personality traits and character development of the gifted have been investigated in some detail. There seems to be general agreement among the early investigators that the gifted, as a group, differ in a favorable direction from unselected children. Terman and others (1925), using a wide range of tests and rating devices, investigated the personal and social characteristics of a group of 500 gifted children and a like number of children in an unselected control group. Witty (1930) studied the characteristics of 100 gifted children. The results of these studies were equally favorable to the gifted, challenging the once widely held belief that intellectual superiority was associated with social and personal maladjustment.

Terman and others (1925) report that gifted children have much more favorable social characteristics than the control group. The gifted showed more favorable social preferences, less boastful exaggeration, less cheating, and greater trustworthiness under stress. From 60 to 80 percent of the gifted exceeded the median scores on the separate tests of the battery employed. The gifted were found to be significantly freer from psychopathic trends and significantly more emotionally stable than were control children. The superiority of the gifted in emotional stability was maintained for a number of years when they were reexamined (Burks, Jensen, and Terman, 1930; Oden, 1968).

The superiority on personality traits of the gifted as a group is supported by other investigations of personality traits in intellectually superior children as compared with children of average IQ. Social adjustment of the gifted as a group tends to be above average. Even children who have been accelerated in school and are young for their grade placement have been reported as well adjusted (Miller, 1957). Sociometric studies indicate that the gifted are more frequently chosen by their peers in regular classes (Gallagher, 1958). On projective tests as well as on rating scales, the lower frequency of emotional problems has held up (Gallagher and Crowder, 1957). Investigations using teachers' rating, sociometric procedures, personality inventories, and projective techniques have reported superiority in emotional stability of the gifted as a group. There is evidence that this superiority continues into adulthood (Barbe, 1957; Terman and Oden, 1959).

The studies so far cited have dealt with gifted children as a group, and various other factors have not been controlled. M. Bonsall and B. Stefflre (1955), working with a group of gifted and a group of nongifted high school boys, found the usual pattern of superiority for the gifted as a group. However, when they analyzed the data so that only gifted and nongifted students from the same economic levels were compared, little or no differences were found between the two groups. Although it is without doubt that the intellectually superior make better personal and social adjustments than do the intellectually average, part of this superiority is apparently due to class differences.

The personality correlates of intelligence and creativity among the gifted is an active area of research (Welsh, 1977).

THE HIGHLY CREATIVE

Adults designated as highly creative by one means or another have been studied rather intensively by several groups of investigators. As a consequence of the investigations of creative scientists, writers, artists, architects, and mathematicians, a rather large body of descriptive material is available. However, a general picture of the highly creative person is difficult to discern, because of the complexity of bright adults in general and because of the diversity of creative endeavor. Individual differences among the highly creative are to be expected.

There does seem to be some agreement among various investigators as to the characteristics of outstanding scientists. They are generally described as being highly intelligent, emotionally sensitive, self-sufficient, of independent judgment, dedicated, introspective, confident, ideationally productive, and somewhat unconventional. On the Allport-Vernon-Lindzey Scale of Values, they score high in "Theoretical and Aesthetic" values and low in "Religious, Social, and Economic" values (Gough, 1961). Barron (1965) presents a unified picture of the productive scientist gleaned from the research of a number of individual investigators. Productive scientists are depicted as having a high degree of intelligence, emotional stability, ego strength, personal dominance, forcefulness of opinion, and liking for precision and order. They are challenged by the unknown, by contradictions, and by apparent disorder. They appear to be somewhat distant and detached in personal relations, and prefer to deal with things or abstractions rather than with people. Productive scientists are further depicted as having a strong need for independence and autonomy. They appear to be self-sufficient and self-directing, and they enjoy abstract thinking. They resist pressure to conform in their thinking. In brief, they seem to be personally strong, dedicated, independent, somewhat adventurous, and scholarly. These characteristics of the productive scientist appear to be those that would rationally be expected (Taylor and Barron, 1963). To be productive or creative, the scientist must be bright, orderly, and thorough. If a contribution to science is to be made efforts must be unique and at the frontiers of knowledge. Novelty and uncertainty are of necessity involved in such endeavors. The scientist must be willing to take risks and be enthusiastically dedicated to the pursuit of unique ideas and directions.

An earlier investigation (Cox, 1926) of the characteristics of 300 geniuses, divided into several subgroups according to area of accomplishment, provides some interesting data for comparing scientists and imaginative writers. Their personal and moral qualities, as well as their intellectual ones, were depicted.

The scientific geniuses were estimated to have an average IQ of over 170. This represents a very high level of intellect, as might be expected. Compared with eminent individuals from all of the subgroups, the scientists had very great strength or force of character and balance, and were very active. They were less sociable, excitable, and sensitive to criticism than the other subgroups. These scientists were described as the strongest, most forceful, and best balanced people in the study.

The artists in the study were estimated to be of somewhat lower, but still very high, intelligence, their average IQ probably being well over 135. They were rated as having a high degree of aesthetic feeling, desire to excel, belief in themselves, originality of ideas, and ability to strive for distant goals.

Imaginative writers (poets, novelists, and dramatists) were judged to have an average IQ of 165. These people were notably high in imaginativeness and aesthetic feeling, effort directed toward pleasure, originality of ideas, strength of memory, and keenness of observation. They ranked lower on common sense and the degree to which their actions and thoughts were dependent on reason than did the other groups.

The most consistent findings in the literature appear to be those of D. W. MacKinnon (1960). Other investigators have since reported essentially the same patterns of interest on the Strong Vocational Interest Blank and the Allport-Vernon-Lindzey Scale of Values. The more original or highly creative rated high on the interest scales for architect, psychologist, author-journalist, and specialization level. They scored low on scales for purchasing agent, office manager, banker, farmer, carpenter, veterinarian, police officer, and mortician. MacKinnon interprets these findings as indicating that creative individuals are less interested in small details or the practical, concrete facets of life, and more concerned with meanings, implications, and the symbolic equivalents of things and ideas.

All of MacKinnon's highly creative groups scored high on theoretical and aesthetic values and high on several scales of the Minnesota Multiphasic Personality Inventory. His groups of highly creative males scored high on the masculinity–femininity scale, although they were *not* effeminate in manner or appearance. Their elevated masculinity–femininity scores apparently derived from their openness to their feelings and emotions, a sensitive awareness of self and others, and a wide range of interests. Their interests included many which are regarded as feminine in our culture.

Various researchers have emphasized conflicting motives among the highly creative (MacKinnon, 1960; Palm, 1959; Torrance, 1962) and their ability to tolerate the tensions arising from such conflicts. Torrance depicts the creative person as one who enjoys intense, sustained, and vigorous effort to surmount difficulties and who has a need to dramatize and display these ideas and prove his or her personal worth. These tendencies are held in check by the creative individual's self-awareness, awareness of the feelings and experiences of others, and detached intellectualization. The total picture is one of a person alive and open to one's own experiences, who tries to organize and see meaning in them.

HIGHLY CREATIVE YOUNG PEOPLE

In the study of the personal characteristics of creative children and adolescents, an assumption must be made about the future creativity of the subjects. Retrospective studies of the childhood of creative adults yields some justification for assuming that creativity in childhood and adolescence is predictive of adult creativity. Such an assumption seems warranted, too, in the light of investigations of other psychological variables. Most psychological variables in adults can be seen to have their roots in earlier development and experience. In essence, the quest is for answers to the question, "What are the early signs of adult creativity?"

An investigation of the personality characteristics of highly creative adolescents was conducted by Getzels and Jackson (1962). In this investigation, the adolescents selected for study and comparison were in grades seven through twelve. They were separated into a high-creative group (26 children) and a high-IQ group (28 children), in the manner previously described. When the two were contrasted, some interesting findings resulted.

The values of the two groups appeared to be grossly different. Both groups were given an Outstanding Traits test. Thirteen descriptions of hypothetical children displaying a desirable personality quality or trait were given to the subjects. They were required to rank the thirteen descriptions of children in three ways. First, they ranked the descriptions according to the degree to which they would like to be like the child described. The data from this procedure provided a measure of the "self-ideal" of the subjects. Second, they ranked the descriptions according to the degree to which they believed the various children would succeed in adult life. A "success image" of the subjects was thus obtained. Third, they ranked the descriptions according to the degree to which they believed the children described would be liked by their teachers. This provided a measure of the subjects' "teacher perception."

Analyses of the data revealed that both groups agreed on the qualities that make for adult success in our society and on the qualities which teachers prefer in their students. However, there was little agreement between the two groups about what qualities they wanted for themselves, despite their agreement about the qualities considered desirable by the adult world. The high-IQ group preferred for themselves the personal traits believed to be predictive of adult success. The high-creative group had but little preference for these traits. In other words, the high-creative group seemed not to be highly success-oriented. The high-IQ group preferred traits for themselves that were highly similar to those personal traits they believed to be favored by teachers. Not so the high-creative group. They tended to place high personal value on qualities which they felt teachers value least! "Sense of humor" was ranked near the top, above "high marks," "high IQ," and "goal directedness." The high-IQ group ranked "sense of humor" near the bottom, below high marks, high IQ, and goal directedness. A sense of humor seems to be highly characteristic of creative adolescents and it is expressed in a variety of ways, but both groups perceived the teachers as ranking it rather low. The highly creative adolescents know what makes for conventional success and what teachers like, but these are not necessarily the qualities they want for themselves.

The same general area of research has been explored by other means with highly similar findings (Halpin, Payne, and Ellet, 1973). G. Halpin and others, using biographical data, found that the more creative adolescent girls regularly read news magazines and other nonrequired reading and that they often watched television news and special reports. These creative girls enjoyed courses in the sciences and music, and were active in dramatic and musical groups. They liked their teachers and felt their high school education had been adequate. They did not often go out on dates, something which was characteristic of their less creative age mates. They daydreamed, sometimes felt downcast, and brooded over the meaning of life more than did their less creative peers.

The results obtained with the male sample were somewhat at variance with those of the girls. The more creative adolescent boys disliked their teachers and school, did less homework, and were not as academically interested as the girls. They seldom engaged in team sports or physical activities and disliked physical education. They did enjoy discussion courses and actively took part in questioning the teacher about topics under discussion. They often wanted to be alone to pursue their thoughts and were regarded as rather radical and unconventional.

A further investigation (Payne and others, 1975), using the Cattell and Eber (1962) Sixteen Personality Factor Questionnaire (16PF) and the What Kind of Person Are You? test (WKPAY) (Torrance and Khatena, 1970), found that the most significant characteristics on the self-report basis, for an academically talented group of gifted youth, were those of willingness to experiment, assertiveness, less intelligence, shrewdness, and reserve. The artistically talented group described themselves as experimenting, assertive, tender-minded, and expedient. The combined group could be described in these terms as experimenting, assertive, less intelligent, shrewd, and reserved.

Torrance (1962) conducted a well-controlled investigation of the personalities of a group of elementary school children. He chose the most creative boy and girl from each of twenty-three classes in grades one through six, and matched them with control subjects in sex, IQ, race, classroom teacher, and age. He states, from an analysis of his data, that certain personality characteristics differentiate the highly creative from the less creative children. Teachers and peers agree that the highly creative, especially boys, have wild and silly ideas. Their work is characterized by the production of ideas "off the beaten track, outside the mold," and by humor, playfulness, relative lack of rigidity, and relaxation. These findings are in essential agreement with those of other investigations of the personality traits of creative children and adolescents.

J. S. Renzulli (1973) has suggested the use of various measures of creativity to identify and develop talent among the culturally different and disadvantaged. This relatively untapped reservoir of talent holds great potential for cultural and individual development (Torrance, 1979).

An investigation of the personalities of highly creative children by P. S. Weisberg and K. J. Springer (1961) is reported by Torrance (1962). This was an extensive investigation, using materials from the Minnesota test battery, psychiatric interviews, Rorschachs, and the Draw-a-Family Technique. As compared with less creative children, the highly creative scored higher on strength of self-image, ease of early recall, humor, availability of Oedipal anxiety, and uneven ego development. The more creative children could recall their earlier experiences more readily even when they were unpleasant. Torrance reports that the same highly creative child might love Shakespeare and dolls, and that self-control appropriate to a young adult might be interspersed with impulsive, almost infantile behavior, during one interview.

SOCIOECONOMIC BACKGROUND

Socioeconomic background must be considered in the educational program for individual gifted children (Renzulli, 1973). It is to be expected that differences in children from contrasting socioeconomic backgrounds will be educationally significant for the gifted. The learning style of disadvantaged gifted students has been described as likely to be content-centered, externally-oriented, physical in nature, problem-oriented, slow, and patient (Riessman, 1962). Disadvantaged gifted children have been described as visual rather than abstract learners who depend on concrete rather than abstract exposure (Gallagher, 1968). Successful teachers of the gifted differ from the less successful in several significant dimensions (Bishop, 1968). Teachers of the gifted should be conscious of the characteristics of the various gifted groups as well as informed of the preferred procedures in working with them (Jordan, 1974).[1]

EDUCATION OF THE GIFTED

Gifted students typically do well in school, and there has been little concern about such matters as their keeping up with the class. They usually have little or no trouble measuring up to age or grade levels for achievement. This, combined with their general tendency to be well behaved and emotionally controlled, may cause them to go unnoticed in the classroom. They create no particular classroom disturbances. They have plenty of ability. They can be left to fend for themselves and will still do all right in school. A common attitude seems to be, "Don't worry about the gifted; they will do all right anyway!"

No immediate and apparent characteristic of the gifted can serve as a basis for an emotional appeal for special consideration. Special consideration for the gifted does not have the emotional appeal or the urgency of training for the physically handicapped, the blind, the deaf, or the mentally retarded. Rarely does one hear a plea for special facilities or programs for the exceptionally brilliant based on democracy in education, a concept that has a strong appeal in this country and has been employed as an argument for special facilities for the handicapped. Contrariwise, it has been argued that special consideration for the gifted would be undemocratic, in that it would give advantage in training and education to those who are already ahead of their classmates and result in a kind of intellectual aristocracy or privileged group. *Guarding against privilege has perhaps absorbed more attention and effort in our educational structure than have plans and procedures for providing for individual differences.* Actually, a desirable slogan for the individual education of students might be "special privilege for all." In the final analysis this is what a program based upon meeting the educational needs of individuals, as well as the culture, strives to do.

In recent years many professionals and laypersons have become genuinely concerned about the education of the gifted, in part because of the rapid advancements in science and technology of the past decade or so. The need to train scientists is obvious in a rapidly expanding scientific

---

[1]The literature in this area is extensive. Several excellent articles have appeared in a volume of *The Journal of Special Education* (Anastasi, 1975; Astin, 1975; Fox, 1975; Keating, 1975; Stanley, 1975). *The Gifted and the Talented: The Seventy-eighth Yearbook of the National Society for the Study of Education.* Part I is an excellent source (Passow, 1979) as is *The Gifted and the Creative* (Stanley, George, and Solano, 1977).

world. Few would deny that we must provide educational facilities that will develop achievement in these areas, as well as in the areas of social and literary accomplishment. However, there is a great deal of disagreement as to how this can best be done. Disagreement among so-called experts on curriculum and methods is easy to find, stemming, no doubt, from our current lack of information in these fields. Research in this area is proceeding. An unfortunate delay in doing anything about the problem stems from our not knowing what to do. In the meantime, various programs are being developed out of a perceived need to do something to insure that society make better use of ability. It seems to be much wiser to develop such programs than to delay doing anything for fear of not doing the "right" thing.

Some interesting results that should encourage giving special attention to the education of the gifted have been reported by R. A. Martinson (1961). The findings of her investigation of various education and administrative programs, special classes, cluster grouping, and independent study are encouraging. In measured results, including academic achievement and social adjustment, children given special services surpassed those who did not receive them. Perhaps any systematic program considered adequate by professionals familiar with the characteristics of the gifted produces better results than no program at all. The percentage of gifted children in the United States, however, who are in special programs or for whom any systematic program is provided has been reported to be amazingly small (Dunn, 1963). Research has indicated that gifted students can develop new problem-solving skills through the use of auto-instructional materials, and teachers can teach gifted students to approach problems creatively (Parnes, 1966). The United States Office of Education has, by policy statement, recognized the education of the gifted and talented as being an integral part of our educational system, and advocates increased educational opportunities for these students. Improvement in evaluative thinking abilities of gifted children who received special instruction for only one month has been reported (Hauck, 1967). Testing the achievement of those of high ability presents special problems and is being given special attention (Keating, 1975b). Although measures of academic skills are used to determine access to many educational opportunities, they tend to lack utility for predicting professional achievement (Wallach, 1976).

Stanley (1979) has advocated acceleration in mathematics and related subjects as a result of experiences with the SMPY project. Acceleration in other areas for children of special abilities in verbal and performance areas is likely to be successful. Daurio (1979), following an extensive review of the research literature, has indicated that acceleration is successful over a wide range of achievement areas and personal growth and indicates no substantial study demonstrating harmful effects of such programs. Even so, educators tend to be strongly opposed to acceleration.

Much of this opposition may stem from beliefs that tend to be unfounded that educational acceleration produces emotional and social problems inhibitory or damaging to personal growth. Other opposition no doubt stems from reluctance to accelerate those whose achievement already may be advanced for fear of being judged to be antidemocratic. However, the stimulation of working with those of equal or better ability rather than working with agemates of lesser achievement status can make a tremendous difference in students' progress and their sense of accomplishment (Stanley, 1979).

Exceptionally capable students can profit from any number of educational arrangements, including highly regarded enrichment programs where students are allowed and encouraged to self-pace their learning, although the challenge and stimulation resulting from acceleration may prove more effective, both academically and personally. Acceleration through grade-skipping (an older practice) may have considerable value for those of high ability, particularly when it results in moving children a year or so early into junior high school, high school, or even college. Many colleges and high schools are cooperating in programs of early part-time college study for the talented. Such programs are deemed highly successful (Solano and George, 1976). Gifted students can advance by gaining credit through such examination programs as the Advanced Placement Program and the College Level Examination Program. Early college entrance and college graduation in fewer than the conventional four years should be given serious consideration by the gifted and those who counsel them.

NURTURING ACHIEVEMENT AND CREATIVITY

To be most effective, the circumstances encouraging creativity must be built into the total context of life. Highly creative activities are nurtured as a way of life rather than by the use of a set of specific devices. Creative activities are fostered by the social climate of the individual's life and are mediated by a complex set of perceptual, conceptual, linguistic, motivational, and attitudinal processes. Some suggestions for fostering achievement and creativity follow.[2]

PERPETUATE CURIOSITY

Children high in curiosity are also generally high in self-esteem. Initially active and highly curious, they have a wealth of experience with their environment, develop competencies, interact successfully with their

[2]Adapted from Sawrey and Telford (1973), Harris and Evans (1974), and others.

external world, develop confidence in themselves, and hence have high self-esteem and are potentially creative. Of course, children with initially equivalent levels of active curiosity may find exploration and manipulation of novel situations and objects differentially rewarding because of their environmental circumstances. Children rewarded for curiosity will continue experimenting. Conversely, children who are punished or, for whatever reason, negatively reinforced when investigating new experiences tend to restrict activity, to limit the experiential world, and to fail to develop those competencies that contribute to self-confidence and creativity. Curiosity, self-esteem, and creativity in children are positively related and probably grow and develop together (Maw and Maw, 1970).

FREE PEOPLE FROM FEAR OF ERROR

Anxiety about the likelihood of making errors hampers originality. Emphasis on the ways in which we learn from errors encourages the playful experimentation with possibilities which is a necessary ingredient of creativity. A relaxed and permissive attitude toward initial errors which are subsequently evaluated and rejected in terms of relevant appropriateness encourages experimentation with alternative possibilities, which is a part of being creatively productive. Labeling errors without providing information leading to correction is minimally useful educationally. Instructional procedures should encourage adventuresomeness and minimize the risks attendant upon exploration. Educational procedures should also maximize the informativeness and minimize the failure component of error.

ENCOURAGE FANTASY AS WELL AS REALITY-ORIENTED COGNITION

Just as severe criticism of errors hampers originality, so an insistence that all judgments be closely tied to reality may discourage the play and fanciful experimentation with wild possibilities that are often fruitful. Periods of relaxed, fanciful concoction of extreme possibilities followed by critical evaluation are reported by most creative people as being highly productive. Free movement from fantasy to reality and a mixture of wild spontaneity and critical evaluation should be encouraged.

ENCOURAGE CONTACTS WITH CREATIVE PEOPLE

High levels of achievement require that people accept and appreciate innovations and innovative people. Contact with such people will contribute to this end. Children will strive to maximize their similarity to others who possess traits or command goals they admire. The child desiring intangible goals and not knowing how to realize them will try to attain these goals by becoming like adult models who possess or command these characteristics or goals (Harris and Evans, 1974). Although highly creative children are less sociable than others, they will often profit from the permissive and rewarding atmosphere provided by the laboratory, workshop, or studio of a highly accomplished and admired person.

ENCOURAGE DIVERSITY AND INDIVIDUALITY

Evidence indicates fairly consistently that most people find their own and others' deviancies in thought and action threatening. A culture, subculture, and family which by precept, as well as by verbal commitment, value diversity and accept and appreciate differences will provide a social environment conducive to high creativity and achievement.

ENCOURAGE INDIVIDUAL INITIATIVE

Providing maximum opportunities for individual study and advancement, and providing flexibility in laboratory and field experiences will assist in accommodating the special needs of gifted and creative students.

AVOID STEREOTYPING THE POTENTIALLY CREATIVE

It is hard to see a member of a socially stigmatized group as having potential for creativity. However, while the statistical probability that recognized creativity will occur in the disadvantaged is less than the probability of its occurrence among the more advantaged, the history of mankind repeatedly documents that a potential Leonardo da Vinci, Isaac Newton, Ludwig von Beethoven, or Albert Einstein may exist in a Hindu untouchable, the son of a slave, or a child in the ghetto. A realization of our verbal commitment to equality of social, economic, and educational opportunity will increase the likelihood that such potential will be realized.

SUMMARY

Concern for the gifted child is not of recent vintage, but quantitative studies of the gifted are a relatively recent development. The pioneering work of Terman and his associates, who investigated the characteristics of gifted children and conducted extensive follow-up studies at later periods in life, has contributed a large body of data to the area. The various definitions of the gifted have contributed to some of the confusion that exists in terminology employed in this area. A definition of the gifted is partially determined by the definition of intelligence that is used. Intelligence has, of course, been defined in a variety of ways.

The importance of potential contributions of the gifted and talented to the culture, as well as a cultural concern for individual welfare, make the problem of identifying the gifted among us imperative. Ability and talent cannot be adequately used unless they are identified. The early detection of superiority among children is essential to make the earliest provisions for their development and education.

Intellectually superior children tend to be superior in a number of ways that are not closely related to intellectual performance. In general they tend to be larger, healthier, happier, and have more extensive interests and hobbies than their normal peers. They particularly enjoy reading and develop this skill rather early and with a minimum of difficulty. Their educational achievement tends to be uniformly high, and they engage in extracurricular activities rather extensively. The gifted tend to have better-educated parents than the average, to come from better socioeconomic backgrounds, and to have parents with higher occupational levels.

The relationship between measured intelligence (IQ) and creativity over the entire range of both variables is not known. Low positive estimates of the size of the correlation may be unrealistically low. Some intelligence is obviously essential for creative activity, but a high level of intelligence does not guarantee creativity.

The personalities of creative adults have been investigated by a number of researchers. Descriptions of the highly creative are complicated, and attention must be paid to the area of creative activity in order to present a meaningful composite of creative persons, even within a given discipline. Tests of creativity have been devised and given to groups of children and adolescents. Descriptions of children and adolescents thus designated as highly creative were presented.

Concern with the development and encouragement of creativity has become widespread. Rapid technological advances have made routine problem solving the province of machines. People can be free from this drudgery to engage in more productive and creative enterprise.

A variety of means has been employed to identify highly creative individuals. In the identification of creative adults, a method of nomination by peers can be used or a listing of culturally relevant productions can be made. Identifying creative children is more tenuous. Teachers may make nominations, or tests designed to measure originality can be employed. A great deal of effort has gone into the development of tests of creativity for both children and adults. The criteria for creativity seem to be elusive, especially among children and adolescents. Long-range studies should improve the validity of measures being developed.

Special educational programs and facilities for the gifted and talented have not developed as rapidly or as extensively as have special programs for the handicapped. The gifted do not create serious problems in the home or school. They are not as noticeable as certain of the handicapped groups, nor do they arouse compassion. Programs for the education of the gifted need to be increased and should be sufficiently flexible so that they can be changed when additional research findings so indicate.

REFERENCES

Abraham, W., *Common Sense about Gifted Children* (New York: Harper and Row, 1958).

Anastasi, A., *Differential Psychology: Individual and Group Differences in Behavior* (New York: Macmillan, 1958).

Barbe, W. B., "What Happens to Graduates of Special Classes for the Gifted," *Educational Research Bulletin*, 1957, *36*, 13–16.

Barnette, W. L., "Advance Credit for the Superior High-school Student," *Journal of Higher Education*, 1957, *28*, 15–20.

Barron, F., *Creativity and Psychological Health* (New York: Van Nostrand Reinhold, 1963).

Barron, F., "The Dream of Art and Poetry," *Psychology Today*, 1968, *2* (7), 18–23, 66.

Barron, F., and others, *New Directions in Psychology*, vol. 2 (New York: Holt, Rinehart and Winston, 1965).

Bishop, W., "Successful Teachers of the Gifted," *Exceptional Children*, 1968, *34*, 317–25.

Bock, R. D. and D. Kolakowski, "Further Evidence of Sex-Linked Major-Gene Influence on Human Spatial Visualizing Ability," *American Journal of Human Genetics*, 1973, *25*, 1–14.

Bonsall, M., and B. Stefflre, "The Temperament of Gifted Children," *California Journal of Educational Research*, 1955, *6*, 195–99.

Burks, B. S., D. W. Jensen, and L. M. Terman, *The Promise of Youth: Follow-up Studies of a Thousand Gifted Children (Genetic Studies of Genius*, vol. 3) (Stanford, Calif.: Stanford University Press, 1930).

Callahan, C. M., "The Gifted and Talented Woman," in A. H. Passow, ed., *The Gifted and Talented: Their Education and Development* (Chicago: University of Chicago Press, 1979).

Cattell, J. M., "Families of American Men of Science," *Popular Science Monthly*, 1915, *86*, 504–15.

Cattell, R. B., *Objective-Analytic Test Battery* (Champaign, Ill.: Institute for Personality and Ability Testing, 1956).

Cattell, R. B. and H. W. Eber, *Handbook for the Sixteen Personality Factor Questionnaire* (Champaign, Ill.: Institute for Personality and Ability Testing, 1962).

Cohler, M. J., "Scholastic Status of Achievers and Nonachievers of Superior Intelligence," *Journal of Educational Psychology,* 1941, *32,* 603–10.

Cox, C., "The Early Mental Traits of 300 Geniuses," in *Genetic Studies in Genius,* vol. 2 (Stanford, Calif.: Stanford University Press, 1926).

Daurio, S. P., "Educational Enrichment versus Acceleration: A Review of the Literature," in W. C. George, S. J. Cohn, and J. C. Stanley, eds., *Acceleration and Enrichment: Strategies for Educating the Gifted* (Baltimore: Study of Mathematically Precocious Youth, Johns Hopkins University, 1979).

De Mille, R., and P. R. Merrifield, "Creativity and Intelligence," *Educational Psychology Measurement,* 1962, *22,* 803–8.

Dunn, L. M., ed., *Exceptional Children in the Schools* (New York: Holt, Rinehart and Winston, 1963).

Gallagher, J. J., "The Disadvantaged Gifted Child," in A. J. Tannenbaum, ed., *Special Education and Programs for Disadvantaged Children and Youth* (Washington, D.C.: NEW, CEC, 1968).

Gallagher, J. J. "Social Status of Children Related to Intelligence, Propinquity, and Social Perception," *Elementary School Journal,* 1958, *58,* 225–31.

Gallagher, J. J. and T. H. Crowder, "Adjustment of Gifted Children in the Regular Classroom," *Exceptional Children,* 1957, *23,* 306–12, 317–19.

Galton, F., *Hereditary Genius* (London: Macmillan, 1869).

Getzels, J. W. and P. W. Jackson, *Creativity and Intelligence* (New York: John Wiley, 1962).

Gough, H. G., "Techniques for Identifying the Creative Research Scientist," in D. W. MacKinnon, ed., *The Creative Person* (Berkeley: University of California Extension, 1961).

Granzin, K. L. and W. J. Granzin, "Peer Group Choice as a Device for Screening Intellectually Gifted Children," *Gifted Child Quarterly,* 1969, *13,* 189–94.

Guilford, J. P., "Creativity," *American Psychologist,* 1950, *5,* 444–54.

Guilford, J. P., "Traits of Creativity," in H. H. Anderson, ed. *Creativity and Its Cultivation* (New York: Harper and Row, 1959).

Guilford, J. P. and P. R. Merrifield, *The Structure of Intellect Model: Its Uses and Implications,* Report of the Psychology Laboratory, No. 24. (Los Angeles: University of Southern California, 1960).

Halpin, G., D. A. Payne, and C. P. Ellett, "Biographical Correlates of the Creative Personality: Gifted Adolescents," *Exceptional Children,* 1973, *39,* 652–53.

Harris, M. B. and R. C. Evans, "The Effects of Modeling and Instruction on Creative Responses," *Journal of Psychology*, 1974, *86*, 3–11.

Hauck, B. B., "A Comparison of Gains in Evaluation Ability Between Gifted and Nongifted Sixth-grade Students," *Gifted Children*, 1967, *11*, 166–71.

Heck, A. O., *The Education of Exceptional Children* (New York: McGraw-Hill, 1953).

Higher Education and National Affairs. Washington, D. C.: American Council on Education, 1975, *24*, (41), 5.

Hildreth, G., "The Educational Achievement of Gifted Children," *Child Development*, 1938, *9*, 365–71.

Holland, J. L., "Creative and Academic Performance Among Talented Adolescents," *Journal of Educational Psychology*, 1961, *52*, 136–47.

Hollingworth, L. S., "How Should Gifted Children Be Educated?" *Baltimore Bulletin of Education*, 1931, *50*, 196.

Hollingworth, L. S. and M. V. Cobb, "Children Clustering at 165 IQ and Children Clustering at 145 IQ Compared for Three Years in Achievement," *Yearbook of the National Society for the Study of Education*, 1928, *27*, 3–33.

Jenkins, M. D., "A Socio-psychological Study of Negro Children of Superior Intelligence," *Journal of Negro Education*, 1936, *5*, 175–90.

Johnson, H. G., "Does the Gifted Child Have a Low IQ?" *Journal of Educational Research*, 1942, *36*, 91–99.

Jones, A. M., "An Analytical Study of One Hundred and Twenty Superior Children," *Psychological Clinic*, 1925, *16*, 19–76.

Jordan, J. B., "Foundation for Exceptional Children Addresses the Needs of the Culturally Gifted Child," *Exceptional Children*, 1974, *40*, 279–83.

Keating, D. P., "The Study of Mathematically Precocious Youth," *The Journal of Special Education*, 1975a, *9*, 45–62.

Keating, D. P., "Testing Those in the Top Percentiles," *Exceptional Children*, 1975b, *11*, 435–36.

Kogan, N., "Creativity and Cognitive Style: A Life Span Perspective," in P. B. Baltes and K. W. Schaie, eds., *Life-span Developmental Psychology: Personality and Socialization* (New York: Academic Press, 1973).

Kough, J. and R. F. DeHaan, *Teacher's Guidance Handbook* (Chicago: Science Research Associates, 1955).

Lewis, W. D., "A Study of Superior Children in the Elementary School," *Peabody College Contributions to Education*, No. 266 (Nashville, Tenn.: Peabody College Press, 1940).

Maccoby, E. E., and C. N. Jacklin, *The Psychology of Sex Differences* (Stanford, Calif.: Stanford University Press, 1974).

MacKinnon, D. W., "The Nature and Nurture of Creative Talent," *American Psychologist*, 1962, *17*, 484–95.

MacKinnon, D. W., "What Do We Mean by Talent and How Do We Test for It?" in *The Search for Talent* (Princeton, N.J.: College Entrance Examination Board, 1960).

MacMeeken, A. M., "The Intelligence of a Representative Group of Scottish Children," *Publication of the Scottish Counsel on Research in Education*, 1939 (15).

McNemar, Q., "Lost: Our Intelligence? Why?" *American Psychologist*, 1964, *19*, 871–82.

Maltzman, I., "On the Training of Originality," *Psychological Review*, 1960, *67*, 229–42.

Marsh, R. W., "A Statistical Re-analysis of Getzels and Jackson's Data," *British Journal of Educational Psychology*, 1964, *34*, 91–93.

Martinson, R. A., *Educational Programs for Gifted Pupils* (Sacramento: California State Department of Education, 1961).

Martinson, R. A. and L. M. Lessinger, "Problems in the Identification of Intellectually Gifted Pupils," *Exceptional Children*, 1960, *26*, 227–31.

Martinson, R. A. and M. V. Seagoe, *The Abilities of Young Children* (Washington, D. C.: Council for Exceptional Children, 1967).

Maslow, A. H., "Creativity in Self-actualizing People," in H. H. Anderson, ed., *Creativity and Its Cultivation* (New York: Harper and Row, 1959).

Maslow, A. H., *Motivation and Personality*, 2nd ed. (New York: Harper and Row, 1970).

Maw, W. H. and E. W. Maw, "Self Concepts of High and Low Curiosity Boys," *Child Development*, 1970, *41*, 123–29.

Mearns, H., *Creative Power: The Education of Youth in the Creative Arts* (New York: Dover Publications, 1958).

Mednick, S., "The Associative Basis of the Creative Process," *Psychological Review*, 1962, *69*, 220–32.

Miles, C. C., "Gifted Children," in L. Carmichael, ed., *Manual of Child Psychology* (New York: John Wiley, 1954).

Miller, V., "Academic Achievement and Social Adjustment of Children Young for Their Grade Placement," *Elementary School Journal*, 1957, *57*, 257–63.

Monahan, J. E. and L. S. Hollingworth, "Neuromuscular Capacity of Children Who Test Above 135 IQ (Stanford-Binet)," *Journal of Educational Psychology*, 1927, *18*, 88–96.

Mullis, I. V. S., *Educational Achievement and Sex Discrimination* (Denver: National Assessment of Education Progress, 1975).

Nicholls, J. G., "Creativity in the Person Who Will Never Produce Anything Original and Useful: The Concept of Creativity as a Normally Distributed Trait," *American Psychologist*, 1972, *27*, 717–27.

Oden, M. H., "The Fulfillment of Promise: 40-Year Follow-up of the Terman Gifted Group," *Genetic Psychology Monographs*, 1968, *77*, 3–93.

Otto, H. J., "Curriculum Adjustment for Gifted Elementary School Children in Regular Classes," Bureau of Laboratory Schools Publication 6 (Austin: University of Texas Press, 1957).

Palm, H. J., "An Analysis of Test-score Differences Between Highly Creative and High Miller Analogies Members of the Summer Guidance Institute," Research Memo., BER–59–13 (Minneapolis: Bureau of Educational Research, University of Minnesota, 1959).

Parnes, S. J., "Programming Creative Behavior," U.S. Department of Health, Education and Welfare, Office of Education, Cooperative Research Project No. 5–0716 (Buffalo: State University of New York, 1966).

Passow, S. H., ed., *The Gifted and the Talented: Their Education and Development* (Chicago: University of Chicago Press, 1979).

Payne, D. A., W. G. Halpin, C. D. Ellett, and J. B. Dale, "General Personality Correlates of Creative Personality in Academically and Artistically Gifted Youth," *The Journal of Special Education*, 1975, *9*, 105–8.

Pegnato, C. V. and J. W. Birch, "Locating Gifted Children in Junior High Schools," *Exceptional Children*, 1959, *25*, 300–304.

Renzulli, J. S., "Talent Potential in Minority Group Students," *Exceptional Children*, 1973, *39*, 437–44.

Riessman, F., *The Culturally Deprived Child* (New York: Harper and Row, 1962).

Ripple, R. E. and F. B. May, "Caution in Comparing Creativity and I.Q.," *Psychological Reports*, 1962, *10*, 229–30.

Robinson, H. A., W. C. Roedell, and N. Jackson, "Early Identification and Intervention," in A. H. Passow, ed., *The Gifted and the Talented: Their Education and Development* (Chicago: University of Chicago Press, 1979).

Rogers, C. R., "Toward a Theory of Creativity," in H. H. Anderson, ed., *Creativity and Its Cultivation* (New York: Harper and Row, 1959).

Sawrey, J. M. and C. W. Telford, *Educational Psychology*, 4th ed. (Boston: Allyn and Bacon, 1973).

Sawrey, J. M. and C. W. Telford, *Adjustment and Personality*, 4th ed. (Boston: Allyn and Bacon, 1975).

Shannon, D. C., "What Research Says about Acceleration," *Phi Delta Kappan,* 1957, *39,* 70–73.

Shaycoft, M. F. and others, *Project Talent: Studies of a Complete Age Group Age 15* (Pittsburgh: University of Pittsburgh, 1963; mimeographed).

Solano, C. H. and W. C. George, "College Courses and Educational Facilitation of the Gifted," *Gifted Child Quarterly,* 1976, *20,* 274–85.

Stanley, J. C., "The Study and Facilitation of Talent for Mathematics," in A. H. Passow, ed., *The Gifted and the Talented: Their Education and Development* (Chicago: University of Chicago Press, 1979).

Stanley, J. C., W. C. George, and C. H. Solano, eds., *The Gifted and The Creative: A Fifty Year Perspective* (Baltimore and London: Johns Hopkins University Press, 1977).

Taylor, C. W. and F. Barron, *Scientific Creativity: Its Recognition and Development* (New York: John Wiley, 1963).

Taylor, C. W. and J. L. Holland, "Development 32 and Application of Tests of Creativity," *Reviews of Educational Research,* 1962, *32,* 91–102.

Terman, L. M., "A Preliminary Study in the Psychology and Pedagogy of Leadership," *Pedagogical Seminary,* 1904, *11,* 413–51.

Terman, L. M., "Genius and Stupidity," *Pedagogical Seminary,* 1906, *13,* 307–73.

Terman, L. M., "The Mental Hygiene of Exceptional Children," *Pedagogical Seminary,* 1915, *22,* 529–37.

Terman, L. M., and others, *Mental and Physical Traits of a Thousand Gifted Children* (Stanford, Calif.: Stanford University Press, 1925).

Terman, L. M., and M. H. Oden, *The Gifted Child Grows Up* (Stanford, Calif.: Stanford University Press, 1947).

Terman, L. M. and M. H. Oden, *The Gifted Group at Mid-Life* (Stanford, Calif.: Stanford University Press, 1959).

Terman, L. M. and L. E. Tyler, "Psychological Sex Differences," in L. Carmichael, ed., *Manual of Child Psychology,* 2nd ed. (New York: John Wiley, 1954).

Torrance, E. P., *Guiding Creative Talent* (Englewood Cliffs, N. J.: Prentice-Hall, 1962).

Torrance, E. P., *Torrance Tests of Creativity* (Princeton, N. J.: Personnel Press, 1966).

Torrance, E. P., "Creatively Gifted and Disadvantaged Gifted Students," in J. C. Stanley, W. C. George, and C. H. Solona, eds., *The Gifted and the Creative* Baltimore and London: Johns Hopkins University Press, 1977).

Torrance, E. P., "Unique Needs of the Creative Child and Adult," in

A. H. Passow, ed., *The Gifted and the Talented: Their Education and Development* (Chicago: University of Chicago Press, 1979).

Torrance, E. P. and J. Khatena, "What Kind of Person Are You?" *Gifted Child Quarterly*, 1970, *14*, 71–75.

Wallach, M. A., "Tests Tell Us Little About Talent," *American Scientist*, 1976, *64* (1) 57–63.

Ward, L. F., *Applied Sociology* (Boston: Ginn, 1906).

Weisberg, P. S. and K. J. Springer, *Environmental Factors Influencing Creative Function in Gifted Children* (Cincinnati: Department of Psychiatry, Cincinnati General Hospital, 1961; mimeographed).

Welsh, G. S., "Personality Correlates of Intelligence and Creativity in Gifted Adolescents," in J. C. Stanley, W. C. George, and C. H. Solano, eds., *The Gifted and the Creative* (Baltimore and London: Johns Hopkins University Press, 1977).

Witty, P. A., "A Genetic Study of Fifty Gifted Children," *Yearbook of the National Society for the Study of Education*, 1940, *39*, 401–8.

Witty, P. A., "A Study of One Hundred Gifted Children," *University of Kansas Bulletin of Education, State Teachers College Studies in Education*, 1930, *1* (13).

Witty, P. A., "Who Are the Gifted?" in N. D. Henry, ed., *Education for the Gifted: Yearbook of the National Society for the Study of Education*, 1958, *57*, Part 2.

SUGGESTIONS FOR STUDENTS AND INSTRUCTORS

1. Discuss the following statement which John Dryden made in the seventeenth century: "Great wits are sure to madness near allied, and thin partitions do their bounds abide."

2. Discuss: "The recipe typically prescribed for the handicapped, consisting of early identification, constant encouragement, properly spaced sequential successes, individualized programming, and personally paced progress, is not appropriate for the intellectually gifted as they are self-starters and internally motivated."

3. Discuss: "Special enriched programs for the gifted are undemocratic."

4. Discuss: "Age-grade acceleration of gifted children does them more harm than good."

5. Discuss: "In the present international tug of war, survival itself depends upon our developing and making the most effective use of the nation's intellectually gifted."

6. How do you think giftedness would have been defined by the fifteenth-century American Indians, Eskimos, and in King Arthur's court?

ADDITIONAL READINGS

> Ginsberg, G. and C. H. Harrison, *How to Help Your Gifted Child: A Handbook for Parents and Teachers* (New York: Monarch Press, 1977). The more than twenty years of experience of the Gifted Child Society is distilled into a practical, readable manual.
>
> Goertzel, V. and M. Goertzel, *Cradles of Eminence* (Boston: Little, Brown, 1962). Biographies of gifted persons.

SELECTED FILMS

> *Gifted Children.* (15 minutes) University of Minnesota Audiovisual Education Service, University of Minnesota, Minneapolis, Minnesota. Defines giftedness and suggests effective guidance procedures.
>
> *The Gifted Child.* (29 minutes) Syracuse University Film Library, 1455 Colvin Street, Syracuse, N. Y. A day in the life of a well-adjusted gifted child.

ORGANIZATIONS AND AGENCIES

> American Association for Gifted Children
> 15 Gramercy Park
> New York, N. Y. 10003
>
> Gifted Child Society, Inc.
> 59 Glen Gray Road
> Oakland, N. J. 07436
>
> National Association for Creative Children and Adults
> 8080 Springvalley Drive
> Cincinnati, Ohio 45236

CHAPTER 8

LOW LEVELS OF COGNITIVE DEVELOPMENT (MENTAL RETARDATION)

Nathan was born prematurely, the last of six children. His early development was slow. He sat up at fifteen months, walked at three years, and did not talk until five and a half years of age. He attended regular kindergarten, tried first grade but was taken out after three months. He made another unsuccessful attempt at the first grade a year later. Following that, he spent three years in regular classes but made little progress. At the age of eleven he was placed in a special class for the educable mentally retarded. Nathan did well in the special class, progressed through the school program, was active in athletics, became a Boy Scout, and participated in the school's work-study program. His work experience included working as a grocery carry-out clerk, a dishwasher, and janitor for a drugstore. All of his employers were pleased with him and his work. With the money he earned he was able to open a bank account and make purchases for his personal needs.

When he left school at the age of eighteen, his teachers estimated his academic skills to be at about a fourth-grade level. He completed his driver education course and was able to get his driver's license. He is currently employed as a stockman and carry-out clerk at a local grocery. He is living in a group home with six other young men. While he has not attained his goal of becoming totally independent, since he is still living in a somewhat restricted environment under supervision, he has achieved far beyond what was thought possible in terms of his slow development in infancy and his early school failures.

DEFINITIONS

The American Association on Mental Deficiency proposes the following definition of mental retardation: "Mental retardation refers to significantly sub-average general intellectual functioning existing concurrently with deficits in adaptive behavior, and manifested during the developmental period" (Grossman, 1977). This definition is very different from the older ones. E. A. Doll (1941), in a widely quoted statement, indicated six criteria essential to an adequate definition of mental deficiency: (1) social incompetence, (2) due to mental subnormality, (3) resulting from developmental arrest, which (4) obtains at maturity, (5) is of constitutional origin, and (6) is essentially incurable.

Although Doll's definition is more than a quarter of a century old and official definitions and conceptions of mental subnormality have been greatly changed in the interval, many popular ideas of mental retardation reflect this type of definition. This is particularly true of the last two components—constitutional origin and incurability.

According to the AAMD all three conditions—subnormal intellectual functioning, originating during the developmental period, and impairment of adaptive behavior—must be present for a person to be designated mentally retarded. Persons cannot be labeled mentally retarded just because their adaptive behavior is impaired. There are many causes other than mental retardation for slow maturational development, poor school progress, and inadequate social and vocational adjustment. Persons likewise cannot be designated as mentally retarded solely because of a low IQ. A low IQ, plus impaired adaptive behavior, which originates before maturity, are all required.

The AAMD's definition is stated in functional terms—impairment in adaptive behavior and low level of intellectual functioning. This impairment may take the forms of: (1) maturational retardation as indicated by slowness in acquiring skills such as sitting, crawling, standing, walking, talking, habit training, and interacting with age peers; (2) deficiencies in learning, principally poor academic achievement; and (3) inadequate social adjustment, principally adult social and economic inadequacy. Adequacy of adjustment must be judged in relation to the individual's peers. This definition makes "mental retardation" a term descriptive of the current status of the individual's adaptive behavior and functional level, irrespective of etiology or curability.

This AAMD definition, as well as several older ones, refers to the current functional status of the individual rather than to any inferred "potential" or future condition. A person may function sufficiently subnormally to meet the criteria at one time in life and not do so at some other time. A person's status may change as the result of changes in level of intellectual functioning, changes in level of adaptive behavior, or changes in cultural demands and expectations. Retardation is purely descriptive of current condition and does not necessarily imply either prognosis or etiology.

Mental retardation is neither a disease nor a medical syndrome with a specific cause. There are more than two hundred specific identified causes (Brewer and Kakalek, 1979). Mentally retarded individuals may function subnormally because of genetic factors (single gene, polygenes, or chromosomal aberrations); organic deficits of environmental origin (infections, toxins, physical trauma, diet, gestational disorders, or irradiation levels); or the social and psycho-social conditions of their lives. Even though the etiologies of mental subnormality are numerous, in the majority of cases the exact causes are not known. In most cases, care, treatment, and educational training procedures are not related to etiology. They are related more directly to the individual's level of functioning and unique patterns of abilities and disabilities than to what caused the condition. Of course, etiology is of paramount importance when the primary concern is prevention rather than remediation and treatment.

Current definitions and conceptions of mental retardation say nothing about curability. Only within the framework of a medical model of mental retardation is this term appropriate. Remediation is always relative to current medical, rehabilitative, and educational methodology. All current programs for the care, treatment, training, and education of the mentally retarded assume that, by appropriate means, the functional levels of these individuals can be significantly altered. Present information concerning a child's current level of functioning, as well as test scores, are used in choosing or devising treatment programs which will maximize the individual's personal and social effectiveness.

IDENTIFICATION OF THE MENTALLY RETARDED

The AAMD definition of mental retardation assumes a psychometric criterion for the determination of the level of intellectual functioning, developmental information to indicate maturational status, school records to indicate learning ability, and evidence of social and economic competence to serve as an index of social adjustment when the person involved is an adult. Socioeconomic competence may also be evaluated by various adaptive behavior scales.

THE PSYCHOMETRIC CRITERION

With the advent of intelligence testing, psychometric criteria came to the fore as diagnostic of mental retardation. The first individual intelligence tests were developed as a means of identifying the mentally retarded so that instructions could be adapted to their stage of mental development. Although at one time mental retardation was defined in terms of either perceived adaptive behavior or test scores, this is no longer true. In practice, psychometric criteria are invoked only when deficiencies of adaptive behavior are judged to be sufficient to indicate possible mental retardation.

MENTAL TESTS AND THE CULTURALLY DIFFERENT CHILD

Over the past decade, people involved in the assessment of children from deviant cultures for possible placement in special education programs have become concerned about the possible "unfairness" of conventional tests. Tests and test scores in themselves are, of course, neither fair nor unfair. Tests have reliability and validity and are appropriate or inappropriate for particular purposes. Only the treatment of individuals on the basis of test scores can be appropriately labeled fair or unfair. Discussions concerning the use and misuse of psychological tests usually focus on intelligence tests. It is unfortunate that they were ever called intelligence tests; they are really scholastic aptitude tests. If we conceive of intelligence as dealing effectively with one's environment, scholastic aptitude tests are devised to indicate an individual's level of competence in dealing with the academic environment, the subworld of formal education. Intelligence is not an entity but an attribute of an individual, like beauty or speed. People function more or less adequately, that is, intelligently, in terms of the demands and expectancies of the culture and situations in which they live.

Starting over a quarter-century ago, and continuing to the present, there have been periodic attempts to develop *culture free, culture fair*, or *culture specific* tests.

CULTURE FREE, CULTURE FAIR, CULTURE SPECIFIC, AND CULTURALLY ADJUSTED TESTS

The makers of *culture free* tests try to devise test items free of cultural content and to eliminate those that are culturally loaded. *Culture fair* tests contain items which are common, and preferably equally common, to all cultures. While these test concepts seem feasible, in practice their use has been disappointing. Attempts to develop culture free tests have convinced most test makers that there is no such thing. There is no way to measure scholastic aptitudes such as memory, learning, perceiving, conceiving, and problem solving apart from content, and content is always culturally related. In this sense, all tests are, to a degree, content or culture specific. Attempts to develop culture fair tests have been no more successful. It was found that in reducing the specifically culturally related content of tests, one also decreases their usefulness in specific social contexts. It was surprising and disappointing to many to discover that disadvantaged children score as low on the supposedly culture free and culture fair tests as they do on the conventional, culturally loaded ones (Grossman, 1977; Jensen, 1973; Barnes, 1973; Arvey, 1972; Williams, 1974).

A more recent proposal is the development of *culture specific* tests (Barnes, 1973; Williams, 1974). These tests would be written from the contexts of particular minority cultures and subcultures and validated in terms of their accuracy in predicting educational, vocational, and social competence within those specific cultures and subcultures. Such tests, of course, will not predict success within the mainstream of society as well as do conventional tests based on mainstream culture (Hobbs, 1975). The argument for culture specific tests is based on the contention that since Anglo-American culture is not necessarily superior to others, modern America should develop alternative "mainstreams" and individuals should have the option of selecting the one within which they will live.

Another attempt to make tests fairer to people from disadvantaged minorities consists in statistically adjusting test scores derived from conventional tests according to the familial-socio-cultural status of the subjects. Such a system has been developed by Jane Mercer, a sociologist at the University of California at Riverside. She calls this a "System of Multicultural Pluralistic Assessment" (SOMPA) (Rice, 1979). The measuring scale has two major components: a parent interview and a personal assessment. From the parent interview three measures are derived: one indicative of adaptive behavior, another of sociocultural status, and the third related to health history. The personal assessment component consists of scores on three standardized tests: the Wechsler Intelligence Scale for Children—Revised (WISC-R), The Bender Visual Motor Gestalt Test, and a Physical Dexterity Test. In addition, visual and auditory acuity and weight by height indices are obtained. The scores on the WISC-R are considered to represent the child's level of intellectual functioning in terms of the dominant white middle-class culture. This score is then "adjusted" in terms of the individual's deviations from that culture in various familial-sociocultural dimensions. Separate norms are provided for whites, blacks, and Hispanics. These adjustments to the original WISC-R scores yield an "adjusted IQ" which represents a person's "learning potential." Thus to use an example provided in the literature, a child with a WISC-R IQ of 68, which would make her eligible for placement in a class for the mentally retarded, has an adjusted score of 77, which places her outside the range of the mentally retarded. According to the author, such an individual can benefit from a regular instructional program that takes the differences between her background and the culture of the school into account. If we have interpreted this correctly, it means that if this student had lived in a familial-sociocultural environment comparable to the WISC-R standardization group, she would have obtained a score of 77 rather than 68. Furthermore the IQ of 77 represents the person's estimated "true inherent learning potential," thus making her ineligible for the special educational services provided for the mentally retarded.

It seems to the writer that the implied definition of mental retardation in terms of "inherent potential" rather than current functional level is a return to the concept of half a century ago. In order for student assessment to facilitate educational planning and contribute to more effective instruction, the child's current repertoire of educationally relevant percepts, concepts, and skills should indicate the starting point for such endeavors. A statistically derived index of inherent learning potential is minimally relevant. The question of whether the "correction" which places a child outside the range of eligibility for special educational services is to that person's advantage depends upon what alternative services are available. If the correction simply makes the child ineligible for special services it is of doubtful value.

When a child is referred for assessment as possibly mentally retarded, someone presumably has already decided that the child's marked and persistent educational retardation is sufficiently great to make him or her eligible for special educational services designed to facilitate the learning of such students. If adjustments applied to the original test scores do nothing but make the child ineligible for such services without making more appropriate services available, it is hard to see how the child benefits.

Presumably, deriving adjusted indices of learning potential in the way proposed by Mercer will have the effect of identifying an *equal proportion* of blacks, whites, Hispanics, and lower social class whites as mentally retarded and this may or may not be to the advantage of the disadvantaged groups.

The writer is reminded of a list of assumptions that he used to list for his classes, in the 1940s and 1950s, if a conventional Stanford-Binet or WISC score were to be taken as indicative of an individual's inherent potential. The list was about as follows: The subject must be cooperative and sufficiently motivated that the test performance represents his or her best performance; the testee must have adequate language facility and an educational and cultural background comparable to the standardization population; the individual must also be free of sensory, motor, and emotional handicaps.

The following additional suggestions were also included: In interpreting test scores, no single test score can be considered indicative of mental retardation; test scores must be interpreted within the context of the child's educational, medical, and family history; when test scores from comparable tests are discrepant, high scores are more likely to be indicative of intellectual potential than are low scores.

Making a distinction between mental retardation as indicated by "adjusted" versus "unadjusted" test scores is analogous to the old distinction between "real" and "pseudo" mental retardation. The pseudo-retarded were defined as persons with normal intellectual potential who obtain test scores and function as mentally retarded because of personality disorganization, environmental deprivation, sensory-motor defects, or idiosyncratic mental growth curves (Clarke and Clarke, 1955). However, during the past two decades, when mental retardation has been defined in terms of current levels of functioning irrespective of cause or progress, the distinction between real and pseudo-retardation has been dropped.

The writer feels that it is unfortunate that the Binet test and its successors ever came to be called "intelligence tests." They were, and have always been, scholastic aptitude tests designed to facilitate the education of children with special educational needs. Calling the aptitudes measured by such a test "intelligence" has produced a host of misunderstandings. When we administer a test, we sample a person's learned repertoire of relevant information, judgments, concepts, and percepts. All of these are acquired and developed by the individual. The individual's level of functioning in these categories undoubtedly has both genetic and environmental components. Inherent capacity never manifests itself independently of environment. Samplings of test behavior together with the child's educational history indicate that the individual is functioning more or less adequately as compared with his or her peers. He or she is acting more or less "intelligently" with reference to some—principally educational—criteria. Reifying "intelligent" behavior as an entity, intelligence, which is postulated to account for the individual's appropriate or inappropriate behavior, is entirely gratuitous and has produced a host of pseudo-problems. Conceiving of intelligence as an "inherent potential" means that it is innate. During the 1920s and 1930s, when this conception was prevalent, intelligence was considered to be an inherited intellectual potential which could be measured and which was also quite resistant to environmental influences—witness the dogma of the "constancy of the IQ." During this period Cyril Burt defined intelligence as "innate, general, cognitive ability" (Hearnshaw, 1979).

Clearly, although Binet was largely responsible for the use of the term "intelligence" in connection with his test, he certainly never subscribed to the "inherent potential" concept. Binet's primary concern was the educational neglect and mistreatment of the children who failed to learn in school. He felt that, by early identification, these children could be saved the years of frustration and failure which instilled in them feelings of helplessness and hopelessness. Binet advocated "mental orthopedics" to develop the cognitive processes underlying school learning. He considered intelligence to be responsive to education. Test scores were to assist in devising preventative and remedial educational programs. Testing was to facilitate educational planning and more effective practice. Most of this seems to have been forgotten in the intervening years.

Another prejudice of the writer is that the widespread use of the intelligence quotient (IQ) rather than mental age as an index of test performances has contributed to many misunderstandings concerning test scores. To the uninitiated, the IQ is a "thing" or quantity, innately given, which remains the same throughout life. In ordinary communication, the mental age concept is less likely to be misunderstood than is the IQ. When we tell parents that their child's test score is equal to that of the average six-year-old, we give them information they can readily understand and can easily compare with the child's level of functioning in other areas. However, when we indicate that the child's IQ is 60, a lot of additional explanation is required and the information is easily misinterpreted.

The persistence of the notion of an inherent potential for learning that can be measured is behind the various attempts to devise culture free, culture fair, and culturally adjusted tests. The devising of such tests is motivated partially by the desire to demonstrate that the disadvantaged minority ethnic groups are equal to middle-class whites in "fairly derived" or "properly adjusted" test scores. Additionally, it is considered desirable that equal proportions of the various ethnic groups and social classes be certified as eligible for the special programs and services provided for the mentally retarded.

It would seem that if all, or most, of the educable mentally retarded children are to be integrated into the regular classrooms (mainstreamed), we can cease categorizing them as mentally retarded. If we simply remove the requirement that mental test scores must be within the normal range for a child to be designated as "learning disabled," or "educationally handicapped," all of the educable mentally retarded can be included in this category. The "learning disabled" children then will include all those whose educational retardation is sufficiently marked to warrant special educational services, irrespective of their scores on scholastic aptitude (intelligence) tests. If we remove the label of mental retardation and make these mildly retarded children eligible for special services as learning disabled, we do not deprive them of the help they need, as will be the case if we keep the criteria as they are now. Keeping the category of educable mental retardation and certifying eligibility on the basis of culture specific or culturally adjusted test performances may deprive many ethnic minority children of the special services they need because their "inherent potential," as indicated by their culturally adjusted test scores, is too high. Adjusting test scores upward does not endow the subjects with additional scholastic aptitude any more than adjusting the reading on the thermometer makes the house warmer. Although scholastic aptitude tests do not measure inherent potential, they do provide a rough index of one's cognitive development and are probably more useful in educational planning than are derived indices of a theoretically hereditary capacity.

One of the most important determinants of scholastic aptitude is previous learning. The amount and nature of previous learning provides the foundation for subsequent learning. Much of formal learning is sequential and hierarchical. Previous learning can either facilitate or inhibit subsequent learning. The survival skills, language patterns, attitudes, and expectancies acquired in the ghetto may be very useful in that context, but may be handicapping in a different subculture within which the individual may later either elect or be forced to live.

Similarly, culture specific tests based on minority cultures may be indicative of one's ability to survive and function within that culture but will have little or no validity when related to a different culture. To be useful, tests must be validated in terms of the task requirements of a particular job or social context. It is doubtful that we will ever be able to devise tests of inherent potential for learning the scores of which are transcultural in their applicability.

It is clearly possible to decrease the specific cultural content in the development and validation of a given test, but in doing so we diminish its usefulness in the social context where it is designed to be used. No single set of aptitudes is a prerequisite for survival and adaptability in all environments. Every society requires individuals capable of performing the necessary social and economic functions of that society, and inevitably will favor and reward aptitudes, behavior, and values contributing to those capabilities.

The intelligent and highly valued person in a hunting society is the person with keen vision and hearing, great strength and endurance, and good motor coordination so that he can detect, track down, and either capture or kill animals of prey. These are the aptitudes upon which survival depends. Successful living on the terms dictated by current industrialized society increasingly requires a background of success in school. Scholastic aptitude tests are designed to tap the scholastically relevant characteristics of the individual for use in educational placement and guidance.

In school, welfare, or court situations where questions of intellectual competence arise, we do not start with mental test scores. We start with inadequacies in adaptive behavior. These inadequacies most often take the form of marked retardation in the development of sensori-motor, language, and self-help skill in the preschool period, failures in school learning during the school-age period, and gross inadequacies in the broad social and economic competence realm in adulthood. We start with the observation that some individuals have acquired markedly fewer socially useful skills and have learned them significantly less well than their peers. Systematic sampling of the individual's perceptual, learning, memory, and reasoning processes and the products of past learning (the person's repertoire of information and linguistic skills) by means of standardized tests helps determine whether these demonstrated failures are due to deficiencies in the cognitive-learning realm.

In the senior author's experience screening children referred by teachers as probably mentally retarded, 20 percent of the children so referred score within normal ranges on conventional mental tests. The educational inadequacies of such children are the result of something other than lack of scholastic aptitude. Scoring within normal ranges on such tests means that: (1) the perceptual, memory, judgmental, and reasoning aptitudes, (2) the fund of information acquired as the result of experiences common to children of comparable age and circumstances, and (3) the repertoire of specifically taught skills and information which are a necessary prerequisite to additional school learning are on too high a level for the individual's difficulties to be due to lack of intellectual competence. Today, children scoring within normal ranges on scholastic aptitude tests but who are markedly retarded in school achievement may be classified as "educationally handicapped" or as having "learning disabilities" and may be provided help, as we indicated earlier. When failures in adaptive behavior are accompanied by evidences of gross cognitive-intellectual inadequacies, the child may be identified as mentally retarded and become eligible for special assistance in a program more appropriate to his or her competencies and level of functioning.

The problem of the relative usefulness of culturally loaded, culture free, culture fair, and culture specific tests usually becomes involved with the question of the *causes* of individual and group differences in test scores. The practical usefulness of test scores in determining children's present status for educational purposes has nothing to do with how they happen to obtain those scores except for pure "chance" factors. Tests can be useful in indicating the individual's *current repertoire* of educationally relevant linguistic, cognitive, and motor skills as well as his or her fund of information and meanings as a starting point for either remediation or further educational development. Except for social and/or biological engineering programs designed to reduce the deficits or improve the functional levels of future generations, the question of the etiology of the deficits is largely irrelevant. Tests should be validated and used in terms of their relevance for their treatment-remediation implications rather than the *causes* of test performances. Very often the causes of a low test score and school failure are the same—organic or social or both—but the causes are not to be found either in the test or in the lack of achievement.

Devising tests tailored to particular minority ethnic groups or to various disadvantaged subcultures will, of course, show differences in favor of the members of the various minorities. Although proposals to develop such tests have recently been presented anew, the senior author is familiar with an "intelligence test" based on the culture of southwestern American Indians, developed in the late 1920s or early 1930s. However, we have been unable to locate a reference to it in the literature. This test, when administered to whites and American Indians, produced the anticipated differences in favor of the Indian children. More recently R. I. Williams (1973) has developed a Black Intelligence Test of Cultural Homogeneity, a hundred-item multiple-choice vocabulary test which was standardized on separate black and white groups, retaining only those words which were easy for blacks and difficult for whites. Test results consequently show a consistent superiority of urban blacks over whites. The Dove Counter-Balance General Intelligence Test is based on general information drawn from a mixture of Mexican-American, black American, and ghetto white cultures. Scores on this test reflect familiarity with these cultures. It is hard to tell to what extent the authors of these tests are seriously trying to develop genuinely useful tests for educational use within these specific cultures, and to what extent they simply wish to demonstrate that tests can be devised which show differences in favor of the supposedly disadvantaged groups.

The Adaptive Behavior Criterion

Adaptive behavior is defined as "the effectiveness or degree with which the individual meets the standards of personal independence and social responsibility expected of his age and cultural group" (Grossman, 1977). During infancy and early childhood, deficits in adaptive behavior may be reflected in:

1. sensori-motor skills (turning, creeping, walking, manual manipulations).

2. communication skills (social smiling, gesturing, speaking).

3. self-help skills (eating, dressing, toileting, bathing).

4. socialization (playing imitatively, playing with others cooperatively or in parallel depending upon age).

During childhood and early adolescence, deficits in adaptive behavior may be reflected in:

1. academic learning.

2. judgment and reasoning in dealing with the environment.

3. social skills (participation in group activities and effective interpersonal relationships).

In late adolescence and adulthood, deficits in adaptive behavior may be reflected in:

1. vocational competence.

2. family and social duties.

Many current discussions imply that the concept of adaptive behavior as a criterion of mental retardation is new (Hobbs, 1975; Leland, 1974; Nihira, 1973). However, a historical survey of definitions and descriptions of this condition discloses that it is essentially a new term for an old concept. Almost from the beginnings of professional concern with subnormal intellectual functioning, there has been either an implicit or an explicit assumption that personal-social competence—the level of behavioral adaptation to one's environment—is the ultimate criterion of mental retardation. In essence, this means that irrespective of the extent of neural damage or intellectual deficits, no person can be considered mentally retarded (mentally deficient, mentally defective, mentally subnormal, or feebleminded) unless that person's personal and socioeconomic competence is significantly inferior to that of the majority of his or her peers. Of course, there is always the assumed or stated limitation that such demonstrated incompetence is the result of intellectual retardation. In other words, historically as now, the dual standard of both personal-social incompetence *and* mental subnormality was necessary to warrant a diagnosis of mental retardation.

The following definitions and descriptions are typical of the early characterizations of mental retardation. Charles Mercier in 1890 stated that only when persons' intellectual deficiency is so extreme that they are unable to learn to be socially competent can they be judged to be mentally retarded. Tredgold (1908) defined mental retardation as "a state of incomplete mental development of such a kind and degree that the individual is incapable of adapting himself to the normal environment of his fellows in such a way as to maintain existence independent of supervision, external control or support." Those who differentiated degrees of mental deficiency did so in terms of personal-social competence. Thus, Tredgold (1908) indicated that adult idiots are unable to guard against common danger, can understand only the simplest commands, and can articulate only a few monosyllables. Binet characterized idiots as being unable to talk or understand language (Peterson, 1925). Tredgold stated that imbeciles, although superior to idiots, are incapable of managing their own affairs. They are capable of performing simple tasks under supervision, but are incapable of contributing materially toward their own support. Binet indicated that imbeciles are unable to learn to read, to comprehend the written word, or to write meaningfully (Peterson, 1925).

The mildly mentally retarded (morons) are individuals whose mental defectiveness is less than that of imbeciles. According to Tredgold (1908) they are capable of earning a living under favorable circumstances, but are incapable of competing on equal terms with their fellows. Binet's description of this degree of mental defectiveness is essentially the same as Tredgold's.

Thus, for the past century, personal-social incompetence due to mental limitations has been considered the basic criterion of mental retardation.

Marked developmental retardation during the preschool period, repeated school failure during the school years, and evidence of gross personal-social incompetence as an adult are the initial observations which lead to the administration of mental tests to determine if levels of intellectual and achievement test performances *are consistent with* a diagnosis of mental retardation. Although verification, by means of psychometric devices, of the initial assessment of the individual as mentally retarded because of achievement deficiencies is perceived as a kind of medical model diagnosis, its real purpose is to determine eligibility for special treatment. This treatment may be special educational placement or assistance, social services, vocational rehabilitation programs, supervised living in a group home, sheltered workshop placement, or—when referred by courts because of delinquency—diminished responsibility and institutionalization instead of a prison sentence. The following case is typical of individuals in which the observed deficiency in adaptive behavior is in the preschool period (developmental retardation).

developmental retardation in mental subnormality

Karen's mother recalls that as an infant her daughter seemed to be quite normal physically. However, at six months she felt that Karen did not respond as her older sister had at the same age. She did not sit up by herself and when her mother sat her up, she just toppled over. At her next regular medical check-up, Karen's mother asked her pediatrician if something was wrong. He assured her that Karen was possibly a little slow in maturing, but it was nothing to worry about. Karen was slow in creeping and crawling and when she could neither stand alone nor walk at eighteen months she was taken to another pediatrician, who told her mother that her bones were too weak to support her weight. Thyroid therapy was tried, but it did not help.

Karen's parents really began to worry when at age two, when other children her age were beginning to talk, their daughter was still cooing and gurgling but had no real speech. Frantically, they trundled Karen from physician to physician and from clinic to clinic seeking reassurance that she was normal. They received no real assistance nor a positive diagnosis, possibly because they focused on speech and walking as the areas of concern. Karen's mother spent endless hours trying to teach her to walk and talk.

Karen's parents were pleased when she was toilet trained effortlessly at three years. At the same age Karen took her first halting steps. Between three and four she began to say single words. At this time Karen's parents really suspected that she was mentally retarded, but no one who had examined her had mentioned the word. When they finally asked their pediatrician if she was retarded he said he really did not know and referred them to a psychologist. When the pediatrician received word from the psychologist that the patient was severely retarded—her Sanford-Binet IQ was 36—his advice was immediate institutionalization.

Karen's mother says, "Although for the past two years I was sure that something was wrong, I had focused on the physical disabilities alone. None of the doctors had mentioned mental retardation and I don't know when I first started linking the concept with my child's condition, but I finally asked my pediatrician if she was mentally retarded. I hoped he wouldn't say 'yes' but at the same time I wanted to know, one way or the other."

When the pediatrician told Karen's mother of the psychologist's diagnosis, she left his office in tears. Heartsick, she took her daughter home. The parents accepted the diagnosis but rejected the suggestion to institutionalize. Friends and relatives continued to hint that Karen would be better off in an institution. However, her parents coolly ignored the hints and made plans to take care of her at home.

THE LEARNING ABILITY CRITERION

Formal education is part of our culture, and intellectual achievement has considerable prestige value. Intellectual skills are also a prerequisite to admittance to many trades and professions. The individual who does not progress in school has failed in an important social area. The school situation is also the first place in which objective comparisons are systematically made, and the child is placed in a rather definite position in a prestige hierarchy based largely on intellectual achievements.

Failure in school is often the first symptom of inadequate intellectual functioning. In view of this, school failure, when not the result of sensory or motor handicaps, severe emotional disturbance, or absence from school, is considered to indicate mental retardation. Two or three years' retardation in school achievement, in the absence of other causes, has traditionally been considered indicative of possible mental retardation. The following case is fairly typical.

Kirk

Kirk was not diagnosed as mentally retarded until he was eleven years old. His developmental history was not exceptional. There were minor feeding problems in infancy. He did not walk until he was nineteen months old. He had frequent earaches during early childhood and his hearing in one ear is moderately impaired. His preschool behavior seems to have been within the normal range. Explicit limitation became evident only in school achievement. Kirk's school history was an accumulation of school failures, repeated grades, and social promotions. There were no special disciplinary problems.

In the first grade, Kirk's teacher noted "immaturity, slowness, and inattentiveness to school tasks." In the second grade his school record indicated "failure to learn to read and lack of number concepts." The parents agreed to Kirk's retention in the second grade. However, his repetition of second grade did not improve his reading and arithmetic skills. He was promoted yearly for the next three years, but his school performance continued on a low level. Kirk was kept in the regular classroom with no special remedial help during this period.

Kirk was described by his teachers as personable and well accepted by the other students. His attitude toward teacher and school was cooperative. He seemed to have no special personality or emotional problems. His first- and second-grade teachers felt that he was capable of doing better than he did. However, the notes left by teachers for the next three years indicated that they suspected mental retardation. At the age of eleven, after a conference of his present and former teachers, the school nurse, and his principal, Kirk was referred to the school psychologist as possibly mentally retarded.

The psychologist found that Kirk read at about a second-grade level. His sight vocabulary was third-grade. His spelling was commensurate with his reading. His spelling errors showed little appreciation of letter-sound associations. He had little understanding of vowel sounds—a second-grade skill. His arithmetic skills were also about second-grade.

On the Stanford-Binet test he obtained an IQ of 62. His specific weaknesses noted in the test situation were (a) general comprehension, (b) inability to handle abstract concepts, (c) difficulty in reasoning and in drawing inferences, and (d) deficiency in dealing with relationships. His strengths were his cooperativeness, his persistence in tasks even after he became aware of errors, and his eagerness to please. Kirk was judged eligible for special class placement, and following a case conference with his parents he was so placed.

At ages fourteen and seventeen Kirk's status was reassessed. At the latter age his academic achievement level was about fourth grade and his IQ was 65—a nonsignificant change. In the three-year interim between fourteen and seventeen Kirk had shown no significant change in achievement level. It was evident that he had reached a plateau in achievement level, and his parents agreed that he should drop out of school. During the following year, Kirk stayed at home. He then returned voluntarily to be placed in the work-study program, a cooperative program between the local schools and the state division of vocational rehabilitation.

Because of Kirk's advanced age and positive personality assets he was assigned full-time job placement with weekly evening training-counseling sessions under adult education auspices. His work-training placement was as stockboy in a grocery store. The school psychologist and counselor agreed that his training should include the development of specific arithmetic skills, improving his handwriting, budgeting, learning how to establish and maintain a savings account, and general work habits. Kirk was jointly supervised by the school's vocational program coordinator and the vocational rehabilitation counselor. Kirk seemed to be doing well. His attitude toward his work and supervisors was excellent. After three months on the job, Kirk felt he should be making more money and began talking about getting a better job. Kirk's counselors encouraged him to stay where he was for a while, and he now seems satisfied to do so. We would predict reasonable success for Kirk in similar work situations.

Kirk's case is typical of the mildly mentally retarded. Physically, they do not differ significantly from their more academically able peers. They may be a little slow, but within the range of normal preschool development. They become identified as mentally retarded only after marked and persistent academic deficiencies and verification by test scores. They continue to be so labeled until they leave school by dropping out or by "graduating." Most of them manage to find jobs, and to a degree they succeed and merge into the general population. Kirk's intellectual limitations are counterbalanced by his pleasing personality, good grooming, and good work habits. He will probably attain and maintain an acceptable minimal level of socioeconomic competence.

The Social Adjustment Criterion

Although it has limitations, the test of social adequacy is the most basic of all. It is the elementary datum from which we start in establishing mental retardation.

Technically, the subject of the following case would not be mentally retarded according to the current AAMD definition, since her condition did not develop before maturity. However, historically, such individuals have been so classified since they function similarly to those retarded from childhood, so we shall use it as an example.

Mrs. J   Mrs. J. was referred to the senior author by the social welfare office because of suspected mental subnormality. The record showed Mrs. J. to be fifty-five years of age, but she looked and acted at least twenty years older. According to the case worker, Mrs. J.'s husband had recently died and she had been left alone and destitute. Consequently, she had been placed on welfare under the supervision of the caseworker.

The social worker found that Mrs. J. was unable to care for herself. Physical examinations had disclosed nothing organically wrong. She seemed fairly well oriented and showed no psychotic symptoms. So, largely by a process of exclusion, mental retardation was suspected and she was referred for psychological evaluation.

The behavior that was considered indicative of mental deficiency included failure to keep herself and her house clean or to cook, inability to keep accounts or to make change, tendency to become lost when she went uptown alone, and the habit of talking childishly. Mrs. J. was brought to the office by her social worker and told to stay there until the social worker returned to take her home. The interview and tests verified the social worker's characterization of the client, except for some inconsistencies. Her vocabulary was largely that of an adult, but the things she said were childish. She could talk about her daughter who had married and moved away, but could not remember her current address. She could remember correctly her place and date of birth, but not her social worker's name. She could remember the recipe for making a cake, but, according to her social worker, would forget that she had placed it in the oven to bake.

The author's initial impression was that Mrs. J. acted like a senile person, and he asked the social worker to verify her age. She seemed closer to eighty than to fifty. Her age was verified as fifty-five.

When a Stanford-Binet test was administered, Mrs. J. obtained a mental age of five years and four months. However, her vocabulary was only slightly below the twelve-year level. On the Goodenough Draw-a-Man test she obtained a mental age of six. Her test scores were consistent with a diagnosis of mental retardation, and her score pattern was characteristic of a person who had previously functioned at a higher level but had deteriorated.

The test performances and subjective impression were indicative of marked mental retardation sufficient to require care and supervision. There was evidence that the client had previously functioned at a much higher level and seemed to be suffering from a premature senility. At that time the author was unfamiliar with Alzheimer's and Pick's diseases, both of which are premature senile conditions characterized by progressive mental deterioration. Both are associated with the deterioration of localized areas of the brain; the causes are unknown. Mrs. J. seemed to fit the clinical descriptions of these disorders.

This case is typical of those in which the initial assessment of possible mental retardation in adulthood is made on the basis of deficiencies in personal-social competences, which are then verified or refuted by tests.

MEASURES OF ADAPTIVE BEHAVIOR

Those persons who perceive of the adaptive behavior criterion of mental retardation as being of recent origin are thinking of the formal AAMD 1959 definition and the development of scales for its measurement. The first of these scales was the Vineland Social Maturity Scale developed by Doll (1936). The Vineland scale is a schedule of 117 items of habitual activities ranging from infantile behavior, such as a baby's laugh and coo, to adult levels involving community activities. The items are arranged into eight loosely defined categories: general self-help, self-help in dressing, self-help in eating, communication, self-direction, socialization, locomotion, and occupation. The required information is elicited in a semistructured interview with a parent, teacher, attendant, or other person who is intimately acquainted with the child. A social quotient (SQ) comparable to the intelligence quotient (IQ) can be obtained. There is a substantial correlation between Stanford-Binet IQs and Vineland SQs, ranging from .40 to .80 depending on the heterogeneity of the group (Hurst, 1962).

At least a half dozen similar scales have been developed. The best-known of these are one developed by the American Association on Mental Deficiency (AAMD) and a similar one compiled by Jane Mercer (1973).

USES OF THE ADAPTIVE BEHAVIOR SCALES

While the original purpose of the scales of adaptive behavior may have been diagnostic, their greatest usefulness will probably be that of identifying the starting points for training-educational programs (Malone and Christian, 1974). These scales can supplement family-reported evidence of developmental retardation in the young child, educational records of the school learning characteristics of the school-age child, and social welfare or court reports of personal-social deficiencies of the adult, and they can indicate specific domains of behavior and particular skills in need of training. Periodic surveys with such scales can be used to indicate improvements and to evaluate remedial programs (Schachter, Rice, Cormier, Christensen, and James, 1978). This was the principal use being made of a similar instrument developed much earlier in England by H. C. Gunzburg. The senior author found Gunzburg's scale in use routinely at the Monybull Hospital, Birmingham, England, when he visited there in 1967 (Gunzburg, 1973).

THE ASSESSMENT OF MENTAL RETARDATION

The assessment of the mentally retarded individual is an inevitable process. It is carried on informally and haphazardly by relatives, friends, and acquaintances. It becomes more systematic and formal when done by teachers, counselors, and psychologists for purposes of school promotion, demotion, or retention, or for placement in special classes or institutions.

Except for very special purposes, the immediate occasion for the assessment of mental status is some social circumstance, and the ultimate purpose of diagnosis is the solution of some social problem. In addition, the final test of the accuracy of diagnosis and the effectiveness of treatment is the extent to which the social circumstance is improved.

THE RELATION OF IDENTIFICATION TO CRITERIA

Identification of the mentally retarded individual involves the acceptance of certain criteria. We have already indicated that, in practice, multiple criteria are commonly used. The relative weight given to the psychometric, educational, social, economic, and developmental criteria will vary with the purpose of the assessment process. Whereas combined school achievement (educational criteria) and mental test scores (psychometric criteria) are most valid for the identification of the mentally retarded of school age when other specialized programs are being considered, the broader criteria of adequate social adjustment and economic sufficiency are more crucial in the evaluation of the out-of-school adult, and general developmental status is the most relevant information for the preschool child.

Since the various criteria do not correlate highly with one another, we can have the paradox of a child who was classed as intellectually retarded while in school and who, as an adult, functions in a socially adequate way. The available data on the incidence of mental retardation according to chronological age suggest that this happens with a fairly large number of individuals. Table 8–1 shows such data based on two different surveys.

Table 8–1 shows that relatively few children below school age are diagnosed as mentally retarded, that the percentage of defective individuals increases tremendously during the school-age period, and that in adulthood the percentage drops to a comparatively low level. Part of the large difference between children and adults is attributed to the higher death rates among the mentally subnormal and the greater ease of case-finding while the children are of school age, but probably the biggest single factor is the lesser weight given to abstract verbal facility in the adult situation. Many retarded individuals of the higher mental levels (the mildly mentally retarded), who probably make up 75 percent of the school-age children so diagnosed, find formal education an insurmountable obstacle, but once they are out of school a large percentage of them are not defective in terms of social and economic criteria (Tarjan and others, 1973; Granat

Table 8–1

INCIDENCE OF MENTAL RETARDATION AND CHRONOLOGICAL AGE
(PER 1,000 OF THE GENERAL POPULATION)

age in years	England and Wales*	Baltimore†
0–4	1.2	0.7
5–9	15.5	11.8
10–14	25.6	43.6
15–19	10.8	30.2
20–29	8.4	7.6
30–39	5.7	8.2
40–49	5.4	7.4
50–59	4.9	4.5
60 and older	2.9	2.2

*Based on Wood Report as reported by N. O'Connor and J. Tizard (1956, p. 22).
†Data from P. C. Lemkau, C. Tietze, and M. Casper (1942).

and Granat, 1973). Other surveys are consistent with the data presented in Table 8–1, showing that the reported incidence of mental retardation rises with increasing age, reaches a peak at about fourteen, and then drops off sharply (Granat and Granat, 1973).

These observations help explain some apparent paradoxes concerning the number of individuals who are "really" mentally retarded. The literature has long asserted that approximately 3 percent of the population are mentally retarded. However, the limited population surveys that have been made show incidences far below this figure. Whenever surveys have been made of "identified" or "certified" cases, the incidence has been found to be nearer 1 percent (Granat and Granat, 1973; Tarjan and others, 1973; Mercer, 1973). When educational and treatment programs are initiated and justified on the basis of the 3 percent figure and it is found that only about one-third of this number are actually identified as retarded, administrators wonder where the other two-thirds are. These individuals are assumed to exist as undiscovered or unidentified cases.

Actually, the 3 percent figure is obtained only from the statistics of test construction and interpretation. As Table 8–1 indicates, the percentage of individuals in the general population scoring two standard deviation units below the mean is slightly less than the 3 percent figure commonly cited. Assuming that the standard deviation of the test is approximately 15 IQ points minus two standard deviation units yields an IQ of 70, the conventional psychometric cutting-off point for mental retardation. Note that this figure will actually be obtained only if the *purely statistical single psychometric criterion is applied.*

We have already stated that in practice, the double criteria of significant impairment in intelligence (indicated by low test scores) *and* below-normal general adaptation (developmental retardation, school failure, or socioeconomic incompetence) are applied. The lower incidence figures are obtained because many of the individuals who meet the psychometric criterion (IQ below 70) are functioning adequately in the classroom as children or are meeting the minimum socioeconomic standards of society as adults and so fail to qualify in terms of general adaptation. Conversely, many individuals who are judged sufficiently impaired in general adaptation to qualify as mentally retarded score too high psychometrically to qualify on this basis.

The senior author, serving as a school psychologist, has found that approximately one-third of the children referred to him by teachers as probably mentally retarded fail to meet the psychometric criteria. D. I. Ashurst and C. E. Meyers (1973), in their study of 269 students referred by teachers as suspected mental retardates, found that 116 were not so classified by school psychologists. In this study, the psychological assessments were not purely psychometric but were based on school records and classroom observations, as well as on test scores.

If we assume that 3 percent of the population meet the psychometric criterion (IQs below 70), at least half of these are not significantly impaired in general adaptation. In Sweden, where all nineteen-year-old males undergo examinations (including an intelligence test) for placement in military service, 1.5 percent obtained test scores sufficiently low as to qualify as mentally retarded, but had never been so identified. It was also found that 0.71 percent of the men had been certified mentally retarded. The two groups combined yield a *psychometrically-defined* prevalence of 2.21 percent, as compared with 0.71 percent certified on the basis of the *double criterion* (Granat and Granat, 1973). Mercer (1973) found that when the double criterion is used, the rates of mental retardation are cut to about half those found by the psychometric criterion alone.

TERMINOLOGY AND CLASSIFICATION

The American Association on Mental Deficiency has recommended a standard set of terms, but there is still great variation in the terminology used in the field of intellectual subnormality, both in the United States and abroad. In the older American terminology, *feebleminded* was the generic term for all persons sufficiently intellectually subnormal to warrant special consideration, and the terms *moron, imbecile,* and *idiot* designated various degrees of subnormality. At a later date, *mental deficiency* replaced *feebleminded* as the generic term, while the older terms were retained for the three subcategories. The AAMD more recently has proposed that *mental retardation* become the preferred generic term, and that the various degrees of subnormality be indicated as *mild, moderate, severe,* and *profound.* Additional sets of roughly equivalent terms are used in Great Britain, by the World Health Organization, and by the American Psychiatric Association. There are also separate educational terminologies, both in Great Britain and in America. Table 8–2 indicates the relationships among these various sets of terms.

The diversity of roughly equivalent terms is the result of the different criteria used to define and identify individuals with intellectual impairments, the varying purposes served by the diagnosis, and the never-ending attempt to get away from the negative connotations of the names given to handicapping conditions. The older terms—*feebleminded, moron, imbecile,* and *idiot*—came to have a clinical and psychometric frame of reference. Definitions were largely in terms of IQ ranges, heredity was considered to be the primary causal factor, and the prognosis was considered to be poor. These terms, descriptive of significant intellectual impairment with connotations of hopelessness, became emotionally toned and stigmatizing. The newer terms—*mental retardation* as the general term and *mild, moderate, severe,* and *profound* as varying degrees—are less emotion-

Table 8–2

SOME TERMINOLOGY FOR MENTAL RETARDATION

organization	generic terms	more specific designation		
American clinics (earlier)	Feebleminded	Moron	Imbecile	Idiot
American clinics (later)	Mental deficiency	Moron	Imbecile	Idiot
American Association on Mental Deficiency	Mentally retarded	Mild	Moderate	Severe Profound
National Association of Retarded Citizens	Mentally retarded	Marginally dependent	Semidependent	Dependent
World Health Organization	Mental subnormality	Mild	Moderate	Severe
American Psychiatric Association	Mental subnormality	Mild	Moderate	Severe
British clinics	Amentia	Feebleminded	Imbecile	Idiot
American, educational	Mentally retarded	Educable	Trainable	Custodial or dependent
British, educational	Amentia	Educational subnormal	Backward	

ally toned and commonly involve the use of multiple criteria. The terms *educable, trainable,* and *custodial* to indicate degrees of mental retardation obviously refer largely to the practical problems of administrative classification. All these terms refer to classes of intellectual subnormality which relate to the degree of impairment. A second classification, which the AAMD calls a biomedical classification, is based on the principal *causes* of the low level of intellectual functioning.

Two Etiological Populations of Mentally Retarded

Current discussions emphasize that the definition and assessment of mental retardation are independent of etiology and prognosis. However, there is a *statistical relationship* between certain etiological categories, on the one hand, and scholastic aptitude, socioeconomic status, and adaptive behavior levels, on the other. For example, some workers have differentiated between a "familial" and an "organic" population of the mentally retarded. Members of the familial population have no demonstrable organic damage or deficit. They represent the lower portion of the normal curve of intellectual ability. These persons are a part of the normal distribution of abilities produced by the multigenic-environmental interactions. (A corresponding number of persons constitute the upper extreme of the normal curve because of more favorable combinations of these same factors.) The majority of the low-level individuals have IQ and adaptive behavior ratings in the mildly retarded levels. Very few score below 50 in IQ (Mercer, 1973).

The "organics," on the other hand, have marked physiological defects and tend to have IQs and adaptive scale SQs below 50. The causes of these individuals' deficiencies are relatively infrequent single genes, chromosomal abnormalities, and/or major neurological defects from such things as dietary deficiencies, infections, toxins, and physical trauma of similar infrequent occurrence.

The "organics" and the small number of "familials" combine to form a disproportionate number of individuals functioning at very low levels. This produces a great excess of low-level cases beyond those theoretically expected from the shape of the "normal curve." While the two populations are not entirely discrete and the relationships are not sufficient to warrant individual diagnosis and prognosis on the basis of etiology alone, some inferences can be drawn from the etiological categories to which a person belongs. The "organics" are much more likely to be severely or profoundly impaired in intellectual functioning and adaptive behavior than are the "familials." Conversely, individuals with IQs below 50 and those with correspondingly low levels of adaptive behavior will show markedly more organic impairment than will persons scoring higher in intellectual and adaptive behavior (Mercer, 1973).

mental retardation caused by a dominant gene Mental retardation due to a single defective dominant gene is rare. Some conditions apparently of this type are Huntington's chorea, tuberous sclerosis, neurofibromatosis, hereditary cerebellar ataxia, and Freidreich's ataxis. It is obvious that severe mental defectiveness due to a single dominant gene will be self-limiting because the parents must also be defective. Since most of the severely mentally retarded do not reproduce, because of either sterility or lack of opportunity, the transmission of the defective dominant gene from one generation to the next is very limited.

The characteristics of mental subnormality determined by a single dominant gene are as follows:

1. The affected and unaffected members of a family are usually sharply differentiated.

2. Every defective individual has at least one affected parent.

3. Where only one parent is affected, and is heterozygous, approximately one-half of the offspring will be affected; when the affected parent is homozygous, all the offspring will be mentally defective.

4. When both parents are affected and are heterozygous, approximately three-fourths of the offspring will be defective (Penrose, 1963; McCusick, 1979).

mental retardation caused by a recessive gene Much more often, mental retardation is due to a single recessive gene. Such defective children typically come of apparently normal parents. The defect is typically the result of the child's receiving two similar recessive genes, one from each parent. The phenotypically normal parents are carriers of the defective gene but are not themselves affected. Some conditions which are generally considered to be due to a single defective recessive gene are: Tay-Sachs disease, gargoylism, galactosuria, phenylketonuria, and genetic microcephaly. Most of these types of mental retardation are found rarely and the sum of all of them does not represent a very large proportion of the total population of the mentally deficient. However, many types have been discovered quite recently, and new ones are currently being identified, which indicates that this category may be larger than was formerly realized.

Many genetically determined mental deficiencies are, in turn, due to inborn defects of metabolism. The genes produce defective metabolism which in turn affects the development and functioning of the nervous system (possibly through other agencies), resulting in lowered mentality.

Where mental deficiency is the result of a single recessive gene,

1. the affected and unaffected members of a family are usually clearly differentiated;

2. many times the parents and immediate ancestors are unaffected;

3. the offspring are more often affected when the parents are related to each other by blood than when they are not;

4. when neither parent is affected, but some of the offspring show the defect, approximately one-fourth of the children will be defective (Penrose, 1963; McCusick, 1979).

chromosomal aberrations Improved techniques for studying chromosomes led to the discovery, in 1956, that the true number of chromosomes in humans was forty-six rather than forty-eight. Soon after this it was disclosed that mongols (Down's syndrome) had forty-seven chromosomes in place of the normal complement of forty-six. It has since been established that mongolism is associated with an extra chromosome (trisomism) at pair number 21. Cases of extra chromosomes in positions other than number 21 have been reported, but almost none of these individuals, although usually mentally retarded, are mongols (Lilienfeld, 1968). Three etiological subtypes of mongolism—nondisjunction, translocation, and mosaicism—have been identified. It is now possible to diagnose Down's syndrome prenatally. Carrier prospective parents can be provided genetic counseling concerning the statistical risks of their offspring being defective and concerning alternative means of satisfying parental needs.

mental retardation involving many genes The ordinary familial, undifferentiated, nonclinical, or common garden variety mental defectives are at the low end of the distribution curve of intelligence. The factors determining the intelligence of these individuals are the same as those affecting the intelligence level of the normal and the superior. It is certainly a mistake to treat this group of mentally retarded as a well-defined and isolated category, for in reality they are simply the arbitrarily defined tail end of a normally distributed population.

Unlike the mentally retarded whose deficiency results from a single gene, the ordinary familial mentally retarded do not differ markedly from their parents or siblings. They have no obvious distinguishing physical characteristics. They are more likely to be smaller in stature, lighter in weight, have defective vision and hearing, poor health, and greater susceptibility to disease than their peers of normal or superior mentality, but many individuals in this group are actually superior in these areas. Postmortem gross and microscopic examinations of the nervous systems have failed to disclose significant special characteristics of the brains of the typical familial mental defective.

ENVIRONMENTAL CAUSES OF MENTAL RETARDATION

There is a wide variety of possible environmental causes of mental retardation. It is easy to list these and to indicate how they may conceivably lower the mental level. It is also possible to find individual cases in which each of these alleged causes is apparently operative. However, when quantitative studies start with a fairly large, heterogeneous group of mentally deficient individuals, and comparisons are made of the incidence of the alleged causes in the deficient group and in a comparable group of intellectually normal people, significant differences often fail to appear. In other words, that various environmental factors produce mental retardation seems to be fairly convincing on the clinical, individual case level, but their functioning as statistically significant factors in causing mental retardation in general is often hard to establish.

We shall list and briefly comment on the more important environmental causes of mental retardation.

PHYSICAL TRAUMA
  PRENATAL
      1. Unsuccessful attempts at abortion
      2. Accidents to the pregnant mother

  NATAL
      1. Complications of pregnancy such as very precipitate or prolonged delivery, breech delivery, and forceps injury
      2. Excessive anesthetics during delivery

  POSTNATAL
      1. Falls, automobile accidents, and gunshot wounds (The annual incidence of significant head injuries in infants and young children is estimated to be 3.3 percent.) (Caveness, 1970).

INFECTIONS
      1. Syphilitic infestion both pre- and postnatal
      2. Rubella in pregnant mothers
      3. Encephalitis and meningitis
      4. Various other protozoan, bacterial, and viral diseases are infrequent causes of mental retardation both pre- and postnatally.

BLOOD INCOMPATIBILITIES
      1. Rh incompatibility
      2. Other mother-fetus incompatibilities may be involved occasionally.

RADIOACTIVITY
      1. Irradiation during pregnancy causes multiple defects including mental retardation.

TOXIC AGENTS
  A wide variety of toxic agents has been identified as probably having a deleterious effect on mental development both pre- and postnatally. These include:

1. Tobacco
2. Alcohol
3. Various metals such as lead
4. A wide variety of drugs taken by pregnant mothers.

PREMATURITY

The premature fetus propelled through an unrelaxed birth canal is highly vulnerable to anoxic and traumatic injury sufficiently serious to produce a fairly high incidence of neurological disorders, including mental retardation.

ASPHYXIA

1. Prenatal; asphyxia during the birth process may occur if the placenta separates too soon, if the umbilical cord kinks for a prolonged period, if the child aspirates excessive amniotic fluid, or if for any reason the newborn does not breathe for some time after delivery.
2. Postnatal; any time the brain is deprived of oxygen for more than a few minutes there is considerable danger of irreversible brain damage. One of the most frequent incidences of brain injury from asphyxia in children is from partial drowning.

DIET

1. In specific instances such as iodine deficiency producing cretinism and high levels of phenylalanine in the diet of a phenylketonuric (PKU) child, the role of diet is critical in producing retardation.
2. Severe protein and some specific vitamin deficiencies seem to produce mental retardation.
3. The role of general nutritional level in affecting mental level is uncertain. While general nutritional status correlates positively with children's IQ the correlation largely disappears when socioeconomic status is controlled (Jones, 1946). However, one study of a fairly socioeconomically homogeneous group of children living close to subsistence level in a slum area found a positive correlation between nutritional status and mental level (O'Hanlon, 1940).

GENERAL SOCIOCULTURAL FACTORS

Research studies over the past forty years have documented quite extensively that intellectual level and educational achievement are influenced by a wide variety of familial, social class, and ethnic variables, as we indicated in Chapter 3.

MILD RETARDATION

Mentally retarded children with IQs above 50 and comparable levels of adaptive behavior have enough in common to warrant discussing them all together. First, the subgroups within this range merge imperceptibly into one another in terms of most social and educationally significant variables. Second, they represent an arbitrarily designated low end of the normal distribution curve of intelligence. Third, their low intellectual status is generally caused by an interacting combination of handicapping multigenic and/or environmental factors. Fourth, although individuals in this broad category are statistically below average in physique and general health, they are not perceptibly different in these respects from the general population. More specifically, they usually lack the physical stigmata often found in the severely retarded. Fifth, most of the mildly mentally retarded are first identified as educational retardates and only after extensive study are labeled mentally retarded. Follow-up studies of children in this category indicate that most of them, as adults, merge into society and adjust to out-of-school situations only slightly less satisfactorily than do their intellectually normal age-mates from the same socioeconomic background.

This category of the mentally retarded has traditionally included many of the children now designated *educationally handicapped* or *learning disabled*. These individuals are handicapped principally by their low academic aptitudes and the ever-increasing demands of their culture.

Identification of the Mildly Mentally Retarded

In the previous chapter we indicated that the severely mentally retarded child is likely to be identified first by the family or the physician because of marked developmental failures. The extent and significance of the retardation may then be verified or questioned psychometrically. The dynamics of the family largely determine whether the child becomes a candidate for foster home or institutional placement or remains in the natural home. We also pointed out that the bulk of the mentally retarded (the mildly or educable mentally retarded) are identified by the school systems. The identification and labeling of the mildly mentally retarded in sizable numbers occurred only when it was deemed desirable to establish special school programs or assistance for certain children, most of whom were essentially normal in most other respects, but who were showing marked and persistent educational retardation. The identification of these children as mentally retarded in a psychological and/or medically clinical sense came about as the result of guidelines and standards made necessary by legislation mandating special educational programs and/or assistance for these children. Clinical—largely psychometric—guidelines were set up to determine eligibility for these excess-cost programs. Note that these populations are never first surveyed to determine which children are clinically eligible for placement in special educational programs. Only when the child fails to perform adequately within a special segment of the social system—the school system—is his or her intellectual adequacy questioned. When the child fails to fulfill the role expectancies as a school learner, he or she *may be referred* to a psychologist to determine whether the intellectual deficiencies are sufficiently global in nature and degree to *make the child eligible* for educational classification as educably mentally retarded. The psychologist is practically never called upon to confirm mental retardation solely on the basis of low test performances, and the current definitions require that both adaptive behavior and psychometric criteria be used.

INCIDENCE

From our earlier discussions, it is clear that estimates of the number of mentally retarded are meaningful only in terms of the criteria applied at a particular time and in a given culture or subculture. Purely psychometric criteria place about 2 to 3 percent in this category. A combined psychometric and adjustive behavior criterion reduces this figure by about one-half. Figure 8–1 shows this percentage distribution according to a normal probability curve.

When theoretical expectations are compared with actual counts from various sources, the two agree very well for the borderline and mildly mentally retarded, but the estimated prevalence greatly exceeds theoretical expectations for the severely mentally retarded, as shown in Table 8–3. The theoretical expectancies are based on the assumption that a person's mental level is produced by a large number of factors combining on the basis of chance. The deviation from normal expectancies at the lower mental levels is thought to reflect the operation of disease, accidents, single dominant or recessive genes, and other infrequently occurring deleterious factors which have massive effects and produce a disproportionate number of severely mentally retarded individuals.

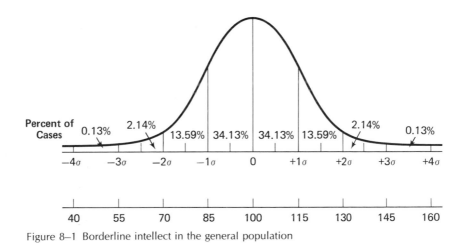

Figure 8–1 Borderline intellect in the general population

PHYSICAL CHARACTERISTICS

We have already indicated that in appearance, physique, and general health the mildly mentally retarded are not noticeably different from their intellectually normal age-mates. However, there is a statistically significant, but low, correlation between intellectual level and various indices of organic status and health (Liese and Lerch, 1974). All studies show the life expectancy of the mentally retarded to be below that of the general population. The incidence of sensory defects and motor disabilities is greater, and the medical histories of the mentally retarded show a higher incidence of disease and development defects than do those of persons of average or more intelligence (Mercer, 1973; Bruininks, 1974).

The mentally retarded approach the normal much more closely in physique and general health than they do intellectually, but they do show some inferiority. The physical handicaps of the mentally subnormal are the result of a variety of causes. In some cases, the mental and physical inferiorities have a common basis such as accident, disease, and maldevelopment, which produce widespread organic and intellectual deficits. Some of the organic deficits of the retarded are the result of their generally low socioeconomic status. A wide variety of health-related factors such as poor diet, inadequate medical care, and greater contact with and less resistance to common communicable diseases and infections are associated with low socioeconomic status.

WORK AND JOB EXPECTANCY

Despite the ever-increasing emphasis on academic training for employment in a good number of situations, it is still safe to say that a large number of employment opportunities are open to those who possess less for-

Table 8–3

DEPARTURES FROM EXPECTATIONS BASED ON THE NORMAL DISTRIBUTION CURVE WHEN 3 PERCENT ARE CONSIDERED MENTALLY RETARDED

IQ	theoretical expectancy	estimated prevalence	excess beyond theoretical expectancies	percentage of excess
0–20	50	92,750	92,700	185,400
20–50	164,861	371,000	206,139	125
50–70	5,537,710	5,593,360	55,650	1

Data from Dingman and Tarjan (1960), and Robinson and Robinson (1976).

mal training. A vast number of industrial jobs can be performed by a person with limited intelligence with a minimum of formal training. Some of the industrial jobs involve a great deal of repetition. With the rapid increases in work mechanization and simplification, the increase in simple jobs has been, and should continue to be, great. The low-level, semiskilled jobs that are constantly created in turn create a great demand for workers of relatively low mental ability. Many workers of relatively limited intelligence do not become bored by the repetitive nature of the task. They gain a high degree of proficiency and tend to stay on the job longer than some people of higher intelligence. Research studies indicate that the dull-normal have sufficient intelligence to pursue successfully a large variety of occupations. Many automotive mechanics, carpenters, cooks, barbers, miners, farmers, and laborers of various kinds have been found to have intelligence test scores equivalent to the dull-normal and borderline categories.

Jobs requiring little training are usually lower-paying jobs, but there are a lot of them. During times of maximum employment, the dull should encounter no particular difficulty in finding jobs. During slack periods, more of these people will be without jobs, and they will probably be less skillful at finding jobs than the more intelligent workers. However, A. S. Halpern (1973) points out some factors which attenuate the perception of the mentally retarded as marginal workers—the last to be hired and the first to be fired. First, the mentally retarded are not always poor workers; second, some employers are committed to employing the handicapped and assume a protective stance toward them. Halpern cites two studies which indicate that when economic conditions deteriorate and unemployment increases, the employed mentally retarded are *not* in jeopardy in disproportionate numbers.

Over the last decade there has been a tremendous proliferation of school, on-the-job, and workshop programs for the mentally retarded. Most of these are cooperative programs operated jointly by school systems and state departments of vocational rehabilitation.

LEARNING CHARACTERISTICS OF THE MILDLY MENTALLY RETARDED

Do the mentally retarded have any distinctive learning characteristics? This is a variation of the question raised in Chapter 1 concerning the qualitative versus quantitative nature of the differences between the handicapped and the nonhandicapped. When applied to the mentally retarded this question usually takes the form of a "defect" versus "developmental" concept of their differentiating characteristics. The separation between special and regular education fostered the notion that handicapped children require special concepts, theories, and treatment—that they are a different kind of people. However, the bulk of the evidence seems strongly to support a developmental rather than a defect concept.

One extensive survey of cognitive development in retarded and non-retarded persons indicates that retarded children pass through the cognitive developmental stages in the same order and in the same way as the nonretarded. They simply pass through them more slowly and attain lower limits relative to nonretarded children (Weisz and Zigler, 1979). Golomb and Barr-Grossman (1977) report that when normal and mildly mentally retarded children are equated for mental age, school attendance, and intact family structure, there are no significant differences in their performances on five different learning tasks. These authors state that their study supports a developmental rather than a defect concept of mental retardation. The development of cognitive tempo (reflectivity-impulsivity) of educable mentally retarded children parallels that of non-retarded children (Rotatori, Cullinan, Epstein, and Lloyd, 1978). Jarman (1978), following a study of patterns of cognitive ability in retarded children, says, "The present research supports the view that fundamentally similar processes are characteristic of educable mentally retarded in comparison with nonretarded children."

Increasingly, mental retardation is recognized as a developmental disorder, a quantitative deviation in functioning from norms established for the general population. The retarded are essentially normal individuals who differ from the nonretarded primarily in their slow rate and lower level of cognitive development. The same developmental and learning principles characterize the retarded and nonretarded. Performance is predominantly a function of developmental level and the retarded are basically similar to chronologically younger nonretarded children.

These facts can be reassuring to teachers of the mentally retarded. No special insights and conceptual framework are required for teaching and handling the retarded. There is no special "psychology" of the retarded. They can be handled and taught basically as the nonretarded who are at comparable levels of mental development and educational achievement. If a given child has the developmental and educational achievement levels of normal eight-year-olds, he or she can be taught and will learn in similar ways and at comparable rates.

All teaching methods are largely variations on a few common themes. If children at different developmental stages do not have unique learning characteristics, they do not require distinctive instructional methods. Methods that are good for the nonexceptional are also good for the exceptional. The differences are largely quantitative ones.

Handicapped individuals are likely to enter into any new situation with a disproportionate number of prior failures and disappointments.

Children whose limitations are principally cognitive will approach new learning problems with apprehension and misgivings. With them the maxim that "Learning should always start where the child is" should perhaps be revised to read, "Start a little below where the child is." It is important that the child who expects failure does not have this expectation confirmed as he or she starts a new learning task. Since we are never sure exactly where the child is, it is better to under- rather than overestimate the level of tasks he or she will find difficult. Once initial success has been achieved, it is easy to move to higher levels and pose successively greater challenges for the learner. When arranging learning tasks for the retarded, it is well to throw in occasional easy items to make sure that the learners will achieve intermittent success as they move to higher levels of difficulty. Some evidence indicates that severely retarded individuals can profit from being provided with error-free experiences in the early stages of learning (O'Brien, 1978). These children are especially in need of prompt and systematic feedback and encouragement. They will also profit from concrete evidence of progress, which can sometimes be provided by charting the child's progress. They need to proceed in small steps, closely related sequences, and with frequent reviews. They need concrete materials; for example, making change rather than learning arithmetic as abstract processes.

CURRICULAR MODIFICATIONS AND GOALS

A survey of the goals of education for the mildly mentally retarded shows the following most commonly listed: (1) basic academic skills, (2) personal and social competence, and (3) occupational skills. Obviously, these goals are not unique; they are equally appropriate for the nonretarded. However, some modifications of curricular requirements must be made for the retarded. This has usually taken one of three forms. One is for the retarded to follow the regular curriculum, simply taking longer to finish. The retarded make slower progress, take longer to attain the same levels of competence as their normal classmates, and finish at a lower level. A second modification is to follow a simplified form of the regular curriculum. This may make it possible for the mentally retarded to pass from grade to grade in step with the nonretarded but to achieve at a lower level. Both of these plans teach essentially the same things to both retarded and nonretarded but at different levels of difficulty and achievement or at different rates.

A third common curricular change is in terms of the relative emphasis given to the various goals. Sometimes the curriculum for the mentally retarded has placed greater emphasis on personal and occupational skills and less on academic skills. Since the mentally retarded are relatively much better in acquiring motor and social skills, the curriculum places greater emphasis on the arts and crafts, industrial arts and homemaking. Since these children can succeed more frequently in these areas, they find them more satisfying. Teachers often use these areas as approaches to the more academic skills. Since most of the mentally retarded will not go on to higher education and prepare for the professions, they are more often prepared to enter the job market out of high school. More vocational courses are taken in school and the children are placed in work-study programs which will facilitate their transition from school to work.

Modified programs pose more problems for teachers of the mainstreamed mentally retarded than they did for teachers of self-contained special classes. The resource teachers will probably have to be responsible for providing the occupational orientation and the work-study programs while the regular teacher remains responsible for the more conventional academic subject matter.

Mainstreaming will pose fewer problems at the junior and senior high school levels than in the elementary grades. The mentally retarded have always been partly mainstreamed in high school. They have already taken some classes with the nonretarded and have had a special teacher for other classes. The special education teacher has also usually been responsible for counseling students, supervising their work-study programs, and assisting them with their work in the regular classes.

ACADEMIC EXPECTANCY

The mildly mentally retarded group is considered *educable*. If the instruction is appropriate and the atmosphere for learning is adequate, these people can be expected to acquire academic skills ranging in level from the second to the fifth or sixth grade. Their maximum academic achievement can be expected to be equal that of the average seven- to ten-year-old child. The mentally retarded child should not be expected to attain this level of accomplishment at the same chronological age as normal children since the mental growth rate is not the same for mentally retarded children as it is for normal ones. The normal child of eleven has a mental age of eleven, whereas the mildly mentally retarded child of eleven has a mental age of seven. This is the conventional age for first or second graders, and in all probability the retarded child will be ready to do first or second grade work by the age of ten or eleven.

The academic progress of a group of 163 children with a median IQ of 60.6 who were admitted to special classes at the age of twelve years and seven months yields what are probably typical data for academic progress (Phelps, 1956). Most of these people left school at sixteen, with work certificates, or at eighteen, without them. The median time spent in the class was three years and four months. A small percentage (2.5) graduated from the eighth grade, and a still smaller percentage (1.2) from junior high school. The median reading grade level on leaving school was 3.9, and the median arithmetic grade level was 4.3. The median age of 12.7, when they were admitted to the special classes, may seem rather high, but it is likely that many of them were not mature enough to have profited much from academic instruction before that age.

MAINSTREAMING THE MENTALLY RETARDED

The mainstreaming or normalization trends discussed in Chapter 5 have focused primarily on the mildly mentally retarded—the educable. Since the first special schools and classes were established in the United States, segregated facilities have been the most popular settings for educating the mildly mentally retarded. However, during the past decade, discontent with segregated facilities has increased and a variety of alternatives have been developed. One focus of this discontent was the "over-representation" of disadvantaged minority children in classes for the mentally retarded. Militant minorities brought pressure on state and local educational agencies to remedy the situation. The courts also played a major role in the "decertification" of minority children previously classified as mentally retarded. These developments, a variety of intertwined political and ethical issues, as well as the deinstitutionalization trend already under way, have led to a widespread movement to provide the most "normalizing" and least restrictive educational programs possible for all the handicapped. This movement is bolstered by a wide array of legal precedents, moral mandates, and philosophical arguments.

THE MORE SEVERELY RETARDED

Many of the problems centering on social attitudes and programs for the mentally retarded arise from the tendency of many people to perceive the mentally retarded as a single homogeneous group. Increasing recognition of the great diversity of the category is evidenced by the misgivings being expressed over the consequences of deinstitutionalizing and/or mainstreaming the severely handicapped.

IDENTIFICATION

The identification of the more severely mentally retarded is comparatively easy as compared with the mildly retarded. Those who belong to one of the many "clinical types" are usually recognized relatively early because of their accompanying physical characteristics or marked behavioral differences. In addition to identifying physical characteristics, these children are usually markedly slow in behavioral development. Difficulties in sucking, slowness in sitting up, creeping, crawling, walking, and talking are almost universal.

Parents, friends, and relatives note these deviations and express concern. Finally, if formal testing seems called for, many developmental scales and adaptive behavior inventories can be used to indicate the breadth and degree of retardation. Although conventional developmental scales are very poor predictors of later intellectual functioning for normal children, they have been found to be quite valid in identifying severely mentally retarded children (DuBose, 1976).

These same scales and inventories can also be used to plan training and educational programs and to indicate progress. Several curricula have been developed which provide a series of objectives and goals together with detailed developmental sequences for children with various degrees of retardation (Johnson and Werner, 1975).

Most of the "clinical types" of mental retardation, which are typically characterized by distinctive patterns of physical symptoms, are severe mental retardation. The causes or accompaniments of severe mental retardation consist, in most cases, of organic brain injury, endocrinological and biochemical deviations of either genetic or environmental origin, and single pathogenic genes.

A tremendous number of such clinical types have been identified. An Atlas published in 1968 listed 166 Mental Retardation Syndromes (Gellis and Feingold, 1968). Undoubtedly, many more are known today. We shall mention and characterize briefly a few of the more common syndromes.

SOME GENETIC SYNDROMES

CHROMOSOMAL ABERRATION

Down's syndrome (mongolism) Mongolism constitutes the largest single clinical category of the severely mentally retarded. From 10 to 20 percent of severely retarded children are of this type. In many cases, from a fourth to a third of the students in the classes for severely mentally retarded are mongoloids. Approximately 1 in every 600 to 900 live babies is a mongoloid. The incidence of mongoloid births varies markedly with the age of the mother: 1 in 1,500 for mothers between fifteen and twenty-four years; 1 in 1,000 for mothers between twenty-five and thirty-four; 1 in 150 for mothers over thirty-five; 1 in 70 for mothers forty to forty-four; and 1 in 38 for mothers over forty-five. Even though young mothers run relatively little risk of having a mongoloid child, 1 in every 4 is born to a mother under thirty. This discrepancy between relative incidence and total number occurs because so many more children are born to younger mothers (Koch and de la Cruz, 1975).

More than fifty physical signs have been listed as characteristic of mongolism. The problem is that none of these stigmata is peculiar to mongoloids, and no single sign is found in all of them. In addition, some of these characteristics do not appear until the child is several years old, while others disappear with aging (Falk and others, 1973). D. Gibson, L. Pozony, and D. E. Zarfas (1964), by applying standards of age stability and assessment reliability, have reduced the number of significant diagnostic signs to the following thirteen: (1) a flattened skull which is shorter than it is wide; (2) abnormally upturned nostrils caused by undeveloped nasal bones; (3) abnormal toe spacing (increased space, particularly between the first and second toes); (4) disproportionate shortness of the fifth finger; (5) a fifth finger which curves inward; (6) a fifth finger which has only one crease instead of the usual two; (7) short and squared hands; (8) epicanthic fold at the inner corners of the eye; (9) large fissured tongue; (10) a single crease across the palm of the hand (simian crease); (11) abnormally "simplified" ear; (12) adherent ear lobule; and (13) abnormal heart.

J. E. Wallin (1949) considers the presence of three or more of these physical anomalies to be indicative of mongolism. If four or more of these anomalies are present, the individual is almost certainly a mongoloid. Despite considerable variability in the individual identifying characteristics, the overall physical impression in mongolism is usually one of striking similarity.

While rare cases with borderline intelligence have been reported, most mongoloids are severely mentally retarded. The mean IQ for various groups is in the 20 to 40 range.

As we indicated earlier, mongolism was first demonstrated to involve a chromosomal abnormality in 1959. Since then, three principal types of chromosomal deviations have been identified in mongolism:

1. A trisomy of chromosome number 21 resulting from *nondisjunction*. This is a genetic disorder but not an inherited one. This type is rarely familial. It is the form most commonly born to older mothers.

2. A *translocation* of a chromosome involving the attachment of an extra number 21 chromosome onto another (usually number 15). This type is familial and occurs in the children of younger parents.

3. A rare chromosomal anomaly in mongolism is known as *mosaicism*. The range of symptoms, including mental level, varies greatly in this condition.

There is evidence that individuals in the three chromosomal sub-categories of mongolism differ in learning ability, mental level, and temperament, as well as in certain biochemical characteristics (Koch and de la Cruz, 1975).

Since the discovery of the chromosomal abnormality in mongolism a large number of chromosomal deviations have been identified. It is estimated that 1 percent of people have such chromosomal deviations. Apparently most chromosomal abnormalities result in early embryonic death. Studies of aborted embryos indicate that approximately one-third display chromosomal aberrations (Bloom, 1970). At least 6.5 percent of newborns possess major chromosome abnormalities sufficient to impair their effectiveness in society (Lubs and Ruddle, 1970).

Samples of amniotic fluid containing cells from the developing fetus can be taken during the first twelve to sixteen weeks of pregnancy to detect chromosomal abnormalities. Translocations of chromosomes in "carrier" parents can also be detected by cytogenic study of suspected individuals. A mother who carries the appropriate chromosomal translocation for mongolism has a 33 percent chance of having a mongol child.

METABOLIC DISORDERS

By 1976 some 150 inborn metabolic disorders had been identified. Nervous system damage and mental retardation occur in many of these (Brady, 1976). Biochemical causes of mental retardation may involve abnormal carbohydrate metabolism or storage, anomalies of protein (amino acid) metabolism or excretion, and similar defects involving lipoid material (fats).

protein metabolism *Phenylketonuria* (PKU) was the first of the metabolic disorders shown to cause mental retardation. It is the result of a single-gene-determined defect of amino acid metabolism. The genetic anomaly produces a deficiency of the liver enzyme which normally catalyzes the breakdown of the amino acid phenylalanine to tyrosine. In this condition, phenylalanine accumulates and is eventually metabolized by an alternate pathway, producing *ketonuria,* the characteristic excretion in the urine of above-average amounts of phenylketones. Approximately 60 percent of untreated PKU children have IQs under 20, more than 80 percent have IQs below 40, while a few are average or above in intelligence. Behavior syndromes similar to those of untreated PKU children have been produced in monkeys by feeding them high levels of phenylalanine from birth to three to six months of age (Chamove, Waisman, and Harlow, 1970).

Phenylketonuria is caused by a single recessive gene, although carriers of the defective gene can be detected. Tests of the blood and urine can detect the condition, and if a diet low in phenylalanine is instituted early enough, development apparently can be normal. Some states now require routine testing of infants for this condition.

metabolism of fats The best-known group of related conditions involving abnormal lipoid metabolism is *amaurotic familial idiocy*. Various forms of this condition have been given different names, depending primarily on the age of onset. The infantile form (Tay-Sachs disease) has an early onset and progresses rapidly. It is characterized by progressive spastic paralysis, blindness, convulsions, and death by the third year. Juvenile forms have a later onset (three to ten years), with mental deterioration and death within ten to fifteen years. A single recessive gene seems to be the primary cause of this condition (Pampeglione, Privett, and Harden, 1974).

MENTAL RETARDATION RESULTING FROM ENDOCRINE DISTURBANCES

cretinism Cretinism is the best-known disorder of endocrine function resulting in mental retardation. Cretinism results from insufficiency of thyroid, which causes irreversible damage to the central nervous system. There is evidence that a fetus suffering from insufficient thyroid may sustain such brain damage prenatally (Lawson, 1955). Cretinism can be either genetic or environmental in origin. The endemic type of cretinism is the result of an iodine-deficient diet and occurs in geographic regions in which the soil, water, and vegetation are deficient in iodine. Cretinism of this type can be prevented by iodine supplements to the diet. Using iodized salt is one way of accomplishing this. Most sporadic cretinism is not genetic.

However, there are at least three separate genetic types of cretinism. All involve recessive genes which seem to interfere with the different enzyme systems of the body involved in the synthesis and secretion of thyroxin. The degree of mental retardation is roughly proportional to the extent of hypothyroidism.

The complex physical syndrome of cretinism involves physical dwarfism and marked delay in bone development, muscular flaccidity, and a shuffling and waddling gait. The head is large, extremities are short and fat, and the fingers are square at the ends. The neck is short and thick, the skin is dry and scaly, the tongue is thick, and the abdomen protrudes. Basal metabolism and blood pressure are both low. The typical cretin is placid, inactive, apathetic, and severely mentally retarded.

Early identification and immediate and properly controlled thyroid medication can prevent the more severe symptoms. In most cases the physical symptoms can be prevented by thyroid treatment, but normal intelligence is seldom attained. Intellectual and physical impairment are generally more severe in the endemic and sporadic forms of cretinism, which are of environmental origin, than in the genetic types. Cretins of the genetic type practically always have goiters, indicating the presence of some thyroid tissue. The genetic types also have not suffered from thyroid deficiency *in utero,* because the normal mother supplies the needs of the fetus.

SYNDROMES OF EXOGENOUS ORIGIN COMMONLY ASSOCIATED WITH SEVERE MENTAL RETARDATION

HYDROCEPHALY

Hydrocephaly (water on the brain) consists of an excessive accumulation of cerebrospinal fluid either in the ventricles of the brain (internal hydrocephalus) or on the outside of the brain in the subarachnoid space (the external form). If the internal form develops before the bones of the skull have fused, the head gradually enlarges, sometimes attaining tremendous size. The extreme conditions of hydrocephalus produce various sensory, motor, and intellectual symptoms, of which mental retardation is one. If the excessive accumulations of fluid develop after the cranial bones are mature and the sutures have fully ossified, enlargement of the head cannot occur, but pressure builds up inside the brain. This pressure produces a thinning of the neural tissue, with resulting motor disability, including paralysis and convulsions, mental deterioration, and eventual death if the condition is progressive.

The mentality of hydrocephalics ranges all the way from low-grade idiocy to superior intelligence. A slight degree of hydrocephaly, if arrested, may be consistent with normal or superior mentality. One of the authors has studied two individuals who, as children, showed pathological head expansion with all of the classical symptoms of hydrocephalus. In neither of these children did the condition progress to a point where any mental effects were noticeable. At maturity, both had test scores comparable to their normal siblings, and the only residual symptoms were poor motor coordination of a nonspecific, generalized sort—including poor articulation. At the other extreme are the severely affected, progressive cases which end up in hospitals and institutions as severely retarded, helpless individuals whose life span is typically short.

Several operative procedures have been developed for early correction of the defect, and treatment with drugs has met with some success. Hydrocephaly is often associated with myelomeningocele, a congenital cleft of the spinal column with spinal cord in protrusion.

CEREBRAL PALSY

Cerebral palsy may occasionally be of genetic origin, but it is usually caused by environmental factors. It is characterized by disturbances of motor function due to brain damage. Cerebral palsy is by far the most common single syndrome associated with severe mental retardation of exogenous origin. Estimates of the total number of cases are in the hundreds of thousands, with an estimated ten thousand new cases added each year (Bailey, 1958). While not all of these are mentally retarded, a sizable percentage are. Since cerebral palsy always involves motor disabilities, this condition is discussed in a later chapter on the orthopedically handicapped.

BRAIN INFECTIONS

Severe mental retardation may be caused by brain infections. Meningitis, encephalitis, and syphilitic brain infections can all result in mental retardation. Untreated syphilitic brain infection is progressive (except for remissions), with a wide variety of physical, personality, and intellectual accompaniments. There is nothing unique about mental defect of syphilitic origin, and with modern methods of treatment syphilis has become a minor cause of mental retardation.

meningitis Meningitis usually responds to modern antibiotics and seldom causes severe mental subnormality. Defects of vision and hearing are probably caused by meningitis more often than is severe mental retardation. One follow-up study of thirty-seven cases of neonatal meningitis showed ten to be apparently normal. The others all had obvious abnormalities of vision, hearing, speech, and motor processes, and intelligence levels below normal (Fitzhardinge, Kazemi, and Stern, 1974).

encephalitis Encephalitis more often results in permanent brain damage and mental retardation than do syphilis and meningitis. Mental deterioration and other postencephalitic effects may follow immediately after the acute attack or they may appear several years later. These chronic effects either remain stationary or become progressively worse.

Paradoxically, the severity of the delayed aftereffects is not closely related to the severity of the acute attack. In fact, many times the symptoms and immunity reactions of postencephalitis develop in the absence of any recognized acute attack.

Postencephalitic symptoms include a large number of motor disorders and character and personality changes, as well as general mental deterioration. The motor symptoms include all of those found in cerebral palsy—paralysis, muscular rigidity, tremors, tic, athetoid and choreiform movements, and the Parkinsonian syndrome. The latter syndrome is said to develop in about 20 percent of postencephalitics. Parkinsonism includes the expressionless, immobile, masklike face, tremors, a stiff and eventually stooped posture, and propulsive gait. Hydrocephalus, epilepsy, and deafness are infrequent sequelae. The incidence of serious aftereffects varies from 10 to 40 percent.

Personality and intellectual changes are more likely to develop when the encephalitis is contracted in infancy or early childhood (DeJong, 1959). In fact, it has been claimed that no child who has encephalitis before the age of three ever escapes some intellectual deficit. About half of the postencephalitics are reported as suffering some mental deficit when encephalitis was contracted before age fourteen. Behavioral and personality changes include increased emotional instability, hyperactivity, sleep reversals, impulsiveness of action, and even psychosis. Some 20 percent are reported to develop psychotic symptoms.

There have been few well-controlled studies of the extent of mental deterioration or arrested intellectual development in postencephalitics. Enough case studies have been reported to indicate that the term *arrested mental development* can appropriately be applied to some of these cases. The mental deficit resulting from encephalitis ranges all the way from no apparent decline to complete arrest or even marked deterioration (Fitzhardinge, Kazemi, and Stern, 1974).

In one survey of ten studies, mean IQs ranged from 73 to 91 and individual scores ranged all the way from low-grade custodial to superior (Pintner, Eisenson, and Stanton, 1940). One study reports a deficit of 16 IQ points in a group of postencephalitic children as compared with their normal siblings (Dawson and Conn, 1926). There seems to be a tendency for the intelligence level to decline in successive testings. The prognosis for postencephalitics is not very good (Brown, Jenkins, and Cisler, 1940).

EDUCATIONAL PROGRAMS FOR THE TRAINABLE (MODERATELY RETARDED)

Since it is expected that most of the trainable mentally retarded will be dependent or semidependent all their lives, the objectives of their school programs are limited. In general terms, their training programs are devised to develop self-help skills, socialization, and elementary oral language.

The self-help skills include independent eating, dressing, toileting, washing, combing hair, brushing teeth, and using a handkerchief. The children are taught to follow directions and to perform simple tasks. In the area of social skills, the children are taught consideration for others (for example, taking turns), common courtesy, and obedience. A good deal of basic sensory and motor training is provided to improve sensory discrimination and develop motor skills. Such household skills as dusting, sweeping, setting and clearing the table, washing and drying dishes, washing and ironing, sewing, elementary homemaking, using common tools, telephoning, and limited traveling in familiar areas are also taught. Considerable time is spent on the development of oral language. Health and safety rules are also taught. The major purposes of these classes are to develop the children's ability to look after themselves and to perform simple tasks about the home or the immediate neighborhood.

Follow-up studies of students after they leave the special classes for the trainable indicate that the outcomes are extremely varied. Practically none of the studies included control or comparison groups of children who did not attend such classes. These studies indicate that, in the years immediately following the termination of their school attendance, about one-fourth of the children are ultimately institutionalized and most of the others live under supervision at home. Interviews with parents indicate that they believe the school programs have been a help in reducing the child's dependency on the family.

One follow-up study of 120 graduates of classes for the trainable mentally retarded found that, when these individuals were nineteen to twenty-one years of age, 94 percent were living at home with their families. About half (48 percent) were in special workshop programs earning less than ten dollars a week for full-time work. The remaining 52 percent were not involved in any work or rehabilitation programs. The parents' stated principal reasons for their children's noninvolvement were the extent of the individual's handicap (50 percent), transportation difficulties (30 percent), and lack of proper post-school programs (20 percent). The parents reported that 94 percent of the handicapped individuals could care for their personal needs. Twenty-three percent of the parents felt confident in leaving their handicapped child for extended periods of time, 56 percent had reservations, and the rest would not leave them. Ninety percent of the children had specific responsibilities for household chores in their homes, 60 percent were independently mobile within the immediate neighborhood, but only 10 percent left their neighborhoods to travel alone. Forty percent never went beyond the front yard of their homes (Stanfield, 1973).

The sheltered workshops have demonstrated that some of the trainable mentally retarded can be productively employed. N. O'Connor and J. Tizard (1956) have provided some optimistic reports of success attained by boys of this mental level in factory work, following systematic on-the-job training. There is some evidence that Great Britain and certain other European countries are more successful with their work programs, which are oriented toward industrial production, than is the United States, which uses a more educational, mental-hygiene, and social-learning approach (O'Connor and Tizard, 1956).

M. W. Gold (1973) has shown that severely mentally retarded persons can be successfully trained to perform simple workshop tasks using conventional operant conditioning procedures. The tasks were broken down into elementary components, and each component, in turn, was taught using modeling and operant reinforcements, both physical and verbal.

A study of the work characteristics of mentally retarded adults in workshop-like situations has shown that: (1) productivity is significantly related to IQ; (2) an IQ of 20 constituted an approximate limit below which such work is not practical; and (3) tolerance for work is positively related to intellectual level, with the most retarded showing the greatest work decrement from boredom and fatigue (Tobias and Gorelick, 1963).

ACADEMIC ACHIEVEMENTS OF THE MODERATELY RETARDED

The educational term *trainable,* applied to this range of mental retardation, defines this population as uneducable in terms of academic skills. However, using highly structured learning situations, proper programming, and consistent reinforcements, academic skills of a relatively low order can be achieved by individuals in this category. Sight vocabulary words, limited reading, writing, counting, making change, and telling time have all been successfully taught to adult trainable subjects. Studies have shown that after five years of academic instruction such persons were able to read simple material and perform simple arithmetic calculations. However, many teachers of such children felt that these slight gains were obtained at a very high cost in terms of time and money and were only minimally useful in the lives of these people (Hirshoren and Burton, 1979). On the other hand, since academic skills are so highly valued, academic instruction will probably continue to be provided to the trainable mentally retarded. Parental demands for higher levels of performance and pressure to normalize these subjects will require that academic instruction be provided. Of course, the ultimate justification for teaching academics must not be simply that it is possible to do so. Rather, the extent to which this learning contributes to the individual's ability to function effectively in society, as compared with the personal, social, and job skills that might be taught instead, measures the program's worth. There is no way of determining whether the price paid in time required and the usefulness of these academic skills justifies formal educational programs for these people.

CUSTODIAL TREATMENT

Until recently, the only alternatives open to parents of the custodial-level mentally retarded child were home care and institutionalization. Day hospitals, day care centers, and boarding or nursing homes are now also becoming alternatives. Public and private residential institutions still take care of the largest group of those profoundly mentally retarded who live outside their own homes.

A 1965 survey of state institutions for the mentally retarded in the United States showed that approximately 192,000 people were residing in such institutions. Table 8–4 shows the resident populations, classified according to degree of retardation.

The data in Table 8–4 indicate that the resident population is pre-

Table 8–4

DISTRIBUTION OF INSTITUTIONAL RESIDENTS ACCORDING TO DEGREE OF MENTAL RETARDATION, COMPARED TO ESTIMATED PREVALENCE (192,493 CASES)

degree of retardation	IQ	percentage of residents	estimated percentage prevalence
Profound	Below 20	27	1.4
Severe	20–35	33 ⎫	6.0
Moderate	36–50	22 ⎭	
Mild	51–67	13	92.6*
Borderline	68–83	5	

*IQs of 50 to 70.
Data from Scheerenberger (1965), and Dingman and Tarjan (1960).

dominantly of the lower mental levels. Eighty-two percent are classified as having IQs below 50, whereas this group represents only 7.4 percent of the estimated total number of mentally retarded. This means that the below-50 IQ group contributes to the resident population between eleven and twelve times its proportional numbers, whereas the above-50 IQ category contributes only 15 percent of its proportional numbers. If we extrapolate from these data and obtain 464,000 as the approximate number of individuals in the United States with IQs below 50 in 1965, and 157,800 as the resident population, only about one-third of the total number were in public institutions for the mentally retarded. Since public institutions house about 90 to 95 percent of the total institutionalized population in the United States, almost two-thirds of this group reside at home. The proportion residing in boarding homes and other similar facilities until recently has been negligible.

THE ROLE OF THE RESIDENTIAL INSTITUTION

In the last ten years, emphasis on the residential institution as the place to take care of the bulk of the mentally retarded has declined. Several developments have contributed to this trend. One, as previously indicated, was the recognition that segregation was not the solution to the problem of mental defectiveness. Another was the increasing cost of institutional care and the practical impossibility of obtaining funds sufficient to provide institutions for any large percentage of the mentally handicapped. It was also recognized that the large residential institution was not the best place to provide care and training for most of the mentally retarded. It is estimated that only about 4 percent of the mentally retarded were ever institutionalized (McCarver and Craig, 1974).

Advances in medicine, as well as social changes, have contributed to the change in the makeup of our institutional population. Medical ad-

vances now keep alive many low-grade mental defectives who would earlier have died. For example, the death rate in New York State institutions
for the mentally retarded decreased from 34.9 per thousand in 1926 to
13.5 per thousand in 1944. Coupled with this decline in death rate are an
increase in the proportion of first admissions in the lower mental level
and a reduction in the age of first admissions. These three factors (increased longevity, reduced admission age, and increasing proportions of
admissions from the lower mental level requiring life-long custodial care)
all combined to give the institutions a predominantly static, custodial, resident population. As a result, the days of trying to provide institutionalization for the bulk of the mentally retarded have passed. The legally-
mandated "least restrictive environment" for the handicapped will limit
institutionalization more and more to a last resort.

However, the total role of residential institutions for the mentally retarded has changed only slightly. As a matter of fact, the deinstitutionalization movement has had relatively little effect on the number of institutionalized mentally retarded in America. The recommendation of the
National Research Council Committee that the large custodial institutions
for the handicapped be abolished, as mentioned in Chapter 5, has been
only partly realized so far as the mentally retarded are concerned.
Whereas the drop in psychiatric hospital populations during the twenty-
year period from 1955 to 1975 was 65 percent, the decline in the mentally retarded population was only about 13 percent (Conroy, 1977). The
big change has been in the number and size of the public institutions. In
the fifteen-year period between 1960 and 1975 the number of institutions
increased from 100 to 250 while the median resident capacity *decreased*
from about 1,000 for institutions built before 1964 to 200 for institutions
built after that date. What has been achieved is the construction of many
smaller institutions and a corresponding reduction of overcrowding in
the older, larger institutions. The total number of institutionalized retarded has changed only slightly, but many residents are now housed in
newer, smaller institutions.

An analysis of population changes in institutions for the mentally retarded shows that over the past two decades institutional releases have increased. However, the number of *readmissions* has also risen dramatically,
largely offsetting the high release rates. This suggests that public and political pressures to get people out of institutions for the retarded have not
been matched by corresponding equally adequate normalizing community services (Conroy, 1977).

Residential institutions have always ranged in quality from humane
treatment centers to warehouses with large resident populations simply
vegetating. As a result of several factors already mentioned, many institutions are modifying their physical environments and programs to make
them more rehabilitation-oriented and "normalizing."

In the writer's experience, many parents have vigorously resisted efforts to deinstitutionalize their children. Their reasons are varied but the most commonly mentioned factors are the availability of resident physicians, skilled nursing care, hospitals, dieticians, and physical therapists in the large institutions. Parents also feel that the institutionalized individuals are assured of life-long care by a permanent staff. Residence with their own parents or relatives, foster families, community residential facilities (halfway houses, group homes, hostels, board-and-care houses, and so forth), nursing homes, and local hospitals is likely to be temporary. Changes in family situations, changes in the needs of the children, as well as the closing of local facilities may necessitate frequent changes in the placement of the handicapped individual. While many of these local facilities may be very good, the mere physical placement of persons in smaller community facilities does not assure the individuals of superior services. Many parents prefer the certainties of permanent residential life-long care for their severely handicapped children to the uncertainties of community-based programs.

Almost from their inception, institutions have made widespread use of patients for the performance of many routine tasks involved in institutional management and upkeep. The performance of such tasks was labeled "work therapy," the patients received little or no pay, and total institutional costs were considerably reduced. However, such peonage was formally outlawed in state hospitals as the result of a 1974 United States District Court ruling in *Souder* v. *Brennan,* which directed institutions to pay all patient-workers minimum wages or at least a portion of the minimum wage contingent upon their productivity (Scharr, 1975). The result of this ruling is that many institutions eliminated "work therapy" jobs altogether and replaced patient help with outside employees. This trend, together with court-mandated improvements in physical facilities and levels of treatment which have resulted from the "right to treatment" lawsuits, have markedly increased institutional costs. Since the financial situation of most state mental health institutions has always been bleak, the additional financial burdens may contribute to their decline.

TRAINING THE CUSTODIAL MENTALLY RETARDED

The conditioning methods that have been used to study learning in the lower animals have also been applied with some success to the training of the low-level custodial mentally retarded. N. R. Ellis (1962, 1963) developed a theoretical analysis of how toilet training could be accomplished using regular operant procedures. M. Dayan (1964) later reported some success with the method. P. Roos (1965) has described an "intensive habit-training unit" established to apply these methods systematically to the training of the profoundly mentally retarded. G. J. Bensberg (1965) has reported considerable success with these methods.

The methods vary from simple toilet training, in which each person was placed on the commode every two hours and was rewarded each time he eliminated while he was on the commode (Dayan, 1964), to the development of many self-care habits by a systematic rewarding of successive approximations to the desired behavior called "behavior shaping" (Bensberg, 1965). N. H. Azrin (1973) has described in detail a procedure which successfully toilet trained ten profoundly mentally retarded individuals in three days.

In the latter methods, simple verbal directions and appropriate gestures were used as cues, and successive approximations of the desired behavior were immediately rewarded. At first food (pieces of cookies and candy) was used. The food reward was always preceded or accompanied by a social reward (such as saying "good boy" or patting the head). As learning progressed, the social rewards were continued but the food was gradually withheld until longer units of behavior occurred and closer approximations to the desired response were attained. Finally the edible rewards were discontinued and only the social rewards were used.

These studies indicate that the principles of operant conditioning can be successfully applied to the low-level custodial mentally retarded. These methods can be used by regular institutional personnel after instruction in behavior-shaping methods (Bensberg, 1965). Studies indicate that intensive training programs can significantly improve the functional levels of the severely retarded. For example, whereas under routine institutional care only 16 percent of the severely retarded improved their ambulatory skills in a three-year follow-up period, 50 percent of those included in an intensive special program did so. Comparable improvement was obtained from toilet training (Tarjan and others, 1973).

DIVERSITY AMONG THE MENTALLY RETARDED

Mental retardation is not a disease, although diseases may accompany or cause it. It is not a unitary thing. Etiologically it is many things and has a bewildering array of causes. Its physical accompaniments are either many and diverse or practically nil, depending upon the etiological type and the level of retardation. The personalities and temperaments of the mentally retarded are almost as diverse as are those of groups of the population at large. Even when the mentally retarded are placed in so-called homogeneous groups for educational purposes, tremendous scholastic differences still exist within these classes. The mentally retarded are a heterogeneous group who are identified, and to some degree segregated and given special consideration because of one characteristic—inadequate adaptive behavior resulting from impairment of intellectual functioning.

When people ask, "What are mentally retarded people like?" they are asking a meaningless question. They would not ask, "What are short or fat people like?" Most people would agree that about the only thing such physically deviant individuals have in common is their diminutive stature or their obesity. While being mentally retarded has more widespread behavioral consequences than being short or being fat, the similarities between mental retardates and intellectually normal people exceed their differences. The mentally retarded are almost as statistically variable and individually distinctive as are people whose intelligence is within the normal range.

SUMMARY

The causes of mental retardation are both hereditary and environmental. A few rare types of mental retardation are caused by a single dominant gene. A larger number of types apparently are due to a single recessive gene. Chromosomal anomalies account for certain types of mental retardation. The hereditary components of the ordinary "familial," or nonclinical, class of mentally retarded are multifactorial or polygenetic and interact with environmental factors.

Environmental causes of mental retardation are prenatal physical trauma, nutritional or toxic infections, blood incompatibility, and radioactivity. Natal causes include prematurity, asphyxia, and physical trauma. Postnatal causes are physical trauma, infections, dietary and extreme sensory deprivation, or general environmental deprivation.

Mental retardation is not a unitary thing. It is not a disease. It has diverse causes and physical accompaniments and embraces a wide range of mental levels.

The exact extent of mental retardation is not known. If a purely psychometric criterion is used—IQs below 70—we arrive at a figure of about six million. However, if we use the combined standard of an IQ below 70 and an equally low relative level of adaptive behavior, the figure obtained is closer to two or three million. Between 80 and 90 percent of these are mildly retarded. An additional one-fifth of the school population is probably sufficiently educationally handicapped to require special consideration.

The mentally retarded are generally found to be under par in physical health and stature. Their life span is shorter and their death rate higher than those of the normal population.

Currently, most mildly mentally retarded school children are either being returned to or retained in regular classes. If these mainstreaming programs are successful in meeting the special needs of these children, the mentally retarded as an educational category may disappear. The educational needs of mentally retarded children as well as of children with "learning disabilities" (to be discussed in Chapter 9) are different only in degree from those of "normal" children, and may likewise be taken care of by more individualized, diagnostic-prescriptive teaching.

Most individuals with IQs below 50 and correspondingly low levels of adaptive behavior are *moderately, severely* or *profoundly* mentally retarded, according to the AAMD classification, and are either *trainable* mentally retarded or *custodial*, in educational terminology. The bulk of the "clinical types" of mentally retarded, the single-gene-determined cases, and most of the more severely environmentally damaged (the exogenous mentally retarded) also fall into these categories.

The genetic syndromes are the result of either chromosomal aberrations or pathogenic single genes. Mongolism (Down's syndrome) is the most common type of chromosomal anomaly accompanying mental retardation. Three subtypes of mongolism are differentiated in terms of the chromosomal mechanism involved.

Biochemical anomalies caused by single genes with accompanying mental retardation may affect carbohydrate, protein, or lipoid (fat) metabolism. Phenylketonuria—a failure to properly metabolize phenylalanine (one of the amino acids which is a constituent of most proteins); and amaurotic familial idiocy—involving abnormal lipoid metabolism, are representative of these conditions. Specific dietary restrictions, if instituted sufficiently early in life, can prevent the physical stigmata and mental retardation characteristic of certain types of untreated cases.

Familial cretinism is a form of severe physical and mental retardation resulting from insufficient thyroid. Cretinism can be of either genetic or environmental origin. Untreated cretins display a characteristic physical syndrome and are severely mentally retarded. Most cretinism can be prevented by early and continued administration of supplementary thyroid extract.

Hydrocephaly (water on the brain) is a syndrome which is usually environmentally caused. The most common cause is an obstruction in the ventricular system of the brain which prevents the normal circulation of the cerebrospinal fluid. The abnormal accumulation of cerebrospinal fluid produces an enlarged head, atrophy of brain tissue, and mental retardation. Some cases can be treated surgically.

Severe mental retardation may accompany or be caused by cerebral palsy and brain infections. General familial and cultural deprivation is not considered an important cause of severe mental retardation, since the familial-cultural background of this type is fairly typical of that of the general population.

The bulk of the severely mentally retarded are cared for in residential institutions, special classes, and at home. A relatively small number work in sheltered workshops and under close supervision in industry. Some are taken care of in boarding homes, halfway houses, and day care centers. Even the low-level custodial mentally retarded can be trained if appropriate methods are employed.

We cannot solve the problem of educational retardation by redefining and de-labeling children. There is always the danger that reclassifying the "misclassified" may simply exclude them from needed services. The immediate task is to design and provide services appropriate to each child's needs. An intermediate goal is the early identification of vulnerable children in order to assist them by early intervention to attain adequate levels of independent living.

Developmental deficits arise from many sources, many of which are deeply imbedded in social values and institutions. Long-range approaches include research and preventative programs centering on the basic organic and psychological causes of retardation. Such programs must focus on the elimination of the "environment of poverty" as one of the root causes of both the socio-psychological and the medical-organic categories of mental retardation.

REFERENCES

Arvey, R. D., "Some Comments on Culture Fair Tests," *Personnel Psychology,* 1972, *25,* 433–48.

Ashurst, D. L. and C. E. Meyers, "Social System and Clinical Model in School Identification of the Educable Mentally Retarded," in G. Tarjan, R. K. Eyman, and C. E. Myers, eds., *Sociobehavioral Studies in Mental Retardation* (Washington, D. C.: American Association on Mental Retardation, 1973).

Azrin, N. H., "On Toilet Training the Severely and Profoundly Retarded," *Journal of Research and Training,* 1973, *1,* 9–13.

Bailey, C. J., "Interrelationships of Asphyxia Neonatorium, Cerebral Palsy, and Mental Retardation: Present Status of the Problem," in W. F. Windle, ed., *Neurological and Psychological Deficits of Asphyxia Neonatorium* (Springfield, Ill.: Charles C Thomas, 1958).

Barnes, E. J., "IQ Testing and Minority School Children: Imperatives for Change," *Journal of Non-White Concerns in Personnel and Guidance,* 1973, *2,* 4–20.

Bensberg, G. J., "Teaching the Profoundly Retarded Self-help Activities by Behavior Shaping Techniques," *American Journal of Mental Deficiency,* 1965, *69,* 674–79.

Bloom, S. E., "Trisomy—3—4 and Triploidy (3A—ZZZW) in Chick Embryos," *Science,* 1970, *170,* 457–58.

Brady, R. Q., "Inherited Metabolic Diseases of the Nervous System," *Science,* 1976, *193,* 733–39.

Brewer, G. D. and J. S. Kakalek, *Handicapped Children: Strategies for Improving Services* (New York: McGraw-Hill, 1979).

Brown, A. W., R. W. Jenkins, and L. E. Cisler, "Influence of Lethargic

Encephalitis on the Intelligence of Children as Determined by Objective Tests," *American Journal of Diseases of Children,* 1940, *59,* 238–54.

Bruininks, R. H., "Physical and Motor Development of Retarded Persons," in N. R. Ellis, ed., *International Review of Research in Mental Retardation* (New York: Academic Press, 1974).

Caveness, W., "Epidemiologic Studies in Head Injury," in C. A. Angle and E. A. Bering, Jr., eds., *Physical Trauma as an Etiological Agent in Mental Retardation* (Washington, D. C.: U. S. Department of Health, Education and Welfare, 1970).

Chamove, A. S., H. Waisman, and H. F. Harlow, "Abnormal Social Behavior in Phenylketonuric Monkeys," *Journal of Abnormal Psychology,* 1970, *76,* 62–68.

Clarke, A. D. B. and A. M. Clarke, "Pseudofeeblemindedness: Some Implications," *American Journal of Mental Deficiency,* 1955, *59,* 507–9.

Conroy, J. W., "Trends in Deinstitutionalization of the Mentally Retarded," *Mental Retardation,* 1977, *15*(4), 44–46.

Dawson, S. and J. C. Conn, "Effects of Encephalitis Lethargica on the Intelligence of Children" Archives of Diseases in Children," 1926, *1,* 357–89.

Dayan, M., "Toilet Training Retarded Children in a State Residential Institution," *Mental Retardation,* 1964, *2,* 116–17.

DeJong, R. N., *"Diseases of the Nervous System"* in D. A. Rytard and W. P. Greger, eds. Annual Review of Medicine (Palo Alto, Ca., Annual Reviews, 1959).

Dingman, H. F. and G. Tarjan, "Mental Retardation and the Normal Probability Distribution Curve," *American Journal of Mental Deficiency,* 1960, *64,* 991–94.

Doll, E. A., *The Vineland Social Maturity Scale: Revised Condensed Manual of Direction* (Vineland, N. J.: Training School, 1936).

Doll, E. A., "The Essentials of an Inclusive Concept of Mental Deficiency," *American Journal of Mental Deficiency,* 1941, *46,* 214–19.

Dorfman, A., ed., *Antenatal Diagnosis* (Chicago: University of Chicago Press, 1972).

Du Bose, R. F., "Predictive Value of Infant Intelligence Scales with Multiply Handicapped Children," *American Journal of Mental Deficiency,* 1976, *81,* 388–90.

Dybwad, G., "Basic Legal Aspects in Providing Medical, Educational, Social, and Vocational Help to the Mentally Retarded," *Journal of Special Education,* 1973, *7,* 39–51.

Ellis, N. R., "Amount of Reward and Operant Behavior in Mental Defectives," *American Journal of Mental Deficiency,* 1962, *66,* 595–99.

Ellis, N. R., "Toilet Training the Severely Defective Patient: An S-R Reinforcement Analysis," *American Journal of Mental Deficiency*, 1963, *68*, 98–103.

Falk, R. E., R. E. Carrel, M. Valente, B. F. Crandall, and R. S. Sparkes, "Partial Trisomy of Chromosome: II. A Case Report," *American Journal of Mental Deficiency*, 1973, 77, 383–88.

Fitzhardinge, P. M., M. Kazemi, and L. Stern, "Long-term Sequelae of Neonatal Meningitis," *Developmental Medicine and Child Neurology*, 1974, *16*, 3–10.

Gellis, S. S. and M. Feingold, *Atlas of Mental Retardation Syndromes*, (Washington, D. C.: U. S. Government Printing Office, 1968).

Gibson, D., "Karyotype Variation and Behavior in Down's Syndrome," *American Journal of Mental Deficiency*, 1973, *78*, 128–33.

Gibson, D., L. Pozony, and D. E. Zarfas, "Dimensions of Mongolism: II. The Interaction of Clinical Indices," American Journal of Mental Deficiency, 1964, *608*, 503–10.

Gold, M. W., "Research on the Vocational Rehabilitation of the Retarded," in N. R. Ellis, ed., *International Review of Research in Mental Retardation*, vol. 6 (New York: Academic Press, 1973).

Golomb, C. and T. Barr-Grossman, "Representational development of the human figure in familial retardates," *Genetic Psychology Monographs*, 1977, *95*, 247–60.

Granat, K. and S. Granat, "Below-average Intelligence and Mental Retardation," *American Journal of Mental Deficiency*, 1973, *78*, 27–32.

Grossman, H. J., ed., *Manual of Terminology and Classification in Mental Retardation* (Baltimore: American Association on Mental Deficiency Special Publication Series, No. 2, 1977).

Gunzburg, H. C., *Social Competence and Mental Handicap* (London: Bailliere Tindal, and Fox, 1973).

Halpern, A. S., "General Unemployment and Vocational Opportunities for EMR Individuals," *American Journal of Mental Deficiency*, 1973, *78*, 123–27.

Hearnshaw, L. S., *Cyril Burt, Psychologist* (Ithaca, N. Y.: Cornell University Press, 1979).

Hirshoren, A. and T. A. Burton, "Teaching Academic Skills to Trainable Mentally Retarded Children: A Study in Tautology," *Mental Retardation*, 1979, *17*, 177–79.

Hobbs, N., *The Futures of Children* (San Francisco: Jossey-Bass, 1975).

Hurst, J. F., "The Meaning and Use of Difference Scores Obtained Between the Performance on the Stanford-Binet Intelligence Scale and the Vineland Social Maturity Scale," *Journal of Clinical Psychology*, 1962, *18*, 153–60.

Jarman, R. F., "Patterns of Cognitive Ability in Retarded Children: A

Reexamination," *American Journal of Mental Deficiency*, 1978, *82*, 344–48.

Jensen, A. R., *Educability and Group Differences* (New York: Harper and Row, 1973).

Jensen, A. R., "How Biased are Culturally-Loaded Tests?" *Genetic Psychology Monographs*, 1975, *91*, 281–98.

Johnson, V. M. and R. A. Werner, *A Step-By-Step Learning Guide for Retarded Infants and Children* (Syracuse, N. Y.: Syracuse University Press, 1975).

Jones, H. E., "Environmental Influences on Mental Development," in L. Carmichael, ed., *Manual of Child Psychology* (New York: John Wiley, 1946).

Koch, R. and F. de la Cruz, eds., *Down's Syndrome (Mongolism): Research, Prevention, and Management* (New York: Brunner/Mazel, 1975).

Lawson, D., "On the Prognosis in Cretinism," *Archives of Diseases in Childhood*, 1955, *30*, 75.

Leland, H., "Adaptive Behavior and Mentally Retarded Behavior," in R. K. Eyman, C. E. Meyers, and G. Tarjan, eds., *Sociobehavioral Studies in Mental Retardation* (Washington, D. C.: American Association on Mental Deficiency, 1974).

Lemkau, P. C., C. Tietze, and M. Casper, "Mental Hygiene Problems in an Urban District: Third Paper," *Mental Hygiene*, 1942, *26*, 275–88.

Liese, J. E. and H. A. Lerch, "Physical Fitness and Intelligence in TMR's," *Mental Retardation*, 1974, *12*(5), 50–51.

Lilienfeld, A. A., *Epidemiology of Mongolism* (Baltimore: Johns Hopkins Press, 1968).

Lubs, H. A. and F. H. Ruddle, "Chromosomal Abnormalities in the Human Population," *Science*, 1970, *189*, 495–97.

Malone, D. R. and W. P. Christian, Jr., "Adaptive Behavior Scale as a Screening Measure for Special Education Placement," *American Journal of Mental Deficiency*, 1974, *79*, 367–71.

McCarver, R. B. and E. M. Craig, "Placement of the Retarded in the Community," in N. R. Ellis, ed., *International Review of Research in Mental Retardation*, vol. 7 (New York: Academic Press, 1974).

McCusick, V. A., *Mendelian Inheritance in Man: Catalog of Antosomal Dominant, Antosomal Recessive, and X-linked Phenotypes* (Sec. Ed.) (Baltimore: Johns Hopkins Press, 1979).

Mercer, J. R., "The Myth of 3% Prevalence," in G. Tarjan, R. K. Eyman, and C. E. Meyers, eds., *Sociobehavioral Studies of Mental Retardation* (Washington, D. C.: American Association on Mental Deficiency, 1973).

Mercier, C., *Sanity and Insanity* (London: Walter Scott, 1890).

Nihira, K., "Importance of Environmental Demands in the Measurement of Adaptive Behavior," in G. Tarjan, R. K. Eyman and C. E. Meyers, eds., *Sociobehavioral Studies in Mental Retardation* (Washington, D. C.: American Association on Mental Retardation, 1973).

O'Brien, F., "An Error-Free, Quick, and Enjoyed Strategy for Teaching Multiple Discriminations to Severely Delayed Students," *Mental Retardation*, 1978, *16*(4), 291–94.

O'Connor, N. and J. Tizard, *The Social Problem of Mental Deficiency* (New York: Pergamon Press, 1956).

O'Hanlon, G. S., "An Investigation into the Relationship Between Fertility and Intelligence," *British Journal of Educational Psychology*, 1940, *10*, 196–211.

Pampeglione, G., G. Privett, and A. Harden, "Tay-Sachs Disease: Neurophysiological Studies in 20 Children," *Developmental Medicine and Child Neurology*, 1974, *16*, 201–8.

Peterson, J., *Early Conceptions and Tests of Intelligence* (Chicago: World Book, 1925).

Phelps, H. R., "Post-school Adjustment of Mentally Retarded Children in Selected Ohio Cities," *Exceptional Children*, 1956, *23*, 58–62.

Pinter, R., J. Eisenson, and N. Stanton, *The Psychology of the Physically Handicapped* (New York: Appleton-Century-Crofts, 1940).

Plummer, G., "Anomalies Occurring in Children Exposed in Utero to the Atomic Bomb in Hiroshima," *Pediatrics*, 1952, *10*, 687–93.

Reynolds, M. C. and J. W. Birch, *Teaching Exceptional Children in all America's Schools*, (Reston, Va.: The Council for Exceptional Children, 1977).

Rice, B., "Brave New World of Intelligence Testing," *Psychology Today*, Sept. 1979, *13*(4), 26–41.

Robinson, H. B. and N. M. Robinson, *The Mentally Retarded Child*, 2nd ed. (New York: McGraw-Hill, 1976).

Roos, P., "Development of an Intensive Habit-training Unit at Austin State School," *Mental Retardation*, 1965, *3*, 12–15.

Rotatori, A., D. Cullinan, M. H. Epstein, and J. Lloyd, "Cognitive Tempo in Mentally Retarded Children," *The Journal of Psychology*, 1978, *99*, 135–37.

Scharr, K., "Minimum Wage Regs Pose Problems," *APA Monitor*, March 1975, *6*(3), 10–11.

Schachter, M., J. A. Rice, H. G. Cormier, P. M. Christensen, and N. J. James, "A Process for Individual Program Planning Based on the Adaptive Behavior Scale," *Mental Retardation*, 1978, *16*(3), 259–63.

Scheerenberger, R. C., "The Current Census of State Institutions for the Mentally Retarded," *Mental Retardation*, 1965, *3*, 3–6.

Stanburg, J. B., *The Metabolic Basis of Inherited Disease* (New York: McGraw-Hill, 1960).

Stanfield, J. S., "Graduation: What Happens to the Retarded Child When He Grows Up," *Exceptional Children,* 1973, *39,* 548–52.

Tarjan, G., S. W. Wright, R. K. Eyman, and C. V. Keeran, "Natural History of Mental Retardation," *American Journal of Mental Deficiency,* 1973, *77,* 369–79.

Tobias, J. and J. Gorelick, "Work Characteristics of Adults at Trainable Level," *Mental Retardation,* 1963, *1,* 338–44.

Tredgold, A. F., *Mental Deficiency* (London: Balliere, Tindall and Cox, 1908).

Wallin, J. E., *Children with Mental and Physical Handicaps* (Englewood Cliffs, N. J.: Prentice-Hall, 1949).

Weisz, J. R. and E. Zigler, "Cognitive Development in Retarded and Non-Retarded Persons: Piagetian Tests of the Similar Sequence Hypothesis," *Psychological Bulletin,* 1979, *86,* 831–51.

Williams, R. I., *Black Intelligence Test of Cultural Homogenity* (St. Louis, Mo.: Williams and Associates, 1973).

Williams, R. I., "Black Pride, Academic Relevance, and Individual Achievement," in R. W. Tyler and R. M. Wolf, eds., *Crucial Issues in Testing* (Berkeley, Calif.: McCutchan Publishing Corp., 1974).

SUGGESTIONS FOR STUDENTS AND INSTRUCTORS

1. Attend a meeting of the local Association for Retarded Citizens or other parent group concerned with the mentally retarded.

2. Visit a local workshop for the mentally retarded.

3. Make a survey of local programs for the mentally retarded.

4. Have a representative of the local vocational rehabilitation facility discuss their program for the mentally retarded.

5. Discuss: "The degree of severity of mental retardation is more significant than is its formal identification."

6. Discuss: "It would be possible to bring about a 50 percent reduction in the incidence of mental retardation if high priority were given to implementing what is known about its prevention."

ADDITIONAL READINGS

Ingalls, R., *Mental Retardation: The Changing Outlook* (Somerset, N. J.: John Wiley and Sons, Inc., 1978). A general text providing a good survey of the biological, psychological, social, and educational problems of the mentally retarded.

Bialer, I. and M. Sternlicht, eds., *The Psychology of Mental Retardation: Issues and Approaches* (New York: Psychological Dimensions, Inc., 1977). A group of experts discuss critically the important issues of mental retardation; comprehensive coverage.

Fotheringham, J. B. and M. Morrison, *Prevention of Mental Retardation* (Toronto, Canada: National Institute on Mental Retardation, 1976). Considers some 200 causes of mental retardation and possible preventive measures.

SELECTED FILMS

A Family of Friends. (26 minutes) Richfield Productions, 8006 Takoma Avenue, Silver Springs, Md. 20910. Depicts the life of seven members of a group home for the retarded.

A Way Out of the Wilderness. (24 minutes) National Audiovisual Center, General Service Administration, Washington, D. C. 20409. The care and training of mentally retarded children at two institutions.

ORGANIZATIONS AND AGENCIES

American Association on Mental Deficiency
5201 Connecticut Avenue, N.W.
Washington, D. C. 20015

Mental Retardation Association of America
211 East Third South, Suite 212
Salt Lake City, Utah 84111

National Association for Retarded Citizens
2709 Avenue E East
Arlington, Tex. 76011

National Association of Private Residential Facilities
for the Mentally Retarded
6269 Leesburg Pike
Falls Church, Va. 22044

CHAPTER 9

LEARNING DISABILITIES

When referred to the resource room Patrick was repeating the third grade and had not learned to read or spell except for a few two-letter words and his own name. Despite his severe learning difficulties, Patrick was still trying to function in a regular classroom with no auxiliary services. However, behind a calm exterior, Patrick was a discouraged and confused boy. His teachers had attempted most of the well-known methods of teaching reading (phonics, phonic-linguistics, look-and-say, language-experience, and Fernald word-tracing) without success.

Testing revealed that Patrick had normal scholastic aptitude. However, he had both auditory and visual perception problems. These included poor sound discrimination, limited figure-ground differentiation, and confused directionality. It was decided that Patrick needed a multisensory reading method that would provide considerable repetition and, if possible, produce rather immediate positive results. A highly structured, sequential introduction of a limited number of words taken from the context of high interest stories would be used.

Patrick was very interested in horses. Consequently, stories about horses were selected from highly illustrated preprimers. The industrial arts instructor devised a simple word imprinting technique for presenting words visually and tactile on cards, and aurally on tape recordings. The tapes contained not only the words selected for study, but also recordings of the entire lessons.

The first lesson consisted of four words taken from the first preprimer lesson and embossed on separate cards. This lesson went somewhat as follows:

1. Seeing and saying the word. The word was both seen and said in imitation of the teacher. "This is the word *ride*. Now you say it." Patrick says, "ride," and moves his finger along under the word in imitation of the teacher. The teacher says, "Fine."

2. Emphasizing word meaning. "Have you ever gone for a ride?" "Yes, I can ride a horse and I also ride my bike." "Fine! Now, look at the word again and read it." Patrick points to the word and says, "Ride."

3. Developing visual and tactile awareness of word configurations. "Look at the word *ride* again. Notice that the first two letters are even, then it goes up for the *d* and down for the *e*. Let's trace around the word with our fingers, saying it as we go." Patrick traces the letters of the word and reads the letters simultaneously. The teacher says, "Fine."

4. Picturing the word. "Now Patrick, look at the word *ride* carefully, then close your eyes and picture in your mind how it looks and feels when you ride a horse. Tell me what you see." "I see myself riding my black pony." "Fine. Now write the word *ride* in the air. That's good."

This procedure took only about ten minutes for four words. The entire lesson was tape-recorded. Patrick was returned to his classroom with his word cards, tape recorder, and headset. He was instructed to listen to the recordings as many times as needed to learn the four words.

The next day Patrick returned to the resource room and was able to both spell and read all four words quickly and confidently. By the end of the week he was able to read the first story in the preprimer which contained the words he had learned individually. Patrick was enthusiastic and wanted more! He was instructed to record new words in the resource room and then practice both in his classroom and at home. Patrick's mother followed up the school lessons by helping him practice his reading.

In the first four weeks Patrick learned thirty-nine new words. This was more than he had accomplished in three years of formal schooling. Appropriately designed learning experiences, based on an analysis of the child's cognitive assets and limitations, enabled this child eventually to perform reasonably normally. Patrick is now in the seventh grade. He reads with good comprehension and enjoyment and is satisfied with his progress (adapted from Carbo, 1978).

There is still a great diversity of opinions concerning the nature and causes of learning disabilities. The validity and usefulness of the category itself is questioned. These uncertainties are matched by the puzzling nature of the disabilities themselves. Children designated as learning disabled typically have strengths as well as weaknesses, and one may obscure the other. They may not be able to read and write, but may speak fluently. They may be unable to read directions but yet can put together and operate complicated model airplanes. They may be able to perform mathematical calculations but be unable to read word problems. Often, although they are unable to read simple words, their scholastic aptitudes, as indicated by test performances, are normal or superior. This discrepancy between educational performance and scholastic aptitude is the most commonly used defining characteristic of the learning disabled.

The typical learning disabled child is a puzzle to him or herself as well as to teachers. Teachers are frustrated because, in a situation where most children learn, this child who is not physically handicapped, emotionally impaired, or mentally retarded does not learn certain things. These children, who may be otherwise gifted and highly talented, cannot learn to read simple words. Learning disabled children may be socially adept and athletically talented. They may even learn to speak a second language or to sing songs but be unable to learn to spell common words or read simple prose. Since these children are intelligent and capable in many ways, people often attribute their learning problems to lack of motivation or to emotional problems. For no apparent reason they fail to learn to read, and because of this failure often experience years of frustration, self-depreciation, and emotional distress. Many more boys than girls have learning disabilities—ratios range from two to one or ten to one, depending on the study. There does seem to be a tendency for learning disabilities to follow certain family lines. A disproportionate number of children in this category are slow in acquiring language. Estimates of the total number of school children with learning disabilities range from 2 to 10 percent.

Historically, and to a degree today, two general approaches are taken to learning disabilities. One assumes a neurological deficit to be the basic cause of the disorder. Many treatment programs have been based on this assumption. The second is a behavioral or education-based approach, assuming that whatever the causes, the problem is primarily the child's failure to learn—an educational problem—and the solution is to find a way to make learning possible for him or her—an educational solution.

HISTORICAL ORIGINS

The Straussian Legacy

The category of learning disabilities as known today has developed out of the concept of the "brain-damaged child," formulated by Alfred A. Strauss and Heinz Werner during their association of more than a decade at a Michigan institution for the mentally retarded then known as the Wayne County Training School. Heinz Werner, a developmental and comparative psychologist, and Alfred A. Strauss, a neuropsychiatrist, both refugees from Nazi Germany, worked together at this school for approximately thirteen years studying the impact of brain injury on the behavior and psychological development of children. Strauss and Werner differentiated the endogenous (largely genetic) from the exogenous (largely brain-damaged) mentally retarded and focused their attention on the latter.

The behavioral symptoms alleged to characterize the minimally brain-damaged child, which came to be known as the Strauss syndrome, had the following principal components: perceptual disorders, perseveration and distractibility, thinking and conceptual disorders, and motor disorders—especially awkwardness, hyperactivity, and disinhibition. These components have been expanded, subdivided, and made more specific but still form the core of the behavioral characteristics of children with "learning disabilities."

Early Work on Dyslexia and Aphasia

Strauss paid relatively little attention to linguistic defects in his characterizations of the brain-injured child. However, the professional literature in the fields of speech, hearing, and neurology had long associated certain linguistic and other types of symbolic representational impairment with brain injury. An impressive list of formidable-sounding terms had been coined to refer to a wide variety of linguistic defects associated with brain injury. These included aphasia and dyslexia. *Aphasia* refers to an impairment of language functions due to brain injury. *Dyslexia* refers to a neurogenic reading disability. The symptoms of dyslexia, in addition to the defining inability to read, include difficulties in writing and spelling, memory disorders, inadequate auditory and visual imagery, deviant motor behavior patterns, and other signs of neurological disturbances.

dyslexia—a
case study

"I seemed to have trouble from the first day of school. I just couldn't make sense out of the material given me to read. I could see the words. I learned to recognize individual letters, but some-

how, I was never able to put them together to spell words or to recognize the words or sentences written on the board or printed in
books. I hated school! I didn't want to go to school. I was sure that
I was dumb. Just plain dumb!

"Even in the third grade I couldn't read at all—even my own
name. I don't blame my teachers. Neither they, nor anyone else,
understood my problem. My teachers would be encouraging. 'Come
on, you know the word, try hard!' But I didn't know the word no
matter how hard I tried. I was sure I was just stupid. The other kids
would make fun of me. That was awful, for if there was anything I
wanted more than being able to read, it was to have friends and be
accepted. When I made 'three wishes,' being able to read was always
second to having the kids like me."

The concept of dyslexia has undergone essentially the same changes
as that of "learning disabilities," and dyslexia is now usually considered a
subclassification of this category. The disorder was originally defined as
a specific linguistic disability of organic origin. Then, because its organic
basis could seldom be independently verified, dyslexia came to be defined
as a behavioral syndrome which was assumed to be the result of a postulated, but not demonstrated, neural impairment. Because many emotionally disturbed and environmentally disadvantaged children showed symptoms indistinguishable from those of dyslectic individuals with demonstrated
brain damage, dyslexia came to be considered not a specific disease entity
but a behavioral syndrome which can result from a number of different
factors, both organic and functional. The concept came to be divorced
from etiology (Marshall and Newcombe, 1973).

BEHAVIORAL TESTS FOR THE IDENTIFICATION OF THE NEUROLOGICALLY IMPAIRED

Strauss and others characterized the behavior patterns of the brain-
damaged child and suggested that when the behavior of a given child *re-
sembles that of diagnosed neurologically impaired children,* the child can be presumed to be brain-damaged even though the medical history is negative
and no positive neurological signs are present. Such a proposal opened
the way for the development of purely behavioral tests for the identification of children of this type. Several tests for the identification of the
brain damaged were developed in the 1930s and 1940s.

It remained for L. Bender (1946) to make available a simple and easily administered test which, while not claiming to be limited in purpose to
the identification of the neurologically impaired, came to be used predominantly for this purpose. The Bender-Gestalt test made use of nine
designs previously developed by K. N. Wertheimer (1923) to demonstrate

the principles of Gestalt psychology involved in perception. Bender postulated that the perception and reproduction of the Gestalt figures are determined by organic factors dependent on the growth patterns and maturational level of the individual and on neurological impairment, either functionally or organically induced.

These tests were important in themselves, but they also contributed significantly to the notion that the neurologically impaired constituted a fairly distinct category of people with differentiating behavioral characteristics. The existence of such tests also indicated that brain-damaged individuals can be differentiated from "normals." The educational program described by Strauss and L. Lehtinen (1947) was specifically designed to remedy the perceptual, cognitive, and behavioral limitations of this category of handicapped children. The category of the brain-injured child thus became, even under its original exponents, a broad, elastic category including children with neurological impairment demonstrated by positive neurological signs as well as those with perceptual and conceptual difficulties with no evidence of brain damage but which were assumed to be the result of a postulated neural impairment. The reasoning behind these assumptions seemed to be as follows: since some children with brain injury show certain perceptual, cognitive, and behavioral characteristics, those children with these same characteristics can be assumed to be brain-damaged.

THE DIVORCE OF THE CATEGORY OF
LEARNING DISABILITIES FROM ETIOLOGY

Skeptics have long insisted that children with functional emotional disturbances display many components of the Strauss syndrome. More recently, a large number of "culturally disadvantaged" children have also been shown to have deficiencies in perceptual discrimination, concept formation, and sustained attention and are hyperactive and emotionally labile, much like the diagnosed brain-damaged. Critics have argued convincingly that these behavioral symptoms do not necessarily indicate central nervous system damage.

Many people today believe that there will be no loss if the concept of presumed neurological impairment as an intervening variable is dropped and each child's particular perceptual, cognitive, and motor deficits and assets are described or defined so that appropriate psycho-educational programming can be developed for him or her. Irrespective of etiology, the critical problem is to determine the individual's areas of relative strength and handicap and then to capitalize on the strengths and remove, diminish, or circumvent the deficits so that the child's intellectual and behavioral functioning may reach the optimal practical level.

THE NEED FOR A NEW CATEGORY

Since the 1940s it has been generally accepted by educators, school psychologists, psychiatrists, and neurologists that there is a group of children of normal or superior intelligence who fail to learn because of neurogenic learning disabilities. These children have been variously characterized as minimally brain-damaged, chronic brain syndrome, minimal brain dysfunction, or psychoneurological learning disabilities. However, paralleling these organically-oriented designations, a corresponding set of *behavioral* terms has been used to identify these groups of children. Dyslexia (marked impairment of the ability to read), dysgraphia (inability to express ideas in written form) and perceptual handicap, difficulties in figure-ground differentiation, and letter and number reversals in reading and writing (poor form recognition) are behavioral syndromes presumably associated with cerebral dysfunction. Although originally the correlation of behavior syndromes and neural impairments was assumed, the evidence supporting this assumption was always tenuous. It soon became clear that: (a) many children with known brain damage do not exhibit the patterns of behavior presumably characteristic of the brain-damaged child; (b) many children exhibiting these behavior patterns do not show independent signs of neurological impairment; (c) most of the behavior characteristics ascribed to the brain-damaged are common manifestations of emotional and presumably functional psychiatric disorders, so these behavior syndromes can arise from *either* functional or organic causes; (d) attaching the qualifying adjective *minimal* to the term *brain damage* does not increase the appropriateness of the organically-oriented designation; (e) there is little to be gained by postulating the existence of nondemonstrable neurological impairment to account for the observed behavioral deficits.

In the early 1960s the term *learning disabilities* began to appear regularly as a substitute for "brain injured." This term referred to behavior rather than to etiology. Although the new term still carried the implications of brain damage, it seemed more logical to call children who displayed symptoms similar to those with certain neurological impairments learning disabled rather than brain-damaged. Although originally the term *learning disability* became the educational alternative to the etiological category of minimal brain dysfunction, there is an increasing tendency to divorce it from etiology and define it entirely in behavioral and educational terms (Hobbs, 1975).

THE SUDDEN POPULARITY OF THE CONCEPT

Before the 1960s the term *learning disabilities*, if used at all in special education, referred in a generic way to all children who were educationally handicapped for whatever reason. In the early 1960s the term began appearing with regularity largely as a substitute for *minimally brain-injured.* Within a few years the acceptance of the term *learning disabilities* by people in the field of special education was widespread. In the early 1960s the term *learning disorders* competed with learning disabilities for acceptance. In 1965 J. Hellmuth published *Learning Disorders,* volume one. The following year the *Review of Educational Research* for the first time reviewed the topic of "Learning Disorders" (Bateman, 1966). The 1969 review of the same area is titled "Learning Disabilities" (Kass, 1969). At the 1965 annual convention of the Council for Exceptional Children, the topic of learning disabilities was second only to mental retardation in the number of sessions and papers dealing with it. The entire December 1964 issue of *Exceptional Children* was devoted to the topic of learning disabilities. In 1965, when the local and state organizations of parents of minimally brain-damaged children formed a national organization, they adopted the name "National Association for Children with Learning Disabilities," and by 1969 they had over two hundred local and state affiliates (McCarthy, 1969). In 1968 the first issue of the *Journal of Learning Disabilities* appeared. During the 1970s the literature on the topic has continued to multiply (Tarnopol, 1974).

LEGAL RECOGNITION OF THE CATEGORY

Early in the 1960s the state legislatures began recognizing the category and started providing additional financial aid for programs so designated. California began providing such state aid in 1963. The designation used for the programs in that state is *educationally handicapped* (EH). What happened in California is probably typical of what happened elsewhere. The California Association for Neurologically Handicapped Children, consisting largely of the parents of minimally brain-damaged children, sponsored and obtained passage of a bill in the state legislature providing special state aid for the establishment of special classes for such children. A 1968 national survey of programs for children with learning disabilities found that over half of the programs were started largely as the result of the activities of parent pressure groups (Clark and Richards, 1968). Since the differentiation between the neurologically handicapped and the emotionally disturbed is not easily made, the authorized programs for the educationally handicapped in California included both categories. California may be unique in the use of the term *educationally handicapped* to refer to this group which, by code, includes both the emotionally disturbed and the neurologically handicapped as etiological categories in the same classes. National legislative recognition for the educational category was first given when HR13310, the Children with Learning Disability Act of 1969, passed the U.S. House of Representatives by a roll call of 350 to 0. The bill provided $6 million for the fiscal year 1971, $12 million for 1972, and $18 million for 1973 to support research, training programs, model centers, and demonstration programs in the area. By 1967 over thirty-five states were reported to have legislation providing financial assistance to school districts for the development and support of special classes or programs for children described as educationally handicapped, perceptually handicapped, neurologically impaired, minimally brain-damaged, and/or emotionally disturbed (Blom, 1969). All such children are now being encompassed within the category of learning disabilities. By the 1970s no area of special education was receiving as much attention as that of learning disabilities. However, some doubts about the usefulness of the category were being expressed (Hobbs, 1975). In 1975 PL 94-170 included the learning disabled among the handicapped for whom special education services were required.

DEFINITIONS AND DELINEATIONS

The distinguishing behavioral characteristics of the category of neurologically impaired children—described by Strauss as *brain-injured,* later known as *Strauss-syndrome children,* and known still later as *children with learning disabilities*—were hyperactivity, distractibility, disinhibition, and perseveration. Educational measures proposed to overcome or compensate for these behavioral disturbances or deficits included spacious rooms to accommodate small groups of children without crowding, bare walls with all extraneous sights eliminated, translucent rather than transparent windows, screens to hide extraneous objects, and sound-absorbent walls and ceilings to reduce distracting sounds. Masking screens for printed matter, which permitted only one line of print to be seen at one time, were used to reduce the distracting effects from the rest of the page. The significant figures in visual material were darkly outlined to aid in the differentiation of figure and ground, in accordance with the principles of Gestalt psychology.

Strauss mentioned the necessity of directed and controlled motor activity to reduce the disinhibition and diffuse hyperactivity. However, it remained for N. C. Kephart (1960) and R. H. Barsch (1965) to develop educational programs which centered primarily on motor activities. Drill was kept to a minimum because of the tendency of these children to perseverate. The teaching of rhythm was recommended. Speech training was required but should be done by specialists.

The Strauss-Lehtinen program and concepts set the patterns and, with shifts in emphasis, still dominates thinking and practice in the field. Some programs for the neurologically impaired or Strauss-syndrome child were established during the 1940s and 1950s, but it was not until the next decade, as already indicated, that the concept really came into its own. Several developments made the period of the 1960s propitious for this great surge of interest. One was the enlarging of the category.

DEFINITIONS

In 1967 the Association for Children with Learning Disabilities adopted the following definition:

> *A child with learning disabilities is one with adequate mental ability, sensory processes, and emotional stability who has a limited number of specific deficits in perceptual, integrative, or expressive processes which severely impair learning efficiency. This includes children who have central nervous system dysfunction which is expressed primarily in impaired learning efficiency.*

The following year, the National Advisory Committee to the Bureau of Education for the Handicapped, Office of Education, formulated the following definition, which provided the basis for the subsequent Children with Specific Learning Disabilities Act of 1969:

> *Children with special learning disabilities exhibit a disorder in one or more of the basic psychological processes involved in understanding or in using spoken or written language. These may be manifested in disorders of listening, thinking, talking, reading, writing, spelling, or arithmetic. They include conditions which have been referred to as perceptual handicaps, brain injury, minimal brain dysfunction, dyslexia, developmental aphasia, etc. They do not include learning problems which are due primarily to visual, hearing, or motor handicaps, to mental retardation, emotional disturbance or to environmental disadvantage. Essentially this same definition is included in PL 94–142.*

Except for the exclusionary provisions, such a concept is divorced from etiology and is characterized largely by a significant educational discrepancy between the individual's capacity for learning and his or her actual functional level. Such a definition will include a sizable group of children in need of special assistance who have previously been denied such help because they failed to meet the specifications of the older conventional categories of exceptional individuals eligible for special aid.

TAKING CARE OF ONE CATEGORY OF "LEFT-OVER" CHILDREN

Educators, psychologists, psychiatrists, and pediatricians, as well as parents, have long recognized that there is a group of children of average or above average intelligence who fail to actualize their potential in school learning. Such children have been a source of puzzlement and frustration to all concerned. They all demonstrate a failure to learn despite apparently adequate intellectual abilities, sensory acuity, and educational opportunities. These are the children who are referred from service to service and from agency to agency in the hope of finding a conventional category for special educational or rehabilitative service where they "fit" and can receive help. The psychologist finds that they are not mentally retarded, the psychiatrist can find no evidence of emotional blockings or other serious disturbance, the neurologist finds no evidence of neural impairment, the internist's findings are negative, and the child is handed back to the regular classroom teachers and/or parents with the admonition, "I guess it is your problem." One reason for the tremendous popularity of the category *learning disabilities* is that a large number of people were waiting in the wings who were eligible and anxious to take advantage of the help that such an additional service offered. It promised to reduce the total number of "left-over" children in need of special help. N. Hobbs (1975) refers to learning disabilities as a catch-all category. Cruickshank (1972) states that some forty terms have been used to describe the conditions encompassed by the category.

THE EDUCATIONAL APPEAL OF THE TERM

Another reason for the popularity of the term and concept of learning disabilities derives from the implications of the term itself. The term and category are educationally oriented. Most of the conventional groupings of children for rehabilitative and special educational purposes have derived from medical and psychological rather than from primarily educational sources. For the most part, quantitative medical, psychological, and legal definitions and criteria have been used in defining and establishing eligibility requirements for educational services. In many cases these criteria and definitions are not maximally useful for identifying educational needs. This often results in interpreting eligibility criteria loosely or strictly and otherwise stretching or redefining terms to make them educationally relevant. This means that many children may be legally and administratively eligible for programs which they do not need while others more in need of the special services are deprived of them because they do not fit the category and are therefore ineligible. The trend toward mainstreaming and noncategorical funding will mitigate this problem.

If the category of learning disabilities can be divorced from etiology, special education is freed from the limitations of the "medical model," which is probably no more appropriate for special education than it is for mental health.

The term *learning disability* implies diagnosis that is primarily educational and remediation that is teacher-learner oriented. The term also suggests a program of positive action: appropriate teaching. It does not suggest an inherent and largely static condition, as does the term *mental retardation.* The name contains a plea for good teaching based on the child's specific needs.

The term is relatively nonstigmatizing, designates a specific deficit in children who are essentially normal, and focuses attention on identifying the child's specific needs and applying appropriate remedial procedures rather than becoming excessively concerned with etiology and proper labeling. Hobbs (1975) says that for cosmetic reasons, it is a "nice" term to have around.

Because the same people are intimately involved in both processes, identification and classification will be more closely tied to the corrective, remedial, educative process. A continuing study and analysis of the child's classroom behavior and learning assets and deficits is crucial in the identification of and response to remedial procedures. Rehabilitative efforts become part of a continuous diagnostic, evaluative process. Diagnosis is concerned with identifying the areas of educational deficit, and response to the proposed educational procedures becomes an integral part of the diagnostic and classifying procedures.

The concept and category of learning disabilities will not break down the rigid artificial barriers between the categories of exceptional individuals for whom special services are provided, nor will they entirely divorce special education from its medical and psychological roots and its excessive concern with formal diagnosis and defining etiologies. Nevertheless, it does constitute a major step in this direction. The broad category of learning disabilities will assist in providing a full circle of services for all who need them. It constitutes a move in the direction of providing a comprehensive, integrated program extending over the entire range of deviants in need of special services and covering the entire age range.

EDUCATIONAL PROGRAMS
FOR CHILDREN WITH LEARNING DISABILITIES

The training and educational techniques involved and the rationale for most of the programs designed for children with learning disabilities are either derived or extrapolated from Strauss and Lehtinen (1947) (McCarthy & McCarthy, 1969; Tarnopol, 1974). The programs are specifically designed to remedy or diminish behavioral deficits arising from the characteristics of such children, presumed to be caused by their postulated, but often nondemonstrable, neural impairment. Breaking down and adding to the original list of the behavioral characteristics provided by Strauss, researchers and writers in the field have listed almost a hundred specific behaviors. J. J. McCarthy and J. F. McCarthy (1969) list the eight most frequently cited:

1. hyperactivity

2. perceptual-motor deficits

3. emotional liability

4. general orientation and laterality defects

5. disorders of attention, such as distractibility and short attention span

6. impulsivity

7. disorders of memory and conceptual thinking

8. specific learning defects, particularly language deficits.

These are the deficits we associate today with learning disabilities.

THE STRAUSS-LEHTINEN-CRUICKSHANK PERCEPTUAL-MOTOR PROGRAM

We have already indicated that the Strauss-Lehtinen conceptualization of the brain-damaged child and their development of a program of education for these children provided the basis for the programs associated today with learning disabilities.

Cruickshank, one of the original group of workers with Werner and Strauss, has written extensively and developed a program of his own which largely follows the Strauss-Lehtinen proposals. Cruickshank (1975a) emphasizes that individuation of instruction is essential to an appropriate educational program. This requires a small teacher–student ratio. Even with a relatively homogeneous group, a full-time teacher and teacher's aide should have no more than eight children. The major element which must be incorporated into the educational programs for brain-injured children is "structure," and many of the details of methods consist of ways in which structure can be used in the training and education of the child. The various components of structure identified by Cruickshank are relationship structure, environmental structure, program structure, and structured teaching material. Motor training is also an essential part of the program.

relationship structure Relationship structure refers to the personal relationship between teacher and child. A satisfactory relationship requires that the teacher understand the child sufficiently well to deal with him or her in ways that will maximize the child's development. Properly structured personal relationships are the basis from which all other structuring emanates. If this relationship is satisfactory the child eventually identifies with the teacher, internalizes goals, and strives to live up to the teacher's expectations. Cruickshank believes that this can best be achieved in a structured teaching situation—an adult-dominated teaching situation. Such a situation is not dominated in the sense of being constricted, but dominated in terms of carefully planned procedures based on the unique needs and nature of the individual child. The adult is the most significant element in the entire concept of structure, and too much emphasis cannot be placed on the nature of this personal relationship. Essential elements incorporated into this child–teacher relationship are: (a) Limits must be set for appropriate behavior. The child must know just what is and what is not acceptable behavior. (b) Within these limitations the teacher must accept the child and his or her behavior at all times in terms of the meaning of the situation to the child. (c) The final essential is that of consistency of attitude and behavior on the part of the teacher.

environmental structure The classroom must be a nonstimulating and nondistracting environment. This is achieved by removing as many visually and auditorily distracting stimuli as possible. Walls, woodwork, and furniture are all painted the same color. No bulletin boards or pictures are on the walls. Indirect lighting or translucent rather than transparent window glass is used. Wall-to-wall carpeting and sound-treated walls and ceilings are used to reduce extraneous sounds.

Individual cubicles for each child are recommended. The sound-deadened cubicle is large enough to permit the child and the teacher to sit side by side. The cubicle prevents the child from being visually distracted by the other children.

Children in such programs should be in a self-contained classroom with their own toilet and lunchroom facilities immediately at hand. The factor of stimuli-reduction is a significant one for the brain-injured child (Cruickshank, 1975a).

program structure Program structuring is a further attempt to bring order into the child's "life space." It is essential that the child's daily program be simplified and definitely structured so that routines can be anticipated. With the school program sufficiently simplified and precisely structured, child and teacher can work together comfortably within a context which ensures the child some degree of success. The program structuring extends to such things as the specific ways in which hats, coats, and overshoes are put on, taken off, and stored; ways of signaling the teacher or assistant for help; the routines established for lunch, toilet, and rest activities; and all the other innumerable routines involved in the course of a normal school day.

structured teaching material Teaching materials and their use must be adapted to the child's individual characteristics regarding attention span, perceptual and conceptual limitations, perseverative and dissociative tendencies, and motor capacities. Much material used by the child will be prepared by the teacher or assistant to meet the child's specific needs. Most of it is expendable. As with all disabled, it is necessary to "teach to the disability." Where figure-ground perceptual difficulties are present, the stimulus value of the perceptual components which require emphasis must be increased by the use of heavy outlining or contrasting colors. Tasks ·must be geared to the child's attention span. For example, to minimize the distracting effects of extraneous stimuli, masking screens which expose only one line of print at a time are prescribed, and instead of giving the child a single page with ten arithmetic problems to be done, he or she is provided ten pages, one at a time, with one problem on each page.

motor training In addition to the personal relationship and environmental structuring, motor training is an integral part of the educational program of the brain-injured child. Daily motor training carried out on an individual basis for approximately thirty minutes is prescribed. It is suggested that properly supervised volunteers can assist in the motor training program. It is also recommended that the total educational program include a speech development or correction program carried out by personnel ancillary to the educational program.

The Cruickshank and similar programs are based on the behavioral characteristics of the learning disabled as listed earlier. However, many people are questioning the validity and usefulness of these characterizations. As we have already indicated, a belief in the universality of neurological impairment in these children has been pretty largely discarded. It seems clear that not all brain-injured individuals have these learning disabilities and only a few—perhaps 10 to 15 percent—of children with learning disabilities have evidence of brain damage.

Those of the behavioral characteristics that have been specifically investigated as characteristics of learning disabled children have not stood up very well. One study which factor-analyzed ratings of children diagnosed as learning disabled disclosed the existence of two independent factors. One was an independent dimension of maladjustive behavior that could reasonably be labeled *hyperactivity*. The other was a more general factor characteristic of the broad category of learning disability (Lahey, Stempniak, Robinson, and Tyroler, 1978). These authors conclude that hyperactivity and learning disabilities are independent dimensions of behavior. By one estimate only about 10 percent of children diagnosed as learning disabled are significantly hyperactive (Yahraes and Pestwich, 1979). In one study comparing learning disabled children with comparable normals in terms of abstract reasoning and perceptual abilities, there were no differences between the two groups in conceptual thinking as indicated by their performances on a series of Piagetian tests. However, in keeping with the usual characterizations of these children, the learning disabled were markedly deficient in perceptual abilities (Meltzer, 1978). Apparently, there is a marked discrepancy between the perceptual and conceptual abilities of the learning disabled. This discrepancy may be related to the corresponding difference between the mental level of these children as measured by conventional scholastic aptitude tests, on the one hand, and school achievement, on the other. Children identified as learning disabled are not deficient in conceptual thinking as the brain disorder hypothesis assumes.

Considerable evidence indicates that emotional and behavioral problems are associated with learning disabilities. However, these problems are also associated with learning deficits not identified as learning disabilities. Although often perceived as primary causes of learning problems, emotional disturbances can also result from repeated academic failure. Studies have found that such emotional problems increase in frequency with increasing age in learning disabled children (Black, 1974). It seems likely that a circular process is involved, in which educational failure and emotional disturbances are mutually reinforcing in children with educational deficits of any nature or etiology. This relationship is not limited to children with learning disabilities.

The writer is convinced that the reason the category of learning disabilities has sparked so much confusion and controversy is the assumption that such a distinctive syndrome actually exists. Clearly, the category of learning disabilities does not encompass a homogeneous group of children in terms of either etiology or behavioral characteristics. We probably have as heterogeneous a population in this category as among the mentally retarded. As we indicated earlier, we no longer try to characterize the more than a hundred different etiological categories of mental retardation as a single syndrome. The only characteristic shared by all the mentally retarded is relatively low cognitive development. Similarly, we probably have a very diverse population identified as learning disabled. If the learning disabled are so diverse, any one educational-remedial program must fail. With children so heterogeneous, no single educational approach will succeed with more than a small percentage.

SOME GENERAL DIAGNOSTIC-REMEDIAL APPROACHES

In the 1890s Lightner Witmer at the University of Pennsylvania and Grace Fernald in the Clinic School at the University of California at Los Angeles were treating educationally handicapped children in a diagnostic-remedial way.

Witmer's psycho-educational approach The establishment by Witmer in 1896 of the first psychological clinic in the world, at the University of Pennsylvania, marked the beginning not only of clinical psychology but also of the diagnostic-remedial approach to problem school children. Each child served by the clinic received an educational program individually designed by an interdisciplinary team in which the teacher was the central figure. Clinical studies were supplemented by classroom observation. Diagnosis was a continuing process growing out of clinical data, classroom experience, and the child's response to treatment. Psychologists, teachers, social workers, and physicians were all involved in the process.

Witmer believed that children with educational problems could not be understood without periods of systematic observation in the school setting during which attempts were made to improve their behavior. Particular emphasis was put on special types of remedial and educative efforts. Much of what Witmer wrote in the journal *The Psychological Clinic,* which he founded and edited, sounds quite modern and many of his procedures are applicable to the child today designated as having learning disabilities. Like many present-day psychologists, Witmer was interested in the physical and neurological aspects of the cases referred to him.

the Fernald contribution Grace Fernald, the first psychologist to work in a child guidance clinic, was dealing in a diagnostic-remedial way with children with learning disabilities in the University of California Clinic School long before these children were separately categorized (Fernald, 1943). She insisted that all educational difficulties in children of normal or superior intelligence can be removed or compensated for if proper techniques are employed.

Fernald is best known for her kinesthetic method of teaching reading, which is still used with children who have failed to learn to read by other methods. The first step in Fernald's method consists in writing in large letters on a card a word chosen by the child. The child then traces the word with a finger while saying it. The child repeats the process until the word can be written from memory. It is important that the child trace the word with a finger, and have cutaneous contact with the paper while saying the word in a natural way. This procedure combines visual, kinesthetic, cutaneous, and auditory factors. In the next step, the tracing is dropped, and the child merely looks at and says the word. From then on, the method is fairly conventional except that Fernald believes that children should select the words they want to learn and should begin writing and reading with their own stories rather than those adults have written for them.

OTHER DIAGNOSTIC-REMEDIAL APPROACHES

Currently, a large number of pragmatic diagnostic-remedial approaches to the problems of children with learning disabilities are being developed (Blanco, 1974; Gearheart, 1973; Hallahan and Cruickshank, 1973; Moran, 1975). As the field of learning disabilities evolves, the pragmatic general diagnostic-remedial approaches may prove to be the dominant ones. The entire range of children designated as having learning disabilities may prove to be so varied that educational programs stemming from a single orientation may not be applicable to more than a small segment of the total population. For children with perceptual-motor problems and children whose problems verge in that direction, programs with this emphasis will be most appropriate. Matching each child's disability to the appropriate program is technically feasible but does involve many practical problems.

The majority of children currently being referred to programs for the educationally handicapped are recommended for individualized instruction in a small class setting. The specific recommendations usually include perceptual training and counseling (Keogh and Becker, 1973). These children show a fairly consistent constellation of classroom behavior. A Pupil Identification Scale based on the classroom behavior of such children has been developed to assist in identifying these problem children (Novack, Bonaventura, and Merendo, 1973). B. K. Keogh and L. D. Becker (1973) provide some cautions and guidelines for the early identification of children with learning problems.

EVALUATIVE STUDIES

A few studies have been concerned with the claim of Strauss and his co-workers that brain-damaged children do actually learn differently from non-brain-damaged children. C. D. Barnett, N. R. Ellis, and M. Pryor (1960) matched brain-damaged and non-brain-damaged children on a variety of variables and compared their learning of six different types of skills in which differences in favor of the neurologically unimpaired group would support the Straussian theory. The brain-damaged children performed less well on two of the learning tasks but no differences were found on the other four. The authors concluded that the proposition that the brain-damaged learn differently from the neurologically unimpaired must be questioned.

D. B. Cruse (1961) found no differences in distractibility between brain-injured and ordinary familial retardates of equal mental levels. Cruickshank and others (1961) and K. J. Rost (1967) found that the use of isolation booths during one semester had no measurable effect on the classroom learning of brain-injured children.

J. W. Somerville, L. S. Warnberg, and D. E. Bost (1973) compared the performances of first-grade boys judged to be either distractible or nondistractible either in cubicles or with increased levels of stimulation and found no effects of the different conditions for either group. They conclude that "the acceptance of stimulus reduction as desirable for distractible children is, at best, premature."

Cruickshank (1975a) has reviewed the research studies evaluating the effects of structuring on the learning of learning disabled children. He concludes that although research support for the efficacy of structuring is meager, the theoretical basis for advocating structuring for these children is so compelling that he continues to recommend it.

On the other hand, M. Levine, G. Spivak, and G. Fernald (1962) did find differences in visual discrimination learning between groups of brain-injured, emotionally disturbed, and normal children, favoring the normal and emotionally disturbed. N. Haring and E. L. Phillips (1962) found that a group of emotionally disturbed, but presumably not neurologically damaged, children profited significantly by a program structured along the lines recommended by Cruickshank for the brain-damaged. This study provides support for the proposition that the highly structured programs designed for the brain-damaged are useful for children with behavioral characteristics similar to those who are positively identified as brain-injured.

D. D. McCormick, J. N. Schnobrick, and S. W. Footlik (1966) provide some support for the Straussian hypothesis. They compared two equated groups of first graders, one of which received perceptual-motor exercises systematically for nine weeks, the other of which received an equivalent amount of physical education activity. Subsequent testing revealed no significant differences between the means of the reading achievement scores of the two groups. However, a subgroup of underachievers in the perceptual-motor-trained group did show significant greater improvement in reading than did those whose achievements were more in keeping with their aptitudes.

The limited research on the effectiveness of the various programs developed for children with learning disabilities is inconclusive. E. M. Koppitz (1971), in a follow-up study of learning disabled children attending special classes, obtained results reminiscent of the findings concerning such classes for the educable mentally retarded or the "slow learners." Some administrators thought of these classes as remedial, short-term assignments; the children would return to their regular classes after they had "caught up." Other administrators perceived of these placements as last resorts for nonlearners and the unmanageable, while still others considered them to be places where vulnerable children could be placed early enough to prevent the development of serious learning, emotional, and behavior problems. Koppitz found that only 17 percent of children so placed (30 of 177) returned successfully to their regular classes. The corresponding figure for the mentally retarded is about 10 percent (Kirk, 1974). Those children who returned to their regular classes had practically all "lost" a year—they did not "catch up."

There is little in the evaluative studies to guide the practitioner in selecting the most effective method to use. Perhaps children with learning disabilities are too heterogeneous a group for all to be helped by any program that is dominantly linguistic, perceptual, or motor. Possibly, further research and practice should be directed at the problem of matching student needs and appropriate remediation.

GENERAL PROCEDURES FOR THE IDENTIFICATION AND
TREATMENT OF CHILDREN WITH LEARNING DISABILITIES

Under the "least restrictive environment" provisions of PL 94-142, regular classroom teachers will have the major responsibility for recognizing, referring, and teaching most children with learning disabilities. When classroom teachers suspect that they have children with learning disabilities, they will usually refer them to a special education specialist for preliminary investigation. The specialist will go over the school records and test scores, observe the children in the classroom, and confer with the teachers. If the preliminary investigation seems to verify the teacher's initial impressions, school authorities will confer with the parents and get their permission to do formal testing and gather other relevant information preparatory to case conferences and the formulation of appropriate educational programs for these children.

Test scores, school, medical, and other records will all be used to determine the children's strengths and weaknesses, and the preferred modalities for learning. After diagnosis, all persons concerned, including the parents, will develop an individualized education program (IEP) as described in an earlier chapter. This program will specify goals, instructional program, and educational methods to be used.

Many learning disabled children can remain in the regular classroom and, with help from a teacher's aide, require relatively little specialized instruction. Others will require additional support by a resource teacher or specialist who will act as a consultant to the regular teacher or take the children to a resource room and teach them for short periods of time. Some of the more severely handicapped children may be enrolled in a self-contained class where they will be taught entirely by special teachers.

DIFFERENTIAL DIAGNOSIS AND PRESCRIPTIVE TEACHING

Some form of psycho-educational diagnosis, so that instructional procedures can be matched to the differential learning needs of individual children, is recommended by most authorities and special education teachers (Arter and Jenkins, 1979). These diagnostic-prescriptive teaching procedures typically take one of two forms. The first is a psychologically oriented basic-abilities approach. The other is a more educationally oriented task-analytic approach.

The basic-abilities approach assumes an identifiable and measurable set of basic abilities which underlie academic learning. These are rather general abilities such as auditory discrimination and memory, visual discrimination and perception of spatial relationships, cross-sensory perceptual ability, psycholinguistic ability, and perceptual-motor abilities. This approach assumes that the failure to master such academic skills as reading and arithmetic is due to deficits in one or more of these underlying abilities. The prescriptive educational procedures generated by the identification of children's relative strengths and weaknesses in these basic abilities takes the form of a program designed either to strengthen the weak abilities or to capitalize on the strong ones. For example, if a child is weak in visual but strong in auditory discrimination, training exercises should be prescribed to remedy the weakness, or instruction should be geared to hearing rather than vision in order to take advantage of the child's strength.

The task-analytic approach perceives of learning as the mastery of a hierarchy of tasks in which each higher and more complex task is dependent upon the mastery of a sequence of simpler, lower-order ones. Accordingly, the teacher's task is to help children master the specific tasks in the hierarchy which make possible their mastery of the higher-level tasks.

The basic-abilities approach views the educational problem as one of developing and strengthening general perceptual, memory, motor, and linguistic abilities. The educational task for the task-analytic approach is to teach specific components of academic skills or tasks. According to Haring and Bateman (1977), the basic-abilities approach has dominated the field of learning disabilities for the past twenty years. Remedial programs have predominantly been of the basic-ability-training type.

Educational publishers have developed and marketed a wide array of general ability assessment instruments and related instructional materials. New tests and training materials appear on the market almost daily. School systems are investing heavily in these materials for their special education programs.

Arter and Jenkins (1979) have evaluated the extensive literature dealing with the relative effectiveness of these various assessment-teaching programs. As a result of their survey, these authors conclude that the abilities measured by the assessment devices have been found to be highly resistant to training by the prescribed procedures and, more often than not, academic performance is not improved by such training. In the majority of studies, control groups without training performed as well on both basis-abilities measures and tests of academic progress as did the trained experimental groups.

If this evaluation is valid, it means that the use of materials closely related to academic skills or their components is a more promising approach to teaching children with learning disabilities than is attempting to strengthen the general perceptual motor-linguistic abilities postulated to be prerequisites to academic progress. This proposal will be resisted by the large proportion of special education teachers who believe that they can and should train the weak basic abilities of children with learning disabilities (Arter and Jenkins, 1979). The basic-ability-improvement approach has also served to differentiate the functions of special and regular education teachers. According to this model, regular education teachers teach the academic skills of reading, arithmetic, and so on, while special education teachers focus on strengthening the more basic underlying processes. The basic-abilities approach is also consistent with the assumption of such early childhood programs as Head Start. In these programs perceptual-motor-linguistic skills are the focus of concern since they are assumed to be the basis for the later acquisition of academic skills.

THE OVERLAPPING CATEGORIES

In Chapter 8 we questioned the usefulness of keeping the mildly mentally retarded (educable mentally retarded) and learning disabled in separate categories. Studies indicate that, in practice, the two populations overlap. One study of 208 children in 23 classrooms for the learning disabled found that 37 percent of the children had WISC-R test scores *below* the legally prescribed limits for such children (Smith, Coleman, Dokechi, and Davis, 1977). Other studies have found that similar percentages of children designated as learning disabled do not meet the most generally accepted prerequisites of normal mental level. The uniqueness and validity of the category is still very much in question. Hallahan and Kauffman (1979) and Gajar (1979) claim that children identified as learning disabled, educable mentally retarded, and emotionally disturbed have many more characteristics in common than they have characteristics that are unique. These authors point out that, while children with learning disabilities and the emotionally disturbed are higher in measured intelligence than the identified mentally retarded, there is considerable overlapping of the groups. The same is true of emotional disturbances. Children designated emotionally disturbed have the highest incidence but the other two groups are also considerably above average in this respect. All three groups are about equally educationally retarded. These authors argue for a noncategorical approach to the education of these children.

Hasazi and York (1978) claim that the steps in good teaching are the same irrespective of the category. Although many of the principles implicit in their list of steps have been mentioned in other contexts, we shall paraphrase and condense them here.

STEPS TO GOOD TEACHING
1. Determine what are the student's interests, ambitions, and self-perceptions.
2. Determine the student's current repertoire of skills and information via formal and informal testing, school and medical records.

3. Determine the skill and informational deficits of the student.
4. Specify the long- and short-term goals of the instructional programs for the children.
5. Break these down into small, measurable, and more immediate objectives.
6. Select instructional procedures and techniques to match the student's learning strengths and weaknesses.
7. Select settings, materials, and procedures to match student characteristics.
8. Carry out the instructional program.
9. Provide for continuous feedback to indicate student progress.
10. Make constant revisions in light of the student's progress.

These proposed steps are consistent with the individualized educational program requirements of Public Law 94-142.

THE PROMISE FOR CHILDREN WITH LEARNING DISABILITIES

Learning disabilities is the most recently designated category of exceptional children. PL 94-142 specifically brings children with learning disabilities under the broad umbrella of handicapped children, making them eligible for financial support for special education and related services. However, this law also places a ceiling on the number of children with learning disabilities who can be counted to receive federal money. Not more than one-sixth of all school-age children (five to seventeen) counted as handicapped under this act (PL 94-142) can be children with learning disabilities. The statute does, however, provide a basis for removing this ceiling without the necessity of further legislation (Brooke, 1977).

At present we have had insufficient time to determine what the long-term outlook is for children in this category. The fragmentary reports and case studies cited in the literature indicate that some of these children will be able to overcome their handicap, move ahead, and progress educationally much as do the unimpaired. Many who are strongly motivated can succeed in spite of their handicap. Many of the more severely handicapped (the dyslectics), as adults, still have trouble with reading and spelling and in perceiving numbers in their right order.

SUMMARY

An increasingly large segment of the schools' special education population is being designated as "children with learning disabilities." The term was seldom heard before the 1960s, but by the 1970s the group was probably receiving more professional attention than any other category of exceptional children. The term *learning disabilities* first appeared as a substitute for *brain-injured* in the sense in which the term was used by Strauss.

The brain-injured, according to Strauss, was a broad and elastic category including children with positive neurological signs and/or a history of neural trauma, on the one hand, but also applicable to children characterized by purely behavioral, perceptual, and conceptual deficits *similar to* those with demonstrated neural pathology. There is an increasing tendency to divorce the category from etiology entirely and to define it in purely behavioral and educational terms.

Strauss and Lehtinen proposed a specific methodology for the education of the brain-injured child; most subsequent programs developed for children with learning disabilities have been derived, either directly or indirectly, from their proposals. Cruickshank's program follows very closely the original Strauss model and emphasizes the importance of "structure."

Learning disabilities are defined largely by exclusion. Children so categorized are those with marked learning deficits who are not sufficiently mentally retarded, emotionally disturbed, physically handicapped, culturally handicapped, or environmentally disadvantaged to account for their educational retardation. Despite the lists of traits alleged to characterize these children, it seems that no consistent pattern of behavior or traits—except their defining characteristics—typify these children. The only ways in which the learning disabled differ significantly from the educable mentally retarded is in their higher mental test scores and greater variability in their aptitude-achievement profiles. Many more boys than girls are learning disabled. There is a familial tendency toward the disorder and many are slow in learning to talk. Because of the heterogeneity of the learning disabled, any uniform educational program will fail. Some form of the diagnostic-prescriptive type of teaching is the most promising approach to the special problems of the learning disabled. This approach utilizes a clinical team which adapts those principles of good teaching, applicable to all, to meet the unique needs of these particular children. Special educational programs for the learning disabled are designed to answer the question applicable to all children: What do the special characteristics of these children require educationally to enable them to function more adequately?

REFERENCES

Arter, J. A. and J. R. Jenkins, "Differential Diagnosis—Prescriptive Teaching: A Critical Appraisal," *Review of Educational Research*, 1979, *49*, 517–56.

Arter, J. A. and J. R. Jenkins, "Examining the Benefits and Modality Considerations in Special Education," *Journal of Special Education*, 1977, *11*, 281–98.

Barnett, C. D., N. R. Ellis and M. Pryor, "Learning in Familial and Brain-injured Defectives," *American Journal of Mental Deficiency*, 1960, *64*, 894–97.

Barsch, R. H., *A Movigenic Curriculum* (Madison, Wis.: Bureau for Handicapped Children, 1965).

Bateman, B., "Learning Disorders," *Review of Educational Research*, 1966, *36*, 93–119.

Bender, L., *Bender Motor Gestalt Test: Cards and Manual of Instruction* (New York: American Orthopsychiatric Association, 1946).

Black, F. W., "Self-concept as Related to Achievement and Age in Learning-Disabled Children," *Child Development*, 1974, *45*, 1137–40.

Blanco, R. F., *Prescriptions for Children with Learning and Adjustment Problems* (Springfield, Ill.: Charles C Thomas, 1974).

Blom, G. E., "The Concept 'Perceptually Handicapped': Its Assets and Limitations," *Seminars in Psychiatry*, 1969, *1*, 253–61.

Brooke, E., "PL 94-142—Getting the Money to Make it Work," *Today's Education*, 1977, *66*(4), 50–52.

Carbo, M. L., "A Word Imprinting Technique for Children with Severe Memory Disorder," *Teaching Exceptional Children* 1978, *11*(1), 3–5.

Clark, A. D. and C. J. Richards, "Learning Disabilities: A National Survey of Existing Public School Programs," *Journal of Special Education*, 1968, *2*, 223–28.

Cruickshank, W. M., "The Education of the Child with Brain Injury," in W. M. Cruickshank and G. O. Johnson, eds., *Education of Exceptional Children and Youth*, 2nd ed. (Englewood Cliffs, N.J.: Prentice-Hall, 1967).

Cruickshank, W. M., "The Learning Environment," in W. M. Cruickshank and D. P. Hallahan, eds., *Perceptual and Learning Disabilities in Children* (Syracuse, N.Y.: Syracuse University Press, 1975a).

Cruickshank, W. M., "The Psychoeducational Match," in W. M. Cruickshank and D. P. Hallahan, eds., *Perceptual and Learning Disabilities in Children* (Syracuse, N.Y.: Syracuse University Press, 1975b).

Cruickshank, W. M., "Some Issues Facing the Field of Learning Disabilities," *Journal of Learning Disabilities*, 1972, *5*, 380–88.

Cruickshank, W. M., F. A. Bentzen, F. H. Ratzeburg, and M. T. Tannhauser, *A Teaching Method for Brain-injured and Hyperactive Children* (Syracuse, N.Y.: Syracuse University Press, 1961).

Cruse, D. B., "Effects of Distraction upon the Performance of Brain-injured and Familial Retarded Children," *American Journal of Mental Deficiency*, 1961, *66*, 86–90.

Fernald, G. M., *Remedial Techniques in Basic School Subjects.* (New York: McGraw-Hill, 1943).

Gajar, A., "Educable Mentally Retarded, Learning Disabled, Emotionally Disturbed: Similarities and Differences," *Exceptional Children,* 1979, *45,* 470–80.

Gearheart, B. R., *Learning Disabilities: Educational Strategies* (St. Louis: C. V. Mosby, 1973).

Hallahan, D. P. and J. B. Kauffman, *Introduction to Learning Disabilities: A Psycho-behavioral Approach* (Englewood Cliffs, N.J.: Prentice-Hall, 1976).

Hallahan, D. P. and W. M. Cruickshank, *Psychoeducational Foundations of Learning Disabilities* (Englewood Cliffs, N.J.: Prentice-Hall, 1973).

Haring, N. G. and B. Bateman, *Teaching the Learning Disabled Child.* (Englewood Cliffs, N. J.: Prentice-Hall, 1977).

Haring, N. and E. L. Phillips, *Educating Emotionally Disturbed Children* (New York: McGraw-Hill, 1962).

Hasazi, S. and R. York, "Eleven Steps in Good Teaching," *Teaching Exceptional Children,* 1978, *10*(3), 63–66.

Hellmuth, J., ed., *Learning Disorders,* vol. 1 (Seattle: Special Child Publications, 1965).

Hobbs, N., *The Futures of Children* (San Francisco: Jossey-Bass, 1975).

Johnson, D. J. and H. R. Myklebust, *Learning Disabilities: Educational Principles and Practices* (New York: Grune & Stratton, 1967).

Kass, C. E., "Learning Disabilities," *Review of Educational Research,* 1969, *39,* 71–82.

Keogh, B. K. and L. D. Becker, "Early Detection of Learning Problems: Questions, Cautions, and Guidelines," *Exceptional Children,* 1973, *40,* 5–11.

Kephart, N. C., *The Slow Learner in the Classroom* (Columbus, Ohio: Charles E. Merrill, 1960).

Kirk, D. L., "The Great Sorting Machine," *Phi Delta Kappan,* 1974, *60*(8), 521–25.

Koppitz, E. M., *Children with Learning Disabilities: A Five-year Follow-up Study* (New York: Grune and Stratton, 1971).

Lahey, B. B., M. Stempniak, E. J. Robinson, and M. J. Tyroler, "Hyperactivity and Learning Disabilities as Independent Dimensions of Child Behavior Problems," *Journal of Abnormal Psychology,* 1978, *87,* 333–40.

Levine, M., G. Spivak, and G. Fernald, "Discrimination in Diffuse Brain Damage," *American Journal of Mental Deficiency,* 1962, *67,* 287–91.

Marshall, J. C. and F. Newcombe, "Patterns of Paralexia: A Psycholinguistic Approach," *Journal of Psycholinguistic Research*, 1973, *2*, 175–99.

McCarthy, J. M., "Learning Disabilities: Where Have We Been? Where Are We Going?" *Seminar in Psychiatry*, 1969, *1*, 354–61.

McCarthy and J. F. McCarthy, *Learning Disabilities* (Boston: Allyn and Bacon, 1969).

McCormick, D. D., J. N. Schnobrick, and S. W. Footlik, *The Effects of Perceptual Motor Training in Reading Achievement* (Chicago: Reading Research Foundation, 1966, mimeographed).

Meltzer, L. J., "Abstract Reasoning in a Specific Group of Perceptually Impaired Children: Namely the Learning Disabled," *The Journal of Genetic Psychology*, 1978, *132*, 185–95.

Moran, M. R., "Nine Steps to the Diagnostic Prescriptive Process in the Classroom," *Focus on Exceptional Children*, 1975, *6*(9), 1–14.

Naidoo, S., "Specific Developmental Dyslexia," *British Journal of Educational Psychology*, 1971, *41*, 19–21.

Novack, H. S., E. Benaventura, and P. F. Merendo, "A Scale for Early Detection of Children with Learning Disabilities," *Exceptional Children*, 1973, *40*, 98–105.

Rost, K. J., "Academic Achievement of Brain-injured and Hyperactive Children in Isolation," *Exceptional Children*, 1967, *28*, 103–7.

Smith, M. D., J. M. Coleman, P. R. Dokechi, and E. E. Davis, "Intellectual Characteristics of School Labeled Learning Disabled Children," *Exceptional Children*, 1977, *43*, 352–57.

Somerville, J. W., L. S. Warnberg, and D. E. Bost, "Effects of Cubicles versus Increased Stimulation on Task Performance by First-grade Males Perceived as Distractible and Nondistractible," *Journal of Special Education*, 1973, *7*, 169–85.

Strauss, A. A. and L. Lehtinen, *Psychopathology and Education of the Brain-injured Child* (New York: Grune and Stratton, 1947).

Tarnopol, L., *Learning Disabilities: Introduction to Educational and Medical Management* (Springfield, Ill.: Charles C Thomas, 1974).

Westheimer, K. N., "Studies in the Theory of Gestalt Psychology," *Psychogische Forschungen*, 1973, *4*, 230–41.

Yahraes, H. and S. Prestwich, *Detection and Prevention of Learning Disorders* (Stockton, Calif.: Institute for the Study and Treatment of Learning Disorders, 1979).

SUGGESTIONS FOR STUDENTS AND INSTRUCTORS

1. Have a student with a learning disability talk to the class.

2. Attend a meeting of the local association of parents of children with learning disabilities.

3. Why have learning disabilities as a category been so long in appearing?

4. Do children in all cultures display learning disabilities?

ADDITIONAL READINGS

Morasky, R. L., *Learning Disabilities* (Boston: Allyn and Bacon, 1977). A good general discussion of the field.

Sapir, S. G. and B. Wilson, *A Professional's Guide to Working with the Learning Disabled Child* (New York: Brunner/Mazel, Inc., 1978). A useful overall reference of immense help to parents, teachers, and clinicians.

The 1976 Directory of Educational Facilities for the Learning Disabled, 6th ed. (San Rafael, Calif.: Academic Therapy Publications, 1976). This edition lists more than 300 residential and day schools, remedial clinics, and diagnostic centers for persons who are intellectually capable but who are underachieving academically.

SELECTED FILMS

Why Can't I Learn? (60 minutes) Capital Cities Television Productions, 4100 City Lane Avenue, Philadelphia, Pa. An overall view of the needs of children with learning disabilities.

The Exceptional Child. (26 minutes) Films Inc., 1144 Wilmette Avenue, Wilmette, Illinois. A documentary about the Adams School in New York, which deals with the problems of the perceptually handicapped.

ORGANIZATION

Association for Children with Learning Disabilities
5225 Grace Street
Pittsburgh, Pa. 15236

THE SENSORIALLY HANDICAPPED

PART III

CHAPTER 10

THE VISUALLY HANDICAPPED

Harold Stockwood guided fifteen people—mostly elderly—who lived in his wing of an apartment house to safety down three flights of stairs in total darkness. An electrical fire had started in the basement and had plunged the entire building into darkness. Stockwood was awakened when the fire alarm sounded briefly and then ceased as the electrical current to the entire building was cut off, making the elevators inoperative. Stockwood quickly went to each apartment, aroused the occupants, and instructed them to assemble in the corridor leading to the staircase. He then lined up the fifteen people, telling each to hold onto the person in front, and saying he would lead. He told them to keep calm and they would all get out. To assist them in following, but also to keep them occupied, he had them count their steps as he directed: "Take ten steps down, then turn left and take three steps forward, take another five steps down, watching for the torn carpet on the third step," and so forth. Stockwood was able to lead his group with assurance for he had usually found it more convenient to use the stairs than the elevator. Nothing was so unusual about the performance for Stockwood except that he had been completely blind for eight years. In the dark the blind man is king.

In many respects the blind have always been a favored group, compared with the other categories of the handicapped. Historically, they have sometimes been assigned useful roles such as serving as guides in the dark and as memorizers and oral transmitters of tribal and religious lore. They were often assumed to have the power of "second sight" in compensation for their lost vision and were revered as prophets and soothsayers. While blindness has occasionally been perceived as a divine visitation, interpreted as benign, more often it was seen as punishment for sin—one's own or one's parents'—and blind people were stigmatized.

Because of the high visibility and the obvious nature of the handicap, blindness has effectively elicited the sympathy and concern of the non-handicapped. Consequently, despite their relatively small number, it is estimated that ten times more legal, social, and educational services have been provided for the blind than for any other handicapped group. R. A. Scott has estimated that in 1960 there were over eight hundred separate organizations, agencies, and programs for the blind in the United States. The total annual expenditures of these agencies were nearly $470 million (Scott, 1969). The first special education programs established were for the visually handicapped.

EARLY HISTORICAL CONCERNS

Several early Christian monasteries and hospitals showed some concern for the blind (Best, 1934). In the fourth century, St. Basil at Caesarea, in Cappadovia (a Roman province in Asia Minor) established a hospice for the blind. In the following century, similar facilities (refuges, asylums, or retreats) were established in Syria, Jerusalem, France, Italy, and Germany. In 1254 Louis IX created an asylum in Paris in which several hundred blind persons found refuge. This asylum was established mainly to care for the large number of blind crusaders returning to Western Europe. Many were said to have lost their sight as punishment at the hands of the Saracens (Best, 1934). This large refuge for the blind attracted considerable attention and similar facilities were subsequently established in many cities of Western Europe.

In the sixteenth century Girolinia Cardano, a physician in Pavia, Italy, conceived the idea that the blind might be taught to read through the sense of touch and attempted to provide some instruction in this way. About the same time, Peter Pontanus, a blind Fleming, and Padre Lana Terzi of Brescia, Italy, wrote books on the education of the blind. A third contemporary anonymous publication on the same subject appeared in Italy. In the eighteenth century, a book on the teaching of mathematics to the blind was published by Jacques Bernovilli in Switzerland. During this time several attempts were made to devise a means for the blind to read the printed word (Best, 1934).

Valentin Haüy of Paris is thought to have established the first school for the blind. In 1784 Haüy took a blind boy he found begging on the streets as his first student. He paid the boy to compensate for his lost alms. Haüy soon increased the number of his students to twelve. In 1791 the school was taken over by the state and continued as a public institution. Other countries soon followed the lead. Between 1891 and 1909 seven schools were started in Great Britain and early in the nineteenth century schools for the blind were started in many of the large cities of Europe.

In 1826 Dr. John D. Fisher of Boston visited the school founded by Haüy in Paris. He was sufficiently impressed to agitate for establishment of a similar school in Massachusetts. As a result, the Massachusetts legislature in 1832 incorporated the New England Asylum for the Purpose of Educating the Blind, later to be known as Perkins Institute and Massachusetts School for the Blind. This school started with six students. Gridly Howe was its first superintendent. About the same time, New York established a similar school (now the New York Institute for the Education of the Blind); Pennsylvania did likewise (now the Overbrook School for the Blind) (Lowenfeld, 1971, 1973). These schools were all private institutions, but shortly thereafter, the first state school for the blind was started in Ohio. Subsequently all of the states established residential public schools where education for the blind was provided essentially free of charge. The first special classes for the blind in American public schools were established in Chicago in 1900 (Lowenfeld, 1971). Thus, private benevolence gave way to public support, and restrictive admission and tuition were replaced by free education for all the blind.

The first private and public schools for the blind were residential, but since the turn of the century, day schools and/or classes for the blind have become an integral part of most school systems. The tendency to integrate the blind into regular classes has accelerated, and today most blind children enrolled in the public schools are partly or completely integrated into regular classes.

SOME DEFINITIONS

Definitions of the visually handicapped are both quantitative and functional. When quantitative definitions are required for legal and administrative purposes, blindness is usually defined as "visual acuity of 20/200 or less in the better eye with proper correction, or a limitation in the fields of vision such that the widest diameter of the visual field subtends an angular distance no greater than 20 degrees" (American Foundation for the Blind, 1961). A person is said to have a visual acuity of 20/200 if he or she must be at a distance of twenty feet to read the standard type which a person with normal vision can read at a distance of two hundred feet. The restriction of the visual field to an angular distance of twenty degrees or less is sometimes called tunnel vision. An individual with such a condition may have normal visual acuity for the area on which he can focus, but his field of vision is so restricted that he can see only a limited area at a time. A person suffering a restriction of either visual acuity or field to this extent is typically considered legally and medically blind.

There has been little demand for medical and legal definitions of *partial blindness* or *partially sighted*. However, the quantitative standard most often accepted is "visual acuity of between 20/70 and 20/200 in the better eye after maximum correction," or comparable visual limitations of other types. A person with 20/70 vision can read letters 1¼ inches high at 20 feet and a person with 20/200 vision, though legally blind, can read letters 2½ inches high at this same distance. Although a person with 20/400 vision cannot read letters of any size at 20 feet, she may be educated as a sighted person with the aid of special lenses and magnifiers.

Functional definitions vary according to the purposes they are intended to serve. Thus we have *travel vision, shadow vision, near vision,* and *distance vision,* as well as *educational blindness* and *occupational blindness.* Because of its practical importance, *educational blindness* has been most systematically studied. The educationally blind are those people whose vision is so defective that they cannot be educated via vision. Their education must be primarily through the auditory, cutaneous, and kinesthetic senses. The educationally blind must read and write in Braille. Functional definitions of the partially sighted or partially blind—we shall use the two terms interchangeably—are less precise. The partially sighted are able to use vision as their main avenue of learning and do not require Braille or have access to such devices as the Optacon or the Kurzweil Reading Machine which convert printed text into synthetic speech or tactile facsimilies of the material. (Goodrich and others, 1979, Bliss and Moore, 1974) But they read only enlarged print, or require magnifying devices, or can read only limited amounts of regular print under special conditions.

Many studies have documented the lack of a close relationship between the quantitative medical and legal definitions and the more functional definitions of visual handicaps. Many legally blind children can read large or even ordinary print. Many more can distinguish large objects sufficiently well to enable them to move around and have a sense of orientation (travel vision), and most have some light perception (shadow vision). Of over seven thousand children enrolled in over six hundred classes for the partially sighted, less than one-third had vision within the limits of visual acuity commonly used in defining partial sight—between 20/70 and 20/200 in the better eye after maximum correction (Kerby, 1952). Table 10–1, based on another study (Jones, 1962), also shows the discrepancies between the quantitative and functional criteria.

Table 10–1

READING PRACTICE AS RELATED TO VISUAL ACUITY

	percentages of children		
visual acuity	reading print	reading Braille	reading both Braille and print
20/200*	82	12	6
15/200*	67	27	6
10/200*	59	32	9

*The fractions indicate that the person must be 20, 15, or 10 feet distant from standard type to read the material which a person with normal vision can read at 200 feet. All these groups are legally blind. Data from Jones (1962).

SYMPTOMS OF VISUAL IMPAIRMENT

Since regular and complete eye examinations for all children are seldom feasible, initial identification of children for more complete examinations is usually based on behavioral symptoms or rough screening tests. The more common symptoms of visual impairment are as follows:

1. Has chronic eye irritations as indicated by watery eyes or by red-rimmed, encrusted, or swollen eyelids.

2. Experiences nausea, double vision, or visual blurring during or following reading.

3. Rubs eyes, frowns, or screws up the face when looking at distant objects.

4. Is overcautious in walking, runs infrequently and falteringly for no apparent reason.

5. Is abnormally inattentive during chalkboard, wall chart, or map work.

6. Complains of visual blurring and attempts to brush away the visual impediments.

7. Is excessively restless, irritable, or nervous following prolonged close visual work.

8. Blinks excessively, especially while reading.

9. Habitually holds the book very close, very far away, or in other unusual positions when reading.

10. Tilts the head to one side when reading.

11. Can read only for short periods at a time.

12. Shuts or covers one eye when reading.

TESTS OF VISUAL IMPAIRMENT

The National Society for the Prevention of Blindness recommends, as a minimum test for school-age children, an annual test with the Snellen chart. The Snellen chart consists of rows of letters, or *E*s, in various positions in lines of different size print. Each row of letters of a given size has a distance designation. For example, the twenty-foot row can be read by people with normal vision at a distance of twenty feet. A person reading the twenty-foot row at this distance is said to have 20/20 vision. A person who can read nothing smaller than the seventy-foot line at the standard twenty-foot distance has 20/70 vision.

The Snellen test is the most widely used because it is simple and can be quickly administered by a nurse or a teacher. Despite its widespread use, however, the Snellen test has decided limitations. It tests central vision only. It does not detect hyperopia (farsightedness), presbyopia (impairment of vision due to diminution of the elasticity of the crystalline lens), or strabismus (a deviation of one of the eyes from its normal direction). While most authorities strongly recommend that visual screening programs include tests such as the Massachusetts Vision Test, the Telebinocular, the Sight Screener, and the Ortho-Rater, studies indicate that, when used by teachers, the Snellen chart does about as well as these much more complicated and expensive devices (Foote and Crane, 1954).

CAUSES OF IMPAIRED VISION

Table 10–2 indicates various causes of visual defects among children of school age, as well as changes in etiology, over a twenty-five-year period. The category of "excessive oxygen" is of special interest because it accounts for one-third of the 1958–59 total. The condition or disease known as retrolental fibroplasia (RLF) was practically unknown before the 1940s. It was identified as a clinical entity and named by Dr. T. L. Terry, a Boston ophthalmologist, in 1942. The condition occurred only in premature infants and its incidence increased rapidly until, in 1952–53, it accounted for over half the blindness of preschool children. In 1952 it was established that the increased concentrations of oxygen to which premature infants were being subjected was the cause. Once the cause was discovered, it was found that the concentration and duration of oxygen administration could be reduced below the critical level without increasing the mortality rate, and blindness of this type has occurred only rarely. However, the impact of the several thousand blind children of this type was felt in the educational systems though the 1970s. By the 1980's these people had largely completed their formal education.

In some respects the RLF blind children are different from children comparably blind from other causes. One study of 263 such children, all legally blind, found that a large number suffered excessive developmental retardation, multiple disabilities, and various behavior disorders including autistic symptoms and "blindisms" (various repetitive hand or body movements, such as rubbing the eyes, waving the fingers before the face, and swaying) (Chase, 1974). When the cause of RLF was discovered, it was thought that oxygen could be administered at levels which would keep the mortality rate and the incidence of hyaline membrane disease and anoxic brain damage low and still not produce blindness. Unfortunately, this has not been found to be true. Consequently there has been a recent increase in RLF blindness when it has been found necessary to keep oxygen levels high enough to prevent brain damage or death (Chase, 1974).

Table 10–2 indicates that, except for the marked increase in the 1958–59 figures due to retrolental fibroplasia, the total incidence of blindness has not changed significantly. However, the relative importance of certain etiologies has changed. Blindness due to infectious diseases has progressively declined, from 6.1 per 100,000 in 1933–34 to 1.3 in 1958–59. There has also been a progressive decline in blindness due to injuries. Unspecified prenatal causes remain the major etiological category of the blind. Heredity is undoubtedly the primary cause in many of these cases. C. E. Kerby (1958) estimates that 14 to 15 percent of blindness results from genetic factors. Heredity as a cause is difficult to establish, but it is thought to be an important etiological agent.

Table 10–2

ESTIMATED PREVALENCE OF LEGAL BLINDNESS OF DIFFERENT ETIOLOGIES IN SCHOOL CHILDREN (PER 100,000)

causes	1933–1934	1943–1944	1954–1955	1958–1959
Infections	6.1	5.0	1.5	1.3
Injuries	1.6	1.5	1.0	0.8
Excessive oxygen	—	—	3.8	11.3
Tumors	0.5	0.8	1.0	0.6
Prenatal causes	10.8	12.1	11.1	16.2
Cause unreported	1.9	2.2	1.3	2.6
Totals per 100,000	21.2	21.9	19.9	34.1
Number of cases	2,702	3,749	4,429	7,757

Data from Hatfield (1973).

As the age composition of the population changes, the incidence of blindness and the relative importance of the various causes of visual impairment change. With increased longevity, glaucoma, cataracts, and diabetic retinopathy increase in importance as causes of blindness. By the mid-1970s these three conditions accounted for one-half of all blindness (Ginsberg, 1973–74). In the late 1960s and early 1970s, the blind population was increasing at a rate nearly twice that of the general population. Between 1940 and 1970 the known blind population of the United States increased 70 percent, while the total population increased 45 percent. In the mid-1970s three out of four blind persons were over forty-five years of age (Ginsberg, 1973–74). (See Table 10–3.) Except for retrolental fibroplasia, most of this increase is the result of the high incidence of glaucoma (2 percent of the adult population are affected) and cataracts (25 percent of the total blind). With more effective controls for diabetes an increasing number of affected persons live to advanced ages, develop diabetic retinopathy, and pass on the genetic potential to succeeding generations. Maturity-onset diabetes (onset after age forty) has a strong genetic component: 60 percent of the children of two such diabetics will develop the condition by age sixty (Lowenstein and Preger, 1976). The number of diabetics in the United States has increased from 1.2 million in 1950 to 5 million in 1975, an increase of more than 300 percent, while the population has increased less than 50 percent (Maugh, 1975). A diabetic is twenty times more likely to become blind than a nondiabetic of the same age. However, the precise course of events leading from diabetes to blindness is not known (Kupfer, 1973; Lowenstein and Preger, 1976).

INCIDENCE OF VISUAL IMPAIRMENT

The incidence of mild visual defects is very high. An estimated one-fifth of the population have some visual anomaly. (Reynolds and Birch, 1977, p. 605.) Of course, the great majority of these defects are correctable and constitute no particular educational or vocational handicap.

Table 10–3
BLINDNESS RATES AND AGE IN ADULTS

age range	rate per 100,000
45–64	200
65–74	440
75–84	900
85 +	2600

Data from Ginsberg (1973–74).

The United States Office of Education estimates that a total of 0.09 percent of school children need special education facilities for the visually impaired. Of these 0.09 percent, two-thirds (0.06 percent) are educationally partially sighted, and one-third (0.03 percent) are educationally blind. As of January 1973, 24,195 blind students were enrolled in educational facilities below college level (Morris, 1974). While this is a sizable group, the visually impaired probably constitute the smallest area of exceptionality. The incidence of blindness increases dramatically with age—particularly beyond early adulthood. Consequently, the total estimated prevalences greatly exceed those given above for children. In 1972, the estimated prevalence of blindness for the United States (including Puerto Rico and the Virgin Islands) was 225 per 100,000 population; that is, a total of 475,200 persons are legally blind, approximately 100,000 are totally blind. The rates of blindness are appreciably higher for nonwhites than for whites in America—252.7 as compared with 127.1. Geographic differences are also marked. The highest rate is 370.1 per 100,000 for Washington, D. C., and the lowest is Hawaii with 139.1 per 100,000 (Hatfield, 1973).

THE HANDICAPS OF THE BLIND

Like all disabilities, the total handicap of the blind person consists of the cumulative effects of the disabilitiy itself and its inherent limitations, the social stigma manifesting itself in cultural stereotypes of the blind, and the self-concept of the blind person.

The inherent limitations of any disability are relative to the extent to which current technology has made available to the handicapped compensatory devices and procedures. Blindness (a) prevents direct access to the printed word, (b) restricts independent mobility in unfamiliar surroundings, (c) limits a person's direct perception of distant environment as well as of objects too large to be apprehended tactually, and (d) deprives the individual of important social cues.

The stigmas of blindness which contribute to the total handicap consist of a set of popular conceptions or misconceptions which result in social practices sufficiently consistent with and supportive of these misconceptions to constitute a self-fulfilling prophecy. The popular stereotypes of blindness contain contradictory components. On the one hand are the presumed traits of docility, dependency, helplessness, and despondency. This stereotype is implicit in the application of the term to the nonhandicapped by expressions such as "You are as helpless as a blind man," "Are you blind?" "He is blind with rage." Blindness also has connotations of "lacking in perceptiveness or judgment," "without intelligent control," and "random." A nationwide poll indicated in 1970 that Americans fear blindness second only to cancer (David, 1970).

The stereotype of helplessness is typified by the blind person on the street corner holding a tin cup. On the other hand, we also have the less common popular conceptions of the unusual and almost miraculous aptitudes of blind people—their alleged insights which more than compensate for their lack of vision, the supposed increased acuity of their other senses, or their possession of a special extra sense or extrasensory perceptiveness. As mentioned earlier, blinded individuals have historically been especially revered as prophets and sages. Because of the dominantly negative stereotype of blindness and the stigmatizing connotations of the term, many people prefer alternative terms such as *sightlessness, visual handicap,* or *visual impairment.* Reflecting this tendency, the International Conference on Education of Blind Youth became the International Council for Education of the Visually Handicapped, and the American Association for Instructors of the Blind became the Association for Education of the Visually Handicapped (Bourgeault, 1974).

Since the popular stereotype of helplessness and dependency is the dominant one, treatment of the blind individual often results in social practices which preclude his or her developing and exercising the skills and competencies which will lead to independence. Nothing inherent in the nature of blindness requires a person to be docile, helpless, and dependent. The individual only becomes so through the same basic processes of learning as do the sighted who develop these characteristics.

Vision plays an important role in interpersonal communication, but the blind person is deprived of important social cues. Instead of maintaining eye contact, as the sighted normally do when conversing, the blind person may turn his or her better ear toward the speaker, thus turning the face away. Turning the face and/or eyes away from the speaker suggests inattentiveness and evasiveness and is disconcerting to the sighted. The blind person is also deprived of the socially communicative cues provided by the facial expressions, gestures, and movements of the other person. Failure to observe and use conventional gestures in communication may result in less complete communication or in the use of gestures which are perceived by others as either contradictory to the oral message or distracting. The blind person uses facial expressions and gestures less often and less appropriately than do the sighted and more often develops stereotyped body movements called "blindisms" which detract from the individual's communicative effectiveness.

MOBILITY OF THE BLIND

One of the most, if not the most, difficult task for the blind person is that of independent travel. However, until recently the problem had never been systematically investigated. The only aspect of the mobility of the blind that has been comprehensively researched is "obstacle sense," which is discussed in the next section. Since, in moving about independently, the blind person makes use of other senses—especially audition—seldom used by the normally sighted for this purpose, the mobility of the blind is influenced markedly by additional handicaps, particularly auditory impairment. It is therefore not surprising to find a significant relationship between the auditory thresholds of blind subjects and their relative mobility. The highest correlations are found with thresholds for the higher frequencies. This relationship probably derives from the crucial role of the higher frequencies in the detection of obstacles (echo reception).

Sight provides us with cues for distance and direction such as motion, color brightness, contrast, depth, and perspective, all of which are involved in the mobility of the sighted. The most obvious limitation of the blind is their limited awareness of distant objects. Other, less obvious problems are in the areas of motivation. The young blind child cannot see objects or people, which he would then set out to reach as does the sighted child. He has to wait for contact, sound, or smell to arouse his curiosity. The blind child cannot see other children moving toward and reaching for toys and other interesting objects and is deprived of visual models to imitate. The visual incentives which stimulate the sighted child to learn to crawl, creep, stand, walk, and run are not present to the blind. The visually impaired child is much more dependent on auditory, principally verbal, sources for motivation to move. The many bumps and bruises he cannot avoid arouse the anxiety of those about him because of real as well as exaggerated dangers. This and the tendency to overprotection add to his inherent disability and increase his handicap. Although independent locomotion—the ability to move about freely and independently at home, in the neighborhood, and in traffic—is of primary importance to the blind, it has only recently begun to receive the attention it warrants. It is obvious that these skills, which the sighted individual learns largely incidentally and with little formal instruction, must become a matter of primary concern in the training of the blind.

Such training begins in the home, where situations must be deliberately contrived to encourage the blind child to become curious and explore her world. The blind child needs a wealth of sounds, objects within reach, and even odors which she is encouraged to find and explore. Stimulation to move about the house, rather than to sit quietly in the crib or playpen, is more essential for the blind than for the sighted child. Keeping furniture in the same places and teaching the child the safe routes around the house will minimize the bumps and bruises which may discourage independent exploration. Permitting her to follow family members about, and encouraging her to use furniture, utensils, and tools and to smell and taste vegetables and fruit are a necessary part of the blind child's education.

Normal playground activities require some modification, but with adequate supervision the blind child can participate in most such programs. The blind child can use the sandbox, jungle gym, and most other playground equipment and can swim, dance, wrestle, and participate in many forms of athletics.

Surveys indicate that most blind adults have relatively little ability to travel independently, are dissatisfied with their level of performance, have not been systematic or purposeful in their mode of travel, have seldom had travel training of any duration, and have no active plans for improvement (Finestone, Lukoff, and Whiteman, 1960).

In 1974, it was estimated that fewer than 10 percent of the blind had achieved independent mobility by using a cane or other similar device (Dobelle, Mladejovsky, and Girvin, 1974).

The goals of programs to aid the blind are not limited to independent travel, but also involve training in dressing, eating, and personal relations. Specific travel training includes instruction in the use of the cane and experience with the seeing-eye dog, as well as more general training in motor and mental orientation in travel. Mobility has come to be recognized as vital to personal independence, independent travel, and vocational success. Consequently, many formal programs have been developed to promote and teach independent mobility to the blind (LaDuke, 1973). The first such program was the "Seeing Eye," founded by Dorothy Harrison Eustis. The use of guide dogs by the blind has received a good deal of popular interest, but its practicability has probably been exaggerated. It is estimated that the use of guide dogs is practical for only about 5 percent of the blind (Robson, 1974). The seeing-eye dog does not guide the blind person to a destination. The person must know the destination and how to get there. His is still the task of orientation. The dog, like the cane, only indicates the spaces into which the blind person can safely move.

The second organized program to teach orientation and increase the independent mobility of the blind was the armed services program developed during and following World War II. The Hines Center in the suburbs of Chicago concentrated on mobility training. One of the products of the Hines program was the long cane, sometimes called the "Hoover cane" after Dr. Richard Hoover, a former physical education instructor, who devised it. Although the introduction of the Hoover cane initially generated considerable resistance among the blind, it is almost universally accepted today as an important aid to mobility. The initial resistance arose because the blind felt that their public and self-images suffered when the cane publicized their disability. Some also argued that the long cane clearing a path through a crowd would endanger the sighted public. These claims have been mostly forgotten, and the Hoover technique is an important part of most programs of mobility training today.

When properly used, the Hoover cane becomes almost an antenna for sensing the environment. It can provide information concerning several things the blind especially fear, such as holes in the ground and ground surfaces which suddenly change steeply upward or downward, like a flight of stairs. The recommended technique for using the Hoover cane is as follows: The dominant hand is held near the center of the body with the index finger pointing straight down along the cane. The wrist is pivoted so that the tip of the can describes an arc in front of the user, touching the ground lightly on each side as it describes the arc. The tip should just clear the ground so that low protruding objects may be detected. The arc must be equidistant from the center on each side to allow for proper coverage of the entire body. The cane tip is moved in a rhythmic motion across the body in step with the feet: when the left foot steps forward, the cane makes its arc to the right, and vice versa (Uslan and Manning, 1974). One study demonstrated that intensive, directed training in the long cane can save about one-half the time usually spent in learning this skill (Peel, 1974).

California and several other states have, by statute, limited the use of the white cane to the legally blind and require all traffic to yield to persons carrying such canes.

Many formal programs provide orientation and mobility training for the visually impaired. In 1973 there were approximately four hundred trained people involved in providing such instruction in the United States (LaDuke, 1973). These programs were reaching out to meet the multiply handicapped, the aged, and those with low vision as well as blind children. J. Armstrong (1975) provides a good survey of current programs.

More than twenty electronic devices have been developed to enhance the mobility of the blind, but only a few have become commercially available. Some which were designed specifically to aid in orientation and mobility include: (a) the "Pathsounder," developed by Lindsay Russell, a unit about the size of a small camera which is suspended from the neck at chest height. It emits warning sounds when an object comes within three to six feet of the user. (b) Ultrasonic spectacles were devised by Dr. Lesley Kay. This device, which uses the principle of sonic radar employed by bats, consists of a modified spectacle frame housing ultrasonic sending and receiving units. The emitted sound is reflected from objects in its path, amplified, and conducted to the user's ears via two plastic tubes inserted in the ears. (c) A laser cane, developed by J. M. Benjamin, Jr., makes use of laser beams. This instrument projects three laser beams up, away, and down from the cane, which is held in front of the user. The presence of an object is signaled by means of a vibrating pin located in the cane's head or by a high-pitched tone. (d) Another mobility aid, which operates somewhat like the laser cane, is a device which projects a narrow beam of invisible infrared rays directly ahead of the user's head. An object within the detection range reflects the rays back to the glasses and is detected by a receiver. The reflected signal is amplified and passed in the form of a musical tone to the ear via a plastic tube. This device weighs less than three ounces and is mounted on ordinary eyeglass frames.[1] L. Kay (1975) analyzes a questionnaire filled out by users of his device and reports that 88 percent found it useful. These electronic aids all make use of hearing. Some other mobility aids use touch as the mediating sense.

Some experimental work has been done with tactile maps of an area which a blind person may wish to traverse. Preliminary work indicates that such maps can use variations in the elevation of symbols as effective coding dimensions. Plastic sheets have been found to work better than paper for such mapping. Raised figures are interpreted more readily than incised ones. Performance can be significantly improved by teaching the subject to scan a map in a systematic way. Overlays on the maps which present supplementary information in Braille have also been tried. Sometimes the Braille is placed on the underside of the map (Gill, 1974; Geldard, 1974). According to J. M. Gill, one limitation of the Braille supplement is that 60 percent of the registered blind population of England cannot read Braille. B. B. Blasch, R. L. Welsh, and T. Davidson (1973) have suggested that an "auditory map" consisting of a tape-recorded description of a particular route or geographic area, indicating landmarks relevant to orientation and independent travel, may supplement the use of a long cane or a guide dog.

Dependence on human guides is seldom satisfactory. It is often costly, and it makes the blind person's mobility contingent on the good health, dependability, and availability of a second person. If he or she can travel independently, the blind person is freed of dependence on the convenience and disposition of family members and friends, or the availability and competence of hired guides. Studies show that blind persons using human guides travel much less than those who use canes or dogs. The blind who use dogs as guides actually travel more than either of the other groups (Finestone, Lukoff, and Whiteman, 1960).

Independent travel involves mental orientation as well as physical locomotion (Lowenfeld, 1971; Warren and Kocon, 1974). Mental orientation is the recognition of an area in terms of its spatial and temporal relations to oneself. This recognition typically consists of a "mental map" or "schema" of the area, within which blind persons orient themselves as they move toward their destination. As they move about, they pick up cues—noises, echoes, changes in ground level, air currents, odors—which either confirm or cast doubt on the accuracy of the mental orientation. The blind person also makes use of "motor memory," the sense of direction and distance, a kind of "muscular memory." A destination is perceived as at a certain distance in terms of time or movement. The blind person perceives distances, not by counting steps, but more in terms of time and movement (Kay, 1974).

Many totally blind individuals can sense obstacles in their paths. This ability has generated the belief that the blind have a supernormal sensory capacity of some sort. Theories to explain the obstacle sense have ranged from the occult, bordering on the supernatural, through a heightened responsiveness of either known or unknown sense organs, indirect response to remote sensory cues (unrecognized cues arouse fear which produces contractions of the pilomotor muscles of the skin, and the person experiences the muscular contractions as an obstacle), to theories which assume a simple direct response to cues from one or more sense organs (auditory, thermal, or pressure).

A series of experiments started in the 1930s and continued over a period of twenty-five years demonstrated fairly well that the "obstacle sense" is largely a reaction to small, unrecognized auditory cues (principally echoes) which warn the individual of obstacles. There is nothing supersensory or mysterious about this responsiveness. A person with vision could accomplish it equally well if he or she had the motivation, training, and experience. In fact, it is probable that a blind person cannot accomplish anything with his remaining senses that a seeing person could not accomplish equally well with the same incentives and experiences. The obstacle sense can function only when conditions are favorable. The noise of wind, rain, and other things interferes with its functioning. When a person is moving rapidly, the auditory cues often cannot be perceived and reacted to quickly enough to be useful.

PERSONAL AND SOCIAL ADJUSTMENT

The earlier discussion of the relationship of exceptionality in general to personal and social adjustment applies to the visually impaired. There is no special "psychology of the blind." The blind are not characterized by any special personality characteristics or types. The adjustment problems of the visually disabled, like those of the normal, range all the way from problems of everyday social contacts to those of economic dependence. Congenitally blind children left to themselves do not live in a world of blackness or eternal night. They do not yearn for light or feel sorry for themselves because they cannot see. The few that do express such attitudes have acquired them from other people. The social and personal effects of impaired vision are nonspecific, most often taking the form of immaturity and insecurity (Bauman, 1964; Schindale, 1974). The fantasies of the blind concern social acceptance, personal achievement, and withdrawal to a simpler and less demanding life. These are analogous to the fantasies of the normally sighted (Cutsforth, 1951).

Certain "blindisms" are commonly listed as occasionally found in the blind. Blindisms are socially irrelevant and often bizarre repetitive activities which are distracting to other people. The most common ones are rocking or weaving, fingering or rubbing the eyes, waving the fingers before the face, and bending the head forward, as well as the twisting, squirming, and posturing which are characteristic of many nervous or mentally retarded sighted children. None of these activities is peculiar to the blind, and they are important only because they add to the person's exceptionality and decrease social acceptability. In most cases these activities disappear as the child grows up, although they persist longer in blind children who are also emotionally disturbed or mentally retarded. The socialization and personal development of the blind are being augmented by such things as special museums, exhibits, and gardens designed especially for them, such as the Mary Duke Biddle Gallery for the Blind, a part of the North Carolina Museum of Art in Raleigh, North Carolina; the Garden of Fragrance in San Francisco's Golden Gate Park; and the traveling museum for the blind sponsored by the California Arts Commission.

SENSORY ACUITY OF THE BLIND

The popular notion that the blind are endowed with hyperacute hearing, touch, taste, and smell or with phenomenal memory is largely erroneous. Studies have consistently shown that persons with vision are either equal or superior to the blind in their ability to identify the direction or distance of the source of a sound, to discriminate the relative intensities of tones, to recognize tactile forms, and to discriminate relative pressures, temperatures, or weights, as well as in their acuteness of smell, taste, and the vibratory sense. The blind have likewise displayed no superiority in either rote or logical memory (Lowenfeld, 1963; Emart and Carp, 1963). Any superiority of the blind in the perceptual areas is the result of increased attention to small cues and greater use of such cues as a source of information and guidance. It is apparently not the result of a lowering of sensory thresholds.

PERCEPTUAL AND CONCEPTUAL PROCESSES OF THE BLIND

It is obvious that the congenitally blind person experiences (perceives) the objects of the universe and builds up knowledge of the world in ways that are different from those of seeing children. That is, the blind person's percepts and concepts derive from different types of stimuli—which does not mean that this cognition is necessarily less adequate or useful.

It is as impossible for the seeing person to experience the world of the congenitally blind as it is for the congenitally blind to conceive of visual experiences, but it does not necessarily follow that the blind individual thereby has a significantly restricted range of concepts. Obviously, a person lacking visual perception will have no visual imagery. Studies indicate that adults who became blind before the age of five have no visual imagery (Lowenfeld, 1973). However, such people do develop and use concepts of forms, space, and distance beyond the range of touch and movement. They function efficiently in conceptual areas which sighted people derive primarily from visual experiences. It is not known if these percepts and concepts, derived primarily from tactile, kinesthetic, and auditory sources, remain on these levels or whether there is a coalescence of impressions and an emergence of concepts from such experiences into something akin to that which the sighted derive from visualization.

The duration of early visual experience prior to becoming blind is also important in the acquisition of manipulatory and locomotive skills. A child who has vision during the period when manual activities normally come under visual control will acquire a basic integration of the manual and visual modes. This provides the basis for a later extrapolation from motor to visual processes in those persons blinded later in life. Vision during the early years of life also seems critical in the development of locomotion.

Knowledge of the spatial qualities of objects is gained by the blind largely through touch and kinesthesis. Audition provides clues to the direction and distance of objects which make sounds, but it gives no idea of the objects as such. Tactile and kinesthetic experiences require direct contact with, or movement around, objects. Thus, distant objects, such as the heavenly bodies, clouds, and the horizon, as well as very large objects such as mountains and other geographical units, or microscopic objects such as bacteria, cannot be perceived and must be conceived only by analogy and extrapolation from objects actually experienced. While this is a limitation, it is probably comparable to the way in which the sighted person conceives of the size of the world and the other planets which cannot be directly perceived or of interplanetary distances which are far beyond direct experience. When interplanetary distances are stated in terms of light years, for example, one's conception of such magnitudes depends largely on verbal or written symbols, or is an extrapolation from distances actually traversed. They are hardly perceived in the way that the distant mountaintop or the corner grocery store are perceived.

EDUCATIONAL ACHIEVEMENT OF THE VISUALLY IMPAIRED

Visual defects of the type found in 25 to 35 percent of school children, most of which are not sufficiently severe to require special educational programs, do not seem to affect education achievement. While hyperopia (farsightedness) and astigmatism (irregularity of the curvature of the cornea) are associated with less than normal progress in reading, myopia (nearsightedness) is associated with above-normal progress in reading (Eames, 1959).

As early as 1918, an educational achievement test was developed for the blind (Hayes, 1941). Since then many achievement tests have been adapted for use with the blind. In addition to offering the tasks in Braille, these tests come with more detailed preliminary instructions, and two and one-half or three times the time is allowed for taking them. Some tests have been adapted for oral administration. Because of these differences, direct comparisons with the norms obtained on the regular tests with the sighted are rather hazardous. However, we can only take achievement test scores as we find them. When seeing and blind children are compared grade by grade, the two groups are about equal except in arithmetic, in which the scores of the blind are generally lower. However, blind children are on the average about two years older than seeing children of the same grade. Consequently, comparisons by either chronological or mental age indicate considerable educational retardation (Hayes, 1941; Lowenfeld, 1973). The greater age of blind children seems to result largely from their late entry to school, their absence from school because of treatment for eye trouble, the lack of appropriate school facilities, and their slower rate of obtaining information from Braille, large type, or audition. Persons interested in testing the blind will find *A Manual for the Psychological Examination of the Adult Blind* (Bauman and Hayes, 1951) very valuable.

Some of the incidental facts relevant to the school achievement of the blind are:

1. The cause of the blindness and the age of becoming blind are unrelated to school achievement (Hayes, 1934).

2. Age of school entrance is negatively correlated with school success (Hayes, 1934).

3. Blind children have particular difficulties in arithmetic (Nolan, 1959).

Currently Braille and large-type editions of the New Stanford Achievement Test series are available for grades two through twelve. These are power rather than speed tests (Morris, 1974).

EDUCATION OF THE VISUALLY IMPAIRED

The aims, content, and subject matter involved in the education of the visually impaired are not essentially different from those involved in normal education. They need a good general education, plus a vocational type of instruction which is in keeping with their special requirements. The education of the visually impaired, like all special education, requires specially trained teachers, special facilities and equipment, and some curricular modifications. Because the educations of the educationally blind and the partially sighted are somewhat different, we will discuss them separately.

SPECIAL EDUCATIONAL NEEDS OF THE BLIND

Ordinary educational experiences, it is estimated, are 85 percent visual. Since blind children are deprived of this type of experience, the adaptation required for their education requires a shift from vision to the auditory, tactile, and kinesthetic senses as avenues of instruction, learning, and guidance. These needs have been met by teaching Braille reading and writing, using many audio aids, and constructing and using models, as well as embossed and relief maps, graphs, and geometric designs. Because of the importance of independent mobility for the blind child, instruction in orientation and training and experiences designed to increase the child's control of the environment and of him or herself in relation to it are becoming part of special education programs for the blind.

the teaching of Braille Learning and developing facility in the Braille system of reading and writing is the greatest single curricular modification required for the education of the blind. In 1829 Louis Braille, a young blind student and later a teacher at the Paris School for the Blind, modified a military code used for night communication so that it could be used by the blind. The system has been further modified under various auspices. At one time three major systems were in use—the New York point system, American Braille, and British Braille. In 1932 a modified British Braille became the Standard English Braille, and since 1950 it has been used consistently as the preferred system. In 1950, UNESCO adapted a Braille system for all languages, but many of its details still have to be worked out.

Braille is the most efficient and useful means of reading and writing

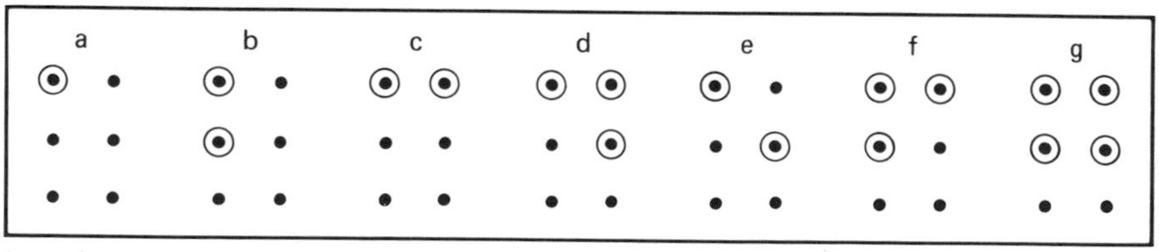

Figure 10–1 Sample of the Braille letter codes

yet devised for the blind. Using the sixty-three possible combinations of six raised dots in the Braille cell, virtually any literary, numerical, or musical material can be presented. Since unmodified Braille takes a lot of space, each Braille cell requires a quarter-inch of line, many abbreviations, contractions, and signs have been developed.

The proficient Braille reader must be familiar with the twenty-six letters of the alphabet, 189 contractions and short-form words, and 31 punctuation and composition marks—a total of 246 different basic elements (Brothers, 1974). The American Printing House for the Blind produces an instructional kit and a set of Braille Code Recognition materials to assist in the development of Braille reading skills.

Mathematics makes use of a special Braille notation system, and most scientific symbols can be written in Braille. A type of Braille shorthand for the blind stenographer has also been developed.

Although Braille is a modified military code, it is not merely a code for the blind reader. It is a complete medium for reading and writing. Braille is taught, learned, and read much the same as ordinary writing and reading. Reading Braille is, in many ways, similar to visual reading. The proficient Braille reader uses both hands in reading, but the two function independently, one ahead of the other. The hands move regularly and smoothly, and horizontally along the line, with few vertical regressive movements. The touch is light, the pressure uniform. The activity is not particularly fatiguing, and there seems to be no decrease in the sensitivity of the touch even after several hours of reading.

Developing facility in reading Braille involves a unifying process in which larger and larger units of material are apprehended at a time in a manner similar to the reading of print by sighted persons. Some Braille readers use lip movements or silent speech, just as do some visual readers.

The limitations of Braille as compared with visual reading are its relative slowness, the large size of books printed in Braille, and the restricted range of material available. A plane geometry textbook, when put into Braille, required over one thousand pages and cost more than ten times the same text in print. Carl Sandburg's biography of Abraham Lincoln is ten volumes in Braille. Braille reading is comparatively slow—about one-third or one-fourth the rate of visual reading. Blind high school students read approximately 90 words per minute in Braille. A really good Braille reader may attain a speed of 150–200 words a minute (Lowenfeld, 1973). Two studies have shown that relatively short periods of rapid reading instruction and practice can double a blind person's rate of reading Braille (Crandell and Wallace, 1974; McBride, 1974).

Braille can be written either by using a mechanical Braille writer or with a slate and stylus. Most schools start children writing with the Braille writer, which is relatively easy and fun to operate. The use of the slate and stylus is more difficult and requires fine motor coordination. The slates come in both pocket and desk sizes. Writing is done by punching holes with a stylus in a paper inserted between two metal strips. Since the material must be read from the underside of the paper, it must be written in reverse by starting at the right margin and writing toward the left. Blind children are also taught to use a standard typewriter, usually in the third or fourth grade. They find it very difficult to write with pen or pencil, and this is no longer emphasized except to teach each child to write his or her name.

Braille reading is so much taken for granted that few people realize a large proportion of the blind—mostly the elderly—are unable to read it. Many of these are diabetics who, as a consequence of their illness, have lost not only their vision, but also much of their fine touch sensitivity. The points of standard Braille are too small and too close together for these diabetics to perceive the characters. It is estimated that fewer than 20 percent of the legally blind persons in the United States can read Braille. A corresponding estimate made in Great Britain was 40 percent. At either value, only a small minority of the blind can read Braille (Dobelle and others, 1974).

OTHER FORMS OF TACTILE COMMUNICATION

Of the score or more systems—other than Braille—that have been devised for tactile communication, only a few have survived (Sherrick, 1975; Geldard,1974). The best-known of these devices is the Optacon, developed by J. C. Bliss and made commercially available by Telesensory Systems in 1971. According to Bliss, there were over a thousand Optacons in use in 1973 (Bliss and Moore, 1974). This machine is still being improved and modified, and plans are underway for a self-contained one-hand model. The Optacon enables the blind to read ordinary printed matter, exposed to a camera and transmitted to the finger pad as an array of vibrating pins which make a tactile facsimile of the printed symbols. However, M. J. Tobin and R. K. James's (1974) evaluation of the Optacon is not very encouraging. They provided thirty-six blind subjects with twelve hours of practice on the Optacon, and a smaller group of seventeen subjects with up to forty-eight hours of practice. The subjects were sixteen to fifty-four years of age and were all professional or semiprofessional people. Most of the subjects could read only ten to twelve words per minute after training. Some, for short periods of time, could reach forty words per minute. Tobin and James conclude that reaching a useful reading level with the Optacon is a long, hard process. They claim that reading machines, such as this one, are only "peripheral aids" where speed is not important, and when no other help is available. The company which manufactures the Optacon is now (1980) developing an attachment for their machine which converts written text into speech.

audio aids for the blind. The education of the blind requires many audio aids. Tape recorders and record players are necessary parts of their school life. Resource or itinerant teachers may give assignments or special instructions on tape. Text material not available in Braille may be taped or recorded. Recordings are normally read at rates of 150 to 170 words per minute—considerably faster than reading Braille. Most of the "talking books" available are fiction or magazines, but school texts are made available through the American Printing House for the Blind, the Library of Congress, and a few private agencies.

A "harmonic compressor" now makes it possible to compress human speech so that it can be played back at twice the normal rate without the usual "Donald Duck" effect which occurs when conventional recordings are reproduced at higher than their recording speeds. Aside from its speed, the reproduction sounds like natural speech. One comparison of Braille reading and listening to both normal and compressed speech recordings showed that Braille reading took twice as long as listening to normal recordings and three times as long as listening to compressed speech. With materials of four different levels of difficulty, no differences in comprehension were found among the three methods. Compressed speech was the most efficient (Tuttle, 1974). The Kurzweil Computer Products Company of Cambridge, Massachusetts has developed a machine which converts standard English text into synthetic speech. The current (1980) version of this device has a maximum reading speed of 250 words per minute (Goodrich and others, 1979). An analagous form of the Optacon was mentioned above.

arithmetic aids for the blind Mental arithmetic is used extensively in the education of the blind. For higher levels of mathematics, calculators, rulers, slide rules, compasses, and protractors have all been adapted for use by the blind. The Braille writer is also used in arithmetical calculations, as are an arithmetic board and adaptations of the abacus. Modeling clay, pins, and rubber bands are used in constructing geometric designs and graphs.

additional educational aids Braille relief and embossed maps and relief globes are useful in teaching geography as well as orientation and space perception to the blind child. Maps of the room, the school grounds, and the town help blind children develop a mental map of their surroundings, assist them in orientation, and aid their independent travel. In addition to mobility training and the special equipment mentioned, special physical education, art, and handicraft activities for the blind are required.

VOCATIONAL TRAINING FOR THE BLIND

The educational needs of the blind are more adequately met today than are their vocational needs. In most of the more advanced countries of the world today, no blind child of normal intelligence need grow up without academic, prevocational, and even some vocational training. Some programmed texts, modified for audio presentation to the blind, have been developed (Dunham and Shelton, 1973). However, many blind people are unable to obtain employment appropriate to their capacities. It is estimated that less than half of the blind individuals capable of working in general occupations are doing so and that only about 20 percent of those who could function adequately in sheltered workshops are so employed (Wilson, 1974).

Specialized vocational training—the teaching of specific skills and knowledge required for employment in regular trades or professions—is seldom provided by agencies for the blind. Only in a few limited areas, such as in work with other blind, in the operation of service stands, and in the teaching of special skills such as chair caning, broom-making, and weaving have the agencies for the blind developed vocational training programs. For the most part, blind people must obtain their vocational training along with the sighted.

a case study

In 1965 Don Harris contracted retinitis. By 1967 he was blind. Prior to this time he had been an auto mechanic. He says he spent the next few years sitting around complaining to his wife and feeling sorry for himself. When he decided he couldn't spend the rest of his life doing nothing, he contacted his state vocational rehabilitation department. His counselor decided that it might be possible for him to return to auto mechanics. He took additional training at the local community college. Two years later he and a sighted friend decided to open their own shop. His banker, after talking to Don's previous employers and his instructors, advanced the partners money enough to start their business.

"There are some things I can't do," says Don, "but most jobs I do by feel and by sound. A lot of car problems can be diagnosed by listening. Since most engines are basically alike, I can locate the various parts fairly easily." He has marked many of his tools in Braille. "When I need a pair of eyes, I use my partner's. No, I am not as fast as most sighted mechanics, but customers are charged in terms of a standard time schedule so they are not penalized because I work slower. When I take an hour and a half for a job that normally takes only an hour, the customer is charged for an hour. I think we will make it and I feel like a whole man again," he summarizes.

There are relatively few occupations and professions in which the blind are not successfully employed. For example, the National Blind

Teachers Association listed eighty blind teachers of the sighted in 1970 (Boykin, 1974). However, the sheltered workshop is still the largest single source of employment for blind people. In the most successful instances of industrial job placement, commitments have been obtained from top management for the employment of a given number of blind workers. It is understood that the workers will meet regular production schedules and standards and be paid at regular rates. As long as the company has jobs which can be satisfactorily performed by blind workers, employment opportunities will be maintained for a specified number or percentage of blind workers. Union commitments are sometimes needed to exempt these people from the seniority provisions of union contracts. Agreements to employ a certain *number* of blind, rather than a particular group of blind workers, prevent the loss of those jobs to other blind workers when a particular employment is terminated. To prevent the blind workers from isolating themselves from the larger working group, many placement officers prefer not to place several blind workers in the same department. H. Rusalem (1973) has provided a good discussion of the vocational problems of the blind.

The federal Rehabilitation Act, particularly section 504, as amended in 1973, prohibits all educational institutions and employers who receive federal funds in any form—and most do—from discriminating against handicapped persons solely on the basis of their handicap. This act also requires these agencies to engage in affirmative action programs for the handicapped.

EDUCATION OF THE PARTIALLY SIGHTED

The education of the partially sighted is much less a problem than is that of the blind. For the most part, the partially sighted are basically people who can see and are educated with and prepared for life as such. At one time a large number of "sight-saving" classes were conducted for the partially sighted. The notion of sight saving has been largely discarded because it is generally recognized that the maximum use of even defective eyes will not cause them to deteriorate. Vision is not saved by not using it. The child with poor vision is now encouraged to use vision to its maximum, to learn to read print, to write, and to acquire as much education as possible by sight. In contrast with the sight-saving emphasis of the old classes for the partially sighted, we now find programs, or at least proposals, for their "sight development" or "sight utilization." In such programs, the children are "learning to see," to make full use of their residual vision (Lowenfeld, 1973).

People working with the visually impaired are becoming increasingly concerned with the most effective use of any residual vision. Many legally blind children have potentially useful but undeveloped near vision. Many such children can develop considerable functional vision even though they have very low measured visual acuity. However, these children require planned opportunities and programs. Teaching procedures specifically directed at this end can significantly increase the visual efficiency of partially sighted children (Barraga, 1970).

The education of partially sighted children makes those adjustments in curriculum and equipment necessary for the education of handicapped children, but otherwise education is not unique. They do not have to learn Braille reading and writing. They are capable of independent travel without acquiring special techniques. Their spatial orientation and concepts are not unique.

educational aids for the partially sighted For the child with borderline vision, minor adjustments, such as sitting near the blackboard, placing the desk in a good light, and being allowed to move about so as to be as close as possible to charts and other wall displays, may be all that is necessary.

For the more severely handicapped child, books in large type and magnifying devices of various types are necessary. Two companies—American Printing House for the Blind and Stanwix Publishing House—publish books in large type for the partially sighted, and a fairly wide variety of reading material is becoming available.

In 1954 the National Association for Visually Handicapped was formed to aid the partially sighted. This agency serves as a clearing-house for large-print books. In addition to distributing large-print books, it also supplies information concerning special aids for the partially sighted and publishes a large-print newsletter. The address of this association is 385 East 24th Street, 17-c, New York, New York 10010.

The simplest way to obtain magnification of print is to bring the book closer to the eyes. To see people holding reading material very close to the eyes is disturbing to many persons because they believe such close reading damages the eyes. Most authorities believe that reading material may safely be held as close to the eyes as necessary. For many partially sighted individuals, however, holding print close to the eyes is not adequate and other means of magnification may be needed.

Optical magnification is achieved in several ways. Magnifying projectors and special lenses—both contact and in conventional frames—are available. Telescopic effects are achieved by using contact lenses along with special lenses in conventional frames. A wide variety of special magnifying devices is produced.

Simple enlargement of print or magnification does not make a normal reader out of the partially sighted person. All means of enlarging print reduce the effective field of vision. This means that the amount of material that can be perceived at one time is reduced, and the rate of reading is correspondingly slow. It is therefore necessary to find the most appropriate type and degree of magnification for each person.

BLIND COLLEGE STUDENTS

Blind college students have special needs. They need to read a large number of technical and highly specialized books. Obtaining access to these books either in Braille or as recordings is often difficult. Recordings for the Blind, Inc., makes tape recordings of such books and is constantly enlarging its free lending library. It serves over 80 percent of the blind college students in the United States and supplies them with several thousand tapes annually. Limited financial support for the organization comes from businesses, foundations, and private contributors. However, the more than 4,000 unpaid volunteers who contribute their time and talent are the greatest asset. The organization is always in need of additional qualified volunteers to keep abreast of the expanding and ever-changing literature. Persons interested in donating their services should contact the organization at 215 East 58th Street, New York, New York 10022. Recording centers are located throughout the United States.

Currently, several psychological journals are available in recorded form by subscription. Interested persons can contact Mari Bull, 219 North Indian Hill Boulevard, Suite 100, Claremont, California 91711.

For materials which are not available in taped form or in Braille, the blind have to depend on readers. In most states limited funds are available to pay such readers. In many cases sighted fellow-students volunteer services. The Kurzweil and Optacon reading machines will be useful aids for college students.

a case study

When word circulated that Rip, our blind classmate, would be unable to continue in graduate school because the state would no longer pay his reader, I (C.W.T.) became involved. I never really knew about the cause or onset of Rip's blindness. I always understood that the condition was congenital. Although he had travel vision and was able to move about independently, he was legally and educationally blind. Rip was bright, sociable, and musically talented. While in college he had some financial help from his family and was able to support himself partially by tuning pianos. He majored in psychology but his primary interest and activity was music. He had a good singing voice and played both the piano and violin.

When word got around about Rip's problem, several of his classmates got together and agreed that those individuals who were in his classes would take turns reading for him. This worked out well for all concerned, despite the readers' occasional consternation when Rip got better grades on an examination than they did. I was graduate assistant in the psychology department and one of my minor duties was to help Rip take his examinations. I would read the examination questions to him as he took them down in Braille. He would then retire to a small cubicle and type out his answers to the questions. When completed, his papers were returned to me. One day the paper he turned in was a complete blank. I discovered that he had failed to fasten the end of his new typewriter ribbon properly and consequently nothing had been typed. He was quite chagrined, for he knew that he should have checked periodically to make sure the ribbon was feeding properly.

Rip was able to function in most ways like a normally sighted person. He would talk about "seeing" things and how things "looked." Often these observations were inferences from remarks he overhead. One time he and I were walking downtown and he remarked about how improved the front of Penney's store was since they had done it over. I laughed and asked him how he knew that. Well, he had heard people remark about the front being renovated. He had also heard work going on for the last several weeks. All was quiet today so he assumed that the work was completed and also that it looked better.

Rip finished his master's degree with the rest of us but felt that there was no future for him in psychology. Consequently, he returned to the small town where he grew up, married, raised a family, and earned a good living teaching music. He and his acquaintances always viewed Rip as a completely "normal" individual who simply lacked normal vision.

A few years ago, the majority of blind persons graduating from college were limited to professional opportunities in the field of work for the blind as home teachers, counselors, and instructors in centers for the blind. Today most of them are finding employment in the world of the sighted.

David Hartman has disproven one preconception concerning the blind by completing, with only minor deviations, all the courses required for the MD degree at the Temple University School of Medicine (Holden, 1976).

RESIDENTIAL VERSUS REGULAR CLASSES

Residential schools were the first, and for a long time practically the only, facilities for the education of the visually impaired. With the development of many local facilities, however, the role of the residential schools has lessened. Most educators today believe that those children who can be educated in regular, unsegregated classrooms should be so placed. Children who can be educated in special classes, or by resource or itinerant teachers, should not be institutionalized. The residential school aims to return the handicapped child to the regular school as quickly as possible. The majority of visually impaired children are in integrated classrooms with their sighted peers, with supplementary services supplied by resource teachers.

Currently all degrees of educational integration of the visually handicapped are found, in all the states and in most communities. These range from complete segregation in residential schools or self-contained special classes, through resource rooms staffed by special teachers where students spend part of each day, regular class placement with special instruction by itinerant teachers, and regular class placement with assistance from consultants, to regular class placement without special assistance from others. All of these levels of segregation-integration are needed and should be available as alternatives (Simon and Gillman, 1979).

Today when a child with serious visual impairment is assigned to a regular classroom, a close relationship will already have been established between the appropriate special education teacher and the regular teacher. The special and regular teachers will decide what adjustments in program and special equipment will be required. There will also be a mutual understanding as to each teacher's duties and responsibilities. Normally this division will be somewhat as follows.

Special education teachers prepared to work with the visually handicapped may serve as consultants, itinerant teachers, resource teachers, or as teachers of self-contained classes. The specialized teacher who works cooperatively with the regular class teacher will usually:

1. see that the children are supplied with and are taught to use all special materials such as magnifiers, large-print material, Braille materials (writers, slates, and so forth), typewriters, tape recorders, abacus, special maps, and so forth.

2. participate in the assessment of, and educational planning for, the visually handicapped.

3. help monitor their progress and deal with special problems that arise.

4. provide mobility training and initial orientation to the classrooms and school grounds as needed.

5. provide and monitor reader and Braille services when needed.

6. regularly confer with, advise, and counsel both parents and teachers.

Special help usually provided the visually impaired by the *regular* teachers will include:

1. making sure that these children have been oriented to the places they must go and the routes to get there. Special alerts should be given concerning obstructions and other danger points.

2. informing the children concerning any *changes* made in routes, room arrangements, and locations of objects.

3. providing a place where the children can store their special equipment. Care of the equipment should be the children's responsibility.

4. assisting the other children in understanding their new classmates by providing information concerning the causes and nature of the special child's impairment and ways of compensating for the handicap.

5. indicating to sighted children when special help is appropriate and how to volunteer it. Warning them against doing more than is necessary.

6. asking one or two other students to assist students with visual handicaps in case of emergencies.

7. insisting on the same standards of conduct, responsibilities, work assignments, and levels of performances for blind children as for the other children.

EDUCATION OF THE BLIND WITH ADDITIONAL HANDICAPS

The negative effects of multihandicaps tend to be multiplicative rather than simply additive. Specifically, the total effects of blindness and deafness together are far more detrimental than the simple additive effects of either occurring separately. One basic difference between a deaf-blind child and a child who is *either* blind *or* deaf is that the former has no concept of the function of language. The deaf child can see other people communicating and can see the effects of communicating. While initially he or she does not understand the process, when language training is started the nature of the oral communication process soon becomes apparent. The blind child, of course, hears and acquires speech as does the sighted, and understands the use of language as an expressive and manipulative device. In contrast, the congenitally deaf-blind child has no awareness of language—either its existence or its functions. So, in addition to acquiring the mechanics of communication, the deaf-blind child must first develop an awareness of communication and a concept of its purposes and functions. He or she must also be motivated to participate in communicative activities.

Dr. Samuel G. Howe and Ann Sullivan Macy's pioneering work with Laura Bridgman and Helen Keller, respectively, focused attention on the education of the deaf-blind in America. The first systematic program for these children was provided at the Perkins Institute for the Blind in Watertown, Massachusetts. Over the past decade there has been a decrease in the proportion of handicapped individuals with single disabilities and an increase in the proportion with multiple handicaps (Nezol, 1975). The rubella epidemic of 1964–65 produced many deaf and blind children and has resulted in an increasing concern for these children in the United States. Whereas in 1970 there were fewer than a dozen programs in the United States specifically for deaf-blind children, by 1975 there were nearly one hundred (Hammer, 1975).

The education of these children is a very demanding, one-to-one, teaching-learning process. The teacher typically becomes a companion to the student and provides constant and intensive social contact and stimulation as well as formal instruction. Education is initially directed at establishing contacts with the world via the cutaneous, kinesthetic, gustatory, and olfactory senses, and arousing a desire for learning. The isolation of the deaf-blind individual is great, and only after effective contact is established can this person's isolation be reduced and formal instruction become possible.

A device potentially useful to the deaf-blind has recently been developed. The instrument applies the "speech feeling" technique made famous by Helen Keller and taught for many years at the Perkins Institute (Kirman, 1973). When using this technique, the deaf-blind person places a hand on the face of the speaker in such a way that one or more fingers can detect lip and jaw movements and oral air pressure. One finger detects throat vibrations, and one finger feels the nasal vibrations. By learning to differentiate these complex cutaneous patterns, the trained person's perception of language becomes remarkably accurate.

The device developed by J. D. Miller, E. M. Engebretson, and C. L. DeFilippo (1974), using this principle, transmits nasal vibrations, throat vibrations, and pressure variations near the speaker's lips to three locations on the skin in the form of tactile vibrations. Initial reports of the use of this device were encouraging (Sherrick, 1975).

One interesting program is provided by the Hadley School for the Blind, founded in 1920 in Winnetka, Illinois, as a correspondence school. The school offers a course called "Independent Living Without Sight and Hearing," designed by Hadley's president, Dr. Richard Kinney, and taught by Geraldine Lawhorn. Both Kinney and Lawhorn are deaf and blind. Hadley has an enrollment of several thousand students. Tuition is free for the legally blind (Crist, 1975).

Special educational programs for the blind–mentally retarded have also been established. While these programs require much less modification than do those for the deaf-blind, the instruction is largely individualized and classes must be limited to three to five children (Williams, 1968, Ellis, 1979).

SELF-HELP AIDS AND SUGGESTIONS
FOR SIGHTED-PERSON ASSISTANCE

Those who live or work with the blind will find useful the wealth of practical suggestions provided by such books as B. Lowenfeld's *Our Blind Children,* now in the third edition, as well as the catalogs and information supplied by The American Foundation for the Blind (15 West 16th Street, New York, New York 10011). Special items invented or modified for the blind by the Foundation include watches with raised dots for numbers, safety-insulated spoons which hook onto the cooking pot, knives with built-in slicing guides for cutting such foods as meat and cheese at desired thicknesses, needle threaders, a hem gauge, pie-cutting guides, carpenter's levels with audible indicators, measuring devices with raised dots indicating dimensions and unit divisions, and a large number of modified popular games.

Suggestions for the sighted who wish to aid the blind include the following: (a) Teach children to use the Continental technique of eating (holding the fork in the left hand and the knife in the right at all times) rather than the American "cross-over" convention. The former makes the act of eating neater and simpler for the blind. (b) Maintain a routine in table arrangements, tell the location of things "by the clock," and use salt and pepper shakers of different sizes or shapes. Teach children to shake salt and pepper into their hand before putting them on food, so as to estimate the amount. Name and indicate the location of food as it is served. (c) To assist in walking, ask the blind person if he or she would like to take your elbow. A gentle but firm grip just above your elbow is best. The blind person can then walk about half a step behind you. Start and stop gradually rather than abruptly, and walk in as straight a line as possible. (d) Let the blind person enter a car by himself after you have placed his hand on the car door. A blind friend of the senior author has humorously described the various ways in which he has been "manhandled" by persons trying to "put" him into a car or bus. (e) In a restaurant, place the blind person's hand either on the chair back or on the seat, and read the menu aloud unless he already knows it. Let him give his order to the waiter. Either touch his hand or tell him the location of such things as ash trays, sugar bowls, salt and pepper shakers. Tell him what his bill is and let him pay the waiter or cashier. (f) When you meet a blind person, shake her hand if she makes a gesture in your direction. Speak directly to her; do not use her sighted companion as an "interpreter." Do not raise your voice.

SUMMARY

The blind were the first handicapped group for whom social provisions were made. Although the numbers involved are comparatively small, they have enjoyed more public concern and special legislation than any other category of the handicapped. Today the quantitative definitions of blindness and partial sight are being either supplemented or replaced by more situationally relevant, functional definitions. While the blind are easily identified, the partially sighted require examinations by specialists.

A wide variety of both genetic and environmental causes produces blindness. Infections and accidents are decreasing in importance as causes, whereas a larger percentage of blindness is attributed to prenatal factors the exact nature of which are largely unknown. It is estimated that among school-age children, one in three thousand meet the medico-legal criterion of blindness, and that one in five hundred have vision in the 20/70 to 20/200 range commonly designated as partially sighted. The United States Office of Education estimates that about half the medico-legally blind children (one out of six thousand) are educationally blind (requiring the bulk of their education to be other than visual) and that about twice this number (one in three thousand) require the special education provided for the partially sighted.

The three major problems of the blind are social understanding, education by other than visual means, and independent mobility. Some type of educational program is available to practically all of the blind in the United States. The problems of social understanding and acceptance of the blind are gradually being reduced. Systematic assistance and training for independent travel are only recently becoming available.

The "obstacle sense" of the blind has been shown to be fundamentally the location of echoes by auditory means. The language of the blind is not noticeably different from that of normal people. Language defects are probably more common, but they are not noticeably different in type from those of the sighted. The same things are true of the personal and social maladjustment of the visually impaired. Their basic intellectual capacities are probably normal. Their restricted sensory input, limited mobility, and greater dependence on other people probably account for any deficits they show in intelligence and on scholastic achievement tests. The blind seem to be capable of compensating for their visual deficit in the perceptual and conceptual areas. While the congenitally blind lack visual percepts and concepts, they do not suffer any significant overall deficiency in this area.

All of the different types of administrative arrangements are used in educating the blind. Most blind school children attend regular integrated classrooms. The special educational needs of the blind are the learning of Braille; the extensive use of auditory, tactile, and kinesthetic experiences; and special mobility training. The partially sighted are educated essentially as are the normally sighted, but with the aid of large print and magnification of various types.

REFERENCES

American Foundation for the Blind, *A Teacher Education Program for Those Who Serve Blind Children and Youth.* (New York: American Foundation for the Blind, 1961).

Armstrong, J., "Blind Mobility: Current Research Programs," *American Foundation for the Blind: Research Bulletin,* June 1975, *29,* 145–48.

Barraga, N. C., "Teaching Children with Low Vision," in R. L. Jones, ed., *New Directions in Special Education* (Boston: Allyn and Bacon, 1970).

Bauman, M. K., "Group Differences Disclosed by Inventory Items," *International Journal of the Education of the Deaf,* 1964, *13,* 101–6.

Bauman, M. K. and S. P. Hayes, *A Manual for the Psychological Examination of the Adult Blind* (New York: The Psychological Corporation, 1951).

Best, H., *Blindness and the Blind in the United States* (New York: Macmillan, 1934).

Blasch, B. B., R. L. Welsh, and T. Davidson, "Auditory Maps: An Orientation Aid for Visually Handicapped Persons," *The New Outlook for the Blind,* 1973, *67,* 145–58.

Bliss, J. C. and M. W. Moore, "The Optacon Reading System," *Education of the Visually Handicapped,* 1974, *6,* 98–102.

Bourgeault, S. E., "Blindness: A Label," *Education of the Visually Handicapped,* 1974, *6,* 1–6.

Boykin, A. O., "There's a Unicorn in the Classroom," *Phi Delta Kappan,* 1974, *60* (8), 593–94.

Brothers, R. J., "Classroom Use of the Braille Code Recognition Materials," *Education of the Visually Handicapped,* 1974, *6,* 6–13.

Brown, C. E., "Defining and Measuring Services to Improve Their Effectiveness," *The New Outlook for the Blind,* 1974, *68,* 241–46.

Chase, J. B., "A Retrospective Study of Retrolental Fibroplasia," *The New Outlook for the Blind,* 1974, *68,* 61–71.

Corbett, M. P., "Professionalism in Mobility," *The New Outlook for the Blind,* 1974, *68,* 104–7, 123–25.

Crandell, J. M. and D. H. Wallace, "Speed Reading in Braille: An Empirical Study," *The New Outlook for the Blind,* 1974, *68,* 13–19.

Crane, M. M., and others, "Study of Procedures for Screening Elementary School Children for Visual Defects," *American Journal of Public Health,* 1952, *42,* 1430–39.

Crist, L. M., "One Who Has Learned to 'See' and 'Hear' Guides Others," *The Christian Science Monitor,* 21 April 1975, 23.

Cutsforth, T. D., *The Blind in School and Society,* rev. ed. (New York: American Foundation for the Blind, 1951).

David, W. D., "Your Health: Eye Care," *Today's Education,* 1970, *59* (3), 10.

Davidson, O. R., "The Accountability of Nonprofit Institutions in a Free Society," *The New Outlook for the Blind,* 1973, *67,* 389–95.

Dobelle, W. H., M. G. Mladejovsky, and J. P. Girvin, "Artificial Vision for the Blind," *Science,* 1974, *183,* 440–43.

Dunham, J. and H. Shelton, "Machine Presented Audible Programmed Instruction for the Blind," *Education of the Visually Handicapped,* 1973, *5,* 117–19.

Eames, T. H., "The Influence of Hypermetropia and Myopia on Reading Achievement," *American Journal of Ophthalmology,* 1955, *39,* 375–77.

Eames, T. H., "Visual Defects in Reading," *Journal of Education,* 1959, *141,* 1–34.

Ellis, D., "Visual Handicaps of Mentally Handicapped People," *American Journal of Mental Deficiency,* 1979, *83,* 497–54.

Emart, A. G. and F. M. Carp, "Recognition of Tactual Forms by Sighted and Blind Subjects," *American Journal of Psychology,* 1963, *76,* 488–91.

Finestone, S., I. Lukoff, and M. Whiteman, *The Demand for Dog Guides and the Travel Adjustment of Blind Persons* (New York: Research Center, Columbia University, 1960).

Foote, F. M. and M. M. Crane, "An Evaluation of Visual Screening," *Exceptional Children,* 1954, *20,* 153–61.

Geldard, F. A., ed., *Conference on Cutaneous Systems and Devices* (Austin, Tex.: The Psychonomic Society, 1974).

Gill, J. M., "Tactual Mapping," *Research Bulletin: American Foundation for the Blind,* October 1974, *28,* 57–80.

Ginsberg, E., "Preventive Health: No Easy Answers," *The Sight-Saving Review,* 1973–74, *43,* 187–95.

Goodrich, G. L., R. R. Bennett, W. R. DeL'aune, H. Laver and L. Mauinski, Kurzweil Reading Machine: A Partial Evaluation of its Optical Character Recognition Error Rate, *Journal of Visual Impairment and Blindness,* 1979, *73,* 389–399.

Hammer, E. K., "What Is Effective Programming for Deaf-blind Children?" *The New Outlook for the Blind,* 1975, *69,* 25, 31.

Hatfield, E. M., "Estimates of Blindness in the United States," *Sight-Saving Review,* 1973, *43,* 69–80.

Hayes, S. P., *Contributions to a Psychology of Blindness* (New York: American Foundation for the Blind, 1941).

Hayes, S. P., "Factors Influencing the School Success of the Blind," *Teachers Forum (Blind),* 1934, *6,* 91–99.

Holden, C., "Blind Medical Student: Overcoming Preconceptions," *Science,* 1976, *191,* 1241–43.

Jones, J. W., "Problems Involved in Defining and Classifying Blindness," *New Outlook for the Blind,* 1962, *56,* 115–21.

Kay, L., "Orientation for Blind Persons: Clear Path Indicators as Environmental Sensor," *The New Outlook for the Blind,* 1974, *68,* 289–96.

Kay, L., "The Sonic Glasses Evaluated," *The New Outlook for the Blind,* 1975, *67,* 7–11.

Kerby, C. E., "A Report on the Visual Handicap of Partially Seeing Children," *Exceptional Children,* 1958, *43,* 137–42.

Kirman, J. H., "Tactile Communication of Speech," *Psychological Bulletin,* 1973, *80,* 54–74.

Kupfer, C., "Evaluation of the Treatment of Diabetic Retinopathy: A Research Project," *The Sight-Saving Review,* 1973, *43,* 17–28.

LaDuke, R. O., "An Analysis of Current Issues and Trends in Orientation and Mobility," *Education of the Visually Handicapped,* 1973, *5,* 20–27.

Lowenfeld, B., *Our Blind Children,* 3rd ed. (Springfield, Ill.: Charles C. Thomas, 1971).

Lowenfeld, B., "The Visually Handicapped," *Review of Educational Research,* 1963, *33,* 38–41.

Lowenfeld, B., ed., *The Visually Handicapped Child in School* (New York: John Day, 1973).

Lowenfeld, B., G. L. Abel, and P. H. Hatten, *Blind Children Learn to Read* (Springfield, Ill.: Charles C Thomas, 1969).

Lowenstein, B. E. and P. D. Preger, Jr., *Diabetes: New Look at an Old Problem* (New York: Harper and Row, 1976).

Maugh, T. H., II, "Diabetes: Epidemiology Suggests a Viral Connection," *Science,* 1975, *188,* 347–51.

McBride, V. G., "Explorations in Rapid Reading in Braille," *The New Outlook for the Blind,* 1974, *68,* 8–12.

Miller, J. D., E. M. Engebretson, and C. L. DeFilippo, "Preliminary Research with a Three-channel Vibrotactile Speech-reception Aid for the Deaf," *Journal of the Acoustical Society of America,* 1974, *55,* Supplement 564.

Morris, J. E., "The 1973 Stanford Achievement Test Series as Adapted for Use by the Visually Handicapped," *Education of the Visually Handicapped,* 1974, *6,* 33–40.

Nezol, A. J., "Reading and the Multiply Handicapped Blind Child," *The New Outlook for the Blind,* 1975, *69,* 39–41.

Nolan, C. Y., "Achievement in Arithmetic Computation: Analysis of School Differences and Identification of Areas of Low Achievement," *International Journal of Education of the Blind,* 1959, *8,* 125–28.

Peel, J. C. F., "Psychological Aspects of Long Cane Orientation Training," *Research Bulletin: American Foundation for the Blind,* October 1974, *28,* 111–24.

Reynolds, M. C. and Birch, J. W., *Teaching Exceptional Children in All America's Schools,* Reston, Va.: The Council for Exceptional Children, 1977.

Robson, H., "The Practice of Guide Dog Mobility in the United Kingdom," *The New Outlook for the Blind,* 1974, *68,* 72–78.

Rusalem, H., *Coping with the Unseen Environment: An Introduction to the Vocational Rehabilitation of Blind Persons* (New York: Teachers College Press, 1973).

Schindale, R., "The Social Adjustment of Visually Handicapped Children in Different Educational Settings," *Research Bulletin: American Foundation for the Blind,* October 1974, *28,* 125–44.

Scott, R. A., *The Making of Blind Men* (New York: Russell Sage Foundation, 1969).

Sherrick, C. E., "The Art of Tactile Communication," *American Psychologist,* 1975, *30,* 353–60.

Simon, E. P. and A. E. Gillman, "Mainstreaming Visually Handicapped Preschoolers," *Exceptional Children,* 1979, *45,* 463–64.

Tobin, M. J. and R. K. James, "Evaluating the Optacon: General Reflections on Reading Machines for the Blind," *Research Bulletin: American Foundation for the Blind,* October 1974, *28,* 145–57.

Tuttle, D. W., "A Comparison of Three Reading Media for the Blind: Braille, Normal Recording, and Compressed Speech," *Research Bulletin: American Foundation for the Blind,* April 1974, *27,* 217–30.

Uslan, M. M. and P. Manning, "A Graphic Analysis of Touch Techniques Safety," *Research Bulletin: American Foundation for the Blind,* October 1974, *28,* 175–80.

Warren, D. H. and I. A. Kocon, "Factors in the Successful Mobility of the Blind: A Review," *Research Bulletin: American Foundation for the Blind,* October 1974, *28,* 191–218.

Williams, D., "Sunland's Program for the Blind," *Mental Retardation,* 1964, *2,* 244–45.

Wilson, E. L., "Assessing the Readiness of Blind Persons for Vocational Placement," *New Outlook for the Blind,* 1974, *65,* 57–60.

Suggestions for Students and Instructors

1. Have class members try some of the suggested stimulation activities such as eating a meal, moving from one classroom to another, or spending longer periods of time blindfolded. Partial blindness can be simulated by reducing the transparency of goggle lenses in varying degrees.

2. Have a blind person talk to the class and demonstrate the use of Braille, the Hoover cane, and other special aids.

3. Visit classes or schools where young visually impaired children are enrolled.

4. Have a person who uses a seeing-eye dog discuss the advantages and limitations of using such dogs.

Additional Readings

International Guide to Aids and Appliances for Blind and Visually Impaired Persons (New York: American Foundation for the Blind, 1979). A comprehensive source of practical information.

Fraiberg, S., *Insights from the Blind: Comparative Studies of Blind and Sighted Infants* (New York: Basic Books, 1977). A detailed study of two cases and a less complete longitudinal study of ten otherwise healthy children who were blind from birth.

Lowenfeld, B., ed., *The Visually Handicapped Child in School* (New York: John Day, 1973). A readable, authoritative book dealing with all aspects of impaired vision, including mainstreaming, and the changing roles of the residential schools and special programs.

Selected Films

Not Without Sight. (19 minutes) American Foundation for the Blind, 15 West 16th Street, New York, N. Y. 10011. Visual impairment as seen by four people with visual defects.

What Color is the Wind? (27 minutes) Allan Grant Productions, 808 Lochearn Street, Los Angeles, Calif. 90049. An award-winning film dealing with the life of twin boys, one of whom is blind.

What Do You Do When You See a Blind Person? (15 minutes) Harvest Films, Inc., 309 Fifth Avenue, New York, N. Y. 10016. This film deals with the stereotypes and expectations of people who encounter the blind. The right and wrong ways of helping are illustrated.

ORGANIZATIONS AND AGENCIES

American Foundation for the Blind, Inc.
15 West 16th Street
New York, N. Y. 10011

American Printing House for the Blind
1839 Frankfort Avenue
Louisville, Ky. 40206

Association for Education of the Visually Handicapped
919 Walnut Street, Fourth Floor
Philadelphia, Pa. 19107

Library of Congress
Division for the Blind and Physically Handicapped
Taylor Street Annex
1291 Taylor Street
Washington, D. C. 20542

National Association for Visually Handicapped
305 East 24th Street, 17-C
New York, N. Y. 10010

National Federation of the Blind
218 Randolph Hotel Building
4th and Court Streets
Des Moines, Iowa 50309

CHAPTER 11

THE AURALLY HANDICAPPED

Our third child June was all right, apparently alert and very cute. There was no reason to suspect that anything could be wrong with her. When she failed to turn toward me when I spoke to her, I was sure she was just not attending. When she learned to walk, her mother remarked that June came readily when you held out your hands toward her but did not come when called. I insisted that she was busy and engrossed in what she was doing. When she was fifteen months I became concerned that she was slow to talk; she was still babbling. When I mentioned it to my pediatrician he said, "The youngest in the family with several other children is often slow in talking because the others anticipate her needs and she gets things without talking."

When my mother stayed with the children for a weekend, she reported that June didn't pay attention when she spoke to her. We took her to our pediatrician for her regular check-up and again voiced our concern. He examined her ears and observed her response to a cricket snapper. He was not sure that she was hearing. He asked if she babbled, and played pat-a-cake. "Yes, she did." He said that he thought the child was too young to be tested. Six months later we pressed the issue with our pediatrician. He used the snapper again and rang some bells and insisted that in his opinion nothing was wrong.

Not until June was thirty months old did our apprehension reach the point where it was evident to us as well as to the other children that something was wrong. We consulted an otolaryngologist. June was finally diagnosed as deaf but with some residual hearing in both ears. We had already lost over two years of precious time when she should have been receiving help.

We were told that even though our daughter was deaf, with properly fitted hearing aids and training, she should be able to function as a partially hearing individual, and for this we should be grateful. We soon learned that for the parents this meant hours, days, weeks, and even years of auditory training. We talked and talked and talked, both with the child's attention focused on our lips to encourage lip reading and with our faces masked to encourage her to use her residual hearing. We would invent and use a wide variety of verbal and tonal games for the same reason. With the fitting of a hearing aid, our auditory training was rewarded by a gush of babbled nonsense, which the professionals told us represented the beginnings of speech. When the babbling developed into recognizable words, we had proof that she was actually using her residual hearing and we were elated.

As the communication barriers lessened, I found myself drawn closer to my daughter. The discovery of our daughter's deafness had come as a lasting shock. I still find that my inability to communicate naturally and effortlessly with her prevents me from banishing completely the ghost of the problem of deafness. I now realize how much we take for granted in communicating with those who hear. With the hearing impaired we must be careful in phrasing, and timing too. I also became aware of the interaction of speech and meanings. I realized that saying, "June, I am going to work, now," was much more readily "heard" after she had been to my office where I worked, observed things that I did, and had some inkling of why I did them. The context and meaning greatly aided her "hearing." Pointing to the door when the doorbell or the telephone rings assists her in hearing these sounds meaningfully. When for the first time she spontaneously said, "I hear a bird," it seemed to mean, "She really cannot be deaf . . . she hears!"

When we sit on the beach and listen, just listen, trying to pick out the sound of a particular bird and she says, "It is a killdeer," it suddenly comes to me that hearing is a priceless gift that we may trade away in some sorry bargain because we fail to sense its true value.

THE SIGNIFICANCE OF AURAL HANDICAPS

Because of the low visibility of auditory defects, and because the hard-of-hearing are often suspected of being unmotivated, inattentive, or mentally retarded, the general public has lacked interest in and sympathy for the aurally handicapped. The normal person can close his or her eyes and move about in total darkness and achieve some conception of the nature of blindness. The average individual has been temporarily orthopedically handicapped and has obtained some idea of the problems of the crippled. However, one cannot close one's ears. Even inserting ear plugs does not approximate the condition of the average person with a serious auditory deficit. The nonhandicapped individual typically is either apathetic or impatient with the acoustically handicapped person.

In many respects, the deaf are a misunderstood, disadvantaged minority. For example, although there are legal precedents requiring courts to provide interpreters without cost for the deaf as well as for those who do not speak English, only a few states have actually legislated this requirement for the deaf. Even with competent interpreters the language gulf presents serious problems. The sign language of the deaf lacks precise equivalent words for many commonplace legal terms. When literal translation is impossible, interpreters attempt to convey the sense of the statements. This often raises the objections of judges and opposing lawyers.

The young child with defective hearing often does not realize the nature of his or her problems, and few nonhandicapped adults are aware of the breadth of the problems of the aurally handicapped. The failure of the congenitally deaf child to acquire speech in the ordinary way, and such a child's inability to hear the speech of others, are the most obvious handicaps. However, the oral and aural handicaps of the deaf and the severely hard-of-hearing are much broader than this. Sharing a common language is a prerequisite to full integration of a child into family, community, and society. To a degree, the problems of the deaf resemble those of minority group members who lack adequate command of English. Adequate hearing and speaking are tremendous aids to cooperative behavior. Sounds—even nonverbal ones—act as guides to behavior and to understanding. Hearing is normally a major source of pleasurable social experience. A common language is our principal means of social interaction. In addition to being two of our prime avenues of information, hearing and speech contribute to social acceptance as well as to one's feeling of personal security, and they also aid in the learning and maintaining of nonverbal skills. That severely and profoundly deaf but otherwise normal children sit up, crawl, and walk later than their normal siblings indicates the importance of hearing and speech in the development of nonverbal habits. The severely aurally handicapped child lacks much more than the ability to hear other people and to acquire speech in the ordinary developmental way. Loss of hearing not only results in an impoverished informational environment; it also entails a restriction of the child's incentives to explore the world, a reduction in the things to become curious about.

DEFINITIONS

Within special education, the deaf and the hard-of-hearing are usually differentiated. These two subgroups are not homogeneous, and further subclassifications are often made. Such subgroups are usually based on the degree of hearing impairment, the cause of the deficit, or the age of the person at the onset of the disability.

The two types of definitions of exceptionality mentioned in earlier chapters—the quantitative and the psychological, educational, and social—are found in the literature on the aurally handicapped. The quantitative definitions typically indicate auditory disability as the degree of hearing loss measured audiometrically in terms of decibels (db). (Hearing loss refers to the deficit in the better ear in the speech range of frequencies.) The following definitions and categorizations are representative of this type.

> *Class 1. Mild losses (20 to 30 db).* People with hearing losses in this range learn to speak by ear in the ordinary developmental way, and are borderline between the hard-of-hearing and the normal.

> *Class 2. Marginal losses (30 to 40 db).* People with such losses usually have some difficulty in hearing speech at a distance of more than a few feet, and in following conversation. Speech can be learned by ear.

> *Class 3. Moderate losses (40 to 60 db).* With amplification of sound and the assistance of vision, people with hearing in this range can learn speech aurally.

> *Class 4. Severe losses (60 to 75 db).* People with hearing losses in this range will not acquire speech without the use of specialized techniques. Most such people are considered "educationally deaf." They are borderline between the hard-of-hearing and the deaf.

> *Class 5. Profound losses (greater than 75 db).* People with hearing in this range seldom learn language by ear alone, even with maximum amplification of sound.

A functional definition identifies the deaf as those whose hearing is nonfunctional for ordinary educational and social purposes. The hard-of-hearing are those whose sense of hearing is defective but functional with a hearing aid.

People in classes 1, 2, and 3 are considered to be *hard-of-hearing,* while those in classes 4 and 5 constitute the *deaf.* The use of subgroups is a recognition that there are tremendous differences between the hard-of-hearing and the deaf, as audiometrically defined.

The aurally handicapped are sometimes subdivided according to whether the hearing loss is purely conductive (conduction deafness) or is the result of sensory-neural impairment (neural deafness). Since conduction deafness usually can be greatly aided by sound amplification systems (hearing aids), whereas sensory-neural impairment is less amenable to such treatment, the difference between the two is of social and educational, as well as of medical, significance.

The aurally impaired, like all other categories of the handicapped, are referred to by a variety of terms with various degrees of stigmatizing connotations. One study found that of several labels commonly used—*deaf, deaf-mute, deaf and dumb, hard-of-hearing,* and *hearing impaired*—the last term, *hearing impaired,* was the least stigmatizing (Wilson, Ross, and Calvert, 1974).

Aurally handicapped, hearing impaired, acoustically impaired or handicapped—all synonyms—are broad categories. They encompass both the deaf and the hard-of-hearing. For all practical purposes, *deafness* means the absence of hearing in both ears. The most important characteristic of the deaf educationally is their inability to hear or to understand speech through audition, with or without a hearing aid. Educationally, the time in life that an individual becomes deaf is of great importance. If deafness develops before the age of two or three, language will not be sufficiently developed to persist and must be taught slowly and laboriously through special educational procedures. The later in life that deafness develops, the greater is the likelihood that oral speech will be retained. This distinction is sometimes made by differentiating between "prelinguistic deafness," which occurs prior to the development of language, and "postlinguistic deafness," which occurs following the development of speech and language.

SOME HEARING LOSS CONDITIONS THAT INFLUENCE EDUCATION

The focus of education today is not so much on audiometric or definitional classifications and labels as it is on the types and varieties of supplementary services and personnel required to maximize the functional level of the individual with hearing impairments. Some of the more educationally significant variables include:

1. the qualitative nature of the impairment. The maximum handicap is when the hearing deficit is in the range of frequencies covered by the human voice in ordinary conversation. Hearing loss is often selective. Many musical tones and other sounds are either below or above those used in ordinary conversation. While missing these high and low tones may be inconvenient, it does not cause the educational and social problems caused by loss of hearing in the normal speaking range.

2. the *degree* of the hearing deficit. This important variable makes the difference between deaf on the one hand or hard-of-hearing on the other. If auditory loss is total, hearing aids will be of no value. If the hearing

loss is less than total, hearing aids are often helpful and make the acquisition of language in the normal developmental way possible. It also simplifies the educational problems tremendously.

3. the *time of onset* of the auditory impairment. This is of major significance, especially when the impairment is extreme.

   Summarizing these three factors: The more serious the hearing loss is in the speech range, the more complete the loss, and the earlier in infancy the hearing loss starts, the more serious are the resulting educational problems.

SYMPTOMS OF HEARING LOSS

An infant severely or profoundly deaf from birth experiences emotion, cries, and initially vocalizes much as does a baby whose hearing is unimpaired. Because such a child seems dominantly normal, an auditory defect may not be suspected—or, if it is suspected, it may not be definitely established for some time. Not until the deaf infant is six months old and starting to babble do sound patterns become differentiated from those of infants who can hear. Often, the failure of the child to speak at the normal age first causes parental concern. Symptoms such as the infant's failure to jump or blink his or her eyes are often not noticed. Being oblivious to ordinary noises may be perceived as evidence that the infant is a "good" baby.

One mother has described her discovery of deafness in her nine-month-old son: "My child was stirring from his nap. His back was toward me and he was looking out the window. I called out to him but he did not respond. Drawing nearer, I called his name louder. Still no response! I approached on the run and by the time I reached the end of his crib I was shouting, but he still did not turn. Then he saw me and held out his arms. Ronnie was deaf!" (Rhodes, 1972).

Many of the symptoms of deafness, such as poor articulation, delayed speech, and lack of responsiveness, are found in mentally retarded, emotionally disturbed, and brain-damaged children, as well as in some otherwise normal children. In the absence of physical signs of pathology, such as malformation of the ears, absence of the ear canal, or chronic discharge from the ears, it is not easy for parents to discover deafness in a child before the age when he or she normally begins to talk.

The general symptoms of auditory deficit in older children are:

1. apparent chronic inattention

2. frequent failure to respond when spoken to

3. marked delay in age of speaking or unusually faulty articulation

4. apparent backwardness in school despite adequate tested intelligence.

TESTS FOR IDENTIFYING THE AURALLY IMPAIRED

Studies have uniformly shown that a relatively small proportion of children who are aurally impaired are identified by behavioral symptoms alone. One research report indicates that teachers do only slightly better than chance in detecting hearing losses among their students (Curry, 1954). Many studies document the need for audiometric testing for the identification of the majority of children with significant hearing losses. The range of testing devices and procedures used in the detection and measurement of auditory loss is very wide.

Unstandardized Tests of Hearing

Noise makers of various types, the oldest devices for testing hearing, are still widely used. For the very young child, a cowbell, a metal cricket which produces a loud snap, or a castanet may be used. The intensity level of the sounds should be fairly high. Responses such as the following are considered indicative of hearing: momentary cessation of random movements, body start (Moro reflex), blinking of the eyes, finger or toe spreading or clenching, and turning the head or eyes in the direction of the sound.

A refinement of this type of test has been developed and used by F. B. Simmons at the Stanford University School of Medicine. The test involves an automated device for recording an infant's movements in its crib when a test sound is applied. The automated system uses an inexpensive motion detector mounted on the frame of the crib, which records the infant's activity on a paper tape before, during, and after a test sound is emitted from a microphone located in the nursery ceiling. The system currently monitors thirty-two cribs simultaneously and is capable of testing six hundred babies an hour. The average cost of screening with this device is said to be only eighty-five cents per child (News and Reports, *Children Today*, 1974).

Pure-Tone Audiometers

The modern audiometers most frequently used are electronic devices which produce tones of variable frequency (pitch) and intensity (loudness) over a wide range. Today, practically every complete test and analysis of a person's hearing involves the use of the pure-tone audiometer. The testing consists of the systematic sounding of a series of tones varying in pitch and loudness. The person being tested hears the tones through earphones and responds by saying "Now" or by pressing a button whenever the tone is heard. The test results are typically plotted on an audiogram which provides a graphic representation of the acuity of each ear for various frequencies. Many audiologists have replaced the manual audiometer with an automatic one devised by G. von Békésy (Sala and Babeghian, 1973).

The Phonographic Audiometer

These devices are phonographs with the desired number (from ten to forty) of telephone receivers attached. Calibrated recordings of both male and female voices are played, and the voices grow gradually less distinct until the material spoken—usually digits or words—can be heard only by people with normal or superior hearing. Each ear is tested separately. The child being tested responds by writing in appropriate blanks, checking the proper word, or marking the picture of the object named. Tests with the phonographic audiometer are calibrated and standardized, and make possible the rapid screening of large numbers of children. More recent developments along this line are usually known as "speech perception tests."

Speech Perception Tests

Speech perception tests measure perception for speech in a manner somewhat like the whisper test and older phonographic audiometric tests. The American Medical Association has developed tests of the threshold of speech perception. These tests use standardized speech material which is presented either on commercial recordings or via the live voice, monitored and controlled for intensity (O'Niell, 1964). The Central Institute for the Deaf in St. Louis has developed a Social Adequacy Index to indicate the degree of difficulty an aurally impaired individual has in ordinary communication (O'Niell, 1964). H. Davis (1973) claims that speech audiometry provides a much better indication of the *functional level* of the ear than does pure-tone audiometry.

A large repertoire of tests has been devised to supplement conventional audiometric methods. These are used largely to test the hard-to-test child, such as the very young, suspected malingerers, persons apparently functionally deaf (psychic deafness), mentally retarded, the hyperactive, and the multihandicapped (Galkowski, 1974).

Other Testing Methods

A large number of ingenious variations of both formal and informal methods of testing auditory acuity have been developed. For example, warbled pure tones have been found to be more effective than steady tones with children who have difficulty in attending (Douglas, Fowler, and Ryan, 1961). One test for children uses a simple Go-Game, in which they make a simple motor response whenever the word "Go!" is heard (Dale, 1962). Music, noise makers, and animal sounds have been used as stimuli, both for measurement and for warm-up exercises which provide rough preliminary assessment of the child's hearing (Reichstein and Rosenstein, 1964).

Conditioned response methods, in which the appropriate response is rewarded, have taken several forms. In one of these, the child looks into a darkened house. When he or she hears a tone, the child pushes a button which illuminates the interior of the house and revolves a group of dolls. Another such device yields candy and knicknacks when the child responds to the auditory stimuli. Studies indicate that children whose responses are rewarded perform significantly better than children who are not rewarded (Reichstein and Rosenstein, 1964). Two Danish researchers have constructed a social-learning handicap index to indicate hearing handicap in daily life (Ewertsen and Birk-Nielsen, 1973).

CAUSES OF AUDITORY DEFECTS

Some auditory defects are inherited. A hereditary type of degenerative nerve deafness may be present at birth or develop later in life. Infections such as German measles (rubella) in early pregnancy, as well as influenza and mumps, may cause congenital deafness which is not hereditary. Occasionally, a child is born with an absence or malformation of the ear canal, ear drum, or the ossicles of the middle ear. Although the development of a vaccine for the prevention of rubella may result in its elimination, currently many rubella-deafened children are in special education and rehabilitation programs. While hearing loss is the most common defect associated with rubella, other anomalies such as cataracts, heart disease, microcephaly, diffuse brain damage, and motor disabilities are also common (Jensema, 1974). Consequently, most of these children have very special educational and rehabilitation needs.

Postnatal causes of auditory defects include most of the childhood diseases—scarlet fever, mumps, measles, and whooping cough. Occasionally, typhoid fever, pneumonia, influenza, and meningitis result in injury to the auditory mechanism. A common but decreasingly important cause of auditory loss is chronic infection of the middle ear (*otitis media*). Among adults, intracranial tumors, cerebral hemorrhage, prolonged exposure to tones of high intensity, and degenerative processes in the auditory mechanism are increasingly important causes of deafness. In approximately one-third of all cases, the causes of deafness are unknown (Schein and

Delk, 1974). It is estimated that occupational noise is responsible for more sensori-neural hearing loss than all other causes combined (Glorig, 1972). Continual or repeated high-intensity noises in the frequency range above 500 Hz (Hz = Hertz = cycles per second) do the most damage to the ear. The passage of the 1970 Occupational Safety and Health Act encouraged employers to become concerned about potentially hazardous noises in their plants (Glorig, 1972). Recent surveys in the British Isles and in Australia find genetic and environmental causes of profound deafness to be of about equal importance (Fraser, 1974).

THE INCIDENCE OF AUDITORY DEFECTS

From 1830 through 1930 the United States Bureau of the Census included an enumeration of deaf persons in each decennial census. Prevalence rates provided by these data were so erratic (a rate of 32.1 per 100,000 in 1900, compared with 67.5 in 1880) that the Bureau discontinued the enumeration of deafness and other disabilities after 1930 and recommended that a separate agency be established for that purpose. Not until forty years later was a federal grant provided to the National Association of the Deaf to make a national census of the deaf population. (Schein and Delk, 1974). According to J. D. Schein and M. T. Delk, Jr., experts had considered the prevalence rates for deafness to be about 1 per 1,000. The Schein and Delk survey estimates deafness at about 2 per 1,000—twice the assumed rate. The Bureau of the Census counted 47 deaf persons per 100,000 in 1930; the Schein and Delk survey estimates 203 per 100,000. The authors doubt that this increase is due to inaccuracies in the two enumerations: "There seems little doubt that there are proportionally, as well as actually, more deaf people today than forty years ago." The 1974 national survey of the deaf estimates that 13.4 million persons in the United States have a significant impairment of hearing. Of these, 1.8 million are deaf. These data indicate that impairment of hearing is the single most prevalent chronic disability in the United States (Schein and Delk, 1974).

Among adults, progressive nerve deterioration (prebycusis) is the most common type of auditory defect. The relationship between age and the incidence of impaired hearing (principally prebycusis) is shown in Table 11–1.

The aging process is said to produce a hearing loss of 160 cycles per year from the upper frequency limits, so that most individuals past middle age have little hearing above 10,000 cycles. There is a more or less normal course of maturation and decline of hearing abilities. Maturation is a gradual process which reaches its maximum between ten and thirteen years with no significant change until late maturity. Statistically the entire

Table 11–1

INCIDENCE OF IMPAIRED HEARING AS RELATED TO AGE (PER 1,000)

age	incidence
45–54	36
55–64	64
65–75	125
Above 75	226

Data from United States Department of Health, Education and Welfare (1961).

population of elderly people have a hearing loss of approximately one decibel a year. This means that between the ages of sixty-five and eighty-five, when this loss becomes significant, the average person will experience a cumulative hearing loss of twenty decibels.

INTELLIGENCE LEVEL OF THE ACOUSTICALLY HANDICAPPED

In the absence of evidence that inferior intelligence and hereditary deafness are genetically linked, we assume that the hereditary determinants of the intellectual level of deaf children are not significantly different from those of their siblings with normal hearing. Differences in their intellectual functioning must then be due to environmental differences. The question of the possible intellectual inferiority of the sensorially handicapped becomes a question of the extent to which the sensory deprivation has influenced the individual's level of intellectual functioning.

Partially because of these considerations, interest has shifted from the general question to that of ways in which the restrictions of auditory input affect the level and pattern of intellectual functioning. In special education, interest focuses primarily on the question of the most effective means of compensating for the auditory deficit. The extent of deficit of intellectual and behavioral functioning in uncomplicated cases of deafness is conceived of as an index of the extent to which the culture has failed to develop or use devices and methods for compensating for the sensory limitations. Special education assumes that specific methods of training and educating handicapped children do make a difference in their functional level. Deaf children learn, or fail to learn, self-help and independence, as well as the fundamental educational and vocational skills, according to the adequacy and availability of the required specialized educational and training resources. In such a frame of reference, the effect of deafness on intelligence becomes part of the question of its effect on achievement.

Some researchers believe that although the general intellectual level of the aurally impaired child may not be inferior to that of comparable children with normal hearing, the perceptual and conceptual processes of congenitally deaf children fail to develop in a comparable way (Myklebust, 1953, 1960; Farrant, 1964). This view is supported by some studies (Hughes, 1959) dealing primarily with *verbal* conceptualization, but the bulk of the investigations indicate that in processes not requiring verbalization, or when the verbalizations required are within the vocabulary range and experience of the subjects, the deaf do as well as hearing subjects in abstract conceptualization (Bornstein and Roy, 1973; Henderson and Henderson, 1973; Ross and Hoemann, 1975; Kates, 1967). Deaf subjects have less adequate verbalization than do hearing subjects, and a larger proportion of adequate conceptual categorizations which are accompanied by inadequate verbalizations than do hearing subjects of the same age and IQ. These differences in verbalization disappear when hearing and deaf subjects are equated as to age, IQ, and educational achievement. Educational attainment probably equates verbalization. These studies also find no evidence of greater rigidity (less flexibility in the strategies of concept attainment) in the deaf subjects.

EDUCATIONAL ACHIEVEMENT OF THE AURALLY IMPAIRED

Studies of educational achievement have uniformly shown the deaf to be retarded from three to five years. The absolute amount of educational retardation increases with age (Schein and Delk, 1974). H. G. Furth (1971) states that the average reading level of deaf pupils is only about grade three. Only 10 percent of the deaf read above the fourth-grade level. Educational retardation is less in the more mechanical skills, such as arithmetic computation and spelling, than in the more intellectual areas, such as paragraph meanings, word meanings, and arithmetic comprehension. Language and communication lag behind the motor and computational skills (Furth, 1971, 1973).

Students applying for admission to the preparatory class at Gallaudet College, who probably represent the best students graduating from the residential schools for the deaf, have a mean age of eighteen years and nine months and obtain a median grade of 9.2 on the Stanford Achievement Test. This level is attained by the average fifteen-year-old hearing child. This group of students, probably highly selected in terms of educational achievement, is retarded by three to four years. About 12 percent of the deaf population twenty-five to sixty-four years of age have gone to college, and half of these earned baccalaureate degrees. These figures are about one-third that of the general population (Schein and Delk, 1974). The educational retardation of deaf children may be partially the result of the excessive amount of school time required for them to learn to speak and their subsequent language deficiencies. The development of improved methods for teaching these children, and the increasing number of children who acquire language in the home, nursery school, and kindergarten prior to beginning their academic education, may help reduce the extent of their educational retardation. M. Vernon (1971) claims that deaf persons who from the first use finger spelling and sign language do better academically than do those children who have been limited to oral communication.

Personal and Social Adjustment of the Aurally Impaired

Statements made in earlier chapters concerning the personal and social adjustment of handicapped people in general hold true for the deaf and the hard-of-hearing. Research studies of the personal and social traits of the aurally impaired show a higher degree of emotional instability, neuroticism, and social maladjustment than do the appropriate norm groups (Schein, 1975). The barriers of deafness and limited language certainly increase the total incidence of frustration, loneliness, helplessness, and despair. However, the deaf child need not be psychologically different from the child who hears. Although the aurally handicapped are more maladjusted than are the normal, they show no distinctive forms or patterns of maladjustment. The adjustment patterns in deaf and hard-of-hearing children are as varied as they are in hearing children. Most of these problems do not derive directly from the hearing loss; they are accentuated by the child's primary handicap but cannot be traced directly to hearing.

Like most other disadvantaged groups, the deaf display a greater tendency than normals to limit their levels of aspiration in the interest of avoiding failure rather than striving for the approval of high achievement (Stinson, 1974). L. R. Bowyer and J. Gillies (1972) find no significant difference between deaf and partially deaf children in terms of their social and emotional adjustment.

When hearing people are unable to communicate with deaf people in a mutually satisfactory way, they often stop trying to do so and either ignore or avoid them altogether. This leaves the aurally handicapped alone and encourages their retreat into isolation. We pointed out in Chapter 2 how the nonhandicapped avoid the handicapped out of a combination of self-consciousness and uncertainty about the right way to act with a deviant person.

SOCIAL ORGANIZATIONS OF THE DEAF

The deaf have been the most active of the handicapped groups in organizing independently on their behalf. The many communities of deaf adults are largely the natural result of people joining with their own kind for mutual pleasure and benefit. The prime reason deaf adults assemble is the relatively free and easy communication they can enjoy. Like most such groups, their mutual problems and interests hold them together. Deaf adults rarely find it possible or enjoyable to integrate wholly with the hearing. The commonalities which bind them also account for the fact that 95 percent of deaf marry other deaf (Jacobs, 1974).

Many national and state organizations of the deaf have local chapters. In 1967 the federal government sponsored the formation of the Council of Organizations Serving the Deaf as a central coordinating agency. There are many local social clubs, with their own athletic teams and leagues. In nearly every large city, there is at least one organization of the deaf which rents social halls for various activities; the only qualification for membership in most of these clubs is deafness.

In many large cities, religious services for the deaf range from providing interpreters to having full-time ministers for deaf members. The Lutheran Church in Los Angeles has provided a successful housing program for deaf senior citizens. In New York City the Jewish deaf have their own synagogues, social clubs, and a senior citizen's housing unit (Tanya Towers). Several television programs are either translated or produced for the deaf. Annually, the *American Annals of the Deaf* publishes a directory of special services and programs.

A device now commercially available allows the deaf to converse on the telephone. It consists of a regular telephone connected to a teletype machine. A light indicates to the deaf person that someone on the other end has picked up the receiver. The caller then types a message on the teletype and waits for the reply. Calls can, of course, be made only to parties with similar devices. A portable machine can be hooked up to any telephone (Leszczynski, 1975). Unfortunately, the equipment costs about $250 minimum and upkeep is fairly expensive (Schein and Delk, 1974).

In February, 1980, three of America's four largest television networks announced that the following month they would begin "closed captioning" about fifteen weekly programs for the benefit of the nation's estimated 14 million deaf and hearing-impaired citizens. Captioning adapter units which sell for about $250 will permit these closed-captioned programs to be seen on any TV set (Deeb, 1980).

MEDICAL ASPECTS OF HEARING LOSS

Medical care and surgery can do a lot to improve certain types of hearing loss. Individuals with middle-ear damage have a very good chance of obtaining improved hearing as a result of appropriate surgery or appropriate hearing aids.

SURGERY

Some of the more common surgical operative procedures are:

1. Fenestration of the labyrinth. A new oval window is made into the horizontal semicircular canal of the inner ear. The artificial window is closed

with a membrane which acts as a sound-sensitive surface, picking up the sound waves directly and bypassing the bones of the inner ear.

2. Mobilization of the stapes. The plate of the stapes (the bone which attaches to the oval window) is loosened by breaking away the excess bone impeding its action. About 80 percent of these operations are said to be successful (Gildston and Gildston, 1972).

3. Artificial replacement of the stapes.

4. Covering tympanic drum perforations with skin grafts.

Today, the otological surgeon can change the shape of the middle ear; rebuild the ossicular chain (the three bones spanning the middle ear); repair, move into a new position, or make a new tympanic membrane; construct new functional membranous windows into the inner ear; and make a bony canal into the middle ear when an infant is born without one.

At present, there is no known medical or surgical means of significantly improving nerve deafness. The approximately 20 percent of deaf children who are deaf because of meningitis, mumps, acute fevers, or other forms of injury to the inner ear or auditory nerve cannot be helped surgically. Because of the constant development of new surgical procedures, however, every person with a serious hearing loss should have a complete otological examination and be advised of the possibilities of medical or surgical treatment.

HEARING AIDS

Modern hearing aids can be used in place of, or in addition to, surgical procedures to improve the hearing of a large percentage of people with conduction deafness. A hearing aid is primarily a sound amplifier. The earphone simply increases the loudness of sounds; a person must have some residual hearing to profit by sound amplification. The person with conduction deafness (outer or middle-ear impairment) can profit more from hearing aids than can the person with perceptive or nerve deafness (injury to the middle ear or auditory nerve).

Improvements in hearing aids are being made continually, and every person with some residual hearing should probably consider their use. It is estimated that not more than one person in three who could be helped by a hearing aid owns and uses one (Schein and Delk, 1974). People with aural impairments fail to use hearing aids for several reasons. Some are unaware of the possibilities offered by modern hearing aids. Many are restrained by vanity or self-consciousness. Some of the deaf and hard-of-hearing have become resigned to their restricted world and are either apathetic or resistant to help. Many people have tried hearing aids and then discarded them. Most of these groups can profit from counseling. The first group may simply need information concerning the nature and avail-ability of hearing aids. Those restrained by vanity may be helped to re-alize that when persons need and can profit by a hearing aid, they are probably more conspicuous when they do not wear one than when they do. The social blunders of the person who hears only half of what is said are much more obvious than is an inconspicuous hearing aid. The ado-lescent girl who will not wear a hearing aid when she needs one makes social errors, the consequences of which are far greater than being rec-ognized as a person with a hearing loss sufficient to require a hearing aid, but otherwise normal. Many people who discard their hearing aids after a short trial expect too much and do not realize that a considerable pe-riod of adjustment and new learning is required before a hearing aid can be tolerated and used effectively.

the limitations of hearing aids Some people cannot profit suffi-ciently from hearing aids to warrant their use, some expect too much from them, and some have developed habits which preclude their effec-tive use. People with certain kinds of inner-ear (nerve) deafness cannot tolerate hearing aids. The person with nerve deafness often has an irreg-ular pattern of auditory loss. A hearing aid with equal amplification of all frequencies will make some sounds unbearably loud while making others just audible. Some earphones provide greater amplification of higher tones, but this often produces intolerable distortion. The accentuation of high tones and suppression of the low frequencies sometimes produce such a radical change in patterns of stimulation that the person's habitual patterns of auditory perception are severely disrupted.

Several attempts have been made to shift or transpose high-frequency speech sounds to lower ranges so as to make them more audi-ble to people with residual hearing in the low frequencies. Since most deaf individuals have some residual hearing in the very low frequencies, the successful devising of practical means of doing this would be of con-siderable significance (Quigley, 1969). Preliminary studies indicate that selective amplification of particular frequencies to fit individual hearing losses is practical and is superior to the flat amplification of a broad band of frequencies as found in most conventional hearing aids (Quigley, 1969).

P. Kuyper (1972) claims that a person with two equally impaired ears should wear two hearing aids. This produces better directional hearing and suppression of acoustical sound shadows. It also produces better un-derstanding of language in an environment of interfering sounds (the "cocktail party effect"). With two-ear hearing, the individual in a crowd feels himself to be in the center of the sources of sound. All sounds do not seem to come from one side, and he feels less threatened by possible unforeseen occurrences. In a group he can quickly identify the person who is speaking and employ lip reading as an aid to understanding.

The average person has to learn to use a hearing aid. Amplification does not restore hearing to normal. It does not necessarily make a hard-of-hearing person hear better. It only provides the possibility of hearing better. The deafened person (one who has lost hearing after having heard normally) has often lost habits of selective hearing. The congenitally deaf person has never acquired these habits. The deaf or hard-of-hearing person must learn or relearn to screen out irrelevant sounds and "hear out" the sounds that are important. The deafened person must also develop a tolerance for the distortions of sound imposed by a hearing aid.

It is advantageous for a person with progressive impairment to begin using a hearing aid before losing the habits of listening and of selective hearing. Distortions imposed by a hearing aid may be tolerated if the device is used with progressively greater amplification as the hearing loss develops, whereas the degree of distortion ultimately involved may be intolerable if the aid is used for the first time after a loss has become acute. Similarly, babies with congenital hearing losses may be fitted with hearing aids so that they will learn in the ordinary developmental way to use sounds as guides to behavior and to understanding. The severely handicapped child, without a hearing aid, may learn to ignore sounds that she can hear because they are too faint to attract her attention and serve as useful guides. She does not become interested in sounds and remains unaware of their significance. If effective amplification is provided, the child will learn to notice and respond to sound. The child who has learned to live in a soundless world is likely to find some sounds disagreeable, and must change from having dominantly visual and cutaneous perception to having dominantly visual and auditory perception.

Economic factors may limit the use of hearing aids. Among the deaf, hearing aid use is directly related to income. Hearing aids are expensive to purchase and maintain (Schein and Delk, 1974).

THE AURALLY IMPAIRED CHILD IN THE FAMILY

In addition to the family problems of handicapped children in general, there are some situations peculiar to the aurally impaired. If the child has any residual hearing—and most children do—every attempt should be made to capitalize on it. After complete otological and audiometric examinations have been made and any surgical or medical treatments completed, hearing aids may be used if there is any useful residual hearing, and training should start immediately.

The child should be raised in a speaking environment. Special efforts should be made to reinforce both the child's responses to sounds and his spontaneous vocalizations. If parents look at the child, go to him, attend to his needs, and play with him when he cries, coos, and gurgles, he will tend to repeat his vocalizing. Talking carefully, distinctly, and slowly to the child when he is watching one's face and when the face is in full light will encourage him to combine looking and listening as sources of cues to meanings. The aurally handicapped child needs the same kind of opportunities to learn and understand speech as the normal child, but needs more of them. Special situations may have to be contrived to emphasize the relationship of dimly heard sounds and visual cues to their meanings by concrete reference to persons, objects, activities, and situations.

When treatment directed at maximizing the child's use of residual hearing and potential for speech is combined with a good home-training program, most aurally handicapped children can come to school as talking children. The majority of deaf children who learn to talk have had good home training from their earliest years (Ewing and Ewing, 1958). A child who is one of the few who are totally deaf must learn to understand speech and to talk via sight and touch.

Phrases and short sentences using the pattern of normal speech—spoken a little more slowly and clearly—while maintaining the normal rhythmic pattern of the sentence are more easily followed than are single words. The home is the place where auditory training, lip reading (or the more recent terms *speech reading, visual communication,* and *visual listening*), and learning to speak all begin (O'Niell, 1964). Proper home training with hearing aids is making it possible for a large percentage of aurally handicapped children to learn to understand language and to talk in the ordinary developmental way.

A list of suggestions to encourage oral speech for the parents of children with severe auditory impairments follows.

1. Talk to your child constantly. Provide a rich speaking atmosphere. Don't use signs with the child, and when the child uses a sign, supply the proper word.

2. Expect your child to learn speech reading and to speak. Start with simple phrases or meaningful words in specific situations or with reference to concrete objects and activities.

3. Work constantly to increase the child's vocabulary. Systematically introduce new words and teach different words for the same thing to avoid the development of a stilted, limited speech pattern.

4. Insist that the child speak for him or herself, first to family members, then to friends and relatives, and later to casual acquaintances and strangers. Don't step in to speak and interpret for your child. Encourage independence and self-confidence.

5. Require and expect the handicapped child to accept responsibility, perform household duties, and participate in family life essentially as do the nonhandicapped. Send the child on errands as soon as he or she has sufficient vocabulary to be understood.

6. Discourage the use of pencil and paper or signs in place of oral speech.

7. Provide as much pleasure and feeling of satisfaction as possible with the use of language. Speech training in the house should never become dull, monotonous, repetitious drill.

Language used spontaneously, in natural situations where it serves a purpose and is meaningful, with the attention, acceptance, and understanding of others operating as rewards, is the ideal situation for the acquisition of speech by the aurally impaired child, just as it is for the non-handicapped. Success in teaching the child to understand and to use oral speech depends on the whole family, the characteristics of the individual child, and the use of specialized facilities and help. But of all these factors, the most important is the parents' attitude toward the child and the handicap.

EDUCATION OF THE AURALLY HANDICAPPED

Although no clear division can be made between the deaf and the hard-of-hearing, many of the problems of their education are sufficiently different to warrant their being educated either separately or by different methods. The primary difference in the education of these two groups is in their learning to speak and to understand speech. Deaf children with no useful residual hearing must depend entirely on vision and the other senses for their education. They must learn to understand speech solely by seeing (lip reading, speech reading, visual communication, or visual listening), and they learn to speak via the visual, cutaneous, and kinesthetic senses. If children with useful residual hearing are taught, like the deaf child, to rely largely or entirely on visual, cutaneous, and kinesthetic cues for understanding speech and for learning to speak, they will eventually neglect their auditory potential and become functionally deaf. Profoundly deaf children acquire oral speech by learning to reproduce what they see on the lips and faces of people talking to them. They can monitor speech only via the cutaneous and kinesthetic sensations from their vocal apparatus. Hard-of-hearing children need auditory training along with speech reading to increase their use of residual hearing, so that they develop a combined visual and auditory perceptual system. Except for the ways in which they acquire their communication skills, the education of the profoundly deaf and the hard-of-hearing is not significantly different.

In France, Abbé de L' Épée (1710–1789) established the first school for deaf children and educated them by the use of signs (manual communication). In Germany, Samuel Heinicke (1723–1790) started the first public school for the deaf, using and teaching the oral methods of communication. By 1800, as the result of these two early developments, there were two opposing schools of thought in Europe on the question of how best to teach deaf children—the French or sign system (manual) and the German oral system (Butterfield, 1971). For over two hundred years the debate concerning these two competing means of communication has continued (Vernon, 1971).

Until recently the education of the deaf in the United States followed the early German lead and was primarily oral. Manual communication was discouraged under the assumption that children who used signs would not be motivated to learn to speak, to use their residual hearing, or to speech read. Manual communication was largely reserved for the "oral failures"—those who failed to develop oral skills. However, this assumption has been challenged; since 1969, a growing number of programs in the United States have used both oral and manual communication (Moores, Weiss, and Goodwin, 1973).

The shift from purely oral to combination methods has resulted from accumulating research evidence indicating that: (a) children taught by purely oral methods use manual communication with their peers despite instructions not to and despite punishment for doing so; (b) only a small percentage—about 17 percent—of students taught by purely oral methods ever become fluent orally; (c) only about 25 percent of the deaf can follow a normal conversation by speech reading, while nearly 75 percent communicate fluently manually, even when use of signs is prohibited in the classroom; (d) early manual communication facilitates, rather than retards, the later development of oral language; (e) children who use finger spelling and sign language do better academically than do comparable children who have been limited to oral communication; (f) deaf children of deaf parents outperform the deaf children of hearing parents on measures of English language skills, suggesting the beneficial effects of early experience with manual communication (Vernon, 1971; Moores, Weiss, and Goodwin, 1973; Hoemann, 1974; Charrow and Fletcher, 1974).

Today there are few advocates of pure "manualism," and the number of pure oralists is also decreasing. The number who advocate the use of oral speech together with finger spelling, sign language, and speech reading (total communication) is increasing (Vernon, 1971; Northcott, 1973; Furfey, 1974).

Speech Reading and Oral Language for the Deaf

Teaching a profoundly deaf child to be fluent in speech reading and in oral speech is one of the most demanding instructional tasks, on the one hand, and the most satisfying accomplishments, on the other. Such instruction requires intensive individualized teaching by a dedicated and resourceful instructor.

some problems of speech or lip reading Speech reading can never be a complete substitute for normal hearing. But lip reading, especially when combined with some residual hearing—either with or without a hearing aid—does promote better communication. The profoundly deaf child often develops some rudimentary lip reading skills spontaneously. However, monitored practice with a trained teacher is necessary for proficiency in lip reading. Most authorities agree that lip reading can benefit people with hearing losses as low as 25 decibels (Broberg, 1971).

Some of the more obvious difficulties the deaf person has in learning speech reading and in oral speech follow. (a) The absence of the auditory feedback, which is necessary for speech acquisition in the normal developmental way, during the early developmental period when the child is apparently optimally capable of language learning, is most handicapping. (b) Whereas hearing children monitor their own speech and perceive the speech of others largely through audition, the deaf must depend mainly on vision to perceive the speech of others and on the cues provided by the feedback from their motor (kinesthetic) and skin (cutaneous) senses to monitor their own speech. (c) Normal speakers cannot observe their mouth and face while talking and consequently do not understand the ambiguities of the visual cues their speech provides. (d) The visual cues provided by oral speech are only the byproducts of articulation and are manipulated so as to produce appropriate sounds rather than visually distinguishable ones.

The person with even minimally useful residual hearing has a great advantage over the profoundly deaf individual in speech reading and the acquisition of oral speech. For such individuals, the auditory and the visual can complement each other. With training, the visual cues can fill in the missing auditory links and the trained ear can bridge the visual gaps. The person with minimally useful residual hearing can often perceive low-pitched sounds and can therefore distinguish most consonants and can understand many words (Erber, 1974). The profoundly deaf person perceives only time and intensity changes in speech and probably does this largely through the vibrotactile receptors in the ears.

SPECIAL AIDS

Many devices have been developed to detect and amplify or code certain features of oral speech as special aids for the deaf (Erber, 1974; Boothroyd and Decker, 1972; Babcock and Wallen, 1974). Some of these devices transform speech into a visual form; others shift the high-frequency components of speech to a lower frequency range and thus bring speech within the perceptual range of those whose auditory losses are primarily for the higher frequencies. A third group of instruments provides articulatory cues to the deaf person via coded light signals. In one of these a microphone picks up sound waves and causes miniature lights set in a frame of glasses to light up in different patterns. These cues provide the wearer with information to supplement the cues provided by the speaker's lips and face.

MANUAL COMMUNICATION

Two systems of manual communication are used by the deaf. One is the manual alphabet, or finger spelling, in which the configurations of the hand correspond to the letters of the alphabet. In this system a spoken language is spelled out manually. The other system consists of sign language, in which manual configurations, movements, and gestures correspond to particular words or concepts. National and regional variations in sign language are comparable to those of spoken languages. The American Sign Language (ASL), with certain regional variations, is used by the deaf in North America and has recently been the subject of formal analysis. The ASL is somewhat like pictograph writing, in which some symbols are arbitrary and some are representational. For example, the sign for "always" is made by holding the hand in a fist, index finger extended as in pointing while rotating the arm at the elbow. This is purely arbitrary. The sign for "flower" is more representational. It is made by holding the fingers of one hand extended, all five fingertips touching (the tapered hand), and touching the fingertips first to one nostril and then to the other as if sniffing a flower. All such signs are arbitrary to a degree. The literate deaf individual typically uses a combination of ASL and finger spelling in manual communication.

Many special and regular teachers as well as students with normal hearing are becoming acquainted with and sometimes even fluent in manual communication. This results from the more extensive use of *total communication* with the hearing impaired. Total communication combines the use of oral speech, speech reading, sign language, and the manual alphabet in communicating with deaf people. Familiarity with manual communication is also facilitated by the trend toward mainstreaming—the inclusion of many more hearing impaired children in the regular classrooms. Daily contact with children who use sign language arouses the interest of other students, who sometimes are encouraged by their teachers to learn it. Regular teachers and hearing students seem to be able to acquire sign language skills quite easily. In some cases, an in-service training unit in manual communication is provided for teachers who have aurally impaired children in their classes. In addition, we are seeing frequent translations of televised news, political speeches, and feature presentations into sign language by superimposing a signing person in a corner of the screen. The high visibility of sign language is increasing public understanding of manual forms of communication and the problems of deafness.

CUED SPEECH FOR THE DEAF

A recently developed aid to total communication with the deaf is called *cued speech*. Basically, this is a manual supplement to lip reading. It was developed in 1966 by R. Orin Cornett at Gallaudet College in Washington, D. C. Cued speech is widely taught in Australia but in only a limited way in the United States. The system combines finger and hand signals with lip reading. It consists of eight hand and finger configurations used in four different positions near the lips. Many speech sounds look alike in terms of lip movements. By cueing with hand and finger gestures, additional information is added to those sounds identifiable by lip reading, so that all the single sounds in the English language may be identified either on the lips or on the hands.

According to Cornett, parents can learn cued speech in twelve to fifteen hours. He states that if the parents of deaf children learn and use cued speech consistently, these children will learn language in a visual way in everyday, normal communication in the home (Barnes, 1978). (For additional information contact the Office of Cued Speech Programs, Gallaudet College, 7th and Florida Avenues, N.E., Washington, D.C. 20002.)

NURSERY SCHOOLS FOR THE AURALLY IMPAIRED CHILD

The young child with useful residual hearing, fitted with a hearing aid and equipped with good home training, will probably develop best in a normal environment where oral speech is experienced all day long and where special efforts are made to talk to the child as much as possible. The profoundly deaf child will require supplementary training by a special teacher of the deaf. The special teacher can also instruct and train the mother and the regular teacher so that they can provide supplementary speech and speech reading training for the child. A good, natural, normal nursery school program, with the aurally handicapped child using a hearing aid, if indicated, and with teachers making special efforts to reach and stimulate the child, is probably the best supplement to the home-training program for the three- to five-year-old.

THE SPECIAL SCHOOL FOR THE DEAF

Deaf children are educated in four settings: residential schools, special day schools, special day classes, and regular classes (Vernon, 1975). In 1960 there were seventy-two public residential schools for children with auditory impairments in the United States, enrolling about 16,000 children. Historically, the residential school was the first type of facility established for the education of the deaf. The advantages and disadvantages of the residential school for the child with auditory impairment are essentially those listed earlier for residential institutions in general. As is true for most other categories of exceptional people, there is a decrease in the percentage of children with hearing impairments being sent to the special schools—both residential and day. In 1972 about half of the deaf aged twenty-four to sixty-four had been educated entirely in residential schools while about one-fourth had attended regular classes for at least part of their education (Schein and Delk, 1974), and about 10 percent had never attended a special school or class for the hearing impaired. The special day school for the aurally impaired child has not been a practical facility except in a few large cities. The relatively low incidence of severe auditory impairment (perhaps 2 per 1,000) requires a school to draw from such a large geographical area that transportation becomes a serious problem.

The residential school will probably always be needed, although attendance at such schools is decreasing. Children with severe hearing impairments living in isolated rural areas, aurally impaired children with additional disabilities, children with unfavorable home situations, and others with special problems can best be educated in residential schools. For some children, short-term programs may be sufficient to develop their special oral and aural skills to the point where they can function satisfactorily in the regular classroom. Since nearly half the children attending residential schools for the hearing impaired go home each weekend, and 12 percent of the children attending such schools are really day students, the majority of the students maintain contact with their homes, communities, and families (Schunhoff, 1964).

The Special Class in a Regular School

The special class, with some integration with the regular classes or a still greater degree of integration with the assistance of resource teachers, consultants, or itinerant teachers, is rapidly becoming the most common educational arrangement for children with auditory impairments. With maximum surgical remediations and the use of improved hearing aids, many children previously considered hopelessly deaf and placed in residential schools can now function adequately in the regular schools.

Although there is a paucity of large-scale and well-controlled studies, the evidence indicates that children in the ordinary school environment mixing with normally hearing children are superior to institutionalized children, except possibly in the area of personal adjustment. When institutionalized and integrated groups of children are equated for degree of auditory impairment, age of onset of the disabilities, and mental level, the children educated in integrated classes are generally superior in fluency of speech and in educational achievement (Johnson, 1962; Brereton, 1957). Recent experience indicates that children can manage in the ordinary school with more severe hearing impairments than has been generally considered possible. Such children do require special help (Hehir, 1973; Northcott, 1973).

SUGGESTIONS TO REGULAR CLASS TEACHERS

Teachers who have never had a deaf or hard-of-hearing child in their classes before are sure to be a little nervous and apprehensive about these new students. The following list of generalizations and specific suggestions may be of assistance. First, some general observations:

1. The range of educational potential among hearing impaired children is about the same as that of the nonhandicapped. Hearing impaired students are roughly the mental equals of their nonhandicapped peers.

2. Most hearing impaired students can learn to read silently, spell, write, handle arithmetic concepts, and perform in other academic areas, in about the same way as do the children with normal hearing.

3. The behavior and mental health problems experienced by the hearing impaired are similar to and are only slightly greater in number than are those of the nonhandicapped.

4. While the ways in which these children learn are basically the same as those with normal hearing, there are three areas in which the severely hearing impaired have special learning problems. These are:
    a. Deaf children first have had to learn that there is such a thing as oral speech. They have also had to learn to employ language to communicate without ever hearing it.
    b. Deaf children have had to learn to communicate with others in nonverbal (largely manual) ways. If they are able to speak, they have acquired this skill in a slow, tedious, and imperfect way.
    c. Hearing impaired children must learn to use vision and other intact senses to compensate for their loss of hearing.

Some specific suggestions to assist regular teachers in teaching hearing impaired children in their classrooms are as follows:

1. Recognize these children's handicap without making unnecessary concessions such as giving them higher grades because they are "poor deaf children." Expect these students to accept the same responsibilities, classroom assignments, and homework commitments as are required of the others.

2. Prepare the other students for the introduction of hearing impaired children to your classes. Tell them about the special problems of hearing im-

pairment, as well as the nature, use, and limitations of hearing aids. Indicate the types of special assistance these children will appreciate and how to provide it. Indicate that these children have acquired almost incredible skills in speech reading and learning to talk. Warn them to expect only limited, imperfect speech.

3. Talk to hearing impaired students in full sentences and remind the other students to do so. Avoid using single words, for meanings are more readily grasped in context than from isolated words. Talk normally, or possibly a little slowly, but at a good moderate rate. Take care to face the child while talking. Do not talk when you are facing the chalkboard or when your face is hidden by a book, papers, or your hands.

4. Natural gestures accompanying speech help, but excessive motions of head, arms, and hands may be distracting.

5. Since lighting arrangements can affect speech reading, light should fall on the speaker's face. This can be facilitated by seating these children so as to take advantage of the lighting arrangements and permitting them to change positions or seats as the light changes. Do not expect lip reading beyond a distance of about ten feet.

6. Remember that hearing aids do not provide these children with normal hearing. Hearing aids simply make sounds louder, but not necessarily clearer. With young children, check occasionally to make sure their hearing aids are working. Keeping the noise level in the classroom down helps hearing impaired children to understand speech. Remember that turning up the hearing aid does not solve the problem of background noise. The hearing aid simple makes *everything* louder and does not help the children to hear selectively.

7. Consider using a buddy system which pairs each hearing impaired child with a compatible companion who agrees to assist his or her buddy in such ways as supplying the child with carbon copies of notes, assisting when fire alarms sound, and in other emergencies.

8. Use a wealth of visual aids such as captioned films, diagrams, and tables. When referring to things in the room, point to them, glance at them, or walk over and touch them.

SUGGESTIONS FOR THE SPECIAL TEACHER OR CONSULTANT

1. See that the children have and use hearing aids. Help the regular teachers understand the operation, functions, and limitations of hearing aids.

2. Inform the regular teachers about the availability of captioned films and other supplementary visual aids.

3. Check with the regular teacher at least once a week and more often if necessary.

4. Reduce the regular teacher's additional load by instructing the special students about school routines, monitoring their own hearing aids, and

being as quiet as possible when moving about and handling materials. Instruct the students what to do in case of such emergencies as fire or accidents.

5. Offer to teach regular class teachers and students the rudiments of signing and the manual alphabet.

6. Encourage regular teachers to institute a buddy system.

7. Become familiar with regular class routines and procedures so as to be able to help orient and arrange for the introduction of the hearing impaired child to the classroom.

8. Be alert to the special problems of first-year and substitute teachers. Help them with lesson plans, special equipment, and problems they may encounter for the first time.

9. Use aids, volunteers, and independent study lessons so as to individualize instruction as much as possible. Avoid having four or five students as passive onlookers while you are working with one child.

10. Consult with parents regularly and in cases of special need.

The Aurally Impaired College Student

In the United States, the deaf high school graduate has a choice of attending a college for the deaf—Gallaudet—or one of the two thousand regular universities and colleges. Gallaudet, a federally sponsored college for the deaf in Washington, D. C., is the only college exclusively for the deaf in the world.

Many problems of the deaf student are magnified in the regular college. There are no special facilities or aids available to him. Classroom instruction is often more oral—sometimes purely lecture or lecture and discussion. The handicapped student is only one among many nonhandicapped, and usually no special consideration is provided him or her. Students with severe auditory impairments usually watch the lecturer to get the general ideas, but depend upon a carbon copy of the notes of helpful classmates and their own outside reading for details. It is very difficult for people who must read speech to follow the rapid flow of conversation in group discussions. They usually have to rely on the help of a thoughtful friend in such situations, for this problem seems insurmountable.

THE MULTIPLY HANDICAPPED DEAF

In the previous chapter we discussed the blind-deaf. Here we will comment on the problems of the *multiply handicapped* deaf. It is conservatively estimated that between a fourth and a third of all deaf children have additional disabilities (Flathouse, 1979). These estimates are based on the individuals enrolled in educational programs for the deaf, who are generally the less severely handicapped, and do not include children not officially identified as multiply handicapped and not being served.

In 1977 approximately 10,000 children enrolled in schools and classes in the United States were identified as multiply handicapped. The largest numbers of these were the deaf-mentally retarded and the deaf-learning disabled (including aphasics). There were about 2,660 of the former and 3,600 of the latter (Flathouse, 1979).

It is generally agreed that these multiply handicapped children have been poorly served. One reason for this is their relatively low incidence. Another is their great diversity. Among them we find all possible combinations of the various disabilities. When a child is multiply handicapped it is very difficult to designate the appropriate service responsibilities. Rarely will a person, clinic, hospital, or school have the facilities and personnel to deal with an individual who is, for example deaf-blind, mentally retarded, and orthopedically handicapped. While there is considerable uncertainty as to the number of these children there is agreement that the population is increasing. The reasons include such factors as improved prenatal care and reduced infant mortality, resulting in a larger number of fetuses that would otherwise be aborted, being born alive and the prolongation of the life span of the more vulnerable multiply handicapped. The increasing number of these children and the legal mandates to search out and provide appropriate services for them will bring about increasing professional concern for this population. This in turn should lead to an emphasis on the early identification of hearing losses in children with other disabilities. Hearing losses are frequently overlooked when they occur in combination with other handicaps. When a child is deaf and unable to communicate, the identification of mental retardation and emotional disturbances as accompanying disabilities becomes very difficult. Because of their unique and severe learning problems, applying the concept of the "least restrictive environment" to these children becomes difficult. The regular classroom is unlikely to be the appropriate least restrictive environment for most multiply handicapped deaf children, since they will require a great deal of one-to-one instruction in communication and self-help skills in special classes, schools, or residential institutions.

VOCATIONAL TRAINING FOR THE IMPAIRED

As compared with the visually impaired, the vocational training of the aurally handicapped poses few problems. Vocational training programs for the aurally handicapped have existed at secondary and post-secondary levels for many years. At the high school level these programs usually involve a work-study coordinator placing handicapped individuals on a job in the school setting or in the community. The work experience is supplemented by related classroom instruction. Post-secondary programs have traditionally been in sheltered workshops or in private vocational training facilities. The passage of Public Law 94-142 and the corresponding vocational education legislation, Public Law 94-482, require that the Individualized Education Plan for each handicapped person have an occupational component. This means the regular vocational educator, the work-study coordinator for the handicapped, the regular teachers, and counselors will all become involved in the vocational training programs for the handicapped. It means that, in so far as possible, the handicapped students will be included in the regular vocational training programs. At the post-secondary level handicapped students will be served in existing regular vocational-technical and professional schools. They will also have access to the appropriate advanced skill training and employment opportunities along with the nonhandicapped.

VOCATIONAL OPPORTUNITIES OF THE AURALLY IMPAIRED

The deaf find employment in almost all vocational areas. Table 11–2 indicates the occupational distribution of the employed deaf in the United States in the late 1950s.

Table 11–2 indicates that the deaf are employed in all major occu-

Table 11–2

PERCENT DISTRIBUTION OF PRINCIPAL OCCUPATIONS OF EMPLOYED DEAF 16 TO 64 YEARS OF AGE IN THE UNITED STATES, 1972

occupation	percent
Professional and technical	8.8
Nonfarm managers and administrators	1.4
Sales	0.5
Clerical	15.0
Craftspersons	21.3
Operatives, nontransit	34.7
Operatives, transit	1.2
Laborers, nonfarm	6.2
Farmers and farm managers	0.8
Farm laborers	0.8
Service workers	9.2
Private household workers	0.2

Data from Schein and Delk (1974).

pational groups. They are underrepresented in the higher professional, managerial, and sales areas, probably because of the greater necessity for facile communication in these occupations. There are relatively greater numbers employed in the intermediate occupational levels (clerical, and semiskilled "operatives"), and a decidedly smaller percentage working as unskilled laborers, as compared with the general population. In the study cited (Lunde and Bogman, 1959), 85 percent of the deaf workers were rated "successful" in their occupations.

Studies of the occupational success of girls who had attended the Lexington School for the deaf indicate that achievement in the language skills was the keystone to successful careers (Connor and Rosenstein, 1963).

The vocational training of the aurally handicapped is not essentially different from that designed for those who hear. Individual differences in special talents and general intelligence are as great among people with hearing defects as among those with normal hearing. Interests, motivation, and realistic levels of personal aspirations and social expectation are no less important to the aurally impaired than to the acoustically normal, and their occupational possibilities are only slightly more restricted.

We mentioned earlier that job success seems to be only slightly related to degree of defect, but is more closely related to personal characteristics (Miller, Kunce, and Getsinger, 1972). In 1972, 3 percent of deaf males were unemployed as compared with 4.9 percent of all males (Schein and Delk, 1974). The overwhelming majority of the deaf are employed. Unfortunately, the deaf are employed predominantly in industrial enterprises, which have a predicted relative decrease of workers, and are underrepresented in the personal service fields, where increasing demands are predicted (Vernon, 1975).

Each state has a vocational rehabilitation office and most states have many branch offices, most of which employ personnel trained to work with the deaf and hard-of-hearing. Also, in many state departments of employment people are selected and trained to work with the handicapped.

THE SOCIAL LIFE OF THE DEAF

The social life of most of the deaf and hard-of-hearing is essentially the same as that of those with normal hearing. The average deaf person has a job, owns a home, marries someone of his or her choice, raises a family of reasonably normal children, and participates in the social life of the community. More than other types of handicapped people, they tend to favor social groups of their own kind. Many deaf people are more relaxed and find great satisfaction from associating with those who share their problems and interests. One evidence or consequence of the tendency of the deaf to associate with those similarly impaired is found in a study of ten thousand married adult deaf, which showed that less than 5 percent had married hearing people (Meadow, 1975).

In addition to social clubs, the deaf have organized the National Fraternal Society of the Deaf, which writes insurance in the millions, publishes a monthly paper, and has a large ladies' auxiliary (Elstad, Frampton, and Gall, 1955). The deaf have organized the National Association of the Deaf, with offices in Silver Spring, Maryland. The Association publishes a monthly magazine. The deaf hold a national basketball tournament yearly; less often, they have bowling and football tournaments. They also stage the World Deaf Olympics.

Since 1967 there has been a National Theater of the Deaf. Cast members communicate on stage by a "sign-mime" language, and two translators speak words for the hearing members of the audience.

The deaf have been a very self-conscious group. They have opposed all types of begging by the deaf. In several states, they have established homes for the aged deaf. The deaf have opposed special preferential legislation for the aurally impaired, just as they have opposed legislation which they feel unrealistically restricts their activities (Elstad, Frampton, and Gall, 1955). The deaf, like many other disadvantaged minorities, have recently become militant in making demands in their own behalf (McCay, 1974; Vernon, 1975). Compared with other categories of the handicapped, the deaf do well economically. The median income of families of employed deaf persons is 85 percent as much as the United States average (Schein and Delk, 1974). Personal earnings are directly related to age at the onset of deafness. Those born deaf have the lowest average.

ACCESSIBILITY AND USABILITY

Newby (1979) points out the important distinction between *accessibility* and *usability* for the deaf. Section 504 of the federal Rehabilitation Act of 1973 states that no handicapped person shall be discriminated against in any program or activity to which that act applies, because the facilities are either *inaccessible* or *unusable* by handicapped persons. The primary problem for the physically handicapped is accessibility; for the deaf, it is usability.

For example, at an information desk or public address system where all information is transmitted orally, the informant does not know sign language, and the deaf recipient cannot speech read, the desk is accessible but not usable for the deaf. The telephone is accessible to the deaf but without a teletypewriter (TTY) it is not usable. All agencies, companies, and facilities should stress the concept of *usability* as well as the more common and popular concept of *accessibility*.

PROSPECTS FOR THE AURALLY IMPAIRED

If we extrapolate from the recent past, the prospect for additional amelioration of the condition of the deaf is good. We can expect continued developments in medical treatment and surgical remediation of the aurally impaired. Further reduction in the incidence of severe aural impairment can result from the decreasing incidence of those diseases of the pregnant mother, or of the child, which may damage the auditory apparatus. We can reasonably expect improvements in hearing aids which reduce the handicap of those with impaired hearing.

There is always the possibility that some major breakthrough may occur—the more effective use of the other senses in perceiving speech, or even bypassing the ordinary sensory inputs to get appropriate neural impulses to the brain.

The social understanding of and vocational outlooks for the deaf are improving.

SUMMARY

Studies of attitudes toward handicapped persons show that while the blind, the orthopedically disabled, the physically ill, and the like are viewed with compassion, the majority of laypeople are either indifferent to the deaf or react unfavorably toward them. The individual deprived of hearing from birth, in addition to being unable to hear the speech of other people and to acquire speech in the ordinary developmental way, lacks an important tool for the acquisition of nonverbal skills, a major source of pleasurable social experience, as well as one of the principal means of social interaction. The deaf and the hearing are most meaningfully differentiated according to whether they have hearing which is functional for the ordinary purposes of life.

Because only a small proportion of the deaf and the hard-of-hearing are identified by parents and teachers unaided, a wide variety of tests has been developed for this purpose. These consist of the watch test, the whisper test, the phonographic audiometer and its modern counterpart, the speech perception tests, tuning fork tests, the galvanic skin response test, and finally and most important, the pure-tone audiometers.

Auditory defects are both endogenous (hereditary) and exogenous (environmental or adventitious) in origin. The causes of a large percentage of cases of impaired hearing are unknown. The exact incidence of impaired hearing is unknown, but conservative estimates indicate that some 300,000 children and 2,300,000 adults are sufficiently aurally impaired to warrant special care and treatment.

There are no personal characteristics or personality patterns peculiar to the aurally impaired. The deaf typically score below the hearing on most intelligence tests, but this can be accounted for in terms other than differences in inherent capacity. The educational retardation of two to three grades commonly found among the severely aurally impaired indicates the extent to which society has failed to develop alternative methods of educating these people. The conceptual deficiencies of the aurally impaired seem to be principally in the verbal areas. Deafness produces no peculiar patterns of personal or social adjustment or maladjustment but, like any other handicap, it creates an excessive number of adjustment problems. Special care and treatment of the acoustically impaired involves medicine, surgery, education, and social work, as well as other disciplines. People with middle- or outer-ear damage (conduction deafness) have a very good chance of having their hearing improved by corrective surgery, appropriate hearing aids, and aural rehabilitation. Those with damage to the inner ear or the auditory nerve have a smaller chance of obtaining help in these ways.

The education of the aurally impaired child begins in the home and is continued in residential schools, special day schools, special classes in regular schools, and integrated classes. The consensus seems to be that the aurally handicapped, like most other exceptional children, should not be sent to special schools if they can be suitably educated in ordinary schools, and that they should not go to boarding schools if they can be suitably educated in day schools near their homes. The acquiring of adequate language and communication skills constitutes the major problem of the aurally handicapped, whether these are acquired by oral speech and speech reading alone or by speech with the aid of finger spelling, either with or without the language of signs.

There is increasing interest in and respect for what can be achieved by manual methods of communication beginning with the very young child. It has been found that learning sign language does not retard the development of speech or speech reading skills. There seems to be little evidence to support the claim that oral speech is necessary for adjusting to a hearing society. Deaf children who learn sign language early in life perform better on speech, speech reading, and psychological adjustment measures than those who do not develop these skills.

The deaf find employment less often than the aurally unimpaired in the professional, managerial, clerical and sales, and personal service areas, and more often in the skilled crafts and in the technical areas. Some find employment in practically all areas.

The social life of the deaf is essentially the same as that of the rest of the population, although there is a greater tendency for them to form social groups of their own kind than is true for the other types of handicapped people. The prospect for improved surgical, remedial, and educational programs for the aurally impaired is good.

Many people with normal hearing are proficient in manual communication. Cued speech, a manual supplement to lip reading, holds some promise for increasing communication with the deaf. Federal legislation mandating that facilities must be *usable* as well as accessible to the handicapped promises to be an improvement for the aurally handicapped.

REFERENCES

Anderson, V. M., "The Incidence and Significance of High-frequency Deafness in Children," *American Journal of Diseases of Children,* 1967, *113,* 560–65.

Babcock, R. and M. K. Wallen, "Visible Speech: Toward Improved Speech for the Hearing Handicapped," *Educational Technology,* 1974, *14,* 52–54.

Barnes, B., "Cued Speech Keeps Deaf Pupils Ahead," *Children Today,* 1978, 7(7), 28–31.

Boothroyd, A. and M. Decker, "Control of Voice Pitch by the Deaf," *Audiology,* 1972, *11,* 343–53.

Bornstein, H. and H. L. Roy, "Comment on 'Linguistic Deficiency and Thinking: Research with Deaf Subjects,'" *Psychological Bulletin,* 1973, *79,* 211–14.

Bowyer, L. R. and J. Gillies, "The Social and Emotional Adjustment of Deaf and Partially Deaf Children." *British Journal of Educational Psychology,* 1972, *42,* 305–8.

Brereton, B. L., *The Schooling of Children with Impaired Hearing* (Sydney, Australia: Commonwealth Office of Education, 1957).

Broberg, R. F., "You've Come a Long Way, Baby: Lipreading in the Early 1970's," *Hearing and Speech News,* 1971, *39* (1), 20–23.

Butterfield, P. H., "The First Training Colleges for Teachers of the Deaf," *British Journal of Educational Studies,* 1971, *19* (1), 51–69.

Charrow, V. R. and J. D. Fletcher, "English as the Second Language of Deaf Children," *Developmental Psychology,* 1974, *10,* 463–70.

Connor, L. E. and J. Rosenstein, "Vocational Status and Adjustment of Deaf Women," *Volta Review,* 1963, *65,* 585–91.

Curry, E. T., "Are Teachers Good Judges of Pupils' Hearing?" *Journal of Exceptional Children,* 1954, *21,* 42, 48.

Dale, D. M., *Applied Audiometry for Children* (Springfield, Ill.: Charles C. Thomas, 1962).

Davis, H., "Sedation of Young Children for Electric Response Audiometry (ERA)," *Audiology,* 1973, *12* (2), 55–57.

Deeb, G., "Nation's 14 million Deaf to Benefit from Network "Closed-Captioning". *San Jose Mercury,* February 22, 1980, P. 11C.

Douglas, F. M., E. P. Fowler, Jr., and G. M. Ryan, *A Differential Study of*

Communication Disorders (New York: Columbia Presbyterian Medical Center, 1961).

Elstad, L. M., M. E. Frampton and E. D. Gall, *The Deaf in Special Education for the Exceptional* (Boston: Porter Sargent, 1955).

Erber, N. P., "Visual Perception of Speech by Deaf Children: Recent Developments and Continuing Needs," *Journal of Speech and Hearing Disorders,* 1974, *39,* 178–85.

Ewertsen, H. W., and H. Birk-Nielsen, "Social Hearing Handicap Index," *Audiology,* 1973, *12,* 180–83.

Ewing, J. R. and A. G. Ewing, *New Opportunities for Deaf Children.* (Springfield, Ill.: Charles C Thomas, 1958).

Farrant, R. H., "The Intellective Ability of Deaf and Hearing Children Compared by Factor Analysis," *American Annals of the Deaf,* 1964, *109,* 306–25.

Flathouse, V. E., "Multiply Handicapped Deaf Children and Public Law 94-142," *Exceptional Children,* 1979, *45,* 560–65.

Fraser, G. R., "Epidemiology of Profound Childhood Deafness," *Audiology,* 1974, *13,* 335–41.

Furfey, P. H., "Total Communication and the Baltimore Deaf Survey," *American Annals of the Deaf,* 1974, *119,* 377–80.

Furth, H. G., "Further Thoughts on Thinking and Language," *Psychological Bulletin,* 1973, *79,* 215–16.

Furth, H. G., "Linguistic Deficiency and Thinking: Research With Deaf Subjects, 1964–1969," *Psychological Bulletin,* 1971, *96,* 58–72.

Galkowski, T., "Auditory Reactions in Mentally Retarded Children by Means of Psychogalvanic Reflexes," *Audiology,* 1974, *13,* 501–5.

Gildston, H., and P. Gildston, "Personality Changes Associated with Surgically Corrected Hypo-acusis," *Audiology,* 1972, *11,* 354–67.

Glorig, A., "Thunderation," *Hearing and Speech News,* 1972, *40* (1), 6–7, 23–26.

Hehir, R. G., "Integrating Deaf Students for Career Education," *Exceptional Children,* 1973, *39,* 611–18.

Henderson, S. E. and L. Henderson, "Levels of Visual-information Processing in Deaf and Hearing Children," *American Journal of Psychology,* 1973, *86,* 507–21.

Hoemann, H. W., "Deaf Children's Use of Finger-spelling to Label Pictures of Common Objects: A Followup Study," *Exceptional Children,* 1974, *40,* 515–20.

Hughes, R. B., "A Comparison of Verbal Conceptualization in Deaf and Hearing Children" (unpublished doctoral dissertation, University of Illinois, 1959).

Jacobs, L., "The Community of the Adult Deaf," *American Annals of the Deaf*, 1974, *119*, 41–46.

Jensema, C., "Post-rubella Children in Special Educational Programs," *The Volta Review*, 1974, 76, 466–73.

Johnson, J. C., *Educating Hearing-impaired Children in Ordinary Schools* (Manchester, England: Manchester University Press, 1962).

Kates, S. L., *Cognitive Structures in Deaf, Hearing, and Psychotic Individuals* (Northampton, Mass.: Clarke School for the Deaf, 1967).

Kuyper, P., "The Cocktail Party Effect," *Audiology*, 1972, *11*, 277–82.

Leszczynski, L., "Device Allows Deaf to Converse on Phone," *San Jose* (California) *Mercury News*, 13 April 1975, 20.

Lunde, A. S. and S. K. Bogman, *Occupational Conditions Among the Deaf* (Washington, D. C.: Gallaudet College Press, 1959).

Maltzman, M., *Clinical Audiology* (New York: Grune and Stratton, 1949).

McCay, V., "Deaf Militancy," *American Annals of the Deaf*, 1974, *119*, 15.

Meadow, K. P., "The Deaf Subculture," *Hearing and Speech Action*, July–August 1975, *43* (9), 16–19.

Miller, D. E., J. T. Kunce, and S. H. Getsinger, "Prediction of Job Success for Clients with Hearing Loss," *Rehabilitation Counseling Bulletin*, 1972, *16* (1), 21–28.

Moores, D. F., K. L. Weiss and M. W. Goodwin, "Receptive Abilities of Deaf Children Across Five Modes of Communication," *Exceptional Children*, 1973, *40*, 22–28.

Myklebust, H. R., "Towards a New Understanding of the Deaf Child," *American Annals of the Deaf*, 1953, *98*, 345–57.

Myklebust, H. R., *The Psychology of Deafness* (New York: Grune and Stratton, 1960).

Newby, J. L., "Usability and Hearing Impairment," *Teaching Exceptional Children*, 1979, *11*, 144–45.

"News and Reports: Detecting Infant's Hearing Loss," *Children Today*, 1974, *3* (1), 30–31.

Northcott, W. H., ed., *The Hearing Impaired Child in a Regular Classroom: Preschool, Elementary, and Secondary Years* (Washington, D. C.: The Alexander Graham Bell Association for the Deaf, 1973).

O'Niell, J. J., *The Hard of Hearing* (Englewood Cliffs, N.J.: Prentice-Hall, 1964).

Quigley, S. P., "The Deaf and the Hard of Hearing," *Review of Educational Research*, 1969, *39*, 103–23.

Reichstein, J. and J. Rosenstein, "Differential Diagnosis of Auditory Deficits: A Review of the Literature," *Journal of Exceptional Children*, 1964, *30*, 73–82.

Rhodes, M. J., "Invisible Barrier," *The Exceptional Parent*, 1972, *1* (6), 10–14.

Ross, B. M., and H. Hoemann, "A Comparison of Probability Concepts in Deaf and Hearing Adolescents," *Genetic Psychology Monographs*, 1975, *91*, 61–120.

Sala, O. and G. Babeghian, "Automatic Versus Standard Audiometry," *Audiology*, 1973, *12* (1), 21–27.

Schein, J. D. "Deaf children with other Disabilities." *American Annals of the Deaf*, 1975, *120*, 92–99.

Schein, J. D. and M. T. Delk, Jr., *The Deaf Population of the United States* (Silver Spring, Md.: National Association of the Deaf, 1974).

Schunhoff, H. F., "Bases of a Comprehensive Program in the Education of the Deaf," *American Annals of the Deaf*, 1964, *109*, 240–47.

Stinson, M. S., "Relations Between Maternal Reinforcement and Help and the Achievement Motive in Normal-Hearing and Hearing-Impaired Sons," *Developmental Psychology*, 1974, *10*, 348–53.

Vernon, M., "Myths in the Education of Deaf Children," *Hearing and Speech News*, 1975, *39* (4), 13–17.

Wilson, G. B., M. Ross, and D. R. Calvert, "An Experimental Study of the Semantics of Deafness," *The Volta Review*, 1974, *76*, 408–14.

SUGGESTIONS FOR STUDENTS AND INSTRUCTORS

1. Using swimmer's ear plugs or earphones, have two students converse on an unfamiliar topic.

2. Have pairs of students watch first a newscast and then a soap opera episode on television with the sound turned off and compare what each thought was being said.

3. Arrange for a deaf person or the parent of a deaf child to talk and be interviewed by class members.

4. Arrange for students to spend a day assisting teachers of the deaf in special schools, special classes, or in regular classes enrolling hearing impaired students.

ADDITIONAL READINGS

Davis, H. and R. Silverman, *Hearing and Deafness* (New York: Holt, Rinehart, and Winston, 1978). A good general text on auditory impairment.

Naiman, D. W. and J. D. Schein, *For Parents of Deaf Children* (Silver Springs, Md.: National Association of the Deaf, 1978). Teachers as well as parents who work with deaf children will find this sensitive and compassionate book invaluable.

International Guide to Aids and Appliances for Blind and Visually Impaired Persons (New York: American Foundation for the Blind, 1979). A comprehensive source of practical information.

Selected Films

That's My Name—Don't Wear it Out. (26 minutes) Learning Corporation of America, 1350 Avenue of the Americas, New York, N.Y. 10019. Provides a good insight into the problems of deafness.

The World of Deaf-Blind Children: How They Communicate. (29 minutes) Campbell Films, Academy Avenue, Saxtons River, Vt. 05154. A good presentation of the complex problems of the deaf-blind.

Free 16 mm motion pictures and educational films are available to groups serving the deaf from Captioned Films for the Deaf Distribution Center, 5034 Wisconsin Avenue, N.W., Washington, D. C. 20016.

ORGANIZATIONS AND AGENCIES

Alexander Graham Bell Association for the Deaf
3417 Volta Place
Washington, D. C.

International Association of Parents of the Deaf
814 Thayer Avenue
Silver Spring, Md. 20910

John Tracy Clinic
(deafness/hearing impairments, deaf-blind)
806 West Adams Boulevard
Los Angeles, Calif. 90007

National Association of the Deaf
814 Thayer Avenue
Silver Spring, Md. 20910

National Hearing Aid Society
20361 Middlebelt Road
Livona, MI 48152

Office of Cued Speech Programs
Gallaudet College
7th and Florida Avenues, N.E.
Washington, D.C. 20020

MOTOR AND COMMUNICATION HANDICAPS

PART IV

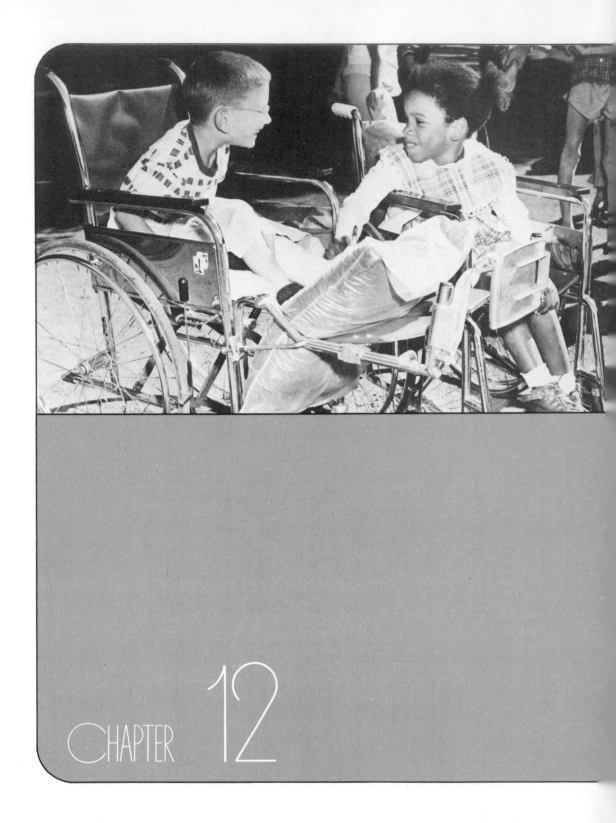

CHAPTER 12

ORTHOPEDIC AND OTHER PHYSICAL IMPAIRMENTS

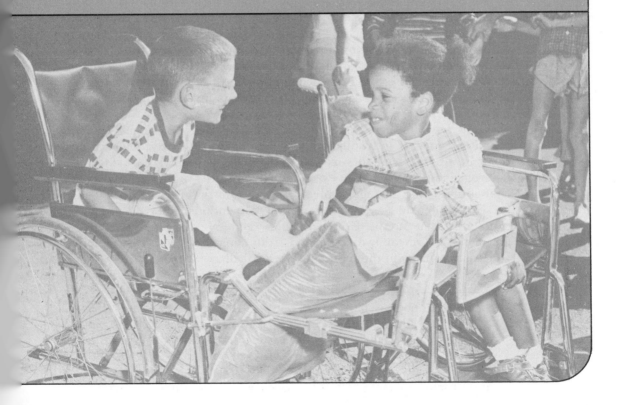

Children and adults with orthopedic impairments have all varieties and degrees of difficulty in physical movement (walking, coordination, and speech). The physical impairment may be due to accidents, disease, or congenital anomalies. Children with cerebral palsy are usually included among those with orthopedic difficulties for educational purposes, because of the severe nature of the physical involvement in cerebral palsy.

It is obvious that the term *orthopedically impaired* designates such a broad category of individuals that to attempt to find psychological and other group characteristics may be an exercise in futility. This extremely heterogeneous category of exceptionality includes individuals who are alike in not being average in physical ability. Beyond this, their likenesses become fewer and fewer because of the tremendous variety of impairing conditions that occur. However, some general characteristics can be gleaned from research findings and from clinical observations, although generalizations from these findings are difficult.

case study _____

Since childhood, Richard Chavez, now thirty-seven years of age, has spent every night in an iron lung. He walks with leg braces and crutches. Technically, he is 100 percent disabled. However, he has founded a rehabilitation institute, fathered two children, and is a licensed private investigator. His hobbies are fishing, disco dancing, and driving his car, which is equipped with special hand controls.

Chavez was born to Spanish-speaking parents in a Los Angeles barrio. He graduated from high school and attended college for two years. When efforts to obtain employment through the Department of Rehabilitation failed, he received federal funds to pay a private investigator as his tutor. He served a two-year apprenticeship, obtained a California special investigator's license, and started his own firm.

He also started a school for the handicapped. His first six students were taught in his garage. Chavez's institute now is a large facility which employs a staff of twenty-two. Governor Jerry Brown appointed him to sit as a judge on the state's Department of Rehabilitation Appeals Board. He also is a member of the Committee for Employment of the Handicapped. (UPI, October 15, 1979).

INCIDENCE OF ORTHOPEDIC IMPAIRMENT

Any estimate of the number of orthopedically impaired in the population is dependent on the manner of their definition. Different definitions and different sources of estimates yield varying prevalence figures.

Wilder (1975) indicates that reports of orthopedic impairment in health interviews run as high as 10 percent. It is generally considered that about 0.5 percent to 1.0 percent of school-age children are afflicted with crippling conditions or health impairment. Some surveys indicate that 0.91 per 1,000 of the general population for certain areas and cities are so afflicted, while others are as high as 9.79 per 1,000.

Physically handicapped students have long received special treatment by elementary and secondary schools, and special provisions for handicapped college students have received increasing attention since the passage of the Education for All Handicapped Children Act (PL 94-142). On September 1, 1978 it became a violation of federal law to deny a free, appropriate, public education to any handicapped child. It was reported that 27 percent of four-year universities and colleges in the United States indicated that they could accept students in wheelchairs (Mahan, 1974).

There has been a continuous increase in the percentage of crippled children being helped by crippled children's programs since 1937 (Saffian, 1962). In 1960, slightly fewer than half the number listed on the states' registers were involved in such programs. The nature of the disabilities of children being served by the programs was varied, with congenital malformations being the most frequent. Handicaps resulting from bone disorders and organs of movement were the second most frequently mentioned, and cerebral palsy was third. Certain crippling factors have noticeably declined. Poliomyelitis accounted for 14.5 percent of children in official programs in 1950, but by 1960 this figure had declined to 7 percent and soon it should disappear entirely if immunization programs become universal. However, in the mid-1970s public health officials expressed concern about the declining numbers of children being vaccinated against polio, and warned that a resurgence of the disease was possible. Vaccine has reduced the incidence of poliomyelitis drastically, and other medical advances hold promise of still further reduction in the incidence of crippling diseases. At the same time, increased medical skill may result in saving from death some orthopedically handicapped infants who heretofore would have died. Some of these children suffer neural damage that results in physical disability of one kind or another.

There has been a significant decrease in the crippling conditions which result from infectious diseases. Such conditions as poliomyelitis, osteomyelitis, tuberculosis of the bones and joints, and arthritis due to infection have been reduced over the years by advancing medical science. Congenital defects, which include a large variety of disorders, have increased among the newborn. However, because of the early correction of many deformities and the development of effective prosthetic devices, large numbers of congenital defects can no longer be considered handicapping.

Although impairment of visual perception is frequent among motor impaired children, it has been suggested that there may be sufficient independence of the two systems that visual impairment should be measured independently of motor functions in the handicapped (Newcomer and Hammill, 1973). An unfortunate trend has been toward increased impairment due to accidents of various kinds. The National Safety Council (1975) indicates that accidents claim more lives of children aged one to fourteen than the five leading diseases combined. Between 11,000 and 15,000 children are accidentally killed in the United States each year, and it is estimated that over 50,000 other children are permanently crippled and disabled by accident.

EMOTIONAL AND SOCIAL ADJUSTMENT

Investigations of the adjustment of physically impaired people are never very satisfactory, for several reasons. The extent and nature of physical disability within a group of the orthopedically impaired are extremely variable. It is difficult to determine their intellectual level, and therefore matching them with control groups is always tenuous. Brain damage may be present in some individuals and not in others, and the extent of damage usually is unknown.

The problems of formulating an adequate self-concept are many for the physically disabled. Self-concept has been considered to be intimately related to adjustment (Sawrey and Telford, 1975). The orthopedically handicapped children are different by reason of the disability. They may suffer pain, fatigue from undue exertion, accidents, and fear of injury or social rejection. These factors make it difficult for them to form realistic perceptions of their adequacies and limitations. As a result of too much parental attention, emotional rejection by parents, or condescending attitudes on the part of society in general, the handicapped child may come to feel inferior and inadequate. The resulting behavior may be maladaptive.

A number of investigators have indicated significant differences in the psychological adjustments of crippled and nonphysically handicapped children, while others have reported that the adjustments of the two groups can be favorably compared (Cruickshank, 1972). There is little doubt that the adjustive problems of crippled children take on different proportions than do those of noncrippled children, although that their adjustive problems are different in kind or process is doubtful. An investigation of the emotional needs of crippled children (Cruickshank and Dolphin, 1949) found no statistically significant differences between them and a group of normal children. Cruickshank (1972) later concluded that many of the objective tests used in the early studies of adjustment of crippled and noncrippled children were not sensitive enough to point up differences even if they did exist. More subtle and less personally threatening projective tests found differences between crippled and normal children (Broida, Izard, and Cruickshank, 1950; Smock and Cruickshank, 1952). The differences reported tend to support the hypothesis that a desire for, and a fear of, social participation constitutes a source of anxiety and fear in crippled children. It is probable that there are characteristic differences in adjustments between crippled and normal children. Delicate measuring instruments and sophisticated research procedures are needed to determine the nature and extent of these differences. Researchers in the field have emphasized that parental and home attitudes may be more significant factors in the adjustment of these children than they are for normal children. Such speculations appear to be reasonable, since the handicapped child is likely to spend more time in the home and be more dependent on the family for social contacts.

The parents with attitudes toward crippled children considered to be most constructive are those that have sufficient understanding to accept the child's handicap and turn their attention and energies toward finding means to compensate for it. Such parents fully realize the implications of the orthopedic problem and can accept the problem and the child both intellectually and emotionally.

LIMITING COVERAGE

There are a great number of crippling conditions from which both children and adults suffer. Cerebral palsy, poliomyelitis, osteomyelitis, arthritis, muscular dystrophy, multiple sclerosis, spina bifida, skeletal deformities, birth defects, and various other debilitating conditions are of concern to the student of exceptionality. Children and adults with special health problems such as epilepsy, heart conditions, asthma, eczema, and diabetes are of concern to educators and psychologists.

It is not our intention to cover each of these conditions and their special problems. We indicated earlier that many problems are shared by normal persons as well as by persons with orthopedic and special health abnormalities, and to cover each condition is beyond the scope of the text. We shall focus our attention on a limited number of conditions.

CEREBRAL PALSY

"Our son has cerebral palsy. He was unable to walk until he was six years old. Today he is twelve and still walks and talks very slowly and laboriously. He can communicate reasonably well with members of his own family but others have great difficulty understanding him. Fortunately he is bright and has good hearing and vision. Relying on these traits, our son is trying to build a satisfactory life for himself despite his physical disability." This brief parental statement reflects the situation of many cerebral palsied individuals and their families. A considerable number of children who are orthopedically handicapped have suffered from early damage to the motor area of the brain. This damage results in motor disturbances and incoordination of various degrees of severity. People exhibiting these motor disturbances as the result of brain damage are said to be suffering from *spastic paralysis*.

Spastic paralysis was first described by W. J. Little in 1843, hence it has been referred to as "Little's disease." Although spastic paralysis was described rather early, intensive work in the area of cerebral palsy was a long time in coming. Serious work in this area got under way during the 1930s, and since that time a great deal of research has been done. A particularly great amount of energy has gone into providing services for the cerebral palsied.

Cerebral palsy is a diagnostic term used to identify those with injury to the brain that affects muscle control in some way (Apgar and Beck, 1974). The major defect of cerebral palsy is disordered tone or muscle control (Johnston and Magrab, 1976). Localization of motor functions and sensory functions in the brain is generally accepted. When there is a motor or sensory dysfunction, it is assumed that damage has occurred to the particular part of the brain controlling this function. Damage to the motor area of the brain results in cerebral palsy. Although it is extremely difficult to determine the extent of any brain damage beyond that to the motor area and that causing concomitant sensory dysfunction, attempts continue in some areas that may be considered sensory/cognitive (Neuringer, Goldstein and Gallaher, 1975; Adams and others, 1975; Holowinsky, 1979).

CLASSIFICATION AND DESCRIPTION

Cerebral palsy may be classified in several different ways. E. Stephen (1958) listed five basic ways in which cerebral palsy may be classified: (1) according to type; (2) according to number of limbs involved; (3) according to time of onset; (4) according to degree of involvement; and (5) according to the extent and nature of the brain damage.

classification according to type Three main types are discerned: the spastic, the athetoid, and the ataxic. They are defined in terms of the dominant symptoms, which in turn are related to the area of the brain that has been damaged.

In *spasticity*, the lesions are in the motor cortex, the premotor area, and the pyramidal tract. Injury to the motor area of the brain results in loss of voluntary muscle control. There appears to be a generalized muscular response to stimulation that results in the simultaneous contraction of both the flexor and extensor muscles. The result is that coordinated movement is extremely difficult. The slightest stimulation causes the person to become very rigid. Jerky and spasmodic movements with "clasp-knife" rigidity and exaggerated reflexes are common. Hypertonicity prevails, and the person can move only with the greatest difficulty. Severe trembling, unsteadiness, and tense and irregular movements are characteristic. Making a deliberate effort to control the jerkiness and incoordination frequently causes them to be worse rather than better.

In *athetosis*, the lesions are in the extrapyramidal system, particularly in the basal ganglia. Athetosis is characterized by involuntary, slow, writhing, serpentine-like movements of the paralyzed member. The shoulders, face, feet, hands, and arms may be involved. Frequently the hands and arms are the seriously involved members. The rhythmical, writhing movement is slow and persistent. If one were to see only an arm and not the rest of the person, it could easily be mistaken for a deliberate, tense movement. The writhing may start in the shoulder and steadily move outward toward the fingers, involving progressively the elbow, the wrist, and then the fingers. Frequently the muscles of the throat and diaphragm are involved, and speech becomes labored, hoarse, and unintelligible. The person may have difficulty in controlling salivation, and thus add to his inconvenience and embarrassment. He may start to do something, like reach for a glass, but spill the contents. This causes excitement and an increased effort for control, which may result in increased tension and spasticity. When the patient relaxes or goes to sleep, the athetoid movements disappear. Athetosis accounts for 15 to 20 percent of the cerebral palsied (Smith and Neisworth, 1975).

More common than a pure case of either spasticity or athetosis is a combination of the two, involving damage to both areas (Sarason, 1959).

In *ataxia*, the area of the brain involved is usually the cerebellum or cerebellar tract. The eighth cranial nerve, which is involved with hearing and equilibrium, is sometimes affected. Ataxia is characterized by a disturbance in balance which is reflected in posture and gait. The person moves at a gait that suggests intoxication. Movements are awkward, speech is slurred, and the person sways and staggers. Locomotion is such that the person appears dizzy and uncertain.

classification according to number of limbs involved W. S. Wyllie (1951) has suggested a sixfold classification according to the number and manner in which the limbs are involved:

1. *congenital symmetrical diplegia,* paralysis in all limbs

2. *congenital paraplegia,* in which only the legs are involved

3. *quadriplegia* or *bilateral hemiplegia,* in which the disturbance is greater in the arms than in the legs

4. *triplegia,* a very rare condition in which three limbs are involved

5. *hemiplegia,* in which both limbs on the same side are involved

6. *monoplegia,* an extremely rare condition in which only one limb is affected.

Such a classification implies a continuum of motor disturbance, rather than clearly defined types of disturbance, and that such a continuum offers a possible explanation for the differences in the reported frequencies of the various involvements.

classification according to time of onset When classification is made according to time of onset, three time periods are usually designated: antenatal, natal, and postnatal. Distinguishing among these is not easy. The antenatal (before birth) and natal (birth) factors are difficult to separate from each other. This is true of natal and postnatal (after birth) factors as well, when the postnatal factors occur shortly after birth.

classification according to degree of involvement Various systems of classification according to degree or severity of involvement are used. F. E. Schonell (1956) classified her subjects as to whether they were slightly, moderately, severely, or very severely handicapped. Even with careful tabulation of the various afflictions common to cerebral palsied children, a great deal of subjective judgment of total severity is still involved. Although such a classification is meaningful within a limited area, it would seem to be lacking in the precision essential to meaningful research. There are so many facets of the cerebral palsied to evaluate that the task of arranging the complexity of variables into a single continuum of severity would seem to be extremely subjective.

classification according to extent and nature of brain damage In that our ability to detect the extent and nature of brain damage is limited, it would seem that such a classification would have to depend largely on the sensory defects concomitant with cerebral palsy. The cerebral palsied are brain-damaged, and they are probably not uniformily so. Our means of detection of brain damage are currently too limited to make meaningful classifications of damage other than through motor and sensory impairment.

INCIDENCE AND ETIOLOGY

The incidence of cerebral palsy is between 3 to 6 infants per 1,000 in the United States (Apgar and Beck, 1974). It is one of the most common crippling disorders of childhood. The total number of children and adults in this country with cerebral palsy has been estimated at 550,000 (Smith and Neisworth, 1975).

Because the causative background of cerebral palsy is complex, we shall attempt only a brief summary of the outstanding features here. The causal factors can be classified as to their time of occurrence in the development of the individual.[1]

prenatal causes Disease in the mother and developmental lesions are considered important factors in the etiology of cerebral palsy. Infections of the fetal brain from diseases of the mother occur. Notable among these are syphilis, meningitis, encephalitis, and German measles. Prenatal factors predisposing the fetus to damage are numerous (Wilson, 1973). Insufficient oxygen in the mother's bloodstream may result in cerebral damage. Anoxia of the brain can occur if the fetus is turned in such a manner as to twist the umbilical cord around its neck. When the oxygen supply is thus disrupted, the brain soon degenerates or fails to develop adequately. Hemorrhages caused by blood incompatibility due to Rh factors may produce brain damage resulting in cerebral palsy. Eight-six percent of cases of cerebral palsy are congenital or present at birth (Bleck, 1975).

natal causes The mode of birth was not found to be of any particular significance in the production of cerebral palsy, according to Benda (1952). Nearly one-fourth of this sample were premature babies. Prolonged labor was reported in eight of his thirty-seven cases, but normal delivery was reported in nine. Prematurity is dangerous to the child because the mother is not actually ready to give birth, and the pressure on the infant during birth is likely to be increased. The child is less mature, and consequently less capable of resisting increased pressure than at maturity. Hemorrhages and asphyxiation occur more easily in the premature.

Various other factors are related to, or can produce, cerebral palsy.

[1]For a more thorough treatment of the background of cerebral palsy, see Benda (1952); Bleck (1975).

Mechanical injury at birth through difficult delivery or from the use of forceps is a factor. However, the role of forceps in the production of cerebral palsy has probably been grossly overestimated. The sudden release of pressure during Caesarean delivery may cause the rupture of blood vessels, as may too rapid a birth or too great pressure during a very difficult birth. Interruptions to the oxygen supply and hemorrhages of the brain membranes and tissue are prominent in birth injury (Wilson, 1973). Sarason (1959) found that cerebral palsy resulting from birth injury of one kind or another comprises about 10 percent of institutionalized cerebral palsied cases. A continuum theory of brain damage, implying that all brains are more or less damaged at birth, indicates the difficulty involved in identifying brain injury at birth.

postnatal causes Injury to the brain after birth may produce cerebral palsy. Such injuries to the motor area of the brain can be produced by injury to the skull through severe accident. High temperature for a prolonged period, which results in a reduced oxygen intake, can also produce brain damage. The separating of natal from postnatal factors is very difficult when it is considered that certain injuries at birth are not detectable for some length of time. Injuries occurring after birth, when the brain has more fully developed, are not associated with mental deficiency to the same extent as are prenatal anomalies. It is estimated that 14 percent of cerebral palsy is postnatally acquired (Bleck, 1975). Cerebral palsy cannot be accounted for adequately by any single factor.

INTELLIGENCE OF CHILDREN WITH CEREBRAL PALSY

The task of measuring the intelligence of cerebal palsied children is fraught with difficulties. The problem of how best to measure the intelligence of children who may have multiple sensory handicaps in addition to paralysis has been attacked by a number of investigators. Most investigators have found it necessary to alter the tasks of standardized intelligence tests in one way or another to fit the handicapped state of the subject involved. Altering standardized tests in any way no doubt has an effect on their validity. In the absence of tests developed particularly for the multiple combinations of disabilities encountered in cerebral palsy, investigators of the intelligence of the cerebral palsied typically have used the Stanford-Binet or other such tests and have prorated the test scores. Inappropriate items are not used, and those that are used count an increasing amount. A certain percentage of cases are found to be untestable. H. V. Bice and Cruickshank (1955) found 15 percent to be untestable.

Studies of the intelligence of the cerebral palsied have yielded consistent results. Two English studies and two in the United States are in fairly close agreement, and all involved a sizable number of cases. Dunsdon (1952) studied the intelligence of 916 cerebral palsied children, largely candidates for special school in England. She reports that the IQs of 58.6 percent were below 70, and that only 8.25 percent scored 100 or better. Schonell (1956), after studying 354 cases of English cerebral palsied children over three years of age, reports that 51 percent had IQs over 70, and that 23 percent had IQs between 50 and 69.

In America, T. Hopkins, H. Bice, and K. Colton (1954) reported on 1,000 cases in New Jersey. They reported that 48.8 percent had IQs below 70; 20.4 percent had IQs between 50 and 69; and 7.9 percent had IQs of 110 or more. E. Miller and G. B. Rosenfeld (1952) studied 330 children with cerebral palsy. They reported that 50 percent of their cases had IQs below 70, and that 4 to 5 percent scored 110 or better. To assess the possibility of an increase in the percentage of mentally defective children due to the large number of children brought to the clinic from a considerable distance as a "last resort," they evaluated this group separately and compared them with the total group. They found "no important differences." (A better control would have been to compare them to the remainder of the group. As it is, they were compared to a group of which they themselves made up more than one-third.)

The four studies presented tend to agree that the incidence of mental deficiency among the cerebral palsied is high. The studies indicate that roughly 50 percent have IQs below 70. The distribution of the intelligence of the cerebral palsied definitely piles up at the lower end of the intellectual continuum. Only 3 or 4 percent have IQs above 115, and less than one-fourth have IQs between 70 and 89. The studies agree, too, that there is no significant difference between the mean IQs of athetoids and spastics, in contrast with the supposition that intelligence is relatively unaffected in athetosis. The damage in athetosis is subcortical (in the basal ganglia), and intelligence was therefore thought to be less impaired. However, there appears to be no significant difference in general intelligence between the two main forms of cerebral palsy.

A. Heilman (1952) reported 59 percent of cerebral palsied children to be mentally retarded; J. W. Wrightstone, J. Justman, and S. Moskowitz (1954) estimated 27 percent; and J. Greenbaum and J. A. Buehler (1960) 45 to 55 percent. These discrepancies no doubt reflect the selection factor operating in the schools from which the samples of students were drawn. If a school is highly selective, it is likely to have fewer low-intellect individuals among its cerebral palsied. While 2 to 3 percent of the general population is considered to be mentally retarded, about 50 percent of cerebral palsied persons can probably be expected to function in the mentally retarded range (Apgar and Beck, 1974).

In view of the range, it is difficult to characterize the intelligence of the cerebral palsied. Intellectually they do not represent a homogeneous group, although the general trend is for intelligence to be low.

Associated Defects

Other than motor paralysis and decreased intellectual efficiency, which are characteristic of the cerebral palsied, a number of defects are commonly found. Roughly 30 percent of children with cerebral palsy are reported to have a history of one or more epileptic seizures (Floyer, 1955; Hopkins, Bice, & Colton, 1954). In a study of certified mentally defective children, B. H. Kirman (1956) reported that children with epilepsy tended to be less intelligent than those not so afflicted. Visual defects and speech disorders are common. Speech defects probably occur in about 70 percent of the cases of cerebral palsy (Stephen, 1958). Hearing disabilities have been reported as more frequent than in other populations. Sensory impairment has been reported in 50 percent of cases of hemiplegia (Tizard, Paine, and Crothers,1954).

Cerebral palsied children, particularly those who are mentally retarded, have a wide variety of concomitant defects. When the additional defects are added to the already existing ones, they represent a tremendous handicap. The cerebral palsied child is typically a multiple handicapped child.

In addition to the 50 percent who are mentally retarded, another 15 to 20 percent can be expected to suffer from some type of specific learning disability.

Treatment and Training

Special facilities for the treatment and training of cerebral palsied and other brain-damaged children have grown rapidly during the past thirty years. The training and subsequent rehabilitation of those who are not mentally retarded are very promising, and a number of physical therapy theories and procedures have been developed.

Surgical and medical treatment of cerebral palsy has not had the curative effects once hoped for. Currently surgery is used only in certain situations to correct deformities. Tranquilizing drugs have been used as muscle relaxants with considerable success with some children (Woods, 1975).

Adolescent youngsters have been successfully trained as paraprofessionals to work with the handicapped (Rouse and Farb, 1974), and approaches to management of cerebral palsy are being evaluated (Heal, 1974). The treatment of learning disabilities among the cerebral palsied is discussed elsewhere in this book. Interested readers also should peruse Rosen, Clark, and Kivitz (1977), and Calhoun and Hawisher (1979).

Children and adults with epilepsy are subject to convulsions. They differ from others principally in that they have convulsive seizures or must take medication in order to prevent or control seizures. The word *epilepsy* is derived from a Greek word that means "to be seized," and modern neurologists consider *epilepsy* to be merely a synonym for "seizure" rather than a term representing a specific disease entity (Folsom, 1968). Convulsive states or seizures that tend to be episodic and recurrent are considered to be symptoms of a disorder, rather than a disorder in and of themselves. When these symptoms occur, they are the result of a functional disturbance in a group of nerve cells in the brain. These nerve cells, for some reason, are discharging their electrical energy at an accelerated rate. The precise reasons for these accelerated discharges are not known, but a variety of factors may be considered contributory. Among these are head injuries, infections, interference with normal blood supply or oxygen to the brain, and prolonged high fever.

Convulsive disorders are not uncommon in early childhood. Early childhood seizures are frequently associated with prolonged high temperatures. It is not uncommon for people to experience an isolated seizure. Any interference with the normal supply of blood and oxygen to the brain may cause certain brain cells to discharge electrical energy at an accelerated rate and bring about a seizure in a healthy person. A seizure reflects the normal reaction of a group of neurones to excessive irritation. A seizure which occurs once and is not repeated within a reasonable period of time does not constitute epilepsy (Sakel, 1958).

Seizures associated with epilepsy are recurrent. There is a relatively persistent functional disturbance of the electrical discharge of cells in the brain. Destroyed cells are no longer functional and do not discharge energy. However, slightly damaged cells, or those which are partially damaged and which surround destroyed cells, may function abnormally and produce seizures. The extent and location of brain cells that discharge excessively are determinants of the nature and severity of epileptic seizures. Periodic disturbances of the rhythm of the brain have been termed "cerebral dysrhythmia" (Lennox, 1941). In many instances it is not possible to identify the contributory factors resulting in cerebral dysrhythmia or to locate areas of brain damage, but the patterns of electrical discharge are disturbed and convulsive behavior does occur. This is *idiopathic epilepsy*. In other instances, contributory factors are identifiable and pathological conditions are present. This is known as *symptomatic epilepsy*.

In symptomatic epilepsy, the convulsions are considered to be a secondary manifestation of a known pathological condition in the brain. Symptomatic epilepsy can be observed in various kinds of mental defectives. The lesions in the brain may be traced to various kinds of injury or infection, or they may represent developmental anomalies. Idiopathic epilepsy is very largely of unknown origin, and by far the greatest number of epileptics are classified as "idiopathic." In these cases there is no detectable structural anomaly. Epileptic seizures are rather common among the mentally retarded, but are considered to be concomitant with the retardism rather than a cause of it.

Epileptic seizures appear in numerous and diverse forms because the electrical disturbance responsible for the seizure may be located within any portion of the brain and may involve few or many abnormally functioning cells. Epileptic seizures of a variety of forms and severity have been described and classified. The typical epileptic seizure comes on suddenly. Unconsciousness occurs, and the person may fall. The patient is unable to control the seizure; it runs its course and is recurrent.

VARIETIES OF EPILEPTIC CONVULSION

Epileptic convulsions vary in a great number of ways. They do not all occur with the same frequency, nor are they all of the same duration, comprehensiveness, or severity. It has already been indicated that this variability has a complex background of concomitant variability in the nervous system. Some of the types of epileptic seizures will be discussed, but it should be remembered that seizures may vary almost infinitely in character and number. The origins of epilepsy are numerous and diagnosis, therefore, is difficult. The presence of overt seizures which are recognizable as epileptic is a guide in the clinical diagnosis of epilepsy. The nature and severity of the seizure determines, in large part, the classification that it is given.

grand mal By far the most frequently reported type of seizure is *grand mal*. A survey of clinic and private patients (Lennox, 1941) reported that of patients having only one type of seizure, 51 percent had *grand mal*. Among the *grand mal* patients, 25 percent had less than five seizures per year, 50 percent less than 15, 75 percent less than 50, 22 percent more than 1,000, and 0.4 percent more than 5,000. Males have more *grand mal* seizures than women. Lennox's data were compiled from questionnaires returned by neurologists, and are based on other than institutional cases.

The typical *grand mal* seizure can be described according to stages, the first of which is an aura. An *aura* may be described as a preliminary experience which constitutes a warning to the patient that he or she is going to have a convulsion. It may consist of nausea, dizziness, flashes of light, sounds, odors, or any sensory experience. About one-half of epileptic patients apparently experience an aura (Lennox and Cobb, 1933), and it has been reported to be less frequent among children than among adults (Kanner, 1935). The aura, or warning, may precede the loss of consciousness by but an instant, but may be as long as few seconds, which would enable the person to prepare for the impending seizure. Children, when asked about their seizures, have been known to confine their comments to the aura. The aura may be a frightening experience for a child.

The aura is followed by a sudden loss of consciousness. The patient pitches or falls to the floor, as if suddenly struck a heavy blow. The person may emit a cry as he or she falls. This is caused by the lungs expelling air and has been called an epileptic cry. The patient quickly stiffens. The muscles are contracted violently, and temporarily are held rigid. This is the *tonic* phase of the seizure. The stiffness or rigidity seems to involve the whole body. The head and eyes may turn. The vigorous contraction may force air from the lungs and inhibit breathing. The skin turns blue and the pupils of the eyes become dilated. The tonic phase of the seizure may last from a few seconds to a minute or two, and is terminated by the beginning of the clonic phase.

The *clonic* phase of the seizure is the most violent portion of it. It is the convulsion proper. It is characterized by the violent alternate contractions and relaxations of the musculature. The legs and arms jerk, the abdominal and chest muscles contort, the face becomes distorted, the chest moves violently as breathing becomes vigorous. Perspiration is often profuse, and the bowels and bladder may be evacuated. This phase of the seizure usually lasts for two or three minutes. The patient may froth at the mouth. This is caused by the violent relaxation and contraction of the facial muscles and the vigorous breathing which may force saliva out of the mouth. It may be blood-stained because the tongue and lips may be bitten during the convulsion. During this phase of the seizure, the patient may be seriously injured by banging the body and limbs against the floor or other objects. People may chew their lips and tongue, and precautions should be taken against injury and strangulation. The frequency and severity of the contractions gradually diminish, and the patient finally relaxes and goes into a deep sleep or coma which is followed by a natural sleep.

The length of the *coma* and of the natural sleep following it will vary according to the state of exhaustion of the individual after the vigorous seizure, and with the time of day. The person awakens not feeling well, may be very tired, and may suffer from headache, sore muscles, vomiting, disorientation, and confusion. The person is confused, has amnesia for the seizure, and frequently feels depressed. Seizures vary greatly from patient to patient in frequency, severity, and aftereffects. The same individual may also show differences among seizures from time to time.

The seizures typically last only a few minutes, but they do not always follow the typical pattern of aura—tonic phase—clonic phase—coma. The patient may go from a semicomatose state back into a tonic phase, followed by a clonic phase, then go back into coma. This may be done several times. This is termed *status epilepticus*, and can be very serious. The attention of a physician is imperative when this occurs. Lennox and Cobb (1933) reported that 40 percent of 1,500 patients studied had seizures both at night and in the daytime. Thirty-six percent had seizures only during the daytime and 15 percent only at night.

petit mal This type of seizure is much less severe than *grand mal*, but may occur much more frequently with a given person. There typically is no aura for this attack. It comes on suddenly and lasts from a few seconds to a half-minute or so. It consists of a short lapse of consciousness. The patient rarely falls or convulses, but suddenly appears dazed, may grow pale, stare fixedly, drop an object being held, and twitch slightly. The eyelids may flicker. The person may continue to do whatever is being done, rather automatically, or may stop for a few moments and then resume the activity. The person is frequently aware of the short lapses of consciousness. *Petit mal* is most frequently found in children. The attacks may range in frequency from 1 to 200 per day (Bridge, 1949). The seizure begins and ends abruptly and may go unnoticed because of the short time involved and the nonspectacular symptoms. *Pyknoepilepsy* is a name frequently applied when children have *petit mal* attacks that seem to cease spontaneously with development. Some varieties of *petit mal* consist of only a single shocklike jerk, without a loss of consciousness (myoclonic jerk). Patients with myoclonic jerks usually also are subject to the more common *petit mal* attacks. Another variety of *petit mal* attack (akinetic epilepsy) involves a sudden postural collapse, with consequent nodding of the head or even falling. Some seizures (autonomic seizures) may consist of periods of sweating, flushing, increased blood pressure, or gagging without apparent cause, with no loss of consciousness. These seizures are rare and can be considered variations of *petit mal*.

Jacksonian Jacksonian seizures are named for the famous English neurologist, Hughlings Jackson. They start in an extremity, or on one side of the face, and gradually move to engulf other portions of the body. If the whole body is involved, it terminates in *grand mal*. In this form of seizure, the extremity starts to convulse or a progressive anesthesia begins to develop. The patient can observe the twitching or jerking from the contractions or feel the numbness as it moves to encompass greater portions of the body. In some cases there is no convulsiveness as such, but a tingling sensation that moves progressively toward greater physiological involvement. These patients sometimes find that they can prevent the continued spread of the muscular twitchings by rapidly engaging themselves in some task requiring large expenditures of physical energy or extensive intellectual involvement.

In some instances the seizure is completely localized. That is, there is no tendency for progressive bodily involvement. One extremity or one side of the body is involved. The attack may be convulsive or simply a sensory phenomenon such as anesthesia (loss of sensation). Sensory seizures may involve various sensations of the body, or they may involve taste, smell, or visual phenomena (Lennox, 1947b). Clonic movements of the face or an extremity are often involved when an attack begins.

psychomotor This is an ill-defined, rare, and poorly understood condition. Mild tonic cramps, a stiffening of the extremities, tightening of the jaws, drooling, and a bluishness of the face may occur. The characteristic part of this seizure is amnesia. The person may act as if drugged, move about rather automatically and deliberately, and may mutter incoherently and go through various apparently meaningless motions or engage in rather complex and complicated behavior as if aware of what was being done. The person may sit motionless or muttering and chewing or may be violently active. The patient does not appear to lose consciousness, but does not seem to be aware of his or her actions. Amnesia is reported for the duration of the seizure. The person may give vent to feelings of hostility through physical violence or abusive language and when resisted, may commit violent aggressive acts without apparent provocation. In some cases, drastic and abrupt alterations in temperament occur, during which time the person is extremely aggressive and impulsive. Crimes of violence may be committed but Turner and Merlis (1962) found only 5 out of 337 epileptics had committed illegal acts during seizures. These attacks may vary in length from a few minutes to several days. It is difficult to tell, in many cases, whether the person is having a psychotic episode of some sort, is emotionally distraught, or is having a seizure. Data about the frequency of such attacks are hard to evaluate because of the failure to make such distinctions. *Epileptic equivalency* has been used as a label for the designation of some such attacks. These attacks have been designated as preceding, taking the place of, or following an epileptic convulsion. The concept of epileptic equivalency has been criticized because the concept may include any kind of pathological behavior in an epileptic individual or in a person with a family history of seizures. Epilepsy thus becomes the scapegoat for pathological behavior.

INCIDENCE

The frequency of epilepsy in the general population is difficult to estimate. The fear and ignorance surrounding epilepsy keep an unknown number of cases from being brought to the attention of medical authorities. Epilepsy has probably existed in all stages of human history, and probably among all races. One-half of one percent is the generally accepted figure for the frequency of epilepsy in the school-age population (United States Office of Education, 1970). However, after reviewing World War I and II draft figures in the United States and some other relevant data, Harlin (1965) indicated that about 7 per 1,000 school children are epileptic. The question of differences in incidence between the sexes has not been answered adequately. Institutions usually have a greater number of epileptic males than females. The fallibility of institutional data for estimating conditions in the general population has been discussed; it is difficult to draw conclusions about sex differences from such data.

Epilepsy essentially is a disorder of children and youth. The onset of seizures has been reported to be before the age of twenty in 71 percent of a large sample of cases, with 63 percent of girls and 52 percent of boys having their first convulsion before age fifteen, and in 47 percent of 4,000 epileptic cases, the first seizure occurred in the first decade of life (Lennox, 1941, 1951). Convulsive disorders are quite common among the mentally deficient. Penrose (1963) has reported that 16 percent of the 1,280 such institutionalized individuals had idiopathic epilepsy.

Probably, in every 1,000 school children, one or two are subject to epileptic seizures. In an investigation of the population of 23 schools, Guerin (1979) found that children with epilepsy constituted 3.65 of each 1,000 pupils. Epileptic seizures in most children can be sufficiently controlled so that perhaps only 10 percent or less of those subject to seizures will actually have a convulsion in school.

ETIOLOGY

The causes of epilepsy are multiple, and not thoroughly understood. A number of sources of brain damage might result in symptomatic epilepsy. So many factors could possibly produce symptomatic epilepsy that no attempt will be made to enumerate them all. Brain lesions traceable to definite natal or postnatal brain injuries to the motor cortical areas are sometimes causative. Brain injury was found in about half of a group of over 700 epileptic patients. One-half of these injuries occurred during the birth process, and the others resulted from various accidents and diseases in childhood (Bridge, 1949). Developmental anomalies which result in maldevelopment of brain tissue may occur. Mechanical injuries of various kinds may produce lesions, as may various infections, hemorrhages, and interruptions in the supply of oxygen to the brain. Brain tissue is very susceptible to interruptions in the supply of oxygen; deterioration sets in rapidly and brain tissue does not regenerate. In older patients, seizures are associated with arteriosclerosis (hardening of the arteries). A great variety of cerebral lesions may result in seizures, but none can be depended upon to do so consistently (Wallin, 1949). Seizures or convulsions are really symptoms which can be produced by a great variety of causes. When it is possible to locate the disturbance in the brain, the epilepsy is termed *focal*. Almost any gross disturbance of cerebral functioning can be accompanied by epileptic convulsions, as is apparent from the large proportion of defectives with cranial malformations who are subject to epilepsy. Generally, the younger the child when seizures first occur, the greater the likelihood of there being a known organic cause. After the age of ten, other causes become more important (Kram, 1963). Forty-four percent of 765 epileptic children in the Detroit school system were reported to have developed their epilepsy during their first four years of life, while only 7 percent started having seizures after the age of twelve (Tenney, 1955). Of 352 epileptic patients in Norway, 40 percent began having seizures before the age of five. In 52 percent of the total sample, possible organic factors were indicated (Mackay, Wortis, and Sugar, 1960). An investigation of epileptic patients in England indicated that most often seizures first occur during the first two years of life (Kram, 1963).

The etiology of idiopathic epilepsy is very perplexing. When there is no detectable structural abnormality and when no other disease condition is present except that the patient is subject to epileptic convulsions, the epilepsy itself has to be regarded as the principal condition.

Investigations of the number of relatives of epileptics who were subject to epilepsy has led to speculations about the hereditary nature of idiopathic epilepsy, but early findings varied considerably. One source of this variance was the closeness of the relationships studied and whether the count was restricted to relatives with epileptic convulsions or included other neuropathic disorders which might be predisposing to epilepsy. Another variable was whether institutional or noninstitutionalized cases were used. Lennox (1954), investigating 20,000 near relatives of approximately 4,000 epileptic patients, found evidences of an inherited predisposition to idiopathic seizures. The incidence of near relatives with a history of one or more seizures was 3.2 percent, and of these about half had chronic epilepsy. This would be more than three times the percentage of chronic epileptics in the general population.

Studies indicate that a greater frequency of epilepsy is found among identical than nonidentical twins (Lennox, 1947a, 1954). Lennox investigated 173 pairs of twins who had seizures. Among the 77 pairs of identical twins, 70 percent were both subject to seizures. Among the 96 pairs of fraternal twins, both were affected only 12.5 percent of the time. In an investigation quoted by Penfield and Erickson (1941), epilepsy was found in both identical twins in 86.3 percent of idiopathic cases, and in both fraternal twins in only 3 percent of the cases.

Studies of the electrical brain activity of epileptics have revealed that they have characteristic brain wave patterns. The highly sensitive device which measures this activity is called an electroencephalograph (EEG). Special training is required for the interpretation of the EEG record, on which is traced the amplitude and frequency of the brain waves. Various convulsive conditions reveal their own unique patterns.

The EEG is not always conclusive in epilepsy. From 5 to 20 percent of clinically diagnosed epileptic patients have been reported to have EEG records within the normal range (Penfield and Erickson, 1941; Hefner, 1960). The situation is further complicated by the observation that 10 to 15 percent of the general population have cerebral dysrhythmia while only 0.5 percent of the population is epileptic (Lennox, Gibbs, and Gibbs, 1940).

Although the EEG is fallible, it is an important diagnostic and research tool. Through its use a great amount of indirect evidence about the heritability of epileptic brain wave patterns has been compiled. EEG records of the families of epileptics early received the attention of Lowenbach (1939). Lennox (1947c) has been an important contributor to this field. He found the incidence of epilepsy to be 2.8 percent among a large sample of the parents, siblings, and children of 2,000 epileptics. This figure is 5.5 times greater than its occurrence in the general population. He found dysrhythmia in nearly all his epileptic subjects. The EEG records of over 90 percent of one or the other of the parents of 55 unselected epileptics were found to be abnormal. Abnormal brain waves were found in both parents of 30 percent of the cases. Sixty percent of the near relatives of 94 epileptics showed abnormal brain waves. In 78 percent of over 2,000 cases, no cause other than an inherited predisposition toward cerebral dysrhythmia could be found. In the remaining 22 percent, various other causes may have produced the seizures or have played only a contributory role.

That seizures are frequently related to emotional factors is rather well agreed (Robinson and Robinson, 1965). There is considerable disagreement that epilepsy is caused by emotional and personality factors. Bridge (1949) feels that there is a possibility that in certain instances emotional and personality factors may be the primary agents. It has been suggested that seizures can be interpreted as release of psychic tensions when other avenues of release are inaccessible. Emotional conflict has been found with a high degree of frequency among epileptic children, and release of hostility in psychotherapy has resulted in a decrease in the number of seizures and required amounts of medication.

The background of epilepsy is not clear. Research is needed into the question of why some, but not all, persons with abnormal EEG records have seizures, and why some who have seizures do not have abnormal EEG records. Psychogenic factors in epilepsy need systematic research, as do the various causes and consequences of cerebral damage.

The importance for educators of the awareness of biological factors in various conditions of physical impairment has been emphasized (Reed, 1979) minimized (Balow, 1979), and critically analyzed (Moss, 1979). Understanding of biological factors in epilepsy, as in other conditions, if not imperative for the educator, at the very least should enhance appreciation and understanding.

It is to be expected that the frequency of seizures can be associated with severity of mental defects, because almost any gross disturbance of cerebral functioning can be accompanied by epileptic manifestations (Penrose, 1963). The influence of epilepsy on intelligence is not clearly understood. Although many epileptics are below average in intelligence, the condition is not inconsistent with average or superior ability.

Some notable men of history are reported to have been subject to epileptic seizures. Such men as Julius Caesar, Alexander the Great, and Napoleon are reported to have been epileptics, as were such literary lights as Charles Lamb and Guy de Maupassant. These men frequently are cited as evidence of the outstanding ability of some epileptics, but the usual findings are that a group of epileptic persons cannot be expected to be of high-level intelligence.

Investigations of the intelligence of epileptics have varied because some researchers have confined their efforts to institutional cases. These cases usually yield lower IQs than do noninstitutional cases, possibly because the most severely afflicted and less brilliant are institutionalized. When epileptics who are not institutionalized have been studied, higher intelligence quotients have been obtained. Some studies, particularly early ones, did not differentiate between symptomatic and idiopathic epileptics. When such distinctions have been made, the lower measured intelligence of the symptomatic group becomes apparent.

Using either the Stanford-Binet, Form L, or the Wechsler-Bellevue, Lennox and Collins (1945) examined 149 nonepileptic twins and obtained a mean IQ of 108. They obtained a mean IQ of 96 for 27 epileptics without evidence of brain lesions, and 77 for 10 epileptics with brain damage. The IQs of 248 Chicago children with convulsive disorders (Mullen, 1953) were spread over a wide range, with 56.7 percent falling between 50 and 79. The mean IQ of the group was 71.8. A review of the studies of the intelligence of noninstitutionalized cases (Broida, 1955) indicated that their intelligence did not differ significantly from that of the general population. Efforts to establish characteristic subtest patterns of epileptics indicate that there is no typical pattern. Numerous studies of the distribution of intelligence among epileptics have reported no significant difference from the normal. A 1962 summary of the psychological test literature (Geist, 1962) concluded that the literature was replete with conflicting evidence.

The question of intellectual deterioration and its relation to epilepsy has been of rather great concern. Pintner, Eisenson, and Stanton (1940) reviewed various studies and indicated that only a small minority of epileptics show marked deterioration. It is rather difficult, in studying deterioration in an institution, to separate the results of institutionalization from those of the seizures (Sarason, 1959). From the data currently available it is impossible to state whether there is a relationship between frequency and severity of seizures and deterioration. Studies have reported less impairment of those with milder seizures, which would seem to be logical when one considers that brain damage is associated with intelligence.

Whether the use of anticonvulsant drugs produces impairment is questionable. Several studies of the various anticonvulsants and intelligence have been made. The results are conflicting, but the better-controlled studies tend to discount the adverse effects of the drugs on intellectual functioning.

PERSONALITY AND EMOTIONAL FACTORS

Early writers in the field described the personality of epileptics in an essentially unfavorable manner. They were described as egocentric, antisocial, unstable, quarrelsome, moody, and criminotic. Enough uniformity in the alleged personality traits was reported so that much consideration was given to the so-called epileptic personality. A stereotype of the personality of people with epilepsy came into being, and the early literature led one to believe that the epileptic was hopelessly antisocial. However, the stereotype of the epileptic personality has not held up under systematic investigation. No doubt some institutionalized epileptics do display unfortunate behavior patterns, but they apparently do not do so with enough consistency to allow for an all-inclusive epileptic pattern.

The theory that differences in personality among epileptics are related to differences in type of epilepsy has, in the case of temporal-lobe epilepsy (excessive electrical discharge from the temporal lobes) received some support (James, 1960). Typically, the behavior of temporal-lobe epileptics has been described in terms of their being underactive, with outbursts of aggressiveness and destructiveness. Personality changes of one kind or another have been identified in as many as 52 percent of temporal-lobe epileptics (Bingley, 1958). In one of the better designed investigations using the EEG to identify the location of discharge focus, frontal-lobe epileptic children were rated as more aggressive than other EEG groups, and their mean "neurotic" score was the lowest (Nuffield, 1961).

The person suffering from the ravages of continuing convulsions has not only the ordinary problems of living to encounter, but the stress and strain of epilepsy as well. Frequently, the epileptic is scorned and discriminated against. The person may have brain damage that is progressive, and the neural pathology may have direct behavioral consequences. The person must take medication to control convulsions. In some cases, the medication may cause general irritability in the patient. In spite of these considerations, the personalities of epileptics are highly diverse. Studies of the personalities of epileptic children, using the Rorschach (a projective test using ink blots), indicate that they have a wide diversity of personality characteristics rather than a single constellation that would comprise a type (Broida, 1955; Tizard, 1962). Studies of the behavior problems of epileptic children indicate that their problems are very similar to those of other children found in a child guidance clinic. Although epileptics are reputed to be destructive, in a study of seventy epileptic children they were found to exhibit less destructive behavior than a comparable group of nonepileptic children (Deutsch and Wiener, 1948). Strong issue has been taken with the concept of an "epileptic personality."

Investigations of the personality characteristics of epileptics are difficult to evaluate for several reasons. Classifications of epilepsy are inadequate; samples have not been representative or adequately observed; bias is hard to avoid; inadequate diagnoses have been employed; the factor of intelligence level has not always been controlled; and personality-measurement devices may lack reliability (Tizard, 1962).

TREATMENT AND PROGNOSIS

The treatment of epilepsy is very largely medical. Sedative and anticonvulsant drugs have proven very effective in diminishing the frequency and severity of the convulsions. Phenobarbital (a sedative) and Dilantin (a nonsedative anticonvulsant) frequently are used to control seizures. Other drugs have been developed, and new ones are constantly being produced in laboratories around the world. Drug therapy is not considered curative of epilepsy. The drugs are used to control and prevent convulsions. They tend to have no intellectually impairing effects, and the relief from convulsions may cause children under sixteen actually to increase in intelligence test performance (Somerfield-Ziskund and Ziskund, 1940).

Some cases of symptomatic epilepsy, particularly the Jacksonian type, can be remedied by surgery. When the convulsions are due to lesions, pressure, or tumor, surgical procedures have proved effective in a limited number of cases. When surgery is effective, the patient is no longer subject to seizures and can function normally.

Psychotherapy, once considered futile with epileptics, holds considerable promise. Emotional problems and conflicts may serve as precipitating factors in the production of seizures. Through psychotherapy those emotional conflicts may be reduced and the frequency of seizures thus reduced. Efron (1956, 1957) reports the arrest of seizures in a woman with temporal-lobe epilepsy through the use of Pavlovian conditioning procedures. Robinson and Robinson (1965) report the case of a girl who had major seizures in spite of medication until she was placed in an institution at the age of fourteen. Following this and without new treatment she had only one seizure during the next year. When she was sent home her seizures returned and were as severe as ever. The role of psychological factors would seem important here. It has been speculated that psychological factors may actually cause seizures (Bridge, 1949). If this is true, considerable improvement might be expected from psychotherapy. Even when the causes of the seizures are rather definitely physiological, psychotherapy may help the patient to live with the epilepsy, its treatment, and the limitations imposed by it.

The control of seizures through the use of drugs has proven to be a tremendous help. People, relieved of their convulsions, function better and adjust more readily. Medical treatment of epilepsy varies from patient to patient. Some patients require different dosages and different drugs than others. Some patients' seizures can be completely prevented through medication; in others, the frequency or severity of the seizures may be reduced. Prolonged use of anticonvulsant drugs is usually necessary, but the prognosis for alleviation of the convulsions is favorable for large numbers of persons.

TEACHER, PARENT, AND COMMUNITY ATTITUDES

Epilepsy is probably one of the older afflictions known to man (Tower, 1960). Its long history is one of interesting contrasts, and the confusions and misunderstandings of the past tend to persist in modified form up to the present time. The persistence of certain attitudes and customs makes the affliction more difficult than it need be. Modern diagnosis and treatment have developed to the point where most people subject to epileptic seizures can be treated so as to control or eliminate the convulsions.

Teachers' attitudes toward epilepsy and the epileptic child in the classroom have improved markedly over the past twenty years. Teachers, however, cannot be of much assistance in the management of epilepsy if they have no way of knowing that a child is epileptic. As parents become better informed, the frequency with which parents of children with epilepsy will inform the teachers of the child's condition will increase.

Public attitudes toward epilepsy have lagged seriously behind scientific information. The result is that many epileptics still face unreasonable discriminatory practices in employment, insurance, automobile driving, and so forth. The public must be brought up-to-date about epilepsy, and research on prevention and treatment must continue. The principal problems for most people with epilepsy are not really in the medical realm. Treatment and control are fairly well advanced. Most problems arise in the area of public understanding and acceptance (Wright, 1975).

The educational problems of children with epilepsy are like those of other children who may be deviant or be so considered. With medical control of seizures and the enlightenment of parents, teachers, and the public, the educational and social problems of the epileptic can be considered essentially those of any other children. Educationally, the most significant problem the disorder, like other chronic health conditions, may present is temporary or chronic lack of strength, vitality, and alertness (Wilson, 1973).

SPINA BIFIDA

Children with spina bifida have multiple physical impairments resulting from damage to the developing nervous system. They suffer from varying degrees of paralysis, sensory loss, bowel and bladder incontinence, and frequently, hydrocephalus (the accumulation of fluid in the ventricles of the brain). These physical conditions may limit independence, mobility, socialization, educational opportunities, and learning.

Spina bifida (Myelodysplasia) is a defect in the bony structure of the spinal column present at birth. In the developmental process some portion of the spinal cord has not closed over properly. Spina bifida literally means "cleft spine." At birth a lesion appears as a swelling or protrusion, with or without a skin cover, at some point along the spine, usually at the lower end. This swelling may contain only the membranes covering the spinal cord or portions of the spinal cord itself. Damage to the spinal cord results in the handicapping condition in these children. It occurs in about 3 in 1,000 live births (Myers, 1975).

When the sac or swelling contains some of the coverings (meninges) of the spinal cord without containing actual neural material, paralysis is not likely; however, muscular weakness and incoordination from the lesion downward are common. Surgical procedures can be utilized to eliminate the sac and recovery without further difficulty is common.

In the more severe form of spina bifida the protruding sac contains not only some of the meninges, but part of the spinal cord. In this instance, the neural pathways connecting the brain with other parts of the body are interrupted. The consequences may include facial paralysis and muscular weakness in the back and legs, as well as insensitivity below the lesion. Bowel and bladder control also are affected. Hydrocephalus, with its concomitant interference with perceptual and cognitive functioning, frequently occurs with spina bifida. These defects present profound medical, personal care, and educational problems. Children with mild forms of spina bifida can be expected to function intellectually within the normal range; however, those where the condition is more severe and accompanied by hydrocephalus are likely to have impaired intellectual functioning (Andersen, 1973). Spina bifida is more common among females than males, and has a greater effect on intelligence in females (Cahoun and Hawisher, 1979).

The majority of children with spina bifida in countries other than the United States are educated in special schools (Smith and Smith, 1973; Woodburn, 1973). However, there is evidence that they do equally well when placed in regular schools (Andersen, 1973b). Children with spina bifida frequently have good verbal ability. This ability may make it difficult for parents and teachers to accept their generally poor performance in reading, spelling, and arithmetic. These children are multiply handicapped and appropriate education is very important for them even though physical and social factors may act as barriers to their full participation in a school program. Their repeated hospitalization may interfere with school attendance and interrupt learning (Lauder, Kanthor, Myers, and Resnick, 1979).

SUMMARY

Children and adults with orthopedic handicaps are those who have problems of physical motility. The orthopedically handicapped include people with a large variety of physical disabilities. Orthopedic handicaps can stem from innumerable causes, and the incidence of such handicaps is relatively high. The relationship between various psychological variables and physical handicap is not a close one. Emotional and social adjustment and intellectual status of the physically handicapped were discussed.

Cerebral palsy is a motor defect present at birth or appearing soon after, and dependent on pathologic abnormalities in the brain. It has been classified and described in a variety of ways, most commonly according to type. Three main types are generally considered: the spastic, athetoid, and ataxic. Spasticity is characterized by jerky, spasmodic movements. Athetosis is characterized by rhythmical, writhing movements, and ataxia by disturbances in balance.

The incidence of cerebral palsy is probably from about 3 to 6 infants per 1,000. It has been estimated that there are about 40 cases under twenty years of age for each 100,000 people.

Cerebral palsy is caused by brain damage of one kind or another. The causes of brain damage are many. They have been divided into prenatal, natal, and postnatal factors. A number of conditions giving rise to injury before, during, or shortly after birth have been studied and reported.

The intelligence of the cerebrally palsied is rather low. Roughly half have IQs below 70. The distribution of intelligence is crowded toward the lower end. However, the range of intelligence among the cerebral palsied is rather large. Sensory defects are common. Concomitant defects in cerebrally palsied mentally deficient are frequent. The cerebrally palsied person typically suffers from a multiplicity of handicaps.

Brain-injured children display a wide variety of physical disabilities and behavioral disorders.

Children and adults with epilepsy differ from others principally in that they are subject to convulsions or must take medication in order to prevent or control seizures. Epilepsy may be termed either *symptomatic* or *idiopathic.* The causes of symptomatic epilepsy frequently can be isolated. The causes of idiopathic epilepsy are essentially unknown. Epilepsy can be classified as to type of seizure. The types of seizure considered were *grand mal, petit mal,* Jacksonian epilepsy, and psychomotor epilepsy. *Grand mal* is the most violent of the varieties of seizure. About 0.5 percent of the general population is probably epileptic. Epileptic convulsions are more common among children and youth than adults. Convulsive disorders are relatively common among the mentally deficient.

The exact causes of epilepsy are not known. Seizures are associated with various forms of brain lesions, but many epileptics have no detectable structural abnormality. An hereditary predisposition is suggested from the measurement of brain waves. An epileptic pattern of brain waves is found in a high percentage of the close relatives of idiopathic epileptics. Seizures frequently are related to emotional factors. There is some disagreement as to whether emotional or personality factors might cause some epilepsy.

The influence of epilepsy on intelligence is not clearly understood. The mean intelligence of epileptics is slightly below that of the general population, but the range of intelligence among epileptics is extreme. Whether epileptic convulsions produce mental deterioration has not been fully determined. Perhaps in a small percentage of cases, when seizures are frequent, severe intellectual deterioration does take place.

The range of personality characteristics among epileptics is such that the concept of the "epileptic personality" appears to be a useless one. Treatment of epilepsy by sedative and anticonvulsant drugs is common practice. A great reduction in the frequency and severity of seizures can be brought about by proper medication. Psychotherapy with epileptics has served to reduce conflicts and anxiety and decrease the number of seizures.

With constantly advancing scientific knowledge and increasing sophistication of parents, educators, and the general public, the life of those afflicted with convulsions should become constantly more nearly normal. Medical control of seizures is now sufficiently adequate that the largest problems faced by the epileptic are those of public misunderstanding and restrictions.

Spina bifida is a defect in the bony structure of the spinal column at birth. Damage to the spinal cord results in the handicapping condition of these children, who suffer from multiple physical impairments.

REFERENCES

Adams, J., T. J. Kenny, R. A. Peterson, and A. Carter, "Age Effects and Revised Scoring of the Canter BIP for Identifying Children with Cerebral Dysfunction," *Journal of Consulting and Clinical Psychology*, 1975, *43*, 117–18.

Andersen, E. M., "Cognitive Deficits in Children with Spina Bifida and Hydrocephalus: A Review of the Literature," *British Journal of Educational Psychology*, 1973, *43*, 257–68 (a).

Andersen, E. M., *The Disabled School Child* (London: Methuen and Co., 1973) (b).

Apgar, V. and J. Beck, *Is My Baby All Right?* (New York: Pocket Books, 1974).

Balow, B., "Biological Defects and Special Education: An Empiricists View," *The Journal of Special Education*, 1979, *13*, 35–40.

Benda, C. E., Developmental Disorders of Mentation and the Cerebral Palsied (New York: Grune & Stratton, 1952).

Bice, H. V. and W. M. Cruickshank, "The Evaluation of Intelligence," in W. M. Cruickshank and S. Raus, eds., *Cerebral Palsy: Its Individual and Community Problems* (Syracuse, N.Y.: Syracuse University Press, 1955).

Bingley, T., "Mental Symptoms in Temporal Lobe Epilepsy and Temporal Gliomas," *Acta Psychiatrica et Neurologica Scandanavia*, Kjφbenhaven, 1958, *33*, Supplementum 120.

Bleck, E. E., "Cerebral Palsy," in E. E. Bleck and D. A. Nagel, eds., *Physically Handicapped Children—A Medical Atlas for Teachers* (New York: Grune and Stratton, 1975).

Bridge, E. M., *Epilepsy and Convulsive Disorders in Children* (New York: McGraw-Hill Book Company, 1949).

Broida, D. C., "Psychological Aspects of Epilepsy," in *Psychology of Exceptional Children and Youth*, ed. W. M. Cruickshank. Englewood Cliffs, N.J.: Prentice-Hall, Inc., 1955.

Broida, D. C., C. E. Izard, and W. M. Cruickshank, "Thematic Apperception Reactions of Crippled Children," *Journal of Clinical Psychology*, 1950, *6*, 243–48.

Cahoun, M. L. and M. Hawisher, *Teaching and Learning Strategies for Physically Handicapped Students* (Baltimore: University Park Press, 1979).

Cruickshank, W. M., ed., *Psychology of Exceptional Children and Youth*, 3rd ed. (Englewood Cliffs, N.J.: Prentice-Hall, 1972).

Cruickshank, W. M. and J. E. Dolphin, "The Emotional Needs of Crippled and Non-crippled Children," *Journal of Exceptional Children,* 1949, *16*, 33–40.

Deutsch, L. and L. L. Wiener, "Children with Epilepsy: Emotional Problems and Treatment," *American Journal of Orthopsychiatry*, 1948, *28*, 65.

Dunsdon, M. I., *The Educability of Cerebral Palsied Children* (London: National Foundation for Educational Research, 1952).

Efron, R., "The Conditioned Inhibition of Uncinate Fits," *Brain*, 1957, 530, 251–62.

Efron, R., "The Effect of Olfactory Stimuli in Arresting Uncinate Fits," *Brain*, 1956, *79*, 267–81.

Floyer, E. B., *A Psychological Study of a City's Cerebral Palsied Children* (Manchester: British Council for the Welfare of Spastics, 1955).

Folsom, A. T., "The Epilepsies," in H. C. Haywood, ed., *Brain Damage in School Age Children* (Washington, D. C.: Council for Exceptional Children, 1968).

Geist, H., *The Etiology of Idiopathic Epilepsy* (New York: Exposition Press, 1962).

Greenbaum, J. and J. A. Buehler, "Further Findings on the Intelligence of Children with Cerebral Palsy," *American Journal of Mental Deficiency*, 1960, *65*, 261–64.

Guerin, G. R., "School Achievement and Behavior of Children with Mild or Moderate Health Conditions," *The Journal of Special Education*, 1979, *13*, 179–86.

Harlin, V. K., "Experiences with Epileptic Children in a Public School Program," *The Journal of School Health*, 1965, *35*, 20–24.

Heal, L. W. "Evaluation of an Integrated Approach to the Management of Cerebral Palsy," *Exceptional Children*, 1974, *40*, 452–53.

Hefner, R., "Some Unusual Varieties of Visceral Epilepsy," *Missouri Medicine*, 1960, *57* (3), 289–92.

Heilman, A., "Intelligence in Cerebral Palsy," *Crippled Child*, 1952, *30*, 12.

Holowinsky, I. Z. "Assessment and Education of Children with Cerebral Palsy in the Soviet Union," *The Journal of Special Education*, 1979, *13*, 209–13.

Hopkins, T., H. V. Bice, and K. Colton, *Evaluation and Education of the Cerebral Palsied Child* (Washington, D. C.: International Council for Exceptional Children, 1954).

James, I. P., "Temporal Lobectomy for Psychomotor Epilepsy," *The Journal of Mental Science*, 1960, *106*, 543–47.

Johnston, R. B. and Magrab, P. R., *Developmental Disorders* (Baltimore: University Park Press, 1976).

Kanner, L., *Child Psychiatry* (Springfield, Ill.: Charles C. Thomas, 1935).

Kirman, B. H., "Epilepsy and Cerebral Palsy," *Archives of Disease in Childhood,* 1956, *31,* 1–7.

Kram, C., "Epilepsy in Children and Youth," in W. M. Cruickshank, ed., *Psychology of Exceptional Children and Youth,* 2nd ed., (Englewood Cliffs, N. J.: Prentice-Hall, Inc., 1963).

Lauder, C. C., H. Kanthor, G. Myers, and J. Resnick, "Educational Placement of Children with Spina Bifida," *Exceptional Children,* March 1979, 432–37.

Lennox, W. G., *Science and Seizures: New Light on Epilepsy and Migraine* (New York: Harper and Row, 1941).

Lennox, W. G., "Sixty-Six Twin Pairs Affected by Seizures," in *Epilepsy and the Convulsive State,* Assoc. for Res. in Nerv. and Ment. Dis., research publication 26 (Baltimore, Md.: The Williams and Wilkins Co., 1947). (a)

Lennox, W. G., "The Treatment of the Epileptic Veteran," *Veterans Administration Technical Bulletin* (Washington, D. C.: Government Printing Office, 1947, pp. 5–9). (b)

Lennox, W. G., "The Genetics of Epilepsy," *American Journal of Psychiatry,* January 1947, *103,* 457–62.(c)

Lennox, W. G., "The Heredity of Epilepsy as Told to Relatives and Twins," *Journal of the American Medical Association,* 1951, *146,* 529–36.

Lennox, W. G., "The Social and Emotional Problems of the Epileptic Child and His Family," *Journal of Pediatrics,* 1954, *44,* 591, 601.

Lennox, W. G. and S. Cobb, "Epilepsy: Aura in Epilepsy: A Statistical Review of 1,359 Cases," *Archives of Neurological Psychiatry,* 1933, *30,* 374–85.

Lennox, W. G. and A. L. Collins, "Intelligence of Normal and Epileptic Twins," *American Journal of Psychiatry,* 1945, *101,* 764–69.

Lennox, W. G., E. L. Gibbs, and F. A. Gibbs, "Inheritance of Cerebral Dysrhythmia and Epilepsy," *Archives of Neurological Psychiatry,* 1940, *44,* 1155–83.

Lowenbach, H., "The Encephalogram in Healthy Relatives of Epileptics," *Bulletin of The Johns Hopkins Hospital,* July 1939, 125–37.

Mackay, R. P., S. B. Wortis, and O. Sugar, *The Year Book of Neurology, Psychiatry and Neurosurgery* (Chicago, Ill.: The Year Book Medical Publishers, Inc., 1960).

Mahan, G. H., "Special Provisions for Handicapped Students in Colleges," *Exceptional Children,* 1974, *41,* 51–53.

Miller, E. and G. B. Rosenfeld, "The Psychologic Evaluation of Children with Cerebral Palsy and Its Implications in Treatment," *Journal of Pediatrics,* 1952, *41,* 613–21.

Moss, J. W., "Neuropsychology: One Way to Go," *The Journal of Special Education,* 1979, *13,* 45–49.

Mullen, F. A., "Convulsive Disorders among Educable Handicapped Pupils," paper presented at Amer. Educ. Res. Assoc., Atlantic City, N.J., February 16, 1953.

Myers, B. A., "The Child With a Chronic Illness," in R.H.A. Haslam and P. J. Valletulti, eds., *Medical Problems in the Classroom* (Baltimore: University Park Press, 1975).

National Safety Council, *Accident Facts* (Chicago: National Safety Council, 1975).

Neuringer, C., G. Goldstein, and R. B. Gallaher, Jr., "Minimal Field Dependency and Minimal Brain Dysfunctions," *Journal of Consulting and Clinical Psychology,* 1975, *43,* 20–21.

Newcomer, P., and D. Hammill, "Visual Perception of Motor Impaired Children: Implications for Assessment," *Exceptional Children,* 1973, *39,* 335–37.

Nuffield, E. J., "Neurophysiology and Behavior Disorders in Epiletic Children," *The Journal of Mental Science,* 1961, *107,* 438–57.

Penfield, W. and T. C. Erickson, *Epilepsy and Cerebral Localization* (Springfield, Ill.: Charles C. Thomas, 1941).

Penrose, L. S., *The Biology of Mental Defect,* 3rd ed., (New York: Grune and Stratton, 1963).

Pintner, R., J. Eisenson, and M. Stanton, *The Psychology of the Physically Handicapped* (New York: Appleton-Century-Crofts, 1940).

Reed, H. B. C., Jr., "Biological Defects and Special Education—An Issue in Personnel Preparation," *The Journal of Special Education,* 1979, *13,* 9–33.

Robinson, H. B. and Robinson, N. M., *The Mentally Retarded Child* (New York: McGraw-Hill, 1965).

Rosen, M., G. R. Clark, and M. S. Kivitz, *Habilitation of the Handicapped* (Baltimore: University Park Press, 1977).

Rouse, B. M. and J. Farb, "Training Adolescents to Use Behavior Modification with the Severely Handicapped," *Exceptional Children,* 1974, *40,* 286–88.

Saffian, S., "Program Trends in Crippling Conditions: 1950–1960's (Washington, D.C.: Child Health Studies Branch, Division of Research, United States Department of Health, Education and Welfare, 1962).

Sakel, M., *Epilepsy* (New York: Philosophical Library, Inc., 1958).

Sarason, S. B. *Psychological Problems in Mental Deficiency* (New York: Harper and Row, 1959).

Sawrey, J. M. and C. W. Telford, *The Psychology of Adjustment*, 4th ed. (Boston: Allyn and Bacon, 1975).

Schonell, F. E., *Educating Spastic Children* (Edinburgh: Oliver and Boyd, 1956).

Smith, G. K. and E. D. Smith, "Selection for Treatment in Spina Bifida Cystica," *British Medical Journal*, 1973, *4*, 189–204.

Smith, R. M. and J. T. Neisworth, *The Exceptional Child: A Functional Approach* (New York: McGraw-Hill, 1975).

Smock, C. and W. M. Cruickshank, "Responses of Handicapped and Normal children to the Rosenzweig P-F Study," *Quarterly Journal of Behavior,* 1952, *4*, 156–64.

Somerfield-Ziskund, E., and E. Ziskund, "Effect of Phenobarbital on the Mentality of Epileptic Patients," *Archives of Neurological Psychiatry*, 1940, *43*, 70–79.

Stephen, E., "Cerebral Palsy and Mental Defect," in A. M. Clarke and A. D. Clarke, eds., *Mental Deficiency: The Changing Outlook* (New York: Free Press, 1958).

Tenney, J. W., "Epileptic Children in Detroit's Special School Program," *Exceptional Children*, 1955, *21*, 162–67.

Tizard, B., "The Personality of Epileptics: A Discussion of the Evidence," *Psychological Bulletin*, 1962, *59*, 196–210.

Tizard, J. P., R. S. Paine, and B. Crothers, "Disturbance of Sensation in Children with Hemiplegia," *Journal of American Medical Association*, 1954, *155*, 628–32.

Tower, D. B., *Neurochemistry and Epilepsy* (Springfield, Ill.: Charles C. Thomas, 1960).

Turner, W. J. and Merlis, S., "Clinical Correlations Between Electroencephalography and Antisocial Behavior," *Medical Times*, 1962, *90*, 505–11.

United States Office of Education, *Better Education for the Handicapped: Annual Report, Fiscal Year, 1969* (Washington, D. C., 1970).

Wallin, J. E., *Children with Mental and Physical Handicaps* (Englewood Cliffs, N.J.: Prentice-Hall, Inc., 1949).

Wilder, C. S., "Prevalence of Selected Impairments," *Vital Health Statistics,* 1975, *99,* 1–64.

Wilson, M., "Children with Crippling and Health Disabilities," in L. M. Dunn, ed., *Exceptional Children in the Schools,* 2nd ed. (New York: Holt, Rinehart and Winston, 1973).

Woodburn, M. F. *Social Implications of Spina Bifida.* (Edinburgh: Scottish Spina Bifida Association, 1973).

Woods, G. E., *The Handicapped Child: Assessment and Management* (Great Britain: Blackwell Scientific Publications, 1975).

Wright, G. N., *Epilepsy Rehabilitation* (Boston: Little, Brown, 1975).

Wrightstone, J. W., J. Justman, and S. Moskowitz, "Studies of Children with Physical Handicaps. II: The Child with Orthopedic Limitations" (New York: Board of Education of the City of New York, Bureau of Educational Research, 1954).

Wyllie, W. S., "Cerebral Palsies in Infancy," in A. Feiling, ed., *Modern Trends in Neurology* (London: Butterworth, 1951).

SUGGESTIONS FOR STUDENTS AND INSTRUCTORS

1. Have the students try some of the simulation exercises mentioned in this chapter.

2. Arrange exercises to demonstrate the special adaptations needed for the use of crutches, walkers, wheelchairs, braces, and similar orthopedic aids.

3. Survey the campus for existing aids and adaptations needed for the orthopedically handicapped.

4. Have an orthopedically handicapped or epileptic person talk to the class.

5. Visit a local workshop for the orthopedically handicapped.

ADDITIONAL READINGS

Mullins, J. B., *A Teacher's Guide to Management of Physically Handicapped Students* (Springfield, Ill.: Charles C. Thomas, 1979). A wealth of good advice and information for the classroom teacher.

Lagos, J. C., *Seizures, Epilepsy, and Your Child: A Handbook for Parents, Teachers, and Epileptics of All Ages* (Boston, Mass.: Exceptional Parent Bookstore, 1979). Diagnosis, treatment, and management of epilepsy.

Anderson, E. M. and B. Spain, *The Child with Spina Bifida* (London: Methuen, 1977). A readable introduction to this complex disorder.

Finnie, N. R., *Handling the Cerebral Palsied Child at Home* (New York: E. P. Dutton, 1975). A practical and clearly written book for all people interacting with cerebral palsied children.

SELECTED FILMS

My Son Kevin. (24 minutes) Wombat Products (FN), 77 Tarrytown Road, White Plains, N.Y. 10607. A thalidomide child as seen by his mother.

The Sun Never Sets. (24 minutes) Muscular Dystrophy Association of America, 1790 Broadway, New York, N.Y. A day in the life of a five-year-old boy with muscular dystrophy.

ORGANIZATIONS AND AGENCIES

Crippled Children's Services
Office of Maternal and Child Health
Bureau of Community Health Services
Health Services Administration
Department of Health, Education, and Welfare
5600 Fishers Lane
Room 7-15 Parklawn Bldg.
Rockville, Md. 20852

Epilepsy Foundation of America
1828 L Street, N.W.
Washington, D. C. 20036

National Association of the Physically Handicapped
76 Elm Street
London, Ohio 43140

National Center for a Barrier Free Environment
8401 Connecticut Avenue #402
Washington, D. C. 20015

National Congress of Organizations of the Physically Handicapped, Inc.
7611 Oakland Avenue
Minneapolis, Minn. 55423

National Epilepsy League
6 North Michigan Avenue
Chicago, Il. 60602

United Cerebral Palsy Associations, Inc.
66 East 34th Street
New York, N. Y. 10016

CHAPTER 13

COMMUNICATION DISORDERS

Wendell Johnson went to the speech clinic at the University of Iowa for therapy because he stuttered severely. There, he received considerable help. He then enrolled as a student and subsequently earned his BA, MA, and PhD degrees. He became a research associate, professor, and director of the speech clinic at the University. At the time of his death, he was a recognized authority on communication disorders. Following are some of his personal comments on his stuttering, abstracted and modified for presentation here.

When I entered kindergarten, at the age of five, I began to stutter, for no apparent reason. My father said I stuttered because I was "thinking ahead of my speech." My mother said that my stuttering was a "kind of nervousness." My older brother insisted that I stuttered because I wanted to.

When I entered school, I did so well my teacher considered advancing me to the second grade but decided not to do so because of my stuttering. When some of my classmates called me "stuttercat" and imitated me, I began arriving at school late so as to avoid them. When my teacher reprimanded me for being tardy, I began fighting with my tormentors. I got to be a good fighter. These experiences brought me my first conscious awarness of my stuttering as a significant part of myself and as a handicap. These convictions I was never able to repudiate. I was bewildered because I could not talk like other children. I asked my mother why. She said she didn't know, and we both cried.

When I was eight, I began regarding my stuttering as something to be concealed. I began to dream of a world in which I did not stutter. This I have never ceased doing. I tried to help my stuttering by talking with pebbles in my mouth, as did Demosthenes, but the attempt was futile. I began to avoid social situations where I would have to talk. My stuttering now involved a real fear, which manifested itself in a halting, shrinking manner of expressing myself. I held myself in because I was afraid I would stutter. Then I felt inadequate and disgusted with myself.

Because I have difficulty with certain words, I tend to substitute one word for another. I often can anticipate stuttering several words in advance and substitute some other word. This anticipation and substitution is a function of my fear of stuttering.

I also discovered that in loud, boisterous company I could make occasional spontaneous remarks without stuttering. It helped to have the attention of the group focused somewhere else. I also found that laughter was an aid, so when blocked on a word, I laughed. Clowning, boisterousness, and humor all made speaking easier, so I became known by my associates as "quite a clown."

Because I was unable to enjoy ordinary social contacts with my peers, I developed an enormous drive to achieve in nonverbal ways. In high school, I became an honor student, captain of the football, basketball, and baseball teams, and editor of the school paper. However, these were only symbols that meant increasingly less to me as I won more and more of them. They were insufficient compensations for my stuttering.

At my mother's insistence, when I was nineteen, I went to an "Institute for the Treatment of Stuttering." There I found, to my delight, that I could talk if I relaxed and drawled my words slowly enough. However, when I left the school to go home and arrived at the railway station, I stuttered to the ticket agent, to the conductor, and to my seat companion. I closed my eyes in despair. This was a shock from which I have never recovered.

To the observer, stuttering is a speech defect. To the stutterer, it is much more than that. It is a constant mental distraction and a physical drain on one's energy. It interferes with social relationships and schoolwork. It forces one to be belligerent, or a clown, or a recluse. The stutterer develops a dislike for social situations where he must speak. For him, the most wonderful thing in the world would be being able to talk freely without others saying, "What? What did

> you say?" I'm sure I have heard that ten thousand times! People
> talk louder as though you are deaf. They nod and say, "Yes," when
> it doesn't make sense. There is hardly an aspect of one's social and
> personal life that is unaffected by a serious speech defect (Johnson,
> 1930).

Concern for the person with a speech defect undoubtedly preceded
by centuries the development of an interest in normal speech. Several
centuries before Christ, Greek physicians were prescribing cures for stuttering. However, it is largely within the present century that systematic
studies of normal speech have been made, and only within the twentieth
century have scientific investigations of the nature, causes, and treatment
of speech defects been systematically pursued. Special community and
school services for persons with communication disorders are relatively
new, compared to the services provided for the more dramatic forms of
disability such as blindness and orthopedic handicaps. The first statutes
in the United States providing special services for speech defectives were
enacted by Wisconsin in 1913. The following year, Dr. Smiley Blanton established the first university clinic for speech problems at the University
of Wisconsin (Irwin, 1955).

Many different professional specialties—general medicine, plastic
surgery, otology, oral surgery, dentistry, psychiatry, psychology, education, and speech therapy—are involved in the diagnosis and treatment of
speech disorders. A wide variety of disciplines is necessarily involved in
speech correction, because anatomical, sociological, psychological, and educational factors all contribute to speech impairment and correction.
Speech defects may be caused by anatomical defects or deviant physiological functioning of the jaws, tongue, or soft palate; by disturbed feelings,
emotions, or attitudes; by inadequate self-concepts; and by faulty language habits arising from unsatisfactory speech models, social pressures,
and misguided efforts at speech training or correction.

DEFINITIONS OF COMMUNICATION DISORDERS

There have been few attempts to define communication impairment
quantitatively. The commonly accepted definitions are all largely functional in nature. Three components seem to be common to most current
answers to the question: What is defective speech? Speech is considered
to be defective when the manner of speaking interferes with communication, when the person's manner of speaking distracts attention from
what is said, or when speech is such that the speaker is unduly self-

conscious or apprehensive about speaking. More concisely, speech is defective whenever the deviant manner of speaking interferes with communication, calls undue attention to itself, or causes the speaker concern to such an extent that special educational or remedial measures are deemed necessary.

These criteria vary according to their social context. The listening ear defines the intelligibility and distractibility of speech. The speaker is the measure of his or her personal concern. One's culture, subculture, and status within the culture, as well as one's age, profession, and role in life, enter into a definition of defective speech. The speech of the average three-year-old is defective by adult standards, but normal for that age group. The adolescent from the slum who says "dese" for "these," "dose" for "those," and "dem" for "them" will not usually be labeled a speech defective. A southern drawl, an eastern twang, or midwestern nasality are normal in those geographic regions and become matters of concern outside these localities only to radio announcers, actors, and public speakers. The listener matches the speech that he or she hears against a varying standard of acceptability and intelligibility, and labels speech as normal or defective accordingly.

There are similarly marked variations in what speakers find objectionable in their own speech. Many people are unable to detect marked impairments in their own speech, while others request therapy for speech which is well within the normal range. The speaker's level of personal concern does not always agree with the listener's judgment.

IDENTIFICATION AND DIAGNOSIS OF COMMUNICATION DISORDERS

Many people are identified as speech defectives by their families, by their peers, or by themselves. Some people who go to speech clinics and speech correctionists are referred by other professional people, such as doctors, psychiatrists, psychologists, and teachers. In schools, many children are referred by their regular classroom teachers. Others are identified by systematic screening procedures. Many schools, in addition to requesting referrals by teachers, systematically screen one or two grades each year.

Individuals thus identified as probably speech defectives usually undergo more thorough diagnostic examinations before treatment is started. Depending on the nature of the referral and the amount of information available, the diagnosis may be made either by a single person—the speech correctionist—or by a team of specialists. A complete diagnostic evaluation involves a complete physical examination, including a dental examination to disclose any oral, dental, or other organic factors contributing to the disorder. An assessment of intellectual level, an audiometric evaluation of hearing, and sometimes a psychiatric examination are also made to disclose any intellectual, auditory, or personality deviations which may complicate the picture.

PREVALENCE OF SPEECH DISORDERS

Surveys of the prevalence of speech disorders are not very reliable because of the varying purpose served by the surveys, the different standards applied, the diverse populations sampled, and the biases of the investigators. When all degrees and categories of speech defects are included, the total of speech impaired school children identified is estimated at around 10 percent. Two committees of the American Speech and Hearing Association (1952, 1959) have independently estimated that a minimum of 5 percent of school-age children have defects of speech sufficiently serious to warrant speech correction or therapy, and that an additional 5 percent suffer from noticeable but less serious defects. A breakdown of the estimated prevalence of speech problems and accompanying disorders is given in Table 13–1.

There are more people with speech defects than with any other type of exceptionality, with the possible exceptions of the emotionally disturbed, the "slow learners," and the culturally disadvantaged. Many more males than females have speech defects—two to five times as many, depending on the type of disorders (Peckham, 1973). The full explanations of these sex differences are not known.

Table 13–1

DISTRIBUTION OF SPEECH DEFECTS OF VARIOUS TYPES AND CAUSES IN PUBLIC SCHOOL CHILDREN

type of defect	percentage
Articulatory defects	81.0
Stuttering	6.5
Delayed speech	4.5
Hard-of-hearing	2.5
Voice problems	2.3
Cleft palate	1.5
Cerebral palsy	1.0
Aphasia Bilinguality Mental retardation	0.7
Total	100.0

Data from American Speech and Hearing Association (1961).

CAUSES OF SPEECH DEFECTS

Speech defects are caused by a wide variety of organic and functional (social and psychological) factors. The organic causes include cleft palate, maldevelopment of other parts of the mouth and jaw, dental irregularities including missing or maloccluded teeth, muscular paralysis of the larynx, tumors or ulcers in or around the larynx, loss of the larynx, brain damage (in cerebral palsy and aphasia), and nasal obstructions. Functional causes include failure to learn adequate speech, fixations, regressive speech patterns, and general personality and emotional disturbances.

Many speech specialists do not find the dichotomy between organic and functional a very useful one. Speech difficulties which are strictly organic in origin usually acquire a large functional component as a result of the way the person reacts to the difficulty, and prolonged functional disorders may have organic consequences. Although it is possible for organic disorders to remain on that level with relatively little functional component, and for functional disorders to continue without any specific organic components, they rarely do so; most speech defects have both functional and organic components.

Recently, attention seems to be shifting from the organic to the functional as the most significant factors in the etiology of most speech defects.

NONLANGUAGE CHARACTERISTICS OF THE SPEECH IMPAIRED

Like most other types of handicapped people, persons with speech defects often have other disabilities. Many of them, at least more than those with normal speech, are mentally retarded, brain-damaged, or have developmental anomalies such as cleft palate and cleft lip. Therefore, in asking what the speech impaired are like, we need to define the population. If all individuals with defective speech are included, we obtain a very heterogeneous population, some subgroups of which are characterized by deviant physiques or intellectual levels—for example, the cerebral palsied and the mentally retarded. Since the group with defective speech contains a disproportionate number of physically and intellectually handicapped individuals, we would expect the mean level of the entire group to be below that of the general population. On the other hand, if we inquire into the physical, intellectual, and personal characteristics of people whose *only* handicap is their speech impairment, the answer may be different. There are few, if any, studies of such groups; consequently, our discussion must deal with the entire group of people with defective speech.

PHYSICAL CHARACTERISTICS OF THE SPEECH IMPAIRED

Most individuals with defective speech are apparently physically normal. That is, most speech defects are primarily functional in nature and are unaccompanied by marked organic impairments. However, about 16 percent of the children with the more serious types of speech defects also have physical disabilities, and this group is large enough to bring the entire group of speech impaired individuals below the norm of the entire population in general physique (Eisenson, 1963).

One intensive study which compared seven-year-old children with marked speech defects and normal hearing to a comparable "normal" control group found that the speech impaired youngsters displayed the following distinguishing characteristics (Sheridan, 1973):

1. A higher proportion were born prematurely.

2. Four times the number of the speech handicapped were not walking at eighteen months.

3. Seven times as many of the special group as of the controls had not spoken in phrases by two years.

4. Four times as many of the handicapped as of controls were visually impaired.

5. Forty-six percent of the special group, as against 13 percent of the controls, were rated by their teachers as "appreciably clumsy."

6. Four times as many of the speech defectives were judged by their teachers to be behaviorally maladjusted.

7. There were ten times the incidence of nonreaders among the speech defectives.

8. There were twice as many boys as girls in the defective group.

Sheridan believes that the marked prevalence of unfavorable neurological and psychological manifestations among the handicapped suggests the involvement of some general "neuro-developmental disorder." The study also found that a disproportionate number of the speech handicapped came from the lower socioeconomic classes.

INTELLIGENCE LEVEL OF SPEECH DEFECTIVES

Studies have consistently found a positive relationship between language proficiency and intelligence level. Therefore, it is not surprising to find that children with speech defects fall below the norms in measured intelligence (Sheridan, 1973). Defects such as the absence of speech, marked delay in acquiring speech, and poor articulation, which may be caused by the child's failure to learn, are, of course, very common among the mentally retarded. However, when the mentally retarded are excluded, there is still a slight relationship between measured intelligence and the incidence of speech defects (Calnan and Richardson, 1977). Possibly, differences in socioeconomic level may be a causal factor here also.

EDUCATIONAL ACHIEVEMENT OF THE SPEECH IMPAIRED

Even excluding the mentally retarded and the cerebral palsied, children with speech defects are relatively retarded in school (Sheridan, 1973). Speech defectives are retarded scholastically even out of proportion to expectations based on their intelligence test scores (Calnan and Richardson, 1977). Social class differences can hardly account for the greater educational than intellectual retardation of children with speech defects. Speech defects would seem to constitute a greater handicap in formal learning than they do in acquiring the more general intellectual skills and information required for satisfactory intelligence test performance.

CLASSIFICATIONS OF SPEECH DISORDERS

Speech defects are classified in several ways, depending on the purpose of the classification and the interest of the researcher. As previously indicated, a broad two-fold classification of speech defects into the organic and the functional is commonly used when etiology is considered. Surveys of speech problems typically classify defects according to the forms they take and according to other associated and causal factors. Accordingly, we have articulatory disorders, disturbances of rhythm, voice disorders, delayed or retarded speech, mutism, and aphonia as types of defects. In a third type of classification, we list speech disorders associated with cleft palate, brain damage (cerebral palsy and aphasia), deafness, and mental retardation.

These various classifications cut across one another. Most of the classes of disorders based on symptoms (articulatory, voice, rhythm, delayed speech, and so forth), with the possible exception of aphasia, can be either organic or functional. Speech disorders of mentally retarded, cleft palated, or cerebral palsied individuals may take any of the forms listed, although certain types are more common than others.

DISORDERS OF ARTICULATION

Disorders of articulation consist of omission ("at" for "cat"), substitution ("gog" for "dog"), and distortion or additions ("furog" for "frog") of speech sounds. They may involve the mispronunciation of an entire word or words.

Certain articulatory disorders are referred to as *immature speech* (baby talk), since all children make these errors in the early stages of language development. Table 13–2 shows the age levels when children are normally able to articulate certain sounds properly. Other studies (Mecham, Berko, and Berko, 1960) indicate that *p, b, m,* and *o* are usually the easiest sounds for children to articulate. Additional sounds, in order of chronological development, are *h, w, d, k, g, j, f, v, t, z, l, s, u,* and *r.* A large percentage of errors of articulation are eliminated by the time children reach the fourth grade, that is, by the age of nine or ten. After this age, defects of articulation seldom diminish without specific remedial measures.

Since most articulation defects seem to be developmental in origin and are not serious, it is important that parents and teachers not become too concerned about them. Children with articulatory difficulties should not be reprimanded and certainly not teased about the way they speak. They should not be singled out nor told that their speech is defective. Individualized corrective exercises are not appropriate for these children. The most that should be done is to strive for speech improvement for all children within the context of speech and language development activities for an entire class.

Table 13–2
AGES AT WHICH CHILDREN ARE NORMALLY ABLE TO ARTICULATE CERTAIN SOUNDS

age (in years)	sounds
3.5	*b, p, m, w, h*
4.5	*t, d, g, k, ng, y*
5.5	*f, v, s, z*
6.5	*sh, l, th* (as in *then*)

Data from Davis (1938).

delayed speech—a case study

Jerry Hansen's parents came for consultation concerning their five-year-old son who wasn't talking. Although the Hansens had realized that Jerry was well beyond the age when he should talk, they were not sufficiently concerned to do anything about it until his kindergarten teacher said that she thought they should be. She suggested that they consult with a psychologist and a pediatrician. Jerry's pediatrician indicated that there were no sensory, perceptual, or neurological problems that could account for Jerry's lack of speech.

The family consisted of the mother who worked half-time, the father, a self-employed auto mechanic, and an older sister, Alice.

Jerry's birth and early development were uneventful. He was a "good baby." He was healthy and slept through the night very early. From an early age, he was able to amuse himself. Jerry's older sister, Alice, took on most of the responsibilities for Jerry's care. She bathed, dressed, fed, and even wanted to cook for him. Sometimes it seemed that Alice was the mother and his mother was an aunt or grandmother.

The last three years had been hard years for Jerry's mother. Her own mother had been sick with terminal cancer and Mrs. Hansen visited her every day—a two-hour trip each way. Jerry's father worked long hours and had little time to spend with his children. He was a quiet, soft-spoken man and thought Jerry was just like him. He said, "My son and I don't have to talk. He just likes to be with me. He sits with me when I watch television or read my paper." According to Mr. Hansen, Jerry would mind well. "If you tell him to stay in the house, he stays. He spends most of his time around the house. Maybe we should let him venture out more on his own."

Although Jerry seemed to be bright and his general development had apparently been normal, his parents insisted that they would like to have him tested. In the testing situation, Jerry was alert and outgoing. He responded well and seemed to enjoy working on the test items. Although he did not speak, he made sounds. When he wished to call the examiner's attention to a bird in a tree outside, he pointed to it and made noises, "m m m m," until the examiner looked at the bird and commented on it. On the basis of the performance test items, Jerry had a mental age of six years four months—somewhat above average. From the accounts given by Jerry's teacher, his pediatrician, and his parents, it seemed clear that Jerry had experienced no undue emotional stress and suffered from no serious psychological disturbances.

The total picture seemed to indicate that the social situation within the family provided Jerry with little opportunity and incentive for speech. There seemed to be a reasonably normal loving regard for Jerry by both parents and his sister. However, direct verbal stimulation was minimal. Mrs. Hanson, employed and preoccupied with her dying mother, had little time to devote to the social needs of her own family. Jerry's father, quiet and taciturn, did little to encourage language. Jerry's older sister took over most of the parenting. She derived considerable satisfaction from playing the parental role and her excessive mothering limited Jerry's social experiences and provided little incentive for speech.

It seemed that the principal need was to change the social context of Jerry's life without concentrating on his lack of speech as a major problem. The Hansens were encouraged to find playmates for Jerry other than his older sister. It was suggested that they find neighbor boys of Jerry's age with whom he could play. They were told of a local community center which provided a range of after-school and weekend activity programs for children Jerry's age. They were encouraged to have Jerry spend more time outside his home and to rely on his own resources. The Hansens were counseled to spend more time talking with Jerry, and to obtain books appropriate to Jerry's age and interests and read aloud to him each day. They were to anticipate Jerry's needs less and cease responding to his gestures. They were told to force him to use sounds to get things he wanted. They were to talk to Jerry continuously about the things they were doing and why they were doing them. Constantly talking and responding to Jerry's vocalizations rather than to his gestures would emphasize the functions and importance of language. Reports received three and six months later indicated that, although the parents were unable to do all of the things suggested, within two months Jerry was using a half dozen recognizable words, and at six months he was speaking quite freely in sentences. No further problems with his speech were anticipated.

The age at which normal children begin to speak varies so widely that it is impossible to set a specific age beyond which delay in speaking is exceptional. However, when a child of three or four does not talk, it should become a matter for study. Causes of delayed speech are many. Table 13–3 indicates the principal causes of delayed speech in a fairly large group of children.

In addition to the major causes of delayed speech listed in Table 13–3, some children do not learn to speak at the usual age because of lack of motivation. When doting parents or nurses anticipate every wish, or when gestures, grunts, or cries are effective in controlling others, children may have no need for words. Children with delayed speech because of insufficient motivation may be otherwise normal. They may be well-behaved and may seem to have made a satisfactory adjustment to the world without speaking. However, some nonverbal children who are not deaf, mentally retarded, brain-damaged, or seriously mentally ill display other patterns of deviant behavior. Some isolate themselves as far as pos-

Table 13–3

DELAYED SPEECH IN 278 CHILDREN

cause of delay	number of children
Deafness	110
Developmental aphasia	72
Mental deficiency	71
Cerebral palsy	22
Mental illness	3

Data from Morley and others. (1955).

sible from other people, and others seek out close physical contact with both adults and inanimate objects. They rub their bodies along the walls or on furniture, rub their faces against toys, climb on laps and snuggle up even to strangers. The significance of these activities is not known, but they are often considered symptomatic of personality disorders.

delayed speech— possibly autistic

Yes, I have heard all the oft-repeated stories about Einstein being such a late talker and about the six-year-old whose first words were, "The soup is cold," and when asked why he had never spoken before replied that, "everything had been all right until now." The story is no longer funny! The child who does not speak was not theirs! I hear a noise at the door and know that Gene's nap is over. I force a smile as he enters the room. He is handsome, the picture of health, but he does not speak.

We had tried to do all the right things. He had his hearing tested; it was normal. His pediatrician could find nothing organically wrong; his vocal apparatus was all right. The psychologist tried to estimate his IQ from his performance on nonverbal tests and thought he was probably of average intelligence. The speech therapists thought that he did not speak for emotional reasons. He could make sounds, repeat syllables, but he could or would not communicate by speech. The psychiatrist also thought that Gene's problem was emotional but this could not be explored without speech.

The only prescription they could offer was, "Love him and talk to him. Talk all the time!" But have you ever tried to talk to someone who not only does not talk back but also gives no sign that he even hears you? I go about describing every object in the room. I discourse on the color and texture of his clothes and mine until I sound ridiculous to myself. Talking becomes increasingly difficult when we are alone. A police siren sounds outside the window and Gene puts his hands over his ears and runs to me crying. He is afraid of loud sounds. I hold him and his sobs subside. I put him down and he clings to my legs. I feel frustrated and angry. I suppress my anger, begin doing the dishes and break a glass against the side of the sink. Sometimes I almost hate him and then feel guilty for doing so. Sometimes I hate myself for having such a child. I put the broken glass in the garbage and return to the sink, deliberately turning my back on Gene. I pretend not to notice when he tugs on my dress.

Why does it have to be this way? Will it always be this way? I try so hard to get him to speak, I so want to show him the world beyond this house, but he will only go as far as the front door. He wants to remain in the safety of his own home. He is terrified by new places and strange sounds. However, I tell myself that I must talk to him, so I begin naming his toys for the hundredth time. I name the colors of everything in the room but I find it more and more difficult until I become almost as mute as Gene. Will it never end?

Although feeling hopeless, I decided to approach, with much apprehension another speech therapist. I will be eternally grateful to this man! He proved to be a friend to Gene and to me. Over a period of six months he developed a relationship with Gene which was very warm and personal. This relationship was the beginning of Gene's emergence. In six months he began to speak. It has been a slow, laborious process, now extending over a period of two years. Enabling Gene to communicate verbally has made it possible for me to enjoy his company. Learning to talk did not solve all of Gene's problems. He still has a long way to go socially but it has done wonders for me. I have learned to maintain a degree of separateness from Gene, to be selfish and feel right about it when I reach the limits of my patience. I have learned to respect my personal needs and not deed my entire time to my son. I see some light at the end of a very dark tunnel!

DISORDERS OF VOICE PRODUCTION: PHONATION

Voice disorders consist of marked deviations in the loudness, pitch, quality, duration, or flexibility of sounds. In addition to the relatively simple variations of each, there are other voice defects, such as breathiness, harshness, hoarseness, and nasality. Voice disorders have the lowest incidence of all categories of speech disorders among children. They are difficult to correct in children, principally because the speech mechanism is still developing and the voice quality is changing. Voice disorders are more often diagnosed and treated in adults than in children, whereas the opposite is true of articulatory disorders and delayed speech.

Although some workers claim that stuttering, stammering, and cluttering should be differentiated, most authors do not discriminate among them. We shall use the term *stuttering* to cover the entire range of rhythmic disorders, and leave any differentiations within the group to the specialists.

Stuttering is one of the more dramatic communication disorders. The American Hearing and Speech Association estimates that somewhere between one and two million Americans stutter. Four of five stutterers recover without professional help—mostly in childhood. The association estimates that probably no more than 10 percent of adult stutterers "recover" (Smith, 1972).

The literature on stuttering is voluminous and often contradictory. More research has been done and more material written on stuttering than on any other type of speech disorder. Theories about the causes of stuttering range from the organic, through social learning, to mental hygiene. Therapy has varied from routine drills and breathing exercises, through behavior modification, through individual and group psychotherapy, to hypnosis and faith cures (see Van Riper, 1973). There are no forms of treatment that cannot claim a sizeable number of successes. We shall briefly summarize the principal research findings and indicate, as best we can, the current theories of stuttering and methods of treatment.

definitions of stuttering It is easier to describe stuttering than to define it. Stuttering is one of the major forms of nonfluency. It is primarily a disturbance of the normal flow and rhythm of speech. It involves blocks, hesitations, and prolongations, and repetitions of sounds, syllables, words, or phrases. It is frequently accompanied by muscular tension, rapid eye-blinking, irregularities of breathing, and facial grimacing. No two stutterers have the same secondary symptoms.

causes of stuttering The alleged causes of stuttering have been as diverse as the theories, and are often related to them. The earlier conceptions stressed organic factors such as heredity and lack of hemispheric brain dominance. The social learning, mental hygiene, or psychological conceptions have stressed habit, personality, and emotional factors as the primary causal factors. No one cause or set of causes has been discovered to date. Stuttering probably has multiple causation.

The types of evidence usually presented in support of the alleged organic etiology, together with some comments, are:

1. The incidence of stuttering in the family lines of stutterers is much greater than in the families of nonstutterers, suggesting a possible genetic basis. (Common family child-rearing practices, attitudes, and expectancies [the self-fulfilling prophecy] may also account for this high incidence.)

2. Stuttering is more frequent among left-handed people and among people shifted from their original left-hand preference. This fact has been used to support a lack-of-brain-dominance conception of the cause of stuttering. (The conflicts involved in changing handedness may induce tensions which may precipitate stuttering. Recent neurological findings also do not support the lack-of-cerebral-dominance concept [Gruber and Powell, 1974].)

3. Stuttering has a number of physiological components or accompaniments (Walker and Walker, 1973; Turton, 1975).

4. Stuttering is associated with multiple births (twinning, and so forth), and with prematurity (Sheridan, 1973).

5. There is a greater-than-chance incidence of central nervous system disorders among stutterers (Sheridan, 1973).

The functional conceptions of stuttering seem to be supported by the following facts:

1. Stuttering varies tremendously as a function of situational factors (Turton, 1975).

2. Stuttering (secondary stuttering) has profound emotional components (Walker and Walker, 1973).

3. Nondirective and psychoanalytic psychotherapy, which improve general adjustment, reduce conflicts, and decrease anxieties, often help or cure stuttering.

4. Stuttering most often develops at times when the child experiences considerable social pressure (when learning to speak, on entering school, and to a lesser degree at adolescence).

5. The parents of stutterers display a characteristic pattern of traits consisting of perfectionism and high levels of aspiration for their children (Goldman and Shames, 1964).

W. Johnson's (1942, 1956) "diagnosogenic" conception of the origin of stuttering is typical of the functional, social-psychological point of view. According to Johnson, when the young child experiences normal nonfluencies while learning to speak, parents often fail to recognize that the child is passing through a normal transitional stage of language learning. They label the child's normal blockings, hesitations, and repetitions as "stuttering," and become concerned about "defective" speech. The label associated with manifestations of parental anxiety becomes a stigma. The child eventually becomes concerned about his or her speech, believing that he is a stutterer. He then becomes fearful of not speaking properly and establishes a vicious cycle of fear–anxiety–nonfluency–increased fear–higher levels of anxiety–greater nonfluency, and so forth. According to this conception, stuttering begins in the mind or ears of the listener, and is transferred to the child as concern for his or her own speech. The child comes to anticipate stuttering, dreads it, tries to avoid it, becomes tense, and so stutters.

Cross-cultural studies lend some support to Johnson's contention. Certain cultures with very tolerant and accepting attitudes toward speech (Ute and Pilagra Indians and native Polynesians) are said to have little, if any, stuttering, and their languages contain no words for it. In cultures with strict standards of speech (the Cowickan and Japanese societies), the incidence of stuttering is high and there are specific names for the disorder (Stewart, 1960; Lemert, 1962).

Studies of the parents of stutterers also report results consistent with Johnson's "diagnosogenic" conception of the origin of stuttering. These studies indicate that the parents of stutterers and nonstutterers differ in their patterns of parent–child interaction. The parents of stutterers are more critical and intolerant of deviant behavior in their children. They are more perfectionistic and hold higher levels of aspiration for their children. Furthermore, these attitudes are specifically related to the speech area (Goodstein, 1958).

primary and secondary stuttering The distinction between primary and secondary stuttering made by C. S. Bluemel in 1932 has proven to be a useful one even though the dichotomy has been criticized by others and has been somewhat modified by Bluemel himself (Bluemel, 1932, 1957; Bloodstein, 1961; Turton, 1975). As we have indicated, all children experience a degree of nonfluency when learning to speak. A large number—some say as many as 30 percent—of children between the ages of two and four show blockings, hesitations, and repetitions of sounds or words. From an objective standpoint, they stutter. However, at this age—the so-called primary stage—the child is not aware of speech difficulties. He or she is not self-conscious about speech and does not experience the secondary symptoms of increased muscular tension, fear, and struggle that characterize the secondary stage of stuttering.

In the secondary stage of stuttering, the individual has been labeled by himself and others as a stutterer. He approaches speech in general, and certain words or sounds in particular, with anxiety. He is afraid that he will stutter. Fear increases the probability of stuttering. In this stage the reactions of listeners become critical when they focus the child's attention on disfluencies. Some speech therapists claim that only secondary stuttering is true stuttering. Primary stuttering is only "normal nonfluency."

Irrespective of their theoretical commitments, all speech specialists agree that social factors are important, if not crucial, in the development of stuttering (Andrews and Cutler, 1974). Most of the psychogenic or social-learning conceptions of stuttering also assign a crucial role to fear or anxiety in the genesis of stuttering (Schwartz, 1974). Social attitudes and anxiety are both essential components of most functional (mental hygiene) conceptions of the origins of stuttering.

Irrespective of the cause, as the child grows older each individual stutterer develops a systematic and fairly predictable pattern of blocking and/or repeating certain sounds or words in certain locations, such as at the beginning of a sentence or phrase. The rate and severity of disfluency in most stutterers will vary with environmental stress. Some typically high-stress situations are responding orally in class, being disciplined or frustrated, and talking on a telephone. Conversely, choral reading or speaking, singing, reciting memorized poems, and casual conversation with a friend are less stressful for most disfluent speakers.

The stutterer's different sensitivities to social situations typically result in developing patterns of specific-situation avoidance. This takes two forms. One is the avoidance of sounds and words which are hard to say. The other is the avoidance of speaking in stressful situations such as speaking orally in class or speaking in public. The individual attempts to deal with the communication problem, not by dealing with disfluent speech, but by manipulating circumstances so as to reduce the personal and social consequences of stuttering.

the treatment of primary stuttering Even though the distinction between primary and secondary stuttering is difficult to make, the initial hesitations, blockings, and repetitions of the two- to four-year-old require different treatment than do the secondary symptoms of the confirmed stutterer. Here are some general suggestions for parents and other adults concerned about the nonfluencies of the child who is in the early stages of language acquisition:

1. Measures taken should be indirect and not concerned with the speech deviations as such.

2. Keep the child in good physical condition.

3. Provide a pleasant, relaxed home atmosphere.

4. Provide as many good speech models as possible.

5. Try to develop feelings of adequacy and self-confidence (a satisfactory self-concept) in the child by emphasizing assets and minimizing liabilities.

6. If referred to, child's nonfluencies should be acknowledged but accepted as normal. The impression that they are bad or that other people are anxious about them should be avoided.

7. Treat children who stutter like all other children. Encourage them to recite and ask questions, and when they do, take time to listen. Do not answer or fill in words for them any more than for any other children.

symptomatic treatment of the secondary stutterer Symptomatic treatment may attempt to teach the person either to stutter in a way that is tolerable to self and to others (controlled stuttering), or to talk without stuttering (inhibition of stuttering).

Controlled stuttering is attained by teaching the stutterer rate-controlled speech techniques of breathing and controlled phrasing, through the repetition of what is said, reading in unison, negative practice (practice in stuttering) and various distracting devices. Remedial procedures are intended to develop tolerance of stuttering, emotional desensitization, anxiety reduction, and controlled speech. Treatment designed to make it possible for individuals to talk without stuttering consists in teaching them analytically, step by step, to articulate properly and gradually to build up fluency. Many of the same techniques used in teaching controlled stuttering may also be used to develop speech which is relatively fluent. A. Irwin (1972) and others claim that they can produce "easy stuttering" simply by slowing down speech. Such stuttering is said to be free of tension. The slow "easy stuttering" can then be speeded up until it approximates normal speech. There are a great many procedures for the control or elimination of stuttering, but no real understanding of how or why they achieve these effects.

Although punishment incident to stuttering would normally be expected to increase the disfluency, it has been shown that operant conditioning involving the administration of mild electric shock to the finger is effective in reducing and/or eliminating stuttering (Beattie, 1973). The contingent application of verbal as well as nonverbal reinforcers—both rewards and punishments—has been used in the treatment of stuttering (Watts, 1973; Patty and Quarrington, 1974).

Pacing speech with a metronome has also been used effectively in the treatment of stuttering, although no satisfactory explanation has been offered for this. The distracting effect of the sound, the slowing up of speech, and the pacemaker effects have all been proposed as the effective variables. However, the fact that rhythmic beats are more effective than irregular ones seems to discount the distraction explanation. While slow beats (seventy-five to ninety-five per minute) are more effective than slow *a-rhythmic ones,* rate alone does not seem to be the crucial variable. The metronome sound must signal the initiation of each word for it to have a positive pacing effect (Berman and Brady, 1973; Watts, 1973). P. A. Berman and J. P. Brady (1973) found that over half of twenty-eight speech clinicians queried regarded metronome conditioning to be a major advance in the treatment of stuttering. Delayed auditory feedback has also been used extensively with stutterers. In this procedure the speaker's own sounds are fed back after a delay of a fraction of a second. Paradoxically, delayed auditory feedback produces disfluencies in normal speakers and increased fluency in stutters. Delayed auditory feedback may constitute a slow rate-controlled and stutter-free speech which can subsequently be increased to a normal speaking rate. R. F. Curlee and W. H. Perkins (1973) report such a delayed auditory feedback program to be effective in substantially reducing stuttering, both in the clinic and in everyday speaking situations, with adolescent and adult stutterers.

The treatment of stuttering, as well as of many other types of speech defects, seems to be shifting away from mechanical drills and devices (speech correction) toward therapeutic relationships (speech therapy). One manifestation of this shift in emphasis is a preference for the term *speech therapist* rather than *speech correctionist*.

psychotherapy for the stutterer Psychotherapy is used with stutterers on the assumption that the nonfluency is either a symptom of, or is accompanied by, personality maladjustment and that the way to handle the stuttering is to deal with the underlying personality defects. Speech pathologists have recommended and used psychotherapy ranging from directive counseling and group discussion to the nondirective, psychoanalytic, and hypnotic therapies. The goals of psychotherapy for stutterers are essentially the same as those for individuals with normal speech. These include the development of insight (self-understanding), changes in the self-concept (ego building), self-acceptance, emotional desensitization (the reduction of fears and anxieties), and the improvement of personal relations.

Psychotherapy attempts to go beyond the removal of the symptom, and deals with the more basic problems and conflicts on the assumption that speech will improve with personality reorientation and improved adjustment. Some clinicians claim that a combination of general psychotherapy and more specific speech training provides optimum treatment potential (Goraj, 1974).

the personality traits of stutterers Prescribing psychotherapy for stutterers implies that they need personality reorganization. However, a survey of the studies of the personality traits and characteristics of stutterers does not show them to be markedly maladjusted. L. D. Goodstein (1958), and J. T. Goraj (1974), surveyed the literature on the topic published over a twenty-five-year period. They found opinions ranging from the contention that stutterers are essentially normal people except in speech, to the notion that stuttering is the manifestation of a basically neurotic personality. These extensive surveys disclosed little evidence to support the contention that either children or adults who stutter have a particular pattern of personality traits, are neurotic, or are otherwise severely maladjusted. Stutterers certainly do not appear to be severely maladjusted when compared with psychiatric patients. However, they are significantly different from nonstutterers in being more tense, anxious, and withdrawn. Certainly in speaking situations and when they are struggling in a stuttering block, they feel different from others and others perceive them as different. Stutterers also have lower levels of aspiration. They have significantly more personal and social problems than nonstutterers, but it is impossible to tell whether these problems were responsible for the stuttering or developed as a consequence of social reactions to the speech defect.

Speech Defects Associated with Neural Impairment

Impairment of brain functioning may be caused by maldevelopment, traumatic injury, hemorrhage, infections, abscesses, and tumors. Such pathology may result in localized injury and the impairment of language functions (aphasia), or it may produce widespread neural damage, with language disorders constituting only a part of a total syndrome which includes widespread muscular paralysis or dysfunction and mental subnormality.

the aphasic child *Aphasia* literally means loss of speech. As a clinical entity, it is an impairment in the understanding or expression of language due to brain injury. Aphasia is a disturbance of one's ability to handle language symbols. Traditionally, the term has been applied to adults and children who have suffered brain damage *after* language has been acquired. Here the meaning is clear, for there is a loss or impairment of a previously acquired habit system. However, the concept of "congenital aphasia" implies something different.

The loss of the language function due to brain injury in a child who has already acquired language skills does not differ from aphasia in adults, except that the language disturbance is milder than in adults with comparable brain damage and recovery is both more rapid and more complete. However, young normal children and adult aphasics make different types of linguistic errors. This indicates that the partial loss of acquired language abilities produces a different pattern of linguistic impairment than does the incomplete acquisition of that ability by a normal child (Gardner, 1974). As expected, the degree of paraphasia (the introduction of inappropriate words into one's speech) is related to the extent of neural damage and the severity of the resulting aphasia (Beyn and Vlasenko, 1974). The prognosis for postnatally acquired aphasia in children is good (Ajax, 1973).

Educators are proposing to substitute the term *verbal communication disorders* for *aphasia,* and to avoid neurological implications by referring to these children simply as "children with learning disabilities." M. A. Mc-Ginnis (1963) has developed a language training program specifically for aphasic children.

speech defects associated with cerebral palsy About 90 percent of children with cerebral palsy are said to have significant speech disorders. Their speech impairments are part of a larger syndrome including abnormal sucking, chewing, swallowing, breathing, and tongue movements. Language training is typically part of their total rehabilitation program. Because of the widespread nature of the neural impairment and the number of accompanying handicaps, speech correction is often difficult. It is recommended that speech training be started when the child normally begins to speak (one to one-and-a-half years of age), and in most cases it will continue for years.

SPEECH DEFECTS ASSOCIATED WITH MENTAL RETARDATION

The relationship between mental retardation and speech level is high. Table 13–4 shows this relationship as indicated by a typical study.

There are several reasons for the close relationship between language proficiency and intellectual level. The most obvious is that individuals with lower levels of intelligence lack the capacity for acquiring language.

Before the advent of intelligence testing, idiots were defined as those individuals who were so low in mental level that they did not learn to speak. In addition to the inability of the most severely mentally retarded to acquire speech, mental retardation and speech defects may both have a common cause: brain damage or defective development of the nervous system. The mentally retarded seem to suffer from the same *types* of speech defects as do the mentally normal, although the frequency of defects is greater (Anastasiow and Stayrook, 1973).

BEHAVIOR PROBLEMS ASSOCIATED WITH SPEECH DEFECTS

What was said about the personality traits of stutterers applies equally well to speech defectives as a group. They are not typically seriously maladjusted or neurotic. However, they do have more than their share of adjustment problems. They tend to be less acceptable to their peers than are children with normal speech (Peckham, 1973). Like stuttering, other functional speech defects are associated with a set of high standards im-

Table 13–4
SPEECH DEFECTS AS RELATED TO DEGREES OF MENTAL RETARDATION

IQ	50–69	21–49	20 and below
Percentage with speech defects	43	73	100

Data from Sirken and Lyon (1941).

---

posed on the children by the parents in an atmosphere of emotional tension (Marge, 1965).

Ways in which children with problems of articulation differ from children with normal speech in the areas of conduct and behavior disorders are shown in Table 13–5.

SCHOOL PROGRAMS FOR SPEECH CORRECTION

Although speech correction is done in hospitals, clinics, and private offices, by far the bulk of speech therapy is done in the schools. Many universities operate speech clinics as both training and service centers, but the largest number of speech correctionists are employed in public school systems.

The most common administrative educational arrangement is to use itinerant teachers. In this type of organization, each teacher serves several schools and the children remain in their regular schools and classes. The itinerant teacher visits each school regularly and provides group or individual therapy as frequently as the workload permits. This plan is easily administered and can be easily adjusted to meet changing needs. The

Table 13–5

THE RELATIVE INCIDENCE OF CONDUCT AND BEHAVIOR DISORDERS AMONG CHILDREN WITH DEFECTS OF ARTICULATION AND AMONG NORMAL CHILDREN

conduct and behavior disorders	frequency of occurrence		
	articulation sample	normal sample	differences between groups
1. Eating and food problems	39	2	37
2. Nervousness	53	22	31
3. Temper tantrums	35	8	27
4. Showing off	30	6	24
5. Refusal to obey	27	7	20
6. Thumb sucking	34	15	19
7. Shyness	31	13	18
8. Destructiveness	18	2	16
9. Fears	21	10	11
10. Jealousy*	6	3	3
11. Sleeplessness	6	1	5
12. Lying	6	1	5
13. Enuresis	9	3	6
14. Fingernail biting	7	11	4
15. Hurting pets	1	0	−1

*All differences above this level are statistically significant at or above the .05 level.
Data from FitzSimons (1958).

teacher's maximum caseload is often specified by state or local codes or regulations. The recommended maximum caseload ranges from 70 to 100. However, a survey made in 1961 found that the average caseload was 130 children. Accepting 100 as the normal caseload means that any school district enrolling 2,000 students could use the services of a speech therapist (Hull, 1963).

In some school systems, speech specialists handle the most difficult cases and train regular teachers to work with the less seriously defective children. The American Speech and Hearing Association has set standard qualifications which speech therapists should meet and has delineated the role of public school therapists in its statement on "Services and Functions of Speech and Hearing Specialists in Public Schools" (1962).

About 75 percent of the children receiving speech therapy in the average school are in the first three grades. Each child is typically seen at least weekly for individual or group work. Maximum carryover from session to session is gained when the regular teachers and the parents cooperate. Very often definite school, home, and private practice exercises are required.

COOPERATION BETWEEN SPECIAL AND REGULAR TEACHERS

No physical plant adaptations or special ancillary service needs arise from the joint responsibilities shared by special and regular teachers dealing with speech problems. However, a certain amount of planning is necessary. If children are to be taken from their regular classes for therapy programs, it should be arranged so that the impact of these absences are minimized. Time for the clinician and the regular class teacher to confer and plan must be built into the week's schedule. Provisions should also be made for those occasions when the regular teacher may wish to sit in or participate in a particular therapy session, or when both may wish to confer with parents or other specialists.

If individualized educational programs are going to be provided for all children with communication disorders, there will be an increasing need for speech therapists. It seems unlikely that enough trained therapists are going to be available to meet this need. Thus regular teachers, teacher aides, and volunteers are going to be needed to supplement the work of the specialists. Available studies indicate that teacher's aides, volunteers, and parents working under the supervision of speech specialists can achieve results equivalent to those of speech clinicians with comparable children (Alvord, 1977; Gray and Barker, 1977).

The use of parents in this connection is significant because of the conviction of most therapists that successes in the clinic and classroom can last only if there is a follow-through and consistency of treatment between clinic and classroom and the home. Parents who have participated in these and similar programs have found that the benefits of their participation were at least three. First, the school benefits from the assistance of willing aides who are eager to learn and have had some contacts with a speech-handicapped child. Second, the additional help permits the specialists to spread their expertise over a larger number of students, thus making the program less costly. Third, the parents are able to use, in their own homes, the techniques they learn in the clinic and classrooms. When doing this the parents become more confident and relaxed with their children because they are sure that they are not working at cross-purposes with the children's therapist or teachers. They also have a sense of accomplishment when contributing to the treatment of their children's problems.

COMMUNICATION BOARDS

Many people who cannot speak are able to communicate by means of a *communication board*. The basic principle of a communication board is simple. The person unable to speak conveys meanings by pointing to a picture, a printed word, a special symbol, a letter, or a syllable according to the contents of the board. Communication boards range from relatively simple display boards, a deck of cards, a notebook, or trays of various sizes, on the one hand, to sophisticated electronic devices on the other. Some boards are available commercially but most are designed and constructed to meet the needs of specific individuals.

A communication board can be used advantageously by individuals with only limited verbal facilities. Speaking with such a board available becomes easier as the individuals become more relaxed because of the diminished pressure and anxiety concerning possible communication failure. A communication board can be an aid in speech therapy by increasing the amount of speaking the person does (Von Bruns-Connolly and Shane, 1978).

One of the most promising electronic communication boards has been developed by Richard Foulds at Tufts University (Boucher, 1979). This aid has rows of letters and a display panel. By operating a switch attached to the machine by an extension cord, the nonvocal operator can communicate with others by spelling words which appear on the display panel. Since many people who cannot talk have limited arm and hand control, the machine minimizes the physical movements required. Operation of the machine requires only vision, control of at least one muscle, and the ability to spell. Research is now focusing on the use of syllables or phonetic groupings to replace single letter spelling (Boucher, 1979).

The Tufts Biomedical Engineering Center is only one of fourteen such regional centers supported by federal funds. Each center has a different core area of research and development. A list of these centers together with their areas of specialization is given in the article by Boucher (1979).

School Programs without a Speech Clinician

In-service training programs can help regular classroom teachers handle children with less serious speech defects, although they probably will not attempt formal therapy. Every teacher is, to a degree, a teacher of speech. Each teacher can be a good speech model. The classroom teacher can make referrals to private, hospital, or university clinics when they are available. The teacher can handle children with all types of speech defects in the ways suggested earlier for the general treatment of the primary stutterer. Some additional suggestions for the classroom handling of the child with a major speech defect are:

1. Complete acceptance of the child as a completely worthy individual is most important.

2. Accept the child's nonfluencies in a relaxed and unembarrassed fashion. Try to get the children to do likewise.

3. Do not look away from the child, or take over and speak for the child.

4. Encourage, but do not force, the child with serious speech defects to speak before the class.

5. Provide the child with nonverbal assignments and responsibilities to keep him from capitalizing on his disability.

6. Capitalize on the child's assets and provide recognition for accomplishments to increase the child's self-confidence.

7. Provide as much group participation as possible for the child. Let those who will not participate verbally participate in a nonverbal way.

8. Provide some daily oral experience for the child, such as group singing, reading in unison, or ordinary conversation.

Language Development Programs

Several movements coalesced during the 1960s to produce a relatively new psycholinguistic concept of language development in general and communication problems in particular. National concern for the educationally disadvantaged—especially the culturally deviant child—and for the mentally retarded provided an atmosphere favorable to the development of new approaches to the language problems of children. A revival of the notion that language is the vehicle of thought, the development of the hypothesis that the restricted or deviant linguistic patterns of the educationally handicapped child may be a critical part of the problem, and the emergence of new theories and approaches to the problems of language acquisition, combined with a heightened public and professional awareness of developmental problems to bring forth a tremendous number of language development programs.

SUMMARY

Speech is defective whenever the manner of speaking interferes with communication, calls undue attention to itself, or causes the speaker concern to the degree that special remedial measures are deemed necessary. Initial identification of speech defects is made both informally and by systematic screening procedures. Diagnosis and treatment may involve parents, teachers, speech therapists, psychologists, psychiatrists, pediatricians, surgeons, dentists, and orthodontists. It is conservatively estimated that 5 percent of school-age children have speech defects sufficiently serious to require therapy, and then an additional 5 percent with less serious disorders should probably receive some speech correction. The causes of speech defects are both organic (cleft palate, auditory defects, brain damage, and so forth) and functional (learning failure and emotional blocking).

As compared with normal people, those with speech defects are slightly inferior in physical characteristics, motor facility, sensory functions, intelligence, school achievement, and general behavioral adequacy. This inferiority is partially the result of the high incidence of speech defects among the organically impaired and of the greater prevalence of speech problems (particularly defects in articulation) among persons of the lower socioeconomic levels.

Speech defects are usually classified according to major symptoms, as disorders of articulation, delayed speech, voice disorders, and disturbances of rhythm. Additional classes of speech disorders are based on accompanying defects. Thus we have speech disorders associated with mental retardation, cleft palate, and brain damage (cerebral palsy, aphasia). On the basis of etiology, speech defects are classified as organic or functional.

Speech disorders are treated in hospitals, clinics, schools, and private offices. The largest number of children are treated in the public schools. Treatment is given both individually and in groups, and concerns itself primarily either with symptoms (speech correction) or with underlying causes (speech therapy). In the schools, the speech therapist typically serves several schools. The therapist's caseload should normally not exceed one hundred.

REFERENCES

Ajax, E. T., "The Aphasic Patient: A Practical Review," *Diseases of the Nervous System,* 1973, *34,* 135–42.

Alvord, D. J., "Innovations in Speech Therapy: A Cost Effective Program," *Exceptional Children,* 1977, *43,* 520–25.

American Speech and Hearing Association, "Services and Functions of Speech and Hearing Specialists in Public Schools," *Journal of Speech and Hearing Disorders,* 1962, *4,* 99–100.

American Speech and Hearing Association, Committee on Legislation, "Need for Speech Pathologists," *Journal of Speech and Hearing Disorders,* 1959, *1,* 138–39, 161–67.

American Speech and Hearing Association, Committee on the Midcentury White House Conference on Children and Youth, "Speech Disorders and Speech Correction," *Journal of Speech and Hearing Disorders,* 1952, *17,* 129–37.

American Speech and Hearing Association, "Public School and Hearing Services," *Journal of Speech and Hearing Disorders,* 1961, Monograph Supplement 8.

Anastasiow, N. J. and N. G. Stayrook, "Miscue Language Patterns of Mildly Retarded and Nonretarded Children," *American Journal of Mental Deficiency,* 1973, *77,* 431–34.

Andrews, G. and J. Cutler, "Stuttering Therapy: The Relation Between Changes in Symptom Level and Attitudes," *Journal of Speech and Hearing Disorders,* 1974, *39,* 312–18.

Beattie, M. S., "A Behavior Therapy Programme for Stuttering," *British Journal of Disorders of Communication,* 1973, *8,* 120–30.

Benton, A. L., "Developmental Aphasia (D.A.)," *Cortex,* 1964, *1,* 40–52.

Berman, P. A. and J. P. Brady, "Miniaturized Metronomes in the Treatment of Stuttering: A Survey of Clinicians' Experience," *Journal of Therapy and Experimental Psychiatry,* 1973, *4,* 117–19.

Beyn, E. S. and I. T. Vlasenko, "Verbal Paraphasia of Aphasic Patients in the Course of Naming Actions," *British Journal of Disorders of Communication,* 1974, *9,* 24–36.

Bloodstein, O., "The Development of Stuttering: III. Theoretical and Clinical Implications," *Journal of Speech and Hearing Disorders,* 1961, *26,* 67–82.

Bluemel, C. S., "Primary and Secondary Stuttering," *Quarterly Journal of Speech,* 1932, *18,* 187–200.

Bluemel, C. S., *The Riddle of Stuttering* (Danville, Ill.: Interstate Publishers, 1957).

Boucher, R. F., "I Have Seen the Future and It Works: The Role of Science," *The Exceptional Parent,* 1979, *9*(1), A13–A17.

Calnan, M. and K. Richardson, "Speech Problems Among Children in a National Survey—Association with Reading, General Ability, Mathematics, and Syntactic Maturity," *Educational Studies,* 1977, *3,* 55–61.

Curlee, R. F. and W. H. Perkins, "Effectiveness of a DAF Conditioning Program for Adolescent and Adult Stutterers," *Behavior Research and Therapy,* 1973, *11,* 395–401.

Davis, J. P., "The Speech Aspects of Reading Readiness: Newer Practices in Reading in the Elementary School," in *Seventeenth Yearbook, Department of Elementary School Principals* (Washington, D. C.: National Educational Association, 1938).

Eisenson, J., "The Nature of Defective Speech," in W. M. Cruickshank, ed., *Psychology of Exceptional Children and Youth,* 2nd ed. (Englewood Cliffs, N.J.: Prentice-Hall, 1963).

FitzSimons, R. M., "Developmental, Psychosocial, and Educational Factors in Children with Articulation Problems," *Child Development,* 1958, *29,* 481–89.

Gardner, H., "The Naming of Objects and Symbols by Children and Aphasic Patients," *Journal of Psycholinguistic Research,* 1974, *3,* 133–49.

Goldman, R. and G. H. Shames, "Comparisons of the Goals that Parents of Stutterers and Parents of Nonstutterers Set for Their Children," *Journal of Speech and Hearing Disorders,* 1964, *29,* 381–89.

Goodstein, L. D., "Functional Speech Disorders and Personality: A Survey of the Literature," *Journal of Speech and Hearing Research,* 1958, *1,* 359–76.

Goraj, J. T., "Stuttering Therapy as Crisis Intervention," *British Journal of Disorders of Communication,* 1974, *9,* 51–57.

Gray, B. B. and K. Barker, "Use of Aides in an Articulation Therapy Program," *Exceptional Children,* 1977, *43,* 534–36.

Gruber, L. and R. L. Powell, "Responses of Stuttering and Nonstuttering Children on a Dichotic Listening Task," *Perceptual and Motor Skills,* 1974, *38,* 263–64.

Hull, F. M., "Speech Impaired Children," in L. M. Dunn, ed., *Exceptional Children in the Schools* (New York: Holt, Rinehart and Winston, 1963).

Irwin, A., "The Treatment and Results of Easy-stammering," *British Journal of Disorders of Communication,* 1972, *7,* 151–56.

Irwin, R. B., "Speech Disorders," in M. E. Frampton and E. D. Gall, eds., *Special Education for the Exceptional,* vol. 2 (Boston: Porter Sargent, 1955).

Johnson, W., "A Study of the Onset and Development of Stuttering," *Journal of Speech and Hearing Disorders,* 1942, 7, 251–57.

Johnson, W., *Because I Stutter* (New York: D. Appleton and Co., 1930).

Johnson, W., *Speech Handicapped School Children* (New York: Harper and Row, 1956).

Lemert, E. M., "Stuttering and Social Structure in Two Pacific Societies," *Journal of Speech and Hearing Disorders,* 1962, *27,* 3–10.

Marge, M., "The Influence of Selected Home Background Variables on the Development of Oral Communication Skills in Children," *Journal of Speech and Hearing Research,* 1965, *8,* 291–309.

McGinnis, M. A., *Aphasic Children: Identification and Education by the Association Method* (Washington, D. C.: Alexander Graham Bell Association for the Deaf, 1963).

Mecham, M. K., M. J. Berko, and F. G. Berko, *Speech Therapy in Cerebral Palsy* (Springfield, Ill.: Charles C. Thomas, 1960).

Morley, M., and others, "Delayed Speech and Developmental Aphasia," *British Medical Journal,* 1955, *20,* 463–67.

Patty, J. and B. Quarrington, "The Effects of Reward on Types of Stuttering," *Journal of Communication Disorders,* 1974, *7,* 65–77.

Peckham, C. S., "Speech Defects in a National Sample of Children Aged Seven Years," *British Journal of Disorders of Communication,* 1973, *8,* 2–8.

Schwartz, M. F., "The Care of the Stuttering Black," *Journal of Speech and Hearing Disorders,* 1974, *39,* 169–77.

Sheehan, J. G., "Conflict Theory of Stuttering," in J. Eisenson, ed., *Stuttering: A Symposium* (New York: Harper and Row, 1958).

Sheridan, M. D., "Children of Seven Years with Marked Speech Defects," *British Journal of Disorders of Communication,* 1973, *8,* 9–16.

Sirken, J. and W. Lyon, "A Study of Speech Defects in Mental Deficiency," *American Journal of Mental Deficiency,* 1941, *46,* 74–80.

Smith, R. C., "You're Not a Person: You're a Stutterer," *Hearing and Speech News,* 1972, *40* (2), 8–9, 20–22.

Stewart, J. L., "The Problems of Stuttering in Certain North American Indian Societies," *Journal of Speech and Hearing Disorders,* Monograph Supplement 6, 1960, 61–87.

Turton, L. J., "Education of Children with Communication Disorders," in W. M. Cruickshank and G. O. Johnson, eds., *Education of Exceptional Children and Youth* (Englewood Cliffs, N. J.: Prentice-Hall, 1975).

Van Riper, C., *The Treatment of Stuttering* (Englewood Cliffs, N. J.: Prentice-Hall, 1973).

Von Bruns-Connolly, S. and H. C. Shane, "Communication Boards: Help for the Child Unable to Talk," *The Exceptional Parent*, 1978, *8*(2), F19–F22.

Walker, S. T. and J. M. Walker, "Differences in Heart-rate Variability Between Stutterers and Nonstutterers Following Arousal," *Perceptual and Motor Skills*, 1973, *36*, 926.

Watts, F., "Mechanisms of Fluency Control in Stutterers," *British Journal of Disorders of Communication*, 1973, *8*, 131–38.

SUGGESTIONS FOR STUDENTS AND INSTRUCTORS

1. Make and then play tape recordings of preschool children and have the students estimate the ages of the speakers.

2. Have the students identify cases of what they consider to be "speech defects" in these same recordings.

3. Play tape recordings of children of various ages after telling the class that the speakers are considerably older than they really are and have them indicate speech defects.

4. Arrange for students to visit a school and either observe or assist a speech clinician or a regular class teacher working with speech handicapped children.

ADDITIONAL READINGS

Cooper, E. B., *Understanding Stuttering: Information for Parents* (Chicago, Ill.: National Easter Seal Society, 1979). This is a valuable source of information for teachers as well as for parents and other nonspecialists.

Caudill, R., *A Certain Small Shepherd* (New York: Holt, Rinehart, and Winston, 1965). Personal account of a person with a speech problem.

Aaronson, D. R. and Rieber, R. W., *Developmental Psycholinguistics and Communication Disorders* (New York: New York Academy of Sciences, 1975). A comprehensive presentation of the development of normal and defective language.

SELECTED FILMS

Speech Disorder—Physical Handicaps. (29 minutes) Indiana University Audio-Visual Center, Bloomington, Ind. Illustrates the variety and causes of speech disorders, as well as techniques of diagnosis and treatment. The film stresses social understanding.

Speech Disorder—Stuttering. (29 minutes) Indiana University Audio-Visual

Center, Bloomington, Ind. Portrays stuttering patterns and shows how therapy is conducted.

ORGANIZATIONS AND AGENCIES

American Speech and Hearing Association
9030 Old Georgetown Road
Washington, D. C. 20014

Orton Society (dyslexia)
8415 Bellona Lane
Towson, Md. 21204

BEHAVIORAL AND EMOTIONAL DISORDERS

PART **V**

CHAPTER 14

BEHAVIORAL AND EMOTIONAL DISORDERS

In the course of daily living, all individuals are subjected to frustration and stress in various forms. Children and adults suffer from fatigue, pain, disease, and injury, as well as from frustration, conflict, anxiety, and fear. The reactions to these facets of life are many and varied. The reactions to the frustrations and stresses of existence are, no doubt, a function of a complex matrix of biological, social, and psychological factors. There are, of course, genetic and constitutional determinants of behavior, but the adaptive behaviors of immediate professional concern to psychologists and educators are those that are learned. Biological considerations establish in part the ease or difficulty with which certain behavior can be acquired and determine the nature of treatment to be employed in behavioral correction, but social-psychological principles of behavior acquisition and modification are applicable within these genetic and biological limitations.

People with differing physiological characteristics have adjustive problems that vary with their physical conditions. Without denying the existence and influence of biological factors, emphasis will be placed on social-psychological factors in this consideration of social deviance.

HABITS OF ADJUSTMENT

Ways of coping with environmental stress and strain are learned in the same general way as other responses. No unique principles of learning are required to account for the acquisition of behavior that is socially or personally unfortunate or inadequate, as opposed to behavior that appears to be essentially adaptive and effective. The *circumstances* of learning will differ for the two, but the *principles* involved are probably identical.

Given the commonality of physical structures of human beings and the commonality of experiences they have as a result of living within a culture, it is not surprising that people develop a number of ways of dealing with the environment that are essentially alike. The means of coping with environmental situations that are learned and employed frequently have been classified and labeled as "mechanisms" (Freud, 1938). Behavioral mechanisms are used by everyone, and nothing really "mechanistic" or "abnormal" is implied by the term. They are behaviors that are learned in the course of ordinary living. When they become extremely routinized and are employed excessively, they become unusual. The various mechanisms were developed within psychoanalytic theory and have subsequently been employed by psychologists in general as labels for describing behavior. The labels designate descriptive categories of behavior and are not intended to be explanatory. The so-called defense mechanisms have become well known, and therefore no detailed treatment of them will be attempted. Defense mechanisms form the basis for the development of certain behaviors that may be considered as deviant; therefore a brief review of them may prove helpful.

MECHANISMS OF BEHAVIOR

Rationalization has been selected to illustrate the operation of mechanisms in general. *Rationalization* is the process of presenting more personally or socially acceptable motives for one's behavior than those that actually exist. Children soon learn that certain reasons for doing things are more acceptable, and therefore better, than others. They learn that rewards and punishments, both obvious and subtle, are frequently administered on the basis of motives underlying their activity rather than the activity itself. The child in our culture learns that to act on the basis of impulse, emotion, desire, or revenge is not socially approved, but that acting on the basis of reason, deliberation, generosity, and kindness is socially approved. In children's attempts to behave in accordance with the demands of society, they learn to offer "rational" excuses for their seemingly inappropriate behavior. If this is done in a sufficient variety of instances, and over a long enough period of time, they may come to believe their own rationalizations. In this case, the rationalizations are self-deceptive as well as socially deceptive. Excessive habits of rationalization derive perhaps from excessive familial, cultural, and social demands for logical, rational motives for behavior, and from our essential unwillingness to accept emotional and irrational excuses.

With practice, children can become quite adept in rationalizing their behavior and in deceiving others. When they come to believe their own rationalizations, they forget what the real and original motives were and lose sight of the fact that their behavior is face-saving and ego-inflating. Their rationalizations then become habitual, unconsciously motivated—a way of life. Verbal expressions of appropriate motives for socially inappropriate behavior are learned because they are rewarded.

There are a goodly number of mechanisms whose development can be understood through essentially this same pattern of learning, reinforcement, social deception, and self-deception. The usual mechanisms—such as projection, identification, sublimation, withdrawal, aggression, daydreaming, regression, compensation, and repression—are to be viewed as usual habits of responding. But they are habits that can get out of hand and become dominant and consistent ways of behaving that are detrimental to society and to personal effectiveness.

EMOTIONAL DISTURBANCE AND SOCIAL MALADJUSTMENT

When socially or personally unsatisfactory modes of behavior are acquired in the course of living, and the manner of acquisition is relatively easy to discern, we generally refer to this as *social maladjustment.* When the reinforcements are subtle and the behavior not obviously adaptive, the individual is said to be *emotionally disturbed.*

Emotionally disturbed children are children with emotional problems severe enough to prevent them from making the necessary adjustments for effective functioning in the culture. They have acquired habits of behavior sufficiently different from other children reared in similar circumstances so that their behavior is considered to be personally and socially deviant. Their behavior may range from aggressive destruction to complete withdrawal. They are unable to do what is expected of their normal peers and are to be found in any social class and in a variety of families. Their social and personal learning has been inappropriate, but the reasons for this are vague.

Socially maladjusted children are chronic violators of broad cultural mores and social values. They have learned to behave in accordance with a set of values and rules that may be shared by their immediate peers, but not by the broader culture. Delinquent gangs are constantly in trouble with constituted authority because the code of conduct acceptable to the immediate group is not accepted by the broader society. Their accepted code of conduct involves truancy, fighting, and defiance of constituted authority. They are handicapped by having learned a provincial pattern of social values, by their conformity to a code that differs from that of the general population. Socially maladjusted children learn their behavior in families and communities that do not conform to the more widely accepted values. The families are typically multiproblem families from the point of view of the rest of society, and many of these families problems are exacerbated by living in urban slum areas.

Some chronic violators of broad cultural mores are emotionally disturbed, and some emotionally disturbed individuals are to be found in gangs of the socially maladjusted. There is some overlap between the two. The same overt behavior can stem from either emotional disturbance or social maladjustment. When the behavior pattern derives rather directly from the obvious social-learning situation and other aspects of personality malfunction are not present, it is generally called "social maladjustment." When the behavior of the individual is unlike that of the immediate peers and it is not apparent how the behavior was learned, it usually comes under the category of "emotionally disturbed." Many children who are delinquent are really victims of unfortunate social situations and have learned inappropriate behavior, but they are not emotionally disturbed. It has been estimated that no more than 25 percent of delinquent acts can be attributed to emotionally disturbed children (Kvaraceus and Miller, 1959). Among groups of delinquent children, it is difficult to discern any distinctive personality patterns (Richardson and Roebuck, 1965).

Children who are problems to themselves and to society, and whose behavior apparently arises from emotional disturbance (inappropriate emotional learning), will be treated under three headings: Anxiety, Withdrawal, and Aggression. Under the heading of Aggression, we shall discuss some aspects of delinquency that may derive from either emotional disturbance or social maladjustment.

ANXIETY

Anxiety is probably basic to all forms of maladjustive behavior, to the so-called behavior mechanisms as well as to the neuroses and the more severe functional psychoses. Certain varieties of behavior which appear to be more directly the consequence of anxiety than others have been designated as anxicty reactions.

Anxiety can be conceptualized as fear with a future reference. If a frightening stimulus is present and observable in the environment, the reaction is usually called "fear." A person can be anxious about an impending circumstance or event and be fearful in the presence of the actual stimuli. The elimination of anxiety-provoking circumstances in the world in which we live is impossible. It is inevitable that the child growing up in our culture is exposed to anxiety-evoking situations. The infant experiences frustration and conflict as an inevitable consequence of being cared for and developing in the family. Inconsistency and incompatibility of disciplinary techniques are bound to occur. Various restrictions are placed on behavior by adults, and some of these restrictions are not consistent with demands placed on the child. Children are encouraged to become independent and to stand up for their rights, but are punished for aggressiveness. Threats are our constant companions throughout childhood, adolescence, and adulthood. Parents and other persons in positions of authority learn that threats are an effective means of controlling behavior, regardless of how much anxiety is evoked by them.

ANXIETY AND CULTURE

The importance of the cultural situation in the development of anxiety reactions has been emphasized by a number of investigators. Karen Horney (1937) emphasized the importance of the feeling of helplessness, isolation, and fear a child experiences in being reared in an essentially hostile world. She referred to the reactions from such stress as "basic anxiety," and considered the feeling of anxiety deriving from such situations basic to the later development of neurosis. The basic causes of anxiety were seen as deriving from the rejection and disapproval a child receives from adults.

Patterns of child rearing in the middle and upper classes have been viewed as a source of anxiety (Lundin, 1965). Among these classes, overprotection, excessive mothering, and pampering are found, and the child is likely to be overly dominated by the parents. When this occurs, the child has little opportunity to learn appropriate methods of adapting to the problems of life. The aggression that usually arises from frustration is discouraged, and expressions of hostility are punished. Striving toward higher social status by the middle class, and the consequent use of children to gratify parental desires for improved social position, may also have a confusing and frustrating effect on children (Seward, 1956).

All individuals are subjected to frustration and punishment from time to time. The anxiety-ridden individual fails to learn adequate means for reducing or avoiding anxiety. The cultural situation may make it nearly impossible for such learning to occur. The subtleties of behavior reinforcement within a given family are such that one child may have sufficient opportunity for such learning while another may not. The possibilities for reduction of anxiety and resolution of conflict in ways condoned by family and society may be more numerous for one child in a family than for another, and such possibilities are more numerous for children from certain social classes than for others.

CHRONIC ANXIETY

Chronically anxious people present a rather complex array of symptoms. They are fearful and apprehensive. They are worried and frightened, without knowing exactly why they feel as they do. The level of anxiety they experience is pathological, in the sense that it appears to be out of proportion to any realistic causal factors. They often recognize their anxiety as unrealistic. The anxiety is often constantly present, though varying in intensity, and it is not tied to any particular situation or set of stimuli. Such anxiety has been termed "free-floating" (Freud, 1936). The anxiety state may be described as a fear, and ascribed by the sufferer to a specific cause or situation; however, the causes and situations shift from time to time and are not the real causes of the anxiety. Chronic anxiety is a persistent nonadaptive reaction arising from a failure to acquire personal and social responses adequate for self-protection.

Chronic anxiety sufferers are jumpy, irritable, and easily upset by irregularities in routine. Trembling sometimes occurs for no apparent reason. Problems of sleep are chronic, with frequent nightmares and anxious dreams of being pursued. Anxious children may awaken in the night frequently, and tell of troubled dreams. Adults are often fatigued, although they have not engaged in excessive activity. Excessive tiredness and feelings of fatigue following sleep and apparent rest are common.

Children's appetites may suffer, and their bladder control may become erratic. Adults may lose interest in food and find that they must urinate frequently. Gastrointestinal disturbances are common. The attention span of anxious children becomes exceedingly short, and concentration becomes difficult for adults. Absentmindedness is rather common in anxious adults, and if heavy demands are placed on them they may become quite confused. Anxious children cry rather readily, many times for no observable reason. Ordinary demands seem excessive to the anxious child and may result in tears.

The neurotically anxious adult reports feelings of apprehension, uncertainty, and dread. The precise situations that produce these reactions cannot be identified, but the feelings are constantly there. Job efficiency may become impaired. They are unhappy and disturbed, and their families are distraught with their ineffectiveness and unhappiness. Anxiety-ridden children suffer from a lack of energy and inability to direct what little they can muster toward the demands of school and home. They are intense and fearful of failure, but cannot direct energy toward its avoidance. School becomes a heavy burden and they are beset by feelings of tension, apprehension, loneliness, and discouragement.

The chronically anxious are made anxious by so many stimuli that the individual cannot discriminate among them and respond in a manner that would be effective in their reduction. The stimuli cannot be identified and, therefore, the person can do little about them. From time to time the chronically anxious person may suffer *acute* anxiety. These anxiety attacks present an exaggerated picture of the chronically anxious person. The individual cannot identify the stimuli or situation that immediately produces these attacks, and they may occur sporadically and be frightening and demoralizing for the person. Their usual feelings of apprehension become magnified; they become suddenly restless, cannot continue what they are doing, and get up and move about; the heart begins to pound; the mouth may feel dry; they begin to perspire; they may gasp for breath, tremble, and wring their hands. They don't know where to go or what to do, and disorganization is quite intense. They may think there is something seriously physically wrong, such as a heart attack, and seek assistance. Subsequently, they suffer embarrassment and doubt when told that there is nothing physically wrong.

If the anxiety attack is particularly severe, the person may become seriously disorganized and disoriented, and may become aggressive and abusive, or self-destructive. The attack may last for a number of days. Such extreme attacks of anxiety have been termed *panic reactions* (Cameron, 1947). They are difficult for the individual to cope with, and psychiatric attention is indicated.

PHOBIC REACTIONS

Phobias are intense, specific fears that have no apparent rational basis. The number of specific phobias that have been given descriptive titles is legion. A phobia is an anxiety reaction, but it differs from chronic anxiety in that the specific stimuli that give rise to the feelings of uneasiness and apprehension are known to the individual. The person does not know why he or she is frightened of these events, however, and the fear is out of all proportion to the real danger. The individual may feel embarrassed and self-conscious about the feelings of panic, but they are very real and intense. When a person is confronted with the phobic object, acute anxiety or even panic may be experienced. In the extreme, phobias may become quite incapacitating; the individual may devote so much time and energy to avoiding the fearful situation that to carry on many usual functions is impossible.

People exhibiting phobic reactions probably have had a goodly number of anxiety-evoking experiences and are thus somewhat predisposed to chronic anxiety. If they encounter situations which are frightening or anxiety-producing for them, their anxiety becomes conditioned to the stimuli of the situation. They usually cannot recall the conditions under which they learned to respond with fear. The fear is perpetuated by avoiding the stimuli that induce it, and the phobic reaction may spread to a variety of tangentially related stimuli. In such instances a person may develop a number of anxiety reactions of sufficient severity and specificity to be called "phobias."

COMPULSIONS AND OBSESSIONS

Some individuals acquire ways of reducing anxiety that are temporary expedients. That is, they learn patterns of thought and action that serve to reduce anxiety, but only on a temporary basis. The behavior keeps overt anxiety at a relatively low level and serves to keep acute anxiety and panic from developing.

Compulsions and obsessions are coercive, recurrent acts, or impulses to act in rather specific ways. The person is quite aware of what he or she is doing or feels compelled to do, recognizes it as irrational, silly, or even dangerous, but is unable to stop doing it (*compulsion*) or get rid of the impulse to perform the act (*obsession*). The impulse to act is sometimes situational, in that it occurs whenever the stimuli are appropriate. In other instances the impulse to act seems to build up as the result of a variety of stimuli, until the act is performed. The individual feels more and more anxious until finally the compulsive act is committed. This affords some measure of anxiety reduction.

An obsession is a thought or idea which keeps recurring to the person. It is usually coercive, irrational, and anxiety-laden, but cannot be disposed of. For example: A mother cannot stop thinking that if she had administered proper medication to her child it would be alive today; the idea that she has killed a loved one keeps recurring. A man is obsessed with the notion that he will lose his keys or wallet, and must reassure himself by checking on their presence every few minutes. An example of the combining of an obsession and compulsion is the behavior of the person who is obsessed by the thought that he or she did not lock the house when leaving in the morning. The person cannot get rid of the idea and feels compelled to return to check. This happens nearly every morning. If the person didn't return to check, he or she would feel uneasy and preoccupied all day.

The list of possible compulsive-obsessive reactions is an imposing one. They range all the way from excessive neatness, excessive cleanliness, and counting steps, posts, and cracks in the sidewalk to criminal acts such as kleptomania (compulsive stealing) and pyromania (compulsive fire setting). The manias are all technically compulsions.

Combinations of phobic and obsessive-compulsive reactions are more common than their occurrence in isolated form. All have a strong component of anxiety. For example: A person may be mysophobic (have a morbid fear of dirt) and be obsessed with the idea of being contaminated with dangerous germs by everything touched. Such a person may have an accompanying handwashing compulsion. These elements are all consistent and mutually supportive. Other combinations of phobia, obsession, and compulsion may occur in the same person.

It has been suggested (Portnoy, 1959) that the anxiety neurotics are really the most psychologically healthy of all neurotics because they are attempting to cope with life in the face of multitudinous threats. They are able to endure great amounts of anxiety without employing the massive defensive reactions and other distorted behavior typical of other psychiatric syndromes. In spite of this contention, a great number of anxious people seek drugs or use alcohol to attain temporary relief from their feelings of anxiety.

WITHDRAWAL

Some people learn to adjust to social situations through withdrawal. Such habits of adjustment are probably learned in the same manner that other social responses are learned. The individual has found that withdrawal and isolation are rewarding. Withdrawal is a relatively easy response to make. It requires less effort than aggressive behavior, and it is rather immediately rewarding. Withdrawal from social contacts can act as a kind of insurance against social failure. If one does not try, one cannot fail, and it is better never to have tried at all than to have tried and failed, as far as the individual involved is concerned.

Withdrawal and timidity are of particular educational concern because they are not as disruptive and attention-getting as aggressive behavior. The child who is overly aggressive and combative stands out as an individual whose adjustment to the school situation is not adequate. The withdrawing students, however, are likely to go unnoticed, because their behavior never disrupts the classroom procedures. They annoy no one, mind their own business, and do their own work. The teacher busy with problems of instruction and classroom control can easily overlook the withdrawn student. Perhaps one reason why psychologists consider seclusiveness so serious is the tendency for it to go unnoticed and undealt with until it becomes very serious. Studies indicate that teachers are becoming more and more aware of the significance of shyness and withdrawal as symptoms of maladjustment (Thompson, 1940). Early studies showed a great discrepancy between the attitudes of teachers and psychologists toward social withdrawal and sensitiveness. The greater agreement between the two shown in later studies (Fitzsimmons, 1958) reflects the teachers' increased understanding of the concepts of mental hygiene.

A word of caution is here in order. Not all quiet and retiring people are pathologically involved in withdrawal. The great emphasis on the possible pathological effects of excessive repression and introversion has led to a tendency, in some circles, to view all quiet, unpretentious and meditative people as emotionally disturbed. Because some of the major psychotic syndromes are dominantly withdrawal behavior patterns, unaggressive and introverted people are sometimes in danger of being considered ill and in need of psychological help. It should be indicated, at this point, that children reared in families where parents are quiet and reflective are likely to learn patterns of behavior that are quiet and reflective. The same thing might be said of children in families where the parents are relatively socially withdrawn and shy. The learning of such responses under such conditions is precisely what is to be expected, and we should not regard behavior of this sort as pathological. Withdrawal becomes of pathological concern when it stems from emotional disturbance rather than from family tradition. Reticent and quiet children may be quite happy, and so long as they are not seriously damaging their own personal effectiveness or do not harm the well-being of others, it would seem that the rubric of "individual differences" should cover the situation.

CAUSES OF WITHDRAWAL

It has been indicated that withdrawal may stem from convention and from family patterns of living. The person whose socially isolated behavior results from a prolonged series of reality-oriented learning experiences is not necessarily maladjusted. For many people, moderate social withdrawal and a certain degree of social isolation may represent good adjustments (Sawrey and Telford, 1975).

The more severe defensive withdrawal stems from emotional maladjustment and serves to reduce anxiety. In the broadest terms, the individual who perceives others as sources of pain and discomfort, and who finds that social isolation is less painful or less threatening than social contact, will develop withdrawn and seclusive habits of adjustment. Abusive discipline, excessive physical punishment, verbal mistreatment, and the withholding or withdrawal of affection as the dominant methods of control in childhood are conducive to the development of fear, timidity, and withdrawal.

Children are very resilient, and they can withstand a good deal in the way of physical punishment, neglect, and abuse. There is some evidence that inconsistencies in treatment are more conducive to anxiety and withdrawal than are perpetually painful or punishing situations. A given level of abuse or punishment is less disturbing when the abuse is part of the social culture to which the child is subjected, than if he or she receives the same treatment as the only individual in the family or community so treated. When punishment is universal and apparently inevitable, it may be perceived as part of a rough world that can and must be endured. When a child is sometimes punished and sometimes rewarded by the same people for the same activity, there is little opportunity to learn how to avoid the punishment. The child can, however, learn to avoid the people who administer it. The child can withdraw as much as possible from them, and the response of withdrawal becomes reinforced by the avoidance of abuse. There is evidence that predictable punishment is more tolerable and less fear-arousing than is random and unpredictable punishment (Sawrey, 1961). Severity and inconsistency would appear to be two aspects of punishment that are particularly conducive to withdrawal. If

the pattern of withdrawal is intense or if the number of persons and circumstances to be avoided is great, a generalized habit of withdrawal can
emerge.

WITHDRAWAL FROM REALITY

schizophrenia The schizophrenias are the most severe varieties of
withdrawal. The term *schizophrenia* currently is used to include a large
number of psychotic reactions in which there are fundamental disturbances in reality relationships and in emotional and intellectual processes.
A variety of symptoms may be displayed and, because of this, some investigators feel that the label *schizophrenia* is relatively meaningless. Nevertheless the term persists, and a constellation of behavior patterns is subsumed under the label. The picture of schizophrenic reactions seems to
be one of emotional apathy, indifference, and withdrawal. There is a
marked reduction of interests and attachments and, of course, an impov-
erishment of human relationships. Delusions and hallucinations may develop. It has been observed that the schizophrenic appears to have withdrawn from reality, constructed his or her own inner reality, and moved
into it.

This reaction is more characteristic of adults than of children, the
typical age of onset being reported as between seventeen and twenty-four
years (Kant, 1948). When a comparable reaction occurs before puberty,
it is often designated as *childhood schizophrenia* and is characterized by severe withdrawal, disorganization, lack of affect, and distorted emotional
reactions. The schizophrenic patient has found ways of reducing or
avoiding anxiety, but the means of doing so are unsatisfactory to others.
Their adjustments are extreme and result in personal and social isolation
and insulation. Childhood schizophrenia is not too common, but quite
dramatic. The symptoms are essentially like those occurring in adolescents and adults, and the withdrawal tends to be quite severe.

---

autism | Grace is an extremely frail, overactive nine-year-old with no speech
beyond a few grunts and cries. She is not toilet-trained and cannot
concentrate on anything for more than a few seconds. Her development has been retarded from the first. She is perpetually in motion and has considerable physical agility. When left alone she oc-
cupies herself by roaming around, throwing her arms about,
hugging herself, and making animal-like sounds. Her interest can
be elicited momentarily by moving or bright colored objects. She is
quite fascinated by bright lights. Grace seems to be quite oblivious
to other people, including her parents. She relates to no one and

makes no apparent distinction among individuals. Grace is an autistic child.

Childhood schizophrenia may not be an appropriate category in which to include some schizophrenic-like behavior by children. As a consequence, some early patterns of behavior have been designated as *autistic* (Rutter, 1977, 1978) and such a distinction has been given considerable support (Eme, 1979). Thus, a pattern of early severe withdrawal in children has been termed *infantile autism* (Kanner and Lesser, 1958). Early infantile autism is rarely diagnosed until the second or third year, when it becomes apparent that something has gone awry. Parents of such children frequently report that the infant did not welcome, or resisted, physical contact from a very early age, or that it was a "good" baby and did not require handling or fondling, and that the baby seldom cried or expressed anger. That is, the child failed to develop normal relationships with others. The vocabulary of such children is small, and they may have developed a language of their own. Frequently, these children repeat words or phrases that are spoken to them but make no other response. Their repetition of words and phrases that they hear appears to be mechanical and without intent to communicate. The child resists changes in routine or in the environment in general. These children arrange their own world the way they want it, without regard to the wishes of others. They frequently become engaged in apparently meaningless, routine activity, and are preoccupied with it. Such children react so inadequately to speech and other noises that they are frequently thought to have impaired hearing. They are quite successful in shutting out the external world and responding only to themselves. Autistic children pay little attention to others, including their parents. There seems to be no emotional or personal relationship between mother and child. The child neither seeks nor accepts the usual comforts of maternal companionship, but may wander about aimlessly, even in strange surroundings.

As autistic children approach school age, their condition begins to resemble mental retardation and they are not infrequently so diagnosed. Interruptions in the child's routine, or attempts to establish new ones may result in temper tantrums and essentially unmanageable behavior. Treatment of such children is difficult, and the prognosis is not very good.

Affectional and social development are almost absent in autistic children. Such behavior is usually considered to be learned very early within the family—particularly in interaction with the mother. It would appear that cold or indifferent personal relationships might be characteristic of the family, and indeed this is reported to be so in a sizable number of cases. Many children grow up in such families, but not all become autistic.

Each child, however, does have a unique climate in which to develop, and each does have unique learning experiences. In spite of our tendency to ascribe a dominant role in personality formation to early learning experience, a review of forty years of research on the problem concluded that the research had identified no factors in the parent-child interaction of schizophrenics, neurotics, or those with behavior disorders which could be identified as unique to them or which could distinguish one group from the others, or any of the groups from the families of control subjects (Frank, 1965).

Infantile autism has been described, by some workers, not as severe emotional disturbance or a form of mental illness but rather as a form of mental retardation (Rimland, 1964). According to this position, the autistic child suffers from a cognitive deficiency, from an inability to relate present sensations to past experience. Thus, the child's bizarre and socially inappropriate behavior stems from neurological impairment, an impairment in the function of the reticular system, possibly produced by neonatal hypoxia resulting in vascular damage to genetically predisposed individuals.

The etiology of infantile autism is vague, the symptoms severe and complex, the diagnosis uncertain, treatment not clearly understood, and the prognosis poor. This is not a very rosy picture! The frequency of occurrence of severe infantile autism is not great, but the dramatic nature of the disorder and its resistance to treatment have caused a great deal of attention to be focused on it. Conditioning the child to respond more appropriately has been used with some success (Ferster and De Myer, 1962), and investigations of these procedures for treatment of autistic children continue. Several investigators have reported varying degrees of success in their treatment (Graziano and Kean, 1967; Lovaas and others, 1966; Rutter, 1977).

regression Other forms of withdrawal that may seriously impair personal and social effectiveness include *regression*. Regression, if defined as a return to earlier or less mature behavior, has been called *retrogression* by some investigators. Regression has also been defined as a manifestation of more primitive behavior after having learned and behaved in a more mature fashion. If "primitive behavior" is conceived as behavior that has not necessarily been in the earlier response repertoire of the individual, but is simply a more primitive or rudimentary response, it is probable that regression in this second sense does not occur. The existence of a reservoir of inherited racial or primitive behavior patterns which are potentially arousable under adequate stress, and which display themselves in an individual for the first time after the person is old enough to "regress," is a doubtful hypothesis.

Regression and *regressive behavior* will be used to designate the occurrence of less mature behavior after having learned more mature forms.

When regression is motivated by the desire to withdraw, the behavior tends to become rigid, compulsive, and persistent. That regression does occur when recent, efficient habits are severely thwarted has been demonstrated in lower animals (Hamilton and Krechevsky, 1933; Mowrer, 1940; Masserman, 1946). Children experimentally frustrated during play have been shown to reduce their subsequent play to a much less mature and constructive level. Children differed tremendously in the extent of their regression, but on the average, they regressed to a play level about one-and-one-half years below their previous play patterns (Barker and others, 1941).

Children, as well as adults, may, when faced with severe stress, adopt previously successful or useful behavior. Children are said to regress when they utilize patterns of behavior under stress that they had previously abandoned. Thus, the child faced with the frustrations of school and separation from mother may cry readily, resume the abandoned habit of thumb-sucking, engage in baby talk, have temper tantrums, wet pants, or do whatever has been heretofore successful in obtaining attention and affection.

At later ages, frustration may produce behavior that was previously used and abandoned. Adults may weep over tragedy and become extremely dependent on others. Adults who were overprotected when young may readily return to their earlier overdependency as a means of avoiding hardship and discouragement. Severe regressive reactions may occur under conditions of great stress, and then the individual regresses to a state of rather infantile dependency and helplessness.

case study

George developed quite normally until he was about six years of age. At that time a second child was born to his mother, and his father deserted the family. He has a good vocabulary and talks in a very precise, stilted manner. George walks on tiptoes and gives one the impression that he is always about to fall. He goes around in a detached, preoccupied fashion, talking to himself, and usually is fingering some small object such as a marble or piece of modeling clay. He seems largely detached from the world and eats very little. He only asks that the outside world always be the same. His reactions even to minor changes in the household are extreme and prolonged. He shouts, thrashes about, and tries to put things back as they were. He maintains a minimal awareness of and contact with people. He will react only with a few very familiar and trusted acquaintances. In brief intervals he will display affection, smile, and laugh. However, his contacts with the external world are meager and sporadic. George is exhibiting a form of autistic regression.

daydreaming and fantasy Daydreaming and fantasy are apparently universal human activities (Singer and McCraven, 1961). Daydreaming and fantasy, in and of themselves, are not to be considered as symptomatic of disturbance. However, when they become excessive and wish-fulfilling (autistic) they become effective ways of withdrawing. One can learn to satisfy many of one's desires by such activity, and they can become dominant ways of reacting to threat and stress. The frequency and popularity of daydreaming is understandable in terms of its availability. It can be engaged in by anyone at anytime, unless one is otherwise preoccupied.

Classrooms are particularly conducive to daydreaming because the presence of many children in the same classroom dictates that all remain relatively inactive and quiet. Children can satisfy vicariously many of their wants, wishes, and desires through imaginary activities and fanciful social situations. Dull children and children with visual or auditory handicaps frequently find that they cannot grasp the instruction and tend to cease trying. Bright children find much extra time with little to do. Daydreaming provides a convenient escape from the possibilities of loss of prestige and self-respect because of failure. It also is an adventurous escape from boredom and monotony. Daydreams are the imaginative fulfillment of wishes and are, therefore, always satisfying. They can be tough competition for school routines. Daydreaming actually does little to aid in the solution of problems, but it serves as an effective temporary escape from the unpleasant impingement of reality. In the extreme, fantasy and daydreaming can provide individuals with a comfortable imaginary world of their own in which to live.

LEARNED HELPLESSNESS

Expectancies concerning the consequences of one's acts and beliefs concerning the causes of those consequences have been established as important determiners of motivation, learning, and achievement (Dweck and Reppucci, 1973). Two types of beliefs concerning relevant expectancies have been dichotomized. One is the expectancy of either negative or positive reinforcements following particular acts. The other refers to the extent that individuals perceive themselves as the important causal agent in determining the observed outcomes. If individuals attribute behavioral outcomes to their own acts, they are said to display internal reinforcement responsibility; if they attribute these outcomes to other forces (other people, the external environment, or chance) they are said to display external reinforcement responsibility (DuCette and Walk, 1973; Nowicki and Strickland, 1974). Some more extreme outcomes of building up minimal expectancies of reinforcement have been conceptualized as "learned helplessness" (Seligman, 1973; Miller and Seligman, 1973).

The phenomenon of learned helplessness was first observed in experimental animals. It had been noted, for some time, that administering inescapable trauma to both animals and humans often resulted in a subsequent complete failure to make any overt response even in situations where the punishment was avoidable (Maier and Seligman, 1976). In other situations, animals, in one case dogs, subjected to less traumatic punishment would not become immobilized, but would take the punishment while simply whining or howling. The animals seemed to give up; they had learned that they were helpless. Subsequent experiments have produced learned helplessness in many kinds of animals, ranging from cockroaches to college students.

Seligman (1973) proposed that passivity, the most prominent symptom of depression, may be the result of prior life experiences in controlling the environment. According to this interpretation, depressed individuals make fewer responses—they become apathetic and, when they do respond, they do not expect to succeed, they misinterpret success as failure, or they perceive success as purely a chance result. The depressives self perception is that of a "born loser."

Research studies have obtained results consistent with this interpretation of depression. In these studies the subjects were given either soluble problems sufficiently easy to ensure successes or insoluble problems and then subsequently provided with either success-possible or success-impossible additional tasks. The response decrements and persistence in the face of repeated failure characteristic of these subjects were then related to their scores on an Intellectual Achievement Responsibility Scale in one study (Dweck and Reppucci, 1973) and to scores on the Beck Depression Inventory in the other (Miller and Seligman, 1973). The results of these studies showed that the subjects who showed the greatest work decrements and least persistence following failure were those who took less personal responsibility for the outcome of their actions (externals), whereas those who accepted more responsibility for the behavioral outcomes (internals) persisted longer and showed less work decrement following failure experiences. The depressed subjects perceived success and failure (reinforcement) as more independent of their personal efforts and acts than did nondepressed subjects. Also, as predicted, the depressed subjects showed less change in expectancies of success following success experiences than did the nondepressed subjects. The more depressed the subjects, the greater were their tendencies to perceive success and failure as independent of their own acts. Depression had a persistent and predictable perceptual-distortion effect on the consequences of their acts.

The results of these studies are consistent with the clinical observation that depressives selectively forget or devalue success experiences and have a high expectation of failure.

Speculating on these research findings, Seligman (1973) suggested that people resistant to depression have probably had extensive success experiences and have been able to control and manipulate many of the sources of satisfaction in their lives. Such individuals are able to view the future optimistically. An unpredictable world without mastery produces vulnerability to pessimism and depression. Seligman (1973) also suggests that the pervasiveness of pessimism and depression may be the result of an affluent society in which reinforcements (things and experiences) are received independently of the behavior of those who receive them—a kind of goodies-from-Heaven attitude. Rewards as well as punishments that come independently of one's efforts can induce an attitude of "learned helplessness" and depression.

Research into the basic mechanisms producing the learned helplessness phenomenon continues (Clifford, 1979; Jackson, Maier, and Coon, 1979) and the relevance of the phenomena among the handicapped has been given emphasis (Rosen, Clark, and Kivitz, 1977).

AGGRESSION

Aggressive behavior may be designated either as a type of overt behavior or as a particular kind of motivated activity. If the emphasis is on the motivation for the activity, as opposed to the overt behavior itself, aggressive behavior implies hostility. It represents activity intended to injure or destroy a person or his possessions. In the broader sense, aggressive behavior can be conceived of as an *approach,* as contrasted with *avoidance* behavior. In this sense, aggressive behavior is not necessarily hostile, and may simply derive from the learning of aggressive (approach and attack) responses from cultural experience.

Much aggressive behavior results from social practices which reinforce the behavior. Behavior may be viewed by the general public as aggressive and hostile, even though it results from social learning and is not necessarily emotion-laden or emotional in origin. Aggressive behavior that exceeds socially approved limits may be the manifestation of response patterns acquired in a family, community, or subculture which encourages such behavior. When patterns of aggression are so acquired, the children are taught to be aggressive. Boys gain status with their parents, family, and peers through aggression and attack. Not only does the boy defend himself aggressively, he may seek out opportunities to assert himself and improve his status by dominating others. Such aggression may become a way of life and a means of seeking status. In the broader culture, the aggressive responses so acquired (fighting, sexual aggressiveness, legal misdemeanors) may meet with resistance and punishment. As a result of such frustration, the person may respond with increased aggression. His increased aggressiveness, resulting from frustration, may be hostile in nature, whereas the original behavior may not have been hostile or emotionally instigated.

HOSTILE AGGRESSION

Hostile aggression is probably always the result of some kind of frustration. It was early hypothesized that frustration invariably resulted in aggressive behavior (Dollard and others, 1939). This position was revised a short time later by the same investigators to allow for other types of responses to frustration (Miller, 1941). Although aggression is not the inevitable consequence of frustration, real or threatened frustrations remain the principal causes of hostile aggression.

frustration A great variety of circumstances are frustrating. Frustrating events and circumstances can be divided into three varieties for purposes of study (Sawrey and Telford, 1975): frustration by delay; frustration by thwarting; and frustration by conflict.

Frustration by *delay* is produced by withholding from an individual the rewards that have previously followed a given sequence of behavior. Small or short delays are more frustrating to children and young adults than to older persons, and they react more dramatically. Delays may result in vigorous protests. Infants particularly, are pretty helpless. They have not yet learned that delay may be unavoidable or that it is only temporary. They may react emphatically, with protest, crying, temper, or attack. As they mature, the severity of the consequences of delay diminish, but delay remains an important cause of frustration. Experimental investigations confirm the frustrating effects of delay of rewards on animals (Amsel, 1958) and on humans (Sears, Hovland, and Miller, 1940).

Frustration by *thwarting* occurs when purposeful behavior is interfered with, interrupted, or prevented. The physically restrained infant struggles and cries. Many rules, regulations, and restrictions imposed by society may prevent or interfere with motivated behavior and result in frustration. Some frustrating obstacles to performance may be physical characteristics of the individual—a physical handicap, being too small or too large, ineptness, obesity, clumsiness, or illness. Social and economic sources of thwarting are many and varied, and constitute important barriers to motivated behavior.

Motivated behavior also may be thwarted by *conflict*. The basic conflictual situation involves the presence of two incompatible possibilities of response in a situation when each, if present alone, would yield a response (Verplank, 1957). Conflict is an inevitable consequence of life. The frustrations resulting from conflict cannot be avoided completely, even in the best organized and regulated of societies. Choices must be made, decisions must be rendered, and behavior frequently may be difficult to reconcile with values. Conflict, as an important source of frustration, has received a great deal of attention from psychologists, and the interested reader will have no difficulty in locating literature relevant to the topic.

As children grow up, they are conditioned to become frustrated by an expanded series of stimuli. Stimuli accompanying or preceding actual physical thwarting agents operate as conditioned stimuli for frustration. Words, gestures, facial expressions, intonations, and threats that accompany or precede thwarting come to act as effective agents of frustration. Thus, actual delay, thwarting, prevention, or conflict need not occur in order to produce the response. The threat of any of these produces frustration.

forms of aggression Aggressive responses to frustration may take a variety of forms. Apparently, the initial and original response to thwarting is a diffuse, chaotic, emotional outburst. This angry outburst seems to be neither purposive nor directive. It consists of squirming, twisting, throwing the arms and legs about, and crying. With maturity and experience, the aggressive response to frustration becomes less random and more *directed, purposeful,* and *retaliative.* The responses come to be directed toward the thwarting agent and are intended to eliminate, remove, or diminish the effectiveness of the restriction. The child physically attacks the restricting agent by hitting, kicking, or biting.

Most children soon learn that an *indirect* attack on the thwarting agent is often more strategic than is a direct attack. Consequently, a child may hide a possession of the mother or father, or may destroy something of theirs, in retaliation for being thwarted. When big brother restricts the child's activities, the child may appeal to mother or father to punish the brother, rather than personally attacking him. Some children learn to feign injury at the hands of a brother or sister in order to get father or mother to punish the older or younger sibling. Children learn to use threats aggressively, as does the two-year-old boy who, on being prevented from doing something by his father, pulls at the lamp cord and pretends that he will tip it over. When orderliness is emphasized by the mother, she may find that her child, when frustrated, will create chaos in a room by moving furniture and throwing or scattering objects around. When children are frustrated, they make indirect physical attacks by engaging in disapproved behavior calculated to annoy their frustrators.

Indirect physical attack may take the form of the well-known temper tantrum. Young children, when frustrated, may cry, scream, fall to the floor, thrash and kick, and even violently bang their heads on the wall or floor. Parental alarm over such behavior may reinforce it, and the behavior may be perpetuated either by their alarm or by their acquiescence to their child's demands. Some severe tantrums may also be interpreted as representing a failure of the child to learn more sophisticated ways of responding to frustration. Viewed in such a fashion, the *diffuse, chaotic, emotional outburst,* characteristic of early responses to frustration, persists as a consequence of immaturity and derives from an absence of social learning rather than resulting from it.

Children usually learn through experience that either direct or indirect physical attack on the person restricting one's activity is not always the wisest approach to the problem. If the person who is causing the frustration is larger, stronger, or more skillful, direct physical attack invites counterattack, resulting in further frustration and increased punishment. Consequently, with the development of language, a verbal attack on the thwarting agent may be substituted for direct or indirect physical retaliation. This really is attack at a symbolic level. Calling the person names, swearing at him, and "cutting him down to size" verbally are symbolic aggressive responses to frustration. In addition to verbal responses to thwarting, other symbolic retaliative aggressive responses, such as making faces, sticking out one's tongue, or thumbing one's nose, may be employed. A further extension of symbolic aggression evolves when it is learned that *indirect symbolic aggression* can serve to damage others without immediately endangering oneself. Instead of swearing at or calling someone names directly, we tell derogatory stories, start malicious rumors, and otherwise undermine their reputation. We attack the status and the good name of the person thwarting us, rather than make a direct attack. We may also attack another person indirectly by belittling or discrediting their possessions, family, friends, beliefs, ideas, or ideals.

In the extreme, indirect hostile responses toward one's own family whom one believes to be thwarting may take the form of personal immorality, delinquency, or criminality. The behavior serves to discredit the family and to besmirch its otherwise good reputation. The delinquency and distressing eccentricity of some adolescents and adults may represent such indirect hostile forms of aggression.

case study   The case of William is illustrative of asocial aggression. William is an extremely well-built, active eleven-year-old boy. He is always active—climbing trees, scaling walls, exploring the attic. He lies a great deal and perpetrates petty thievery for things he can afford and does not need. He leads boys older than himself in escapades that are dangerous, illegal, and carry considerable likelihood of detection. His relationships with people are superficial. He asks little of others but can be quite ingratiating at times and can lie himself out of most incriminating situations. When caught in delinquencies he shows no remorse. His escapades seem to provide an opportunity to demonstrate his physical prowess and his adroitness in manipulating others.

pathological aggression Children displaying pathological aggressiveness as a way of life have been described dramatically by Bettelheim (1950) and by Redl and Wineman (1951, 1952). The children described by these authors are largely incapable of rational control of their own behavior. They have either failed to develop any inner controls, or their normal behavior controls have been destroyed by the inconsistencies of their social environment when they were young. They have become victims of their own aggressive impulses and are largely controlled by them. Aggression seems to be their only way of reacting to life and its stresses. They erupt into reckless destruction or blind rage at the slightest provocation. Their anxieties, fears, and guilt feelings all manifest themselves in aggressiveness which often involves repeating the same acts which produced their guilt feelings in the first place.

Having had a pleasurable social experience, they do not seem to be able to remember it and realize the possibility of its repetition. They seem incapable of profiting from social experience despite normal intelligence. They cannot delay satisfaction. If their desires are not immediately gratified, they react with hostility and violence. The causes of their failures and their hostilities are all projected outward, in paranoid fashion. Everyone and everything is perceived as threatening, and they react to the perceived hostile and punishing world with counterhostility.

Manifestations of affection and good will toward these individuals are interpreted either as signs of an enemy's weakness or as tricks designed to deceive them. Offers of assistance are met with unreasonable demands for more and, if the demands are not met, the inevitable explosion of hate is set off. They neither request nor accept help. These "psychopaths" have proved to be resistant to treatment because of the consolidation of their intense hostility into a pattern of defensive reactions against any offers of help from others. They are seriously emotionally disturbed, behave in ways that are socially and personally destructive, and resist treatment and overtures of assistance.

familial correlates of aggression Overaggressive, antisocial individuals consistently have been reported to have come from early environments characterized by parental rejection, permissiveness of aggression, lack of parental supervision, a low level of parental expectation, parental social deviance, parental dissatisfaction with the child's role in life, family discord, inconsistent treatment, and the use of physically painful punishment or threats of physical punishment (Glueck and Glueck, 1950; Bandura and Walters, 1959; McCord, McCord, and Zola, 1959; McCord, McCord, and Howard, 1961; Berkowitz, 1958, 1962).

These research findings are consistent with the interpretation of overaggression as either a reaction to excessive frustration or a product of social learning. The list of parental practices found in the background of aggressive children provides a picture of a background for the learning of aggression as a way of life. Patterns of aggression developing under such conditions can be considered essentially nonhostile in nature and social in origin. Several of the familial correlates of aggression also constitute excessive frustration of a kind that instigate hostile aggression. The use of physically painful punishment, frequent threats, parental rejection, and parental bickering and disagreement about methods of child rearing with resulting inconsistencies in treatment, provide a favorable background for the development of hostile, retaliative aggression.

The studies of aggression in children uniformly disclose that both social learning and excessive aggression-instigating factors in the home contribute to the development of overaggressiveness in the child. When aggressive behavior is thwarted by the broader society, the person's cultural aggressiveness may become confounded with hostile and retaliative behavior. The result is both personally and culturally damaging. A more complete discussion of aggression can be found in Sawrey and Telford, 1975.

DELINQUENCY

Delinquency may derive essentially from the social learning of deviant patterns of response or from hostility arising from frustration. The two are probably never discrete categories of delinquent behavior, but the social aspects have been emphasized by certain researchers (Cloward and Ohlin, 1960; Gibbons and Garrity, 1962) and the essentially psychological factors by others (Glueck and Glueck, 1950; Argyle, 1961). No doubt both psychological and sociological factors are significant in the etiology of juvenile delinquency (Hathaway and Monachesi, 1963). It is extremely difficult to determine when the principal influences are sociological factors and when they are psychological, because of the difficulties in distinguishing between the two classes of factors. It would seem that when the social-learning factors considered to be primarily responsible for the subsequent behavior are readily discernible, there is a tendency to call the delinquency social. When the factors are subtle and cannot be readily identified, psychological or personality variables are invoked. One method of classification has to do with whether the delinquency can be classified as "social" or "solitary." However, some delinquents are neither purely social nor purely solitary in their delinquent acts.

If the delinquent comes from a background of social, economic, and educational deprivation where delinquency is common (a "bad" family background), social-learning factors are invoked and it is found that such delinquents are more likely to commit delinquent acts in groups or gangs (social delinquency). If the delinquent comes from a family which provides adequate social, economic, and educational opportunities (a "good" family background), psychological explanations are offered, and it is found that there is a tendency for such delinquency to be solitary. But the "good" family may be providing a social-learning situation that is no better than that of the "bad" family. The two familial situations are grossly different, but each may be the training ground for social deviance.

THE COMPLEXITY OF DELINQUENCY

Whether juvenile delinquency be defined in a legalistic manner (behavior on the part of a child between seven and seventeen which violates existing law) or simply as engaging in antisocial or asocial aggressive behavior unapproved by the community, the problem is a complex one. As we have already indicated, overaggressiveness and delinquency may stem from either social learning or frustration. The available statistics on delinquency pose problems both of reliability and validity. There is tremendous variation in the laws of the several states, policies of courts, police, schools, and other social agencies. There is no universally accepted method of identifying, classifying, or treating delinquent behavior. The incidence of hidden, or undiscovered, delinquency is not known. Many, if not most adult males tell tales of their youth that involve undetected delinquent acts. In a study by Murphy, Shirley, and Witmer (1946), case studies of 114 boys over a five-year period were reported. Of these boys, only thirteen had been involved in no delinquent activity, to the case worker's knowledge. The remaining 101 had been involved in 6,416 legal infractions, although only 95 of these infractions had led to legal complaints involving police or court action. Other investigators report essentially the same sort of findings. In an investigation of 1,700 law-abiding men and women, it was reported that almost all admit to having committed illegal offenses, and two-thirds had engaged in behavior legally defined as felonious (Wallerstein and Wyle, 1947). It is contended that although all juvenile delinquents participate in some kind of antisocial behavior, the majority mature into socially conforming adults.

It has already been indicated that delinquency involves both social and psychological factors. Factors in the home, the family, the school, and the community, as well as the psychological factors of frustration, hostility, and aggressive retaliation, are all involved. There seems to be no one clear picture of delinquency or the delinquent. Children from lower, middle, and upper classes become delinquent, as do both sexes. Boys are much more frequently identified as delinquent than are girls—four or five times as frequently.

One of the problems of the delinquent is the social climate of the American culture. We place great emphasis on achievement and competition. Aggressiveness is thus rewarded, but at the same time our culture insists on conformity and cooperation. Learning when and how to compete and to conform is not an easy task for many children, or for adults.

Early investigators saw delinquency as being spawned in the underprivileged and lower-class environments. Others have emphasized faulty home factors, child-rearing practices, and parent-child relationships as productive of delinquency. Still others have emphasized the excessive competitive striving in our culture. Personality variables have been studied, with conflicting results. Attempts to predict delinquency and to develop delinquency-predicting instruments have been less than promising (Bothman, Hartinger, and Richardson, 1965). Delinquency is becoming more common in the so-called better homes and communities. New patterns of delinquency are attributed to our changing times. Communications media are said to influence the young toward greater competitiveness, aggressiveness, and delinquency. A search for simple causes of delinquent behavior seems doomed to failure, for the causes appear to be many.

Considering the many-faceted background of the development of delinquency, it would appear that corrective approaches and preventive approaches will also have to be many-faceted. Recent emphasis on the education and behavior correction of delinquents has been on the individual treatment of the individual deviate. Although there may be a certain commonality of background among overly aggressive and delinquent youngsters, each still has his or her own wants, wishes, desires, frustrations, and ambitions. Emphasis on understanding the individual delinquent in his or her unique circumstance should prove helpful in both corrective and educational practice.

THE HYPERACTIVE CHILD

case study "I would just like to give up and run away from my problem," said Mrs. Ellis. "Today our son, Erik, was kicked off his soccer team. I don't know what to do next! He has to have something to do weekends and after school. If he stays at home he drives us all crazy. I called the Y but they said that he would not fit into their program. Last year they sent him home from summer camp because the counselors couldn't handle him. They said he had too many problems! Last week his report card arrived. It gets worse every term. According to the school psychologist, Erik is a bright, intelligent boy capable of doing excellent work, but unable to do so because of his incessant overactivity and destructiveness. He has always been a problem. His father and I have hardly had a full night's sleep since he was born. He always slept little and was very restless—always crying and wanting something else. His father thinks he will out-grow it. He says I don't understand boys. However, when I see Erik playing soccer or at school I think I understand why others react to him as they do. He always has to be first. He has to be boss. He will not let others take their turns. Everything must go his way. When things don't go his way, he changes the rules to suit himself. In school he is unable to sit still for a minute and is continually getting up, moving around the room, and bothering the other children. He is unable to concentrate on his schoolwork and consequently never finishes his assignments. The intensity and constancy of his hyper-activity arouses strong feelings and counterreactions in everyone with whom he comes in contact."

Following a thorough psychiatric and neurological examination Erik was started on very small doses of medication. He also was placed in a therapeutic activity program with five other children with similar problems. Mr. and Mrs. Ellis agreed to participate in a series of conferences for parents whose children had school-related problems.

At the end of the school year Erik's overactivity was consider-ably diminished, his school work had improved, and he had been accepted back on the soccer team. Mrs. Ellis was feeling much better about herself and her son. Mr. Ellis was skeptical about the value of the parents' group but reluctantly agreed to participate again in the fall. Erik is considered to be a hyperactive child.

Many children are termed *hyperactive* by their parents and other non-professional observers and it is probably true that most such designations result from the tendency toward high levels of activity by children in gen-eral, and adult lack of understanding or impatience with this aspect of child behavior. These, typically, are not the children who are considered to be hyperactive or hyperkinetic by professionals. The American Psychi-atric Association (1980) *Diagnostic and Statistical Manual (DSMIII)* has changed the designation of this disorder to "attention disorder deficit with hyperactivity." This, in effect, serves to emphasize the importance of the problem of attending in the general syndrome.

Although at different ages different symptoms appear as the more exaggerated in that particular developmental period of the hyperactive child, in general the characteristics of hyperactivity are considered to be as follows:

1. excessive general hyperactivity for the child's age. This hyperactivity may take the forms of incessant haphazard, impulsive, climbing, crawling, or

running, as well as fidgeting and inability to sit still. These behaviors differ from the norm for the ages of the child both in quantity and quality.

2. difficulty in sustaining attention and forgetfulness. The child has difficulty sustaining attention adequately to complete tasks, or approaches tasks in a disorganized manner and attends inadequately to tasks in unsupervised situations. The child frequently "forgets" to carry out assignments or to do things that are expected or demanded.

3. impulsive behavior. Such behavior, typically, is manifested in at least two of the following ways: sloppy work even when effort appears adequate; frequently speaking out of turn or making inappropriate noises in class; frequent interruption of other children's activities or conversations; difficulty in "taking turns" in games and group situations; low frustration tolerance, and fighting with others because of low frustration tolerance.

4. the duration of the hyperactive behavior is at least one year. Excessive activity resulting from situational or transient environmental circumstances is common to children but hyperactive children exhibit excessive activity over an extended period.

Few children display all of the above enumerated characteristics. Hyperactive children, typically, exhibit many but not all of these behaviors. Some hyperactive children have attentional problems with schoolwork but are capable of giving sustained attention to tasks they enjoy doing at home. Indeed, hyperactivity is not a homogeneous syndrome but there do appear to be sufficient common elements in the condition to make the category meaningful (Loney, Langhorne, and Paternite, 1978).

Regardless of any labels used to identify or classify the hyperkinetic child, one major symptom apparent even to the untrained observer is hyperactivity. The hyperactivity is of quality as well as quantity. The hyperactive child seems driven—as if there were an "inner tornado" so that the behavior is beyond the child's control. In addition to the predominance of hyperactivity and short attention span, such children often are described as being temperamental, impulsive, and demonstrate perceptual and/or motor impairment. Although hyperactive children may be normal or superior in intellectual ability they are extremely distractable.

INCIDENCE AND ETIOLOGY

The United States Office of Child Development estimates that 3 percent of elementary school children exhibit the symptoms of this syndrome sufficiently to be classified as "hyperkinetic." No geographic region or social class seems to be without such children. The problem appears to be mainly that of young children in that all but the most severe cases seem to improve significantly by early adulthood. More males than females are affected. It is not known why this is true but it may be an exaggeration of the male propensity for higher activity levels. Boys over girls affected have been reported in ratios of 5:1 to 9:1 (Weiss and Hechtman, 1979). The etiology of hyperactivity is unknown. Various factors are probably operative, some of which are social, some biological, and some psychological. Different factors may predominate in any given case and thus the necessity of taking into account the complex interactions among the child's environment, psychological factors, and biological status has been emphasized (Weiss and Hechtman, 1979). Emphasis has been given biological factors (Waldrop, Bell, McLaughlin, and Halverson, 1978); however, the familial and school environment are crucial variables affecting the child's behavioral aberrations (Weiss and Hechtman, 1979).

TREATMENT AND OUTCOME

The use of medication, particularly certain stimulants, in the treatment of such children has been common (Cole, 1975), although the efficacy of these drugs in the treatment of all hyperactive children has been questioned. It is generally accepted that certain drugs, such as dextroamphetamine and methylphenidate (Ritalin), improve various symptoms in a majority of hyperactive children. The use of stimulants with hyperactive children to reduce their hyperactivity was referred to as a paradoxical effect because such stimulants usually tend to increase rather than decrease general activity (Campbell and Randall, 1977). However, even among normal children a single dose of these stimulants tends to reduce rather than increase activity level (Rapoport and others, 1979). The paradox may be more of a developmental phenomenon than one related specifically to the syndrome. The mechanisms by which these drugs produce behavioral changes is not known. Stimulant medication is probably not sufficient in its effect to produce long-term favorable outcomes unless combined with other forms of therapy, such as behavioral or psychological therapy, and counseling. The prognosis for hyperactive children is not particularly good as they mature into adolescents, although significant changes tend to occur by early adulthood. Few hyperactive children become grossly disturbed or criminal adults; however, they do continue to have various symptoms of hyperactivity (Weiss and Hechtman, 1979).

School presents a particular problem for the hyperactive. They can do quite well in most preschool situations where considerable individualized attention is given and activity and freedom of movement are permitted. As the child moves into the elementary school less freedom is permitted, more directed attention and sustained effort are required, and demands become more specific. This results in a very real pressure situation for the child and school achievement and behavior are affected. With the cooperation of medical, psychological, and educational personnel, satisfactory programs of treatment, training, and education can be worked out for these children in the school and the home.

SUMMARY

All individuals are subjected to frustration and stress in the course of daily living. People develop a variety of means for coping with frustration and stress. The more routinized of these have come to be known as defense mechanisms. If this behavior does not become too rigid or exclusive, it can be considered as a portion of adaptive living. If it becomes a dominant way of responding to social stimuli, it is symptomatic of emotional disturbance.

A distinction is generally made between the emotionally disturbed and the socially maladjusted. The emotionally disturbed exhibit patterns of behavior sufficiently different from other children reared in similar circumstances so that their behavior is considered personally and socially deviant. Their behavior may range from aggressive destructiveness to rather complete social withdrawal. Socially maladjusted children are chronic violators of broad cultural mores and social values. They acquire their behavior patterns through social learning. They behave according to the standards of their subgroup, but those standards and values are deviant from those of the broader culture.

Responses generated by emotional disturbance were grouped under three broad headings: anxiety; withdrawal; and aggression.

Chronically anxious people present a complex array of symptoms. The individuals are fearful and apprehensive, without really knowing why. Chronic anxiety sufferers are irritable, jumpy, and easily upset by disturbances in their routine. They have problems in sleeping, suffer from chronic fatigue and gastrointestinal disturbances, and may tremble or perspire for no apparent reason. Many stimuli produce anxiety in the chronically anxious. They may suffer attacks of acute anxiety. Phobic reactions—acute, specific fears—are not uncommon among the highly anxious. Compulsions to commit particular acts and obsessive thoughts are also common among persons suffering from anxiety.

Withdrawal is learned in the same way that other social responses are learned. In withdrawal, the individual learns to avoid social contacts. Withdrawal and timidity have received extra attention because they may be symptomatic of severe emotional problems. It should be remembered, however, that shy, unobtrusive behavior may be learned in families that are essentially quiet and withdrawn. Not all withdrawn persons are emotionally disturbed. They may have learned to live a less socially oriented existence and be quite well-adjusted to it.

Serious withdrawal may be precipitated by abusive discipline, excessive physical punishment, verbal mistreatment, and the withholding of affection. The most serious form of withdrawal is withdrawal from reality, as in schizophrenia. A pattern of early severe withdrawal in children has been termed *infantile autism*. Such withdrawal patterns are extremely personally damaging and resistant to treatment. The background of both schizophrenia and infantile autism is but vaguely understood.

Daydreaming and fantasy were treated as minor forms of withdrawal. Withdrawal in the form of regression to earlier modes of acquired responding has been experimentally demonstrated. It is a not uncommon, transient phenomenon in children who are frustrated and overly dependent on parents for emotional support.

Learned helplessness was discussed in relation to withdrawal and depression and as a result of reinforced helpless behavior.

Much aggressive behavior results from social practices that reinforce aggression. Such patterns of behavior are best understood as social aggression that does not necessarily entail frustration or hostility. It is simply a learned way of coping with the world. Some subcultural patterns of social behavior are predominantly aggressive, and overt aggression is a way of life in such subcultures.

Hostile aggression is a result of frustration. It has an emotional basis and may be retaliative. Frustration can be divided into three classes for purposes of study. Basically, frustration is produced by delay, thwarting, and conflict.

The initial response to thwarting is a diffuse, chaotic, emotional outburst. As development and learning take place, direct attack and means of indirect attack are acquired. The temper tantrum may be conceived of as either an indirect physical attack or as a primitive emotional outburst. Symbolic and indirect symbolic aggression develop as the person becomes more sophisticated. Aggressiveness can develop into a severely damaging way of life. Such pathological aggression has received a good deal of investigative attention. Psychopathic behavior, once developed, is difficult to change.

The familial correlates of aggression have been extensively investigated. Researchers are fairly well agreed about the kinds of family relationships giving rise to excessively aggressive behavior. Studies of aggression in children uniformly disclose that both social learning and excessive aggression-instigating factors in the home contribute to overaggressiveness in children.

Delinquency, like aggressive behavior in general, can be understood as aggressive, hostile behavior or as a culturally acquired way of life. *Social delinquency* is the label usually applied to the latter form. Delinquency is an ill-defined research area, and one to which a variety of disciplines can and do contribute. The phenomenon is not well understood, and a great deal of research is needed to clarify the concept and shed better light on its etiology, prevention, and treatment.

Much recent emphasis has been given the hyperactive child and a good deal of research literature as well as polemic writing has resulted. Hyperactive children present very real problems for themselves, their families, and the school.

REFERENCES

American Psychiatric Association, *Diagnostic and Statistical Manual DSM III* (Washington, D. C.: American Psychiatric Association, 1980).

Amsel, A., "The Role of Frustrative Nonreward in Noncontinuous Reward Situations," *Psychological Bulletin,* 1958, *55,* 102–19.

Argyle, M., "A New Approach to the Classification of Delinquents with Implications for Treatment," *Inquiries Concerning Kinds of Treatment for Kinds of Delinquents,* Monog. 2, Board of Corrections, State of California, July 1961, 15–26.

Bandura, A. and R. Walters, *Adolescent Aggression* (New York: The Ronald Press Company, 1959).

Barker, R., T. Dembo, and K. Lewin, "Frustration and Regression: An Experiment with Young Children," *University of Iowa Study of Child Welfare,* 1941, *18,* no. 1.

Berkowitz, L., *Aggression: A Social Psychological Analysis* (New York: McGraw-Hill, 1962).

Berkowitz, L., "The Expression and Reduction of Hostility," *Psychological Bulletin,* 1958, *55,* 257–83.

Bettelheim, B., *Love Is Not Enough* (New York: The Free Press, 1950).

Bothman, R. W., W. Hartinger, and H. Richardson, "A Comparison of Two Delinquency Predicting Instruments," *Journal of Research of Crime and Delinquency,* 1965, *2,* 45–48.

Cameron, N., *The Psychology of Behavior Disorders* (Boston: Houghton Mifflin, 1947).

Campbell, B. A. and P. J. Randall, "Paradoxical Effects of Amphetamine on Preweanling and Postweanling Rats," *Science,* 1977, *195,* 888–91.

Clifford, M., "Effects of Failure: Alternative Explanations and Possible Implications," *Educational Psychologist,* 1979, *14,* 44–52.

Cloward, R. A. and L. E. Ohlin, *Delinquency and Opportunity* (New York: The Free Press, 1960).

Cole, S. O., "Hyperactive Children, The Use of Stimulant Drugs Evaluated," *American Journal of Orthopsychiatry,* 1975, *45,* 28–37.

Dweck, C. S. and D. Reppucci, "Learned Helplessness and Reinforcement Responsibility in Children," *Journal of Personality and Social Psychology,* 1973, *25,* 109–16.

Dollard, J., L. W. Doob, N. E., Miller, O. H. Mowrer, and R. R. Sears, *Frustration and Aggression* (New Haven: Yale University Press, 1939).

Ducette, J. and S. Walk, "Cognitive and Motivational Correlates of Generalized Expectancies for Control," *Journal of Personality and Social Psychology,* 1973, *26,* 420–26.

Eme, R. F., "Sex Differences in Childhood Psychopathology: A Review," *Psychological Bulletin,* 1979, *86,* 574–95.

Ferster, C. B. and M. K. De Myer, "A Method for the Experimental Analysis of the Behavior of Autistic Children," *American Journal of Orthopsychiatry,* 1962, *32,* 89–98.

Fitzsimmons, M. J., "The Predictive Value of Teachers' Referrals," in M. Krugman, ed., *Orthopsychiatry and the School* (New York: American Orthopsychiatric Association, 1958).

Frank, G. H., "The Role of the Family in the Development of Psychopathology," *Psychological Bulletin,* 1965, *69,* 191–205.

Freud, S., *Inhibition, Symptoms and Anxiety* (London: The Hogarth Press, Ltd., 1936).

Freud, S., *A General Introduction to Psychoanalysis* (Garden City, N. Y.: Garden City Publishing Company, 1938).

Gibbons, D. C. and D. L. Garrity, "Definition and Analysis of Certain Criminal Types," *Journal of Criminal Law, Criminology, Police Science,* 1962, *53,* 27–35.

Glueck, S. and E. Glueck, *Unraveling Juvenile Delinquency* (New York: Commonwealth Fund, 1950).

Graziano, A. M. and J. E. Kean, "Programmed Relaxation and Reciprocal Inhibition with Psychotic Children," in *Proceedings of the 75th Annual Convention of the American Psychological Association,* 1967, *2,* 253–54.

Hamilton, J. A. and I. Krechevsky, "Studies on the Effects of Shock upon Behavior Plasticity in the Rat," *Journal of Comparative and Physiological Psychology,* 1933, *16,* 237–53.

Hathaway, S. R. and E. D. Monachesi, *Adolescent Personality and Behavior: MMPI Patterns of Normal, Delinquent, Dropout, and Other Outcomes* (Minneapolis, Minn.: University of Minnesota Press, 1963).

Hollingshead, A. B. and R. C. Redlich, *Social Class and Mental Illness* (New York: John Wiley, 1958).

Horney, K., *The Neurotic Personality of Our Time* (New York: W. W. Norton, 1937).

Jackson, R. L., S. F. Maier, and D. J. Coon, "Long-term Analgesic Effects of Inescapable Shock and Learned Helplessness," *Science*, 1979, *206*, 91–93.

Kanner, L. and L. Lesser, "Early Infantile Autism," *Pediatric Clinics of North America*, 1958, *5*, 711–30.

Kant, O., "Clinical Investigations of Simple Schizophrenia," *Psychiatric Quarterly*, 1948, *22*, 141–51.

Kvaraceus, W. C. and W. B. Miller, *Delinquent Behavior: Culture and the Individual* (Washington, D. C.: National Education Association, Juvenile Delinquency Project, 1959).

Kvaraceus, W. C. and W. C. Ulrich, *Delinquent Behavior: Principles and Practices* (Washington, D. C.: National Education Association, Juvenile Delinquency Project, 1959).

Loney, J., L. Langhorne, and C. Paternite, "An Empirical Basis for Subgrouping the Hyperkinetic/Minimal Brain Dysfunction Syndrome," *Journal of Abnormal Psychology*, 1978, *87*, 431–41.

Lovaas, O. I., G. Freitag, M. I. Kinder, B. D. Rubenstein, B. Schaeffer, and J. Q. Simmons, "Establishment of Social Reinforcing in Two Schizophrenic Children on the Basis of Food," *Journal of Experimental Child Psychology*, 1966, *4*, 109–25.

Lundin, R. W., *Principles of Psychopathology* (Columbus, O.: Charles E. Merrill, 1965).

Maier, S. F. and M. E. P. Seligman, "Learned Helplessness: Theory and Evidence," *Journal of Experimental Psychology: General*, 1976, *105*, 3–46.

Masserman, J. J., *Principles of Dynamic Psychiatry* (Philadelphia, Pa.: W. B. Saunders Co., 1946).

McCord, W., J. S. McCord, and A. Howard, "Familial Correlates of Aggression in Nondelinquent Male Children," *Journal of Abnormal and Social Psychology*, 1961, *62*, 79–93.

McCord, W., J. S. McCord, and I. Zola, *Origins of Crime* (New York: Columbia University Press, 1959).

Miller, N. E., "The Frustration-Aggression Hypothesis," *Psychological Review*, 1941, *38*, 337–42.

Miller, W. R. and M. E. P. Seligman, "Depression and the Perception of Reinforcement," *Journal of Abnormal Psychology*, 1973, *82*, 62–63.

Mowrer, O. H., "An Experimental Analogue of 'Regression' with Incidental Observations on 'Reaction-Formation,'" *Journal of Abnormal and Social Psychology*, 1940, *35*, 56–87.

Murphy, F. J., M. M. Shirley, and H. L. Witmer, "The Incidence of Hidden Delinquency," *American Journal of Orthopsychiatry*, 1946, *16*, 686–96.

Nowicki, S. J. and B. R. Strickland, "A Locus of Control Scale for Children," *Journal of Consulting and Clinical Psychology,* 1974, *40,* 148–54.

Portnoy, I., "The Anxiety States," in S. Arieti., ed., *American Handbook of Psychiatry* (New York: Basic Books, 1959).

Rapoport, J. L., M. S. Buchsbaum, T. P. Zahn, H. Weingartner, C. Ludlow, and E. J. Mikkelsen, "Dextroamphetamine: Cognitive and Behavioral Effects in Normal Prepubertal Boys," *Science,* 1979, *199,* 560–63.

Redl, F., *Controls from Within* (New York: The Free Press, 1952).

Redl, F., and D. Wineman, *Children Who Hate: The Disorganization and Breakdown of Behavior Controls* (New York: The Free Press, 1951).

Richardson, H. and J. Roebuck, "Minnesota Multiphasic Personality Inventory and California Psychological Inventory Differences between Delinquents and Their Nondelinquent Siblings," in *Proceedings of the 73rd Annual Convention of American Psychological Association,* 1965, 255–56.

Rimland, B., *Infantile Autism: The Syndrome and Its Implications for a Neural Theory of Behavior* (New York: Appleton-Century-Crofts, 1964).

Rosen, M., G. R. Clark, and M. S. Kivitz, *Habilitation of the Handicapped,* (Baltimore-London-Tokyo: University Park Press, 1977).

Rutter, M., "Diagnosis and Definition of Childhood Autism," *Journal of Autism and Childhood Schizophrenia,* 1978, *8,* 139–161.

Rutter, M., "Infantile Autism and Other Child Psychoses," in M. Rutter and L. Hersov, eds., *Child Psychiatry* (London: Blackwell Scientific, 1977).

Sawrey, J. M. and C. W. Telford, *Adjustment and Personality,* 4th ed., (Boston: Allyn and Bacon, Inc., 1975).

Sawrey, W. L., "Conditioned Responses of Fear in Relationship to Ulceration," *Journal of Comparative and Physiological Psychology,* 1961, *54,* 347–49.

Sears, R. R., C. I. Hovland, and N. E. Miller, "Minor Studies of Aggression: I. Measurement of Aggressive Behavior," *Journal of Psychology,* 1940, *9,* 275–95.

Seligman, M. E. P., "Fall into Helplessness," *Psychology Today,* 1973, 7 (1), 43–49.

Seward, G., *Psychotherapy and Culture Conflict* (New York: The Ronald Press Company, 1956).

Singer, J. J. and V. G. McCraven, "Some Characteristics of Adult Daydreaming," *Journal of Psychology,* 1961, *51,* 151–64.

Thompson, C. E., "The Attitudes of Various Groups toward Behavior

Problems in Children," *Journal of Abnormal and Social Psychology,* 1940, *35,* 120–25.

Verplank, W. S., "A Glossary of Some Terms Used in the Objective Science of Behavior," *Psychological Review,* 1957, suppl. *8,* no. 6, part 2, 1–42.

Waldrop, M. F., R. Q. Bell, Jr., B. McLaughlin, and C. F. Halverson, Jr., "Newborn Minor Physical Anomalies Predict Short Attention Span, Peer Aggression, and Impulsivity at Age 3," *Science,* 1978, *199,* 563–65.

Wallerstein, J. S. and C. J. Wyle, "Our Law-abiding Law Breakers," *Probation,* 1947, *25,* 107–12.

Weiss, G. and L. Hechtman, "The Hyperactive Child Syndrome," *Science,* 1979, *205,* 1348–54.

Wine, J. J. and G. Haginava, "Dextroamphetamine: Cognitive and Behavioral Effects in Normal Prepubertal Boys," *Science,* 1978, *199.*

SUGGESTIONS FOR STUDENTS AND INSTRUCTORS

1. If there is a local chapter of the National Society for Autistic Children, have a representative of that group meet with the class.

2. Arrange for students to attend a meeting of the local group.

3. Have a pediatrician discuss the use of medication in the handling and treatment of autistic, schizophrenic, and hyperactive children.

4. Make an informal survey of fears, phobias, and chronic anxieties that class members are currently subject to, or can recall from their childhood.

ADDITIONAL READINGS

Erickson, M. T., *Child Psychopathology: Assessment, Etiology, and Treatment* (Englewood Cliffs, N.J.: Prentice-Hall, 1978). A comprehensive survey of all aspects of child psychopathology.

Hamilton-Paterson, J., *The House in the Waves* (New York: Phillips, 1970). A sensitively written story of a disturbed boy struggling to overcome his tendency to flee from reality. An accurate account of institutional life and therapy.

SELECTED FILMS

Jennifer Is a Lady: Education of an Autistic Child. (26 minutes) New York University Film Library (FN), Press Annex, 26 Washington Square

West, New York, N. Y. 10003. Typical symptoms of autism together with treatment and progress.

As We Are. (29 minutes) Phoenix Films, Inc. (FN), 470 Park Avenue, New York, N. Y. 10016. Margaret, the subject of this film, showed many symptoms of mental retardation but is finally diagnosed as autistic. The role of trained teachers in her treatment is shown.

ORGANIZATIONS AND AGENCIES

National Association for Mental Health, Inc.
1800 North Kent Street
Arlington, Va. 22209

National Society for Autistic Children
306 31st Street
Huntington, W. Va. 25702

AUTHOR INDEX

SUBJECT INDEX